myPerspectives™
ENGLISH LANGUAGE ARTS

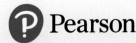

Pearson

NEW YORK, NEW YORK • BOSTON, MASSACHUSETTS
CHANDLER, ARIZONA • GLENVIEW, ILLINOIS

COVER: © Lee Powers/Stone/Getty Images

Acknowledgments of third-party content appear on page R75, which constitutes an extension of this copyright page.

ISBN-13: 978-0-328-92099-0
ISBN-10: 0-328-92099-1

5 18

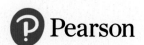

Welcome!

*my*Perspectives™ *English Language Arts* is a student-centered learning environment where you will analyze text, cite evidence, and respond critically about your learning. You will take ownership of your learning through goal-setting, reflection, independent text selection, and activities that allow you to collaborate with your peers.

Each unit of study includes selections of different genres—including multimedia—all related to a relevant and meaningful Essential Question. As you read, you will engage in activities that inspire thoughtful discussion and debate with your peers allowing you to formulate, and defend, your own perspectives.

*my*Perspectives *ELA* offers a variety of ways to interact directly with the text. You can annotate by writing in your print consumable, or you can annotate in your digital Student Edition. In addition, exciting technology allows you to access multimedia directly from your mobile device and communicate using an online discussion board!

We hope you enjoy using *my*Perspectives *ELA* as you develop the skills required to be successful throughout college and career.

Authors' Perspectives

*my*Perspectives is informed by a team of respected experts whose experiences working with students and study of instructional best practices have positively impacted education. From the evolving role of the teacher to how students learn in a digital age, our authors bring new ideas, innovations, and strategies that transform teaching and learning in today's competitive and interconnected world.

" The teaching of English needs to focus on engaging a new generation of learners. How do we get them excited about reading and writing? How do we help them to envision themselves as readers and writers? And, how can we make the teaching of English more culturally, socially, and technologically relevant? Throughout the curriculum, we've created spaces that enhance youth voice and participation and that connect the teaching of literature and writing to technological transformations of the digital age."

Ernest Morrell, Ph.D.

is the Macy professor of English Education at Teachers College, Columbia University, a class of 2014 Fellow of the American Educational Research Association, and the Past-President of the National Council of Teachers of English (NCTE). He is also the Director of Teachers College's Institute for Urban and Minority Education (IUME). He is an award-winning author and in his spare time he coaches youth sports and writes poems and plays. Dr. Morrell has influenced the development of *my*Perspectives in Assessment, Writing & Research, Student Engagement, and Collaborative Learning.

Elfrieda Hiebert, Ph.D.

is President and CEO of TextProject, a nonprofit that provides resources to support higher reading levels. She is also a research associate at the University of California, Santa Cruz. Dr. Hiebert has worked in the field of early reading acquisition for 45 years, first as a teacher's aide and teacher of primary-level students in California and, subsequently, as a teacher and researcher. Her research addresses how fluency, vocabulary, and knowledge can be fostered through appropriate texts. Dr. Hiebert has influenced the development of *my*Perspectives in Vocabulary, Text Complexity, and Assessment.

> " The signature of complex text is challenging vocabulary. In the systems of vocabulary, it's important to provide ways to show how concepts can be made more transparent to students. We provide lessons and activities that develop a strong vocabulary and concept foundation—a foundation that permits students to comprehend increasingly more complex text."

Kelly Gallagher, M.Ed.

teaches at Magnolia High School in Anaheim, California, where he is in his thirty-first year. He is the former co-director of the South Basin Writing Project at California State University, Long Beach. Mr. Gallagher has influenced the development of *my*Perspectives in Writing, Close Reading, and the Role of Teachers.

> " The *my*Perspectives classroom is dynamic. The teacher inspires, models, instructs, facilitates, and advises students as they evolve and grow. When teachers guide students through meaningful learning tasks and then pass them ownership of their own learning, students become engaged and work harder. This is how we make a difference in student achievement—by putting students at the center of their learning and giving them the opportunities to choose, explore, collaborate, and work independently."

> " It's critical to give students the opportunity to read a wide range of highly engaging texts and to immerse themselves in exploring powerful ideas and how these ideas are expressed. In *my*Perspectives, we focus on building up students' awareness of how academic language works, which is especially important for English language learners."

Jim Cummins, Ph.D.

is a Professor Emeritus in the Department of Curriculum, Teaching and Learning of the University of Toronto. His research focuses on literacy development in multilingual school contexts as well as on the potential roles of technology in promoting language and literacy development. In recent years, he has been working actively with teachers to identify ways of increasing the literacy engagement of learners in multilingual school contexts. Dr. Cummins has influenced the development of *my*Perspectives in English Language Learner and English Language Development support.

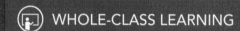

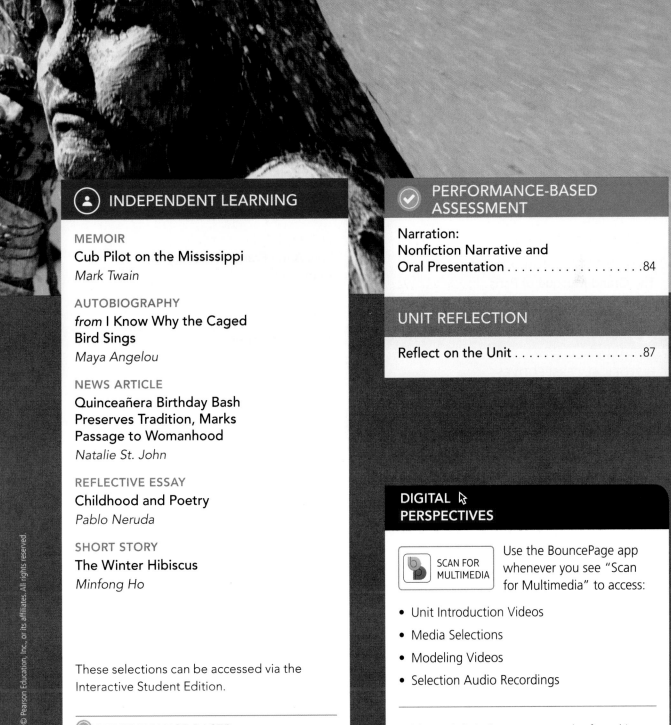

INDEPENDENT LEARNING

These selections can be accessed via the Interactive Student Edition.

PERFORMANCE-BASED ASSESSMENT

UNIT REFLECTION

DIGITAL PERSPECTIVES

SCAN FOR MULTIMEDIA

Use the BouncePage app whenever you see "Scan for Multimedia" to access:

- Unit Introduction Videos
- Media Selections
- Modeling Videos
- Selection Audio Recordings

Additional digital resources can be found in:

- Interactive Student Edition
- *my*Perspectives+

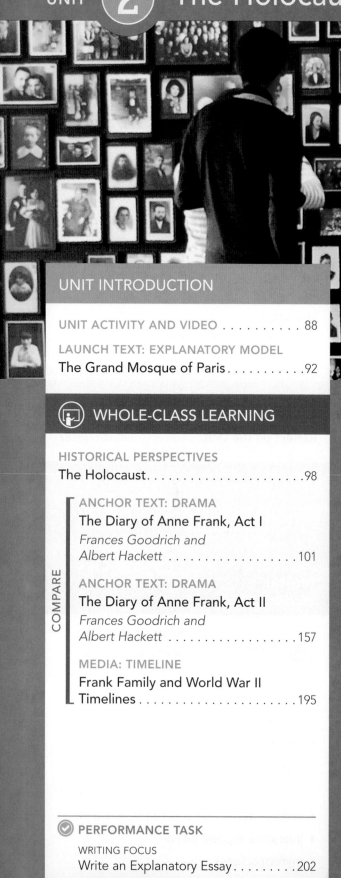

UNIT 2 The Holocaust

(icon) INDEPENDENT LEARNING

These selections can be accessed via the
Interactive Student Edition.

(icon) PERFORMANCE-BASED ASSESSMENT PREP

(icon) PERFORMANCE-BASED ASSESSMENT

UNIT REFLECTION

DIGITAL (cursor) PERSPECTIVES

SCAN FOR
MULTIMEDIA

Use the BouncePage app
whenever you see "Scan
for Multimedia" to access:

- Unit Introduction Videos
- Media Selections
- Modeling Videos
- Selection Audio Recordings

Additional digital resources can be found in:

- Interactive Student Edition
- *my*Perspectives+

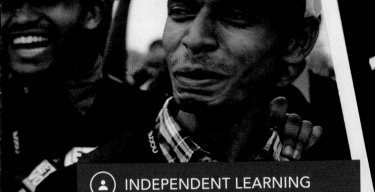

INDEPENDENT LEARNING

These selections can be accessed via the Interactive Student Edition.

 PERFORMANCE-BASED ASSESSMENT PREP

✓ PERFORMANCE-BASED ASSESSMENT

UNIT REFLECTION

DIGITAL ⌕ PERSPECTIVES

 SCAN FOR MULTIMEDIA

Use the BouncePage app whenever you see "Scan for Multimedia" to access:

- Unit Introduction Videos
- Media Selections
- Modeling Videos
- Selection Audio Recordings

Additional digital resources can be found in:

- Interactive Student Edition
- *my*Perspectives+

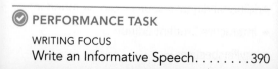

INDEPENDENT LEARNING

ARGUMENT

Is Personal Intelligence Important?

John D. Mayer

BLOG POST

Why Is Emotional Intelligence Important for Teens?

Divya Parekh

EXPLANATORY ESSAY

The More You Know, the Smarter You Are?

Jim Vega

EXPOSITORY NONFICTION

from **The Future of the Mind**

Michio Kaku

These selections can be accessed via the Interactive Student Edition.

 PERFORMANCE-BASED ASSESSMENT PREP

Review Evidence for an an Informative Essay

 PERFORMANCE-BASED ASSESSMENT

UNIT REFLECTION

DIGITAL PERSPECTIVES

 SCAN FOR MULTIMEDIA

Use the BouncePage app whenever you see "Scan for Multimedia" to access:

• Unit Introduction Videos

• Media Selections

• Modeling Videos

• Selection Audio Recordings

Additional digital resources can be found in:

• Interactive Student Edition

• *my*Perspectives+

UNIT 5 Invention

 INDEPENDENT LEARNING

These selections can be accessed via the
Interactive Student Edition.

PERFORMANCE-BASED ASSESSMENT PREP

PERFORMANCE-BASED ASSESSMENT

UNIT REFLECTION

DIGITAL PERSPECTIVES

 Use the BouncePage app
whenever you see "Scan
for Multimedia" to access:

- Unit Introduction Videos
- Media Selections
- Modeling Videos
- Selection Audio Recordings

Additional digital resources can be found in:

- Interactive Student Edition
- *my*Perspectives+

...ctives is completely interactive because you can work ... your digital or print Student Edition.

...s that you complete in your ... Student Edition are saved ...ly. You can access your notes ...hat reviewing work to prepare ...d projects is easy!

Enter answers to p... right in your digita... Notebook and "tu... to your teacher.

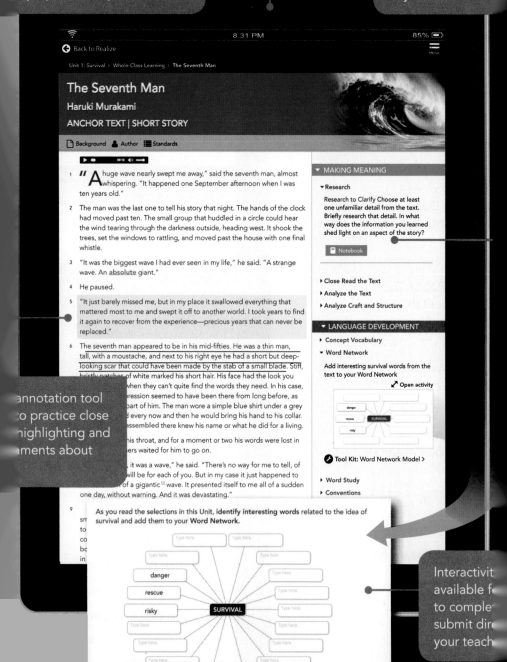

The Seventh Man
Haruki Murakami
ANCHOR TEXT | SHORT STORY

...annotation tool ...o practice close ...highlighting and ...ments about

Interactivit... available f... to comple... submit dir... your teach...

the shops in town lowered their shutters in preparation for the storm. Starting early in the morning, my father and brother went around the house nailing shut all the storm-doors, while my mother spent the day in the kitchen cooking emergency provisions. We filled bottles and canteens with water, and packed our most important possessions in rucksacks[2] for possible evacuation. To the adults, typhoons were an annoyance and a threat they had to face almost annually, but to the kids, removed as we were from such practical concerns, it was just a great big circus, a wonderful source of excitement.

12   Just after noon the color of the sky began to change all of a sudden. There was something strange and unreal about it. I stayed outside on the porch, watching the sky, until the wind began to howl and the rain began to beat against the house with a weird dry sound, like handfuls of sand. Then we closed the last storm-door and gathered together in one room of the darkened house, listening to the radio. This particular storm did not have a great deal of rain, it said, but the winds were doing a lot of damage, blowing roofs off houses and capsizing ships. Many people had been killed or injured by flying debris. Over and over again, they warned people against leaving their homes. Every once in a while, the house would creak and shudder as if a huge hand were shaking it, and sometimes there would be a great crash of some heavy-sounding object against a storm-door. My father guessed that these were tiles blowing off the neighbors' houses. For lunch we ate the rice and omelettes my mother had cooked, waiting for the typhoon to blow past.

13   But the typhoon gave no sign of blowing past. The radio said it had lost momentum[3] almost as soon as it came ashore at S. Province, and now it was moving north-east at the pace of a slow runner. The wind kept up its savage howling as it tried [...] stood on land.

14   Perhaps an hour had gone by with the [...] when a hush fell over everything. All of a [...] could hear a bird crying in the distance. M[...] door a crack and looked outside. The win[...] rain had ceased to fall. Thick, gray clouds [...] [...] showed here and th[...]

THE SEVENTH MAN

NOTES

This sentence is leading up to an exciting story.

CLOSE READ
ANNOTATE: In paragraph 12, annotate at least four vivid details about the storm. Underline those that compare one thing to another.

QUESTION: What is being compared? What picture does each detail create in the reader's mind?

CONCLUDE: How do these descriptions help you visualize the typhoon?

Typhoons are powerful, scary storms that can do a lot of damage.

Use the close-read prompts to guide you through an analysis of the text. You can highlight, circle, and underline the text right in your print Student Edition.

Respond to questions and activities directly in your book!

WORD NETWORK

Add interesting survival words from the text to your Word Network.

LANGUAGE DEVELOPMENT

Concept Vocabulary

desperate	hallucination	profound
entranced	premonition	meditative

Why These Words? These concept words help to reveal the emotional state of the seventh man. For example, when the wave approaches, the seventh man is *entranced*, waiting for it to attack. After the wave hits, the seventh man believes he sees his friend K. in the wave and claims that this experience was no *hallucination*. Notice that both words relate to experiences that occur only in the mind of the seventh man.

1. How does the concept vocabulary sharpen the reader's understanding of the mental or emotional state of the seventh man?
   These words are descriptive and precise.

2. What other words in the selection connect to this concept?
   ominous, overcome, nightmares

Practice

Notebook The concept vocabulary words appear in "The Seventh Man."

1. Use each concept word in a sentence that demonstrates your understanding of the word's meaning.

2. Challenge yourself to replace the concept word with one or two synonyms. How does the word change affect the meaning of your sentence? For example, which sentence is stronger? Which has a more positive meaning?

Word Study

Latin suffix: -tion The Latin suffix *-tion* often indicates that a word is a noun. Sometimes this suffix is spelled *-ion* or *-ation*. These related suffixes mean "act, state, or condition of." In "The Seventh Man," the word *premonition* means "the state of being forewarned."

1. Record a definition of *hallucination* based on your understanding of its root word and the meaning of the suffix *-tion*.
   The condition of seeing something that is not real

2. Look back at paragraphs 37–40 and find two other words that use the suffix *-tion*. Identify the root word that was combined with the suffix. Record a definition for each word.

Digital Resources

You can access digital resources from your print Student Edition, or from Pearson Realize™.

To watch videos or listen to audio from your print Student Edition, all you need is a device with a camera and Pearson's BouncePages app!

ANCHOR TEXT | SHORT STORY

The
Seventh Man

Haruki Murakami

SCAN FOR MULTIMEDIA

BACKGROUND

Hurricanes that originate in the northwest Pacific Ocean are called typhoons. They can stretch up to 500 miles in diameter and produce high winds, heavy rains, enormous waves, and severe flooding. On average, Japan is hit by three severe typhoons each year due to its location and climatic conditions.

1 "A huge wave nearly swept me away," said the seventh man, almost whispering. "It happened one September afternoon when I was ten years old."

2 The man was the last one to tell his story that night. The hands of the clock had moved past ten. The small group that huddled in

NOTES

CLOSE READ
ANNOTATE: Mark details in paragraph 2 that

How to watch a video or listen to audio:

1. Download Pearson's BouncePages App from the Apple App or Google Play Store.

2. Open the app on your mobile device.

3. Aim your camera so the page from your Student Edition is viewable on your screen.

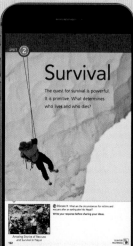

4. Tap the screen to scan the page.

5. Press the "Play" button on the page that appears on your device.

6. View the video or listen to the audio directly from your device!

Amazing Stor
and Surviv
122

Digital resources, including audio and video, can be accessed in the Interactive Student Edition. Your teacher might also assign activities for you to complete online.

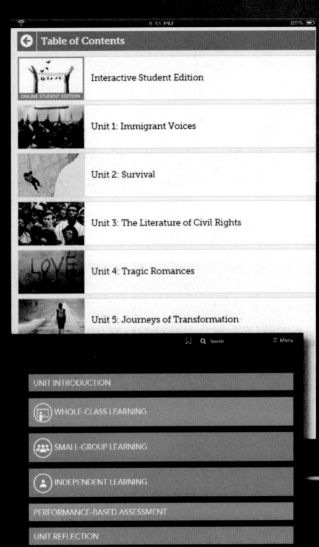

Table of Contents

Interactive Student Edition

Unit 1: Immigrant Voices

Unit 2: Survival

Unit 3: The Literature of Civil Rights

Unit 4: Tragic Romances

Unit 5: Journeys of Transformation

Unit 2: Survival

UNIT 2
Survival

The quest for survival is powerful. It is primitive. What determines who lives and who dies?

UNIT INTRODUCTION

WHOLE-CLASS LEARNING

SMALL-GROUP LEARNING

INDEPENDENT LEARNING

PERFORMANCE-BASED ASSESSMENT

UNIT REFLECTION

You will also find digital novels, interactive lessons, and games!

The Scarlet Letter *By* NATHANIEL HAWTHORNE

THE SCARLET LETTER
By Nathaniel Hawthorne

Illustrated by Hugh Thomson
This book was originally published in 1850 and is in the public domain.

TABLE OF CONTENTS

Standards Overview

English Language Arts will prepare you to succeed in college and your future career. The College and Career Readiness Anchor Standards define what you need to achieve by the end of high school, and the grade-specific Standards define what you need to know by the end of your current grade level.

The following provides an overview of the Standards.

Standards for Reading

College and Career Readiness Anchor Standards for Reading

Key Ideas and Details

1. Read closely to determine what the text says explicitly and to make logical inferences from it; cite specific textual evidence when writing or speaking to support conclusions drawn from the text.

2. Determine central ideas or themes of a text and analyze their development; summarize the key supporting details and ideas.

3. Analyze how and why individuals, events, and ideas develop and interact over the course of a text.

Craft and Structure

4. Interpret words and phrases as they are used in a text, including determining technical, connotative, and figurative meanings, and analyze how specific word choices shape meaning or tone.

5. Analyze the structure of texts, including how specific sentences, paragraphs, and larger portions of the text (e.g., a section, chapter, scene, or stanza) relate to each other and the whole.

6. Assess how point of view or purpose shapes the content and style of a text.

Integration of Knowledge and Ideas

7. Integrate and evaluate content presented in diverse formats and media, including visually and quantitatively, as well as in words.

8. Delineate and evaluate the argument and specific claims in a text, including the validity of the reasoning as well as the relevance and sufficiency of the evidence.

9. Analyze how two or more texts address similar themes or topics in order to build knowledge or to compare the approaches the authors take.

Range of Reading and Level of Text Complexity

10. Read and comprehend complex literary and informational texts independently and proficiently.

Grade 8 Reading Standards for Literature

Standard

Key Ideas and Details

Cite the textual evidence that most strongly supports an analysis of what the text says explicitly as well as inferences drawn from the text.

Determine a theme or central idea of a text and analyze its development over the course of the text, including its relationship to the characters, setting, and plot; provide an objective summary of the text.

Analyze how particular lines of dialogue or incidents in a story or drama propel the action, reveal aspects of a character, or provoke a decision.

Craft and Structure

Determine the meaning of words and phrases as they are used in a text, including figurative and connotative meanings; analyze the impact of specific word choices on meaning and tone, including analogies or allusions to other texts.

Compare and contrast the structure of two or more texts and analyze how the differing structure of each text contributes to its meaning and style.

Analyze how differences in the points of view of the characters and the audience or reader (e.g., created through the use of dramatic irony) create such effects as suspense or humor.

Integration of Knowledge and Ideas

Analyze the extent to which a filmed or live production of a story or drama stays faithful to or departs from the text or script, evaluating the choices made by the director or actors.

Analyze how a modern work of fiction draws on themes, patterns of events, or character types from myths, traditional stories, or religious works such as the Bible, including describing how the material is rendered new.

Range of Reading and Level of Text Complexity

By the end of the year, read and comprehend literature, including stories, dramas, and poems, at the high end of grades 6–8 text complexity band independently and proficiently.

Standards Overview

Grade 8 Reading Standards for Informational Text

Standard

Key Ideas and Details

Cite the textual evidence that most strongly supports an analysis of what the text says explicitly as well as inferences drawn from the text.

Determine a central idea of a text and analyze its development over the course of the text, including its relationship to supporting ideas; provide an objective summary of the text.

Analyze how a text makes connections among and distinctions between individuals, ideas, or events (e.g., through comparisons, analogies, or categories).

Craft and Structure

Determine the meaning of words and phrases as they are used in a text, including figurative, connotative, and technical meanings; analyze the impact of specific word choices on meaning and tone, including analogies or allusions to other texts.

Analyze in detail the structure of a specific paragraph in a text, including the role of particular sentences in developing and refining a key concept.

Determine an author's point of view or purpose in a text and analyze how the author acknowledges and responds to conflicting evidence or viewpoints.

Integration of Knowledge and Ideas

Evaluate the advantages and disadvantages of using different mediums (e.g., print or digital text, video, multimedia) to present a particular topic or idea.

Delineate and evaluate the argument and specific claims in a text, assessing whether the reasoning is sound and the evidence is relevant and sufficient; recognize when irrelevant evidence is introduced.

Analyze a case in which two or more texts provide conflicting information on the same topic and identify where the texts disagree on matters of fact or interpretation.

Range of Reading and Level of Text Complexity

By the end of the year, read and comprehend literary nonfiction at the high end of the grades 6–8 text complexity band independently and proficiently.

Standards for Writing

College and Career Readiness Anchor Standards for Writing

Text Types and Purposes

1. Write arguments to support claims in an analysis of substantive topics or texts, using valid reasoning and relevant and sufficient evidence.

2. Write informative/explanatory texts to examine and convey complex ideas and information clearly and accurately through the effective selection, organization, and analysis of content.

3. Write narratives to develop real or imagined experiences or events using effective technique, well-chosen details, and well-structured event sequences.

Production and Distribution of Writing

4. Produce clear and coherent writing in which the development, organization, and style are appropriate to task, purpose, and audience.

5. Develop and strengthen writing as needed by planning, revising, editing, rewriting, or trying a new approach.

6. Use technology, including the Internet, to produce and publish writing and to interact and collaborate with others.

Research to Build and Present Knowledge

7. Conduct short as well as more sustained research projects based on focused questions, demonstrating understanding of the subject under investigation.

8. Gather relevant information from multiple print and digital sources, assess the credibility and accuracy of each source, and integrate the information while avoiding plagiarism.

9. Draw evidence from literary or informational texts to support analysis, reflection, and research.

Range of Writing

10. Write routinely over extended time frames (time for research, reflection, and revision) and shorter time frames (a single sitting or a day or two) for a range of tasks, purposes, and audiences.

Grade 8 Writing Standards

Standard

Text Types and Purposes

Write arguments to support claims with clear reasons and relevant evidence.

Introduce claim(s), acknowledge and distinguish the claim(s) from alternate or opposing claims, and organize the reasons and evidence logically.

Standards Overview

Standard

Text Types and Purposes (continued)

Support claim(s) with logical reasoning and relevant evidence, using accurate, credible sources and demonstrating an understanding of the topic or text.

Use words, phrases, and clauses to create cohesion and clarify the relationships among claim(s), counterclaims, reasons, and evidence.

Establish and maintain a formal style.

Provide a concluding statement or section that follows from and supports the argument presented.

Write informative/explanatory texts to examine a topic and convey ideas, concepts, and information through the selection, organization, and analysis of relevant content.

Introduce a topic clearly, previewing what is to follow; organize ideas, concepts, and information into broader categories; include formatting (e.g., headings), graphics (e.g., charts, tables), and multimedia when useful to aiding comprehension.

Develop the topic with relevant, well-chosen facts, definitions, concrete details, quotations, or other information and examples.

Use appropriate and varied transitions to create cohesion and clarify the relationships among ideas and concepts.

Use precise language and domain-specific vocabulary to inform about or explain the topic.

Establish and maintain a formal style.

Provide a concluding statement or section that follows from and supports the information or explanation presented.

Write narratives to develop real or imagined experiences or events using effective technique, relevant descriptive details, and well-structured event sequences.

Engage and orient the reader by establishing a context and point of view and introducing a narrator and/or characters; organize an event sequence that unfolds naturally and logically.

Use narrative techniques, such as dialogue, pacing, description, and reflection, to develop experiences, events, and/or characters.

Use a variety of transition words, phrases, and clauses to convey sequence, signal shifts from one time frame or setting to another, and show the relationships among experiences and events.

Grade 8 Writing Standards

Standard

Text Types and Purposes (continued)

Use precise words and phrases, relevant descriptive details, and sensory language to capture the action and convey experiences and events.

Provide a conclusion that follows from and reflects on the narrated experiences or events.

Production and Distribution of Writing

Produce clear and coherent writing in which the development, organization, and style are appropriate to task, purpose, and audience. (Grade-specific expectations for writing types are defined in standards 1–3 above.)

With some guidance and support from peers and adults, develop and strengthen writing as needed by planning, revising, editing, rewriting, or trying a new approach, focusing on how well purpose and audience have been addressed. (Editing for conventions should demonstrate command of Language standards 1–3 up to and including grade 8.)

Use technology, including the Internet, to produce and publish writing and present the relationships between information and ideas efficiently as well as to interact and collaborate with others.

Research to Build and Present Knowledge

Conduct short research projects to answer a question (including a self-generated question), drawing on several sources and generating additional related, focused questions that allow for multiple avenues of exploration.

Gather relevant information from multiple print and digital sources, using search terms effectively; assess the credibility and accuracy of each source; and quote or paraphrase the data and conclusions of others while avoiding plagiarism and following a standard format for citation.

Draw evidence from literary or informational texts to support analysis, reflection, and research.

Apply grade *8 Reading standards* to literature (e.g., "Analyze how a modern work of fiction draws on themes, patterns of events, or character types from myths, traditional stories, or religious works such as the Bible, including describing how the material is rendered new").

Apply *grade 8 Reading standards* to literary nonfiction (e.g., "Delineate and evaluate the argument and specific claims in a text, assessing whether the reasoning is sound and the evidence is relevant and sufficient; recognize when irrelevant evidence is introduced").

Range of Writing

Write routinely over extended time frames (time for research, reflection, and revision) and shorter time frames (a single sitting or a day or two) for a range of discipline-specific tasks, purposes, and audiences.

Standards Overview

Standards for Speaking and Listening

Grade 8 Standards for Speaking and Listening

Standard

Comprehension and Collaboration

Engage effectively in a range of collaborative discussions (one-on-one, in groups, and teacher-led) with diverse partners on *grade 8 topics, texts, and issues,* building on others' ideas and expressing their own clearly.

Come to discussions prepared, having read or researched material under study; explicitly draw on that preparation by referring to evidence on the topic, text, or issue to probe and reflect on ideas under discussion.

Follow rules for collegial discussions and decision-making, track progress toward specific goals and deadlines, and define individual roles as needed.

Pose questions that connect the ideas of several speakers and respond to others' questions and comments with relevant evidence, observations, and ideas.

Acknowledge new information expressed by others, and, when warranted, qualify or justify their own views in light of the evidence presented.

Analyze the purpose of information presented in diverse media and formats (e.g., visually, quantitatively, orally) and evaluate the motives (e.g., social, commercial, political) behind its presentation.

Delineate a speaker's argument and specific claims, evaluating the soundness of the reasoning and relevance and sufficiency of the evidence and identifying when irrelevant evidence is introduced.

Presentation of Knowledge and Ideas

Present claims and findings, emphasizing salient points in a focused, coherent manner with relevant evidence, sound valid reasoning, and well-chosen details; use appropriate eye contact, adequate volume, and clear pronunciation.

Integrate multimedia and visual displays into presentations to clarify information, strengthen claims and evidence, and add interest.

Adapt speech to a variety of contexts and tasks, demonstrating command of formal English when indicated or appropriate. (See grade 8 Language standards 1 and 3 for specific expectations.)

Standards Overview

Standards for Language

College and Career Readiness Anchor Standards for Language

Conventions of Standard English

1. Demonstrate command of the conventions of standard English grammar and usage when writing or speaking.

2. Demonstrate command of the conventions of standard English capitalization, punctuation, and spelling when writing.

Knowledge of Language

3. Apply knowledge of language to understand how language functions in different contexts, to make effective choices for meaning or style, and to comprehend more fully when reading or listening.

Vocabulary Acquisition and Use

4. Determine or clarify the meaning of unknown and multiple-meaning words and phrases by using context clues, analyzing meaningful word parts, and consulting general and specialized reference materials, as appropriate.

5. Demonstrate understanding of figurative language, word relationships, and nuances in word meanings.

6. Acquire and use accurately a range of general academic and domain-specific words and phrases sufficient for reading, writing, speaking, and listening at the college and career-readiness level; demonstrate independence in gathering vocabulary knowledge when considering a word or phrase important to comprehension or expression.

Grade 8 Standards for Language

Standard

Conventions of Standard English

Demonstrate command of the conventions of standard English grammar and usage when writing or speaking.

Explain the function of verbals (gerunds, participles, infinitives) in general and their function in particular sentences.

Form and use verbs in the active and passive voice.

Form and use verbs in the indicative, imperative, interrogative, conditional, and subjunctive mood.

Recognize and correct inappropriate shifts in verb voice and mood.*

Demonstrate command of the conventions of standard English capitalization, punctuation, and spelling when writing.

Grade 8 Standards for Language

Standard

Conventions of Standard English (continued)

Use punctuation (comma, ellipsis, dash) to indicate a pause or break.

Use an ellipsis to indicate an omission.

Spell correctly.

Knowledge of Language

Use knowledge of language and its conventions when writing, speaking, reading, or listening.

Use verbs in the active and passive voice and in the conditional and subjunctive mood to achieve particular effects (e.g., emphasizing the actor or the action; expressing uncertainty or describing a state contrary to fact).

Vocabulary Acquisition and Use

Determine or clarify the meaning of unknown and multiple-meaning words or phrases based on *grade 8 reading and content*, choosing flexibly from a range of strategies.

Use context (e.g., the overall meaning of a sentence or paragraph; a word's position or function in a sentence) as a clue to the meaning of a word or phrase.

Use common, grade-appropriate Greek or Latin affixes and roots as clues to the meaning of a word (e.g., *precede, recede, secede*).

Consult general and specialized reference materials (e.g., dictionaries, glossaries, thesauruses), both print and digital, to find the pronunciation of a word or determine or clarify its precise meaning or its part of speech.

Verify the preliminary determination of the meaning of a word or phrase (e.g., by checking the inferred meaning in context or in a dictionary).

Demonstrate understanding of figurative language, word relationships, and nuances in word meanings.

Interpret figures of speech (e.g., verbal irony, puns) in context.

Use the relationship between particular words to better understand each of the words.

Distinguish among the connotations (associations) of words with similar denotations (definitions) (e.g., *bullheaded, willful, firm, persistent, resolute*).

Acquire and use accurately grade-appropriate general academic and domain-specific words and phrases; gather vocabulary knowledge when considering a word or phrase important to comprehension or expression.

Rites of Passage

You can't get from childhood to adulthood without encountering some powerful experiences.

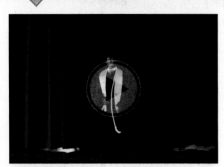

Dear Graduates—A Message from Kid President

Discuss It In what way is graduation a rite of passage, or significant milestone that indicates growth? What other rites of passage are you familiar with?

Write your response before sharing your ideas.

SCAN FOR MULTIMEDIA

UNIT 1

ESSENTIAL QUESTION: # What are some milestones on the path to growing up?

LAUNCH TEXT
NONFICTION
NARRATIVE MODEL
Red Roses

WHOLE-CLASS LEARNING

COMPARE

ANCHOR TEXT: SHORT STORY

The Medicine Bag
Virginia Driving Hawk Sneve

MEDIA: VIDEO

Apache Girl's Rite of Passage
National Geographic

SMALL-GROUP LEARNING

LETTERS

You Are the Electric Boogaloo
Geoff Herbach

Just Be Yourself!
Stephanie Pellegrin

POETRY COLLECTION

Hanging Fire
Audre Lorde

Translating Grandfather's House
E. J. Vega

SHORT STORY

The Setting Sun and the Rolling World
Charles Mungoshi

▸ MEDIA CONNECTION: Stories of Zimbabwean Women

INDEPENDENT LEARNING

MEMOIR

Cub Pilot on the Mississippi
Mark Twain

AUTOBIOGRAPHY

from I Know Why the Caged Bird Sings
Maya Angelou

NEWS ARTICLE

Quinceañera Birthday Bash Preserves Tradition, Marks Passage to Womanhood
Natalie St. John

REFLECTIVE ESSAY

Childhood and Poetry
Pablo Neruda

SHORT STORY

The Winter Hibiscus
Minfong Ho

PERFORMANCE TASK

WRITING FOCUS:
Write a Nonfiction Narrative

PERFORMANCE TASK

SPEAKING AND LISTENING FOCUS:
Present Nonfiction Narratives

PERFORMANCE-BASED ASSESSMENT PREP

Review Evidence for a Nonfiction Narrative

PERFORMANCE-BASED ASSESSMENT

Narrative: Nonfiction Narrative and Oral Presentation

PROMPT: What rite of passage has held the most significance for you or for a person you know well?

Unit Goals

Throughout this unit you will deepen your perspective about rites of passage by reading, writing, speaking, listening, and presenting. These goals will help you succeed on the Unit Performance-Based Assessment.

Rate how well you meet these goals right now. You will revisit your ratings later when you reflect on your growth during this unit.

SCALE	1 NOT AT ALL WELL	2 NOT VERY WELL	3 SOMEWHAT WELL	4 VERY WELL	5 EXTREMELY WELL

READING GOALS

	1	2	3	4	5
• Read and analyze how authors express point of view in nonfiction narrative.	○—○—○—○—○				
• Expand your knowledge and use of academic and concept vocabulary.	○—○—○—○—○				

WRITING AND RESEARCH GOALS

	1	2	3	4	5
• Write a nonfiction narrative in which you develop experiences or events using effective techniques.	○—○—○—○—○				
• Conduct research projects of various lengths to explore a topic and clarify meaning.	○—○—○—○—○				

LANGUAGE GOAL

	1	2	3	4	5
• Demonstrate command of the conventions of standard English grammar and usage, including the usage of the different moods of verbs.	○—○—○—○—○				

SPEAKING AND LISTENING GOALS

	1	2	3	4	5
• Collaborate with your team to build on the ideas of others, develop consensus, and communicate.	○—○—○—○—○				
• Integrate audio, visuals, and text in presentations.	○—○—○—○—○				

📋 STANDARDS

Language
Acquire and use accurately grade-appropriate general academic and domain-specific words and phrases; gather vocabulary knowledge when considering a word or phrase important to comprehension or expression.

SCAN FOR MULTIMEDIA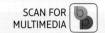

Academic Vocabulary: Nonfiction Narrative

Academic terms appear in all subjects and can help you read, write, and discuss with more precision. Nonfiction narratives are based on true events and written in a story form to engage and keep readers' interest. Here are five academic words that will be useful to you in this unit as you analyze and write nonfiction narratives.

Complete the chart.

1. Review each word, its root, and the mentor sentences.

2. Use the information and your own knowledge to predict the meaning of each word.

3. For each word, list at least two related words.

4. Refer to the dictionary or other resources if needed.

TIP

FOLLOW THROUGH
Study the words in this chart, and mark them or their forms wherever they appear in the unit.

WORD	MENTOR SENTENCES	PREDICT MEANING	RELATED WORDS
attribute ROOT **-trib-** "give"	**1.** I *attribute* my success to hard work. **2.** People *attribute* this song to Bill, but, actually, Shana wrote it.		contribute; tribute
gratifying ROOT **-grat-** "thankful" or "pleasing"	**1.** It was *gratifying* to get an A on the test after studying all week. **2.** Getting praise from her co-workers for a job well done was *gratifying* to Lisa.		
persistent ROOT **-sist-** "stand"	**1.** The East Coast experienced *persistent* rain for days. **2.** The dog's barking from inside the house was *persistent*.		
notable ROOT **-not-** "mark"	**1.** Mrs. Smith's garden was *notable* for its bright flowers. **2.** The book club asked a *notable* writer to speak to their group about his achievements.		
inspire ROOT **-spir-** "breathe"	**1.** This poster will *inspire* people to vote. **2.** If you want to *inspire* me, you'll have to say something positive about my work.		

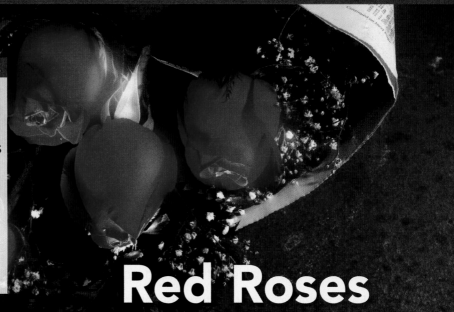

LAUNCH TEXT | NONFICTION NARRATIVE

This text presents a **nonfiction narrative,** a type of writing in which an author explores an experience using descriptive details and events. This is the type of writing you will develop in the Performance-Based Assessment at the end of the unit.

As you read, look at the way the girl's reactions change as she understands the situation better.

Red Roses

NOTES

1 When I was in middle school what I wanted most was to fit in. That's all anybody wants in middle school. In middle school, you're suspicious of anyone who stands out for any reason. Derek stood out. We all avoided him.

2 My mom had always told us never to make fun of people, so I never did. I can't say the same for my friends. Not that they were outright *mean* or anything, but they'd whisper behind their hands, and it was obvious who they were whispering about. I took no part in this, as I said, but I have to admit I steered clear of Derek like everyone else.

3 Despite my standoffishness, Derek started leaving me little gifts: every couple of days, something new—treasures out of a cereal box or a gum machine would turn up in my locker, in my desk, in the pocket of my jacket. I did not acknowledge these things, and immediately tossed them into the back of my closet when I got home. I guess I could have told my mother, but I didn't. Sometimes you have to figure things out for yourself.

4 The weeks passed. I continued to ignore Derek, and made sure to stay out of his way. Still, the presents continued, a different one each time. I resented the fact that he spent so much time thinking up ways to get my attention. Didn't he have better things to do?

5 My friends teased me. "Oooooh, Lila has a boyfriend! Lila has a boyfriend!" they sang out. It didn't seem fair. I'd tried so hard to fit in, to fade into the woodwork, but here I was, being teased, the butt of a joke. The center of attention.

6 One day Derek strode up to me in the lunchroom and presented me with a dozen roses—red, long-stemmed, in a fluted paper wrapper with a note tucked inside: *I know I'm not the coolest kid/But take these roses/You'll be glad you did.*

SCAN FOR MULTIMEDIA

7   I should have been flattered, but I was good and angry. The fact that he stood there grinning lopsidedly, roses in hand, with that hopeful look in his eyes, made me even angrier. I wanted to squash him like a bug.

8   "Leave me alone," I growled. "Don't you get it? GO AWAY!"

9   "Ooooooooh!" sang the chorus of girls. I wanted to crawl under a rock. Derek looked as miserable as I did. And then—horrors!—I saw his bottom lip quiver. He looked like he was going to cry. He *couldn't* cry! If he cried they'd call him a crybaby. *Derek is a crybaby* would follow him around for the rest of his life!

10   I decided I would not, could not let that happen. No one was going to make me. Not even my friends!

11   I took the roses. I carried them around all day.

12   I never did talk to Derek after that. We nodded politely to each other in the hallway, but I never pretended to like him, and he never gave me another present. Somehow we'd worked it out. I lost track of Derek when his family moved away.

13   I guess you could say this was the first time I did something I didn't want to do just to protect someone else's feelings from getting hurt. Maybe you could call this growth or maturity, I honestly don't know.

14   Even though it happened a long time ago, I can picture myself on that day, striding through the corridor proudly, the dozen roses clenched tightly in my hand, walking tall, feeling like no one could touch me. ❧

NOTES

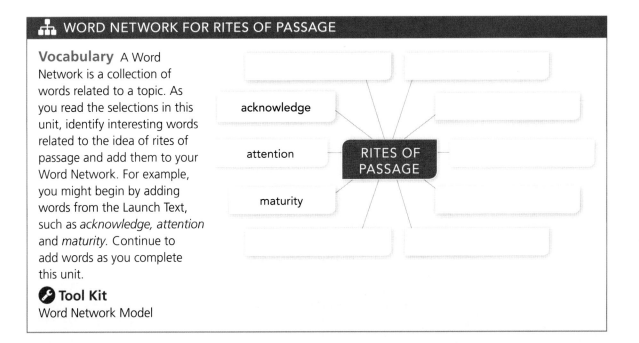

WORD NETWORK FOR RITES OF PASSAGE

Vocabulary A Word Network is a collection of words related to a topic. As you read the selections in this unit, identify interesting words related to the idea of rites of passage and add them to your Word Network. For example, you might begin by adding words from the Launch Text, such as *acknowledge, attention* and *maturity.* Continue to add words as you complete this unit.

acknowledge

attention

maturity

RITES OF PASSAGE

🔧 **Tool Kit**
Word Network Model

Summary

Write a summary of "Red Roses." A **summary** is a concise, complete, and accurate overview of a text. It should not include a statement of your opinion or an analysis of the text.

Launch Activity

Create a Timeline Consider this statement: **The journey into adulthood is marked by life-changing events and observations.**

Work with your class to complete the following activity:

- With your classmates, brainstorm for and list milestones that many people experience. Milestones may include sports events, social or religious events, or academic or work-related events.

- After listing types of milestones, take turns with other students to put a star next to each of the five they deem most important.

- Work with the class to create a timeline of the chosen milestones. Are the milestones scattered, or do they seem to occur during a specific time of life?

QuickWrite

Consider class discussions, presentations, the video, and the Launch Text as you think about the prompt. Record your first thoughts here.

PROMPT: **What rite of passage has held the most significance for you or for a person you know well?**

EVIDENCE LOG FOR RITES OF PASSAGE

Review your QuickWrite and summarize your ideas in one sentence to record in your Evidence Log. Then, record details from "Red Roses" that provide insights about rites of passage.

After each selection, use your Evidence Log to record the details you gather and the connections you make. This graphic shows what your Evidence Log looks like.

🔧 **Tool Kit**
Evidence Log Model

Title of Text: _____ Date: _____

CONNECTION TO PROMPT	TEXT EVIDENCE/DETAILS	ADDITIONAL NOTES/IDEAS

How does this text change or add to my thinking? Date: _____

SCAN FOR
MULTIMEDIA

ESSENTIAL QUESTION:

What are some milestones on the path to growing up?

The path to growing up is lined with milestones; some are universal, but others are meaningful only to you. Often you don't recognize them as milestones until later, after you've passed them. As you read, you will work with your whole class to explore a wide range of milestones on the path to growing up.

Whole-Class Learning Strategies

Throughout your life, in school, in your community, and in your career, you will continue to learn and work in large-group environments.

Review these strategies and the actions you can take to practice them as you work with your whole class. Add ideas of your own for each category for each step. Get ready to use these strategies during Whole-Class Learning.

STRATEGY	ACTION PLAN
Listen actively	• Eliminate distractions. For example, put your cellphone away. • Keep your eyes on the speaker. •
Clarify by asking questions	• If you're confused, other people probably are, too. Ask a question to help your whole class. • If you see that you are guessing, ask a question instead. •
Monitor understanding	• Notice what information you already know and be ready to build on it. • Ask for help if you are struggling. •
Interact and share ideas	• Share your ideas and answer questions, even if you are unsure. • Build on the ideas of others by adding details or making a connection. •

SCAN FOR
MULTIMEDIA

CONTENTS

PERFORMANCE TASK

WRITING FOCUS

Write a Nonfiction Narrative

The Whole-Class reading and video describe some traditional rites of passage. After reading and viewing, you will write a nonfiction narrative in which you relate an experience that you or someone you know had that might be considered a rite of passage.

THE MEDICINE BAG

Comparing Text to Media

In this lesson, you will compare "The Medicine Bag" and "Apache Girl's Rite of Passage." First, you will complete the first-read and close-read activities for "The Medicine Bag."

APACHE GIRL'S RITE OF PASSAGE

About the Author

Virginia Driving Hawk Sneve (b. 1933) grew up on the Rosebud Reservation in South Dakota. Her grandmothers were storytellers, sharing traditional Sioux legends and folk tales that became an inspiration for Sneve's work. She realized that American Indians were often misrepresented in children's books, and she has worked throughout her writing career to portray American Indians realistically. In 2000, President Bill Clinton awarded Sneve a National Humanities Medal.

 **Tool Kit**
First-Read Guide and Model Annotation

☰ STANDARDS

Reading Literature
By the end of the year, read and comprehend literature, including stories, dramas, and poems, at the high end of the grades 6–8 text complexity band independently and proficiently.

The Medicine Bag

Concept Vocabulary

You will encounter the following words as you read "The Medicine Bag." Before reading, note how familiar you are with each word. Then, rank the words in order from most familiar (1) to least familiar (5).

WORD	YOUR RANKING
wearily	
straggled	
fatigue	
frail	
sheepishly	

After completing the first read, come back to the concept vocabulary and review your rankings. Mark any changes to your original rankings.

First Read FICTION

Refer to the information below as you conduct your first read. You will have an opportunity to complete the close-read notes after your first read.

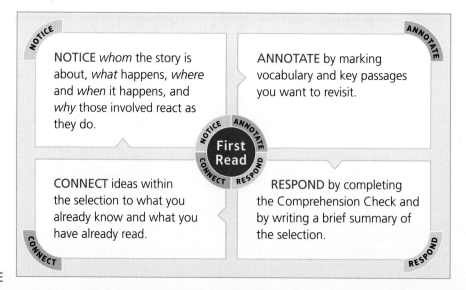

NOTICE *whom* the story is about, *what* happens, *where* and *when* it happens, and *why* those involved react as they do.

ANNOTATE by marking vocabulary and key passages you want to revisit.

First Read

CONNECT ideas within the selection to what you already know and what you have already read.

RESPOND by completing the Comprehension Check and by writing a brief summary of the selection.

The Medicine Bag

Virginia Driving Hawk Sneve

BACKGROUND

The Lakota Indians are part of the Sioux Nation, an indigenous people of the Great Plains region of North America. Today there are about 170,000 Sioux Indians living in the United States. About one-fifth of the American Indian population live on *reservations,* which are designated pieces of land ruled by tribal law.

SCAN FOR MULTIMEDIA

NOTES

1 Grandpa wasn't tall and stately like TV Indians. His hair wasn't in braids; it hung in stringy, gray strands on his neck, and he was old. He was my great-grandfather, and he didn't live in a tipi[1]; he lived all by himself in a part log, part tar-paper shack on the Rosebud Reservation in South Dakota.

2 My kid sister, Cheryl, and I always bragged about our Lakota[2] grandpa, Joe Iron Shell. Our friends, who had always lived in the city and only knew about Indians from movies and TV, were impressed by our stories. Maybe we exaggerated and made Grandpa and the reservation sound glamorous, but when we returned home to Iowa after our yearly summer visit to Grandpa, we always had some exciting tale to tell.

3 We usually had some authentic Lakota article to show our listeners. One year Cheryl had new moccasins[3] that Grandpa had

---

1. **tipi** *n.* cone-shaped tent traditionally made of animal skins or bark.
2. **Lakota** *adj.* belonging to a Native American tribe from the Great Plains region (present-day North and South Dakota).
3. **moccasins** (MOK uh suhnz) *n.* soft shoes traditionally made from animal hide.

made. On another visit he gave me a small, round, flat rawhide drum decorated with a painting of a warrior riding a horse. He taught me a Lakota chant to sing while I beat the drum with a leather-covered stick that had a feather on the end. Man that really made an impression.

4   We never showed our friends Grandpa's picture. Not that we were ashamed of him but because we knew that the glamorous tales we told didn't go with the real thing. Our friends would have laughed, so when Grandpa came to visit us, I was so ashamed and embarrassed I could have died.

5   There are a lot of yippy poodles and other fancy little dogs in our neighborhood, but they usually barked singly at the mailman from the safety of their own yards. Now it sounded as if a whole pack of mutts were barking together in one place.

6   I walked to the curb to see what the commotion was. About a block away I saw a crowd of little kids yelling, with the dogs yipping and growling around someone who was walking down the middle of the street.

7   I watched the group as it slowly came closer and saw that in the center of the strange procession was a man wearing a tall black hat. He'd pause now and then to peer at something in his hand and then at the houses on either side of the street. I felt cold and hot at the same time. I recognized the man. "Oh, no!" I whispered, "It's Grandpa!"

8   I stood on the curb, unable to move even though I wanted to run and hide. Then I got mad when I saw how the yippy dogs were growling and nipping at the old man's baggy pant legs and how **wearily** he poked them away with his cane. "Stupid mutts," I said as I ran to rescue Grandpa.

9   When I kicked and hollered at the dogs to get away, they put their tails between their legs and scattered. The kids ran to the curb where they watched me and the old man.

10   "Grandpa," I said and reached for his beat-up old tin suitcase tied shut with a rope. But he set it down right in the street and shook my hand.

11   "*Hau, Takoza,* Grandchild," he greeted me formally in Lakota.

12   All I could do was stand there with the whole neighborhood watching and shake the hand of the leather-brown old man. I saw how his gray hair **straggled** from under his big black hat, which had a drooping feather in its crown. His rumpled black suit hung like a sack over his stooped frame. As he shook my hand, his coat fell open to expose a bright red satin shirt with a beaded bolo tie under the collar. His getup wasn't out of place on the reservation, but it sure was here, and I wanted to sink right through the pavement.

wearily (WEER uh lee) *adv.* in a tired way

straggled (STRAG uhld) *v.* hung in messy strands

13   "Hi," I muttered with my head down. I tried to pull my hand away when I felt his bony hand trembling and then looked up to see fatigue in his face. I felt like crying. I couldn't think of anything to say so I picked up Grandpa's suitcase, took his arm, and guided him up the driveway to our house.

14   Mom was standing on the steps. I don't know how long she'd been watching, but her hand was over her mouth and she looked as if she couldn't believe what she saw. Then she ran to us.

15   "Grandpa," she gasped. "How in the world did you get here?"

16   She checked her move to embrace Grandpa and I remembered that such a display of affection is unseemly to the Lakota and would have embarrassed him.

17   "*Hau*, Marie," he said as he shook Mom's hand. She smiled and took his other arm.

18   As we supported him up the steps, the door banged open and Cheryl came bursting out of the house. She was all smiles and was so obviously glad to see Grandpa that I was ashamed of how I felt.

19   "Grandpa!" she yelled happily. "You came to see us!"

20   Grandpa smiled, and Mom and I let go of him as he stretched out his arms to my ten-year-old sister, who was still young enough to be hugged.

21   "*Wicincila*, little girl," he greeted her and then collapsed.

22   He had fainted. Mom and I carried him into her sewing room, where we had a spare bed.

23   After we had Grandpa on the bed, Mom stood there patting his shoulder. "You make Grandpa comfortable, Martin," she decided, "while I call the doctor."

24   I reluctantly moved to the bed. I knew Grandpa wouldn't want to have Mom undress him, but I didn't want to either. He was so skinny and **frail** that his coat slipped off easily. When I loosened his tie and opened his shirt collar, I felt a small leather pouch that hung from a thong around his neck. I left it alone and moved to remove his boots. The scuffed old cowboy boots were tight, and he moaned as I put pressure on his legs to jerk them off.

25   I put the boots on the floor and saw why they fit so tight. Each one was stuffed with money. I looked at the bills that lined the boots and started to ask about them, but Grandpa's eyes were closed again.

26   Mom came back with a basin of water. "The doctor thinks Grandpa may be suffering from heat exhaustion," she explained as she bathed Grandpa's face. Mom gave a big sigh, "Oh *hinh*, Martin. How do you suppose he got here?"

27   We found out after the doctor's visit. Grandpa was angrily sitting up in bed while Mom tried to feed him some soup.

28   "Tonight you let Marie feed you, Grandpa," said my dad, who had gotten home from work. "You're not really sick," he said as

NOTES

fatigue (fuh TEEG) *n.* physical or mental exhaustion

CLOSE READ
ANNOTATE: Mark details in paragraphs 12–13 and 18–21 that show how the narrator and Cheryl each greet Grandpa.

QUESTION: Why are their greetings so different?

CONCLUDE: What can you conclude about Martin and his sister by the way they greet Grandpa?

frail (frayl) *adj.* delicate; weak

The Medicine Bag **15**

sheepishly (SHEEP ihsh lee) *adv.* in an embarrassed way

CLOSE READ

ANNOTATE: Note the language the author uses in paragraphs 31–32 that shows the difficulty of Grandpa's journey.

QUESTION: Why does the author provide so much detail about the journey?

CONCLUDE: What can you conclude about Grandpa from the journey he took?

he gently pushed Grandpa back against the pillows. "The doctor thinks you just got too tired and hot after your long trip."

29   Grandpa relaxed, and between sips of soup, he told us of his journey. Soon after we visited him, Grandpa decided that he would like to see where his only living descendants lived and what our home was like. Besides, he admitted **sheepishly**, he was lonesome after we left.

30   I knew that everybody felt as guilty as I did—especially Mom. Mom was all Grandpa had left. So even after she married my dad, who's not an Indian, and after Cheryl and I were born, Mom made sure that every summer we spent a week with Grandpa.

31   I never thought that Grandpa would be lonely after our visits, and none of us noticed how old and weak be had become. But Grandpa knew, so he came to us. He had ridden on buses for two and a half days. When he arrived in the city, tired and stiff from sitting for so long, he set out walking to find us.

32   He had stopped to rest on the steps of some building downtown, and a policeman found him. The officer took Grandpa to the city bus stop, waited until the bus came, and then told the driver to let Grandpa out at Bell View Drive. After Grandpa got off the bus, he started walking again. But he couldn't see the house numbers on the other side when he walked on the sidewalk, so he walked in the middle of the street. That's when all the little kids and dogs followed him.

33   I knew everybody felt as bad as I did. Yet I was so proud of this eighty-six-year-old man who had never been away from the reservation but who had the courage to travel so far alone.

34   "You found the money in my boots?" he asked Mom.

35   "Martin did," she answered and then scolded, "Grandpa, you shouldn't have carried so much money. What if someone had stolen it from you?"

36   Grandpa laughed. "I would've known if anyone tried to take the boots off my feet. The money is what I've saved for a long time—a hundred dollars—for my funeral. But you take it now to buy groceries so that I won't be a burden to you while I am here."

37   "That won't be necessary, Grandpa," Dad said. "We are honored to have you with us, and you will never be a burden. I am only sorry that we never thought to bring you home with us this summer and spare you the discomfort of a long bus trip."

38   Grandpa was pleased. "Thank you," he answered. "But don't feel bad that you didn't bring me with you, for I would not have come then. It was not time." He said this in such a way that no one could argue with him. To Grandpa and the Lakota, he once told me, a thing would be done when it was the right time to do it, and that's the way it was.

39   "Also," Grandpa went on, looking at me. "I have come because it is soon time for Martin to have the medicine bag."

40   We all knew what that meant. Grandpa thought he was going to die, and he had to follow the tradition of his family to pass the medicine bag, along with its history, to the oldest male child.

41   "Even though the boy," he said, still looking at me, "doesn't have an Indian name, the medicine bag will be his."

42   I didn't know what to say. I had the same hot and cold feeling that I had when I first saw Grandpa in the street. The medicine bag was the dirty leather pouch I had found around his neck. "I could never wear it," I almost said aloud. I thought of having my friends see it in gym class or at the swimming pool and could imagine the smart things they would say. But I just swallowed hard and took a step toward the bed. I knew I would have to take it.

43   But Grandpa was tired. "Not now, Martin," he said waving his hand in dismissal. "It is not time. Now I will sleep."

44   So that's how Grandpa came to be with us for two months. My friends kept asking to come see the old man, but I put them off. I told myself that I didn't want them laughing at Grandpa. But even as I made excuses, I knew it wasn't Grandpa I was afraid they'd laugh at.

45   Nothing bothered Cheryl about bringing her friends to see Grandpa. Every day after school started, there'd be a crew of giggling little girls or round-eyed little boys crowded around the

old man on the porch, where he'd gotten in the habit of sitting every afternoon.

46   Grandpa smiled in his gentle way and patiently answered their questions, or he'd tell them stories of brave warriors, ghosts, and animals, and the kids listened in awed silence. Those little guys thought Grandpa was great.

47   Finally, one day after school, my friends came home with me because nothing I said stopped them. "We're going to see the great Indian of Bell View Drive," said Hank, who was supposed to be my best friend. "My brother has seen him three times so he oughta be well enough to see us."

48   When we got to my house, Grandpa was sitting on the porch. He had on his red shirt, but today he also wore a fringed leather vest trimmed with beads. Instead of his usual cowboy boots, he had solidly beaded moccasins on his feet. Of course, he had his old black hat on—he was seldom without it. But it had been brushed, and the feather in the beaded headband was proudly erect, its tip a bright white. His hair lay in silver strands over the red shirt collar.

49   I stared just as my friends did, and I heard one of them murmur, "'Wow!"

50   Grandpa looked up, and when his eyes met mine they twinkled as if he were laughing inside. He nodded to me, and my face got all hot. I could tell that he had known all along I was afraid he'd embarrass me in front of my friends.

51   "*Hau, hoksilas*, boys," he greeted and held out his hand.

52   My buddies passed in single file and shook his hand as I introduced them. They were so polite I almost laughed. "How, Grandpa," and even a "How . . . do . . . you . . . do, sir."

53   "You look fine, Grandpa," I said as the guys sat down.

54   "*Hanh*, yes," he agreed. "When I woke up this morning, it seemed the right time to dress in the good clothes. I knew that my grandson would be bringing his friends."

55   "You guys want a soda or . . . ?" I offered, but no one answered. They were listening to Grandpa as he told how he'd killed the deer from which his vest was made.

56   Grandpa did most of the talking. I was proud of him and amazed at how respectfully quiet my friends were. Mom had to chase them home at supper time. As they left, they shook Grandpa's hand again and said to me, "Can we come back?"

57   But after they left, Mom said, "no more visitors for a while, Martin. Grandpa won't admit it, but his strength hasn't returned. He likes having company, but it tires him."

CLOSE READ
ANNOTATE: Mark details in paragraphs 50 and 51 that describe Grandpa's actions.

QUESTION: What do these actions suggest about Grandpa's character?

CONCLUDE: What is the effect of readers learning more about Grandpa at the same time Martin does?

58 That evening Grandpa called me to his room before he went to sleep. "Tomorrow," he said, "when you come home, it will be time to give you the medicine bag."

59 I felt a hard squeeze from where my heart is supposed to be and was scared, but I answered, "OK, Grandpa."

60 All night I had weird dreams about thunder and lightning on a high hill. From a distance I heard the slow beat of a drum. When I woke up in the morning, I felt as if I hadn't slept at all. At school it seemed as if the day would never end, and when it finally did, I ran home.

61 Grandpa was in his room, sitting on the bed. The shades were down, and the place was dim and cool. I sat on the floor in front of Grandpa, but he didn't even look at me. After what seemed a long time, he spoke.

62 "I sent your mother and sister away. What you will hear today is only for your ears. What you will receive is only for your hands." He fell silent. I felt shivers down my back.

63 "My father in his early manhood," Grandpa began, "made a vision quest[4] to find a spirit guide for his life. You cannot understand how it was in that time, when the great Teton Lakota were first made to stay on the reservation. There was a strong need for guidance from *Wakantanka*,[5] the Great Spirit. But too many of the young men were filled with despair and hatred. They thought it was hopeless to search for a vision when the glorious life was gone and only the hated confines of a reservation lay ahead. But my father held to the old ways.

64 "He carefully prepared for his quest with a purifying sweat bath, and then he went alone to a high butte[6] top to fast and pray. After three days he received his sacred dream—in which he found, after long searching, the white man's iron. He did not understand his vision of finding something belonging to the white people, for in that time they were the enemy. When he came down from the butte to cleanse himself at the stream below, he found the remains of a campfire and broken shell of an iron kettle. This was a sign that reinforced his dream. He took a piece of the iron for his medicine bag, which he had made of elk skin years before, to prepare for his quest.

65 "He returned to his village, where he told his dream to the wise old men of the tribe. They gave him the name *Iron Shell*, but they did not understand the meaning of the dream either. At first Iron Shell kept the piece of iron with him at all times and believed it gave him protection from the evils of those unhappy days.

NOTES

CLOSE READ
ANNOTATE: Mark the details in paragraphs 59 and 60 that show how Martin feels.

QUESTION: Why might the author have chosen to include this information?

CONCLUDE: What do these details suggest about Martin?

---

4. **vision quest** *n.* in Native American cultures, a difficult search for spiritual guidance.
5. **Wakantanka** (WAH kuhn tank uh) Lakota religion's most important spirit—the creator of the world.
6. **butte** (byoot) *n.* isolated mountaintop with steep sides.

CLOSE READ

ANNOTATE: Mark details the author uses in paragraph 66 that describe Iron Shell's experience.

QUESTION: What important information does this passage reveal?

CONCLUDE: What can you conclude about Grandpa's belief in fate and destiny?

66   "Then a terrible thing happened to Iron Shell. He and several other young men were taken from their homes by the soldiers and sent to a boarding school far from home. He was angry and lonesome for his parents and for the young girl he had wed before he was taken away. At first Iron Shell resisted the teachers' attempts to change him, and he did not try to learn. One day it was his turn to work in the school's blacksmith shop. As he walked into the place, he knew that his medicine had brought him there to learn and work with the white man's iron.

67   "Iron Shell became a blacksmith and worked at the trade when he returned to the reservation. All his life he treasured the medicine bag. When he was old and I was a man, he gave it to me."

68   Grandpa quit talking, and I stared in disbelief as he covered his face with his hands. His shoulders shook with quiet sobs. I looked away until he began to speak again.

69   "I kept the bag until my son, your mother's father, was a man and had to leave us to fight in the war across the ocean. I gave him the bag, for I believed it would protect him in battle, but he did not take it with him. He was afraid he would lose it. He died in a faraway land."

70   Again Grandpa was still, and I felt his grief around me.

71   "My son," he went on after clearing his throat, "had no sons, only one daughter, your mother. So the medicine bag must be passed to you."

72   He unbuttoned his shirt, pulled out the leather pouch, and lifted it over his head. He held it in his hand, turning it over and over as if memorizing how it looked.

73   "In the bag," he said, as he opened it and removed two objects, "is the broken shell of the iron kettle, a pebble from the butte, and a piece of the sacred sage.⁷" He held the pouch upside down and fine dust drifted out.

74   "After the bag is yours you must put a piece of prairie sage within and never open it again until you pass it on to your son." He replaced the pebble and the piece of iron and tied the bag.

75   I stood up, somehow knowing I should. Grandpa slowly rose from the bed and stood upright in front of me holding the bag before my face. I closed my eyes and waited for him to slip it over my head. But he spoke.

76   "No, you need not wear it." He placed the soft leather bag in my right hand and closed my other hand over it. "It would not be right to wear it in this time and place where no one will understand. Put it safely away until you are again on the reservation. Wear it then, when you replace the sacred sage."

77   Grandpa turned and sat again on the bed. Wearily he leaned his head against the pillow. "Go," he said. "I will sleep now."

---

7. **sage** (sayj) *n.* type of herb.

78   "Thank you, Grandpa," I said softly and left with the bag in my hands.

NOTES

79   That night Mom and Dad took Grandpa to the hospital. Two weeks later I stood alone on the lonely prairie of the reservation and put the sacred sage in my medicine bag. ❧

Comprehension Check

Complete the following items after you finish your first read.

1. What makes Grandpa sound glamorous to the narrator's friends?

2. What happens when Grandpa arrives at Martin's house?

3. Why does Grandpa want Martin to have the medicine bag?

4. What is in the medicine bag, and what does Martin add to it at the end of the story?

📓 **Notebook** Write a three-sentence summary of "The Medicine Bag."

RESEARCH

Research to Clarify Choose at least one unfamiliar detail from the text. Briefly research that detail. In what way does the information you learned shed light on an aspect of the story?

Research to Explore Choose something that interested you from the text and formulate a research question.

THE MEDICINE BAG

Close Read the Text

1. This model, from paragraph 38 of the text, shows two sample annotations, along with questions and conclusions. Close read the passage, and find another detail to annotate. Then, write a question and your conclusion.

Close Read
ANNOTATE · QUESTION · CONCLUDE

ANNOTATE: These details hint at Grandpa's personality.

QUESTION: Why does the writer reveal two sides of Grandpa's personality?

CONCLUDE: Creating a compassionate but firm character makes Grandpa seem real.

ANNOTATE: The author repeats the word *time*.

QUESTION: What effect does the repetition create?

CONCLUDE: The repetition stresses the Lakota belief in doing things only when the time is right.

"But don't feel bad that you didn't bring me with you, for I would not have come then. It was not time." He said this in such a way that no one could argue with him. To Grandpa and the Lakota, he once told me, a thing would be done when it was the right time to do it....

2. For more practice, go back into the text and complete the close-read notes.

3. Revisit a section of the text you found important. Read this section closely and **annotate** what you notice. Ask yourself **questions** such as "Why did the author make this choice?" What can you **conclude**?

🔧 **Tool Kit**
Close-Read Guide and Model Annotation

Analyze the Text

CITE TEXTUAL EVIDENCE
to support your answers.

📓 **Notebook** Respond to these questions.

1. **Evaluate** Do you think Grandpa made the right decision to travel and visit his family? Use details from the story to support your answer.

2. **Interpret** Summarize the story Grandpa tells about his father. Why do you think Grandpa tells Martin this story at this time?

3. **Draw Conclusions** What happens to Grandpa and to Martin at the end of the story? Cite story details to support your conclusion.

4. **Essential Question:** *What are some milestones on the path to growing up?* What have you learned about the path to growing up by reading this story?

▤ STANDARDS
Reading Literature
Determine the meaning of words and phrases as they are used in a text, including figurative and connotative meanings; analyze the impact of specific word choices on meaning and tone, including analogies or allusions to other texts.

Analyze Craft and Structure

Figurative Meaning: Symbolism A **symbol** is anything that stands for or represents something else. **Symbolism** is the use of symbols.

- Symbols are common in everyday life as well as in literature. For example, a dove with an olive branch in its beak is a symbol of peace.
- In literature, symbolism can highlight certain ideas the author wishes to emphasize.
- Symbolism can also add levels of meaning to a text.

Most Native American cultures show deep respect for nature, and the natural world is considered to have profound spiritual qualities. Symbols of nature play an important role in Native American traditions, especially religious ones. In "The Medicine Bag," the medicine bag is an important symbol. Think about other symbols connected with Grandpa in the story.

Practice

CITE TEXTUAL EVIDENCE to support your answers.

🗐 **Notebook** **Respond to these questions.**

1. **(a)** What details in the story suggest that the medicine bag is a symbol and is important to Grandpa? **(b)** Why do you think the author wants readers to understand Grandpa's connection to the medicine bag?

2. **(a)** How does Martin's view of the medicine bag change? What changes his mind? **(b)** How do Martin's changing feelings about the medicine bag help show what it represents?

3. **(a)** The medicine bag is not the only symbol in the story. Record in the chart two other details from the story that serve as symbols and what each one represents. **(b)** What is the purpose of each symbol? Write your answers in the chart.

THE MEDICINE BAG: SYMBOLS		
SYMBOL	WHAT IT REPRESENTS	PURPOSE IN THE STORY

THE MEDICINE BAG

Concept Vocabulary

wearily	fatigue	sheepishly
straggled	frail	

Why These Words? These concept vocabulary words show someone who is not at full strength or does not look his or her best. For example, Grandpa *wearily* pokes his cane at the dogs that are chasing him. When he arrives at the house, Martin can see the *fatigue* in his face. Notice that both words emphasize how tired Grandpa seems.

1. How does the concept vocabulary sharpen the reader's understanding of Grandpa's state of health and his appearance?

2. What other words in the selection connect to the concept of Grandpa's state of health and his appearance?

⬡ WORD NETWORK

Add words related to the topic of rites of passage from the text to your Word Network.

Practice

CITE TEXTUAL EVIDENCE to support your answers.

📓 **Notebook** The concept words appear in "The Medicine Bag."

1. Use each concept word in a sentence that demonstrates your understanding of the word's meaning.

2. With a partner, come up with an **antonym**, a word with the opposite meaning, for each of the following words: *wearily, frail,* and *sheepishly*. How would Grandpa seem different if the author had used the antonyms to describe him instead of the original words?

Word Study

Animal Words In "The Medicine Bag," the narrator describes Grandpa as *sheepishly* admitting he was lonely after his family finished their visit and drove away from the reservation. Grandpa is acting like a sheep—suddenly bashful and shy—because he is embarrassed to admit his true feelings. Comparing him with a sheep presents a vivid image of Grandpa's behavior.

There are many words that acquire their meanings from the characteristics we associate with certain animals. Guess the meanings of each of the following words based on the characteristics of the animal: *doggedly, bullheaded, lionize, elephantine*. Then, verify their actual definitions using a dictionary or thesaurus.

≣ STANDARDS

Language
Determine or clarify the meaning of unknown and multiple-meaning words or phrases based on *grade 8 reading and content,* choosing flexibly from a range of strategies.

  c. Consult general and specialized reference materials, both print and digital, to find the pronunciation of a word or determine or clarify its precise meaning or its part of speech.
  d. Verify the preliminary determination of the meaning of a word or phrase.

Conventions

Verbs in Active and Passive Voice It's important to learn and use active and passive voice of verbs in your writing. The **voice** of a verb shows whether the subject of the verb is performing the action or receiving it. A verb is in the **active voice** when its subject performs the action. A verb is in the **passive voice** when its subject receives the action.

A passive verb is a verb phrase made from a form of *be* with the past participle of an action verb, as shown in the chart:

ACTIVE VOICE	PASSIVE VOICE
We **filled** the bucket.	The bucket **was filled**. (***Filled*** is the past participle of ***fill***.)
Alison **is winning** the race.	The race **is being won** by Alison. (***Won*** is the past participle of ***win***.)

Generally, the active voice is considered a better choice for writers. The active voice communicates ideas in a more engaging, concise way. It also put the emphasis on the person performing the action.

Passive voice should be used when the performer of the action is unknown or when it is desirable to stress the action instead of its performer. In general, avoid passive voice to keep your writing from sounding vague.

Read It

1. Identify whether each sentence uses the active or the passive voice.

   a. Our friends were impressed by our stories about Grandpa.

   b. Grandpa taught me a Lakota chant to sing.

   c. Grandpa's old black hat had been brushed.

2. Reread paragraph 66 of "The Medicine Bag." Mark and then label one example of passive voice and one of active voice.

Write It

Revise each sentence to use the active voice, to stress the performer of each verb's action.

> EXAMPLE
> Grandpa was brought to Martin's neighborhood by the bus.
> **The bus brought Grandpa to Martin's neighborhood.**

1. Martin was embarrassed by the way Grandpa looked.

2. Grandpa's father was given the name Iron Shell by the wise old men.

3. The medicine bag was given to Martin by Grandpa.

STANDARDS

Language
- Demonstrate command of the conventions of standard English grammar and usage when writing or speaking.
  b. Form and use verbs in the active and passive voice.
- Use knowledge of language and its conventions when writing, speaking, reading, or listening.
  a. Use verbs in the active and passive voice and in the conditional and subjunctive mood to achieve particular effects.

The Medicine Bag **25**

THE MEDICINE BAG

Writing to Sources

Short stories, like "The Medicine Bag," have a narrator—the character or voice that relates story events. **Point of view** is the perspective, or vantage point, from which a narrator tells a story. "The Medicine Bag" is told from Martin's point of view. How would the story be different if it were told from another character's point of view?

Assignment

Write a **retelling** of the story "The Medicine Bag" from Grandpa's point of view: Based on the details provided in the story, imagine Grandpa's journey to see his family. What are his impressions of Martin and his friends? How does he feel about giving the medicine bag to Martin to preserve a sacred Lakota tradition?

Draft your retelling of the story. Make sure to do the following:

- Make Grandpa the narrator, the character who tells the story using the pronoun "I."

- Include details, thoughts, feeling, and insights from Grandpa's point of view.

Vocabulary and Conventions Connection You may want to include several of the concept vocabulary words in your retelling. Also, remember to use the active voice to keep your sentences lively.

wearily	fatigue	sheepishly
straggled	frail	

Reflect on Your Writing

After you have written your retelling of the story, answer the following questions.

1. How well do you think your retelling expressed Grandpa's point of view?

2. What was the most challenging part of retelling the story from Grandpa's point of view?

3. **Why These Words?** The words you choose make a difference in your writing. Which words did you specifically choose to add power to your retelling?

≡ STANDARDS

Writing
Write narratives to develop real or imagined experiences or events using effective technique, relevant descriptive details, and well-structured event sequences.

a. Engage and orient the reader by establishing a context and point of view and introducing a narrator and/or characters; organize an event sequence that unfolds naturally and logically.
b. Use narrative techniques, such as dialogue, pacing, description, and reflection, to develop experiences, events, and/or characters.
d. Use precise words and phrases, relevant descriptive details, and sensory language to capture the action and convey experiences and events.
e. Provide a conclusion that follows from and reflects on the narrated experiences or events.

Speaking and Listening
Present claims and findings, emphasizing salient points in a focused, coherent manner with relevant evidence, sound valid reasoning, and well-chosen details; use appropriate eye contact, adequate volume, and clear pronunciation.

Speaking and Listening

Assignment

A **monologue** is a speech given by a character that expresses that character's point of view. Imagine you are the narrator of "The Medicine Bag." Write and present a monologue in which you reflect on how you came to understand the importance of the Lakota tradition of the medicine bag.

1. **Plan Your Interpretation** As you write your monologue, plan how you want to express the narrator's thoughts and feelings about the medicine bag. Answer the following questions to help guide your delivery.

   - How does the narrator think and feel about the medicine bag tradition when Grandpa first mentions it?

   - Did the narrator's thoughts and feelings change over the course of the story? How? What caused these changes?

   - What word choices can help you sound as if you are speaking from the narrator's point of view?

2. **Prepare Your Delivery** Practice reciting your monologue before you present it to your class. Include the following performance techniques to help you achieve the desired effect.

   - Use details from the story about the importance of the medicine bag.

   - Make appropriate eye contact with the audience.

   - Speak at adequate volume.

   - Pronounce each word clearly so your audience can easily understand what you are saying.

3. **Evaluate Presentations** As your classmates deliver their presentations, listen attentively. Use a presentation evaluation guide like the one shown to analyze their presentations.

PRESENTATION EVALUATION GUIDE
Rate each statement on a scale of 1 (not demonstrated) to 5 (demonstrated).
☐ The monologue reflects the narrator's voice and character.
☐ The details used convey insights about the importance of the Lakota tradition.
☐ The speaker made appropriate eye contact with the audience.
☐ The speaker spoke at an appropriate volume.
☐ The speaker's pronunciation was clear.

EVIDENCE LOG

Before moving on to a new selection, go to your Evidence Log and record what you learned from "The Medicine Bag."

THE MEDICINE BAG

Comparing Text to Media

The video you will watch features an Apache girl participating in tests of strength and endurance. As you watch the selection, compare the public rite with the personal experience of the boy in "The Medicine Bag."

APACHE GIRL'S RITE OF PASSAGE

About National Geographic

The National Geographic Society was founded in 1888 and is one of the largest nonprofit scientific and educational institutions in the world. Its magazine *National Geographic* allows people to read about places and cultures that they might otherwise never experience. In addition to the magazine, the National Geographic Society produces films, videos, and television shows.

Apache Girl's Rite of Passage

Media Vocabulary

The following words or concepts will be useful to you as you analyze, discuss, and write about the video.

narration: commentary that accompanies a film	• The narration may clarify events or add background and further information.
audio: relating to the sound of a film	• Audio includes narration, music, and real-world sounds that are part of the video.
close-up: camera shot taken from a short distance	• Close-ups are used to show facial expressions and details.
contrast: amount of difference between bright and dark elements in filming and viewing	• The use of contrast can create atmosphere and change the mood.
pan: vertical or horizontal camera motion used to follow a subject	• A pan allows a cameraperson to follow action through a scene, or to show a wider or taller expanse on the screen.
synchronization (sync): coordination of motion and sound	• It's important that sounds and actions are in sync, as they would be in real life.

First Review MEDIA: VIDEO

Refer to the information below as you watch the video. As you watch, write down your observations and questions, noting time codes so you can revisit sections later.

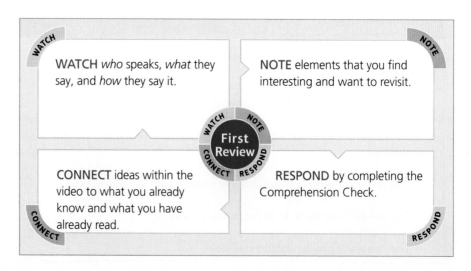

WATCH *who* speaks, *what* they say, and *how* they say it.

NOTE elements that you find interesting and want to revisit.

First Review

CONNECT ideas within the video to what you already know and what you have already read.

RESPOND by completing the Comprehension Check.

Apache Girl's Rite of Passage

National Geographic

BACKGROUND

For hundreds of years, the Mescalero Apaches were nomadic hunters and warriors who roamed throughout the American Southwest and northern Mexico. Today, this Native American tribe lives on a major reservation in New Mexico, in what was once the center of their homelands. The ceremony in this video is one of their most important and sacred traditions.

SCAN FOR MULTIMEDIA

NOTES

Comprehension Check

Complete the following items after you finish your first review of the video.

1. What is the purpose of Dachina's coming-of-age ritual?

2. What symbols are part of the ritual, and what does each represent?

3. What special places, events, and tasks are part of the ritual?

4. What happens to Dachina at the end of the four-day ritual?

🔲 **Notebook** Confirm your understanding of the video "Apache Girl's Rite of Passage" by writing a description of the setting, people, and events the video portrays.

Close Review

Watch the video again. Write down any new observations that seem important. What **questions** do you have? What can you **conclude**?

Analyze the Media

CITE TEXTUAL EVIDENCE
to support your answers.

Notebook Respond to these questions.

1. **(a) Analyze** In what order are the events presented in the video? **(b) Connect** What is the advantage of using this organizational structure for this piece?

2. **(a) Analyze** Who is narrating the video? **(b) Evaluate** Would the video have been more effective or less effective if the story had been told by Dachina? Explain.

3. **Essential Question:** *What are some milestones on the path to growing up?* How does Dachina's coming-of-age ritual symbolize the milestones she has reached on her path to adulthood? How do you think the ritual helps her achieve this goal? Support your response with evidence from the video.

LANGUAGE DEVELOPMENT

Media Vocabulary

narration	close-up	pan
audio	contrast	synchronization

Use the vocabulary words in your responses to the questions.

1. **(a)** How is the sequence of events conveyed in the video? **(b)** How is this different from the way the sequence of events is conveyed in the story "The Medicine Bag"?

2. **(a)** What tools does the video use to emphasize different parts of the ritual? **(b)** How does the video use each tool?

EVIDENCE LOG

Before moving on to a new selection, go to your Evidence Log and record what you learned from the "Apache Girl's Rite of Passage" video.

THE MEDICINE BAG

APACHE GIRL'S RITE OF PASSAGE

Writing to Compare

You have reviewed two selections about rites of passage for young Native Americans, a short story titled "The Medicine Bag" and a documentary video titled "Apache Girl's Rite of Passage." Now, deepen your analysis of the two selections, and express your observations in writing.

Assignment

Write a **comparison-and-contrast essay** in which you compare the rites of passage in the two selections about young Native Americans. Your essay should focus on the following:

- How the Lakota rite of passage and the Apache rite of passage are similar and different
- The advantages and disadvantages of text versus video for presenting the material

Prewriting

Gathering Evidence Use this chart to analyze how the text and the video each describe a young person's rite of passage. Think about the strengths and weaknesses of each medium.

	WHAT I LEARNED FROM THE SHORT STORY	WHAT I LEARNED FROM THE VIDEO	HOW TEXT COMPARES WITH VIDEO
Choice of narrator and impact on audience			
Story details that are emphasized			
How the young person feels about the rite of passage			

🗨 **Notebook** Respond to these questions.

1. **(a)** In what ways are the two rites of passage most similar? **(b)** In what ways are they most different?

2. How does seeing the Apache rite of passage on video help you to understand it more fully?

≣ STANDARDS
Speaking and Listening
Analyze the purpose of information presented in diverse media and formats and evaluate the motives behind its presentation.

Drafting

As you draft your essay, consider factors such as the presence of a narrator, as well as differences in how each medium shares the experience and shows the action. Then, evaluate the advantages and disadvantages of how each medium presents the ritual.

Structuring the Body of Your Essay You have two subtopics to write about in your essay. One involves similarities and differences. The other topic involves advantages and disadvantages. You may want to structure the body of your essay using this format.

I. Similarities and Differences

    A. Similarities between rites of passage

    B. Differences between rites of passage

II. Advantages and Disadvantages

    A. Advantages and Disadvantages of Text

    B. Advantages and Disadvantages of Video

Writing the Introduction The introduction of an essay should not only introduce your central idea but also engage the reader. Think of an image or a piece of information that you can work into your introduction to "hook" the reader's interest.

It is often a good idea to wait to write your introduction until after you have written the other parts of the essay. That way you will be able to clearly identify your central idea.

Review, Revise, and Edit

Once you have finished drafting, review your comparison-and-contrast essay.

- Ensure that your introduction and conclusion are closely related and that you have stated and supported your central idea.
- Add additional details, if needed, to support your statements.
- Add transitions to clearly indicate relationships among ideas.
- Proofread to ensure your essay is free from errors in spelling, punctuation, and grammar.

✐ EVIDENCE LOG

Before moving on to a new selection, go to your Evidence Log and record what you learned from the "Apache Girl's Rite of Passage" video.

☰ STANDARDS

Reading Informational Text
Evaluate the advantages and disadvantages of using different mediums to present a particular topic or idea.

Writing
Write informative/explanatory texts to examine a topic and convey ideas, concepts, and information through the selection, organization, and analysis of relevant content.

    a. Introduce a topic clearly, previewing what is to follow; organize ideas, concepts, and information into broader categories; include formatting, graphics, and multimedia when useful to aiding comprehension.

WRITING TO SOURCES

- THE MEDICINE BAG

- APACHE GIRL'S RITE OF PASSAGE

🔧 Tool Kit

Student Model of a
Nonfiction Narrative

ACADEMIC VOCABULARY

As you craft your narrative, consider using some of the academic vocabulary you learned in the beginning of the unit.

attribute
gratifying
persistent
notable
inspire

STANDARDS

Writing
Write narratives to develop real or imagined experiences or events using effective technique, relevant descriptive details, and well-structured event sequences.

Write a Nonfiction Narrative

You have just read a text and watched a video about rites of passage. In the short story "The Medicine Bag," a boy learns about his great-great-grandfather's vision quest—and he himself takes on the responsibility of family and Lakota tradition. In the "Apache Girl's Rite of Passage" video, a young woman goes through a four-day coming-of-age ritual to become an Apache woman.

Assignment

You have learned about two people who experience changes, learn about their heritage, and begin to think differently. Think about an event that changed your ideas and feelings or an event that changed the life of someone you know. Write a **nonfiction narrative** that answers this question:

> What event changed your understanding of yourself, or that of someone you know?

Elements of a Nonfiction Narrative

A **nonfiction narrative** tells the true story of events the writer or someone else has experienced. Writers adopt the first-person point of view (using *I* and *me*) to tell about their own experience. Writers adopt the third-person point of view (using *he* and *him, she* and *her, they* and *them,* etc.) to tell someone else's experience.

An effective nonfiction narrative contains these elements:

- characterizations of people who play different roles in the event
- a description of the impact of the event on the different people involved
- a clear sequence of events that unfolds naturally and logically
- narrative techniques such as dialogue, description, and pacing that effectively build the action
- a variety of transitional words, phrases, and clauses
- precise words, well-chosen quotations, vivid descriptive details, and powerful sensory language
- a conclusion reflecting on the experiences in the narrative

Model Nonfiction Narrative For a model of a well-crafted nonfiction narrative, see the Launch Text, "Red Roses."

Challenge yourself to find all the elements of an effective nonfiction narrative in the text. You will have an opportunity to review these elements as you prepare to write your own.

Prewriting / Planning

Choose Your Topic Reread the assignment. Consider the person and event you would like to highlight in your narrative. State your main idea in a sentence.

_____ changed how

(event or experience)

_____ viewed or felt about

(person)

_____ .

(something in life or the world)

Gather Evidence Evidence for a nonfiction narrative comes mainly from memories and experiences. A photo album or a conversation with a friend or relative may stimulate your memory and help you find a topic. There are many different types of evidence you can use to craft your nonfiction narrative.

TYPE OF EVIDENCE	EXPLANATION	YOUR EVIDENCE
anecdotes	brief stories that illustrate a point or key idea	
quotations	statements from personal interviews or conversations with the subjects of your narrative	
examples	facts, ideas, and events that support an idea or insight	

Connect Across Texts To effectively develop your nonfiction narrative, look again at the Launch Text and Anchor Texts. Understanding how an author uses narrative techniques will enable you to apply those techniques to your own writing. Ask yourself these questions and take notes on your findings:

- How does dialogue help you understand the people in the narrative better?

- How does the pacing of the story—how slowly or quickly it moves— add interest and convey the sequence of events?

- How does the author use description to help you appreciate what he or she experienced?

EVIDENCE LOG

Review your Evidence Log and identify key details you may want to cite in your nonfiction narrative.

STANDARDS

Writing
Write narratives to develop real or imagined experiences or events using effective technique, relevant descriptive details, and well-structured event sequences.

a. Engage and orient the reader by establishing a context and point of view and introducing a narrator and/or characters; organize an event sequence that unfolds naturally and logically.

b. Use narrative techniques, such as dialogue, pacing, description, and reflection, to develop experiences, events, and/or characters.

Drafting

Organize a Sequence of Events In a nonfiction narrative, the writer often sequences events in **chronological order** so that one event proceeds to the next in the order in which they actually happened.

- Use a timeline to organize your narrative so that it flows in chronological order.
- Start by introducing important people, as well as the setting and the background of the story.
- Then, add details in the order in which they occur.

The timeline here shows key events in the Launch Text. Think about how each event supports the message of the narrative.

LAUNCH TEXT

MODEL: "Red Roses" Personal Narrative Timeline

INTRODUCTION

The narrator, Lila, remembers a boy named Derek that no one liked, herself included.

1. Lila finds little presents from Derek hidden in her locker, desk, and jacket pocket.

2. She is annoyed and ignores Derek.

3. Her friends tease her about having a "boyfriend."

4. Derek presents her with a dozen roses.

5. Lila snaps at him; then she sees that he's about to cry.

CONCLUSION

Lila accepts the flowers to protect Derek from being called a crybaby, and she feels good about it.

Nonfiction Narrative Timeline

INTRODUCTION

1.

2.

3.

4.

5.

CONCLUSION

STANDARDS

Writing
Write narratives to develop real or imagined experiences or events using effective technique, relevant descriptive details, and well-structured event sequences.

a. Engage and orient the reader by establishing a context and point of view and introducing a narrator and/or characters; organize an event sequence that unfolds naturally and logically.
c. Use a variety of transition words, phrases, and clauses to convey sequence, signal shifts from one time frame or setting to another, and show the relationships among experiences and events.

Write a First Draft Refer to your prewriting notes and timeline, and then begin drafting your narrative. As you draft, strive to engage your audience by:

- Beginning with an exciting detail that hints at the story's conclusion.
- Keeping your audience's interest by showing, not telling.
- Interspersing dialogue to bring people's personalities to life.
- Concluding with an original observation about the importance of the event.

LANGUAGE DEVELOPMENT: AUTHOR'S STYLE

Create Cohesion: Transitions

Transitions are words and phrases that connect and show relationships among events and ideas. Transitional words and phrases perform an essential function in a narrative. They help the writer guide the reader through the sequence of events and show the relationships among ideas.

Read It

These sentences from the Launch Text use transitions to show specific connections among ideas and events.

- *Despite* **my standoffishness, Derek started leaving me little gifts.** (shows contrast)
- *And then*—**horrors!—I saw his bottom lip quiver.** (shows time order)
- **I** *immediately* **tossed them into the back of my closet when I got home.** (emphasizes)

Write It

As you draft your nonfiction narrative, choose transitions that accurately show specific relationships among your ideas. Transitions are especially important when connecting one paragraph to the next.

If you want to . . .	consider using one of these transitions
list or add ideas	*first of all, second, next, last, in addition*
show time order	*before, after, the next day, then*
compare	*also, equally, likewise*
contrast	*although, however, on the other hand, despite*
emphasize	*most of all, immediately, in fact*
show effect	*therefore, as a result, so, consequently*
illustrate or show	*for example, for instance, specifically*

PUNCTUATION

Make sure to punctuate transitional expressions correctly.

- Some transitional expressions at the beginning of a sentence should be followed by a comma; e.g., *In addition, The next day, Most of all.*

- Some transitional expressions in the middle of a sentence should be preceded by a comma (or a semicolon) and followed by a comma; e.g., *however, therefore, for example.*

▤ STANDARDS

Writing
Use a variety of transition words, phrases, and clauses to convey sequence, signal shifts from one time frame or setting to another, and show the relationships among experiences and events.

Revising

Evaluating Your Draft

Use the following checklist to evaluate the effectiveness of your first draft. Then, use your evaluation and the instructions on this page to guide your revision.

FOCUS AND ORGANIZATION	EVIDENCE AND ELABORATION	CONVENTIONS
☐ Describes a change in the life, ideas, or feelings of the writer or of another person.	☐ Develops the people in the narrative through dialogue and description.	☐ Attends to the norms and conventions of the discipline, especially the correct use and punctuation of transitions.
☐ Describes the experience that caused the writer's or another person's life, ideas, or feelings to change.	☐ Builds the action through dialogue, description, and pacing.	
☐ Has a clear sequence of events that unfolds naturally and logically.	☐ Captures the action and illustrates experiences and events using precise words, descriptive details, and sensory language.	
☐ Includes a conclusion that follows from and reflects on the experiences in the narrative.		

WORD NETWORK

Include interesting words from your Word Network in your narrative.

Revising for Focus and Organization

Clear Conclusion The conclusion of a nonfiction narrative clarifies the essay's overall message and provides readers with a sense of **resolution**, or completion. It resolves any conflicts or questions presented in the narrative. Reread the conclusion in the Launch Text, and then review your own conclusion. To increase clarity, begin by summarizing the relationship between the events and experiences that you present and the overall message that you would like to communicate. Strengthen your conclusion by reflecting on this relationship and sharing any insights you have gained from making these connections.

Revising for Evidence and Elaboration

Precise Language In order to craft a lively narrative that engages readers, avoid words and language that leave the reader with questions such as *What kind? How? In what way? How often?* and *To what extent?* As you review your draft, identify vague words that do not provide specific answers to those questions. As you revise, replace vague words with specific, precise words that convey your ideas more vividly and accurately. Here are some examples.

vague noun: *stuff*   use   *souvenirs, gifts, photos*

vague verb: *said*   use   *exclaimed, whispered, declared*

vague adjective: *pretty*   use   *attractive, exquisite, adorable*

vague adverb: *greatly*   use   *enormously, incredibly, remarkably*

STANDARDS

Writing
Write narratives to develop real or imagined experiences or events using effective technique, relevant descriptive details, and well-structured event sequences.

d. Use precise words and phrases, relevant descriptive details, and sensory language to capture the action and convey experiences and events.

e. Provide a conclusion that follows from and reflects on the narrated experiences or events.

PEER REVIEW

Exchange narratives with a classmate. Use the checklist to evaluate your classmate's nonfiction narrative and provide supportive feedback.

1. Is the point of view clear and are the people in the narrative well developed?

☐ yes ☐ no   If no, suggest how the writer might improve them.

2. Is there a clear sequence of events that unfolds chronologically and is clarified by transitions?

☐ yes ☐ no   If no, explain what confused you.

3. Does the narrative end with a conclusion that connects to and reflects on the events and experiences presented?

☐ yes ☐ no   If no, tell what you think might be missing.

4. What is the strongest part of your classmate's narrative? Why?

_____

_____

_____

Editing and Proofreading

Edit for Conventions Reread your draft for accuracy and consistency. Correct errors in grammar and word usage. Be sure you have included a variety of transitions to make connections among events.

Proofread for Accuracy Read your draft carefully, looking for errors in spelling and punctuation. As you proofread, make sure that any **dialogue**—the actual words spoken by people—is enclosed in quotation marks. A split dialogue is a quotation that is interrupted by additional information, such as the identification of the speaker. Refer to the Launch Text for examples of each type of dialogue.

Publishing and Presenting

Create a final version of your narrative. Share it with a small group so that your classmates can read it and make comments. In turn, review and comment on your classmates' work. As a group, discuss what your narratives have in common and the ways in which they are different. Always maintain a polite and respectful tone when commenting.

Reflecting

Reflect on what you learned as you wrote your narrative. In what ways did writing about past experiences and events help to heighten your understanding of them?

STANDARDS
Writing
• Produce clear and coherent writing in which the development, organization, and style are appropriate to task, purpose, and audience.
• With some guidance and support from peers and adults, develop and strengthen writing as needed by planning, revising, editing, rewriting, or trying a new approach, focusing on how well purpose and audience have been addressed.

ESSENTIAL QUESTION:

What are some milestones on the path to growing up?

Roads to adulthood may differ around the world, but they all have some recognizable landmarks in common. Learning about rites of passage in different cultures may echo your own experiences or may introduce you to a challenge you never considered. You will work in a group to continue your exploration of the experiences that change and define people as they grow up.

Small-Group Learning Strategies

Throughout your life, in school, in your community, in college, and in your career, you will continue to learn and work with others.

Look at these strategies and the actions you can take to practice them as you work in teams. Add ideas of your own for each step. Use these strategies during Small-Group Learning.

STRATEGY	ACTION PLAN
Prepare	• Complete your assignments so that you are prepared for group work. • Organize your thinking so you can contribute to your group's discussion. •
Participate fully	• Make eye contact to signal that you are listening and taking in what is being said. • Use text evidence when making a point. •
Support others	• Build off ideas from others in your group. • Invite others who have not yet spoken to do so. •
Clarify	• Paraphrase the ideas of others to ensure that your understanding is correct. • Ask follow-up questions. •

SCAN FOR MULTIMEDIA

CONTENTS

Working as a Team

1. **Discuss the Topic** In your group, discuss the following question:

   What defines an event in a young person's life as a milestone or rite of passage?

   As you take turns sharing your positions, be sure to provide examples for your choice. After all group members have shared, discuss the similarities and differences in your responses.

2. **List Your Rules** As a group, decide on the rules that you will follow as you work together. Two samples are provided. Add two more of your own. You may add or revise rules based on your experience together.

   - Everyone should participate in group discussions.
   - People should not interrupt.

   - _____

     _____

   - _____

     _____

3. **Apply the Rules** When you share what you have learned about growing up, make sure each person in the group contributes and follows the group's rules.

4. **Name Your Group** Choose a name that reflects the unit topic.

   Our group's name: _____

5. **Create a Communication Plan** Decide how you want to communicate with one another. For example, you might use online collaboration tools, email, or instant messaging.

   Our group's decision: _____

   _____

Making a Schedule

First, find out the due dates for the Small-Group activities. Then, preview the texts and activities with your group and make a schedule for completing the tasks.

SELECTION	ACTIVITIES	DUE DATE
You Are the Electric Boogaloo Just Be Yourself!		
Hanging Fire Translating Grandfather's House		
The Setting Sun and the Rolling World		

Working on Group Projects

Different projects require different roles. As your group works together, you'll find it more effective if each person has a specific role. Before beginning a project, discuss the necessary roles and choose one for each group member. Here are some possible roles; add your own ideas.

Project Manager: monitors the schedule and keeps everyone on task

Researcher: organizes research activities

Recorder: takes notes during group meetings

_____

_____

_____

_____

_____

_____

_____

LETTERS

You Are the Electric Boogaloo
Just Be Yourself!

Concept Vocabulary

As you perform your first read of "You Are the Electric Boogaloo" and "Just Be Yourself!" you will encounter these words.

immense	majestic	numerous

Context Clues To find the meaning of unfamiliar words, look for clues in the context, which is made up of the words that surround the unknown word in a text. Consider the following examples.

> **Example:** They **emblazoned** the crew's name on the T-shirts.
>
> **Context clue:** To get the name on the T-shirt, they **emblazoned** it.
>
> **Possible meaning: Emblazoned** means "inscribed" or "displayed a name on something."
>
> **Example:** It's about finding out who you really are on your own **terms** and in your own way.
>
> **Context clue:** You do it on your own **terms** and in your own way.
>
> **Possible meaning: Terms** means "conditions."

Apply your knowledge of context clues and other vocabulary strategies to determine the meanings of unfamiliar words you encounter during your first read.

First Read NONFICTION

Apply these strategies as you conduct your first read. You will have an opportunity to complete a close read after your first read.

:≡ STANDARDS

Reading Informational Text
By the end of the year, read and comprehend literary nonfiction at the high end of the grades 6–8 text complexity band independently and proficiently.

Language
Determine or clarify the meaning of unknown and multiple-meaning words or phrases based on *grade 8 reading and content,* choosing flexibly from a range of strategies.

  a. Use context as a clue to the meaning of a word or phrase.

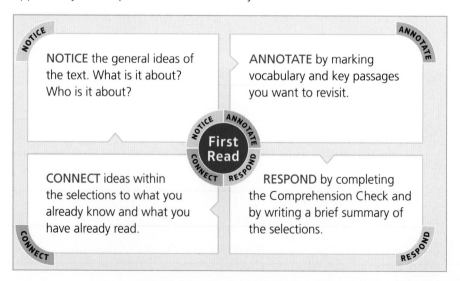

NOTICE the general ideas of the text. What is it about? Who is it about?

ANNOTATE by marking vocabulary and key passages you want to revisit.

CONNECT ideas within the selections to what you already know and what you have already read.

RESPOND by completing the Comprehension Check and by writing a brief summary of the selections.

First Read

NOTICE · ANNOTATE · CONNECT · RESPOND

Meet the Authors

Geoff Herbach is the author of the series *Stupid Fast* and other works of literature for young adults. His books have won the 2011 Cybils Award for best YA novel and the Minnesota Book Award. He lives in a log cabin in Minnesota and teaches creative writing.

Stephanie Pellegrin was in second grade when she wrote her first book. Pellegrin lives in Austin, Texas, and is involved with the Austin chapter of the Society of Children's Book Writers and Illustrators.

Backgrounds

You Are the Electric Boogaloo

Break dancing, or "breaking," is an athletic style of street dance that originated in New York City in the 1970s. Break dancing has continued to grow in popularity and is now performed in many different countries.

Just Be Yourself!

There is so much to learn, and no way to tell what the future will hold! This author writes a reassuring letter to her younger self saying that it will all work out in the end.

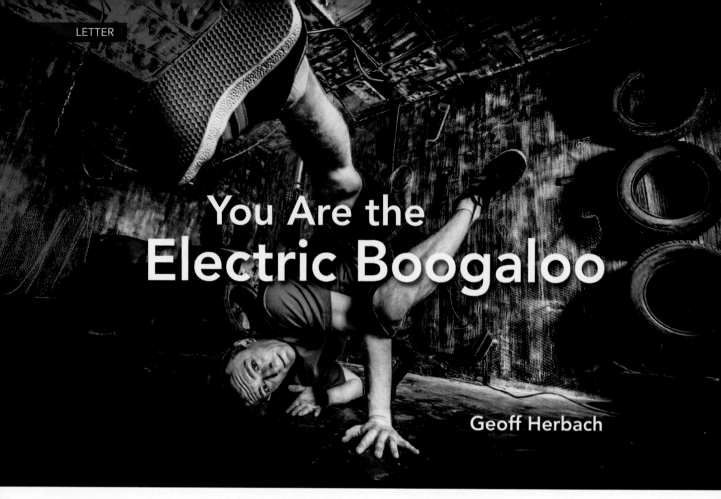

You Are the
Electric Boogaloo

Geoff Herbach

SCAN FOR
MULTIMEDIA

NOTES

1 Dear Teen Me,

2   Humiliation and hilarity are closely linked, my little friend. Don't lie there in bed, your guts churning, as you replay the terrible scene. I'm *glad* your shirt stuck to the floor.

3   I love your break-dancing crew, okay? You and your friends from the rural Wisconsin hills have that K-Tel how-to album (including posters and diagrams). You pop. You worm. You spin on your backs. You windmill. In fact, you're not even that bad!

4   I love your silver "butterfly" pants (with forty-six zippers) that burst red fabric when you spin. Beautiful.

5   I love it when you take your giant piece of cardboard (mobile dance floor) down the corner of Kase Street and Highway 81 to dance for traffic. Maybe you're right. Maybe a talent scout will be driving between Stitzer and Hazel Green. Maybe you *will* be discovered . . . Keep at it!

6   I love it that you have the guts to go into Kennedy Mall in Dubuque, Iowa, to dance across from Hot Sam's Pretzels. You and your buddies go for broke in front of a small, glum crowd (who all eat Hot Sam's pretzels), and when security comes to escort you out, you scream, "Dancing is not a crime!" I love that.

7   I especially love what happened at Dubuque's Five Flags Center a few months later. You and your crew (Breakin Fixation) challenged Dubuque's 4+1 Crew to a dance-off. You practiced. You got T-shirts with your crew name emblazoned on them. You worked hard, and you daydreamed harder. You imagined the roaring crowd lifting you onto their shoulders. You didn't expect the Five Flags floor to be so sticky. You didn't expect to sweat through your new shirt. You didn't expect the flesh of your back to be gripped and twisted so that it felt like it was on fire. You didn't expect it, but that's how it was, and it hurt so bad that instead of spinning into a windmill—the main part of your routine—you just writhed on the floor, howling.

8   So okay, sure, people laughed at you—and you know why? Because you looked really funny.

9   Don't stay awake worrying about it, though. Don't wonder what you should have done differently. Don't beat yourself up, gut boiling with embarrassment. Don't imagine punching out the members of 4+1—you can't blame them for wearing slick Adidas tracksuits that didn't grip the floor. Just go to sleep, kid, and get ready for the next dance. It's all going to be great, okay?

10   How do I know?

11   Because now, so many years later, you can barely remember your victories (although there were some). What you think about now are the high-wire acts, the epic falls, and the punishing jeers of your classmates. You think about how excellent it is that you got up, dusted yourself off and, with utter seriousness of purpose, tried again.

12   Your **immense** dorkiness as a teen will be the center of your artistic life, the center of your sense of humor, the center of ongoing friendships with so many of the kids you knew back then. (You guys never discuss the relatively boring victories—you only talk about the grand, **majestic**, hilarious failures.)

13   What if you hit it big at that contest? Would you be a professional break-dancer now? Would success have gone to your head? Or would you be a rich banker? Or a lawyer? Terrible!

14   But instead, you stuck to that floor, with your back on fire with the pain, and you screamed.

15   Don't beat yourself up over it, okay? Just relax. Keep dancing by the highway, you splendid little dork. ❧

Mark context clues or indicate another strategy you used that helped you determine meaning.

immense (ih MEHNS) *adj.*

MEANING:

majestic (muh JEHS tihk) *adj.*

MEANING:

Just Be Yourself!

Stephanie Pellegrin

SCAN FOR
MULTIMEDIA

NOTES

Mark context clues or indicate
another strategy you used that
helped you

numerous (NOO muhr uhs)
adj.

MEANING:

1   Dear Teen Me,

2   Psst! Hey! You in the corner of the library with your nose stuck in a book. Yes, you. Don't recognize me without that awful perm, do you? (Remind me again why you thought that was a good idea?)

3   Anyway, I hope you don't mind if I sit with you for a minute, but we need to talk. Don't worry about the "no talking in the library" rule. I'm sure we'll be fine. Librarians aren't as bad as they seem.

4   Judging from the hair and braces I'd have to guess you're in your junior year. Yes? Thought so. I'd forgotten how many lonely lunch hours you spent in the school library. You have some friends in the cafeteria that you could sit with, but you don't feel like you really fit in, do you? That's why you joined every school club you could. I just counted and you're in eighteen, not to mention the **numerous** after-school activities you're involved in. I mean honestly, you joined the ROTC.[1] You don't even *like* ROTC! And I won't even bother bringing up that time you tried ballet. I'm still having nightmares about the fifth position!

5   Let me ask you, how's it all working out? Not very well, am I right? By spending so much time trying to *find* yourself, you're slowly *losing* yourself. We don't all have one single rock-star talent, and honestly, I think those of us who don't are the lucky ones. Life isn't about finding the one thing you're good at and never doing anything else; it's about exploring yourself and

---

1. **ROTC** *n.* abbreviation for Reserve Officers Training Corps, a college-based training program for the U.S. military.

finding out who you really are on your own terms and in your own way. You don't have to exhaust yourself to do that.

6   Oh, don't be so down in the dumps about it. You'll eventually find something you're good at, I promise. It's a long, winding road to get there, but you'll find it. Being able to spend all day doing what you love (or one of the things that you love) is the most amazing feeling in the world. And no, I won't tell you what it is, so don't even ask me. Just remember to always be yourself, because there's nobody else who can do it for you. I think E. E. Cummings put it best when he said, "It takes courage to grow up and become who you really are."

7   Looks like the bell is about to ring so I'll leave you to your book. What are you reading, anyway? Oh, *The Last Battle* by C. S. Lewis. I should have guessed. You should give those Harry Potter books a try. I saw you roll your eyes! I know they seem like just another fad, but trust me, they're better than you think. They've got a real future! ❧

NOTES

Comprehension Check

Complete the following items after you finish your first read. Review and clarify details with your group.

YOU ARE THE ELECTRIC BOOGALOO

1. What activity does the author focus on in his letter to his teenage self?

2. What does the teen author scream when security comes to escort him out of the mall?

JUST BE YOURSELF!

3. Why did the author join so many clubs when she was a teenager?

4. What does the author tell her teen self is happening as a result of all the time she is spending trying to find herself?

5. 🗐 **Notebook** Confirm your understanding by writing a short summary of each letter.

- -

RESEARCH

Research to Clarify Choose at least one unfamiliar detail from one of the letters. Briefly research that detail. In what way does the information you learned shed light on an aspect of the letter?

YOU ARE THE ELECTRIC
BOOGALOO | JUST BE YOURSELF!

💡 TIP

GROUP DISCUSSION

As you discuss the letters, compare your own experiences with those of the authors.

🔗 WORD NETWORK

Add interesting words related to rites of passage from the text to your Word Network.

≔ STANDARDS

Reading Informational Text
Determine the meaning of words and phrases as they are used in a text, including figurative, connotative, and technical meanings; analyze the impact of specific word choices on meaning and tone, including analogies or allusions to other texts.

Language
• Determine or clarify the meaning of unknown and multiple-meaning words or phrases based on *grade 8 reading and content,* choosing flexibly from a range of strategies.
  b. Use common, grade-appropriate Greek or Latin affixes and roots as clues to the meaning of a word.
  c. Consult general and specialized reference materials, both print and digital, to find the pronunciation of a word or determine or clarify its precise meaning or its part of speech.
• Demonstrate understanding of figurative language, word relationships, and nuances in word meanings.
  c. Distinguish among the connotations of words with similar denotations.

Close Read the Text

With your group, revisit sections of the text you marked during your First Read. **Annotate** what you notice. What **questions** do you have? What can you **conclude**?

Close Read

- -

Analyze the Text

> **CITE TEXTUAL EVIDENCE**
> to support your answers.

📓 **Notebook** Complete the activities.

1. **Review and Clarify** With your group, reread paragraph 13 of "You Are the Electric Boogaloo." What do you think the author means by asking these questions? What is he trying to say about the importance of failure?

2. **Present and Discuss** Now, work with your group to share the passages from the text that you found especially important. Take turns presenting your passages. Discuss what you noticed in the text, what questions you asked, and what conclusions you reached.

3. **Essential Question:** *What are some milestones on the path to growing up?* What kinds of milestones do the letters include? Why are they important? Discuss with your group.

LANGUAGE DEVELOPMENT

Concept Vocabulary

immense	majestic	numerous

Why These Words? The concept vocabulary words from the text are related. With your group, determine what the words have in common. Record your ideas, and add another word that fits the category.

Practice

📓 **Notebook** Confirm your understanding of the concept vocabulary words by using each word in a sentence.

Word Study

Latin Suffix: -ous The Latin suffix *-ous* means "characterized by" or "full of" and often indicates that a word is an adjective. In "Just Be Yourself!," the author uses the word *numerous* to describe the after-school activities she was involved in as a teen. Based on your understanding of the suffix *-ous,* write a definition for the word *numerous.* Then, explain how the suffix contributes to the meanings of the following words: *continuous, desirous, prosperous.*

Analyze Craft and Structure

Author's Word Choice: Tone An author's **tone** is his or her attitude toward a subject or audience. An author's tone may be described using adjectives such as *serious, humorous, casual,* or *formal.* The tone of a literary work is often conveyed through the author's **word choice,** or the individual words as well as the phrases and expressions he or she uses.

To develop the tone of a literary work, an author considers the **connotations** of the words he or she uses, or the ideas and feelings associated with the words. Connotations often suggest meaning beyond the word's dictionary definition, or **denotation**. A word's connotations may be positive or negative. For example, the words *postpone* and *procrastinate* have similar denotations—"to put off until a later time." However, the word *postpone* has a more positive connotation that suggests that something is being rescheduled due to circumstances beyond one's control. In contrast, the word *procrastinate* has the negative connotation of putting something off because one doesn't feel like doing it.

TIP

PROCESS

As you work with your group to analyze the authors' word choices, discuss any differences in the connotations you have for specific words.

Practice

CITE TEXTUAL EVIDENCE to support your answers.

Work with your group to analyze the authors' word choices and how these choices work together to convey the tone of each letter. Use the charts to take notes as you review each letter. Consult a dictionary to determine the precise denotation of each word.

YOU ARE THE ELECTRIC BOOGALOO	
WORD AND ITS DENOTATION	CONNOTATIONS
Writer's tone:	

JUST BE YOURSELF!	
WORD AND ITS DENOTATION	CONNOTATIONS
Writer's tone:	

Conventions

Verb Moods Verbs can express different **moods**. Speakers and writers express their attitudes through the verbs they use, as Geoff Herbach shows in "You Are the Electric Boogaloo."

- Verbs in the **indicative mood** state facts and opinions.
- Verbs in the **imperative mood** issue commands or make requests. This mood can also be used to give a strong suggestion or advice.
- Verbs in the **interrogative mood** pose, or ask, questions.

Types of Verb Moods Use the chart to review three types of verb moods.

INDICATIVE	IMPERATIVE	INTERROGATIVE
States, or declares, an idea	Gives a command or direction	Asks a question
Librarians aren't as bad as they seem.	Just be yourself!	What are you reading, anyway?

Read It

Work individually. Find an example of one sentence in the indicative, one in the interrogative, and one in the imperative mood in "You Are the Electric Boogaloo."

Write It

Sometimes writers and speakers shift between indicative and imperative moods in a jarring or confusing way. Review the example below, and then correct the improper mood shift in the following sentences.

> EXAMPLE
>
> Students should come to class prepared. Arrive on time. *[improper shift to imperative]*
>
> Students should come to class prepared. They should arrive on time.

1. Dancers should try to perform in public. Wear colorful costumes!

2. Authors may write about themselves, and use what you know.

STANDARDS

Writing
Conduct short research projects to answer a question, drawing on several sources and generating additional related, focused questions that allow for multiple avenues of exploration.

Speaking and Listening
- Present claims and findings, emphasizing salient points in a focused, coherent manner with relevant evidence, sound valid reasoning, and well-chosen details; use appropriate eye contact, adequate volume, and clear pronunciation.
- Integrate multimedia and visual displays into presentations to clarify information, strengthen claims and evidence, and add interest.

Language
Demonstrate command of the conventions of standard English grammar and usage while writing or speaking.

c. Form and use verbs in the indicative, imperative, interrogative, conditional, and subjunctive mood.
d. Recognize and correct inappropriate shifts in verb voice and mood.

Speaking and Listening

Assignment

Work with your group to conduct research for a **visual presentation** on one of the following topics:

☐ Write and present **illustrated instructions** in which you explain how to perform one of the break-dancing steps mentioned in "You Are the Electric Boogaloo."

☐ Write and deliver an **illustrated informational report** on the history and culture of break-dancing.

Project Plan Make a list of tasks that your group will need to perform. Decide which group members will carry out each task. Use this chart to organize your plans.

TASK	WHO	PART IN PRESENTATION

📝 EVIDENCE LOG

Before moving on to a new selection, go to your Evidence Log, and record what you learned from "You Are the Electric Boogaloo" and "Just Be Yourself!"

Conduct Research As you conduct research, be sure to use a variety of reliable print and digital sources. Remember to find useful visual aids that will help your audience understand and visualize the information in your presentation.

Present and Evaluate After you have rehearsed your presentation, deliver it to the class. Remember to speak clearly and make eye contact with your audience regularly. After your presentation, evaluate your performance as well as the performances of other groups.

Hanging Fire
Translating Grandfather's House

Concept Vocabulary

As you perform your first read of "Hanging Fire" and "Translating Grandfather's House," you will encounter these words.

horizon	awakenings	beaming

Context Clues If these words are unfamiliar to you, try using context clues—other words and phrases that appear in a text—to help you determine their meanings. Here are three types of context clues that might help you as you read.

Synonym Gregory has one **sibling,** his <u>brother</u> Anthony.

Contrast of Ideas: The winner was **elated,** but the loser was <u>filled with sadness.</u>

Explanation: The **cupola** on the roof looked like a <u>little dog house.</u>

Apply your knowledge of context clues and other vocabulary strategies to determine the meanings of unfamiliar words you encounter during your first read.

First Read POETRY

Apply these strategies as you conduct your first read. You will have an opportunity to complete a close read after your first read.

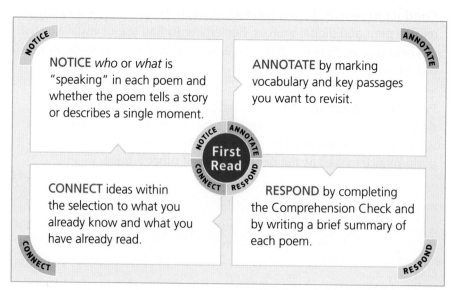

NOTICE *who* or *what* is "speaking" in each poem and whether the poem tells a story or describes a single moment.

ANNOTATE by marking vocabulary and key passages you want to revisit.

CONNECT ideas within the selection to what you already know and what you have already read.

RESPOND by completing the Comprehension Check and by writing a brief summary of each poem.

First Read

STANDARDS

Reading Literature
By the end of the year, read and comprehend literature, including stories, dramas, and poems, at the high end of grades 6–8 text complexity band independently and proficiently.

Language
Determine or clarify the meaning of unknown and multiple-meaning words or phrases based on *grade 8 reading and content,* choosing flexibly from a range of strategies.
a. Use context as a clue to the meaning of a word or phrase.

Meet the Poets

Audre Lorde (1934–1992) was a Caribbean American poet and civil rights activist. Her poetry and writing addresses social prejudices and injustices. She was the Poet Laureate of New York from 1991 until her death.

E.J. Vega (b. 1961) is an award-winning poet, novelist, and journalist. He was born in Cuba and worked as a sailor on tugboats and ocean barges. He has degrees in writing, literature, and journalism from Brooklyn College and Columbia University. He lives in New York City.

Backgrounds

Hanging Fire

Adolescence can be a challenging stage of life, with childhood left behind but adulthood not yet achieved. In "Hanging Fire," Audre Lorde explores the frustrating feelings that can arise from the contradictions of being a "young adult."

Translating Grandfather's House

In the poem, E.J. Vega mentions Zorro, a popular fictional character, originally created in 1919 by writer Johnston McCulley. In McCulley's novel, Zorro is a heroic outlaw and a skilled sword fighter who wears a mask to hide his true identity—he is actually a wealthy noble named Diego de la Vega.

Hanging Fire

Audre Lorde

I am fourteen
and my skin has betrayed me
the boy I cannot live without
still sucks his thumb
5 in secret
how come my knees are
always so ashy
what if I die
before morning
10 and momma's in the bedroom
with the door closed.

I have to learn how to dance
in time for the next party
my room is too small for me
15 suppose I die before graduation
they will sing sad melodies
but finally
tell the truth about me
There is nothing I want to do
20 and too much
that has to be done
and momma's in the bedroom
with the door closed.

Nobody even stops to think
25 about my side of it
I should have been on Math Team
my marks were better than his
why do I have to be
the one
30 wearing braces
I have nothing to wear tomorrow
will I live long enough
to grow up
and momma's in the bedroom
35 with the door closed.

Translating
Grandfather's
House

E. J. Vega

According to my sketch,
Rows of lemon & mango
Trees frame the courtyard
Of Grandfather's stone
5   And clapboard home;
The shadow of a palomino[1]
Gallops on the lip
Of the horizon.

The teacher says
10 The house is from
Some Zorro
Movie I've seen.

"Ask my mom," I protest.
"She was born there—
15 Right there on the second floor!"

Crossing her arms she moves on.

Memories once certain as rivets
Become confused as awakenings
In strange places and I question
20 The house, the horse, the wrens
Perched on the slate roof—
The roof Oscar Jartín
Tumbled from one hot Tuesday,
Installing a new weather vane;
25 (He broke a shin and two fingers).
Classmates finish drawings of New York City
Housing projects[2] on Navy Street.
I draw one too, with wildgrass
Rising from sidewalk cracks like widows.
30 In big round letters I title it:

GRANDFATHER'S HOUSE

Beaming, the teacher scrawls
An A+ in the corner and tapes
It to the green blackboard.

To the green blackboard.

---

1. **palomino** (pal uh MEE noh) *n.* horse with a light golden coat and a white mane and tail.
2. **housing projects** *n.* apartment buildings subsidized by the government, usually for low-income households.

NOTES

Mark context clues or indicate another strategy you used that helped you determine meaning.

horizon (huh RY zuhn) *n.*
MEANING:

awakenings
(uh WAY kuhn ihngz) *n.*
MEANING:

beaming (BEEM ihng) *v.*
MEANING:

Comprehension Check

Complete the following items after you finish your first read. Review and clarify details with your group.

HANGING FIRE

1. In the first stanza, what is the speaker unhappy about?

2. Where is momma in the poem?

3. What does the speaker have to learn before the next party?

TRANSLATING GRANDFATHER'S HOUSE

4. What is the subject of the speaker's first drawing?

5. What is the teacher's reaction to the speaker's first drawing?

6. What grade does the speaker receive on the second drawing?

7. ⊟ **Notebook** Confirm your understanding by writing a short summary of each poem.

RESEARCH

Research to Clarify Choose one unfamiliar detail from one of the poems. Briefly research that detail. In what way does the information you learned shed light on an aspect of the poem?

Research to Explore Choose something that interests you from the texts, and perform research on it. Share your findings with your group.

POETRY COLLECTION

TIP

GROUP DISCUSSION

Allow each member of the group to share reactions to the poems. Discuss the similarities and differences in group members' reactions.

⊹ WORD NETWORK

Add interesting words related to rites of passage from the text to your Word Network.

☰ STANDARDS

Reading Literature
• Determine a theme or central idea of a text and analyze its development over the course of the text, including its relationship to the characters, setting, and plot; provide an objective summary of the text.
• Compare and contrast the structure of two or more texts and analyze how the differing structure of each text contributes to its meaning and style.

Language
Determine or clarify the meaning of unknown and multiple-meaning words or phrases based on *grade 8 reading and content*, choosing flexibly from a range of strategies.
 b. Use common, grade-appropriate Greek or Latin affixes and roots as clues to the meaning of a word.

Close Read the Text

With your group, revisit sections of the text you marked during your first read. **Annotate** what you notice. What **questions** do you have? What can you **conclude**?

Analyze the Text

CITE TEXTUAL EVIDENCE to support your answers.

🗒 **Notebook** Complete the activities.

1. **Review and Clarify** With your group, reread "Hanging Fire." Identify the lines that are repeated throughout the poem. What does this repetition suggest about the relationship between the speaker and the mother?

2. **Present and Discuss** Now, work with your group to share the passages from the poems that you found especially important. Take turns presenting your passages. Discuss what you noticed in the text, what questions you asked, and what conclusions you reached.

3. **Essential Question:** *What are some milestones on the path to growing up?* What have you learned about growing up by reading these poems? Discuss with your group.

LANGUAGE DEVELOPMENT

Concept Vocabulary

horizon	awakenings	beaming

Why These Words? The concept vocabulary words from the text are related. With your group, determine what the words have in common. Write your ideas, and add another word that fits the category.

Practice

🗒 **Notebook** Confirm your understanding of these words from the text by using them in sentences. Provide context clues for each word.

Word Study

Etymology: *horizon* In "Translating Grandfather's House," the author uses the word *horizon*. The etymology, or word origin, of *horizon* can be traced back to the Greek word *horos,* meaning "boundary marker." The related Greek word *horizon* means "limiting" or "creating a boundary." How does understanding the origin of the word horizon help you to better understand its meaning? How does this knowledge enhance your appreciation of the poem?

Analyze Craft and Structure

Forms of Poetry Two major **forms of poetry** are lyric poetry and narrative poetry. Understanding a poem's structure and style will help you to analyze the meaning of a poem and identify a **theme,** or insight about life that it conveys.

- The purpose of **lyric poetry** is to create a single, vivid impression of an object, person, or moment in time. Lyric poems are generally short. They may be rhymed or unrhymed, but most lyric poems contain musical qualities that help to convey meaning. These musical effects are created through the repetition of words and sounds as well as the rhythm created by the strong and weak stresses a reader naturally places on words.

- A **narrative poem** tells a story and includes the main elements of a short story—characters, setting, conflict, and plot. A narrative poem may also include musical effects, but generally not to the same degree that a lyric poem does.

Practice

> **CITE TEXTUAL EVIDENCE**
> to support your answers.

Analyze the poems and fill in the charts with your findings. Then, answer the questions that follow. Share your responses with your group.

HANGING FIRE	
ELEMENTS OF LYRIC POETRY	**EXAMPLES/EVIDENCE**
musical effects (repetition of words and sounds; rhythms)	
expresses thoughts and feelings	
details create a single, vivid impression	

TRANSLATING GRANDFATHER'S HOUSE	
ELEMENTS OF NARRATIVE POETRY	**EXAMPLES/EVIDENCE**
characters	
setting	
conflict	

1. **(a)** What overall impression does "Hanging Fire" create? **(b)** What theme is conveyed by the poem?

2. **(a)** How is the conflict resolved in "Translating Grandfather's House"? **(b)** What theme does the poem suggest?

POETRY COLLECTION

Author's Style

Word Choice Writers carefully choose words to create meaning. The poems you have just read are carefully crafted to convey each speaker's personality, situation, and attitude. When you analyze poetry, pay attention to word choice and ask the following:

- Has the poet used figurative language, like similes or metaphors, or more straightforward descriptions?
- Has the poet used slang, informal language, or formal language?
- Has the poet repeated ideas, words, or phrases?

Once you have examined the word choices, draw conclusions about how the word choices help to build the speaker's character and enhance the overall meaning of the poem.

Read It

In the chart, mark words from each passage that are descriptive or interesting in some way. Describe how the word choice helps reveal the speaker's personality and situation. Then, find one more passage from each poem that reveals something about the speaker, and share it with your group.

PASSAGE FROM THE TEXT	WHAT WORD CHOICE REVEALS ABOUT THE SPEAKER
I am fourteen / and my skin has betrayed me / the boy I cannot live without / still sucks his thumb / in secret . . . ("Hanging Fire," lines 1–5)	
Memories once certain as rivets / Become confused as awakenings / In strange places and I question / The house, the horse, the wrens / Perched on the slate roof— . . . ("Translating Grandfather's House," lines 17–21)	

Write It

Choose one stanza from either "Hanging Fire" or "Translating Grandfather's House." Rewrite the stanza as if it were spoken by a different speaker. Choose words that help to reveal your speaker's distinct personality. Then, share your stanzas with the group, and discuss how your versions create a new tone that fits the speakers you created.

STANDARDS

Reading Literature
Determine the meaning of words and phrases as they are used in a text, including figurative and connotative meanings; analyze the impact of specific word choices on meaning and tone, including analogies or allusions to other texts.

Speaking and Listening
Engage effectively in a range of collaborative discussions with diverse partners on grade 8 topics, texts, and issues, building on others' ideas and expressing their own clearly.

a. Come to discussions prepared, having read or researched material under study; explicitly draw on that preparation by referring to evidence on the topic, text, or issue to probe and reflect on ideas under discussion.

c. Pose questions that connect the ideas of several speakers and respond to others' questions and comments with relevant evidence, observations, and ideas.

d. Acknowledge new information expressed by others, and, when warranted, qualify or justify their own views in light of the evidence presented.

Speaking and Listening

Assignment

Conduct a **group discussion** about "Hanging Fire" and "Translating Grandfather's House." Draw on the texts to explore and reflect on ideas. Choose one of the following topics.

☐ Explore the **aspects of growing up** that are described in each poem. Are these experiences specific to the speakers or more universal in nature? Support your ideas with details from the poems as well as your own experiences.

☐ **Compare and contrast the speakers** in the two poems. In what ways are they similar? How do they differ? Would the two become friends if they were to meet? Use details from the poems to support your analysis.

Discussion Preparation Identify examples from the text that support your ideas. Record the examples in the chart, and write notes and ideas related to the discussion topic. Then, join with others in your group and compare notes:

HANGING FIRE	TRANSLATING GRANDFATHER'S HOUSE

Holding the Discussion As your group discusses the information in the chart, take turns asking each other questions. Look for connections among the various ideas. Listen carefully to other group members and clarify anything you do not understand. Be open to changing your opinions, and at all times be respectful of others' ideas.

EVIDENCE LOG

Before moving on to a new selection, record what you learned from "Hanging Fire" and "Translating Grandfather's House" in your Evidence Log.

The Setting Sun and the Rolling World

Concept Vocabulary

As you perform your first read of "The Setting Sun and the Rolling World," you will encounter these words.

patronized	obligations	psychological

Base Words If these words are unfamiliar to you, analyze each one to see if it contains a base word, or "inside" word, you know. Then, use your knowledge of the "inside" word, to determine the meaning of the unfamiliar word. Here is an example of how to apply this strategy.

Unfamiliar Word: *murkiness*

Familiar "Inside" Word: *murky*

Context: But just as dust quickly settles over a glittering pebble revealed by a hoe, so a **murkiness** hid the gleam . . .

Conclusion: The word **murkiness** must mean something dusty or cloudy that makes it hard to see.

Apply your knowledge of base words and other vocabulary strategies to determine the meanings of unfamiliar words you encounter during your first read of "The Setting Sun and the Rolling World."

First Read FICTION

Apply these strategies as you conduct your first read. You will have an opportunity to complete a close read after your first read.

NOTICE *whom* the *story* is about, *what* happens, *where* and *when* it happens, and *why* those involved react as they do.

ANNOTATE by marking vocabulary and key passages you want to revisit.

First Read

CONNECT ideas within the selection to what you already know and what you have already read.

RESPOND by completing the Comprehension Check and by writing a brief summary of the selection.

About the Author

Charles Mungoshi (b. 1947) is a Zimbabwean writer. He grew up working on his father's farm, where the time he spent alone inspired him to start creating stories. He writes in both English and Shona, one of the main languages spoken in Zimbabwe. His works have won the International PEN Award and the Commonwealth Writers Prize.

STANDARDS

Reading Literature
By the end of the year, read and comprehend literature, including stories, dramas, and poems, at the high end of grades 6–8 text complexity band independently and proficiently.

Language
Demonstrate understanding of figurative language, word relationships, and nuances in word meanings.

b. Use the relationship between particular words to better understand each of the words.

The *Setting* Sun *and* the **Rolling World**

Charles Mungoshi

BACKGROUND

Zimbabwe is a landlocked country in Africa. Traditionally, many Zimbabweans have made a living farming the land. When farming goes well, food is plentiful, but farmers are always at the mercy of unpredictable rainfall and weather.

SCAN FOR MULTIMEDIA

NOTES

1　Old Musoni raised his dusty eyes from his hoe and the unchanging stony earth he had been tilling and peered into the sky. The white speck whose sound had disturbed his work and thoughts was far out at the edge of the yellow sky, near the horizon. Then it disappeared quickly over the southern rim of the sky and he shook his head. He looked to the west. Soon the sun would go down. He looked over the sunblasted land and saw the shadows creeping east, blearier and taller with every moment that the sun shed each of its rays. Unconsciously wishing for rain and relief, he bent down again to his work and did not see his son, Nhamo, approaching.

2　Nhamo crouched in the dust near his father and greeted him. The old man half raised his back, leaning against his hoe, and said what had been bothering him all day long.

3　"You haven't changed your mind?"

4　"No, father."

5　There was a moment of silence. Old Musoni scraped earth off his hoe.

6　"Have you thought about this, son?"

7　"For weeks, father."

8　"And you think that's the only way?"

9　"There is no other way."

10　The old man felt himself getting angry again. But this would be the last day he would talk to his son. If his son was going away, he must not be angry. It would be equal to a curse. He himself had taken chances before, in his own time, but he felt too much of a father. He had worked and slaved for his family and the land had not betrayed him. He saw nothing now but disaster and death for his son out there in the world. Lions had long since vanished but he knew of worse animals of prey, animals that wore redder claws than the lion's, beasts that would not leave an unprotected homeless boy alone. He thought of the white metal bird and he felt remorse.

11   "Think again. You will end dead. Think again, of us, of your family. We have a home, poor though it is, but can you think of a day you have gone without?"

12   "I have thought everything over, father, I am convinced this is the only way out."

13   "There is no only way out in the world. Except the way of the land, the way of the family."

14   "The land is overworked and gives nothing now, father. And the family is almost broken up."

15   The old man got angry. Yes, the land is useless. True, the family tree is uprooted and it dries in the sun. True, many things are happening that haven't happened before, that we did not think would happen, ever. But nothing is more certain to hold you together than the land and a home, a family. And where do you think you are going, a mere beardless kid with the milk not yet dry on your baby nose? What do you think you will do in the great treacherous world where men twice your age have gone and returned with their backs broken—if they returned at all? What do you know of life? What do you know of the false honey bird that leads you the whole day through the forest to a snake's nest? But all he said was: "Look. What have you asked me and I have denied you? What, that I have, have I not given you for the asking?"

16   "All. You have given me all, father." And here, too, the son felt hampered, **patronized** and his pent-up fury rolled through him. It showed on his face but stayed under control. You have given me damn all and nothing. You have sent me to school and told me the importance of education, and now you ask me to throw it on the rubbish heap and scrape for a living on this tired cold shell of the moon. You ask me to forget it and muck around in this slow dance of death with you. I have this one chance of making my own life, once in all eternity, and now you are jealous. You are afraid of your own death. It is, after all, your own death. I shall be around a while yet. I will make my way home if a home is what I need. I am armed more than you think and wiser than you can dream of. But all he said, too, was:

17   "Really, father, have no fear for me. I will be all right. Give me this chance. Release me from all **obligations** and pray for me."

Mark base words or indicate another strategy you used that helped you determine meaning.

patronized (PAY truh nyzd) *v.*

MEANING:

obligations (ob lih GAY shuhnz) *n.*

MEANING:

18   There was a spark in the old man's eyes at these words of his son. But just as dust quickly settles over a glittering pebble revealed by the hoe, so a murkiness hid the gleam in the old man's eye. Words are handles made to the smith's[1] fancy and are liable to break under stress. They are too much fat on the hard unbreaking sinews of life.

19   "Do you know what you are doing, son?"

20   "Yes."

21   "Do you know what you will be a day after you leave home?"

22   "Yes, father."

23   "A homeless, nameless vagabond living on dust and rat's droppings, living on thank-yous, sleeping up a tree or down a ditch, in the rain, in the sun, in the cold, with nobody to see you, nobody to talk to, nobody at all to tell your dreams to. Do you know what it is to see your hopes come crashing down like an old house out of season and your dreams turning to ash and dung without a tang of salt in your skull? Do you know what it is to live without a single hope of ever seeing good in your own lifetime?" And to himself: Do you know, young bright ambitious son of my loins, the ruins of time and the pains of old age? Do you know how to live beyond a dream, a hope, a faith? Have you seen black despair, my son?

24   "I know it, father. I know enough to start on. The rest I shall learn as I go on. Maybe I shall learn to come back."

25   The old man looked at him and felt: Come back where? Nobody comes back to ruins. You will go on, son. Something you don't know will drive you on along deserted plains, past ruins and more ruins, on and on until there is only one ruin left: yourself. You will break down, without tears, son. You are human, too. Learn to the *haya*—the rain bird, and heed its warning of coming storm: plow no more, it says. And what happens if the storm catches you far, far out on the treeless plain? What, then, my son?

26   But he was tired. They had taken over two months discussing all this. Going over the same ground like animals at a drinking place until, like animals, they had driven the water far deep into the stony earth, until they had sapped all the blood out of life and turned it into a grim skeleton, and now they were creating a stampede on the dust, groveling for water. Mere thoughts. Mere words. And what are words? Trying to grow a fruit tree in the wilderness.

27   "Go son, with my blessings. I give you nothing. And when you remember what I am saying you will come back. The land is still yours. As long as I am alive you will find a home waiting for you."

28   "Thank you, father."

---

1. **smith** *n.* blacksmith; artisan who creates objects out of iron.

Mark base words or indicate another strategy you used that helped you determine meaning.

psychological (sy kuh LAHJ ih kuhl) *adj.*

MEANING:

29   "Before you go, see Chiremba. You are going out into the world. You need something to strengthen yourself. Tell him I shall pay him. Have a good journey, son."

30   "Thank you, father."

31   Nhamo smiled and felt a great love for his father. But there were things that belonged to his old world that were just lots of humbug[2] on the mind, empty load, useless scrap. He would go to Chiremba but he would burn the charms as soon as he was away from home and its sickening environment. A man stands on his feet and guts. Charms were for you—so was God, though much later. But for us now the world is godless, no charms will work. All that is just the opium you take in the dark in the hope of a light. You don't need that now. You strike a match for a light. Nhamo laughed.

32   He could be so easily light-hearted. Now his brain worked with a fury only known to visionaries. The **psychological** ties were now broken, only the biological tied him to his father. He was free. He too remembered the aeroplane which his father had seen just before their talk. Space had no bounds and no ties. Floating laws ruled the darkness and he would float with the fiery balls. He was the sun, burning itself out every second and shedding tons of energy which it held in its power, giving it the thrust to drag its brood wherever it wanted to. This was the law that held him. The mystery that his father and ancestors had failed to grasp and which had caused their being wiped off the face of the earth. This thinking reached such a pitch that he began to sing, imitating as intimately as he could Satchmo's[3] voice: "What a wonderful world." It was Satchmo's voice that he turned to when he felt buoyant.

33   Old Musoni did not look at his son as he left him. Already, his mind was trying to focus at some point in the dark unforeseeable future. Many things could happen and while he still breathed he would see that nothing terribly painful happened to his family, especially to his stubborn last born, Nhamo. Tomorrow, before sunrise, he would go to see Chiremba and ask him to throw bones over the future of his son. And if there were a couple of ancestors who needed appeasement, he would do it while he was still around.

34   He noticed that the sun was going down and he scraped the earth off his hoe.

35   The sun was sinking slowly, bloody red, blunting and blurring all the objects that had looked sharp in the light of day. Soon a chilly wind would blow over the land and the cold cloudless sky would send down beads of frost like white ants over the unprotected land. ❧

---

2. **humbug** *n.* nonsense.
3. **Satchmo** nickname for famous American jazz musician Louis Armstrong (1901–1971).

Discuss It How does this video help you understand more about life in a rural village like the one where Nhamo lived?

Write your response before sharing your ideas.

STORIES OF ZIMBABWEAN WOMEN

SCAN FOR MULTIMEDIA

Comprehension Check

Complete the following items after you finish your first read.
Review and clarify details with your group.

1. Why does Nhamo want to leave his family?

2. Why does Old Musoni want him to stay?

3. How does Nhamo feel about getting charms from Chiremba?

4. **Notebook** Confirm your understanding of the story by writing a short summary.

- -

RESEARCH

Research to Clarify Choose at least one unfamiliar detail from the story. Briefly research that detail. How does the information you learned shed light on an aspect of the story?

THE SETTING SUN AND THE
ROLLING WORLD

WORD NETWORK

Add interesting words
about growing up from the
text to your Word Network.

STANDARDS

Reading Literature
Analyze how differences in the
points of view of the characters
and the audience or reader create
such effects as suspense or humor.
Language
Determine or clarify the meaning
of unknown and multiple-meaning
words or phrases based on
grade 8 reading and content,
choosing flexibly from a range of
strategies.

　b. Use common, grade-
　appropriate Greek or Latin
　affixes and roots as clues to the
　meaning of a word.

　c. Consult general and
　specialized reference materials,
　both print and digital, to find
　the pronunciation of a word or
　determine or clarify its precise
　meaning or its part of speech.

Close Read the Text

With your group, revisit sections of the text you marked
during your First Read. **Annotate** what you notice. What
questions do you have? What can you **conclude**?

Analyze the Text

CITE TEXTUAL EVIDENCE
to support your answers.

📋 **Notebook** **Complete the activities.**

1. **Review and Clarify** With your group, reread paragraph 10 of "The
Setting Sun and the Rolling World." What does the author mean
when he says that Musoni "felt too much of a father"? What "animals
of prey" do you think the father worries about?

2. **Present and Discuss** Now, work with your group to share the
passages from the text that you found especially important. Take turns
presenting your passages. Discuss what you noticed in the text, what
questions you asked, and what conclusions you reached.

3. **Essential Question:** *What are some milestones on the path to
growing up?* What kind of milestone does the story explore? Why is
it important? Discuss with your group.

LANGUAGE DEVELOPMENT

Concept Vocabulary

patronized	obligations	psychological

Why These Words? The concept vocabulary words from the text are
related. With your group, determine what the words have in common.
Write your ideas, and add another word that fits the category.

Practice

📋 **Notebook** Confirm your understanding of these words from the
text by using each in a sentence. Provide context clues for the words.

Word Study

Greek Root: *-psych-* In "The Setting Sun and the Rolling World," the
narrator observes that the "psychological ties" with his father were
broken. The word *psychological* contains the Greek root *-psych-* which
means "mind" or "spirit." Use a dictionary or thesaurus to identify
several other words that have the same root. Write the words and
their meanings.

Analyze Craft and Structure

Point of View in Fiction The perspective from which a story is told is its **point of view.** Using point of view, authors can control the information readers receive. Most stories are told from the first-person or third-person point of view.

- **First-person point of view** presents the story from the perspective of a character in the story. This character is the narrator and participates in the story's action. The narrator uses the pronouns *I*, *me*, and *my* to communicate what he or she sees, knows, thinks, or feels.

- **Third-person point of view** tells the story from the perspective of a narrator outside the story. The narrator uses pronouns such as *he*, *she*, and *they* to refer to the characters in the story. An **omniscient** third-person narrator knows everything that happens and reveals what each character thinks and feels. A **limited** third-person narrator reveals only the thoughts and feelings of a single character.

⊟ Notebook Work with your group to identify the point of view the author uses in "The Setting Sun and the Rolling World." Then, use a chart like the one shown to compare and contrast the points of view of Old Musoni and his son Nhamo. In the chart, note key passages from the story that show each character's thoughts and feelings. Then, answer the questions that follow.

OLD MUSONI'S POINT OF VIEW	NHAMO'S POINT OF VIEW

1. (a) Use the details in your chart to identify key differences in the points of view of Old Musoni and Nhamo. (b) How do these differences develop the plot?

2. How would the story be different if it were told from a different point of view?

TIP

GROUP DISCUSSION
As you analyze a story, discuss the ways in which the story would change if it were told from a different point of view. How would these changes impact readers' understanding?

THE SETTING SUN AND
THE ROLLING WORLD

STANDARDS

Writing
• Write informative/explanatory texts to examine a topic and convey ideas, concepts, and information through the selection, organization, and analysis of relevant content.

   b. Develop the topic with relevant, well-chosen facts, definitions, concrete details, quotations, or other information and examples.

   f. Provide a concluding statement or section that follows from and supports the information or explanation presented.

• Conduct short research projects to answer a question, drawing on several sources and generating additional related, focused questions that allow for multiple avenues of exploration.

• Gather relevant information from multiple print and digital sources, using search terms effectively; assess the credibility and accuracy of each source; and quote or paraphrase the data and conclusions of others while avoiding plagiarism and following a standard format for citation.

Language
Demonstrate command of the conventions of standard English grammar and usage when writing or speaking.

   c. Form and use verbs in the indicative, imperative, interrogative, conditional, and subjunctive mood.

   d. Recognize and correct inappropriate shifts in verb voice and mood.

Conventions

Verb Moods To write effectively and precisely, writers use a variety of **verb moods.**

VERB MOOD	WRITERS USE IT TO	EXAMPLE
Interrogative	ask a question	*Is Nhamo happy about leaving?*
Imperative	give a command	***Do not** leave!*
Indicative	declare a fact or opinion	*The land **is** dry.*
Conditional	refer to something that may or may not happen	*I **could** go see Chiremba.*
	express uncertainty	*I **might** travel by plane.*
Subjunctive	express a wish, a hope, or a statement contrary to fact	*If Musoni **were** traveling, he would walk.*
	express a request, demand, or proposal	*Musoni asks that Nhamo **be** cautious.*

Read It

Work individually to find in the text an example of an interrogative verb, an imperative verb, a conditional verb, and a subjunctive verb. When you have finished, compare your findings with the group.

Write It

Writers sometimes use verb moods incorrectly. For example, writers may shift improperly between the **indicative** and the **imperative**.

> **Incorrect:** Travelers <u>must be</u> cautious and <u>don't get</u> lost!
> **Correct:** Travelers <u>must be</u> cautious and <u>not get</u> lost.

Writers sometimes use **indicative** when they should use **subjunctive**.

> **Incorrect:** If I <u>was</u> Nhamo, I would be sad.
> **Correct:** If I <u>were</u> Nhamo, I would be sad.

Work with your group to rewrite each sentence correctly.

1. If Musoni was younger, he **would understand Nhamo better.**

2. Sons should listen to their fathers and don't talk back!

Research

Assignment

Deepen your understanding of the story by conducting research on Zimbabwean culture and writing an **informational report**. With your group, choose one of the following topics.

☐ In the story, Old Musoni tells his son to see Chiremba, a traditional Zimbabwean healer. Conduct research, and write an informational report about **Zimbabwean healers.** Conclude your report by explaining whether you think Nhamo's rejection of this traditional aspect of his culture is justified.

☐ Conduct research to learn more about **traditional family life in Zimbabwe.** Then, write an informational report in which you describe the customs and traditions. Conclude your report by explaining the ways in which your research increased your understanding of the perspectives of Old Musoni and Nhamo.

Project Plan Using effective search terms, find multiple print and digital sources of information for your report. Make sure to evaluate each of your sources for credibility and accuracy. With your group, use the following checklist to evaluate your sources.

Does the source go into enough depth to cover the subject?	☐ yes	☐ no
Does the publisher have a good reputation?	☐ yes	☐ no
Is the author an authority on the subject?	☐ yes	☐ no
Do at least two other sources agree with this source?	☐ yes	☐ no
Is the information current? (Check publication date or date it was posted.)	☐ yes	☐ no

Once you have found valid sources, use the facts they provide to develop your report. Paraphrase information and properly credit your sources to avoid plagiarism. Follow a standard format to cite your sources.

Work with your group to organize the information you have found and to create a final draft of your informational report.

✎ **EVIDENCE LOG**

Before moving on to a new selection, go to your Evidence Log, and record what you learned from "The Setting Sun and the Rolling World."

Present Nonfiction Narratives

Assignment

You have read about characters facing different milestones on the path to growing up. Work with your group to create a **series of nonfiction narratives** about rites of passage to present to the class. Use the following prompt to guide you as you develop your presentation:

> What defines an event or experience in a young person's life as a milestone or rite of passage?

Plan With Your Group

Analyze the Texts With your group, discuss the various milestones that characters in the selections face. Use the chart to list your ideas. For each selection, identify the rite of passage that the main character undergoes and why it is important to the character's growth. Talk more generally about rites of passage that you or people you know have undergone, and identify how the event or experience has helped each person on the road to maturity. Then, have each group member select a different type of rite of passage, such as a journey or ritual, to focus on in the presentation. You may choose a rite of passage explored in one of the selections or one from a different experience.

TITLE	RITE OF PASSAGE
You Are the Electric Boogaloo	
Just Be Yourself!	
Hanging Fire	
Translating Grandfather's House	
The Setting Sun and the Rolling World	
Your Rite of Passage:	

Gather Evidence and Media Examples Review the selections and your notes to determine what information is relevant to your presentation. Then, discuss multimedia, such as illustrations and audio, that you can use to enhance your presentation.

STANDARDS

Speaking and Listening
- Present claims and findings, emphasizing salient points in a focused, coherent manner with relevant evidence, sound valid reasoning, and well-chosen details; use appropriate eye contact, adequate volume, and clear pronunciation.
- Integrate multimedia and visual displays into presentations to clarify information, strengthen claims and evidence, and add interest.

Draft and Organize Work individually to craft a brief nonfiction narrative for the rite of passage you chose. Make sure that your narrative has an introduction, a clear sequence of events, and a meaningful conclusion. Then, work as a group to sequence your individual narratives into a cohesive whole for your presentation. Finally, add multimedia to highlight important points and add interest.

Rehearse With Your Group

Practice With Your Group As you prepare to deliver your presentation, use this checklist to evaluate the effectiveness of your group's rehearsal. Then, use your evaluation and the instructions here to guide your revision.

CONTENT	USE OF MEDIA	PRESENTATION TECHNIQUES
☐ Each narrative has an introduction, a clear sequence of events, and a meaningful conclusion. ☐ Individual narratives are sequenced to create a cohesive presentation.	☐ Multimedia highlights the main points in the presentation. ☐ Multimedia adds interest to the presentation.	☐ The speaker makes eye contact and speaks clearly.

Fine-Tune the Content To make your narrative stronger, you may need to work on the sequence of events to make sure that the importance of your rite of passage is clear. Work as a group to identify ideas that may be unclear, and revise these sections by rewording them or adding clarifying information.

Improve Your Use of Media Double-check that your multimedia elements are effective and that they add to the narrative. If any element is not helpful to your presentation, work to replace it with a more useful item.

Brush Up on Your Presentation Techniques Practice a few times with your group before you deliver your narratives to a wider audience. Make sure that you make eye contact and pronounce words correctly.

Present and Evaluate

When you present as a group, be sure that each member has taken into account each of the checklist items. As you watch other groups, evaluate how well their presentations meet the checklist criteria.

ESSENTIAL QUESTION:

What are some milestones on the path to growing up?

There are many different kinds of events and experiences in a young person's life that can be thought of as milestones. What makes an event or experience a milestone? Why are milestones important in our lives? In this section, you will complete your study of major events on the path to adulthood by exploring an additional selection related to the topic. You'll then share what you learn with classmates. To choose a text, follow these steps.

Look Back Think about the selections you have already read. What more do you want to know about the topic of rites of passage?

Look Ahead Preview the selections by reading the descriptions. Which one seems most interesting and appealing to you?

Look Inside Take a few minutes to scan through the text you chose. Make another selection if this text doesn't meet your needs.

Independent Learning Strategies

Throughout your life, in school, in your community, and in your career, you will need to rely on yourself to learn and work on your own. Review these strategies and the actions you can take to practice them during Independent Learning. Add ideas of your own for each category.

STRATEGY	ACTION PLAN
Create a schedule	• Understand your goals and deadlines. • Make a plan for what to do each day. •
Practice what you've learned	• Use first-read and close-read strategies to deepen your understanding. • Evaluate the usefulness of the evidence to help you understand the topic. • Consider the quality and reliability of the source. •
Take notes	• Record important ideas and information. • Review your notes before preparing to share with a group. •

SCAN FOR
MULTIMEDIA

CONTENTS

Choose one selection. Selections are available online only.

SCAN FOR MULTIMEDIA

First-Read Guide

Use this page to record your first-read ideas.

Selection Title: _____

🔧 **Tool Kit**
First-Read Guide and
Model Annotation

NOTICE new information or ideas you learned about the unit topic as you first read this text.

ANNOTATE by marking vocabulary and key passages you want to revisit.

First Read

NOTICE · ANNOTATE · CONNECT · RESPOND

CONNECT ideas within the selection to other knowledge and the selections you have read.

RESPOND by writing a brief summary of the selection.

⊞ **STANDARD**

Reading Read and comprehend complex literary and informational texts independently and proficiently.

Close-Read Guide

Use this page to record your close-read ideas.

Selection Title: _____

Close Read the Text

Revisit sections of the text you marked during your first read. Read these sections closely and **annotate** what you notice. Ask yourself **questions** about the text. What can you **conclude**? Write down your ideas.

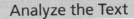

Analyze the Text

Think about the author's choices of patterns, structure, techniques, and ideas included in the text. Select one, and record your thoughts about what this choice conveys.

QuickWrite

Pick a paragraph from the text that grabbed your interest. Explain the power of this passage.

▤ STANDARD
Reading Read and comprehend complex literary and informational texts independently and proficiently.

Share Your Independent Learning

Prepare to Share

What are some milestones on the path to growing up?

Even when you read something independently, your understanding continues to grow by sharing what you've learned with others. Reflect on the text you explored independently and write notes about its connection to the unit. In your notes, consider why this text belongs in this unit.

Learn From Your Classmates

◉ Discuss It Share your ideas about the text you explored on your own. As you talk with others in your class, jot down ideas that you learn from them.

Reflect

Review your notes, and underline the most important insight you gained from these writing and discussion activities. Explain how this idea adds to your understanding of the topic.

▤ STANDARDS

Speaking and Listening
Engage effectively in a range of collaborative discussions with diverse partners on *grade 8 topics, texts, and issues*, building on others' ideas and expressing their own clearly.

Review Evidence for a Nonfiction Narrative

At the beginning of this unit you identified evidence and examples to support the following question:

What rite of passage has held the most significance for you or for a person you know well?

✏ EVIDENCE LOG

Review your Evidence Log and your QuickWrite from the beginning of the unit. Did you learn anything new?

NOTES

Identify three details that most interested you about rites of passage in a young person's life.

1.

2.

3.

Identify a real-life experience that illustrates one of your ideas about a life-changing rite of passage you experienced or know about.

_____

Develop your thoughts into an introduction for a nonfiction narrative. Complete this sentence starter:
An example of a life-changing milestone or rite of passage in a person's life is

_____

_____

Evaluate the Strength of Your Evidence Consider your point of view. How did the texts you read impact your point of view?

≡ STANDARDS

Writing
Write narratives to develop real or imagined experiences or events using effective technique, relevant descriptive details, and well-structured event sequences.

SOURCES

- WHOLE-CLASS
  SELECTIONS

- SMALL-GROUP
  SELECTIONS

- INDEPENDENT-LEARNING
  SELECTION

🔗 WORD NETWORK

As you write and revise your nonfiction narrative, use your Word Network to help vary your word choices.

PART 1
Writing to Sources: Nonfiction Narrative

In this unit, you read about various fictional characters and real-life people and their rites of passage. Some went through experiences that were confusing and difficult, while others felt joy at the changes in their lives.

Assignment

Write a **nonfiction narrative** in which you respond to the following prompt:

> What rite of passage has held the most significance for you or for a person you know well?

Narrate the events leading up to and following the rite of passage. If writing about yourself, use the first-person point of view. If writing about someone else, use the third-person. Use transition words to make your narrative easy to follow, and use sensory language to convey notable experiences. Conclude with a reflection that inspires readers and shares what you have learned about rites of passage.

Reread the Assignment Review the assignment to be sure you fully understand it. The assignment may reference some of the academic words presented at the beginning of the unit. Be sure you understand each of the words here in order to complete the assignment correctly.

Academic Vocabulary

attribute	persistent	inspire
gratifying	notable	

Review the Elements of Nonfiction Narrative Before you begin writing, read the Nonfiction Narrative Rubric. Once you have completed your first draft, check it against the rubric. If one or more of the elements are missing or not as strong as they could be, revise your essay to add or strengthen those components.

📊 STANDARDS

Writing
- Write narratives to develop real or imagined experiences or events using effective technique, relevant descriptive details, and well-structured event sequences.
- Produce clear and coherent writing in which the development, organization, and style are appropriate to task, purpose, and audience.
- Write routinely over extended time frames and shorter time frames for a range of discipline-specific tasks, purposes, and audiences.

Nonfiction Narrative Rubric

	Focus and Organization	Evidence and Elaboration	Conventions
4	The introduction is engaging and introduces the characters and situation in a way that appeals to readers. Events in the narrative progress in logical order and are linked by clear transitions. The conclusion follows from and reflects on what is related in the rest of the narrative.	The narrative includes techniques such as dialogue and description to add interest and to develop the characters and events. The narrative includes vivid adjectives, verbs, and sensory language to convey the experiences and to help the reader imagine the characters and scenes.	The narrative consistently uses standard English conventions of usage and mechanics.
3	The introduction is somewhat engaging and clearly introduces the characters and situation. Events in the narrative progress logically and are frequently linked by transition words. The conclusion follows from the rest of the narrative and provides some reflection on the experiences related in the narrative.	The narrative includes some dialogue and description to add interest and develop experiences and events. The narrative includes precise words and some sensory language to convey experiences and to describe the characters and scenes.	The narrative demonstrates accuracy in standard English conventions of usage and mechanics.
2	The introduction is not engaging but introduces the characters and situation. Events in the narrative progress somewhat logically and are sometimes linked by transition words. The conclusion adds very little to the narrative and does not provide reflection on the experiences related in the narrative.	The narrative includes some dialogue and descriptions. The words in the narrative vary between vague and precise, and some sensory language is included.	The narrative demonstrates some accuracy in standard English conventions of usage and mechanics.
1	The introduction does not introduce characters and a situation, or there is no clear introduction. The events in the narrative do not progress logically. The ideas seem disconnected and the sentences are not linked by transitional words and phrases. The conclusion does not connect to the narrative, or there is no conclusion.	Dialogue and descriptions are not included in the narrative. The narrative does not incorporate sensory language or precise words to convey experiences and to develop characters.	The narrative contains mistakes in standard English conventions of usage and mechanics.

PART 2
Speaking and Listening: Oral Presentation

Assignment
After completing the final draft of your nonfiction narrative, use it as the foundation for a brief **oral presentation.**

Do not simply read your narrative aloud. Take the following steps to make your presentation lively and engaging.

- Review your narrative, and annotate the main parts of the story and the parts that provide reflection on the experiences you are describing.
- Refer to the annotations to guide your presentation.
- Choose visuals that add interest to your presentation.
- Maintain eye contact with your audience. Make sure to speak loud enough for people to hear you, and pronounce words clearly.

Review the Rubric The criteria by which your nonfiction narrative will be evaluated appear in the rubric. Review these criteria before presenting to ensure that you are prepared.

▤ STANDARDS
Speaking and Listening
• Present claims and findings, emphasizing salient points in a focused, coherent manner with relevant evidence, sound valid reasoning, and well-chosen details; use appropriate eye contact, adequate volume, and clear pronunciation.
• Integrate multimedia and visual displays into presentations to clarify information, strengthen claims and evidence, and add interest.

	Content	Use of Media	Presentation Techniques
3	The presentation has an engaging introduction, a logical sequence of events, and a meaningful conclusion. The presentation includes narrative techniques and a variety of transitions for clarity. The presentation includes descriptive details relevant to the story.	The images in the presentation connect well to all parts of the narrative. The images enhance and add interest to the narrative. The timing of the images matches the timing of the narrative.	The speaker maintains effective eye contact and speaks clearly and with adequate volume. The speaker varies tone and volume to create an engaging presentation.
2	The presentation has an introduction, a somewhat logical sequence of events, and a conclusion. The presentation includes some narrative techniques and some transitions for clarity. The presentation includes some descriptive details.	The images in the presentation connect to some parts of the narrative. The images somewhat enhance and add interest to the narrative. The timing of the images somewhat matches the timing of the narrative.	The speaker sometimes maintains effective eye contact and speaks somewhat clearly and with adequate volume. The speaker sometimes varies tone and emphasis to create an engaging presentation.
1	The presentation does not have a logical sequence of events, and lacks an introduction or conclusion. The presentation does not include narrative techniques and transitions. The presentation does not include descriptive details.	The images in the presentation do not connect to the narrative. The images do not enhance and add interest to the narrative. The timing of the images does not match the timing of the narrative.	The speaker does not maintain effective eye contact or speak clearly with adequate volume. The speaker does not vary tone and emphasis to create an engaging presentation.

Reflect on the Unit

Now that you've completed the unit, take a few moments to reflect on your learning.

Reflect on the Unit Goals

Look back at the goals at the beginning of the unit. Use a different colored pen to rate yourself again. Think about readings and activities that contributed the most to the growth of your understanding. Record your thoughts.

Reflect on the Learning Strategies

Discuss It Write a reflection on whether you were able to improve your learning based on your Action Plans. Think about what worked, what didn't, and what you might do to keep working on these strategies. Record your ideas before a class discussion.

Reflect on the Text

Choose a selection that you found challenging and explain what made it difficult.

Explain something that surprised you about a text in the unit.

Which activity taught you the most about childhood? What did you learn?

SCAN FOR
MULTIMEDIA

The Holocaust

Some events from the past are too horrendous
for the world to forget—or to let happen again.

The Holocaust

💬 **Discuss It** How might the Nazis' treatment of
European Jews have affected everyone else?

Write your response before sharing your ideas.

SCAN FOR
MULTIMEDIA

UNIT 2

UNIT INTRODUCTION

ESSENTIAL QUESTION:

How do we remember the past?

LAUNCH TEXT
EXPLANATORY MODEL
The Grand
Mosque of Paris

COMPARE

WHOLE-CLASS LEARNING

ANCHOR TEXT: DRAMA

The Diary of Anne Frank, Act I
Frances Goodrich and Albert Hackett

ANCHOR TEXT: DRAMA

The Diary of Anne Frank, Act II
Frances Goodrich and Albert Hackett

MEDIA: TIMELINE

Frank Family and World War II Timeline

PERFORMANCE TASK

WRITING FOCUS:
Write an Explanatory Essay

SMALL-GROUP LEARNING

DIARY ENTRIES

from Anne Frank: The Diary of a Young Girl
Anne Frank

SPEECH

Acceptance Speech for the Nobel Peace Prize
Elie Wiesel

MEDIA: GRAPHIC NOVEL

from Maus
Art Spiegelman

PERFORMANCE TASK

SPEAKING AND LISTENING FOCUS:
Deliver a Multimedia Presentation

INDEPENDENT LEARNING

TELEVISION TRANSCRIPT

Saving the Children
Bob Simon

REFLECTIVE ESSAY

A Great Adventure in the Shadow of War
Mary Helen Dirkx

INFORMATIVE ARTICLE

Irena Sendler: Rescuer of the Children of Warsaw
Chana Kroll

HISTORICAL WRITING

Quiet Resistance
from Courageous Teen Resisters
Ann Byers

NEWS ARTICLE

Remembering a Devoted Keeper of Anne Frank's Legacy
Moni Basu

FIRST-PERSON ACCOUNT

I'll Go Fetch Her Tomorrow
from Hidden Like Anne Frank
Bloeme Emden with Marcel Prins

PERFORMANCE-BASED ASSESSMENT PREP

Review Evidence for an Explanatory Essay

PERFORMANCE-BASED ASSESSMENT

Explanatory Text: Essay and Oral Presentation

PROMPT:

How can literature help us remember and honor the victims of the Holocaust?

Unit Goals

Throughout this unit, you will deepen your understanding of the Holocaust by reading, writing, speaking, listening, and presenting. These goals will help you succeed on the Unit Performance-Based Assessment.

Rate how well you meet these goals right now. You will revisit your ratings later when you reflect on your growth during this unit.

SCALE

1	2	3	4	5
NOT AT ALL WELL	NOT VERY WELL	SOMEWHAT WELL	VERY WELL	EXTREMELY WELL

READING GOALS
1 2 3 4 5

- Read and analyze how authors discuss a cause, event, or condition that produces a specific result.

- Expand your knowledge and use of academic and concept vocabulary.

WRITING AND RESEARCH GOALS
1 2 3 4 5

- Write an explanatory essay in which you show the connections between historical events and a dramatic adaptation of a historical document.

- Conduct research projects of various lengths to explore a topic and clarify meaning.

LANGUAGE GOAL
1 2 3 4 5

- Demonstrate command of the conventions of standard English grammar and usage, including correct usage of verbs and conjunctions.

SPEAKING AND LISTENING GOALS
1 2 3 4 5

- Collaborate with your team to build on the ideas of others, develop consensus, and communicate.

- Integrate audio, visuals, and text in presentations.

STANDARDS

Language
Acquire and use accurately grade-appropriate general academic and domain-specific words and phrases; gather vocabulary knowledge when considering a word or phrase important to comprehension or expression.

SCAN FOR MULTIMEDIA

Academic Vocabulary: Explanatory Text

Academic terms appear in all subjects and can help you read, write, and discuss with more precision. Explanatory writing relies on facts to inform or explain. Here are five academic words that will be useful to you in this unit as you analyze and write explanatory texts.

Complete the chart.

1. Review each word, its root, and the mentor sentences.

2. Use the information and your own knowledge to predict the meaning of each word.

3. For each word, list at least two related words.

4. Refer to the dictionary or other resources if needed.

TIP

FOLLOW THROUGH
Study the words in this chart, and mark them or their forms wherever they appear in the unit.

WORD	MENTOR SENTENCES	PREDICT MEANING	RELATED WORDS
theorize ROOT: **-theo-/-thea-** "view"; "consider"	1. When you *theorize*, you think of possible explanations for an idea or fact. 2. Since they could not agree on the true cause, doctors could only *theorize* about the illness.		theory; theoretical
sustain ROOT: **-tain-** "hold"	1. It is difficult to *sustain* a pose long enough for an artist to paint your portrait. 2. Those sandwiches will *sustain* us until dinner.		
declaration ROOT: **-clar-** "clear"	1. The country's *declaration* of peace made all the citizens happy that the war was finally over. 2. Congress issued a *declaration* in which the new election laws were explained.		
pronounce ROOT: **-nounc-/-nunc-** "declare"; "report"	1. If you don't *pronounce* your words clearly, people might not be able to understand your ideas. 2. "I now *pronounce* this game officially over," said the referee.		
enumerate ROOT: **-numer-** "number"	1. I have created a list in which I *enumerate* the tasks that should be completed. 2. In her book, the author tries to *enumerate* all the possible explanations for the conflict.		

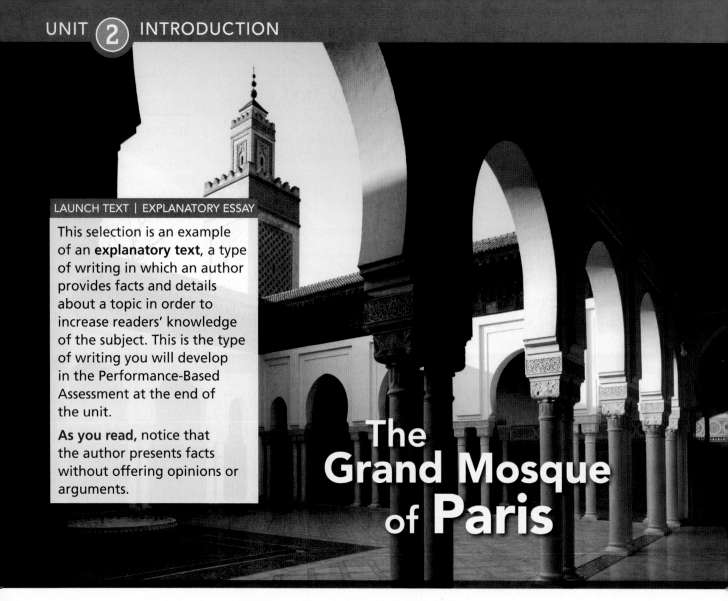

This selection is an example of an **explanatory text**, a type of writing in which an author provides facts and details about a topic in order to increase readers' knowledge of the subject. This is the type of writing you will develop in the Performance-Based Assessment at the end of the unit.

As you read, notice that the author presents facts without offering opinions or arguments.

The Grand Mosque of Paris

NOTES

1   After the Nazis conquered France in 1940, the country fell under the control of the Vichy government. This regime supported Hitler's plan to rid the world of Jews and other "undesirables."

2   In Paris, it was a terrifying time. No Jew was safe from arrest and deportation. Few Parisians were willing to come to their aid, as there was too much risk involved. Despite the deadly campaign, many Jewish children living in Paris at the time survived. Some of those children found refuge in the Grand Mosque of Paris, where heroic Muslims saved Jews from the Nazis.

3   The Grand Mosque of Paris is a fortress-like structure the size of a city block. It was built in 1926 as an expression of France's thanks to the many North African Muslims who fought with the French during World War I. In 1940, it provided an ideal hiding place and escape route for Jews on the run.

4   The rescue involved an extensive network of men and women of all religions and political persuasions. Rescuers took the children from detention centers or homes. They got them false

SCAN FOR MULTIMEDIA

papers, found them temporary shelter in safe houses, and raised funds to pay for their care.

5   Rescuers kept records of the children's real names and fake names, as well as their hiding places. They escorted the children to these locations in small groups. Many who participated were themselves arrested and deported.

6   The Grand Mosque was the perfect cover. Not just a place of worship, it was a community center. Visitors could walk through its doors without attracting a lot of attention. Under these conditions, it was possible for a Jew to pass as a Muslim.

7   Directly beneath the mosque's grounds lay the sewer system of Paris. This complicated web of underground passages now served as a hiding place and escape route. It also reached the Seine. From there, barges were used to smuggle human cargo to ports in the South of France and then to Algeria or Spain.

8   Many believe that the "soul" of the rescue effort was the mosque's rector, Si Kaddour Benghabrit. Benghabrit wrote out false birth certificates for Jewish children, claiming they were Muslim. He is thought to have set up an alarm system warning fugitives to run into the women's section of the prayer room, where men were normally not allowed.

9   Other Muslims also took a stand against the Nazi oppressors by refusing to reveal the whereabouts of fugitives. Some helped Jews avoid detection by coaching them to speak and act like Arabs. Albert Assouline, a North African Jew who found refuge at the Paris mosque, wrote that in life and death situations, there are always people who can be counted on to do the right thing. There may not be a better way to describe the heroic actions of Paris's Muslim community during a horrific time in world history. ❧

NOTES

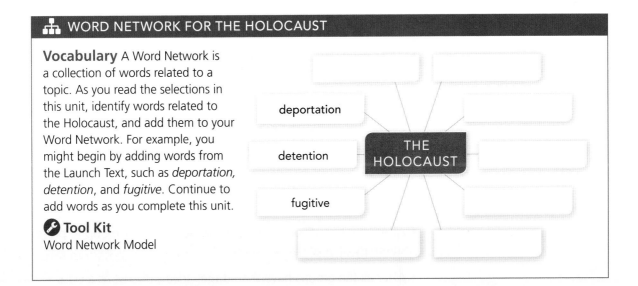

⛛ WORD NETWORK FOR THE HOLOCAUST

Vocabulary A Word Network is a collection of words related to a topic. As you read the selections in this unit, identify words related to the Holocaust, and add them to your Word Network. For example, you might begin by adding words from the Launch Text, such as *deportation*, *detention*, and *fugitive*. Continue to add words as you complete this unit.

🔧 **Tool Kit**
Word Network Model

deportation

detention   THE HOLOCAUST

fugitive

Summary

Write a summary of "The Grand Mosque of Paris." A **summary** is a concise, complete, and accurate overview of a text. It should not include a statement of your opinion or an analysis.

Launch Activity

Conduct a Discussion Consider this statement: **There are always people who can be counted on to do the right thing.**

- Write what you think about the question. Briefly explain your thinking.

  _____

  _____

- Get together with a small group of students, and discuss your responses. Support your ideas with examples from stories you have heard or read, including the Launch Text. Consider how your ideas are similar and different.

- After your discussion, choose someone from your group to present a summary of your conversation.

- After all the groups have shared their ideas, discuss as a class similarities and differences among the views presented.

QuickWrite

Consider class discussions, the video, and the Launch Text as you think about the prompt. Record your first thoughts here.

PROMPT: **How can literature help us remember and honor the victims of the Holocaust?**

EVIDENCE LOG FOR THE HOLOCAUST

Review your QuickWrite. Summarize your thoughts in one sentence to record in your Evidence Log. Then, record textual details and evidence from "The Grand Mosque of Paris" that support your thinking.

Prepare for the Performance-Based Assessment at the end of the unit by completing the Evidence Log after each selection.

🔧 **Tool Kit**
Evidence Log Model

Title of Text: _____ Date: _____

CONNECTION TO PROMPT	TEXT EVIDENCE/DETAILS	ADDITIONAL NOTES/IDEAS

How does this text change or add to my thinking? Date: _____

SCAN FOR MULTIMEDIA

ESSENTIAL QUESTION:

How do we remember the past?

There are many ways to remember the past: We can honor it, study it, analyze it, and learn from it. In the case of the Holocaust, we can work to make sure it never happens again. As you read, you will work with your whole class to explore some of the ways we remember the past.

Whole-Class Learning Strategies

Throughout your life, in school, in your community, and in your career, you will continue to learn and work in large-group environments.

Review these strategies and the actions you can take to practice them as you work with your whole class. Add ideas of your own for each step. Get ready to use these strategies during Whole-Class Learning.

STRATEGY	ACTION PLAN
Listen actively	• Eliminate distractions. For example, put your cellphone away. • Keep your eyes on the speaker. •
Clarify by asking questions	• If you're confused, other people probably are, too. Ask a question to help your whole class. • If you see that you are guessing, ask a question instead. •
Monitor understanding	• Notice what information you already know and be ready to build on it. • Ask for help if you are struggling. •
Interact and share ideas	• Share your ideas and answer questions, even if you are unsure. • Build on the ideas of others by adding details or making a connection. •

SCAN FOR
MULTIMEDIA

CONTENTS

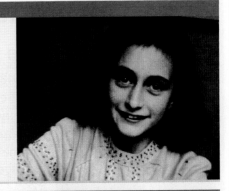

PERFORMANCE TASK

WRITING FOCUS

Write an Explanatory Essay

The Whole-Class readings focus on the events in history that are collectively known
as the Holocaust. After reading, you will write an explanatory essay in which you
discuss the ways in which the events of World War II are reflected in the drama *The
Diary of Anne Frank*.

The Holocaust

The Nazi Rise to Power

In 1918, the First World War came to an end and Germany was defeated. The Treaty of Versailles set harsh terms for Germany's surrender—the country had to make huge payments, give up territory, and severely limit the size of its armed forces.

One of the surviving soldiers was a man named Adolf Hitler, who was outraged by the terms of the treaty and determined that they should be overturned. In 1921, Hitler became the leader of a small political party, the National Socialist German Workers Party, also known as the Nazi Party. At first, the party had little influence, but it quickly gained support as the Great Depression of 1929 began to devastate the German economy and impoverish German citizens. Many Germans were desperate for change, and Hitler was a charismatic speaker who promised to make Germany prosperous and powerful again.

In 1933, Hitler became chancellor—head of the government. From the very beginning, Nazis made it their goal to control all aspects of German life. All newspapers and radio stations that did not support the party were censored, bookstores and libraries were raided, and thousands of books were burned. All other political parties and social organizations except the Nazi Party and Hitler Youth were banned, and Hitler's opponents were arrested or killed. This all happened within the first few months of 1933.

Nazi Ideology

Nazis believed in the superiority of the "Aryan" race—an invented category of "pure" Germans that excluded Jews, gypsies, and the

∧ Adolf Hitler was in firm control of Nazi Germany from 1933 until his suicide in 1945. His actions and ideas led to the deaths of an estimated 40 million people.

∨ Throughout the late 1930s, German power was on display at massive rallies, such as this Nazi rally at Nuremberg.

‹ Hungarian Jewish prisoners arrive at Auschwitz-Birkenau, the largest of the extermination camps. About one million Jews were killed there.

descendants of immigrants from Eastern Europe. They targeted German Jews in particular for violence and persecution. Nazis forced Germans to boycott Jewish-run businesses, banned Jews from many professions, and prevented Jews from marrying those they considered Aryan or "pure" Germans. Schools taught that Jews were "polluting" German society and culture.

In 1938, the Nazis organized a rampage, "The Night of Broken Glass," against German Jews, destroying homes, businesses, and synagogues. More than 90 Jews were killed, and 30,000 were imprisoned in concentration camps. The message to German Jews was clear—leave everything behind and flee Germany, or face persecution.

^ The words *Arbeit Macht Frei*—"work makes you free"—appeared at the entrance to every concentration camp. Meant to give false hope, the slogan became a cruel joke in camps where prisoners were gassed, starved, or worked to death.

The Final Solution

In 1939, Germany invaded Poland, starting World War II. As the Nazis overran much of Europe, their plans for Jews became increasingly extreme. They rounded them up and relocated them to sealed ghettos, in which overcrowding and starvation were common.

Even treatment this harsh rapidly intensified, as German plans grew more organized and deadly. In 1942, the Nazis began to transport millions of Jews from all across Europe to forced labor camps and extermination camps they had established. In two camps in Poland, perhaps a quarter of the prisoners were worked to death. The rest were sent immediately to gas chambers to be killed. In the other four camps, all of the prisoners were gassed as soon as they arrived.

When the Allied forces finally occupied Germany and Poland in 1945, the camps were liberated, and the Nazis' horrific plans were stopped. But the "Final Solution" had already resulted in the deaths of about six million Jews—two-thirds of Europe's prewar Jewish population.

About the Playwrights

Frances Goodrich (1890–1984) and **Albert Hackett** (1900–1995) began working together in 1927 and were married in 1931. The couple's writings include screenplays for such classic films as *The Thin Man* (1934), *It's a Wonderful Life* (1946), and *Father of the Bride* (1950). Goodrich and Hackett spent two years writing *The Diary of Anne Frank*, which went on to win many awards, including the Pulitzer Prize for Drama.

🔧 **Tool Kit**

First-Read Guide and Model Annotation

The Diary of Anne Frank, Act I

Concept Vocabulary

As you conduct your first read of *The Diary of Anne Frank*, Act I, you will encounter these words. Before reading, note how familiar you are with each word. Then rank the words in order from most familiar (1) to least familiar (6).

WORD	YOUR RANKING
anxiously	
tension	
restraining	
quarrels	
bickering	
hysterically	

After completing the first read, come back to the concept vocabulary and review your rankings. Mark changes to your original rankings as needed.

First Read DRAMA

Apply these strategies as you conduct your first read. You will have an opportunity to complete the close-read notes after your first read.

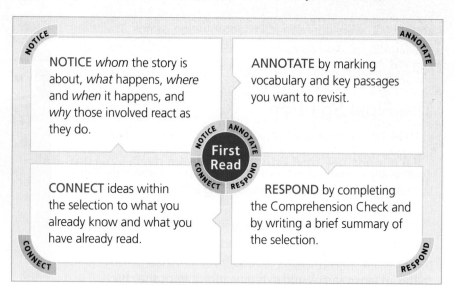

NOTICE *whom* the story is about, *what* happens, *where* and *when* it happens, and *why* those involved react as they do.

ANNOTATE by marking vocabulary and key passages you want to revisit.

First Read

CONNECT ideas within the selection to what you already know and what you have already read.

RESPOND by completing the Comprehension Check and by writing a brief summary of the selection.

STANDARDS

Reading Literature
By the end of the year, read and comprehend literature, including stories, dramas, and poems, at the high end of grades 6–8 text complexity band independently and proficiently.

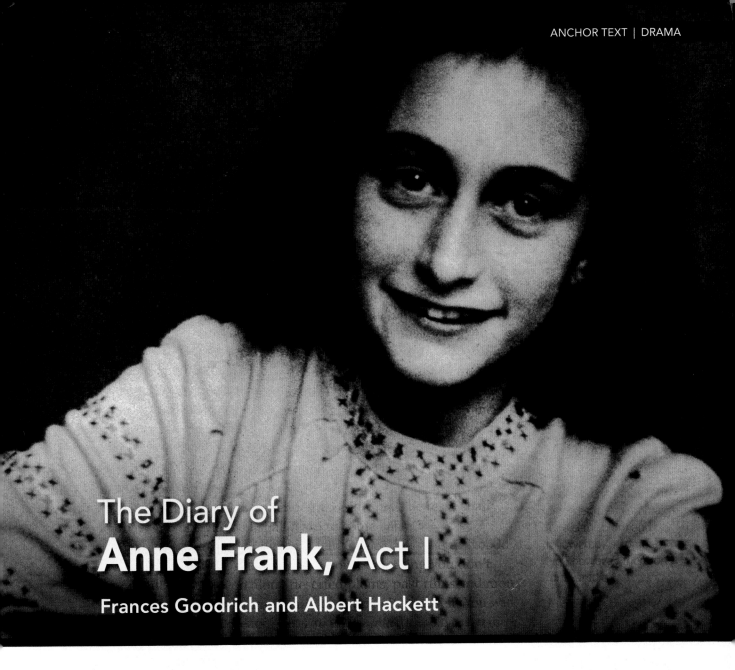

The Diary of Anne Frank, Act I

Frances Goodrich and Albert Hackett

BACKGROUND

Anne Frank was a young Jewish girl living in Amsterdam during the Nazi occupation of the Netherlands in World War II. Fearing for their lives, the Frank family was forced into hiding. The diary that Anne kept during their time in hiding is one of the most famous and heartbreaking pieces of literature from the Holocaust. Anne's diary gained recognition both for its historical significance and for her incredible talent as a writer and storyteller. Tragically, Anne died in a concentration camp just weeks before it was liberated by British soldiers. The play you will read was based on her life and diary.

SCAN FOR MULTIMEDIA

NOTES

Characters

Anne Frank	Miep Gies	Mrs. Van Daan
Otto Frank	Mr. Kraler	Mr. Van Daan
Edith Frank	Mr. Dussel	
Margot Frank	Peter Van Daan	

Act I

Scene 1

1   *[The scene remains the same throughout the play. It is the top floor of a warehouse and office building in Amsterdam, Holland. The sharply peaked roof of the building is outlined against a sea of other rooftops, stretching away into the distance. Nearby is the belfry of a church tower, the Westertoren, whose carillon[1] rings out the hours. Occasionally faint sounds float up from below: the voices of children playing in the street, the tramp of marching feet, a boat whistle from the canal.*

2   *The three rooms of the top floor and a small attic space above are exposed to our view. The largest of the rooms is in the center, with two small rooms, slightly raised, on either side. On the right is a bathroom, out of sight. A narrow steep flight of stairs at the back leads up to the attic. The rooms are sparsely furnished with a few chairs, cots, a table or two. The windows are painted over, or covered with makeshift blackout curtains.[2] In the main room there is a sink, a gas ring for cooking and a woodburning stove for warmth.*

3   *The room on the left is hardly more than a closet. There is a skylight in the sloping ceiling. Directly under this room is a small steep stairwell, with steps leading down to a door. This is the only entrance from the building below. When the door is opened we see that it has been concealed on the outer side by a bookcase attached to it.*

4   *The curtain rises on an empty stage. It is late afternoon, November 1945.*

5   *The rooms are dusty, the curtains in rags. Chairs and tables are overturned.*

6   *The door at the foot of the small stairwell swings open.* **Mr. Frank** *comes up the steps into view. He is a gentle, cultured European in his middle years. There is still a trace of a German accent in his speech.*

7   *He stands looking slowly around, making a supreme effort at self-control. He is weak, ill. His clothes are threadbare.*

8   *After a second he drops his rucksack on the couch and moves slowly about. He opens the door to one of the smaller rooms, and then abruptly closes it again, turning away. He goes to the window at the back, looking off at the Westertoren as its carillon strikes the hour of six, then he moves restlessly on.*

9   *From the street below we hear the sound of a barrel organ[3] and children's voices at play. There is a many-colored scarf hanging from a nail.* **Mr. Frank** *takes it, putting it around his neck. As he starts back for his rucksack, his eye is caught by something lying on the floor. It is a woman's white glove. He holds it in his hand and suddenly all of his self-control is gone. He breaks down, crying.*

---

1. **carillon** (KAR uh lon) *n.* set of bells, each producing one note of the scale.

2. **blackout curtains** dark curtains that conceal all lights that might be visible to bombers from the air.

CLOSE READ

ANNOTATE: Mark details in paragraphs 1–5 that describe the dimensions, or sizes, of the various rooms.

QUESTION: Why do the playwrights note these details of the setting?

CONCLUDE: What is the effect of these details?

3. **barrel organ** mechanical musical instrument often played by street musicians in past decades.

10 *We hear footsteps on the stairs.* Miep Gies *comes up, looking for* Mr. Frank. Miep *is a Dutch girl of about twenty-two. She wears a coat and hat, ready to go home. She is pregnant. Her attitude toward* Mr. Frank *is protective, compassionate.*]

11 **Miep.** Are you all right, Mr. Frank?

12 **Mr. Frank.** [*Quickly controlling himself*] Yes, Miep, yes.

13 **Miep.** Everyone in the office has gone home . . . It's after six. [*Then pleading*] Don't stay up here, Mr. Frank. What's the use of torturing yourself like this?

14 **Mr. Frank.** I've come to say good-bye . . . I'm leaving here, Miep.

15 **Miep.** What do you mean? Where are you going? Where?

16 **Mr. Frank.** I don't know yet. I haven't decided.

17 **Miep.** Mr. Frank, you can't leave here! This is your home! Amsterdam is your home. Your business is here, waiting for you . . . You're needed here . . . Now that the war is over, there are things that . . .

18 **Mr. Frank.** I can't stay in Amsterdam, Miep. It has too many memories for me. Everywhere there's something . . . the house we lived in . . . the school . . . that street organ playing out there . . . I'm not the person you used to know, Miep. I'm a bitter old man. [*Breaking off*] Forgive me. I shouldn't speak to you like this . . . after all that you did for us . . . the suffering . . .

19 **Miep.** No. No. It wasn't suffering. You can't say we suffered. [*As she speaks, she straightens a chair which is overturned.*]

20 **Mr. Frank.** I know what you went through, you and Mr. Kraler. I'll remember it as long as I live. [*He gives one last look around.*] Come, Miep. [*He starts for the steps, then remembers his rucksack, going back to get it.*]

21 **Miep.** [*Hurrying up to a cupboard*] Mr. Frank, did you see? There are some of your papers here. [*She brings a bundle of papers to him.*] We found them in a heap of rubbish on the floor after . . . after you left.

22 **Mr. Frank.** Burn them. [*He opens his rucksack to put the glove in it.*]

23 **Miep.** But, Mr. Frank, there are letters, notes . . .

24 **Mr. Frank.** Burn them. All of them.

25 **Miep.** Burn *this*? [*She hands him a paperbound notebook.*]

26 **Mr. Frank.** [*Quietly*] Anne's diary. [*He opens the diary and begins to read.*] "Monday, the sixth of July, nineteen forty-two." [*To Miep*] Nineteen forty-two. Is it possible, Miep? . . . Only three years ago. [*As he continues his reading, he sits down*

on the couch.] "Dear Diary, since you and I are going to be great friends, I will start by telling you about myself. My name is Anne Frank. I am thirteen years old. I was born in Germany the twelfth of June, nineteen twenty-nine. As my family is Jewish, we emigrated to Holland when Hitler came to power."

27 [As Mr. Frank *reads on, another voice joins his, as if coming from the air. It is* Anne's Voice.]

28 **Mr. Frank and Anne.** "My father started a business, importing spice and herbs. Things went well for us until nineteen forty. Then the war came, and the Dutch capitulation,[4] followed by the arrival of the Germans. Then things got very bad for the Jews."

29 [Mr. Frank's Voice *dies out.* Anne's Voice *continues alone. The lights dim slowly to darkness. The curtain falls on the scene.*]

30 **Anne's Voice.** You could not do this and you could not do that. They forced Father out of his business. We had to wear yellow stars.[5] I had to turn in my bike. I couldn't go to a Dutch school any more. I couldn't go to the movies, or ride in an automobile, or even on a streetcar, and a million other things. But somehow we children still managed to have fun. Yesterday Father told me we were going into hiding. Where, he wouldn't say. At five o'clock this morning Mother woke me and told me to hurry and get dressed. I was to put on as many clothes as I could. It would look too suspicious if we walked along carrying suitcases. It wasn't until we were on our way that I learned where we were going. Our hiding place was to be upstairs in the building where Father used to have his business. Three other people were coming in with us . . . the Van Daans and their son Peter . . . Father knew the Van Daans but we had never met them . . .

31 [*During the last lines the curtain rises on the scene. The lights dim on.* Anne's Voice *fades out.*]

⌘ ⌘ ⌘

Scene 2

1 [*It is early morning, July 1942. The rooms are bare, as before, but they are now clean and orderly.*

2 Mr. Van Daan, *a tall portly[6] man in his late forties, is in the main room, pacing up and down, nervously smoking a cigarette. His clothes and overcoat are expensive and well cut.*

4. **capitulation** (kuh pihch uh LAY shuhn) *n.* surrender.

5. **yellow stars** Stars of David, the six-pointed stars that are symbols of Judaism. The Nazis ordered all Jews to wear them on their clothing.

6. **portly** (PAWRT lee) *adj.* large and heavy.

3   Mrs. Van Daan *sits on the couch, clutching her possessions, a hatbox, bags, etc. She is a pretty woman in her early forties. She wears a fur coat over her other clothes.*

4   Peter Van Daan *is standing at the window of the room on the right, looking down at the street below. He is a shy, awkward boy of sixteen. He wears a cap, a raincoat, and long Dutch trousers, like "plus fours."[7] At his feet is a black case, a carrier for his cat.*

5   *The yellow Star of David is conspicuous on all of their clothes.*]

6   **Mrs. Van Daan.** [*Rising, nervous, excited*] Something's happened to them! I know it!

7   **Mr. Van Daan.** Now, Kerli!

8   **Mrs. Van Daan.** Mr. Frank said they'd be here at seven o'clock. He said . . .

9   **Mr. Van Daan.** They have two miles to walk. You can't expect . . .

10   **Mrs. Van Daan.** They've been picked up. That's what's happened. They've been taken . . .

11   [Mr. Van Daan *indicates that he hears someone coming.*]

12   **Mr. Van Daan.** You see?

13   [Peter *takes up his carrier and his schoolbag, etc., and goes into the main room as* Mr. Frank *comes up the stairwell from below.* Mr. Frank *looks much younger now. His movements are brisk, his manner confident. He wears an overcoat and carries his hat and a small cardboard box. He crosses to the* Van Daans, *shaking hands with each of them.*]

NOTES

7. **plus fours** *n.* short pants worn for active sports.

CLOSE READ

ANNOTATE: In paragraphs 6–10, mark punctuation that suggests the characters are anxious or being interrupted.

QUESTION: Why might the playwrights have used these punctuation marks?

CONCLUDE: What **mood**, or feeling, does this punctuation help convey?

Anne in happier times, out for a stroll with her family and friends.

8. **Green Police** Dutch Gestapo, or Nazi police, who wore green uniforms and were known for their brutality. Those in danger of being arrested or deported feared the Gestapo, especially because of their practice of raiding houses to round up victims in the middle of the night—when people are most confused and vulnerable.

9. **mercurial** (muhr KYUR ee uhl) *adj.* quick or changeable in behavior.

10. **ration** (RASH uhn) **books** books of stamps given to ensure the equal distribution of scarce items, such as meat or gasoline, in times of shortage.

14 **Mr. Frank.** Mrs. Van Daan, Mr. Van Daan, Peter. [*Then, in explanation of their lateness*] There were too many of the Green Police[8] on the streets . . . we had to take the long way around.

15 [*Up the steps come* Margot Frank, Mrs. Frank, Miep (*not pregnant now*) *and* Mr. Kraler. *All of them carry bags, packages, and so forth. The Star of David is conspicuous on all of the* Franks' *clothing.* Margot *is eighteen, beautiful, quiet, shy.* Mrs. Frank *is a young mother, gently bred, reserved. She, like* Mr. Frank, *has a slight German accent.* Mr. Kraler *is a Dutchman, dependable, kindly.*

16 *As* Mr. Kraler *and* Miep *go upstage to put down their parcels,* Mrs. Frank *turns back to call* Anne.]

17 **Mrs. Frank.** Anne?

18 [Anne *comes running up the stairs. She is thirteen, quick in her movements, interested in everything, mercurial[9] in her emotions. She wears a cape, long wool socks and carries a schoolbag.*]

19 **Mr. Frank.** [*Introducing them*] My wife, Edith. Mr. and Mrs. Van Daan [Mrs. Frank *hurries over, shaking hands with them.*] . . . their son, Peter . . . my daughters, Margot and Anne.

20 [Anne *gives a polite little curtsy as she shakes* Mr. Van Daan's *hand. Then she immediately starts off on a tour of investigation of her new home, going upstairs to the attic room.*

21 Miep *and* Mr. Kraler *are putting the various things they have brought on the shelves.*]

22 **Mr. Kraler.** I'm sorry there is still so much confusion.

23 **Mr. Frank.** Please. Don't think of it. After all, we'll have plenty of leisure to arrange everything ourselves.

24 **Miep.** [*To* Mrs. Frank] We put the stores of food you sent in here. Your drugs are here . . . soap, linen here.

25 **Mrs. Frank.** Thank you, Miep.

26 **Miep.** I made up the beds . . . the way Mr. Frank and Mr. Kraler said. [*She starts out.*] Forgive me. I have to hurry. I've got to go to the other side of town to get some ration books[10] for you.

27 **Mrs. Van Daan.** Ration books? If they see our names on ration books, they'll know we're here.

28 **Mr. Kraler.** There isn't anything . . .

29 **Miep.** Don't worry. Your names won't be on them. [*As she hurries out*] I'll be up later.

30 **Mr. Frank.** Thank you, Miep.

31 **Mrs. Frank.** [*To Mr. Kraler*] It's illegal, then, the ration books? We've never done anything illegal.

32 **Mr. Frank.** We won't be living here exactly according to regulations.

33 [*As Mr. Kraler reassures Mrs. Frank, he takes various small things, such as matches, soap, etc., from his pockets, handing them to her.*]

34 **Mr. Kraler.** This isn't the black market,[11] Mrs. Frank. This is what we call the white market . . . helping all of the hundreds and hundreds who are hiding out in Amsterdam.

11. **black market** illegal way of buying scarce items.

35 [*The carillon is heard playing the quarter-hour before eight. Mr. Kraler looks at his watch. Anne stops at the window as she comes down the stairs.*]

36 **Anne.** It's the Westertoren!

37 **Mr. Kraler.** I must go. I must be out of here and downstairs in the office before the workmen get here. [*He starts for the stairs leading out.*] Miep or I, or both of us, will be up each day to bring you food and news and find out what your needs are. Tomorrow I'll get you a better bolt for the door at the foot of the stairs. It needs a bolt that you can throw yourself and open only at our signal. [*To Mr. Frank*] Oh . . . You'll tell them about the noise?

38 **Mr. Frank.** I'll tell them.

39 **Mr. Kraler.** Good-bye then for the moment. I'll come up again, after the workmen leave.

40 **Mr. Frank.** Good-bye, Mr. Kraler.

41 **Mrs. Frank.** [*Shaking his hand*] How can we thank you?

42 [*The others murmur their good-byes.*]

43 **Mr. Kraler.** I never thought I'd live to see the day when a man like Mr. Frank would have to go into hiding. When you think—

44 [*He breaks off, going out. Mr. Frank follows him down the steps, bolting the door after him. In the interval before he returns, Peter goes over to Margot, shaking hands with her. As Mr. Frank comes back up the steps, Mrs. Frank questions him anxiously.*]

anxiously (ANGK shuhs lee) *adv.* in a nervous or worried way

45 **Mrs. Frank.** What did he mean, about the noise?

46 **Mr. Frank.** First let us take off some of these clothes.

47 [*They all start to take off garment after garment. On each of their coats, sweaters, blouses, suits, dresses, is another yellow Star of David. Mr. and Mrs. Frank are underdressed quite simply.*

The others wear several things: sweaters, extra dresses, bathrobes, aprons, nightgowns, etc.]

48 **Mr. Van Daan.** It's a wonder we weren't arrested, walking along the streets . . . Petronella with a fur coat in July . . . and that cat of Peter's crying all the way.

49 **Anne.** [*As she is removing a pair of panties*] A cat?

50 **Mrs. Frank.** [*Shocked*] Anne, please!

51 **Anne.** It's alright. I've got on three more.

52 [*She pulls off two more. Finally, as they have all removed their surplus clothes, they look to* Mr. Frank, *waiting for him to speak.*]

53 **Mr. Frank.** Now. About the noise. While the men are in the building below, we must have complete quiet. Every sound can be heard down there, not only in the workrooms, but in the offices too. The men come at about eight-thirty, and leave at about five-thirty. So, to be perfectly safe, from eight in the morning until six in the evening we must move only when it is necessary, and then in stockinged feet. We must not speak above a whisper. We must not run any water. We cannot use the sink, or even, forgive me, the w.c.[12] The pipes go down through the workrooms. It would be heard. No trash . . .

54 [Mr. Frank *stops abruptly as he hears the sound of marching feet from the street below. Everyone is motionless, paralyzed with fear.* Mr. Frank *goes quietly into the room on the right to look down out of the window.* Anne *runs after him, peering out with him. The tramping feet pass without stopping. The* **tension** *is relieved.* Mr. Frank, *followed by* Anne, *returns to the main room and resumes his instructions to the group.*] . . . No trash must ever be thrown out which might reveal that someone is living up here . . . not even a potato paring. We must burn everything in the stove at night. This is the way we must live until it is over, if we are to survive.

55 [*There is silence for a second.*]

56 **Mrs. Frank.** Until it is over.

57 **Mr. Frank.** [*Reassuringly*] After six we can move about . . . we can talk and laugh and have our supper and read and play games . . . just as we would at home. [*He looks at his watch.*] And now I think it would be wise if we all went to our rooms, and were settled before eight o'clock. Mrs. Van Daan, you and your husband will be upstairs. I regret that there's no place up there for Peter. But he will be here, near us. This will be our common room, where we'll meet to talk and eat and read, like one family.

CLOSE READ

ANNOTATE: In paragraph 54, mark the sound that causes the characters to feel afraid.

QUESTION: Why do the playwrights include this detail?

CONCLUDE: How does this detail clarify the characters' situation?

12. **w.c.** water closet; bathroom.

tension (TEHN shuhn) *n.* nervous, worried, or excited condition that makes relaxation impossible

58 **Mr. Van Daan.** And where do you and Mrs. Frank sleep?

59 **Mr. Frank.** This room is also our bedroom.

60 [*Together*] {
Mrs. Van Daan. That isn't right. We'll sleep here and you take the room upstairs.

Mr. Van Daan. It's your place.
}

61 **Mr. Frank.** Please. I've thought this out for weeks. It's the best arrangement. The only arrangement.

62 **Mrs. Van Daan.** [*To* Mr. Frank] Never, never can we thank you. [*Then to* Mrs. Frank] I don't know what would have happened to us, if it hadn't been for Mr. Frank.

63 **Mr. Frank.** You don't know how your husband helped me when I came to this country . . . knowing no one . . . not able to speak the language. I can never repay him for that. [*Going to* Mr. Van Daan] May I help you with your things?

64 **Mr. Van Daan.** No. No. [*To* Mrs. Van Daan] Come along, *liefje.*[13]

65 **Mrs. Van Daan.** You'll be all right, Peter? You're not afraid?

66 **Peter.** [*Embarrassed*] Please, Mother.

67 [*They start up the stairs to the attic room above.* Mr. Frank *turns to* Mrs. Frank.]

68 **Mr. Frank.** You too must have some rest, Edith. You didn't close your eyes last night. Nor you, Margot.

69 **Anne.** I slept, Father. Wasn't that funny? I knew it was the last night in my own bed, and yet I slept soundly.

70 **Mr. Frank.** I'm glad, Anne. Now you'll be able to help me straighten things in here. [*To* Mrs. Frank *and* Margot] Come with me . . . You and Margot rest in this room for the time being.

71 [*He picks up their clothes, starting for the room on the right.*]

72 **Mrs. Frank.** You're sure . . . ? I could help . . . And Anne hasn't had her milk . . .

73 **Mr. Frank.** I'll give it to her. [*To* Anne *and* Peter] Anne, Peter . . . it's best that you take off your shoes now, before you forget.

74 [*He leads the way to the room, followed by* Margot.]

75 **Mrs. Frank.** You're sure you're not tired, Anne?

76 **Anne.** I feel fine. I'm going to help Father.

77 **Mrs. Frank.** Peter, I'm glad you are to be with us.

78 **Peter.** Yes, Mrs. Frank.

13. *liefje* (LEEF yuh) Dutch for "little love."

Jews were regularly rounded up and forced to leave their homes without notice.

79 [Mrs. Frank *goes to join* Mr. Frank *and* Margot.]

80 [*During the following scene* Mr. Frank *helps* Margot *and* Mrs. Frank *to hang up their clothes. Then he persuades them both to lie down and rest. The* Van Daans *in their room above settle themselves. In the main room* Anne *and* Peter *remove their shoes.* Peter *takes his cat out of the carrier.*]

81 **Anne.** What's your cat's name?

82 **Peter.** Mouschi.

83 **Anne.** Mouschi! Mouschi! Mouschi! [*She picks up the cat, walking away with it. To* Peter] I love cats. I have one . . . a darling little cat. But they made me leave her behind. I left some food and a note for the neighbors to take care of her . . . I'm going to miss her terribly. What is yours? A him or a her?

84 **Peter.** He's a tom. He doesn't like strangers. [*He takes the cat from her, putting it back in its carrier.*]

85 **Anne.** [*Unabashed*] Then I'll have to stop being a stranger, won't I? Is he fixed?

86 **Peter.** [*Startled*] Huh?

87 **Anne.** Did you have him fixed?

88 **Peter.** No.

89 **Anne.** Oh, you ought to have him fixed—to keep him from—you know, fighting. Where did you go to school?

90 **Peter.** Jewish Secondary.

91 **Anne.** But that's where Margot and I go! I never saw you around.

92 **Peter.** I used to see you . . . sometimes . . .

93 **Anne.** You did?

94 **Peter.** . . . In the school yard. You were always in the middle of a bunch of kids. [*He takes a penknife from his pocket.*]

95 **Anne.** Why didn't you ever come over?

96 **Peter.** I'm sort of a lone wolf. [*He starts to rip off his Star of David.*]

97 **Anne.** What are you doing?

98 **Peter.** Taking it off.

99 **Anne.** But you can't do that. They'll arrest you if you go out without your star.

100 [*He tosses his knife on the table.*]

NOTES

101 **Peter.** Who's going out?

102 **Anne.** Why, of course! You're right! Of course we don't need them any more. [*She picks up his knife and starts to take her star off.*] I wonder what our friends will think when we don't show up today?

103 **Peter.** I didn't have any dates with anyone.

104 **Anne.** Oh, I did. I had a date with Jopie to go and play ping-pong at her house. Do you know Jopie de Waal?

105 **Peter.** No.

106 **Anne.** Jopie's my best friend. I wonder what she'll think when she telephones and there's no answer? . . . Probably she'll go over to the house . . . I wonder what she'll think . . . we left everything as if we'd suddenly been called away . . . breakfast dishes in the sink . . . beds not made . . . [*As she pulls off her star, the cloth underneath shows clearly the color and form of the star.*] Look! It's still there! [Peter *goes over to the stove with his star.*] What're you going to do with yours?

107 **Peter.** Burn it.

108 **Anne.** [*She starts to throw hers in, and cannot.*] It's funny, I can't throw mine away. I don't know why.

109 **Peter.** You can't throw . . . ? Something they branded you with . . . ? That they made you wear so they could spit on you?

110 **Anne.** I know. I know. But after all, it *is* the Star of David, isn't it?

111 [*In the bedroom, right,* Margot *and* Mrs. Frank *are lying down.* Mr. Frank *starts quietly out.*]

112 **Peter.** Maybe it's different for a girl.

113 [Mr. Frank *comes into the main room.*]

114 **Mr. Frank.** Forgive me, Peter. Now let me see. We must find a bed for your cat. [*He goes to a cupboard.*] I'm glad you brought your cat. Anne was feeling so badly about hers. [*Getting a used small washtub*] Here we are. Will it be comfortable in that?

115 **Peter.** [*Gathering up his things*] Thanks.

116 **Mr. Frank.** [*Opening the door of the room on the left*] And here is your room. But I warn you, Peter, you can't grow any more. Not an inch, or you'll have to sleep with your feet out of the skylight. Are you hungry?

117 **Peter.** No.

118 **Mr. Frank.** We have some bread and butter.

NOTES

CLOSE READ

ANNOTATE: In paragraphs 94–107, mark details that show what Peter is doing and why.

QUESTION: Think about what the yellow star represents during World War II. Why do the playwrights include the details of Peter's actions?

CONCLUDE: What do Peter's actions show about his character?

119 **Peter.** No, thank you.

120 **Mr. Frank.** You can have it for luncheon then. And tonight we will have a real supper . . . our first supper together.

121 **Peter.** Thanks. Thanks. [*He goes into his room. During the following scene he arranges his possessions in his new room.*]

122 **Mr. Frank.** That's a nice boy, Peter.

123 **Anne.** He's awfully shy, isn't he?

124 **Mr. Frank.** You'll like him, I know.

125 **Anne.** I certainly hope so, since he's the only boy I'm likely to see for months and months.

126 [Mr. Frank *sits down, taking off his shoes.*]

14. **Annele** (AHN eh leh) nickname for "Anne."

127 **Mr. Frank.** Annele,[14] there's a box there. Will you open it?

128 [*He indicates a carton on the couch.* Anne *brings it to the center table. In the street below there is the sound of children playing.*]

129 **Anne.** [*As she opens the carton*] You know the way I'm going to think of it here? I'm going to think of it as a boarding house. A very peculiar summer boarding house, like the one that we—[*She breaks off as she pulls out some photographs.*] Father! My movie stars! I was wondering where they were! I was looking for them this morning . . . and Queen Wilhelmina![15] How wonderful!

15. **Queen Wilhelmina** (vihl hehl MEE nah) Queen of the Netherlands from 1890 to 1948.

130 **Mr. Frank.** There's something more. Go on. Look further. [*He goes over to the sink, pouring a glass of milk from a thermos bottle.*]

131 **Anne.** [*Pulling out a pasteboard-bound book*] A diary! [*She throws her arms around her father.*] I've never had a diary. And I've always longed for one. [*She looks around the room.*] Pencil, pencil, pencil, pencil. [*She starts down the stairs.*] I'm going down to the office to get a pencil.

CLOSE READ

ANNOTATE: In paragraphs 129–135, mark details that show the changes in Anne's mood.

QUESTION: Why do the playwrights include these details?

132 **Mr. Frank.** Anne! No! [*He goes after her, catching her by the arm and pulling her back.*]

133 **Anne.** [*Startled*] But there's no one in the building now.

134 **Mr. Frank.** It doesn't matter. I don't want you ever to go beyond that door.

CONCLUDE: How do these details help readers appreciate the extreme nature of the Franks' situation?

135 **Anne.** [*Sobered*] Never . . . ? Not even at nighttime, when everyone is gone? Or on Sundays? Can't I go down to listen to the radio?

136 **Mr. Frank.** Never. I am sorry, Anneke.[16] It isn't safe. No, you must never go beyond that door.

16. **Anneke** (AHN eh keh) another nickname for "Anne."

137 [*For the first time* Anne *realizes what "going into hiding" means.*]

138 **Anne.** I see.

139 **Mr. Frank.** It'll be hard, I know. But always remember this, Anneke. There are no walls, there are no bolts, no locks that anyone can put on your mind. Miep will bring us books. We will read history, poetry, mythology. [*He gives her the glass of milk.*] Here's your milk. [*With his arm about her, they go over to the couch, sitting down side by side.*] As a matter of fact, between us, Anne, being here has certain advantages for you. For instance, you remember the battle you had with your mother the other day on the subject of overshoes? You said you'd rather die than wear overshoes? But in the end you had to wear them? Well now, you see, for as long as we are here you will never have to wear overshoes! Isn't that good? And the coat that you inherited from Margot, you won't have to wear that any more. And the piano! You won't have to practice on the piano. I tell you, this is going to be a fine life for you!

140 [Anne's *panic is gone.* Peter *appears in the doorway of his room, with a saucer in his hand. He is carrying his cat.*]

141 **Peter.** I . . . I . . . I thought I'd better get some water for Mouschi before . . .

142 **Mr. Frank.** Of course.

143 [*As he starts toward the sink the carillon begins to chime the hour of eight. He tiptoes to the window at the back and looks down at the street below. He turns to* Peter, *indicating in pantomime that it is too late.* Peter *starts back for his room. He steps on a creaking board. The three of them are frozen for a minute in fear. As* Peter *starts away again,* Anne *tiptoes over to him and pours some of the milk from her glass into the saucer for the cat.* Peter *squats on the floor, putting the milk before the cat.* Mr. Frank *gives* Anne *his fountain pen, and then goes into the room at the right. For a second* Anne *watches the cat, then she goes over to the center table, and opens her diary.*

144 *In the room at the right,* Mrs. Frank *has sat up quickly at the sound of the carillon.* Mr. Frank *comes in and sits down beside her on the settee, his arm comfortingly around her.*

145 *Upstairs, in the attic room,* Mr. *and* Mrs. Van Daan *have hung their clothes in the closet and are now seated on the iron bed.* Mrs. Van Daan *leans back exhausted.* Mr. Van Daan *fans her with a newspaper.*

146 Anne *starts to write in her diary. The lights dim out, the curtain falls.*

147 *In the darkness* Anne's Voice *comes to us again, faintly at first, and then with growing strength.*]

148 **Anne's Voice.** I expect I should be describing what it feels like to go into hiding. But I really don't know yet myself. I only know it's funny never to be able to go outdoors . . . never to breathe fresh air . . . never to run and shout and jump. It's the silence in the nights that frightens me most. Every time I hear a creak in the house, or a step on the street outside, I'm sure they're coming for us. The days aren't so bad. At least we know that Miep and Mr. Kraler are down there below us in the office. Our protectors, we call them. I asked Father what would happen to them if the Nazis found out they were hiding us. Pim said that they would suffer the same fate that we would . . . Imagine! They know this, and yet when they come up here, they're always cheerful and gay as if there were nothing in the world to bother them . . . Friday, the twenty-first of August, nineteen forty-two. Today I'm going to tell you our general news. Mother is unbearable. She insists on treating me like a baby, which I loathe. Otherwise things are going better. The weather is . . .

149 [*As* Anne's Voice *is fading out, the curtain rises on the scene.*]

⌘ ⌘ ⌘

Scene 3

1 [*It is a little after six o'clock in the evening, two months later.*

2 Margot *is in the bedroom at the right, studying.* Mr. Van Daan *is lying down in the attic room above.*

3 *The rest of the "family" is in the main room.* Anne *and* Peter *sit opposite each other at the center table, where they have been doing their lessons.* Mrs. Frank *is on the couch.* Mrs. Van Daan *is seated with her fur coat, on which she has been sewing, in her lap. None of them are wearing their shoes.*

4 *Their eyes are on* Mr. Frank, *waiting for him to give them the signal which will release them from their day-long quiet.* Mr. Frank, *his shoes in his hand, stands looking down out of the window at the back, watching to be sure that all of the workmen have left the building below.*

5 *After a few seconds of motionless silence,* Mr. Frank *turns from the window.*]

6 **Mrs. Frank.** [*Quietly, to the group*] It's safe now. The last workman has left.

7 [*There is an immediate stir of relief.*]

8 **Anne.** [*Her pent-up energy explodes.*] WHEE!

© Pearson Education, Inc., or its affiliates. All rights reserved.

CLOSE READ

ANNOTATE: In paragraphs 4–8, mark details that relate to quiet or confinement. Mark other details that relate to being free or letting go.

QUESTION: Why do the playwrights go into such detail about this moment?

CONCLUDE: What do these details suggest about the characters' daily lives?

9 **Mr. Frank.** [*Startled, amused*] Anne!

10 **Mrs. Van Daan.** I'm first for the w.c.

11 [*She hurries off to the bathroom.* Mrs. Frank *puts on her shoes and starts up to the sink to prepare supper.* Anne *sneaks* Peter's *shoes from under the table and hides them behind her back.* Mr. Frank *goes in to* Margot's *room.*]

12 **Mr. Frank.** [*To* Margot] Six o'clock. School's over.

13 [Margot *gets up, stretching.* Mr. Frank *sits down to put on his shoes. In the main room* Peter *tries to find his.*]

14 **Peter.** [*To* Anne] Have you seen my shoes?

15 **Anne.** [*Innocently*] Your shoes?

16 **Peter.** You've taken them, haven't you?

17 **Anne.** I don't know what you're talking about.

18 **Peter.** You're going to be sorry!

19 **Anne.** Am I?

20 [Peter *goes after her.* Anne, *with his shoes in her hand, runs from him, dodging behind her mother.*]

21 **Mrs. Frank.** [*Protesting*] Anne, dear!

22 **Peter.** Wait till I get you!

23 **Anne.** I'm waiting! [Peter *makes a lunge for her. They both fall to the floor.* Peter *pins her down, wrestling with her to get the shoes.*] Don't! Don't! Peter, stop it. Ouch!

24 **Mrs. Frank.** Anne! . . . Peter!

25 [*Suddenly* Peter *becomes self-conscious. He grabs his shoes roughly and starts for his room.*]

26 **Anne.** [*Following him*] Peter, where are you going? Come dance with me.

27 **Peter.** I tell you I don't know how.

28 **Anne.** I'll teach you.

29 **Peter.** I'm going to give Mouschi his dinner.

30 **Anne.** Can I watch?

31 **Peter.** He doesn't like people around while he eats.

32 **Anne.** Peter, please.

33 **Peter.** No! [*He goes into his room.* Anne *slams his door after him.*]

34 **Mrs. Frank.** Anne, dear, I think you shouldn't play like that with Peter. It's not dignified.

35 **Anne.** Who cares if it's dignified? I don't want to be dignified.

36 [Mr. Frank *and* Margot *come from the room on the right.* Margot *goes to help her mother.* Mr. Frank *starts for the center table to correct* Margot's *school papers.*]

37 **Mrs. Frank.** [*To* Anne] You complain that I don't treat you like a grownup. But when I do, you resent it.

38 **Anne.** I only want some fun . . . someone to laugh and clown with . . . After you've sat still all day and hardly moved, you've got to have some fun. I don't know what's the matter with that boy.

39 **Mr. Frank.** He isn't used to girls. Give him a little time.

40 **Anne.** Time? Isn't two months time? I could cry. [*Catching hold of* Margot] Come on, Margot . . . dance with me. Come on, please.

41 **Margot.** I have to help with supper.

42 **Anne.** You know we're going to forget how to dance . . . When we get out we won't remember a thing.

43 [*She starts to sing and dance by herself.* Mr. Frank *takes her in his arms, waltzing with her.* Mrs. Van Daan *comes in from the bathroom.*]

44 **Mrs. Van Daan.** Next? [*She looks around as she starts putting on her shoes.*] Where's Peter?

45 **Anne.** [*As they are dancing*] Where would he be!

46 **Mrs. Van Daan.** He hasn't finished his lessons, has he? His father'll kill him if he catches him in there with that cat and his work not done. [Mr. Frank *and* Anne *finish their dance. They bow to each other with extravagant formality.*] Anne, get him out of there, will you?

47 **Anne.** [*At* Peter's *door*] Peter? Peter?

48 **Peter.** [*Opening the door a crack*] What is it?

49 **Anne.** Your mother says to come out.

50 **Peter.** I'm giving Mouschi his dinner.

51 **Mrs. Van Daan.** You know what your father says. [*She sits on the couch, sewing on the lining of her fur coat.*]

52 **Peter.** For heaven's sake, I haven't even looked at him since lunch.

53 **Mrs. Van Daan.** I'm just telling you, that's all.

54 **Anne.** I'll feed him.

55 **Peter.** I don't want you in there.

56 **Mrs. Van Daan.** Peter!

57 **Peter.** [*To* Anne] Then give him his dinner and come right out, you hear?

58 [*He comes back to the table.* Anne *shuts the door of* Peter's *room after her and disappears behind the curtain covering his closet.*]

59 **Mrs. Van Daan.** [*To* Peter] Now is that any way to talk to your little girl friend?

60 **Peter.** Mother . . . for heaven's sake . . . will you please stop saying that?

61 **Mrs. Van Daan.** Look at him blush! Look at him!

62 **Peter.** Please! I'm not . . . anyway . . . let me alone, will you?

63 **Mrs. Van Daan.** He acts like it was something to be ashamed of. It's nothing to be ashamed of, to have a little girl friend.

64 **Peter.** You're crazy. She's only thirteen.

65 **Mrs. Van Daan.** So what? And you're sixteen. Just perfect. Your father's ten years older than I am. [*To* Mr. Frank] I warn you, Mr. Frank, if this war lasts much longer, we're going to be related and then . . .

66 **Mr. Frank.** *Mazel tov!*[17]

67 **Mrs. Frank.** [*Deliberately changing the conversation*] I wonder where Miep is. She's usually so prompt.

68 [*Suddenly everything else is forgotten as they hear the sound of an automobile coming to a screeching stop in the street below. They are tense, motionless in their terror. The car starts away. A wave of relief sweeps over them. They pick up their occupations again.* Anne *flings open the door of* Peter's *room, making a dramatic entrance. She is dressed in* Peter's *clothes.* Peter *looks at her in fury. The others are amused.*]

69 **Anne.** Good evening, everyone. Forgive me if I don't stay. [*She jumps up on a chair.*] I have a friend waiting for me in there. My friend Tom. Tom Cat. Some people say that we look alike. But Tom has the most beautiful whiskers, and I have only a little fuzz. I am hoping . . . in time . . .

70 **Peter.** All right, Mrs. Quack Quack!

71 **Anne.** [*Outraged—jumping down*] Peter!

72 **Peter.** I heard about you . . . How you talked so much in class they called you Mrs. Quack Quack. How Mr. Smitter made you write a composition . . . "'Quack, Quack,' said Mrs. Quack Quack."

17. *Mazel tov* (MAH zuhl tohv) "good luck" in Hebrew and Yiddish; a phrase used to offer congratulations.

73 **Anne.** Well, go on. Tell them the rest. How it was so good he read it out loud to the class and then read it to all his other classes!

74 **Peter.** Quack! Quack! Quack . . . Quack . . . Quack . . .

75 [Anne *pulls off the coat and trousers.*]

76 **Anne.** You are the most intolerable, insufferable boy I've ever met!

77 [*She throws the clothes down the stairwell. Peter goes down . . . after them.*]

78 **Peter.** Quack, quack, quack!

79 **Mrs. Van Daan.** [*To* Anne] That's right, Anneke! Give it to him!

80 **Anne.** With all the boys in the world . . . Why I had to get locked up with one like you!

81 **Peter.** Quack, quack, quack, and from now on stay out of my room!

82 [*As* Peter *passes her,* Anne *puts out her foot, tripping him. He picks himself up, and goes on into his room.*]

83 **Mrs. Frank.** [*Quietly*] Anne, dear . . . your hair. [*She feels* Anne's *forehead.*] You're warm. Are you feeling all right?

84 **Anne.** Please, Mother. [*She goes over to the center table, slipping into her shoes.*]

85 **Mrs. Frank.** [*Following her*] You haven't a fever, have you?

86 **Anne.** [*Pulling away*] No. No.

87 **Mrs. Frank.** You know we can't call a doctor here, ever. There's only one thing to do . . . watch carefully. Prevent an illness before it comes. Let me see your tongue.

88 **Anne.** Mother, this is perfectly absurd.

89 **Mrs. Frank.** Anne, dear, don't be such a baby. Let me see your tongue. [*As* Anne *refuses,* Mrs. Frank *appeals to* Mr. Frank] Otto . . . ?

90 **Mr. Frank.** You hear your mother, Anne.

91 [Anne *flicks out her tongue for a second, then turns away.*]

92 **Mrs. Frank.** Come on—open up! [*As* Anne *opens her mouth very wide*] You seem all right . . . but perhaps an aspirin . . .

93 **Mrs. Van Daan.** For heaven's sake, don't give that child any pills. I waited for fifteen minutes this morning for her to come out of the w.c.

94 **Anne.** I was washing my hair!

95 **Mr. Frank.** I think there's nothing the matter with our Anne that a ride on her bike, or a visit with her friend Jopie de Waal wouldn't cure. Isn't that so, Anne?

96 [Mr. Van Daan *comes down into the room. From outside we hear faint sounds of bombers going over and a burst of ack-ack.*[18]]

97 **Mr. Van Daan.** Miep not come yet?

98 **Mrs. Van Daan.** The workmen just left, a little while ago.

99 **Mr. Van Daan.** What's for dinner tonight?

100 **Mrs. Van Daan.** Beans.

101 **Mr. Van Daan.** Not again!

102 **Mrs. Van Daan.** Poor Putti! I know. But what can we do? That's all that Miep brought us.

103 [Mr. Van Daan *starts to pace, his hands behind his back.* Anne *follows behind him, imitating him.*]

104 **Anne.** We are now in what is known as the "bean cycle." Beans boiled, beans en casserole, beans with strings, beans without strings . . .

105 [Peter *has come out of his room. He slides into his place at the table, becoming immediately absorbed in his studies.*]

106 **Mr. Van Daan.** [*To* Peter] I saw you . . . in there, playing with your cat.

107 **Mrs. Van Daan.** He just went in for a second, putting his coat away. He's been out here all the time, doing his lessons.

108 **Mr. Frank.** [*Looking up from the papers*] Anne, you got an excellent in your history paper today . . . and very good in Latin.

109 **Anne.** [*Sitting beside him*] How about algebra?

110 **Mr. Frank.** I'll have to make a confession. Up until now I've managed to stay ahead of you in algebra. Today you caught up with me. We'll leave it to Margot to correct.

111 **Anne.** Isn't algebra *vile*, Pim!

112 **Mr. Frank.** Vile!

113 **Margot.** [*To* Mr. Frank] How did I do?

114 **Anne.** [*Getting up*] Excellent, excellent, excellent, excellent!

115 **Mr. Frank.** [*To* Margot] You should have used the subjunctive[19] here . . .

This photo shows the front of the building that held the Secret Annex.

NOTES

18. *ack-ack* (AK AK) *n.* slang for an anti-aircraft gun's fire.

19. **subjunctive** (suhb JUHNGK tihv) *n.* form of a verb that is used to express doubt or uncertainty.

CLOSE READ

ANNOTATE: In paragraphs 123–133, mark words and phrases that show Mrs. Van Daan's words and actions.

QUESTION: What do these words and phrases reveal about her personality?

CONCLUDE: How do Mrs. Van Daan's actions affect Peter and Mr. Van Daan?

116 **Margot.** Should I? . . . I thought . . . look here . . . I didn't use it here . . .

117 [*The two become absorbed in the papers.*]

118 **Anne.** Mrs. Van Daan, may I try on your coat?

119 **Mrs. Frank.** No, Anne.

120 **Mrs. Van Daan.** [*Giving it to* Anne] It's all right . . . but careful with it. [Anne *puts it on and struts with it.*] My father gave me that the year before he died. He always bought the best that money could buy.

121 **Anne.** Mrs. Van Daan, did you have a lot of boy friends before you were married?

122 **Mrs. Frank.** Anne, that's a personal question. It's not courteous to ask personal questions.

123 **Mrs. Van Daan.** Oh I don't mind. [*To* Anne] Our house was always swarming with boys. When I was a girl we had . . .

124 **Mr. Van Daan.** Oh, God. Not again!

125 **Mrs. Van Daan.** [*Good-humored*] Shut up! [*Without a pause, to* Anne, Mr. Van Daan *mimics* Mrs. Van Daan, *speaking the first few words in unison with her.*] One summer we had a big house in Hilversum. The boys came buzzing round like bees around a jam pot. And when I was sixteen! . . . We were wearing our skirts very short those days and I had good-looking legs. [*She pulls up her skirt, going to* Mr. Frank.] I still have 'em. I may not be as pretty as I used to be, but I still have my legs. How about it, Mr. Frank?

126 **Mr. Van Daan.** All right. All right. We see them.

127 **Mrs. Van Daan.** I'm not asking you. I'm asking Mr. Frank.

128 **Peter.** Mother, for heaven's sake.

129 **Mrs. Van Daan.** Oh, I embarrass you, do I? Well, I just hope the girl you marry has as good. [*Then to* Anne] My father used to worry about me, with so many boys hanging round. He told me, if any of them gets fresh, you say to him . . . "Remember, Mr. So-and-So, remember I'm a lady."

130 **Anne.** "Remember, Mr. So-and-So, remember I'm a lady."

131 [*She gives* Mrs. Van Daan *her coat.*]

132 **Mr. Van Daan.** Look at you, talking that way in front of her! Don't you know she puts it all down in that diary?

133 **Mrs. Van Daan.** So, if she does? I'm only telling the truth!

134 [Anne *stretches out, putting her ear to the floor, listening to what is going on below. The sound of the bombers fades away.*]

135 **Mrs. Frank.** [*Setting the table*] Would you mind, Peter, if I moved you over to the couch?

136 **Anne.** [*Listening*] Miep must have the radio on.

137 [Peter *picks up his papers, going over to the couch beside* Mrs. Van Daan.]

138 **Mr. Van Daan.** [*Accusingly, to* Peter] Haven't you finished yet?

139 **Peter.** No.

140 **Mr. Van Daan.** You ought to be ashamed of yourself.

141 **Peter.** All right. All right. I'm a dunce. I'm a hopeless case. Why do I go on?

142 **Mrs. Van Daan.** You're not hopeless. Don't talk that way. It's just that you haven't anyone to help you, like the girls have. [*To* Mr. Frank] Maybe you could help him, Mr. Frank?

143 **Mr. Frank.** I'm sure that his father . . . ?

144 **Mr. Van Daan.** Not me. I can't do anything with him. He won't listen to me. You go ahead . . . if you want.

145 **Mr. Frank.** [*Going to* Peter] What about it, Peter? Shall we make our school coeducational?

146 **Mrs. Van Daan.** [*Kissing* Mr. Frank] You're an angel, Mr. Frank. An angel. I don't know why I didn't meet you before I met that one there. Here, sit down, Mr. Frank . . . [*She forces him down on the couch beside* Peter.] Now, Peter, you listen to Mr. Frank.

147 **Mr. Frank.** It might be better for us to go into Peter's room.

148 [Peter *jumps up eagerly, leading the way.*]

149 **Mrs. Van Daan.** That's right. You go in there, Peter. You listen to Mr. Frank. Mr. Frank is a highly educated man.

150 [*As* Mr. Frank *is about to follow* Peter *into his room,* Mrs. Frank *stops him and wipes the lipstick from his lips. Then she closes the door after them.*]

151 **Anne.** [*On the floor, listening*] Shh! I can hear a man's voice talking.

152 **Mr. Van Daan.** [*To* Anne] Isn't it bad enough here without your sprawling all over the place?

153 [Anne *sits up.*]

154 **Mrs. Van Daan.** [*To* Mr. Van Daan] If you didn't smoke so much, you wouldn't be so bad-tempered.

155 **Mr. Van Daan.** Am I smoking? Do you see me smoking?

CLOSE READ

ANNOTATE: In paragraphs 138–148, mark words and phrases that suggest disappointment, anger, and blame.

QUESTION: Why do the playwrights include these details?

CONCLUDE: What is the effect of these details, especially in making Peter and Mr. Van Daan's relationship clearer?

156 **Mrs. Van Daan.** Don't tell me you've used up all those cigarettes.

157 **Mr. Van Daan.** One package. Miep only brought me one package.

158 **Mrs. Van Daan.** It's a filthy habit anyway. It's a good time to break yourself.

159 **Mr. Van Daan.** Oh, stop it, please.

160 **Mrs. Van Daan.** You're smoking up all our money. You know that, don't you?

161 **Mr. Van Daan.** Will you shut up?

162 [*During this,* Mrs. Frank *and* Margot *have studiously kept their eyes down. But* Anne, *seated on the floor, has been following the discussion interestedly.* Mr. Van Daan *turns to see her staring up at him.*] And what are you staring at?

163 **Anne.** I never heard grownups quarrel before. I thought only children quarreled.

164 **Mr. Van Daan.** This isn't a quarrel! It's a discussion. And I never heard children so rude before.

165 **Anne.** [*Rising, indignantly*] I, rude!

166 **Mr. Van Daan.** Yes!

167 **Mrs. Frank.** [*Quickly*] Anne, will you get me my knitting? [Anne *goes to get it.*] I must remember, when Miep comes, to ask her to bring me some more wool.

168 **Margot.** [*Going to her room*] I need some hairpins and some soap. I made a list. [*She goes into her bedroom to get the list.*]

169 **Mrs. Frank.** [*To Anne*] Have you some library books for Miep when she comes?

170 **Anne.** It's a wonder that Miep has a life of her own, the way we make her run errands for us. Please, Miep, get me some starch. Please take my hair out and have it cut. Tell me all the latest news, Miep. [*She goes over, kneeling on the couch beside* Mrs. Van Daan] Did you know she was engaged? His name is Dirk, and Miep's afraid the Nazis will ship him off to Germany to work in one of their war plants. That's what they're doing with some of the young Dutchmen . . . they pick them up off the streets—

171 **Mr. Van Daan.** [*Interrupting*] Don't you ever get tired of talking? Suppose you try keeping still for five minutes. Just five minutes.

172 [*He starts to pace again. Again* Anne *follows him, mimicking him.* Mrs. Frank *jumps up and takes her by the arm up to the sink, and gives her a glass of milk.*]

173　**Mrs. Frank.** Come here, Anne. It's time for your glass of milk.

176　**Mr. Van Daan.** Talk, talk, talk. I never heard such a child. Where is my . . . ? Every evening it's the same talk, talk, talk. [*He looks around.*] Where is my . . . ?

175　**Mrs. Van Daan.** What're you looking for?

176　**Mr. Van Daan.** My pipe. Have you seen my pipe?

177　**Mrs. Van Daan.** What good's a pipe? You haven't got any tobacco.

178　**Mr. Van Daan.** At least I'll have something to hold in my mouth! [*Opening* Margot's *bedroom door*] Margot, have you seen my pipe?

179　**Margot.** It was on the table last night.

180　[Anne *puts her glass of milk on the table and picks up his pipe, hiding it behind her back.*]

181　**Mr. Van Daan.** I know. I know. Anne, did you see my pipe? . . . Anne!

182　**Mrs. Frank.** Anne, Mr. Van Daan is speaking to you.

183　**Anne.** Am I allowed to talk now?

184　**Mr. Van Daan.** You're the most aggravating . . . The trouble with you is, you've been spoiled. What you need is a good old-fashioned spanking.

185　**Anne.** [*Mimicking* Mrs. Van Daan] "Remember, Mr. So-and-So, remember I'm a lady." [*She thrusts the pipe into his mouth, then picks up her glass of milk.*]

186　**Mr. Van Daan.** [*Restraining himself with difficulty*] Why aren't you nice and quiet like your sister Margot? Why do you have to show off all the time? Let me give you a little advice, young lady. Men don't like that kind of thing in a girl. You know that? A man likes a girl who'll listen to him once in a while . . . a domestic girl, who'll keep her house shining for her husband . . . who loves to cook and sew and . . .

187　**Anne.** I'd cut my throat first! I'd open my veins! I'm going to be remarkable! I'm going to Paris . . .

188　**Mr. Van Daan.** [*Scoffingly*] Paris!

189　**Anne.** . . . to study music and art.

190　**Mr. Van Daan.** Yeah! Yeah!

191　**Anne.** I'm going to be a famous dancer or singer . . . or something wonderful.

192　[*She makes a wide gesture, spilling the glass of milk on the fur coat in* Mrs. Van Daan's *lap.* Margot *rushes quickly over with a towel.* Anne *tries to brush the milk off with her skirt.*]

restraining (rih STRAY nihng) *v.* holding back; controlling one's emotions

The Diary of Anne Frank, Act I　**123**

193 Mrs. Van Daan. Now look what you've done . . . you clumsy little fool! My beautiful fur coat my father gave me . . .

194 Anne. I'm so sorry.

195 Mrs. Van Daan. What do you care? It isn't yours . . . So go on, ruin it! Do you know what that coat cost? Do you? And now look at it! Look at it!

196 Anne. I'm very, very sorry.

197 Mrs. Van Daan. I could kill you for this. I could just kill you!

198 [Mrs. Van Daan *goes up the stairs, clutching the coat.* Mr. Van Daan *starts after her.*]

199 Mr. Van Daan. Petronella . . . *Liefje! Liefje!* . . . Come back . . . the supper . . . come back!

200 Mrs. Frank. Anne, you must not behave in that way.

201 Anne. It was an accident. Anyone can have an accident.

202 Mrs. Frank. I don't mean that. I mean the answering back. You must not answer back. They are our guests. We must always show the greatest courtesy to them. We're all living under terrible tension. [*She stops as* Margot *indicates that* Mr. Van Daan *can hear. When he is gone, she continues.*] That's why we must control ourselves . . . You don't hear Margot getting into arguments with them, do you? Watch Margot. She's always courteous with them. Never familiar. She keeps her distance. And they respect her for it. Try to be like Margot.

203 Anne. And have them walk all over me, the way they do her? No, thanks!

204 Mrs. Frank. I'm not afraid that anyone is going to walk all over you, Anne. I'm afraid for other people, that you'll walk on them. I don't know what happens to you, Anne. You are wild, self-willed. If I had ever talked to my mother as you talk to me . . .

205 Anne. Things have changed. People aren't like that any more. "Yes, Mother." "No, Mother." "Anything you say, Mother." I've got to fight things out for myself! Make something of myself!

206 Mrs. Frank. It isn't necessary to fight to do it. Margot doesn't fight, and isn't she . . . ?

207 Anne. [*Violently rebellious*] Margot! Margot! Margot! That's all I hear from everyone . . . how wonderful Margot is . . . "Why aren't you like Margot?"

208 Margot. [*Protesting*] Oh, come on, Anne, don't be so . . .

CLOSE READ

ANNOTATE: In paragraphs 202–207, mark details related to control and calm. Mark other details related to lack of control or strong emotions.

QUESTION: Why do the playwrights use these contrasting details?

CONCLUDE: What is the effect of these details, especially in portraying Anne's character and relationships with her family?

209 **Anne.** [*Paying no attention*] Everything she does is right, and everything I do is wrong! I'm the goat around here! . . . You're all against me! . . . And you worst of all!

210 [*She rushes off into her room and throws herself down on the settee, stifling her sobs.* Mrs. Frank *sighs and starts toward the stove.*]

211 **Mrs. Frank.** [*To* Margot] Let's put the soup on the stove . . . if there's anyone who cares to eat. Margot, will you take the bread out? [Margot *gets the bread from the cupboard.*] I don't know how we can go on living this way . . . I can't say a word to Anne . . . she flies at me . . .

212 **Margot.** You know Anne. In half an hour she'll be out here, laughing and joking.

213 **Mrs. Frank.** And . . . [*She makes a motion upwards, indicating the* Van Daans.] . . . I told your father it wouldn't work . . . but no . . . no . . . he had to ask them, he said . . . he owed it to him, he said. Well, he knows now that I was right! These **quarrels**! . . . This **bickering**!

214 **Margot.** [*With a warning look*] Shush. Shush.

215 [*The buzzer for the door sounds.* Mrs. Frank *gasps, startled.*]

216 **Mrs. Frank.** Every time I hear that sound, my heart stops!

217 **Margot.** [*Starting for* Peter's *door*] It's Miep. [*She knocks at the door.*] Father?

218 [Mr. Frank *comes quickly from* Peter's *room.*]

219 **Mr. Frank.** Thank you, Margot. [*As he goes down the steps to open the outer door*] Has everyone his list?

220 **Margot.** I'll get my books. [*Giving her mother a list*] Here's your list. [Margot *goes into her and* Anne's *bedroom on the right.* Anne *sits up, hiding her tears, as* Margot *comes in.*] Miep's here. [Margot *picks up her books and goes back.* Anne *hurries over to the mirror, smoothing her hair.*]

221 **Mr. Van Daan.** [*Coming down the stairs*] Is it Miep?

222 **Margot.** Yes. Father's gone down to let her in.

223 **Mr. Van Daan.** At last I'll have some cigarettes!

224 **Mrs. Frank.** [*To* Mr. Van Daan] I can't tell you how unhappy I am about Mrs. Van Daan's coat. Anne should never have touched it.

225 **Mr. Van Daan.** She'll be all right.

226 **Mrs. Frank.** Is there anything I can do?

227 **Mr. Van Daan.** Don't worry.

quarrels (KWAWR uhlz) *n.* arguments; disagreements

bickering (BIHK uhr ihng) *n.* arguing over unimportant things

228 [*He turns to meet* Miep. *But it is not* Miep *who comes up the steps. It is* Mr. Kraler, *followed by* Mr. Frank. *Their faces are grave.* Anne *comes from the bedroom.* Peter *comes from his room.*]

229 **Mrs. Frank.** Mr. Kraler!

230 **Mr. Van Daan.** How are you, Mr. Kraler?

231 **Margot.** This is a surprise.

232 **Mrs. Frank.** When Mr. Kraler comes, the sun begins to shine.

233 **Mr. Van Daan.** Miep is coming?

234 **Mr. Kraler.** Not tonight.

235 [Mr. Kraler *goes to* Margot *and* Mrs. Frank *and* Anne, *shaking hands with them.*]

236 **Mrs. Frank.** Wouldn't you like a cup of coffee? . . . Or, better still, will you have supper with us?

237 **Mr. Frank.** Mr. Kraler has something to talk over with us. Something has happened, he says, which demands an immediate decision.

238 **Mrs. Frank.** [*Fearful*] What is it?

239 [Mr. Kraler *sits down on the couch. As he talks he takes bread, cabbages, milk, etc., from his briefcase, giving them to* Margot *and* Anne *to put away.*]

240 **Mr. Kraler.** Usually, when I come up here, I try to bring you some bit of good news. What's the use of telling you the bad news when there's nothing that you can do about it? But today something has happened . . . Dirk . . . Miep's Dirk, you know, came to me just now. He tells me that he has a Jewish friend living near him. A dentist. He says he's in trouble. He begged me, could I do anything for this man? Could I find him a hiding place? . . . So I've come to you . . . I know it's a terrible thing to ask of you, living as you are, but would you take him in with you?

241 **Mr. Frank.** Of course we will.

242 **Mr. Kraler.** [*Rising*] It'll be just for a night or two . . . until I find some other place. This happened so suddenly that I didn't know where to turn.

243 **Mr. Frank.** Where is he?

244 **Mr. Kraler.** Downstairs in the office.

245 **Mr. Frank.** Good. Bring him up.

246 **Mr. Kraler.** His name is Dussel . . . Jan Dussel.

247 **Mr. Frank.** Dussel . . . I think I know him.

248 **Mr. Kraler.** I'll get him.

249 [*He goes quickly down the steps and out.* Mr. Frank *suddenly becomes conscious of the others.*]

250 **Mr. Frank.** Forgive me. I spoke without consulting you. But I knew you'd feel as I do.

251 **Mr. Van Daan.** There's no reason for you to consult anyone. This is your place. You have a right to do exactly as you please. The only thing I feel . . . there's so little food as it is . . . and to take in another person . . .

252 [Peter *turns away, ashamed of his father.*]

253 **Mr. Frank.** We can stretch the food a little. It's only for a few days.

254 **Mr. Van Daan.** You want to make a bet?

255 **Mrs. Frank.** I think it's fine to have him. But, Otto, where are you going to put him? Where?

256 **Peter.** He can have my bed. I can sleep on the floor. I wouldn't mind.

257 **Mr. Frank.** That's good of you, Peter. But your room's too small . . . even for *you.*

258 **Anne.** I have a much better idea. I'll come in here with you and Mother, and Margot can take Peter's room and Peter can go in our room with Mr. Dussel.

259 **Margot.** That's right. We could do that.

260 **Mr. Frank.** No, Margot. You mustn't sleep in that room . . . neither you nor Anne. Mouschi has caught some rats in there. Peter's brave. He doesn't mind.

261 **Anne.** Then how about *this?* I'll come in here with you and Mother, and Mr. Dussel can have my bed.

262 **Mrs. Frank.** *No. No. No!* Margot will come in here with us and he can have her bed. It's the only way. Margot, bring your things in here. Help her, Anne.

263 [Margot *hurries into her room to get her things.*]

264 **Anne.** [*To her mother*] Why Margot? Why can't I come in here?

265 **Mrs. Frank.** Because it wouldn't be proper for Margot to sleep with a . . . Please, Anne. Don't argue. Please.

266 [Anne *starts slowly away.*]

This photograph shows the stairway to the Secret Annex that was hidden behind a swinging bookcase.

NOTES

267 **Mr. Frank.** [*To* Anne] You don't mind sharing your room with Mr. Dussel, do you, Anne?

268 **Anne.** No. No, of course not.

269 **Mr. Frank.** Good. [Anne *goes off into her bedroom, helping* Margot. Mr. Frank *starts to search in the cupboards.*] Where's the cognac?

270 **Mrs. Frank.** It's there. But, Otto, I was saving it in case of illness.

271 **Mr. Frank.** I think we couldn't find a better time to use it. Peter, will you get five glasses for me?

272 [Peter *goes for the glasses.* Margot *comes out of her bedroom, carrying her possessions, which she hangs behind a curtain in the main room.* Mr. Frank *finds the cognac and pours it into the five glasses that* Peter *brings him.* Mr. Van Daan *stands looking on sourly.* Mrs. Van Daan *comes downstairs and looks around at all the bustle.*]

273 **Mrs. Van Daan.** What's happening? What's going on?

274 **Mr. Van Daan.** Someone's moving in with us.

275 **Mrs. Van Daan.** In here? You're joking.

276 **Margot.** It's only for a night or two . . . until Mr. Kraler finds him another place.

277 **Mr. Van Daan.** Yeah! Yeah!

278 [Mr. Frank *hurries over as* Mr. Kraler *and* Dussel *come up.* Dussel *is a man in his late fifties, meticulous, finicky . . . bewildered now. He wears a raincoat. He carries a briefcase, stuffed full, and a small medicine case.*]

279 **Mr. Frank.** Come in, Mr. Dussel.

280 **Mr. Kraler.** This is Mr. Frank.

281 **Dussel.** Mr. Otto Frank?

282 **Mr. Frank.** Yes. Let me take your things. [*He takes the hat and briefcase, but* Dussel *clings to his medicine case.*] This is my wife, Edith . . . Mr. and Mrs. Van Daan . . . their son, Peter . . . and my daughters, Margot and Anne.

283 [Dussel *shakes hands with everyone.*]

284 **Mr. Kraler.** Thank you, Mr. Frank. Thank you all. Mr. Dussel, I leave you in good hands. Oh . . . Dirk's coat.

285 [Dussel *hurriedly takes off the raincoat, giving it to* Mr. Kraler. *Underneath is his white dentist's jacket, with a yellow Star of David on it.*]

286 **Dussel.** [*To* Mr. Kraler] What can I say to thank you . . . ?

287 **Mrs. Frank.** [*To* Dussel] Mr. Kraler and Miep . . . They're our life line. Without them we couldn't live.

288 **Mr. Kraler.** Please. Please. You make us seem very heroic. It isn't that at all. We simply don't like the Nazis. [*To* Mr. Frank, *who offers him a drink*] No, thanks. [*Then going on*] We don't like their methods. We don't like . . .

289 **Mr. Frank.** [*Smiling*] I know. I know. "No one's going to tell us Dutchmen what to do with our damn Jews!"

290 **Mr. Kraler.** [*To* Dussel] Pay no attention to Mr. Frank. I'll be up tomorrow to see that they're treating you right. [*To* Mr. Frank] Don't trouble to come down again. Peter will bolt the door after me, won't you, Peter?

291 **Peter.** Yes, sir.

292 **Mr. Frank.** Thank you, Peter. I'll do it.

293 **Mr. Kraler.** Good night. Good night.

294 **Group.** Good night, Mr. Kraler. We'll see you tomorrow, etc., etc.

295 [Mr. Kraler *goes out with* Mr. Frank. Mrs. Frank *gives each one of the "grownups" a glass of cognac.*]

296 **Mrs. Frank.** Please, Mr. Dussel, sit down.

297 [Mr. Dussel *sinks into a chair.* Mrs. Frank *gives him a glass of cognac.*]

298 **Dussel.** I'm dreaming. I know it. I can't believe my eyes. Mr. Otto Frank here! [*To* Mrs. Frank] You're not in Switzerland then? A woman told me . . . She said she'd gone to your house . . . the door was open, everything was in disorder, dishes in the sink. She said she found a piece of paper in the wastebasket with an address scribbled on it . . . an address in Zurich. She said you must have escaped to Zurich.

299 **Anne.** Father put that there purposely . . . just so people would think that very thing!

300 **Dussel.** And you've been *here* all the time?

301 **Mrs. Frank.** All the time . . . ever since July.

302 [Anne *speaks to her father as he comes back*]

303 **Anne.** It worked, Pim . . . the address you left! Mr. Dussel says that people believe we escaped to Switzerland.

304 **Mr. Frank.** I'm glad . . . And now let's have a little drink to welcome Mr. Dussel.

305 [*Before they can drink,* Mr. Dussel *bolts his drink.* Mr. Frank *smiles and raises his glass.*]

306 To Mr. Dussel. Welcome. We're very honored to have you with us.

307 **Mrs. Frank.** To Mr. Dussel, welcome.

308 [*The* Van Daans *murmur a welcome. The "grownups" drink.*]

309 **Mrs. Van Daan.** Um. That was good.

310 **Mr. Van Daan.** Did Mr. Kraler warn you that you won't get much to eat here? You can imagine . . . three ration books among the seven of us . . . and now you make eight.

311 [Peter *walks away, humiliated. Outside a street organ is heard dimly.*]

312 **Dussel.** [*Rising*] Mr. Van Daan, you don't realize what is happening outside that you should warn me of a thing like that. You don't realize what's going on . . . [*As Mr. Van Daan starts his characteristic pacing,* Dussel *turns to speak to the others.*] Right here in Amsterdam every day hundreds of Jews disappear . . . They surround a block and search house by house. Children come home from school to find their parents gone. Hundreds are being deported . . . people that you and I know . . . the Hallensteins . . . the Wessels . . .

313 **Mrs. Frank.** [*In tears*] Oh, no. No!

314 **Dussel.** They get their call-up notice . . . come to the Jewish theater on such and such a day and hour . . . bring only what you can carry in a rucksack. And if you refuse the call-up notice, then they come and drag you from your home and ship you off to Mauthausen.[20] The death camp!

315 **Mrs. Frank.** We didn't know that things had got so much worse.

316 **Dussel.** Forgive me for speaking so.

317 **Anne.** [*Coming to* Dussel] Do you know the de Waals? . . . What's become of them? Their daughter Jopie and I are in the same class. Jopie's my best friend.

318 **Dussel.** They are gone.

319 **Anne.** Gone?

320 **Dussel.** With all the others.

321 **Anne.** Oh, no. Not Jopie!

322 [*She turns away, in tears.* Mrs. Frank *motions to* Margot *to comfort her.* Margot *goes to* Anne, *putting her arms comfortingly around her.*]

323 **Mrs. Van Daan.** There were some people called Wagner. They lived near us . . . ?

CLOSE READ

ANNOTATE: Mark details in paragraphs 312–322 that show how the characters react to Dussel's news of the outside world.

QUESTION: Why do the playwrights include these details?

CONCLUDE: What is the effect of these details?

20. **Mauthausen** (MOW tow zuhn) village in Austria that was the site of a Nazi concentration camp.

324 **Mr. Frank.** [*Interrupting, with a glance at* Anne] I think we should put this off until later. We all have many questions we want to ask . . . But I'm sure that Mr. Dussel would like to get settled before supper.

325 **Dussel.** Thank you. I would. I brought very little with me.

326 **Mr. Frank.** [*Giving him his hat and briefcase*] I'm sorry we can't give you a room alone. But I hope you won't be too uncomfortable. We've had to make strict rules here . . . a schedule of hours . . . We'll tell you after supper. Anne, would you like to take Mr. Dussel to his room?

327 **Anne.** [*Controlling her tears*] If you'll come with me, Mr. Dussel? [*She starts for her room.*]

328 **Dussel.** [*Shaking hands with each in turn*] Forgive me if I haven't really expressed my gratitude to all of you. This has been such a shock to me. I'd always thought of myself as Dutch. I was born in Holland. My father was born in Holland, and my grandfather. And now . . . after all these years . . . [*He breaks off.*] If you'll excuse me.

329 [Dussel *gives a little bow and hurries off after* Anne. Mr. Frank *and the others are subdued.*]

330 **Anne.** [*Turning on the light*] Well, here we are.

331 [Dussel *looks around the room. In the main room* Margot *speaks to her mother.*]

332 **Margot.** The news sounds pretty bad, doesn't it? It's so different from what Mr. Kraler tells us. Mr. Kraler says things are improving.

333 **Mr. Van Daan.** I like it better the way Kraler tells it.

334 [*They resume their occupations, quietly.* Peter *goes off into his room. In* Anne's *room,* Anne *turns to* Dussel.]

335 **Anne.** You're going to share the room with me.

336 **Dussel.** I'm a man who's always lived alone. I haven't had to adjust myself to others. I hope you'll bear with me until I learn.

337 **Anne.** Let me help you. [*She takes his briefcase.*] Do you always live all alone? Have you no family at all?

338 **Dussel.** No one. [*He opens his medicine case and spreads his bottles on the dressing table.*]

339 **Anne.** How dreadful. You must be terribly lonely.

340 **Dussel.** I'm used to it.

341 **Anne.** I don't think I could ever get used to it. Didn't you even have a pet? A cat, or a dog?

342 **Dussel.** I have an allergy for fur-bearing animals. They give me asthma.

343 **Anne.** Oh, dear. Peter has a cat.

344 **Dussel.** Here? He has it here?

345 **Anne.** Yes. But we hardly ever see it. He keeps it in his room all the time. I'm sure it will be all right.

346 **Dussel.** Let us hope so. [*He takes some pills to fortify himself.*]

347 **Anne.** That's Margot's bed, where you're going to sleep. I sleep on the sofa there. [*Indicating the clothes hooks on the wall*] We cleared these off for your things. [*She goes over to the window.*] The best part about this room . . . you can look down and see a bit of the street and the canal. There's a houseboat . . . you can see the end of it . . . a bargeman lives there with his family . . . They have a baby and he's just beginning to walk and I'm so afraid he's going to fall into the canal some day. I watch him . . .

348 **Dussel.** [*Interrupting*] Your father spoke of a schedule.

349 **Anne.** [*Coming away from the window*] Oh, yes. It's mostly about the times we have to be quiet. And times for the w.c. You can use it now if you like.

350 **Dussel.** [*Stiffly*] No, thank you.

351 **Anne.** I suppose you think it's awful, my talking about a thing like that. But you don't know how important it can get to be, especially when you're frightened . . . About this room, the way Margot and I did . . . she had it to herself in the afternoons for studying, reading . . . lessons, you know . . . and I took the mornings. Would that be all right with you?

352 **Dussel.** I'm not at my best in the morning.

353 **Anne.** You stay here in the mornings then. I'll take the room in the afternoons.

354 **Dussel.** Tell me, when you're in here, what happens to me? Where am I spending my time? In there, with all the people?

355 **Anne.** Yes.

356 **Dussel.** I see. I see.

357 **Anne.** We have supper at half past six.

358 **Dussel.** [*Going over to the sofa*] Then, if you don't mind . . . I like to lie down quietly for ten minutes before eating. I find it helps the digestion.

359 **Anne.** Of course. I hope I'm not going to be too much of a bother to you. I seem to be able to get everyone's back up.

360 [Dussel *lies down on the sofa, curled up, his back to her.*]

361 **Dussel.** I always get along very well with children. My patients all bring their children to me, because they know I get on well with them. So don't you worry about that.

362 [Anne *leans over him, taking his hand and shaking it gratefully.*]

363 **Anne.** Thank you. Thank you, Mr. Dussel.

364 [*The lights dim to darkness. The curtain falls on the scene.* Anne's Voice *comes to us faintly at first, and then with increasing power.*]

365 **Anne's Voice.** . . . And yesterday I finished Cissy Van Marxvelt's latest book. I think she is a first-class writer. I shall definitely let my children read her. Monday the twenty-first of September, nineteen forty-two. Mr. Dussel and I had another battle yesterday. Yes, Mr. Dussel! According to him, nothing, I repeat . . . nothing, is right about me . . . my appearance, my character, my manners. While he was going on at me I thought . . . sometime I'll give you such a smack that you'll fly right up to the ceiling! Why is it that every grownup thinks he knows the way to bring up children? Particularly the grownups that never had any. I keep wishing that Peter was a girl instead of a boy. Then I would have someone to talk to. Margot's a darling, but she takes everything too seriously. To pause for a moment on the subject of Mrs. Van Daan. I must tell you that her attempts to flirt with Father are getting her nowhere. Pim, thank goodness, won't play.

366 [*As she is saying the last lines, the curtain rises on the darkened scene.* Anne's Voice *fades out.*]

❈ ❈ ❈

Scene 4

1 [*It is the middle of the night, several months later. The stage is dark except for a little light which comes through the skylight in* Peter's *room.*

2 *Everyone is in bed.* Mr. *and* Mrs. Frank *lie on the couch in the main room, which has been pulled out to serve as a makeshift double bed.*

3 Margot *is sleeping on a mattress on the floor in the main room, behind a curtain stretched across for privacy. The others are all in their accustomed rooms.*

4 *From outside we hear two drunken soldiers singing "Lili Marlene." A girl's high giggle is heard. The sound of running feet is heard*

CLOSE READ

ANNOTATE: In paragraph 361, mark details that relate to Dussel's feelings toward children. Mark details in paragraph 365 that refer to his feelings toward Anne.

QUESTION: Why do the playwrights include these contrasting details?

CONCLUDE: What do these details show about Mr. Dussel's character and conflicts that arise as the story continues?

Anne's Dutch passport and samples of her writing.

coming closer and then fading in the distance. Throughout the scene there is the distant sound of airplanes passing overhead.

5 *A match suddenly flares up in the attic. We dimly see* Mr. Van Daan. *He is getting his bearings. He comes quickly down the stairs, and goes to the cupboard where the food is stored. Again the match flares up, and is as quickly blown out.*

6 *The dim figure is seen to steal back up the stairs.*

7 *There is quiet for a second or two, broken only by the sound of airplanes, and running feet on the street below.*

8 *Suddenly, out of the silence and the dark, we hear* Anne *scream.*]

9 **Anne.** [*Screaming*] No! No! Don't . . . don't take me!

10 [*She moans, tossing and crying in her sleep. The other people wake, terrified.* Dussel *sits up in bed, furious.*]

11 **Dussel.** Shush! Anne! Anne, for God's sake, shush!

12 **Anne.** [*Still in her nightmare*] Save me! Save me!

13 [*She screams and screams.* Dussel *gets out of bed, going over to her, trying to wake her.*]

14 **Dussel.** For God's sake! Quiet! Quiet! You want someone to hear?

15 [*In the main room* Mrs. Frank *grabs a shawl and pulls it around her. She rushes in to Anne, taking her in her arms.* Mr. Frank *hurriedly gets up, putting on his overcoat.* Margot *sits up, terrified.* Peter's *light goes on in his room.*]

16 **Mrs. Frank.** [*To* Anne, *in her room*] Hush, darling, hush. It's all right. It's all right. [*Over her shoulder to* Dussel] Will you be kind enough to turn on the light, Mr. Dussel? [*Back to* Anne] It's nothing, my darling. It was just a dream.

17 [Dussel *turns on the light in the bedroom.* Mrs. Frank *holds* Anne *in her arms. Gradually* Anne *comes out of her nightmare still trembling with horror.* Mr. Frank *comes into the room, and goes quickly to the window, looking out to be sure that no one outside has heard* Anne's *screams.* Mrs. Frank *holds* Anne, *talking softly to her. In the main room* Margot *stands on a chair, turning on the center hanging lamp. A light goes on in the* Van Daans' *room overhead.* Peter *puts his robe on, coming out of his room.*]

18 **Dussel.** [*To* Mrs. Frank, *blowing his nose*] Something must be done about that child, Mrs. Frank. Yelling like that! Who knows but there's somebody on the streets? She's endangering all our lives.

19 **Mrs. Frank.** Anne, darling.

20 **Dussel.** Every night she twists and turns. I don't sleep. I spend half my night shushing her. And now it's nightmares!

21 [Margot *comes to the door of* Anne's *room, followed by* Peter. Mr. Frank *goes to them, indicating that everything is all right.* Peter *takes* Margot *back.*]

22 **Mrs. Frank.** [*To* Anne] You're here, safe, you see? Nothing has happened. [*To* Dussel] Please, Mr. Dussel, go back to bed. She'll be herself in a minute or two. Won't you, Anne?

23 **Dussel.** [*Picking up a book and a pillow*] Thank you, but I'm going to the w.c. The one place where there's peace!

24 [*He stalks out.* Mr. Van Daan, *in underwear and trousers, comes down the stairs.*]

25 **Mr. Van Daan.** [*To* Dussel] What is it? What happened?

26 **Dussel.** A nightmare. She was having a nightmare!

27 **Mr. Van Daan.** I thought someone was murdering her.

28 **Dussel.** Unfortunately, no.

29 [*He goes into the bathroom.* Mr. Van Daan *goes back up the stairs.* Mr. Frank, *in the main room, sends* Peter *back to his own bedroom.*]

30 **Mr. Frank.** Thank you, Peter. Go back to bed.

31 [Peter *goes back to his room.* Mr. Frank *follows him, turning out the light and looking out the window. Then he goes back to the main room, and gets up on a chair, turning out the center hanging lamp.*]

32 **Mrs. Frank.** [*To* Anne] Would you like some water? [Anne *shakes her head.*] Was it a very bad dream? Perhaps if you told me . . . ?

33 **Anne.** I'd rather not talk about it.

34 **Mrs. Frank.** Poor darling. Try to sleep then. I'll sit right here beside you until you fall asleep. [*She brings a stool over, sitting there.*]

35 **Anne.** You don't have to.

36 **Mrs. Frank.** But I'd like to stay with you . . . very much. Really.

37 **Anne.** I'd rather you didn't.

38 **Mrs. Frank.** Good night, then. [*She leans down to kiss* Anne. Anne *throws her arm up over her face, turning away.* Mrs. Frank, *hiding her hurt, kisses* Anne's *arm.*] You'll be all right? There's nothing that you want?

39 **Anne.** Will you please ask Father to come.

40 **Mrs. Frank.** [*After a second*] Of course, Anne dear. [*She hurries out into the other room.* Mr. Frank *comes to her as she comes in.*] *Sie verlangt nach Dir!*[21]

41 **Mr. Frank.** [*Sensing her hurt*] Edith, *Liebe, schau*[22] . . .

42 **Mrs. Frank.** *Es macht nichts! Ich danke dem lieben Herrgott, dass sie sich wenigstens an Dich wendet, wenn sie Trost braucht! Geh hinein, Otto, sie ist ganz hysterisch vor Angst.*[23] [*As* Mr. Frank *hesitates*] *Geh zu ihr.*[24] [*He looks at her for a second and then goes to get a cup of water for* Anne. Mrs. Frank *sinks down on the bed, her face in her hands, trying to keep from sobbing aloud.* Margot *comes over to her, putting her arms around her.*] She wants nothing of me. She pulled away when I leaned down to kiss her.

43 **Margot.** It's a phase . . . You heard Father . . . Most girls go through it . . . they turn to their fathers at this age . . . they give all their love to their fathers.

44 **Mrs. Frank.** You weren't like this. You didn't shut me out.

45 **Margot.** She'll get over it . . .

46 [*She smooths the bed for* Mrs. Frank *and sits beside her a moment as* Mrs. Frank *lies down. In* Anne's *room* Mr. Frank *comes in, sitting down by* Anne. Anne *flings her arms around him, clinging to him. In the distance we hear the sound of ack-ack.*]

47 **Anne.** Oh, Pim. I dreamed that they came to get us! The Green Police! They broke down the door and grabbed me and started to drag me out the way they did Jopie.

48 **Mr. Frank.** I want you to take this pill.

49 **Anne.** What is it?

50 **Mr. Frank.** Something to quiet you.

21. ***Sie verlangt nach Dir*** (zee FER langt nokh DIHR) German for "She is asking for you."

22. ***Liebe, schau*** (LEE buh SHOW) German for "Dear, look."

23. ***Es macht . . . vor Angst*** German for "It's all right. I thank dear God that at least she turns to you when she needs comfort. Go in, Otto, she is hysterical because of fear."

24. ***Geh zu ihr*** (GAY tsoo eer) German for "Go to her."

51 [*She takes it and drinks the water. In the main room* Margot *turns out the light and goes back to her bed.*]

52 **Mr. Frank.** [*To* Anne] Do you want me to read to you for a while?

53 **Anne.** No. Just sit with me for a minute. Was I awful? Did I yell terribly loud? Do you think anyone outside could have heard?

54 **Mr. Frank.** No. No. Lie quietly now. Try to sleep.

55 **Anne.** I'm a terrible coward. I'm so disappointed in myself. I think I've conquered my fear . . . I think I'm really grownup . . . and then something happens . . . and I run to you like a baby . . . I love you, Father. I don't love anyone but you.

56 **Mr. Frank.** [*Reproachfully*] Annele!

57 **Anne.** It's true. I've been thinking about it for a long time. You're the only one I love.

58 **Mr. Frank.** It's fine to hear you tell me that you love me. But I'd be happier if you said you loved your mother as well . . . She needs your help so much . . . your love . . .

59 **Anne.** We have nothing in common. She doesn't understand me. Whenever I try to explain my views on life to her she asks me if I'm constipated.

60 **Mr. Frank.** You hurt her very much just now. She's crying. She's in there crying.

61 **Anne.** I can't help it. I only told the truth. I didn't want her here . . . [*Then, with sudden change*] Oh, Pim, I was horrible, wasn't I? And the worst of it is, I can stand off and look at myself doing it and know it's cruel and yet I can't stop doing it. What's the matter with me? Tell me. Don't say it's just a phase! Help me.

62 **Mr. Frank.** There is so little that we parents can do to help our children. We can only try to set a good example . . . point the way. The rest you must do yourself. You must build your own character.

63 **Anne.** I'm trying. Really I am. Every night I think back over all of the things I did that day that were wrong . . . like putting the wet mop in Mr. Dussel's bed . . . and this thing now with Mother. I say to myself, that was wrong. I make up my mind, I'm never going to do that again. Never! Of course I may do something worse . . . but at least I'll never do *that* again! . . . I have a nicer side, Father . . . a sweeter, nicer side. But I'm scared to show it. I'm afraid that people are going to laugh at me if I'm serious. So the mean Anne comes to the

CLOSE READ

ANNOTATE: In paragraph 63, mark the details that suggest the kinds of mischief Anne carries out against adults in the Annex.

QUESTION: Why might the playwrights have chosen to include this detail—but no others—about Anne's bad behavior?

CONCLUDE: What does this detail reveal about Anne's character?

The Diary of Anne Frank, Act I **137**

outside and the good Anne stays on the inside, and I keep on trying to switch them around and have the good Anne outside and the bad Anne inside and be what I'd like to be . . . and might be . . . if only . . . only . . .

64 [*She is asleep.* Mr. Frank *watches her for a moment and then turns off the light, and starts out. The lights dim out. The curtain falls on the scene.* Anne's Voice *is heard dimly at first, and then with growing strength.*]

65 **Anne's Voice** . . . The air raids are getting worse. They come over day and night. The noise is terrifying. Pim says it should be music to our ears. The more planes, the sooner will come the end of the war. Mrs. Van Daan pretends to be a fatalist. What will be, will be. But when the planes come over, who is the most frightened? No one else but Petronella! . . . Monday, the ninth of November, nineteen forty-two. Wonderful news! The Allies have landed in Africa. Pim says that we can look for an early finish to the war. Just for fun he asked each of us what was the first thing we wanted to do when we got out of here. Mrs. Van Daan longs to be home with her own things, her needlepoint chairs, the Beckstein piano her father gave her . . . the best that money could buy. Peter would like to go to a movie. Mr. Dussel wants to get back to his dentist's drill. He's afraid he is losing his touch. For myself, there are so many things . . . to ride a bike again . . . to laugh till my belly aches . . . to have new clothes from the skin out . . . to have a hot tub filled to overflowing and wallow in it for hours . . . to be back in school with my friends . . .

66 [*As the last lines are being said, the curtain rises on the scene. The lights dim on as* Anne's Voice *fades away.*]

⌘ ⌘ ⌘

Scene 5

1 [*It is the first night of the Hanukkah*[25] *celebration.* Mr. Frank *is standing at the head of the table on which is the Menorah.*[26] *He lights the Shamos,*[27] *or servant candle, and holds it as he says the blessing. Seated listening is all of the "family," dressed in their best. The men wear hats,* Peter *wears his cap.*]

2 **Mr. Frank.** [*Reading from a prayer book*] "Praised be Thou, oh Lord our God, Ruler of the universe, who has sanctified us with Thy commandments and bidden us kindle the Hanukkah lights. Praised be Thou, oh Lord our God, Ruler of

25. **Hanukkah** (HAH nu kah) Jewish celebration that lasts eight days.

26. **Menorah** (muh NAWR uh) *n.* candleholder with nine candles, used during Hanukkah.

27. **Shamos** (SHAH muhs) *n.* candle used to light the others in a menorah.

This still image from a film version of the play shows the Hanukkah scene.

the universe, who has wrought wondrous deliverances for our fathers in days of old. Praised be Thou, oh Lord our God, Ruler of the universe, that Thou has given us life and sustenance and brought us to this happy season." [*Mr. Frank lights the one candle of the Menorah as he continues.*] "We kindle this Hanukkah light to celebrate the great and wonderful deeds wrought through the zeal with which God filled the hearts of the heroic Maccabees, two thousand years ago. They fought against indifference, against tyranny and oppression, and they restored our Temple to us. May these lights remind us that we should ever look to God, whence cometh our help." Amen.

3 **All.** Amen.

4 [Mr. Frank *hands* Mrs. Frank *the prayer book.*]

5 **Mrs. Frank.** [*Reading*] "I lift up mine eyes unto the mountains, from whence cometh my help. My help cometh from the Lord who made heaven and earth. He will not suffer thy foot to be moved. He that keepeth thee will not slumber. He that keepeth Israel doth neither slumber nor sleep. The Lord is thy keeper. The Lord is thy shade upon thy right hand. The sun shall not smite thee by day, nor the moon by night. The Lord shall keep thee from all evil. He shall keep thy soul. The Lord shall guard thy going out and thy coming in, from this time forth and forevermore." Amen.

CLOSE READ

ANNOTATE: In paragraph 2, mark the sentences that explain why the Hanukkah candles are lit.

QUESTION: Why might the playwrights have included this explanation of the Hanukkah story?

CONCLUDE: What is the effect of this explanation?

6 **All.** Amen.

7 [Mrs. Frank *puts down the prayer book and goes to get the food and wine.* Margot *helps her.* Mr. Frank *takes the men's hats and puts them aside.*]

8 **Dussel.** [Rising] That was very moving.

9 **Anne.** [*Pulling him back*] It isn't over yet!

10 **Mrs. Van Daan.** Sit down! Sit down!

11 **Anne.** There's a lot more, songs and presents.

12 **Dussel.** Presents?

13 **Mrs. Frank.** Not this year, unfortunately.

14 **Mrs. Van Daan.** But always on Hanukkah everyone gives presents . . . everyone!

15 **Dussel.** Like our St. Nicholas's Day.[28]

16 [*There is a chorus of "no's" from the group.*]

17 **Mrs. Van Daan.** No! Not like St. Nicholas! What kind of a Jew are you that you don't know Hanukkah?

18 **Mrs. Frank.** [*As she brings the food*] I remember particularly the candles . . . First one, as we have tonight. Then the second night you light two candles, the next night three . . . and so on until you have eight candles burning. When there are eight candles it is truly beautiful.

19 **Mrs. Van Daan.** And the potato pancakes.

20 **Mr. Van Daan.** Don't talk about them!

21 **Mrs. Van Daan.** I make the best *latkes* you ever tasted!

22 **Mrs. Frank.** Invite us all next year . . . in your own home.

23 **Mr. Frank.** God willing!

24 **Mrs. Van Daan.** God willing.

25 **Margot.** What I remember best is the presents we used to get when we were little . . . eight days of presents . . . and each day they got better and better.

26 **Mrs. Frank.** [*Sitting down*] We are all here, alive. That is present enough.

27 **Anne.** No, it isn't. I've got something . . . [*She rushes into her room, hurriedly puts on a little hat improvised from the lamp shade, grabs a satchel bulging with parcels and comes running back.*]

28 **Mrs. Frank.** What is it?

29 **Anne.** Presents!

30 **Mrs. Van Daan.** Presents!

31 **Dussel.** Look!

28. **St. Nicholas' Day** December 6, the day Christian children in the Netherlands receive gifts.

32 **Mr. Van Daan.** What's she got on her head?

33 **Peter.** A lamp shade!

34 **Anne.** [*She picks out one at random.*] This is for Margot. [*She hands it to* Margot, *pulling her to her feet.*] Read it out loud.

35 **Margot.** [*Reading*]
"You have never lost your temper.
You never will, I fear,
You are so good.
But if you should,
Put all your cross words here."

36 [*She tears open the package.*] A new crossword puzzle book! Where did you get it?

37 **Anne.** It isn't new. It's one that you've done. But I rubbed it all out, and if you wait a little and forget, you can do it all over again.

38 **Margot.** [*Sitting*] It's wonderful, Anne. Thank you. You'd never know it wasn't new.

39 [*From outside we hear the sound of a streetcar passing.*]

40 **Anne.** [*With another gift*] Mrs. Van Daan.

41 **Mrs. Van Daan.** [*Taking it*] This is awful . . . I haven't anything for anyone . . . I never thought . . .

42 **Mr. Frank.** This is all Anne's idea.

43 **Mrs. Van Daan.** [*Holding up a bottle*] What is it?

44 **Anne.** It's hair shampoo. I took all the odds and ends of soap and mixed them with the last of my toilet water.

45 **Mrs. Van Daan.** Oh, Anneke!

46 **Anne.** I wanted to write a poem for all of them, but I didn't have time. [*Offering a large box to* Mr. Van Daan] Yours, Mr. Van Daan, is really something . . . something you want more than anything. [*As she waits for him to open it*] Look! Cigarettes!

47 **Mr. Van Daan.** Cigarettes!

48 **Anne.** Two of them! Pim found some old pipe tobacco in the pocket lining of his coat . . . and we made them . . . or rather. Pim did.

49 **Mrs. Van Daan.** Let me see . . . Well, look at that! Light it, Putti! Light it.

50 [Mr. Van Daan *hesitates.*]

51 **Anne.** It's tobacco, really it is! There's a little fluff in it, but not much.

© Pearson Education, Inc., or its affiliates. All rights reserved.

52 [*Everyone watches intently as* Mr. Van Daan *cautiously lights it. The cigarette flares up. Everyone laughs.*]

53 **Peter.** It works!

54 **Mrs. Van Daan.** Look at him.

55 **Mr. Van Daan.** [*Spluttering*] Thank you, Anne. Thank you.

56 [Anne *rushes back to her satchel for another present.*]

57 **Anne.** [*Handing her mother a piece of paper*] For Mother, Hanukkah greeting.

58 [*She pulls her mother to her feet.*]

59 **Mrs. Frank.** [*She reads*] "Here's an I.O.U. that I promise to pay. Ten hours of doing whatever you say. Signed, Anne Frank." [Mrs. Frank, *touched, takes* Anne *in her arms, holding her close.*]

60 **Dussel.** [*To Anne*] Ten hours of doing what you're told? Anything you're told?

61 **Anne.** That's right.

62 **Dussel.** You wouldn't want to sell that, Mrs. Frank?

63 **Mrs. Frank.** Never! This is the most precious gift I've ever had!

64 [*She sits, showing her present to the others.* Anne *hurries back to the satchel and pulls out a scarf, the scarf that* Mr. Frank *found in the first scene.*]

65 **Anne.** [*Offering it to her father*] For Pim.

66 **Mr. Frank.** Anneke . . . I wasn't supposed to have a present!

67 [*He takes it, unfolding it and showing it to the others.*]

68 **Anne.** It's a muffler . . . to put round your neck . . . like an ascot, you know. I made it myself out of odds and ends . . . I knitted it in the dark each night, after I'd gone to bed. I'm afraid it looks better in the dark!

69 **Mr. Frank.** [*Putting it on*] It's fine. It fits me perfectly. Thank you, Annele.

70 [Anne *hands* Peter *a ball of paper with a string attached to it.*]

71 **Anne.** That's for Mouschi.

72 **Peter.** [*Rising to bow*] On behalf of Mouschi, I thank you.

73 **Anne.** [*Hesitant, handing him a gift*] And . . . this is yours . . . from Mrs. Quack Quack. [*As he holds it gingerly in his hands*] Well . . . open it . . . Aren't you going to open it?

CLOSE READ

ANNOTATE: Mark details in paragraphs 57–63 that show Mrs. Frank's reaction to Anne's gift.

QUESTION: Why do the playwrights include these details?

CONCLUDE: What is the effect of this scene, especially in showing growth in Anne's character?

74 **Peter.** I'm scared to. I know something's going to jump out and hit me.

75 **Anne.** No. It's nothing like that, really.

76 **Mrs. Van Daan.** [*As he is opening it*] What is it, Peter? Go on. Show it.

77 **Anne.** [*Excitedly*] It's a safety razor!

78 **Dussel.** A what?

79 **Anne.** A razor!

80 **Mrs. Van Daan.** [*Looking at it*] You didn't make that out of odds and ends.

81 **Anne.** [*To* Peter] Miep got it for me. It's not new. It's secondhand. But you really do need a razor now.

82 **Dussel.** For what?

83 **Anne.** Look on his upper lip . . . you can see the beginning of a mustache.

84 **Dussel.** He wants to get rid of that? Put a little milk on it and let the cat lick it off.

85 **Peter.** [*Starting for his room*] Think you're funny, don't you.

86 **Dussel.** Look! He can't wait! He's going in to try it!

87 **Peter.** I'm going to give Mouschi his present!

88 [*He goes into his room, slamming the door behind him.*]

89 **Mr. Van Daan.** [*Disgustedly*] Mouschi, Mouschi, Mouschi.

90 [*In the distance we hear a dog persistently barking.* Anne *brings a gift to* Dussel.]

91 **Anne.** And last but never least, my roommate, Mr. Dussel.

92 **Dussel.** For me? You have something for me?

93 [*He opens the small box she gives him.*]

94 **Anne.** I made them myself.

95 **Dussel.** [*Puzzled*] Capsules! Two capsules!

96 **Anne.** They're ear-plugs!

97 **Dussel.** Ear-plugs?

98 **Anne.** To put in your ears so you won't hear me when I thrash around at night. I saw them advertised in a magazine. They're not real ones . . . I made them out of cotton and

candle wax. Try them . . . See if they don't work . . . see if you can hear me talk . . .

99 **Dussel.** [*Putting them in his ears*] Wait now until I get them in . . . so.

100 **Anne.** Are you ready?

101 **Dussel.** Huh?

102 **Anne.** Are you ready?

103 **Dussel.** Good God! They've gone inside! I can't get them out! [*They laugh as* Mr. Dussel *jumps about, trying to shake the plugs out of his ears. Finally he gets them out. Putting them away*] Thank you, Anne! Thank you!

104 [*Together*]

Mr. Van Daan. A real Hanukkah!

Mrs. Van Daan. Wasn't it cute of her?

Mrs. Frank. I don't know when she did it.

Margot. I love my present.

105 **Anne.** [*Sitting at the table*] And now let's have the song, Father . . . please . . . [*To* Dussel] Have you heard the Hanukkah song, Mr. Dussel? The song is the whole thing! [*She sings.*] "Oh, Hanukkah! Oh, Hanukkah! The sweet celebration . . ."

106 **Mr. Frank.** [*Quieting her*] I'm afraid, Anne, we shouldn't sing that song tonight. [*To* Dussel] It's a song of jubilation, of rejoicing. One is apt to become too enthusiastic.

107 **Anne.** Oh, please, please. Let's sing the song. I promise not to shout!

108 **Mr. Frank.** Very well. But quietly now . . . I'll keep an eye on you and when . . .

109 [*As* Anne *starts to sing, she is interrupted by* Dussel, *who is snorting and wheezing.*]

110 **Dussel.** [*Pointing to* Peter] You . . . You! [Peter *is coming from his bedroom, ostentatiously holding a bulge in his coat as if he were holding his cat, and dangling* Anne's *present before it.*] How many times . . . I told you . . . Out! Out!

111 **Mr. Van Daan.** [*Going to* Peter] What's the matter with you? Haven't you any sense? Get that cat out of here.

112 **Peter.** [*Innocently*] Cat?

In this photograph, the common room of the Secret Annex appears much as it did when Anne Frank lived there.

113 **Mr. Van Daan.** You heard me. Get it out of here!

114 **Peter.** I have no cat. [*Delighted with his joke, he opens his coat and pulls out a bath towel. The group at the table laugh, enjoying the joke.*]

115 **Dussel.** [*Still wheezing*] It doesn't need to be the cat, his clothes are enough . . . when he comes out of that room . . .

116 **Mr. Van Daan.** Don't worry. You won't be bothered any more. We're getting rid of it.

117 **Dussel.** At last you listen to me. [*He goes off into his bedroom.*]

118 **Mr. Van Daan.** [*Calling after him*] I'm not doing it for you. That's all in your mind . . . all of it! [*He starts back to his place at the table.*] I'm doing it because I'm sick of seeing that cat eat all our food.

119 **Peter.** That's not true! I only give him bones . . . scraps . . .

120 **Mr. Van Daan.** Don't tell me! He gets fatter every day! Damn cat looks better than any of us. Out he goes tonight!

121 **Peter.** No! No!

122 **Anne.** Mr. Van Daan, you can't do that! That's Peter's cat. Peter loves that cat.

123 **Mrs. Frank.** [*Quietly*] Anne.

124 **Peter.** [*To* Mr. Van Daan] If he goes, I go.

125 **Mr. Van Daan.** Go! Go!

126 **Mrs. Van Daan.** You're not going and the cat's not going! Now please . . . this is Hanukkah . . . Hanukkah . . . this is the time to celebrate . . . What's the matter with all of you? Come on, Anne. Let's have the song.

127 **Anne.** [*Singing*]
"Oh, Hanukkah! Oh, Hanukkah! The sweet celebration."

128 **Mr. Frank.** [*Rising*] I think we should first blow out the candle . . . then we'll have something for tomorrow night.

129 **Margot.** But, Father, you're supposed to let it burn itself out.

130 **Mr. Frank.** I'm sure that God understands shortages. [*Before blowing it out*] "Praised be Thou, oh Lord our God, who hast sustained us and permitted us to celebrate this joyous festival."

131 [*He is about to blow out the candle when suddenly there is a crash of something falling below. They all freeze in horror, motionless. For a few seconds there is complete silence.* Mr. Frank *slips off his shoes. The others noiselessly follow his example.* Mr. Frank *turns out a light near him. He motions to* Peter *to turn off the center lamp.* Peter *tries to reach it, realizes he cannot and gets up on a chair. Just as he is touching the lamp he loses his balance. The chair goes out from under him. He falls. The iron lamp shade crashes to the floor. There is a sound of feet below, running down the stairs.*]

132 **Mr. Van Daan.** [*Under his breath*] God Almighty! [*The only light left comes from the Hanukkah candle.* Dussel *comes from his room.* Mr. Frank *creeps over to the stairwell and stands listening. The dog is heard barking excitedly.*] Do you hear anything?

133 **Mr. Frank.** [*In a whisper*] No. I think they've gone.

134 **Mrs. Van Daan.** It's the Green Police. They've found us.

135 **Mr. Frank.** If they had, they wouldn't have left. They'd be up here by now.

136 **Mrs. Van Daan.** I know it's the Green Police. They've gone to get help. That's all. They'll be back!

137 **Mr. Van Daan.** Or it may have been the Gestapo,[29] looking for papers . . .

138 **Mr. Frank.** [*Interrupting*] Or a thief, looking for money.

139 **Mrs. Van Daan.** We've got to do something . . . Quick! Quick! Before they come back.

140 **Mr. Van Daan.** There isn't anything to do. Just wait.

CLOSE READ

ANNOTATE: In paragraphs 133–140, mark sentences of four words or less.

QUESTION: Why do the characters speak in a series of short sentences during this scene?

CONCLUDE: How does the series of short sentences add to the scene's tension?

29. **Gestapo** (guh STAH poh) *n.* secret police force of Nazi Germany, known for its brutality.

141 [Mr. Frank *holds up his hand for them to be quiet. He is listening intently. There is complete silence as they all strain to hear any sound from below. Suddenly* Anne *begins to sway. With a low cry she falls to the floor in a faint.* Mrs. Frank *goes to her quickly, sitting beside her on the floor and taking her in her arms.*]

142 **Mrs. Frank.** Get some water, please! Get some water!

143 [Margot *starts for the sink.*]

144 **Mr. Van Daan.** [*Grabbing* Margot] No! No! No one's going to run water!

145 **Mr. Frank.** If they've found us, they've found us. Get the water. [Margot *starts again for the sink.* Mr. Frank, *getting a flashlight*] I'm going down.

146 [Margot *rushes to him, clinging to him.* Anne *struggles to consciousness.*]

147 **Margot.** No, Father, no! There may be someone there, waiting . . . It may be a trap!

148 **Mr. Frank.** This is Saturday. There is no way for us to know what has happened until Miep or Mr. Kraler comes on Monday morning. We cannot live with this uncertainty.

149 **Margot.** Don't go, Father!

150 **Mrs. Frank.** Hush, darling, hush. [Mr. Frank *slips quietly out, down the steps and out through the door below.*] Margot! Stay close to me. [Margot *goes to her mother.*]

151 **Mr. Van Daan.** Shush! Shush!

152 [Mrs. Frank *whispers to* Margot *to get the water.* Margot *goes for it.*]

153 **Mrs. Van Daan.** Putti, where's our money? Get our money. I hear you can buy the Green Police off, so much a head. Go upstairs quick! Get the money!

154 **Mr. Van Daan.** Keep still!

155 **Mrs. Van Daan.** [*Kneeling before him, pleading*] Do you want to be dragged off to a concentration camp? Are you going to stand there and wait for them to come up and get you? Do something, I tell you!

156 **Mr. Van Daan.** [*Pushing her aside*] Will you keep still!

157 [*He goes over to the stairwell to listen.* Peter *goes to his mother, helping her up onto the sofa. There is a second of silence, then* Anne *can stand it no longer.*]

158 **Anne.** Someone go after Father! Make Father come back!

159 **Peter.** [*Starting for the door*] I'll go.

160 **Mr. Van Daan.** Haven't you done enough?

161 [*He pushes* Peter *roughly away. In his anger against his father* Peter *grabs a chair as if to hit him with it, then puts it down, burying his face in his hands.* Mrs. Frank *begins to pray softly.*]

162 **Anne.** Please, please, Mr. Van Daan. Get Father.

163 **Mr. Van Daan.** Quiet! Quiet!

164 [Anne *is shocked into silence.* Mrs. Frank *pulls her closer, holding her protectively in her arms.*]

165 **Mrs. Frank.** [*Softly, praying*] "I lift up mine eyes unto the mountains, from whence cometh my help. My help cometh from the Lord who made heaven and earth. He will not suffer thy foot to be moved . . . He that keepeth thee will not slumber . . ."

166 [*She stops as she hears someone coming. They all watch the door tensely.* Mr. Frank *comes quietly in.* Anne *rushes to him, holding him tight.*]

167 **Mr. Frank.** It was a thief. That noise must have scared him away.

168 **Mrs. Van Daan.** Thank God.

169 **Mr. Frank.** He took the cash box. And the radio. He ran away in such a hurry that he didn't stop to shut the street door. It was swinging wide open. [*A breath of relief sweeps over them.*] I think it would be good to have some light.

170 **Margot.** Are you sure it's all right?

171 **Mr. Frank.** The danger has passed. [Margot *goes to light the small lamp.*] Don't be so terrified, Anne. We're safe.

172 **Dussel.** Who says the danger has passed? Don't you realize we are in greater danger than ever?

173 **Mr. Frank.** Mr. Dussel, will you be still!

174 [Mr. Frank *takes* Anne *back to the table, making her sit down with him, trying to calm her.*]

175 **Dussel.** [*Pointing to* Peter] Thanks to this clumsy fool, there's someone now who knows we're up here! Someone now knows we're up here, hiding!

176 **Mrs. Van Daan.** [*Going to* Dussel] Someone knows we're here, yes. But who is the someone? A thief! A thief! You think

a thief is going to go to the Green Police and say . . . I was robbing a place the other night and I heard a noise up over my head? You think a thief is going to do that?

177 **Dussel.** Yes. I think he will.

178 **Mrs. Van Daan.** [*Hysterically*] You're crazy!

hysterically (hihs TEHR ihk lee) *adv.* in a way that shows uncontrolled emotion

179 [*She stumbles back to her seat at the table.* Peter *follows protectively, pushing* Dussel *aside.*]

180 **Dussel.** I think some day he'll be caught and then he'll make a bargain with the Green Police . . . If they'll let him off, he'll tell them where some Jews are hiding!

181 [*He goes off into the bedroom. There is a second of appalled silence.*]

182 **Mr. Van Daan.** He's right.

183 **Anne.** Father, let's get out of here! We can't stay here now . . . Let's go . . .

184 **Mr. Van Daan.** Go! Where?

185 **Mrs. Frank.** [*Sinking into her chair at the table*] Yes. Where?

186 **Mr. Frank.** [*Rising, to them all*] Have we lost all faith? All courage? A moment ago we thought that they'd come for us. We were sure it was the end. But it wasn't the end. We're alive, safe. [Mr. Van Daan *goes to the table and sits.* Mr. Frank *prays.*]

187 "We thank Thee, oh Lord our God, that in Thy infinite mercy Thou hast again seen fit to spare us." [*He blows out the candle, then turns to* Anne.] Come on, Anne. The song! Let's have the song!

188 [*He starts to sing.* Anne *finally starts falteringly to sing, as* Mr. Frank *urges her on. Her voice is hardly audible at first.*]

189 **Anne.** [*Singing*]
"Oh, Hanukkah! Oh, Hanukkah! The sweet . . . celebration . . ."

190 [*As she goes on singing, the others gradually join in, their voices still shaking with fear.* Mrs. Van Daan *sobs as she sings.*]

191 **Group.** Around the feast . . . we . . . gather
In complete . . . jubilation . . .
Happiest of sea . . . sons
Now is here.
Many are the reasons for good cheer.

192 [Dussel *comes from the bedroom. He comes over to the table, standing beside* Margot, *listening to them as they sing.*]

CLOSE READ

ANNOTATE: In paragraphs 194 and 198, mark details related to the characters' singing and the stage lights.

QUESTION: Why do the playwrights set up a contrast between the singing and the lights?

CONCLUDE: What is the effect of this final scene of Act I?

193 "Together
We'll weather
Whatever tomorrow may bring."

194 [*As they sing on with growing courage, the lights start to dim.*]

195 "So hear us rejoicing
And merrily voicing
The Hanukkah song that we sing.
Hoy!"

196 [*The lights are out. The curtain starts slowly to fall.*]

197 "Hear us rejoicing
And merrily voicing
The Hanukkah song that we sing."

198 [*They are still singing, as the curtain falls.*] 🕯

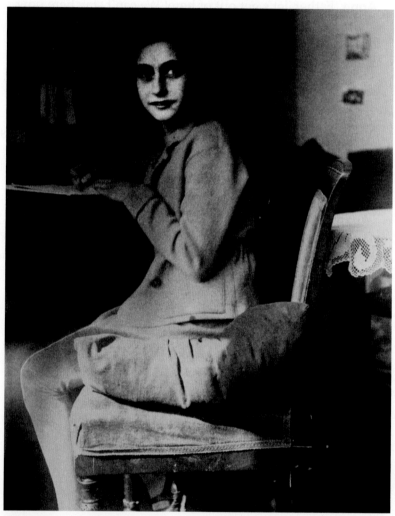

This photo of Anne Frank was taken before she and her family went into hiding.

Comprehension Check

Complete the following items after you finish your first read.

1. In Scene 1, what year is it?

2. How does the time period change in Scene 2?

3. Why must the Franks and the Van Daans be quiet during the day?

4. Why does Mr. Dussel join the group in the attic?

5. What happens to interrupt the Hanukkah celebration?

6. 🖫 **Notebook** Write a summary of *The Diary of Anne Frank,* Act I.

- -

RESEARCH

Research to Clarify Choose at least one unfamiliar detail from the text. Briefly research that detail. In what way does the information you learned shed light on an aspect of the play?

Research to Explore Choose something that interested you from the text, and formulate a research question.

THE DIARY OF ANNE FRANK, ACT I

Close Read the Text

1. The model—from Act I, Scene 1, paragraph 18—shows two sample annotations, along with questions and conclusions. Close read the passage, and find another detail to annotate. Then, write a question and your conclusion.

ANNOTATE: These details show why Mr. Frank feels he must leave Amsterdam.

QUESTION: Why might the playwrights have included these details?

CONCLUDE: These details show what Mr. Frank has lost, and why he feels that he is a different person.

ANNOTATE: The playwrights use many ellipses in this dialogue.

QUESTION: Why have the playwrights punctuated the dialogue in this way?

CONCLUDE: The ellipses show hesitation and the difficulty of speaking. They hint at Mr. Frank's sorrow and pain.

Mr. Frank. I can't stay in Amsterdam, Miep. It has too many memories for me. Everywhere there's something … the house we lived in … the school … that street organ playing out there … I'm not the person you used to know, Miep. I'm a bitter old man. [*Breaking off*] Forgive me. I shouldn't speak to you like this … after all that you did for us … the suffering …

2. For more practice, go back into the text, and complete the close-read notes.

3. Revisit a section of the text you found important during your first read. Read this section closely, and **annotate** what you notice. Ask yourself **questions** such as "Why did the author make this choice?" What can you **conclude**?

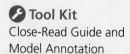
Tool Kit
Close-Read Guide and Model Annotation

Analyze the Text

CITE TEXTUAL EVIDENCE to support your answers.

Notebook Respond to these questions.

1. **Compare and Contrast** How is Anne's response to her confinement different from her sister's?

2. **Make a Judgment** Many of the adults in the play become frustrated with Anne's behavior. Do you think they are being unfair? Explain.

3. **(a) Draw Conclusions** What insights does the Hanukkah scene suggest about the different ways in which people deal with crisis?

4. **Essential Question: *How do we remember the past?*** What has this selection taught you about how people remember the past?

STANDARDS
Reading Literature
• Analyze how particular lines of dialogue or incidents in a story or drama propel the action, reveal aspects of a character, or provoke a decision.
• Analyze how differences in the points of view of the characters and the audience or reader create such effects as suspense or humor.

152 UNIT 2 • THE HOLOCAUST

Analyze Craft and Structure

Text Structures in Drama Dialogue is the conversation between or among characters. In a play, dialogue serves three main functions:

- helping readers learn about the characters, their relationships, and their goals
- setting the **mood** or emotional quality, of a scene in order to prompt the desired feeling or response in readers
- developing the plot and subplots—**Conflicts**, or problems and struggles, come to life as characters confide in friends, argue with enemies, and plan their actions.

Dialogue also helps playwrights create **dramatic irony,** a situation in which the audience knows more than the characters do. For example, in a play based on tragic historical events, such as *The Diary of Anne Frank,* the audience knows the characters' fates. That knowledge contributes to the suspense and tension of the story.

Practice

CITE TEXTUAL EVIDENCE
to support your answers.

Notebook Review *The Diary of Anne Frank,* Act I. For each item in the chart, identify passages of dialogue that serve that purpose. Explain each choice.

PURPOSE OF DIALOGUE	EXAMPLES FROM ACT I	EXPLANATION
shows what characters are like and what they want		
sets the mood		
shows conflicts and action, moving the plot forward		

1. Reread Scene 2, paragraph 139. What does Mr. Frank mean when he says, "There are . . . no locks that anyone can put on your mind"? What does this dialogue show about Mr. Frank as a father and as the leader of the group in hiding?
2. Reread Scene 3, paragraphs 40–45. What subplot, or secondary conflict, does this dialogue develop?
3. Review the Background for Act I, and consider what you know about Anne's fate. How does this knowledge add dramatic irony to the end of Act I?

THE DIARY OF ANNE FRANK, ACT I

Concept Vocabulary

anxiously	restraining	bickering
tension	quarrels	hysterically

Why These Words? These concept vocabulary words are used to describe feelings of stress and conflict. For example, the *bickering* between Mr. and Mrs. Van Daan shows how small issues can expand into heated *quarrels* for people experiencing extreme *tension*.

1. How does the concept vocabulary help the reader understand the experiences of the characters?

2. What other words in the selection connect to this concept?

Practice

🗐 **Notebook** The six concept vocabulary words appear in Act I of *The Diary of Anne Frank*.

1. Write a paragraph about this part of the play, using as many of the concept words as possible.

2. Work with a partner. Take turns listing **synonyms**, or words with similar meanings, for each concept word. When you have finished, take turns listing **antonyms**, or words with opposite meanings, for each concept word.

Word Study

Latin Suffix: –*ion* The Latin suffix *-ion* means "act or condition of." In the play *The Diary of Anne Frank*, the characters feel *tension* when they hear noise outside.

1. Using your knowledge of the suffix *-ion*, write a definition of the word *tension*.

2. Use your understanding of the suffix *-ion*, to write definitions for the following words: *aggression, confusion, possession*. Then, use a dictionary to verify your definitions.

⛓ WORD NETWORK

Add words related to the Holocaust from the text to your Word Network.

☷ STANDARDS

Language
• Demonstrate command of the conventions of standard English grammar and usage when writing or speaking.
• Determine or clarify the meaning of unknown and multiple-meaning words or phrases based on *grade 8 reading and content,* choosing flexibly from a range of strategies.

  b. Use common, grade-appropriate Greek or Latin affixes and roots as clues to the meaning of a word.

  d. Verify the preliminary determination of the meaning of a word or phrase.

• Demonstrate understanding of figurative language, word relationships, and nuances in word meanings.

  b. Use the relationship between particular words to better understand each of the words.

Conventions

Principal Parts of Verbs A **verb** is a word that expresses an action or state of being. All verbs have four **principal parts,** or forms. Most verbs are **regular,** but some common verbs are **irregular**—their past and past participle do not follow a single predictable pattern.

The chart below shows the four principal parts of one regular verb, *ask*, and one irregular verb, *write*.

PRINCIPAL PART	HOW TO FORM	EXAMPLES
Present	Basic form. Add -s or -es for third-person singular.	Peter asks her to be quiet. Anne writes in her diary each night.
Present Participle	Add -ing. Use after a form of *be* (*is, are, was, were, will be*, etc.).	They **are** asking if there is more food. She **was** writing about her experiences.
Past	REGULAR: Add -d or -ed. IRREGULAR: No one predictable pattern.	Mr. Dussel asked to be left alone. Mr. Frank wrote a list of items.
Past Participle	REGULAR: Add -d or -ed. Use after a form of *have* (*have, has, had*). IRREGULAR: No one predictable pattern. Use after a form of *have*.	Mrs. Van Daan **has** asked for her coat. Margot **had** written in her book.

Read It

1. Mark the verb form in each sentence. Then, label it present, present participle, past, or past participle.

   a. Yesterday, I finished her latest book.

   b. Margot is sleeping on a mattress on the floor.

   c. Nothing has happened.

2. Read the stage directions at the beginning of Scene 5. Mark the verb form in each sentence. Then, label each one present or present participle.

Write It

📓 **Notebook** Reread the stage directions at the beginning of Scene 5. Then, rewrite them using the past and past participle.

Playwrights

**Frances Goodrich and
Albert Hackett**

The Diary of Anne Frank, Act II

Concept Vocabulary

As you conduct your first read of *The Diary of Anne Frank*, Act II, you will encounter these words. Before reading, note how familiar you are with each word. Then, rank the words in order from most familiar (1) to least familiar (6).

WORD	YOUR RANKING
foreboding	
apprehension	
intuition	
mounting	
rigid	
insistent	

After completing the first read, come back to the concept vocabulary and review your rankings. Mark changes to your original rankings as needed.

First Read DRAMA

Apply these strategies as you conduct your first read. You will have an opportunity to complete the close-read notes after your first read.

NOTICE *whom* the story is about, *what* happens, *where* and *when* it happens, and *why* those involved react as they do.

ANNOTATE by marking vocabulary and key passages you want to revisit.

First Read

CONNECT ideas within the selection to what you already know and what you have already read.

RESPOND by completing the Comprehension Check and by writing a brief summary of the selection.

Tool Kit
First-Read Guide and
Model Annotation

STANDARDS

Reading Literature
By the end of the year, read and comprehend literature, including stories, dramas, and poems, at the high end of grades 6–8 text complexity band independently and proficiently.

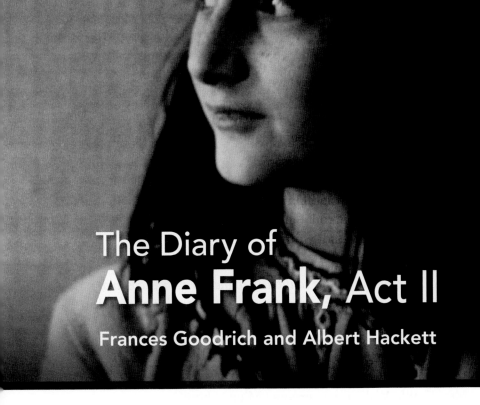

The Diary of
Anne Frank, Act II

Frances Goodrich and Albert Hackett

BACKGROUND
In Act I, Anne Frank's father visits the attic where his family and four others hid from the Nazis during World War II. As he holds his daughter's diary, Anne's offstage voice draws him into the past as the families begin their new life in hiding. As the months drag on, fear and lack of privacy in the attic rooms contribute to increasing tension among the family members.

SCAN FOR MULTIMEDIA

Scene 1

1 [*In the darkness we hear Anne's Voice, again reading from the diary.*]

2 **Anne's Voice.** Saturday, the first of January, nineteen forty-four. Another new year has begun and we find ourselves still in our hiding place. We have been here now for one year, five months and twenty-five days. It seems that our life is at a standstill.

3 [*The curtain rises on the scene. It is late afternoon. Everyone is bundled up against the cold. In the main room* Mrs. Frank *is taking down the laundry which is hung across the back.* Mr. Frank

---

NOTES

CLOSE READ
ANNOTATE: In paragraph 2, mark words that refer to date and time.

QUESTION: Why do the playwrights include these details?

CONCLUDE: What is the effect of these details?

sits in the chair down left, reading. **Margot** *is lying on the couch with a blanket over her and the many-colored knitted scarf around her throat.* **Anne** *is seated at the center table, writing in her diary.* **Peter, Mr.** *and* **Mrs. Van Daan** *and* **Dussel** *are all in their own rooms, reading or lying down.*

4 *As the lights dim on,* **Anne's Voice** *continues, without a break.]*

5 **Anne's Voice.** We are all a little thinner. The Van Daans' "discussions" are as violent as ever. Mother still does not understand me. But then I don't understand her either. There is one great change, however. A change in myself. I read somewhere that girls of my age don't feel quite certain of themselves. That they become quiet within and begin to think of the miracle that is taking place in their bodies. I think that what is happening to me is so wonderful . . . not only what can be seen, but what is taking place inside. Each time it has happened I have a feeling that I have a sweet secret.

6 [*We hear the chimes and then a hymn being played on the carillon outside. The buzzer of the door below suddenly sounds. Everyone is startled.* **Mr. Frank** *tiptoes cautiously to the top of the steps and listens. Again the buzzer sounds, in* **Miep's** *V-for-Victory signal.*[1]]

7 **Mr. Frank.** It's Miep!

8 [*He goes quickly down the steps to unbolt the door.* **Mrs. Frank** *calls upstairs to the* **Van Daans** *and then to* **Peter.**]

9 **Mrs. Frank.** Wake up, everyone! Miep is here! [**Anne** *quickly puts her diary away.* **Margot** *sits up, pulling the blanket around her shoulders.* **Mr. Dussel** *sits on the edge of his bed, listening, disgruntled.* **Miep** *comes up the steps, followed by* **Mr. Kraler.** *They bring flowers, books, newspapers, etc.* **Anne** *rushes to* **Miep,** *throwing her arms affectionately around her.*] Miep . . . and Mr. Kraler . . . What a delightful surprise!

10 **Mr. Kraler.** We came to bring you New Year's greetings.

11 **Mrs. Frank.** You shouldn't . . . you should have at least one day to yourselves. [*She goes quickly to the stove and brings down teacups and tea for all of them.*]

12 **Anne.** Don't say that, it's so wonderful to see them! [*Sniffing at* **Miep's** *coat*] I can smell the wind and the cold on your clothes.

13 **Miep.** [*Giving her the flowers*] There you are. [*Then to* **Margot,** *feeling her forehead*] How are you, Margot? . . . Feeling any better?

14 **Margot.** I'm all right.

15 **Anne.** We filled her full of every kind of pill so she won't cough and make a noise. [*She runs into her room to put the*

1. **V-for-Victory signal** three short rings and one long one (the letter *V* in Morse code).

flowers in water. Mr. and Mrs. Van Daan come from upstairs. Outside there is the sound of a band playing.]

16 **Mrs. Van Daan.** Well, hello, Miep. Mr. Kraler.

17 **Mr. Kraler.** [*Giving a bouquet of flowers to* Mrs. Van Daan] With my hope for peace in the New Year.

18 **Peter.** [*Anxiously*] Miep, have you seen Mouschi? Have you seen him anywhere around?

19 **Miep.** I'm sorry, Peter. I asked everyone in the neighborhood had they seen a gray cat. But they said no.

20 [Mrs. Frank *gives* Miep *a cup of tea.* Mr. Frank *comes up the steps, carrying a small cake on a plate.*]

21 **Mr. Frank.** Look what Miep's brought for us!

22 **Mrs. Frank.** [*Taking it*] A cake!

23 **Mr. Van Daan.** A cake! [*He pinches* Miep's *cheeks gaily and hurries up to the cupboard.*] I'll get some plates.

24 [Dussel, *in his room, hastily puts a coat on and starts out to join the others.*]

25 **Mrs. Frank.** Thank you, Miepia. You shouldn't have done it. You must have used all of your sugar ration for weeks. [*Giving it to* Mrs. Van Daan] It's beautiful, isn't it?

26 **Mrs. Van Daan.** It's been ages since I even saw a cake. Not since you brought us one last year. [*Without looking at the cake, to* Miep] Remember? Don't you remember, you gave us one on New Year's Day? Just this time last year? I'll never forget it because you had "Peace in nineteen forty-three" on it. [*She looks at the cake and reads*] "Peace in nineteen forty-four!"

27 **Miep.** Well, it has to come sometime, you know. [*As Dussel comes from his room*] Hello, Mr. Dussel.

28 **Mr. Kraler.** How are you?

29 **Mr. Van Daan.** [*Bringing plates and a knife*] Here's the knife, *liefje.* Now, how many of us are there?

30 **Miep.** None for me, thank you.

31 **Mr. Frank.** Oh, please. You must.

32 **Miep.** I couldn't.

33 **Mr. Van Daan.** Good! That leaves one . . . two . . . three . . . seven of us.

34 **Dussel.** Eight! Eight! It's the same number as it always is!

35 **Mr. Van Daan.** I left Margot out. I take it for granted Margot won't eat any.

CLOSE READ

ANNOTATE: In paragraph 26, mark details that show what Miep wrote on two cakes she brought to the Secret Annex.

QUESTION: Why do the playwrights include these details?

CONCLUDE: What do these details show about the war, the characters' situation, and Miep's character?

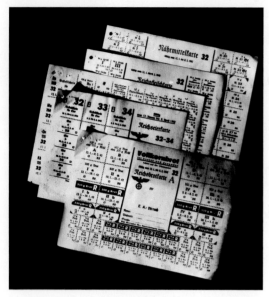

Ration cards, the kind Miep Gies might have used to get food for the Franks.

36 **Anne.** Why wouldn't she!

37 **Mrs. Frank.** I think it won't harm her.

38 **Mr. Van Daan.** All right! All right! I just didn't want her to start coughing again, that's all.

39 **Dussel.** And please, Mrs. Frank should cut the cake.

40 [*Together*] {
Mr. Van Daan. What's the difference?
Mrs. Van Daan. It's not Mrs. Frank's cake, is it, Miep? It's for all of us.
}

41 **Dussel.** Mrs. Frank divides things better.

42 [*Together*] {
Mrs. Van Daan. [*Going to* Dussel] What are you trying to say?
Mr. Van Daan. Oh, come on! Stop wasting time!
}

43 **Mrs. Van Daan.** [*To* Dussel] Don't I always give everybody exactly the same? Don't I?

44 **Mr. Van Daan.** Forget it, Kerli.

45 **Mrs. Van Daan.** No. I want an answer! Don't I?

46 **Dussel.** Yes. Yes. Everybody gets exactly the same . . . except Mr. Van Daan always gets a little bit more.

47 [Mr. Van Daan *advances on* Dussel, *the knife still in his hand*.]

48 **Mr. Van Daan.** That's a lie!

49 [Dussel *retreats before the onslaught of the* Van Daans.]

50 **Mr. Frank.** Please, please! [*Then to* Miep] You see what a little sugar cake does to us? It goes right to our heads!

51 **Mr. Van Daan.** [*Handing* Mrs. Frank *the knife*] Here you are, Mrs. Frank.

52 **Mrs. Frank.** Thank you. [*Then to* Miep *as she goes to the table to cut the cake*] Are you sure you won't have some?

53 **Miep.** [*Drinking her tea*] No, really, I have to go in a minute.

54 [*The sound of the band fades out in the distance.*]

55 **Peter.** [*To* Miep] Maybe Mouschi went back to our house . . . they say that cats . . . Do you ever get over there . . .? I mean . . . do you suppose you could . . .?

56 **Miep.** I'll try, Peter. The first minute I get I'll try. But I'm afraid, with him gone a week . . .

57 **Dussel.** Make up your mind, already someone has had a nice big dinner from that cat!

58 [Peter *is furious, inarticulate. He starts toward* Dussel, *as if to hit him.* Mr. Frank *stops him.* Mrs. Frank *speaks quickly to ease the situation.*]

59 **Mrs. Frank.** [*To* Miep] This is delicious, Miep!

60 **Mrs. Van Daan.** [*Eating hers*] Delicious!

61 **Mr. Van Daan.** [*Finishing it in one gulp*] Dirk's in luck to get a girl who can bake like this!

62 **Miep.** [*Putting down her empty teacup*] I have to run. Dirk's taking me to a party tonight.

63 **Anne.** How heavenly! Remember now what everyone is wearing, and what you have to eat and everything, so you can tell us tomorrow.

64 **Miep.** I'll give you a full report! Good-bye, everyone!

65 **Mr. Van Daan.** [*To* Miep] Just a minute. There's something I'd like you to do for me.

66 [*He hurries off up the stairs to his room.*]

67 **Mrs. Van Daan.** [*Sharply*] Putti, where are you going? [*She rushes up the stairs after him, calling hysterically.*] What do you want? Putti, what are you going to do?

68 **Miep.** [*To* Peter] What's wrong?

69 **Peter.** [*His sympathy is with his mother.*] Father says he's going to sell her fur coat. She's crazy about that old fur coat.

70 **Dussel.** Is it possible? Is it possible that anyone is so silly as to worry about a fur coat in times like this?

71 **Peter.** It's none of your darn business . . . and if you say one more thing . . . I'll, I'll take you and I'll . . . I mean it . . . I'll . . .

72 [*There is a piercing scream from* Mrs. Van Daan *above. She grabs at the fur coat as* Mr. Van Daan *is starting downstairs with it.*]

73 **Mrs. Van Daan.** No! No! No! Don't you dare take that! You hear? It's mine! [*Downstairs* Peter *turns away, embarrassed, miserable.*] My father gave me that! You didn't give it to me. You have no right. Let go of it . . . you hear?

74 [Mr. Van Daan *pulls the coat from her hands and hurries downstairs.* Mrs. Van Daan *sinks to the floor, sobbing. As* Mr. Van Daan *comes into the main room the others look away, embarrassed for him.*]

75 **Mr. Van Daan.** [*To* Mr. Kraler] Just a little—discussion over the advisability of selling this coat. As I have often reminded Mrs. Van Daan, it's very selfish of her to keep it when people

NOTES

CLOSE READ

ANNOTATE: Mark words and phrases in paragraphs 67–74 that show Mrs. Van Daan's reaction to her husband's decision to sell her coat.

QUESTION: Why do the playwrights include these details?

CONCLUDE: What conflicts do these details reveal?

outside are in such desperate need of clothing . . . [*He gives the coat to* Miep.] So if you will please to sell it for us? It should fetch a good price. And by the way, will you get me cigarettes. I don't care what kind they are . . . get all you can.

76 **Miep.** It's terribly difficult to get them, Mr. Van Daan. But I'll try. Good-bye.

77 [*She goes.* Mr. Frank *follows her down the steps to bolt the door after her.* Mrs. Frank *gives* Mr. Kraler *a cup of tea.*]

78 **Mrs. Frank.** Are you sure you won't have some cake, Mr. Kraler?

79 **Mr. Kraler.** I'd better not.

80 **Mr. Van Daan.** You're still feeling badly? What does your doctor say?

81 **Mr. Kraler.** I haven't been to him.

82 **Mrs. Frank.** Now, Mr. Kraler! . . .

83 **Mr. Kraler.** [*Sitting at the table*] Oh, I tried. But you can't get near a doctor these days . . . they're so busy. After weeks I finally managed to get one on the telephone. I told him I'd like an appointment . . . I wasn't feeling very well. You know what he answers . . . over the telephone . . . Stick out your tongue! [*They laugh. He turns to* Mr. Frank *as* Mr. Frank *comes back.*] I have some contracts here . . . I wonder if you'd look over them with me . . .

84 **Mr. Frank.** [*Putting out his hand*] Of course.

85 **Mr. Kraler.** [*He rises*] If we could go downstairs . . . [Mr. Frank *starts ahead;* Mr. Kraler *speaks to the others.*] Will you forgive us? I won't keep him but a minute. [*He starts to follow* Mr. Frank *down the steps.*]

86 **Margot.** [*With sudden foreboding*] What's happened? Something's happened! Hasn't it, Mr. Kraler?

87 [Mr. Kraler *stops and comes back, trying to reassure* Margot *with a pretense of casualness.*]

88 **Mr. Kraler.** No, really. I want your father's advice . . .

89 **Margot.** Something's gone wrong! I know it!

90 **Mr. Frank.** [*Coming back, to* Mr. Kraler] If it's something that concerns us here, it's better that we all hear it.

91 **Mr. Kraler.** [*Turning to him, quietly*] But . . . the children . . . ?

92 **Mr. Frank.** What they'd imagine would be worse than any reality.

93 [*As* Mr. Kraler *speaks, they all listen with intense apprehension.* Mrs. Van Daan *comes down the stairs and sits on the bottom step.*]

foreboding (fawr BOH dihng) *n.* sudden feeling that something bad is going to happen

apprehension (ap rih HEHN shuhn) *n.* fearful feeling about what will happen next

94 **Mr. Kraler.** It's a man in the storeroom . . . I don't know whether or not you remember him . . . Carl, about fifty, heavy-set, nearsighted . . . He came with us just before you left.

95 **Mr. Frank.** He was from Utrecht?

96 **Mr. Kraler.** That's the man. A couple of weeks ago, when I was in the storeroom, he closed the door and asked me . . . how's Mr. Frank? What do you hear from Mr. Frank? I told him I only knew there was a rumor that you were in Switzerland. He said he'd heard that rumor too, but he thought I might know something more. I didn't pay any attention to it . . . but then a thing happened yesterday . . . He'd brought some invoices to the office for me to sign. As I was going through them, I looked up. He was standing staring at the bookcase . . . your bookcase. He said he thought he remembered a door there . . . Wasn't there a door there that used to go up to the loft? Then he told me he wanted more money. Twenty guilders[2] more a week.

97 **Mr. Van Daan.** Blackmail!

98 **Mr. Frank.** Twenty guilders? Very modest blackmail.

99 **Mr. Van Daan.** That's just the beginning.

100 **Dussel.** [*Coming to Mr. Frank*] You know what I think? He was the thief who was down there that night. That's how he knows we're here.

101 **Mr. Frank.** [*To Mr. Kraler*] How was it left? What did you tell him?

102 **Mr. Kraler.** I said I had to think about it. What shall I do? Pay him the money? . . . Take a chance on firing him . . . or what? I don't know.

103 **Dussel.** [*Frantic*] Don't fire him! Pay him what he asks . . . keep him here where you can have your eye on him.

104 **Mr. Frank.** Is it so much that he's asking? What are they paying nowadays?

105 **Mr. Kraler.** He could get it in a war plant. But this isn't a war plant. Mind you. I don't know if he really knows . . . or if he doesn't know.

106 **Mr. Frank.** Offer him half. Then we'll soon find out if it's blackmail or not.

107 **Dussel.** And if it is? We've got to pay it, haven't we? Anything he asks we've got to pay!

108 **Mr. Frank.** Let's decide that when the time comes.

109 **Mr. Kraler.** This may be all my imagination. You get to a point, these days, where you suspect everyone and

© Pearson Education, Inc., or its affiliates. All rights reserved.

NOTES

2. **guilders** (GIHL duhrz) *n.* monetary unit of the Netherlands at the time.

CLOSE READ

ANNOTATE: In paragraphs 97–109, mark details that show the characters' responses to Mr. Kraler's news.

QUESTION: Why do the playwrights include this range of reactions?

CONCLUDE: How does this passage increase suspense for readers?

everything. Again and again . . . on some simple look or word, I've found myself . . .

110 [*The telephone rings in the office below.*]

111 **Mrs. Van Daan.** [*Hurrying to* Mr. Kraler] There's the telephone! What does that mean, the telephone ringing on a holiday?

112 **Mr. Kraler.** That's my wife. I told her I had to go over some papers in my office . . . to call me there when she got out of church. [*He starts out.*] I'll offer him half then. Goodbye . . . we'll hope for the best!

113 [*The group calls their good-byes halfheartedly.* Mr. Frank *follows* Mr. Kraler *to bolt the door below. During the following scene,* Mr. Frank *comes back up and stands listening, disturbed.*]

114 **Dussel.** [*To* Mr. Van Daan] You can thank your son for this . . . smashing the light! I tell you, it's just a question of time now.

115 [*He goes to the window at the back and stands looking out.*]

116 **Margot.** Sometimes I wish the end would come . . . whatever it is.

117 **Mrs. Frank.** [*Shocked*] Margot!

118 [Anne *goes to* Margot, *sitting beside her on the couch with her arms around her.*]

119 **Margot.** Then at least we'd know where we were.

120 **Mrs. Frank.** You should be ashamed of yourself! Talking that way! Think how lucky we are! Think of the thousands dying in the war, every day. Think of the people in concentration camps.

121 **Anne.** [*Interrupting*] What's the good of that? What's the good of thinking of misery when you're already miserable? That's stupid!

122 **Mrs. Frank.** Anne!

123 [*As* Anne *goes on raging at her mother,* Mrs. Frank *tries to break in, in an effort to quiet her.*]

124 **Anne.** We're young, Margot and Peter and I! You grownups have had your chance! But look at us . . . If we begin thinking of all the horror in the world, we're lost! We're trying to hold onto some kind of ideals . . . when everything . . . ideals, hopes . . . everything, are being destroyed! It isn't our fault that the world is in such a mess! We weren't around when all this started! So don't try to take it out on us! [*She rushes off to her room, slamming the door after her. She picks up a brush from the chest and hurls it to the floor. Then she sits on the settee, trying to control her anger.*]

125 **Mr. Van Daan.** She talks as if we started the war! Did we start the war?

126 [*He spots* Anne's *cake. As he starts to take it,* Peter *anticipates him.*]

127 **Peter.** She left her cake. [*He starts for* Anne's *room with the cake. There is silence in the main room.* Mrs. Van Daan *goes up to her room, followed by* Mr. Van Daan. Dussel *stays looking out the window.* Mr. Frank *brings* Mrs. Frank *her cake. She eats it slowly, without relish.* Mr. Frank *takes his cake to* Margot *and sits quietly on the sofa beside her.* Peter *stands in the doorway of* Anne's *darkened room, looking at her, then makes a little movement to let her know he is there.* Anne *sits up, quickly, trying to hide the signs of her tears.* Peter *holds out the cake to her.*] You left this.

128 **Anne.** [*Dully*] Thanks.

129 [Peter *starts to go out, then comes back.*]

130 **Peter.** I thought you were fine just now. You know just how to talk to them. You know just how to say it. I'm no good . . . I never can think . . . especially when I'm mad . . . That Dussel . . . when he said that about Mouschi . . . someone eating him . . . all I could think is . . . I wanted to hit him. I wanted to give him such a . . . a . . . that he'd . . . That's what I used to do when there was an argument at school . . . That's the way I . . . but here . . . And an old man like that . . . it wouldn't be so good.

131 **Anne.** You're making a big mistake about me. I do it all wrong. I say too much. I go too far. I hurt people's feelings . . .

132 [Dussel *leaves the window, going to his room.*]

133 **Peter.** I think you're just fine . . . What I want to say . . . if it wasn't for you around here, I don't know. What I mean . . .

134 [Peter *is interrupted by* Dussel's *turning on the light.* Dussel *stands in the doorway, startled to see* Peter. Peter *advances toward him forbiddingly.* Dussel *backs out of the room.* Peter *closes the door on him.*]

135 **Anne.** Do you mean it, Peter? Do you really mean it?

136 **Peter.** I said it, didn't I?

137 **Anne.** Thank you, Peter!

138 [*In the main room* Mr. *and* Mrs. Frank *collect the dishes and take them to the sink, washing them.* Margot *lies down again on the couch.* Dussel, *lost, wanders into* Peter's *room and takes up a book, starting to read.*]

139 **Peter.** [*Looking at the photographs on the wall*] You've got quite a collection.

NOTES

CLOSE READ

ANNOTATE: In paragraphs 127–135, mark details that relate to Peter's struggle to express himself in words. Mark other details that show what he does—his actions.

QUESTION: Why have the playwrights included these details?

CONCLUDE: What is the effect of these details, especially in showing how Peter has changed?

140 **Anne.** Wouldn't you like some in your room? I could give you some. Heaven knows you spend enough time in there . . . doing heaven knows what . . .

141 **Peter.** It's easier. A fight starts, or an argument . . . I duck in there.

142 **Anne.** You're lucky, having a room to go to. His lordship is always here . . . I hardly ever get a minute alone. When they start in on me, I can't duck away. I have to stand there and take it.

143 **Peter.** You gave some of it back just now.

144 **Anne.** I get so mad. They've formed their opinions . . . about everything . . . but we . . . we're still trying to find out . . . We have problems here that no other people our age have ever had. And just as you think you've solved them, something comes along and bang! You have to start all over again.

145 **Peter.** At least you've got someone you can talk to.

146 **Anne.** Not really. Mother . . . I never discuss anything serious with her. She doesn't understand. Father's all right. We can talk about everything . . . everything but one thing. Mother. He simply won't talk about her. I don't think you can be really intimate with anyone if he holds something back, do you?

147 **Peter.** I think your father's fine.

148 **Anne.** Oh, he is, Peter! He is! He's the only one who's ever given me the feeling that I have any sense. But anyway, nothing can take the place of school and play and friends of your own age . . . or near your age . . . can it?

149 **Peter.** I suppose you miss your friends and all.

150 **Anne.** It isn't just . . . [*She breaks off, staring up at him for a second.*] Isn't it funny, you and I? Here we've been seeing each other every minute for almost a year and a half, and this is the first time we've ever really talked. It helps a lot to have someone to talk to, don't you think? It helps you to let off steam.

151 **Peter.** [*Going to the door*] Well, any time you want to let off steam, you can come into my room.

152 **Anne.** [*Following him*] I can get up an awful lot of steam. You'll have to be careful how you say that.

153 **Peter.** It's all right with me.

154 **Anne.** Do you mean it?

155 **Peter.** I said it, didn't I?

156 [*He goes out.* Anne *stands in her doorway looking after him. As* Peter *gets to his door he stands for a minute looking back at her. Then he goes into his room.* Dussel *rises as he comes in, and quickly passes him, going out. He starts across for his room.* Anne *sees him coming, and pulls her door shut.* Dussel *turns back toward* Peter's *room.* Peter *pulls his door shut.* Dussel *stands there, bewildered, forlorn.*]

157 *The scene slowly dims out. The curtain falls on the scene.* Anne's Voice *comes over in the darkness . . . faintly at first, and then with growing strength.*]

158 **Anne's Voice.** We've had bad news. The people from whom Miep got our ration books have been arrested. So we have had to cut down on our food. Our stomachs are so empty that they rumble and make strange noises, all in different keys. Mr. Van Daan's is deep and low, like a bass fiddle. Mine is high, whistling like a flute. As we all sit around waiting for supper, it's like an orchestra tuning up. It only needs Toscanini[3] to raise his baton and we'd be off in the Ride of the Valkyries.[4] Monday, the sixth of March, nineteen forty-four. Mr. Kraler is in the hospital. It seems he has ulcers. Pim says we are his ulcers. Miep has to run the business and us too. The Americans have landed on the southern tip of Italy. Father looks for a quick finish to the war. Mr. Dussel is waiting every day for the warehouse man to demand more money. Have I been skipping too much from one subject to another? I can't help it. I feel that spring is coming. I feel it in my whole body and soul. I feel utterly confused. I am longing . . . so longing . . . for everything . . . for friends . . . for someone to talk to . . . someone who understands . . . someone young, who feels as I do . . .

159 [*As these last lines are being said, the curtain rises on the scene. The lights dim on.* Anne's Voice *fades out.*]

❊ ❊ ❊

Scene 2

1 [*It is evening, after supper. From outside we hear the sound of children playing. The "grownups," with the exception of* Mr. Van Daan, *are all in the main room.* Mrs. Frank *is doing some mending.* Mrs. Van Daan *is reading a fashion magazine.* Mr. Frank *is going over business accounts.*

NOTES

CLOSE READ
ANNOTATE: A **soliloquy** is a speech in which a character, usually alone on stage, expresses his or her private thoughts or feelings aloud. In paragraphs 157–159, mark words that indicate how the stage should look and sound during Anne's soliloquy.

QUESTION: Why might the playwrights have included these details?

CONCLUDE: What mood do these stage directions create?

3. **Toscanini** (TOS kuh NEE nee) Arturo Toscanini, a famous Italian orchestra conductor.

4. **Ride of the Valkyries** (VAL kih reez) stirring selection from an opera by Richard Wagner, a German composer.

2   Dussel, *in his dentist's jacket, is pacing up and down, impatient to get into his bedroom.* Mr. Van Daan *is upstairs working on a piece of embroidery in an embroidery frame.*

3   *In his room* Peter *is sitting before the mirror, smoothing his hair. As the scene goes on, he puts on his tie, brushes his coat and puts it on, preparing himself meticulously for a visit from* Anne. *On his wall are now hung some of* Anne's *motion picture stars.*

4   *In her room* Anne *too is getting dressed. She stands before the mirror in her slip, trying various ways of dressing her hair.* Margot *is seated on the sofa, hemming a skirt for* Anne *to wear.*

5   *In the main room* Dussel *can stand it no longer. He comes over, rapping sharply on the door of his and* Anne's *bedroom.*]

6   **Anne.** [*Calling to him*] No, no, Mr. Dussel! I am not dressed yet. [Dussel *walks away, furious, sitting down and burying his head in his hands.* Anne *turns to* Margot.] How is that? How does that look?

7   **Margot.** [*Glancing at her briefly*] Fine.

8   **Anne.** You didn't even look.

9   **Margot.** Of course I did. It's fine.

10 **Anne.** Margot, tell me, am I terribly ugly?

11 **Margot.** Oh, stop fishing.

12 **Anne.** No. No. Tell me.

13 **Margot.** Of course you're not. You've got nice eyes . . . and a lot of animation, and . . .

14 **Anne.** A little vague, aren't you?

15 [*She reaches over and takes a brassiere out of* Margot's *sewing basket. She holds it up to herself, studying the effect in the mirror. Outside,* Mrs. Frank, *feeling sorry for* Dussel, *comes over, knocking at the girls' door.*]

16 **Mrs. Frank.** [*Outside*] May I come in?

17 **Margot.** Come in, Mother.

18 **Mrs. Frank.** [*Shutting the door behind her*] Mr. Dussel's impatient to get in here.

19 **Anne.** [*Still with the brassiere*] Heavens, he takes the room for himself the entire day.

20 **Mrs. Frank.** [*Gently*] Anne, dear, you're not going in again tonight to see Peter?

21 **Anne.** [*Dignified*] That is my intention.

22 **Mrs. Frank.** But you've already spent a great deal of time in there today.

This photo shows a re-creation of the room Anne shared with Mr. Dussel.

23 **Anne.** I was in there exactly twice. Once to get the dictionary, and then three-quarters of an hour before supper.

24 **Mrs. Frank.** Aren't you afraid you're disturbing him?

25 **Anne.** Mother, I have some **intuition**.

26 **Mrs. Frank.** Then may I ask you this much, Anne. Please don't shut the door when you go in.

27 **Anne.** You sound like Mrs. Van Daan! [*She throws the brassiere back in* Margot's *sewing basket and picks up her blouse, putting it on.*]

28 **Mrs. Frank.** No. No. I don't mean to suggest anything wrong. I only wish that you wouldn't expose yourself to criticism . . . that you wouldn't give Mrs. Van Daan the opportunity to be unpleasant.

29 **Anne.** Mrs. Van Daan doesn't need an opportunity to be unpleasant!

30 **Mrs. Frank.** Everyone's on edge, worried about Mr. Kraler. This is one more thing . . .

31 **Anne.** I'm sorry, Mother. I'm going to Peter's room. I'm not going to let Petronella Van Daan spoil our friendship.

32 [Mrs. Frank *hesitates for a second, then goes out, closing the door after her. She gets a pack of playing cards and sits at the center table, playing solitaire. In* Anne's *room* Margot *hands the finished skirt to* Anne. *As* Anne *is putting it on,* Margot *takes off her high-heeled shoes and stuffs paper in the toes so that* Anne *can wear them.*]

intuition (ihn too IHSH uhn) *n.* ability to see the truth of something immediately without reasoning

33 **Margot.** [*To* Anne] Why don't you two talk in the main room? It'd save a lot of trouble. It's hard on Mother, having to listen to those remarks from Mrs. Van Daan and not say a word.

34 **Anne.** Why doesn't she say a word? I think it's ridiculous to take it and take it.

35 **Margot.** You don't understand Mother at all, do you? She can't talk back. She's not like you. It's just not in her nature to fight back.

36 **Anne.** Anyway . . . the only one I worry about is you. I feel awfully guilty about you. [*She sits on the stool near* Margot, *putting on* Margot's *high-heeled shoes.*]

37 **Margot.** What about?

38 **Anne.** I mean, every time I go into Peter's room, I have a feeling I may be hurting you. [Margot *shakes her head.*] I know if it were me, I'd be wild. I'd be desperately jealous, if it were me.

39 **Margot.** Well, I'm not.

40 **Anne.** You don't feel badly? Really? Truly? You're not jealous?

41 **Margot.** Of course I'm jealous . . . jealous that you've got something to get up in the morning for . . . But jealous of you and Peter? No.

42 [Anne *goes back to the mirror.*]

43 **Anne.** Maybe there's nothing to be jealous of. Maybe he doesn't really like me. Maybe I'm just taking the place of his cat . . . [*She picks up a pair of short white gloves, putting them on.*] Wouldn't you like to come in with us?

44 **Margot.** I have a book.

45 [*The sound of the children playing outside fades out. In the main room* Dussel *can stand it no longer. He jumps up, going to the bedroom door and knocking sharply.*]

46 **Dussel.** Will you please let me in my room!

47 **Anne.** Just a minute, dear, dear Mr. Dussel. [*She picks up her mother's pink stole and adjusts it elegantly over her shoulders, then gives a last look in the mirror.*] Well, here I go . . . to run the gauntlet.[5]

48 [*She starts out, followed by* Margot.]

49 **Dussel.** [*As she appears—sarcastic*] Thank you so much.

50 [Dussel *goes into his room.* Anne *goes toward* Peter's *room, passing* Mrs. Van Daan *and her parents at the center table.*]

5. **run the gauntlet** (GAWNT liht) literally, to pass between two rows of men who struck at the offender with clubs as he passed; here, a series of troubles or difficulties.

51 **Mrs. Van Daan.** My God, look at her! [Anne *pays no attention. She knocks at* Peter's *door*.] I don't know what good it is to have a son. I never see him. He wouldn't care if I killed myself. [Peter *opens the door and stands aside for* Anne *to come in*.] Just a minute, Anne. [*She goes to them at the door.*] I'd like to say a few words to my son. Do you mind? [Peter *and* Anne *stand waiting.*] Peter, I don't want you staying up till all hours tonight. You've got to have your sleep. You're a growing boy. You hear?

52 **Mrs. Frank.** Anne won't stay late. She's going to bed promptly at nine. Aren't you, Anne?

53 **Anne.** Yes, Mother . . . [*To* Mrs. Van Daan] May we go now?

54 **Mrs. Van Daan.** Are you asking me? I didn't know I had anything to say about it.

55 **Mrs. Frank.** Listen for the chimes, Anne dear.

56 [*The two young people go off into* Peter's *room, shutting the door after them.*]

57 **Mrs. Van Daan.** [*To* Mrs. Frank] In my day it was the boys who called on the girls. Not the girls on the boys.

58 **Mrs. Frank.** You know how young people like to feel that they have secrets. Peter's room is the only place where they can talk.

59 **Mrs. Van Daan.** Talk! That's not what they called it when I was young.

60 [Mrs. Van Daan *goes off to the bathroom.* Margot *settles down to read her book.* Mr. Frank *puts his papers away and brings a chess game to the center table. He and* Mrs. Frank *start to play. In* Peter's *room,* Anne *speaks to* Peter, *indignant, humiliated.*]

61 **Anne.** Aren't they awful? Aren't they impossible? Treating us as if we were still in the nursery.

62 [*She sits on the cot.* Peter *gets a bottle of pop and two glasses.*]

63 **Peter.** Don't let it bother you. It doesn't bother me.

64 **Anne.** I suppose you can't really blame them . . . they think back to what *they* were like at our age. They don't realize how much more advanced we are . . . When you think what wonderful discussions we've had! . . . Oh, I forgot. I was going to bring you some more pictures.

65 **Peter.** Oh, these are fine, thanks.

66 **Anne.** Don't you want some more? Miep just brought me some new ones.

67 **Peter.** Maybe later. [*He gives her a glass of pop and, taking some for himself, sits down facing her.*]

CLOSE READ

ANNOTATE: In paragraph 68, mark the details that reveal Anne's self-described change in perspective as well as her attitude toward the future.

QUESTION: Why might Anne's perspective have changed?

CONCLUDE: What does Anne's attitude toward the future reveal about her character?

68 **Anne.** [*Looking up at one of the photographs.*] I remember when I got that . . . I won it. I bet Jopie that I could eat five ice-cream cones. We'd all been playing ping-pong . . . We used to have heavenly times . . . we'd finish up with ice cream at the Delphi, or the Oasis, where Jews were allowed . . . there'd always be a lot of boys . . . we'd laugh and joke . . . I'd like to go back to it for a few days or a week. But after that I know I'd be bored to death. I think more seriously about life now. I want to be a journalist . . . or something. I love to write. What do you want to do?

69 **Peter.** I thought I might go off some place . . . work on a farm or something . . . some job that doesn't take much brains.

70 **Anne.** You shouldn't talk that way. You've got the most awful inferiority complex.

71 **Peter.** I know I'm not smart.

72 **Anne.** That isn't true. You're much better than I am in dozens of things . . . arithmetic and algebra and . . . well, you're a million times better than I am in algebra. [*With sudden directness*] You like Margot, don't you? Right from the start you liked her, liked her much better than me.

73 **Peter.** [*Uncomfortably*] Oh, I don't know.

74 [*In the main room* Mrs. Van Daan *comes from the bathroom and goes over to the sink, polishing a coffee pot.*]

75 **Anne.** It's all right. Everyone feels that way. Margot's so good. She's sweet and bright and beautiful and I'm not.

76 **Peter.** I wouldn't say that.

77 **Anne.** Oh, no, I'm not. I know that. I know quite well that I'm not a beauty. I never have been and never shall be.

78 **Peter.** I don't agree at all. I think you're pretty.

79 **Anne.** That's not true!

80 **Peter.** And another thing. You've changed . . . from at first, I mean.

81 **Anne.** I have?

82 **Peter.** I used to think you were awful noisy.

83 **Anne.** And what do you think now, Peter? How have I changed?

84 **Peter.** Well . . . er . . . you're . . . quieter.

85 [*In his room* Dussel *takes his pajamas and toilet articles and goes into the bathroom to change.*]

86 **Anne.** I'm glad you don't just hate me.

87 **Peter.** I never said that.

88 **Anne.** I bet when you get out of here you'll never think of me again.

89 **Peter.** That's crazy.

90 **Anne.** When you get back with all of your friends, you're going to say . . . now what did I ever see in that Mrs. Quack Quack.

91 **Peter.** I haven't got any friends.

92 **Anne.** Oh, Peter, of course you have. Everyone has friends.

93 **Peter.** Not me. I don't want any. I get along all right without them.

94 **Anne.** Does that mean you can get along without me? I think of myself as your friend.

95 **Peter.** No. If they were all like you, it'd be different.

96 [*He takes the glasses and the bottle and puts them away. There is a second's silence and then* Anne *speaks, hesitantly, shyly.*]

97 **Anne.** Peter, did you ever kiss a girl?

98 **Peter.** Yes. Once.

99 **Anne.** [*To cover her feelings*] That picture's crooked. [Peter *goes over, straightening the photograph.*] Was she pretty?

100 **Peter.** Huh?

101 **Anne.** The girl that you kissed.

102 **Peter.** I don't know. I was blindfolded. [*He comes back and sits down again.*] It was at a party. One of those kissing games.

103 **Anne.** [*Relieved*] Oh. I don't suppose that really counts, does it?

104 **Peter.** It didn't with me.

105 **Anne.** I've been kissed twice. Once a man I'd never seen before kissed me on the cheek when he picked me up off the ice and I was crying. And the other was Mr. Koophuis, a friend of Father's who kissed my hand. You wouldn't say those counted, would you?

106 **Peter.** I wouldn't say so.

107 **Anne.** I know almost for certain that Margot would never kiss anyone unless she was engaged to them. And I'm sure too that Mother never touched a man before Pim. But I don't know . . . things are so different now . . . What do you think? Do you think a girl shouldn't kiss anyone except if she's engaged or something? It's so hard to try to think what to do, when here we are with the whole world falling around our ears and you think . . . well . . . you don't know what's going to happen tomorrow and . . . What do you think?

108 **Peter.** I suppose it'd depend on the girl. Some girls, anything they do's wrong. But others . . . well . . . it wouldn't necessarily be wrong with them. [*The carillon starts to strike nine o'clock.*] I've always thought that when two people . . .

109 **Anne.** Nine o'clock. I have to go.

110 **Peter.** That's right.

111 **Anne.** [*Without moving*] Good night.

112 [*There is a second's pause, then* Peter *gets up and moves toward the door.*]

113 **Peter.** You won't let them stop you coming?

114 **Anne.** No. [*She rises and starts for the door.*] Sometimes I might bring my diary. There are so many things in it that I want to talk over with you. There's a lot about you.

115 **Peter.** What kind of things?

116 **Anne.** I wouldn't want you to see some of it. I thought you were a nothing, just the way you thought about me.

117 **Peter.** Did you change your mind, the way I changed my mind about you?

118 **Anne.** Well . . . You'll see . . .

CLOSE READ

ANNOTATE: In paragraph 119, mark details that relate to feelings. Mark other details that relate to silence or quiet.

QUESTION: Why do the playwrights present this incident in stage directions rather than in dialogue?

CONCLUDE: What is the effect of these details?

119 [*For a second* Anne *stands looking up at* Peter, *longing for him to kiss her. As he makes no move she turns away. Then suddenly* Peter *grabs her awkwardly in his arms, kissing her on the cheek.* Anne *walks out dazed. She stands for a minute, her back to the people in the main room. As she regains her poise she goes to her mother and father and* Margot, *silently kissing them. They murmur their good nights to her. As she is about to open her bedroom door, she catches sight of* Mrs. Van Daan. *She goes quickly to her, taking her face in her hands and kissing her first on one cheek and then on the other. Then she hurries off into her room.* Mrs. Van Daan *looks after her, and then looks over at* Peter's *room. Her suspicions are confirmed.*]

120 **Mrs. Van Daan.** [*She knows.*] Ah hah!

121 [*The lights dim out. The curtain falls on the scene. In the darkness* Anne's Voice *comes faintly at first and then with growing strength.*]

122 **Anne's Voice.** By this time we all know each other so well that if anyone starts to tell a story, the rest can finish it for him. We're having to cut down still further on our meals. What makes it worse, the rats have been at work again. They've carried off some of our precious food. Even

Mr. Dussel wishes now that Mouschi was here. Thursday, the twentieth of April, nineteen forty-four. Invasion fever is **mounting** every day. Miep tells us that people outside talk of nothing else. For myself, life has become much more pleasant. I often go to Peter's room after supper. Oh, don't think I'm in love, because I'm not. But it does make life more bearable to have someone with whom you can exchange views. No more tonight. P.S. . . . I must be honest. I must confess that I actually live for the next meeting. Is there anything lovelier than to sit under the skylight and feel the sun on your cheeks and have a darling boy in your arms? I admit now that I'm glad the Van Daans had a son and not a daughter. I've outgrown another dress. That's the third. I'm having to wear Margot's clothes after all. I'm working hard on my French and am now reading *La Belle Nivernaise*.

123 [*As she is saying the last lines—the curtain rises on the scene. The lights dim on, as Anne's Voice fades out.*]

⌘ ⌘ ⌘

Scene 3

1 [*It is night, a few weeks later. Everyone is in bed. There is complete quiet. In the Van Daans' room a match flares up for a moment and then is quickly put out. Mr. Van Daan, in bare feet, dressed in underwear and trousers, is dimly seen coming stealthily down the stairs and into the main room, where Mr. and Mrs. Frank and Margot are sleeping. He goes to the food safe and again lights a match. Then he cautiously opens the safe, taking out a half-loaf of bread. As he closes the safe, it creaks. He stands rigid. Mrs. Frank sits up in bed. She sees him.*]

2 **Mrs. Frank.** [*Screaming.*] Otto! Otto! *Komme schnell!* [6]

3 [*The rest of the people wake, hurriedly getting up.*]

4 **Mr. Frank.** *Was ist los? Was ist passiert?* [7]

5 [Dussel, *followed by* Anne, *comes from his room.*]

6 **Mrs. Frank.** [*As she rushes over to* Mr. Van Daan] *Er stiehlt das Essen!* [8]

7 **Dussel.** [*Grabbing* Mr. Van Daan] You! You! Give me that.

8 **Mrs. Van Daan.** [*Coming down the stairs*] Putti . . . Putti . . . what is it?

9 **Dussel.** [*His hands* on Van Daan's *neck*] You dirty thief . . . stealing food . . . you good-for-nothing . . .

NOTES

mounting (MOWN tihng) *adj.* increasing gradually; building up

rigid (RIHJ ihd) *adj.* stiff and unbending

6. ***Komme schnell!*** (KOHM uh SHNEHL) German for "Come quick!"

7. ***Was ist los? Was ist passiert?*** (VAHS ihst LOS VAHS ihst PAHS eert) German for "What's the matter? What happened?"

8. ***Er stiehlt das Essen!*** (ehr SHTEELT dahs EHS uhn) German for "He steals food!"

10 **Mr. Frank.** Mr. Dussel! For God's sake! Help me, Peter!

11 [Peter *comes over, trying, with* Mr. Frank, *to separate the two struggling men.*]

12 **Peter.** Let him go! Let go!

13 [Dussel *drops* Mr. Van Daan, *pushing him away. He shows them the end of a loaf of bread that he has taken from* Van Daan.]

14 **Dussel.** You greedy, selfish . . . !

15 [Margot *turns on the lights.*]

16 **Mrs. Van Daan.** Putti . . . what is it?

17 [*All of* Mrs. Frank's *gentleness, her self-control, is gone. She is outraged, in a frenzy of indignation.*]

18 **Mrs. Frank.** The bread! He was stealing the bread!

19 **Dussel.** It was you, and all the time we thought it was the rats!

20 **Mr. Frank.** Mr. Van Daan, how could you!

21 **Mr. Van Daan.** I'm hungry.

22 **Mrs. Frank.** We're all of us hungry! I see the children getting thinner and thinner. Your own son Peter . . . I've heard him moan in his sleep, he's so hungry. And you come in the night and steal food that should go to them . . . to the children!

23 **Mrs. Van Daan.** [*Going to* Mr. Van Daan *protectively*] He needs more food than the rest of us. He's used to more. He's a big man.

24 [Mr. Van Daan *breaks away, going over and sitting on the couch.*]

25 **Mrs. Frank.** [*Turning on* Mrs. Van Daan] And you . . . you're worse than he is! You're a mother, and yet you sacrifice your child to this man . . . this . . . this . . .

26 **Mr. Frank.** Edith! Edith!

27 [Margot *picks up the pink woolen stole, putting it over her mother's shoulders.*]

28 **Mrs. Frank.** [*Paying no attention, going on to* Mrs. Van Daan] Don't think I haven't seen you! Always saving the choicest bits for him! I've watched you day after day and I've held my tongue. But not any longer! Not after this! Now I want him to go! I want him to get out of here!

29 [*Together*] {
Mr. Frank. Edith!
Mr. Van Daan. Get out of here?
Mrs. Van Daan. What do you mean?
}

30 **Mrs. Frank.** Just that! Take your things and get out!

31 **Mr. Frank.** [*To* Mrs. Frank] You're speaking in anger. You cannot mean what you are saying.

32 **Mrs. Frank.** I mean exactly that!

33 [Mrs. Van Daan *takes a cover from the* Franks' *bed, pulling it about her.*]

34 **Mr. Frank.** For two long years we have lived here, side by side. We have respected each other's rights . . . we have managed to live in peace. Are we now going to throw it all away? I know this will never happen again, will it, Mr. Van Daan?

35 **Mr. Van Daan.** No. No.

36 **Mrs. Frank.** He steals once! He'll steal again!

Anne Frank [R] with her sister, Margot [L].

37 [Mr. Van Daan, *holding his stomach, starts for the bathroom.* Anne *puts her arms around him, helping him up the step.*]

38 **Mr. Frank.** Edith, please. Let us be calm. We'll all go to our rooms . . . and afterwards we'll sit down quietly and talk this out . . . we'll find some way . . .

39 **Mrs. Frank.** No! No! No more talk! I want them to leave!

40 **Mrs. Van Daan.** You'd put us out, on the streets?

41 **Mrs. Frank.** There are other hiding places.

42 **Mrs. Van Daan.** A cellar . . . a closet. I know. And we have no money left even to pay for that.

43 **Mrs. Frank.** I'll give you money. Out of my own pocket I'll give it gladly. [*She gets her purse from a shelf and comes back with it.*]

44 **Mrs. Van Daan.** Mr. Frank, you told Putti you'd never forget what he'd done for you when you came to Amsterdam. You said you could never repay him, that you . . .

45 **Mrs. Frank.** [*Counting out money.*] If my husband had any obligation to you, he's paid it, over and over.

46 **Mr. Frank.** Edith, I've never seen you like this before. I don't know you.

47 **Mrs. Frank.** I should have spoken out long ago.

48 **Dussel.** You can't be nice to some people.

NOTES

49 **Mrs. Van Daan.** [*Turning on* Dussel] There would have been plenty for all of us, if *you* hadn't come in here!

50 **Mr. Frank.** We don't need the Nazis to destroy us. We're destroying ourselves.

51 [*He sits down, with his head in his hands.* Mrs. Frank *goes to* Mrs. Van Daan.]

52 **Mrs. Frank.** [*Giving* Mrs. Van Daan *some money*] Give this to Miep. She'll find you a place.

53 **Anne.** Mother, you're not putting Peter out. Peter hasn't done anything.

54 **Mrs. Frank.** He'll stay, of course. When I say I must protect the children, I mean Peter too.

55 [Peter *rises from the steps where he has been sitting.*]

56 **Peter.** I'd have to go if Father goes.

57 [Mr. Van Daan *comes from the bathroom.* Mrs. Van Daan *hurries to him and takes him to the couch. Then she gets water from the sink to bathe his face.*]

58 **Mrs. Frank.** [*While this is going on*] He's no father to you . . . that man! He doesn't know what it is to be a father!

59 **Peter.** [*Starting for his room*] I wouldn't feel right. I couldn't stay.

60 **Mrs. Frank.** Very well, then. I'm sorry.

61 **Anne.** [*Rushing over* to Peter] No. Peter! No! [Peter *goes into his room, closing the door after him.* Anne t*urns back to her mother, crying.*] I don't care about the food. They can have mine! I don't want it! Only don't send them away. It'll be daylight soon. They'll be caught . . .

62 **Margot.** [*Putting her arms comfortingly around* Anne] Please, Mother!

63 **Mrs. Frank.** They're not going now. They'll stay here until Miep finds them a place. [*To* Mrs. Van Daan] But one thing I insist on! He must never come down here again! He must never come to this room where the food is stored! We'll divide what we have . . . an equal share for each! [Dussel *hurries over to get a sack of potatoes from the food safe.* Mrs. Frank *goes on, to* Mrs. Van Daan] You can cook it here and take it up to him.

64 [Dussel *brings the sack of potatoes back to the center table.*]

65 **Margot.** Oh, no. No. We haven't sunk so far that we're going to fight over a handful of rotten potatoes.

66 **Dussel.** [*Dividing the potatoes into piles*] Mrs. Frank, Mr. Frank, Margot, Anne, Peter, Mrs. Van Daan, Mr. Van Daan, myself . . . Mrs. Frank . . .

67 [*The buzzer sounds in* Miep's *signal.*]

68 **Mr. Frank.** It's Miep! [*He hurries over, getting his overcoat and putting it on.*]

69 **Margot.** At this hour?

70 **Mrs. Frank.** It is trouble.

71 **Mr. Frank.** [*As he starts down to unbolt the door*] I beg you, don't let her see a thing like this!

72 **Mr. Dussel.** [*Counting without stopping*] . . . Anne, Peter, Mrs. Van Daan, Mr. Van Daan, myself . . .

73 **Margot.** [*To* Dussel] Stop it! Stop it!

74 **Dussel.** . . . Mr. Frank, Margot, Anne, Peter, Mrs. Van Daan, Mr. Van Daan, myself, Mrs. Frank . . .

75 **Mrs. Van Daan.** You're keeping the big ones for yourself! All the big ones . . . Look at the size of that! . . . And that! . . .

76 [Dussel *continues on with his dividing.* Peter, *with his shirt and trousers on, comes from his room.*]

77 **Margot.** Stop it! Stop it!

78 [*We hear* Miep's *excited voice speaking to* Mr. Frank *below.*]

79 **Miep.** Mr. Frank . . . the most wonderful news! . . . The invasion has begun!

80 **Mr. Frank.** Go on, tell them! Tell them!

81 [Miep *comes running up the steps ahead of* Mr. Frank. *She has a man's raincoat on over her nightclothes and a bunch of orange-colored flowers in her hand.*]

82 **Miep.** Did you hear that, everybody? Did you hear what I said? The invasion has begun! The invasion!

83 [*They all stare at* Miep, *unable to grasp what she is telling them.* Peter *is the first to recover his wits.*]

84 **Peter.** Where?

85 **Mrs. Van Daan.** When? When, Miep?

86 **Miep.** It began early this morning . . .

87 [*As she talks on, the realization of what she has said begins to dawn on them. Everyone goes crazy. A wild demonstration takes place.* Mrs. Frank *hugs* Mr. Van Daan.]

88 **Mrs. Frank.** Oh, Mr. Van Daan, did you hear that?

NOTES

CLOSE READ

ANNOTATE: Mark details in paragraph 81 that describe Miep's appearance.

QUESTION: Why do the playwrights include these specific details?

CONCLUDE: What is the effect of these details?

89 [Dussel *embraces* Mrs. Van Daan. Peter *grabs a frying pan and parades around the room, beating on it, singing the Dutch National Anthem.* Anne *and* Margot *follow him, singing, weaving in and out among the excited grown-ups.* Margot *breaks away to take the flowers from* Miep *and distribute them to everyone. While this pandemonium is going on* Mrs. Frank *tries to make herself heard above the excitement.*]

9. **B.B.C.** British Broadcasting
   Corporation.

90 **Mrs. Frank.** [*To* Miep] How do you know?

91 **Miep.** The radio . . . The B.B.C.! [9] They said they landed on the coast of Normandy!

92 **Peter.** The British?

93 **Miep.** British, Americans, French, Dutch, Poles, Norwegians . . . all of them! More than four thousand ships! Churchill spoke, and General Eisenhower! D-Day they call it!

94 **Mr. Frank.** Thank God, it's come!

95 **Mrs. Van Daan.** At last!

96 **Miep.** [*Starting out*] I'm going to tell Mr. Kraler. This'll be better than any blood transfusion.

97 **Mr. Frank.** [*Stopping her*] What part of Normandy did they land, did they say?

98 **Miep.** Normandy . . . that's all I know now . . . I'll be up the minute I hear some more! [*She goes hurriedly out.*]

99 **Mr. Frank.** [*To* Mrs. Frank] What did I tell you? What did I tell you?

100 [Mr. Frank *indicates that he has forgotten to bolt the door after* Miep. *He hurries down the steps.* Mr. Van Daan, *sitting on the couch, suddenly breaks into a convulsive*[10] *sob. Everybody looks at him, bewildered.*]

10. **convulsive** (kuhn VUHL sihv)
    adj. having an uncontrolled
    muscular spasm; shuddering.

101 **Mrs. Van Daan.** [*Hurrying to him*] Putti! Putti! What is it? What happened?

102 **Mr. Van Daan.** Please, I'm so ashamed.

103 [Mr. Frank *comes back up the steps.*]

104 **Dussel.** Oh, for God's sake!

105 **Mrs. Van Daan.** Don't, Putti.

106 **Margot.** It doesn't matter now!

107 **Mr. Frank.** [*Going to* Mr. Van Daan] Didn't you hear what Miep said? The invasion has come! We're going to be liberated! This is a time to celebrate! [*He embraces* Mrs. Frank *and then hurries to the cupboard and gets the cognac and a glass.*]

108 **Mr. Van Daan.** To steal bread from children!

109 **Mrs. Frank.** We've all done things that we're ashamed of.

110 **Anne.** Look at me, the way I've treated Mother . . . so mean and horrid to her.

111 **Mrs. Frank.** No, Anneke, no.

112 [Anne *runs to her mother, putting her arms around her.*]

113 **Anne.** Oh, Mother, I was. I was awful.

114 **Mr. Van Daan.** Not like me. No one is as bad as me!

115 **Dussel.** [*To* Mr. Van Daan] Stop it now! Let's be happy!

116 **Mr. Frank.** [*Giving* Mr. Van Daan a *glass of cognac*] Here! Here! *Schnapps! L'chaim!*[11]

117 [Van Daan *takes the cognac. They all watch him. He gives them a feeble smile.* Anne *puts up her fingers in a V-for-Victory sign. As* Van Daan *gives an answering V-sign, they are startled to hear a loud sob from behind them. It is* Mrs. Frank, *stricken with remorse. She is sitting on the other side of the room.*]

118 **Mrs. Frank.** [*Through her sobs*] When I think of the terrible things I said . . .

119 [Mr. Frank, Anne *and* Margot *hurry to her, trying to comfort her.* Mr. Van Daan *brings her his glass of cognac.*]

120 **Mr. Van Daan.** No! No! You were right!

121 **Mrs. Frank.** That I should speak that way to you! . . . Our friends! . . . Our guests! [*She starts to cry again.*]

122 **Dussel.** Stop it, you're spoiling the whole invasion!

123 [*As they are comforting her, the lights dim out. The curtain falls.*]

124 **Anne's Voice.** [*Faintly at first and then with growing strength*] We're all in much better spirits these days. There's still excellent news of the invasion. The best part about it is that I have a feeling that friends are coming. Who knows? Maybe I'll be back in school by fall. Ha, ha! The joke is on us! The warehouse man doesn't know a thing and we are paying him all that money! . . . Wednesday, the second of July, nineteen forty-four. The invasion seems temporarily to be bogged down. Mr. Kraler has to have an operation, which looks bad. The Gestapo have found the radio that was stolen. Mr. Dussel says they'll trace it back and back to the thief, and then, it's just a matter of time till they get to us. Everyone is low. Even poor Pim can't raise their spirits. I have often been downcast myself . . . but never in despair. I can shake off everything if I write. But . . . and that is the great question . . . will I ever be able to write well? I want to so much. I want to go on living even after my death. Another birthday has gone by, so now I

11. *Schnapps!* (SHNAHPS) German for "a drink." *L'chaim!* (luh KHAH yihm) Hebrew toast meaning "To life!"

am fifteen. Already I know what I want. I have a goal, an opinion.

125 [*As this is being said—the curtain rises on the scene, the lights dim on, and* Anne's Voice *fades out.*]

⌘ ⌘ ⌘

Scene 4

1 [*It is an afternoon a few weeks later . . . Everyone but* Margot *is in the main room. There is a sense of great tension.*

2 *Both* Mrs. Frank *and* Mr. Van Daan *are nervously pacing back and forth,* Dussel *is standing at the window, looking down fixedly at the street below.* Peter *is at the center table, trying to do his lessons.* Anne *sits opposite him, writing in her diary.* Mrs. Van Daan *is seated on the couch, her eyes on* Mr. Frank *as he sits reading.*

3 *The sound of a telephone ringing comes from the office below. They all are* rigid, *listening tensely.* Dussel *rushes down to* Mr. Frank.]

4 **Dussel.** There it goes again, the telephone! Mr. Frank, do you hear?

5 **Mr. Frank.** [*Quietly*] Yes. I hear.

6 **Dussel.** [*Pleading, insistent*] But this is the third time, Mr. Frank! The third time in quick succession! It's a signal! I tell you it's Miep, trying to get us! For some reason she can't come to us and she's trying to warn us of something!

7 **Mr. Frank.** Please. Please.

8 **Mr. Van Daan.** [*To* Dussel] You're wasting your breath.

9 **Dussel.** Something has happened, Mr. Frank. For three days now Miep hasn't been to see us! And today not a man has come to work. There hasn't been a sound in the building!

10 **Mrs. Frank.** Perhaps it's Sunday. We may have lost track of the days.

11 **Mr. Van Daan.** [*To* Anne] You with the diary there. What day is it?

12 **Dussel.** [*Going to* Mrs. Frank] I don't lose track of the days! I know exactly what day it is! It's Friday, the fourth of August. Friday, and not a man at work. [*He rushes back to* Mr. Frank. *Pleading with him, almost in tears.*] I tell you Mr. Kraler's dead. That's the only explanation. He's dead and they've closed down the building, and Miep's trying to tell us!

insistent (ihn SIHS tuhnt) *adj.* demanding that something should happen

13 **Mr. Frank.** She'd never telephone us.

14 **Dussel.** [*Frantic*] Mr. Frank, answer that! I beg you, answer it!

15 **Mr. Frank.** No.

16 **Mr. Van Daan.** Just pick it up and listen. You don't have to speak. Just listen and see if it's Miep.

17 **Dussel.** [*Speaking at the same time*] For God's sake . . . I ask you.

18 **Mr. Frank.** No. I've told you, no. I'll do nothing that might let anyone know we're in the building.

19 **Peter.** Mr. Frank's right.

20 **Mr. Van Daan.** There's no need to tell us what side you're on.

21 **Mr. Frank.** If we wait patiently, quietly, I believe that help will come.

22 [*There is silence for a minute as they all listen to the telephone ringing.*]

23 **Dussel.** I'm going down. [*He rushes down the steps.* Mr. Frank *tries ineffectually to hold him.* Dussel *runs to the lower door, unbolting it. The telephone stops ringing.* Dussel *bolts the door and comes slowly back up the steps.*] Too late. [Mr. Frank *goes to* Margot *in* Anne's *bedroom.*]

24 **Mr. Van Daan.** So we just wait here until we die.

25 **Mrs. Van Daan.** [*Hysterically*] I can't stand it! I'll kill myself! I'll kill myself!

26 **Mr. Van Daan.** For God's sake, stop it!

27 [*In the distance, a German military band is heard playing a Viennese waltz.*]

28 **Mrs. Van Daan.** I think you'd be glad if I did! I think you want me to die!

29 **Mr. Van Daan.** Whose fault is it we're here? [Mrs. Van Daan *starts for her room. He follows, talking at her.*] We could've been safe somewhere . . . in America or Switzerland. But no! No! You wouldn't leave when I wanted to. You couldn't leave your things. You couldn't leave your precious furniture.

30 **Mrs. Van Daan.** Don't touch me!

31 [*She hurries up the stairs, followed by* Mr. Van Daan. Peter, *unable to bear it, goes to his room.* Anne *looks after him, deeply concerned.* Dussel *returns to his post at the window.* Mr. Frank *comes back into the main room and takes a book, trying to read.* Mrs. Frank *sits near the sink, starting to peel some potatoes.* Anne *quietly goes to* Peter's *room closing the door after her.* Peter *is lying face down on the cot.* Anne *leans over him, holding him in her arms, trying to bring him out of his despair.*]

CLOSE READ
ANNOTATE: In paragraph 32, mark sensory details—words and phrases related to sight, hearing, touch, smell, or taste.

QUESTION: Why might the playwrights have included these details?

CONCLUDE: What is the effect of these details? What do they show about Anne's character?

12. **Orthodox** (AWR thuh doks) *adj.* strictly observing the rites and traditions of Judaism.

13. **purgatory** (PUR guh tawr ee) *n.* state or place of temporary punishment.

32 **Anne.** Look, Peter, the sky. [*She looks up through the skylight.*] What a lovely, lovely day! Aren't the clouds beautiful? You know what I do when it seems as if I couldn't stand being cooped up for one more minute? I *think* myself out. I think myself on a walk in the park where I used to go with Pim. Where the jonquils and the crocus and the violets grow down the slopes. You know the most wonderful part about *thinking* yourself out? You can have it any way you like. You can have roses and violets and chrysanthemums all blooming at the same time . . . It's funny . . . I used to take it all for granted . . . and now I've gone crazy about everything to do with nature. Haven't you?

33 **Peter.** I've just gone crazy. I think if something doesn't happen soon . . . if we don't get out of here . . . I can't stand much more of it!

34 **Anne.** [*Softly*] I wish you had a religion, Peter.

35 **Peter.** No, thanks! Not me!

36 **Anne.** Oh, I don't mean you have to be Orthodox[12] . . . or believe in heaven and hell and purgatory[13] and things . . . I just mean some religion . . . it doesn't matter what. Just to believe in something! When I think of all that's out there . . . the trees . . . and flowers . . . and seagulls . . . when I think of the dearness of you, Peter . . . and the goodness of the people we know . . . Mr. Kraler, Miep, Dirk, the vegetable man, all risking their lives for us every day. . . When I think of these good things, I'm not afraid any more . . . I find myself, and God, and I . . .

37 [Peter *interrupts, getting up and walking away.*]

38 **Peter.** That's fine! But when I begin to think, I get mad! Look at us, hiding out for two years. Not able to move! Caught here like . . . waiting for them to come and get us . . . and all for what?

39 **Anne.** We're not the only people that've had to suffer. There've always been people that've had to . . . sometimes one race . . . sometimes another . . . and yet . . .

40 **Peter.** That doesn't make me feel any better!

41 **Anne.** [*Going to him*] I know it's terrible, trying to have any faith . . . when people are doing such horrible . . . But you know what I sometimes think? I think the world may be going through a phase, the way I was with Mother. It'll pass, maybe not for hundreds of years, but some day . . . I still believe, in spite of everything, that people are really good at heart.

42 **Peter.** I want to see something now . . . Not a thousand years from now! [*He goes over, sitting down again on the cot.*]

43 **Anne.** But, Peter, if you'd only look at it as part of a great pattern . . . that we're just a little minute in the life . . . [*She breaks off.*] Listen to us, going at each other like a couple of stupid grownups! Look at the sky now. Isn't it lovely? [*She holds out her hand to him. Peter takes it and rises, standing with her at the window looking out, his arms around her.*] Some day, when we're outside again, I'm going to . . .

44 [*She breaks off as she hears the sound of a car, its brakes squealing as it comes to a sudden stop. The people in the other rooms also become aware of the sound. They listen tensely. Another car roars up to a screeching stop. Anne and Peter come from Peter's room. Mr. and Mrs. Van Daan creep down the stairs. Dussel comes out from his room. Everyone is listening, hardly breathing. A doorbell clangs again and again in the building below. Mr. Frank starts quietly down the steps to the door. Dussel and Peter follow him. The others stand rigid, waiting, terrified.*]

45 *In a few seconds* Dussel *comes stumbling back up the steps. He shakes off* Peter's *help and goes to his room.* Mr. Frank *bolts the door below, and comes slowly back up the steps. Their eyes are all on him as he stands there for a minute. They realize that what they feared has happened.* Mrs. Van Daan *starts to whimper.* Mr. Van Daan *puts her gently in a chair; and then hurries off up the stairs to their room to collect their things.* Peter *goes to comfort his mother. There is a sound of violent pounding on a door below.*]

46 **Mr. Frank.** [*Quietly*] For the past two years we have lived in fear. Now we can live in hope.

47 [*The pounding below becomes more insistent. There are muffled sounds of voices, shouting commands.*]

48 **Men's Voices.** *Auf machen! Da drinnen! Auf machen! Schnell! Schnell! Schnell!*[14] etc., etc.

49 [*The street door below is forced open. We hear the heavy tread of footsteps coming up.* Mr. Frank *gets two school bags from the shelves, and gives one to* Anne *and the other to* Margot. *He goes to get a bag for* Mrs. Frank. *The sound of feet coming up grows louder.* Peter *comes to* Anne, *kissing her good-bye, then he goes to his room to collect his things. The buzzer of their door starts to ring.* Mr. Frank *brings* Mrs. Frank *a bag. They stand together, waiting. We hear the thud of gun butts on the door, trying to break it down.*

NOTES

14. ***Auf machen!. . . Schnell!*** German for "Open up, you in there, open up, quick, quick, quick!"

50 Anne *stands, holding her school satchel, looking over at her father and mother with a soft, reassuring smile. She is no longer a child, but a woman with courage to meet whatever lies ahead.*

51 *The lights dim out. The curtain falls on the scene. We hear a mighty crash as the door is shattered. After a second* Anne's Voice *is heard.*]

52 **Anne's Voice.** And so it seems our stay here is over. They are waiting for us now. They've allowed us five minutes to get our things. We can each take a bag and whatever it will hold of clothing. Nothing else. So, dear Diary, that means I must leave you behind. Good-bye for a while. P.S. Please, please, Miep, or Mr. Kraler, or anyone else. If you should find this diary, will you please keep it safe for me, because some day I hope . . .

53 [*Her voice stops abruptly. There is silence. After a second the curtain rises.*]

⌘ ⌘ ⌘

Scene 5

1 [*It is again the afternoon in November, 1945. The rooms are as we saw them in the first scene.* Mr. Kraler *has joined* Miep *and* Mr. Frank. *There are coffee cups on the table. We see a great change in* Mr. Frank. *He is calm now. His bitterness is gone. He slowly turns a few pages of the diary. They are blank.*]

2 **Mr. Frank.** No more. [*He closes the diary and puts it down on the couch beside him.*]

3 **Miep.** I'd gone to the country to find food. When I got back the block was surrounded by police . . .

4 **Mr. Kraler.** We made it our business to learn how they knew. It was the thief . . . the thief who told them.

5 [Miep *goes up to the gas burner, bringing back a pot of coffee.*]

6 **Mr. Frank.** [*After a pause*] It seems strange to say this, that anyone could be happy in a concentration camp. But Anne was happy in the camp in Holland where they first took us. After two years of being shut up in these rooms, she could be out . . . out in the sunshine and the fresh air that she loved.

7 **Miep.** [*Offering the coffee to* Mr. Frank] A little more?

8 **Mr. Frank.** [*Holding out his cup to her*] The news of the war was good. The British and Americans were sweeping through France. We felt sure that they would get to us in time. In

September we were told that we were to be shipped to Poland . . . The men to one camp. The women to another. I was sent to Auschwitz.[15] They went to Belsen.[16] In January we were freed, the few of us who were left. The war wasn't yet over, so it took us a long time to get home. We'd be sent here and there behind the lines where we'd be safe. Each time our train would stop . . . at a siding, or a crossing . . . we'd all get out and go from group to group . . . Where were you? Were you at Belsen? At Buchenwald?[17] At Mauthausen? Is it possible that you knew my wife? Did you ever see my husband? My son? My daughter? That's how I found out about my wife's death . . . of Margot, the Van Daans . . . Dussel. But Anne . . . I still hoped . . . Yesterday I went to Rotterdam. I'd heard of a woman there . . . She'd been in Belsen with Anne . . . I know now.

9 [*He picks up the diary again, and turns the pages back to find a certain passage. As he finds it we hear* Anne's Voice.]

10 **Anne's Voice.** In spite of everything, I still believe that people are really good at heart. [Mr. Frank *slowly closes the diary.*]

11 **Mr. Frank.** She puts me to shame.

12 [*They are silent.*] ❧

NOTES

15. **Auschwitz** (OWSH vihts) Nazi concentration camp in Poland at which approximately 1.1 million Jews were murdered.

16. **Belsen** (BEL zuhn) village in Germany that, with the village of Bergen, was the site of Bergen-Belsen, a Nazi concentration camp; another name for this camp.

17. **Buchenwald** (BOO kuhn wawld) Nazi concentration camp in central Germany.

Comprehension Check

Complete the following items after you finish your first read.

📓 **Notebook** Respond to the questions.

1. How long have the characters been in hiding at the beginning of Act II?

2. What happens to Mr. Kraler that prevents him from coming to the attic?

3. What does Anne give Peter to decorate his room?

4. What does Mr. Van Daan do that upsets the others?

5. At the end of the war, what happened to all the members of the Frank family except Mr. Frank?

6. Write a summary of *The Diary of Anne Frank*, Act II.

- -

RESEARCH

Research to Clarify Choose at least one unfamiliar detail from the text. Briefly research that detail. In what way does the information you learned shed light on an aspect of the play?

Research to Explore Choose something that interested you from the text, and formulate a research question you might use to learn more about it.

Close Read the Text

1. The model—from Act II, Scene 4, paragraph 44—shows two sample annotations, along with questions and conclusions. Close read the passage, and find another detail to annotate. Then, write a question and your conclusion.

ANNOTATE: These details identify sounds coming from outside the Secret Annex.

QUESTION: Why do the playwrights include these details in the stage directions?

CONCLUDE: These details build suspense as readers' wonder what the sounds imply about future events.

ANNOTATE: These sentences describe characters' reactions to the alarming noises.

QUESTION: Why do the playwrights include these descriptions?

CONCLUDE: These details convey the characters' sense of dread.

[*She breaks off as she hears* the sound of a car, its brakes squealing as it comes to a sudden stop. *The people in the other rooms also become aware of the sound.* They listen tensely. *Another car roars up to a screeching stop....* Everyone is listening, hardly breathing. A doorbell clangs again and again *in the building below.*]

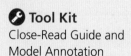

Tool Kit
Close-Read Guide and Model Annotation

2. For more practice, go back into the text, and complete the close-read notes.

3. Revisit a section of the text you found important during your first read. Read this section closely, and **annotate** what you notice. Ask yourself **questions** such as "Why did the author make this choice?" What can you **conclude**?

Analyze the Text

CITE TEXTUAL EVIDENCE to support your answers.

📓 **Notebook** Respond to these questions.

1. **(a)** What disturbing news does Mr. Kraler bring on New Year's Day? **(b) Connect** What hint does this news give about the play's ending?

2. **Analyze** How is Anne able to preserve her dignity and hope despite her suffering?

3. **Essential Question: *How do we remember the past?*** What has the play taught you about how we remember the past?

⊟ STANDARDS

Reading Literature
• Cite the textual evidence that most strongly supports an analysis of what the text says explicitly as well as inferences drawn from the text.
• Analyze how particular lines of dialogue or incidents in a story or drama propel the action, reveal aspects of a character, or provoke a decision.

Analyze Craft and Structure

Characters' Motivations A character's motivation is the reason he or she takes a particular action. The reason may be internal, external, or a combination of the two.

- **Internal motivations** include emotions, such as jealousy or loneliness.
- **External motivations** include factors in the setting or situation, such as war or poverty.

Playwrights reveal characters' motivation through their dialogue and actions, as well as by including revealing details in the stage directions. To identify characters' motivations in a drama, make **inferences,** or educated guesses, about their behavior. Consider what characters say and how they say it. Take note of what they do, and what their attitudes are toward their actions. Also, think about descriptive details or explanations that are given in stage directions.

Practice

CITE TEXTUAL EVIDENCE to support your answers.

📓 **Notebook** Analyze the characters' motivations in Act II. Use the chart to gather your observations. Then, respond to the questions.

ACTION	MOTIVATION	INTERNAL OR EXTERNAL?
Mr. Kraler tells those in hiding about Carl.		
Mr. Van Daan steals bread.		
Peter offers to leave.		

1. (a) What is Anne's motivation for keeping a diary? (b) Cite at least two details from the play that support your inference.

2. What can you infer from details in Act II about why an informer might be motivated to tell authorities about a family in hiding?

3. Identify at least three ways in which the setting contributes the characters' motivations. For each item, cite specific details from the text that support your thinking.

THE DIARY OF ANNE FRANK, ACT II

Concept Vocabulary

foreboding	intuition	rigid
apprehension	mounting	insistent

Why These Words? These concept words are used to reveal feelings about the future—hopes, fears, and a sense of anticipation. For example, when Mr. Kraler comes to tell Mr. Frank about Carl, Margot can sense his *apprehension* about telling the group. As a result, she experiences a sense of *foreboding*. Notice that both of these words relate to the characters' feelings of fear and anxiety about the future.

1. How does the concept vocabulary help the reader understand the characters' experiences?

2. What other words in the selection connect to this concept?

Practice

🔲 **Notebook** The first word in each pair is a concept vocabulary word. For each pair, write a sentence in which you correctly use both words.

1. *apprehension,* unknown

2. *mounting,* future

3. *insistent,* voice

4. *foreboding,* tension

5. *intuition,* guess

6. *rigid,* movement

Word Study

Latin Suffix: -ent The Latin suffix -*ent* can make a verb or a noun into an adjective. Adding the suffix -*ent* to the verb *insist* changes the verb into the adjective *insistent*. In Act II, Scene 4, Mr. Dussel's pleading with Mr. Frank to investigate the ringing telephone downstairs is described as *insistent*.

1. Write a sentence in which you correctly use the adjective *insistent*.

2. Based on your understanding of the suffix -*ent,* write a definition for each of the following words: *adherent, dependent, excellent, intelligent*. Then, identify the part of speech for each word. Use a dictionary to verify each word's part of speech and definition.

🔲 WORD NETWORK

Add words related to the Holocaust from the text to your Word Network.

🔳 STANDARDS

Language
• Demonstrate command of the conventions of standard English grammar and usage when writing or speaking.
• Determine or clarify the meaning of unknown and multiple-meaning words or phrases based on *grade 8 reading and content*, choosing flexibly from a range of strategies.

   b. Use common, grade-appropriate Greek or Latin affixes and roots as clues to the meaning of a word.

   c. Consult general and specialized reference materials, both print and digital, to find the pronunciation of a word or determine or clarify its precise meaning or its part of speech.

   d. Verify the preliminary determination of the meaning of a word or phrase.

• Use knowledge of language and its conventions when writing, speaking, reading, or listening.

Conventions

Simple Tenses of Verbs The **tense** of a verb shows the time of an action or a condition. Writers need verb tenses to tell when the events they write about took place. There are three **simple tenses** of verbs: *past*, *present*, and *future*.

The chart below shows how to form these tenses. Note that the past and future forms are the same for all persons.

PRESENT TENSE	PAST TENSE	FUTURE TENSE
Use the base form; add *-s* or *-es* for the third person.	For regular verbs, add *-d* or *-ed* to base form. For irregular verbs, there is no predictable pattern, so you need to memorize their forms.	Use *will* before base form.
I **wait** You **wait** He, she, it **waits** We **wait** They **wait**	REGULAR: I **waited** IRREGULAR: I **ran**, you **came**, we **went**	I **will wait** You **will wait** He, she, it **will wait** We **will wait** They **will wait**

When telling a sequence of events, do not shift tense unnecessarily.

> **Incorrect:** I *walked* to the door and *open* it.
> **Correct:** I *walked* to the door and *opened* it.

In some cases, however, it is necessary to shift tense to show the order of events.

> **Incorrect:** Because I *run* yesterday, I *ache* today.
> **Correct:** Because I *ran* yesterday, I *ache* today.

Read It

1. Label the underlined verb in each sentence from the selection *past*, *present*, or *future*.

   a. We came to bring you New Year's greetings.

   b. If we wait patiently, quietly, I believe that help will come.

   c. Mr. Van Daan always gets a little bit more.

2. Rewrite the underlined verb in each sentence using the correct tense.

   a. They ate dinner together tomorrow night.

   b. The war happens decades ago, but for some, it could have been yesterday.

Write It

Reread the stage directions at the end of Scene 1. Rewrite the stage directions so that they are in the simple past tense.

THE DIARY OF ANNE FRANK, ACT II

Speaking and Listening

Assignment
With a partner, deliver a **dramatic reading** of a scene from *The Diary of Anne Frank*. As you perform, use your voice as well as gestures and movements to accurately re-create the scene and convey meaning.

1. **Choose a Scene and a Character** With a partner, choose a scene from either Act I or Act II of the play. Then, decide who will portray each character. If you choose a scene with more than two characters, decide how you will make the shifts from one character to another clear for your audience.

2. **Analyze the Scene** Analyze the scene you chose, considering how each character contributes to the emotions and actions. Use this analysis to decide how to perform the scene. Think about the following questions:

   - How does the scene fit into the play as a whole?
   - What does the scene reveal about the characters' perspectives, personalities, and motivations?

3. **Rehearse** As you practice your performance, use these guidelines to make your delivery effective:

   - Speak the dialogue as it is written. Adjust your tone according to the instructions provided in the stage directions.
   - Use your voice, gestures, and movements to portray your character accurately and to show your interpretation of the playwrights' intentions.

4. **Evaluate Presentations** As your classmates deliver their scenes, listen and watch attentively. Use an evaluation guide like the one shown to evaluate their dramatic readings. You will use this evaluation to write a drama review during the Writing to Sources activity.

STANDARDS

Speaking and Listening
• Engage effectively in a range of collaborative discussions with diverse partners on *grade 8 topics, texts, and issues,* building on others' ideas and expressing their own clearly.

a. Come to discussions prepared, having read or researched materials under study; explicitly draw on that preparation by referring to evidence on the topic, text, or issue to probe and reflect on issues under discussion.

b. Follow rules for collegial discussions and decision-making, track progress toward specific goals and deadlines, and define individual roles as needed.

• Present claims and findings, emphasizing salient points in a focused, coherent manner with relevant evidence, sound valid reasoning, and well-chosen details; use appropriate eye contact, adequate volume, and clear pronunciation.

DRAMATIC READING EVALUATION GUIDE

Rate each statement on a scale of 1 (not demonstrated) to 5 (demonstrated).

☐ The actors spoke the lines clearly.

☐ The actors spoke in a way that captured the characters' personalities.

☐ The actors interacted in a way that was believable and true to the play's meaning.

☐ The actors used gestures and movements effectively.

Writing to Sources

A **drama review** is an evaluation of a dramatic performance. In a review, a writer describes a performance and evaluates its quality. The writer states an opinion and then supports it with specific details. For example, it is not enough to say that an actor did a good job portraying a character. The reviewer must explain what, specifically, made the actor's portrayal successful.

Assignment

During the Speaking and Listening activity, classmates delivered dramatic readings of scenes from the play, and you evaluated those performances. Now, write a **drama review** of one of the performances. Prepare to write your review by considering these questions:

- How did watching the performance differ from reading the text?
- Did the actors make effective choices that captured the emotions, personalities, and motivations of the characters?
- Was the performance faithful to the text?
- Did the performance reveal something about the text that was new or surprising?

Draft a review in which you analyze the similarities and differences between the written text and the dramatic reading. In your conclusion, explain whether the dramatic reading effectively captured the written version of the scene. Be sure to support your analysis and evaluation with relevant details from both the text and the performance.

✐ EVIDENCE LOG

Before moving on to a new selection, go to your Evidence Log and record what you learned from *The Diary of Anne Frank*.

▤ STANDARDS

Reading Literature
Analyze the extent to which a filmed or live production of a story or drama stays faithful to or departs from the text or script, evaluating the choices made by the director or actors.

Writing
Write informative/explanatory texts to examine a topic and convey ideas, concepts, and information through the selection, organization, and analysis of relevant content.
  b. Develop the topic with relevant, well-chosen facts, definitions, concrete details, quotations, or other information and examples.
  f. Provide a concluding statement or section that follows from and supports the information or explanation presented.

THE DIARY OF ANNE FRANK

Comparing Text to Media

In this lesson, you will examine a timeline showing how events in the Frank family correspond to events in history. You will then compare the information in the timeline and the play *The Diary of Anne Frank*.

FRANK FAMILY AND WORLD WAR II TIMELINE

About the Frank Family

Otto and Edith Frank were born in Germany, where they were married and had two daughters—Margot in 1926 and Anne in 1929. The Franks began to worry about the increasing persecution of the Jews under the Nazis. In 1933, when Anne was four, the family emigrated to the Netherlands. There, at least for a while, they felt safe and free. On May 10, 1940, Germany invaded the Netherlands, and the Franks—along with all the other Jews of Holland—were in danger once more.

Frank Family and World War II Timeline

Media Vocabulary

The following words or concepts will be useful to you as you analyze, discuss, and write about timelines.

annotated: containing explanatory notes	• An annotated timeline lists events and the dates on which they occurred. • It may also include brief descriptions or explanations.
chronological: arranged in a sequence that follows the time order of events	The events in a timeline appear in chronological order, with the earliest events on the left and more recent events on the right.
parallel: similar and happening at the same time	Parallel timelines show events that are related to each other and happen during the same time period.

First Read NONFICTION

Apply these strategies as you conduct your first read. You will have an opportunity to complete a close read after your first read.

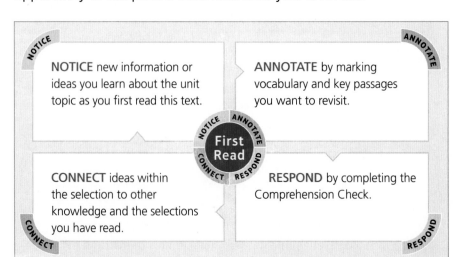

NOTICE new information or ideas you learn about the unit topic as you first read this text.

ANNOTATE by marking vocabulary and key passages you want to revisit.

First Read

CONNECT ideas within the selection to other knowledge and the selections you have read.

RESPOND by completing the Comprehension Check.

≣ STANDARDS

Reading Informational Text
By the end of the year, read and comprehend literary nonfiction at the high end of the grades 6–8 text complexity band independently and proficiently.

Frank Family and World War II Timeline

BACKGROUND

When you study historical events, it is important to consult a wide variety of text types. There are two broad categories of text type: primary sources and secondary sources.

A **primary source** offers a firsthand, eyewitness view of an event. Primary sources include a wide variety of text types, such as diaries, speeches, and official records. Photographs, maps, and artifacts are also types of primary sources.

- A **secondary source** interprets or analyzes a primary source. Secondary sources are one or more steps removed from an event. Such sources include textbooks, commentaries, encyclopedias, and histories. Interestingly, the play *The Diary of Anne Frank* is a secondary source. However, it is based closely on a primary source—Anne Frank's actual diary.

The annotated timeline on these pages is a secondary source because it pulls together and interprets other texts and images. Some of those texts and images are primary sources. As you read the annotations and look at the images, consider how the various types of texts help you build a deeper understanding of the Frank family, World War II, and the Holocaust. Think about how the events depicted here continue to shape the world today. Use the Notes boxes to make connections and to capture your observations.

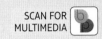

SCAN FOR MULTIMEDIA

NOTES

Frank Family and World War II Timeline

1941: Growing Nazi restrictions on the daily lives of Dutch Jews force the Frank girls to attend an all-Jewish school.

June 12, 1942: Otto gives Anne a diary for her thirteenth birthday.

July 6, 1942: The Franks go into hiding after receiving an order for Margot to report to a forced labor camp. They hide in the attic rooms above Mr. Frank's workplace with the help of close friends. Another family, the Van Pels (called the "Van Daans" in her diary), joins them, followed by Fritz Pfeffer ("Dussel"), months later.

1934: Anne starts kindergarten at the Montessori school in Amsterdam.

Summer 1933: Alarmed by Nazi actions in Germany, Otto Frank begins the process of moving his family to safety in the Netherlands.

1929: Anne Frank is born in Frankfurt, Germany.

1930   **1935**   **1940**

January 1933: Adolf Hitler comes to power in Germany. Over the next few months, all political parties, except the Nazi Party, are banned. Jews are dismissed from medical, legal, government, and teaching positions.

1935: The Nuremberg Laws are passed in Germany, stripping Jews of their rights as German citizens. Laws passed over the next several years further isolate Jews, including the requirement to wear a yellow Star of David.

September 1, 1939: Germany invades Poland, triggering the beginning of World War II.

May 1940: The Nazis invade the Netherlands. Once in control, they set up a brutal police force, the Gestapo, to administer laws to isolate Dutch Jews from the rest of the Dutch population.

NOTES

August 4, 1944: The hiding place of the Franks is discovered and the families are arrested.

September 3, 1944: All eight of those who hid in the attic are deported from the Netherlands to Auschwitz death camp.

March 1945:* Anne and Margo die of the disease typhus in the Bergan-Belsen concentration camp.

1947: Anne's diary is published in Dutch. Over the next few years it is translated and published in France, Germany, the United States, Japan, and Great Britain.

1960: The hiding place of the Franks is converted into a permanent museum that tells the story of Anne and those who hid with her.

1945   **1950**   **1955**   **1960**

May 1945: The Allies win as the war in Europe ends.

1960: Adolf Eichmann, one of the last major Nazi figures to be tried, is captured and put on trial in Israel. He is convicted and executed for his role in arranging the transport of Jews to concentration camps and ghettoes, where an estimated six million Jews died.

January 1943: The Battle of Stalingrad marks the turning of the tide against the Nazis.

June 1944: The Allies carry out a successful invasion of France. Their success gives many who live under Nazi occupation hope that the end of the war is near.

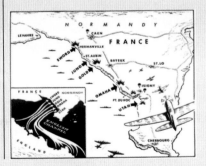

NOTES

Comprehension Check

Complete the following items after you finish your first read.

1. What was happening to Jews in Germany around the time the Frank family fled to the Netherlands?

2. What happens to Jews when the Nuremberg Laws are passed in 1935?

3. What event prompted the Franks to go into hiding in 1942?

4. What was the cause of death of Anne and her sister Margot?

5. How long after Anne's death did the war in Europe end?

6. 🗒 **Notebook** Describe the situation for Dutch Jews at the time the Frank family went into hiding.

- -

RESEARCH

Research to Clarify Choose at least one unfamiliar detail from the timeline. Briefly research that detail. In what way does the information you learned shed light on an aspect of the Holocaust?

Research to Explore Choose something that interested you from the timeline, and formulate a research question you might use to find out more about it.

Close Read

Read the timeline again. Write down any new observations that seem important. What **questions** do you have? What can you **conclude**?

Close Read

ANNOTATE · QUESTION · CONCLUDE

FRANK FAMILY AND WORLD WAR II TIMELINE

- -

Analyze the Media

CITE TEXTUAL EVIDENCE to support your answers.

Notebook Respond to these questions.

1. **(a)** What events in the lives of Anne and her family are recorded in the timeline? **(b) Connect** How do these events relate to the World War II events in the timeline?

2. **Analyze** Describe the organization of the timeline.

3. The timeline entry for July 6, 1942, notes that Anne Frank changed the names of the Van Daans and Dussel in her diary. Why might she have made this choice? Explain your thinking.

4. **Essential Question:** *How do we remember the past?* Consider the two timeline entries from 1960. What do these two events suggest about the ways in which we remember the past?

LANGUAGE DEVELOPMENT

Media Vocabulary

annotated	chronological	parallel

1. Choose one of the timeline entries with an illustration. How do the text and illustration combine to express the significance of the entry?

2. **(a)** Which timeline entries identify the beginning of the end for the Nazi war effort? **(b)** What is happening to the Frank family around the same time?

3. Choose a year that is represented with an entry in both timelines. What do the entries suggest about the relationship between the experiences of the Frank family and the events of World War II?

WORD NETWORK

Add words related to the Holocaust from the timeline to your Word Network.

THE DIARY OF ANNE FRANK

FRANK FAMILY AND WORLD
WAR II TIMELINE

Writing to Compare

Both the play *The Diary of Anne Frank* and the Frank Family and World
War II Timeline describe aspects of the same topic, the Holocaust.
Deepen your understanding of the topic by comparing what you learn
from literature with what you learn from factual information and
pictures.

Assignment

Goodrich and Hackett's play *The Diary of Anne Frank* is a dramatic
adaptation of the events described in Anne Frank's real-life diary.
The play and the timeline use different strategies to combine
information about historical events and personal family issues. Write
a **comparison-and-contrast essay** in which you explain similar and
different information you learned from the two texts. Explain how
each text might be useful for different reading purposes.

Planning and Prewriting

Compare Play and Timeline Techniques Think about the kinds of
information you learned from reading the play and from reading and
looking at the timeline. Use the chart to capture your thoughts.

WHAT I LEARNED ABOUT...	FROM THE PLAY	FROM THE TIMELINE
Historical Events		
Causes of Events		
Effects of Events		

📓 **Notebook** Respond to these questions.

1. Which medium presents historical details more accurately and
   effectively? Explain.

2. Which medium is better at revealing **motivations,** the reasons for
   people's actions? Explain.

Drafting

Outline Decide the order in which you will present details in your essay. Block organization will work well for this task, allowing you to explain what you learned and did not learn from one text and then the other. Complete the outline to organize your ideas.

I. **Introduction** State your central idea and the two works you will compare.

_____

II. **Play: *The Diary of Anne Frank***

   A. What I learned from the play _____

   _____

   B. What I did or could not learn from the play _____

   _____

III. **Timeline: Frank Family and World War II Timeline**

   A. What I learned from the timeline _____

   _____

   B. What I did or could not learn from the timeline _____

IV. **Conclusion** Explain how each type of text offers information that is useful in different ways.

   _____

   _____

Choose Strong Examples Scan or reread both sources to make sure you have chosen passages and details that clearly support your ideas. You should have at least one strong supporting detail for every point you make.

Support Your Conclusion In the final paragraph, present a broad statement about the advantages and disadvantages of using different types of texts for different purposes.

Reviewing and Revising After drafting your essay, review the assignment, and then reread your essay. Make sure you have met the requirements of the assignment. Ask yourself the following questions:

- Do I clearly explain what I learned from each text?
- Do I present information in a clear and logical order?
- Do I clearly explain how the two types of texts are useful in different ways?

EVIDENCE LOG

Before moving on to a new selection, go to your Evidence Log and record what you have learned from the play *The Diary of Anne Frank* and the Frank Family and World War II Timeline.

STANDARDS

Reading Informational Text
Evaluate the advantages and disadvantages of using different mediums to present a particular topic or idea.
Writing
Write informative/explanatory texts to examine a topic and convey ideas, concepts, and information through the selection, organization, and analysis of relevant content.
a. Introduce a topic clearly, previewing what is to follow; organize ideas, concepts, and information into broader categories; include formatting, graphics, and multimedia when useful to aiding comprehension.
b. Develop the topic with relevant, well-chosen facts, definitions, concrete details, quotations, or other information and examples.

Write an Explanatory Essay

The characters in the play *The Diary of Anne Frank* are based on real people who faced the terrifying threat of discovery, arrest, persecution, and death. In this unit, background information about the time period and a timeline of historical events provide context for the action of the play.

Assignment

Drawing on information from the Historical Perspectives feature and the Frank Family and World War II Timeline, write an **explanatory essay** addressing the following question:

> **How are historical events reflected in the play** *The Diary of Anne Frank?*

Cite specific historical events, and explain how the playwrights choose to filter them through the action in key scenes of the play. Explain how outside events affected the moods of the residents of the Secret Annex and their relationships with one another. Conclude your essay with a judgment about how well the playwrights capture the relationship between the outside world of the war and the inside world of the attic.

✎ Tool Kit
Student Model of an
Explanatory Text

ACADEMIC VOCABULARY

As you craft your explanatory essay, consider using some of the academic vocabulary you learned in the beginning of the unit.

theorize
sustain
declaration
pronounce
enumerate

Elements of an Explanatory Essay

An **explanatory essay** provides information about a subject. A well-written essay is organized so that the controlling idea is supported by reasons, facts, and examples.

An effective explanatory essay contains these elements:

- an introduction with a clear thesis statement
- a logical organization and effective conclusion
- valid reasoning and evidence, including relevant facts, details, and examples that support the thesis
- appropriate transitions to clarify relationships among ideas
- precise language and vocabulary
- formal language
- varied sentences that include accurate punctuation

Model Explanatory Essay For a model of a well-crafted explanatory essay, see the Launch Text, "The Grand Mosque of Paris."

Challenge yourself to find all of the elements of an explanatory essay in the text. You will have an opportunity to review these elements as you prepare to write your own essay.

LAUNCH TEXT

The Grand Mosque of Paris

STANDARDS

Writing
• Write informative/explanatory texts to examine a topic and convey ideas, concepts, and information through the selection, organization, and analysis of relevant content.
• Write routinely over extended time frames and shorter time frames for a range of discipline-specific tasks, purposes, and audiences.

Prewriting / Planning

Draft a Working Thesis A strong thesis does more that just state the topic of an essay—it introduces a controlling idea that sparks readers' curiosity. Notice how the opening paragraphs of the Launch Text build to an effective thesis:

> *Some of those children found refuge in the Grand Mosque of Paris, where heroic Muslims saved Jews from the Nazis.*
>
> —"The Grand Mosque of Paris"

After reading this thesis, readers might ask themselves, "What is the Grand Mosque of Paris?" or "How did Muslims save Jews?" The rest of the essay provides the answers.

Drafting a working thesis can help you develop ideas and choose supporting evidence from the selections. You will take a position on how well the playwrights of *The Diary of Anne Frank* capture the influence of historical events on the families hidden in the attic, as well as explaining what that relationship was. As you continue to write your essay, you may revise your thesis or even change it entirely.

Working Thesis: _____

_____ .

Gather Evidence from Sources Your essay will explain how historical events are reflected in the play *The Diary of Anne Frank*. Review the sources to find evidence that supports your thesis. A chart can help you identify useful evidence and make connections among the background information, timeline, and play.

EVIDENCE LOG

Review your Evidence Log and identify key details you may want to cite in your explanatory essay.

FACTS AND DETAILS Events described in Historical Perspectives and the Timeline	EXAMPLES Characters' actions, descriptions of the setting, and other details from the play that reflect each event

Take Accurate Notes While you collect evidence for your essay, think about how you might use each detail you find. Use these strategies to cite evidence you collect:

- **Exact quotations:** If the precise words from the source are important, use exact quotations. Use quotation marks in your notes, and identify the source.

- **Paraphrase:** Restate ideas in your own words to clarify.

STANDARDS

Writing
Write informative/explanatory texts to examine a topic and convey ideas, concepts, and information through the selection, organization, and analysis of relevant content.

a. Introduce a topic clearly, previewing what is to follow; organize ideas, concepts, and information into broader categories; include formatting, graphics, and multimedia when useful to aiding comprehension.

b. Develop the topic with relevant, well-chosen facts, definitions, concrete details, quotations, or other information and examples.

Drafting

Evaluate Your Evidence Take time to consider the strength of the evidence you collect. Ask yourself these questions:

- Do I have enough evidence? _____

   _____

- Which evidence provides the strongest support for my thesis? Why?

   _____

- Will I be able to answer most of the questions my readers are likely to have? If not, what other information do I need? _____

   _____

- Did I find any evidence that contradicts, or goes against, my thesis? If so, should I revise my thesis? If so, how?_____

   _____

Choose a Logical Organization Use an organizational structure that makes sense for your essay. You might consider one of the following structures:

- **Chronology:** Explain events in the order in which they happened. Your essay might begin by explaining how historical events that took place before the beginning of the play are reflected in the opening scene. Then, continue to write about events following time order.

- **Subject:** You might organize your essay by general topics. For example, you might begin by explaining how historical events are reflected in the play's setting. In the next sections of your essay, you might talk about the play's characters and their actions.

After choosing your organization, create an outline to follow as you write.

Build to a Strong Conclusion The assignment contains specific requirements for writing an effective conclusion. It asks you to make a judgment about how well Frances Goodrich and Albert Hackett, the authors of the play, show the influence of large historical events in the outside world on the interior world of the attic. Be sure that your conclusion follows logically from the evidence you present in the body of your essay.

Write a First Draft Use your outline to guide your first draft. While writing, you may think of additional ideas to include, but be sure they are relevant and are clearly connected to the topic. Finally, end your draft with a strong conclusion.

© Pearson Education, Inc., or its affiliates. All rights reserved.

STANDARDS

Writing
Write informative/explanatory texts to examine a topic and convey ideas, concepts, and information through the selection, organization, and analysis of relevant content.
   b. Develop the topic with relevant, well-chosen facts, definitions, concrete details, quotations, or other information and examples.
   f. Provide a concluding statement or section that follows from and supports the information or explanation presented.

Revising Sentences by Combining With Conjunctions

Compound sentences are made up of two or more independent clauses, which—if separated—could each form a complete sentence.

Coordinating conjunctions are words that can join independent clauses into a compound sentence. The conjunctions *and, but, or, nor, so, yet*, and *for* can help make your writing smoother by connecting too closely related ideas. You can also use coordinating conjunctions to revise run-on sentences or to improve two short, choppy sentences.

Read It

These sentences based on *The Diary of Anne Frank* show coordinating conjunctions used to join closely related independent clauses.

- *The residents of the Secret Annex must remain silent, <u>or</u> the Gestapo will discover them* (shows alternatives)
- *Anne constantly annoys Dussel, <u>yet</u> they manage to live together.* (shows contrast)
- *Mrs. Frank nearly evicts the Van Daans, <u>for</u> Mr. Van Daan has been stealing food.* (shows cause)

Write It

As you draft your essay, choose coordinating conjunctions that help you connect important ideas and make your writing smoother.

ORIGINAL	COORDINATING CONJUNCTION	REVISION
In 1933, Germany stopped Jewish involvement in the medical profession. Jewish doctors lost their jobs.	*so* (shows effect)	In 1933, Germany stopped Jewish involvement in the medical profession, <u>so</u> Jewish doctors lost their jobs.
Nuremburg Laws were targeted at Jews. Even Christians with Jewish grandparents were considered Jews.	*but* (shows contrast)	Nuremburg Laws were targeted at Jews, <u>but</u> even Christians with Jewish grandparents were considered Jews.
In 1938, Jews were excluded from public schools. They were barred from cinemas and theaters.	*and* (shows addition)	In 1938, Jews were excluded from public schools, *and* they were barred from cinemas and theaters.

PUNCTUATION

Make sure to correctly punctuate sentences with coordinating conjunctions.

- Use a comma before a coordinating conjunction in a compound sentence.
- If the clauses are very short, the comma that precedes the coordinating conjunction may be omitted.

≡ STANDARDS

Language
- Demonstrate command of the conventions of standard English grammar and usage when writing or speaking.
- Demonstrate command of the conventions of standard English capitalization, punctuation, and spelling when writing.
- Use knowledge of language and its conventions when writing, speaking, reading, or listening.

Revising

Evaluating Your Draft

Use this checklist to evaluate the effectiveness of your first draft. Then, use your evaluation and the instruction on this page to guide your revision.

FOCUS AND ORGANIZATION	EVIDENCE AND ELABORATION	CONVENTIONS
☐ Begins with an introduction that presents a clear thesis.	☐ Supports the thesis and makes clear connections among ideas.	☐ Attends to the norms and conventions of the discipline, especially the correct use and punctuation of transitions.
☐ Includes valid reasoning and evidence, including relevant facts and details.	☐ Provides adequate support for all of the main points in the essay.	
☐ Provides a concluding section that logically completes the essay.	☐ Explains ideas clearly and completely.	☐ Uses coordinating conjunctions to ensure smooth sentences and connections between important ideas.
☐ Follows a logical and effective organization.	☐ Uses vocabulary that clearly informs and explains.	
☐ Uses transitions to show the connections between ideas.	☐ Establishes and maintains a formal style.	

⊞ WORD NETWORK

Include words from your Word Network in your explanatory essay.

☰ STANDARDS

Writing
Write informative/explanatory texts to examine a topic and convey ideas, concepts, and information through the selection, organization, and analysis of relevant content.
c. Use appropriate and varied transitions to create cohesion and clarify the relationships among ideas and concepts.
d. Use precise language and domain-specific vocabulary to inform about or explain the topic.
e. Establish and maintain a formal style.

Revising for Focus and Organization

Logical Organization Reread your draft, paying attention to the organization of ideas. Is each main point stated clearly? Does each main point connect to the thesis? Do any ideas or evidence seem out of place? If so, do they belong in another section or should they be deleted?

Transitions When you transition from one idea to the next, do you use words and phrases such as *therefore, on the other hand, in contrast, similarly,* and *next* to show the relationship between ideas? If not, revise to make it easier on your readers to follow the path of your ideas.

Revising for Evidence and Elaboration

Depth of Support Review your draft. Identify your main points by underlining them. Then, read the information that follows. Have you provided at least one strong detail to support your point? Have you provided at least one example from the selections? If not, add support.

Revising for Word Choice and Style

Formal Style An explanatory essay is a formal piece of writing. To write formally, avoid slang words, imprecise words, and contractions. Use precise words that are appropriate for the topic. Consider these examples:

Informal and Imprecise: *A lot of important things went down during World War II.*

Formal and Precise: *Many significant events happened during World War II.*

PEER REVIEW

Exchange essays with a classmate. Use the checklist to evaluate your classmate's explanatory essay and provide supportive feedback.

1. Does the thesis state a controlling idea and make readers curious about the subject?

☐ yes ☐ no If no, explain what element the thesis is missing.

2. Are ideas clearly stated and supported by facts and examples?

☐ yes ☐ no If no, point out which ideas need more support.

3. Does the conclusion logically wrap up the essay?

☐ yes ☐ no If no, tell why the conclusion needs improvement.

4. What is the strongest part of your classmate's essay?

_____

Editing and Proofreading

Edit for Conventions Reread your draft for accuracy and consistency. Correct errors in grammar and word usage. Then, check to make sure that commas precede coordinating conjunctions linking independent clauses.

Proofread for Accuracy Read your draft carefully, looking for errors in spelling and punctuation. Check quotations to be sure you have used quotation marks around the exact words from the original source. Review spellings of proper nouns, including the names of people and places.

Publishing and Presenting

Create a final version of your essay. Trade essays with a partner and read each other's work. Review and comment on your partner's essay, maintaining a polite and respectful tone. Discuss your thesis statements and the evidence you each used to support your points.

Reflecting

Think about what you learned by writing your essay and what you learned by reading your partner's essay. What could you do differently the next time you need to write an explanatory essay?

:: STANDARDS

Writing
With some guidance and support from peers and adults, develop and strengthen writing as needed by planning, revising, editing, rewriting, or trying a new approach, focusing on how well purpose and audience have been addressed.

ESSENTIAL QUESTION:

How do we remember the past?

Much of what we know about the Holocaust comes from the writings and recollections of those who experienced the events firsthand. You will work in a group to continue your explorations into this time in history, focusing on the important role of personal accounts.

Small-Group Learning Strategies

Throughout your life, in school, in your community, and in your career, you will continue to learn and work with others.

Review these strategies and the actions you can take to practice them. Add ideas of your own for each step. Use these strategies during Small-Group Learning.

STRATEGY	ACTION PLAN
Prepare	• Complete your assignments so that you are prepared for group work. • Organize your thinking so you can contribute to your group's discussion. •
Participate fully	• Make eye contact to signal that you are listening and taking in what is being said. • Use text evidence when making a point. •
Support others	• Build on ideas from others in your group. • Invite others who have not yet spoken to do so. •
Clarify	• Paraphrase the ideas of others to ensure that your understanding is correct. • Ask follow-up questions. •

SCAN FOR
MULTIMEDIA

CONTENTS

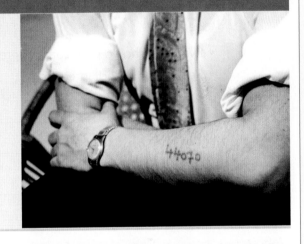

PERFORMANCE TASK

SPEAKING AND LISTENING FOCUS
Deliver a Multimedia Presentation

After reading, your group will plan and deliver an explanatory multimedia presentation based on the selections in this section and your own research.

Working as a Team

1. Discuss the Topic In your group, discuss the following question:

> **What do you think you can learn about the Holocaust from diaries, interviews, and personal accounts?**

As you take turns sharing your positions, be sure to provide reasons for your choice. After all group members have shared, discuss some of the strengths and weaknesses of information from these types of accounts.

2. List Your Rules As a group, decide on the rules that you will follow as you work together. Two samples are provided. Add two more of your own. You may add or revise rules based on your experience together.

- Everyone should participate in group discussions.
- People should not interrupt.

- _____

  _____

- _____

  _____

3. Apply the Rules Practice working as a group. Share what you have learned about the Holocaust. Make sure each person in the group contributes. Take notes on and be prepared to share one thing you learned from another member of your group.

4. Name Your Group Choose a name that reflects the unit topic.

Our group's name: _____

5. Create a Communication Plan Decide how you want to communicate with one another. For example, you might use online collaboration tools, email, or instant messaging.

Our group's decision: _____

_____

Making a Schedule

First, find out the due dates for the Small-Group activities. Then, preview the texts and activities with your group and make a schedule for completing the tasks.

SELECTION	ACTIVITIES	DUE DATE
from Anne Frank: The Diary of a Young Girl		
Acceptance Speech for the Nobel Peace Prize		
from Maus		

Working on Group Projects

As your group works together, you'll find it more effective if each person has a specific role. Different projects require different roles. Before beginning a project, discuss the necessary roles, and choose one for each group member. Some possible roles are listed here. Add your own ideas to the list.

Project Manager: monitors the schedule and keeps everyone on task

Researcher: organizes research activities

Recorder: takes notes during group meetings

_____

_____

_____

_____

SCAN FOR MULTIMEDIA

About the Author

Anne Frank (1929–1945) was a young girl who lived in Amsterdam with her family during World War II. Fleeing Nazi persecution of Jews, the Franks went into hiding, where Anne began writing her thoughts, experiences, and observations in a diary. She was 15 when the family was found and sent to the concentration camps. Anne and her sister died at Bergen-Belsen, just weeks before the camp was liberated.

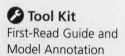 **Tool Kit**
First-Read Guide and Model Annotation

☰ STANDARDS

Reading Informational Text
By the end of the year, read and comprehend literary nonfiction at the high end of the grades 6–8 text complexity band independently and proficiently.

Language
Determine or clarify the meaning of unknown and multiple-meaning words or phrases based on *grade 8 reading and content,* choosing flexibly from a range of strategies.

  a. Use context as a clue to the meaning of a word or phrase.

from Anne Frank: The Diary of a Young Girl

Concept Vocabulary

You will encounter the following words as you read the excerpt from *Anne Frank: The Diary of a Young Girl.*

forbidden	restrictions	sacrifices

Context Clues If these words are unfamiliar to you, try using **context clues**—other words and phrases that appear nearby in the text—to help you determine their meanings. There are various types of context clues that may help you unlock word meanings.

Synonyms: The **bifurcated** tree branch looked remarkably similar to a snake's <u>forked</u> tongue.

Restatement: A healthful breakfast can **invigorate** you, <u>giving you the energy you need</u> to get through your morning.

Contrast of Ideas: The first crate looked **cumbersome**, so I grabbed the second one, which was <u>small and easy to handle</u>.

Apply your knowledge of context clues and other vocabulary strategies to determine the meanings of unfamiliar words you encounter during your first read.

First Read NONFICTION

Apply these strategies as you conduct your first read. You will have an opportunity to complete a close read after your first read.

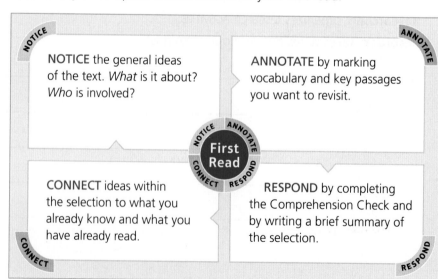

NOTICE the general ideas of the text. *What* is it about? *Who* is involved?

ANNOTATE by marking vocabulary and key passages you want to revisit.

CONNECT ideas within the selection to what you already know and what you have already read.

RESPOND by completing the Comprehension Check and by writing a brief summary of the selection.

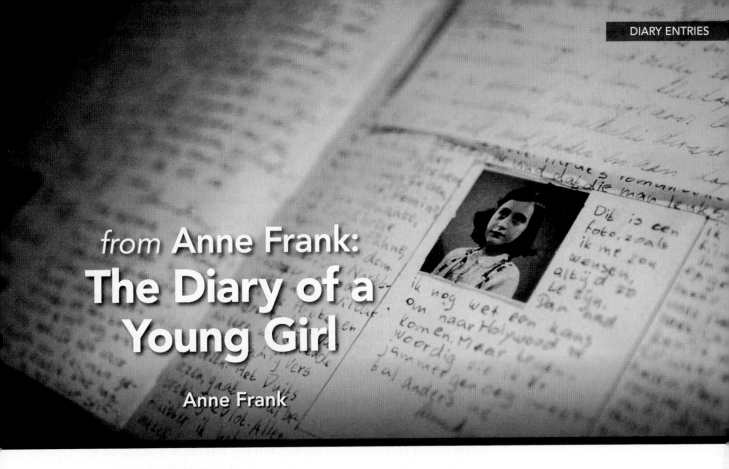

from Anne Frank: The Diary of a Young Girl

Anne Frank

BACKGROUND

Otto Frank was the only member of the Frank family to survive the concentration camps. He discovered that his daughter Anne's diary had been salvaged by Miep Gies, a close friend who had been a great help to the family during their time in hiding. He decided to publish Anne's diary as a way to honor her memory and share her story with the world.

SCAN FOR MULTIMEDIA

Saturday, 20 June, 1942

NOTES

1   . . . There is a saying that "paper is more patient than man"; it came back to me on one of my slightly melancholy days, while I sat chin in hand, feeling too bored and limp even to make up my mind whether to go out or stay at home. Yes, there is no doubt that paper is patient and as I don't intend to show this cardboard-covered notebook, bearing the proud name of "diary," to anyone, unless I find a real friend, boy or girl, probably nobody cares. And now I come to the root of the matter, the reason for my starting a diary: it is that I have no such real friend.

2   Let me put it more clearly, since no one will believe that a girl of thirteen feels herself quite alone in the world, nor is it so. I have darling parents and a sister of sixteen. I know about thirty people whom one might call friends—I have strings of boy friends, anxious to catch a glimpse of me and who, failing that, peep at me through mirrors in class. I have relations, aunts and uncles, who are darlings too, a good home, no—I don't seem to lack anything. But it's the same with all my friends, just fun and

joking, nothing more. I can never bring myself to talk of anything outside the common round. We don't seem to be able to get any closer, that is the root of the trouble. Perhaps I lack confidence, but anyway, there it is, a stubborn fact and I don't seem to be able to do anything about it.

3   Hence, this diary. In order to enhance in my mind's eye the picture of the friend for whom I have waited so long, I don't want to set down a series of bald facts in a diary like most people do, but I want this diary itself to be my friend, and I shall call my friend Kitty. No one will grasp what I'm talking about if I begin my letters to Kitty just out of the blue, so, albeit[1] unwillingly, I will start by sketching in brief the story of my life.

4   My father was thirty-six when he married my mother, who was then twenty-five. My sister Margot was born in 1926 in Frankfort-on-Main, I followed on June 12, 1929, and, as we are Jewish, we emigrated to Holland in 1933, where my father was appointed Managing Director of Travies N.V. This firm is in close relationship with the firm of Kolen & Co. in the same building, of which my father is a partner.

5   The rest of our family, however, felt the full impact of Hitler's anti-Jewish laws, so life was filled with anxiety. In 1938 after the pogroms,[2] my two uncles (my mother's brothers) escaped to the U.S.A. My old grandmother came to us, she was then seventy-three. After May 1940 good times rapidly fled: first the war, then the capitulation,[3] followed by the arrival of the Germans, which is when the sufferings of us Jews really began. Anti-Jewish decrees followed each other in quick succession. Jews must wear a yellow star, Jews must hand in their bicycles, Jews are banned from trains and are **forbidden** to drive. Jews are only allowed to do their shopping between three and five o'clock and then only in shops which bear the placard "Jewish shop." Jews must be indoors by eight o'clock and cannot even sit in their own gardens after that hour. Jews are forbidden to visit theaters, cinemas, and other places of entertainment. Jews may not take part in public sports. Swimming baths, tennis courts, hockey fields, and other sports grounds are all prohibited to them. Jews may not visit Christians. Jews must go to Jewish schools, and many more **restrictions** of a similar kind.

Mark context clues or indicate another strategy you used that helped you determine meaning.

forbidden (fuhr BIHD uhn) *v.*

MEANING:

restrictions (rih STRIHK shuhnz) *n.*

MEANING:

---

1. **albeit** (awl BEE iht) *conj.* although.
2. **pogroms** (POH gruhmz) *n.* organized killings and other persecution of Jews.
3. **capitulation** (kuh pihch uh LAY shuhn) *n.* act of surrendering.

6   So we could not do this and were forbidden to do that. But life went on in spite of it all. Jopie[4] used to say to me, "You're scared to do anything, because it may be forbidden." Our freedom was strictly limited. Yet things were still bearable.

7   Granny died in January 1942; no one will ever know how much she is present in my thoughts and how much I love her still.

8   In 1934 I went to school at the Montessori Kindergarten and continued there. It was at the end of the school year, I was in form 6B, when I had to say good-by to Mrs. K. We both wept, it was very sad. In 1941 I went, with my sister Margot, to the Jewish Secondary School, she into the fourth form[5] and I into the first.

9   So far everything is all right with the four of us and here I come to the present day.

Thursday, 19 November, 1942

10   Dear Kitty,

11   Dussel is a very nice man, just as we had all imagined. Of course he thought it was all right to share my little room.

12   Quite honestly I'm not so keen that a stranger should use my things, but one must be prepared to make some **sacrifices** for a good cause, so I shall make my little offering with a good will. "If we can save someone, then everything else is of secondary importance," says Daddy, and he's absolutely right.

13   The first day that Dussel was here, he immediately asked me all sorts of questions: When does the charwoman[6] come? When can one use the bathroom? When is one allowed to use the lavatory?[7] You may laugh, but these things are not so simple in a hiding place. During the day we mustn't make any noise that might be heard downstairs; and if there is some stranger—such as the charwoman for example—then we have to be extra careful. I explained all this carefully to Dussel. But one thing amazed me: he is very slow on the uptake. He asks everything twice over and still doesn't seem to remember. Perhaps that will wear off in time, and it's only that he's thoroughly upset by the sudden change.

14   Apart from that, all goes well. Dussel has told us a lot about the outside world, which we have missed for so long now. He had very sad news. Countless friends and acquaintances have gone to a terrible fate. Evening after evening the green and gray army

---

4. **Jopie** (YOH pee) Jacqueline van Maarsen, Anne's best friend.
5. **fourth form** here, a grade in secondary school.
6. **charwoman** *n.* cleaning woman.
7. **lavatory** *n.* toilet.

NOTES

Mark context clues or indicate another strategy you used that helped you determine meaning.

sacrifices (SAK ruh fys ihz) *n.*

MEANING:

lorries trundle past.[8] The Germans ring at every front door to inquire if there are any Jews living in the house. If there are, then the whole family has to go at once. If they don't find any, they go on to the next house. No one has a chance of evading them unless one goes into hiding. Often they go around with lists, and only ring when they know they can get a good haul. Sometimes they let them off for cash—so much per head. It seems like the slave hunts of olden times. But it's certainly no joke; it's much too tragic for that. In the evenings when it's dark, I often see rows of good, innocent people accompanied by crying children, walking on and on, in charge of a couple of these chaps, bullied and knocked about until they almost drop. No one is spared—old people, babies, expectant mothers, the sick—each and all join in the march of death.

15   How fortunate we are here, so well cared for and undisturbed. We wouldn't have to worry about all this misery were it not that we are so anxious about all those dear to us whom we can no longer help.

16   I feel wicked sleeping in a warm bed, while my dearest friends have been knocked down or have fallen into a gutter somewhere out in the cold night. I get frightened when I think of close friends who have now been delivered into the hands of the cruelest brutes that walk the earth. And all because they are Jews!

17   Yours, Anne ❧

---

8. **lorries trundle past** trucks move along.

Comprehension Check

Complete the following items after you finish your first read. Review and clarify details with your group.

1. What does the author say is her reason for starting a diary?

2. Why does Anne start her diary entries with the words *Dear Kitty*?

3. How old were Anne's parents when they got married?

4. In the beginning of her entry from November 1942, how does Anne describe Dussel?

5. 🗐 **Notebook** Confirm your understanding of the text by writing a summary of the diary excerpt.

- -

RESEARCH

Research to Clarify Choose at least one unfamiliar historical detail from the text. Briefly research that detail. In what way does the information you learned shed light on an aspect of the diary entries?

Research to Explore These diary entries may inspire you to learn more about young people affected by war. Formulate a research question about the subject, and briefly research it. Share what you discover with your group.

Close
Read

Close Read the Text

With your group, revisit sections of the text you marked during your first read. **Annotate** what you notice. What **questions** do you have? What can you **conclude**?

Analyze the Text

CITE TEXTUAL EVIDENCE to support your answers.

Notebook Complete the activities.

1. **Review and Clarify** With your group, review the diary entries. Though Anne died during the Holocaust, do you think she lives on through her diary? Explain.

2. **Present and Discuss** Now, work with your group to share the passages from the text that you found especially important. Take turns presenting your passages. Discuss what you noticed in the text, what questions you asked, and what conclusions you reached.

3. **Essential Question:** *How do we remember the past?* What has this diary excerpt taught you about how we remember the past? Discuss your thoughts with your group.

LANGUAGE DEVELOPMENT

Concept Vocabulary

forbidden	restrictions	sacrifices

Why These Words? The concept vocabulary words from the text are related. With your group, determine what the words have in common. Record your ideas, and add another word that fits the category.

Practice

Notebook Confirm your understanding of the vocabulary words by using a dictionary to verify the meaning of each word.

Word Study

Latin Root: -strict- In her diary entry for Saturday, June 20, Anne Frank mentions the many *restrictions* Jewish people were subjected to. The word *restriction* includes the Latin root *-strict-*, which means "draw tight." Find another word that contains the root *-strict-*, and explain how the root contributes to the meaning of the word.

Analyze Craft and Structure

Central Idea and Supporting Details Informational texts are often organized according to a central idea and supporting details. The **central idea** is the most important idea about the topic that a paragraph or an entire selection conveys. The central idea may either be directly stated or implied using the details provided.

- To find a **stated central idea** in a paragraph or section of text, identify the **topic,** or what it is about. Then, look for the **topic sentence**—the sentence that states the author's central idea about the topic. Often, the first sentence of a paragraph expresses its central idea.

- To determine an **implied central idea** in a paragraph or section of text, make an inference based on details in the text. An **inference** is an educated guess that you reach by analyzing the details in the text and making connections among them. For example, if someone walks into a room with a wet umbrella, you can infer that it is raining outside without needing the person with the umbrella to tell you that directly.

Practice

CITE TEXTUAL EVIDENCE to support your answers.

📓 **Notebook** Work individually to fill in this chart for paragraph 5 of the excerpt from *Anne Frank: The Diary of a Young Girl.*

PARAGRAPH 5
Topic:
Central Idea:
Supporting Detail:
Supporting Detail:
Supporting Detail:
Supporting Detail:
Supporting Detail:
Supporting Detail:

When you have finished, share your completed chart with your group, and come to a consensus about the topic, central idea, and supporting details.

from ANNE FRANK: THE DIARY
OF A YOUNG GIRL

Author's Style

Word Choice An author's **style** is his or her way of using language. Style includes a writer's **word choice**, or **diction**, and sentence structure. The author of a diary often uses an informal, conversational style. Anne Frank is no exception. In her diary, her style is conversational and even intimate, as if she were speaking to a trusted friend. In fact, she even gives this friend a name—Kitty. Notice the unique qualities of her style in the passages from her diary shown here:

Passage 1: Notice her use of a contraction, as well as plain, straightforward words.

I don't want to set down a series of bald facts in a diary like most people do, but I want this diary itself to be my friend, and I shall call my friend Kitty.

Passage 2 Notice how her sentence has a natural flow rather than a stiff formality.

Perhaps I lack confidence, but anyway, there it is, a stubborn fact and I don't seem to be able to do anything about it.

Read It

Work with your group to identify two additional examples of Anne Frank's style. Explain specific ways in which her diction and syntax create an informal, conversational style. Use the chart to record your notes.

PASSAGE FROM THE DIARY	DICTION AND/OR SYNTAX

Write It

Notebook Write a diary entry in which you use diction and syntax to create an informal, friendly style. Your diary entry can simply be about your day or about an interesting event in your life. Avoid any personal subjects that you do not want to share with a wider audience.

⊞ STANDARDS

Reading Informational Text
Determine the meaning of words and phrases as they are used in a text, including figurative, connotative, and technical meanings; analyze the impact of specific word choices on meaning and tone, including analogies or allusions to other texts.

Speaking and Listening

> **Assignment**
>
> Reread the excerpt from *Anne Frank: The Diary of a Young Girl.* Then, engage in a **collaborative group discussion** in which you discuss what you learned from Anne Frank's diary entries.

Prepare for the Discussion To prepare for your group discussion, reread the diary entries. Then, briefly respond to the following questions:

- What does Anne mean when she says "I have no such real friend"?

- How might learning Anne's thoughts add to readers' understanding of the horror of the Holocaust?

- Otto Frank decided to publish his daughter's private thoughts and feelings. Was that the right thing to do?

During the Discussion Use the questions and your responses to guide your group discussion. During the discussion, follow these guidelines:

- Ask questions of other group members. For example, you may ask someone to elaborate on an idea, or explain it more thoroughly. You may also ask someone to clarify a point.

- Respond to other group members' questions with relevant observations and new ideas.

- Think about new ideas or information expressed by others, and consider the ways in which these ideas and information confirm your views or change your perspective.

- Use evidence from Anne Frank's diary entries to support your ideas during the discussion.

✎ EVIDENCE LOG

Before moving on to a new selection, go to your Evidence Log and record what you learned from the excerpt from *Anne Frank: The Diary of a Young Girl.*

▤ STANDARDS

Speaking and Listening
Engage effectively in a range of collaborative discussions with diverse partners on *grade 8 topics, texts, and issues,* building on others' ideas and expressing their own clearly.

a. Come to discussions prepared, having read or researched material under study; explicitly draw on that preparation by referring to evidence on the topic, text, or issue to probe and reflect on ideas under discussion.

c. Pose questions that connect the ideas of several speakers and respond to others' questions and comments with relevant evidence, observations, and ideas.
d. Acknowledge new information expressed by others, and, when warranted, qualify or justify their own views in light of the evidence presented.

About the Author

Elie Wiesel (1928–2016) was a Nobel Prize–winning writer, activist, orator, and teacher, best known for his internationally acclaimed memoir *Night*, in which he recounts his experiences surviving the Holocaust. Wiesel became a revered figure of peace over the years, speaking out against persecution and injustice all across the globe.

🔧 **Tool Kit**

First-Read Guide and Model Annotation

☰ STANDARDS

Reading Informational Text
By the end of the year, read and comprehend literary nonfiction at the high end of the grades 6–8 text complexity band independently and proficiently.

Language
Determine or clarify the meaning of unknown and multiple-meaning words or phrases *based on grade 8 reading and content,* choosing flexibly from a range of strategies.

c. Consult general and specialized reference materials, both print and digital, to find the pronunciation of a word or determine or clarify its precise meaning or its part of speech.
d. Verify the preliminary determination of the meaning of a word or phrase.

Acceptance Speech for the Nobel Peace Prize

Concept Vocabulary

As you read Elie Wiesel's Nobel Peace Prize acceptance speech, you will encounter these words.

humiliation	persecuted	traumatized

Using a Dictionary and Thesaurus When you come across an unfamiliar word and cannot determine its meaning from context clues alone, it's a good idea to look up the word in a **dictionary** or **thesaurus.**

When you look up a word in a dictionary, you will find its meaning, part of speech, and pronunciation. In a thesaurus, you will find **synonyms** for a word, or words with similar meaning. A thesaurus can be helpful when you're looking to vary your word choices in your writing.

Compare these two entries for the word *verdict*:

Dictionary

ver•dict (VUR dihkt) *n.*
1. decision arrived at by a jury at the end of a trial
2. any decision or judgment

Thesaurus

verdict *n.* judgment, finding, decision, answer, opinion, sentence, determination

Notice that a thesaurus does not provide definitions. Before you use a word you find in a thesaurus, check a dictionary to verify its meaning.

First Read NONFICTION

Apply these strategies as you conduct your first read. You will have an opportunity to complete a close read after your first read.

NOTICE

ANNOTATE

NOTICE the general ideas of the text. *What* is it about? *Who* is involved?

ANNOTATE by marking vocabulary and key passages you want to revisit.

First Read

CONNECT ideas within the selection to what you already know and what you have already read.

RESPOND by completing the Comprehension Check and by writing a brief summary of the selection.

CONNECT

RESPOND

Acceptance Speech for the
Nobel Peace Prize

Elie Wiesel

BACKGROUND

Elie Wiesel wrote more than sixty books, many of which are about his experiences in the Buchenwald and Auschwitz concentration camps. He was honored with a Nobel Peace Prize in 1986 for his commitment to serving people around the world who have been persecuted or currently face persecution.

SCAN FOR MULTIMEDIA

NOTES

1　It is with a profound sense of humility that I accept the honor you have chosen to bestow upon me. I know: Your choice transcends me. This both frightens and pleases me.

2　It frightens me because I wonder: Do I have the right to represent the multitudes who have perished? Do I have the right to accept this great honor on their behalf? . . . I do not. That would be presumptuous. No one may speak for the dead, no one may interpret their mutilated dreams and visions.

3　It pleases me because I may say that this honor belongs to all the survivors and their children, and through us, to the Jewish people with whose destiny I have always identified.

4　I remember: It happened yesterday or eternities ago. A young Jewish boy discovered the kingdom of night. I remember his bewilderment, I remember his anguish. It all happened so fast. The ghetto. The deportation. The sealed cattle car. The fiery altar upon which the history of our people and the future of mankind were meant to be sacrificed.

5　I remember: He asked his father, "Can this be true?" This is the twentieth century, not the Middle Ages. Who would allow such crimes to be committed? How could the world remain silent?

6　And now the boy is turning to me: "Tell me," he asks. "What have you done with my future? What have you done with your life?"

7　And I tell him that I have tried. That I have tried to keep memory alive, that I have tried to fight those who would forget. Because if we forget, we are guilty, we are accomplices.

NOTES

Use a dictionary or thesaurus or indicate another strategy you used that helped you determine meaning.

humiliation (hyoo mihl ee AY shuhn) *n.*

MEANING:

persecuted (PUR suh kyoo tihd) *v.*

MEANING:

traumatized (TRAW muh tyzd) *adj.*

MEANING:

8   And then I explained to him how naive we were, that the world did know and remain silent. And that is why I swore never to be silent whenever and wherever human beings endure suffering and **humiliation**. We must always take sides. Neutrality helps the oppressor, never the victim. Silence encourages the tormentor, never the tormented. Sometimes we must interfere. When human lives are endangered, when human dignity is in jeopardy, national borders and sensitivities become irrelevant. Wherever men or women are **persecuted** because of their race, religion, or political views, that place must—at that moment—become the center of the universe.

9   Of course, since I am a Jew profoundly rooted in my people's memory and tradition, my first response is to Jewish fears, Jewish needs, Jewish crises. For I belong to a **traumatized** generation, one that experienced the abandonment and solitude of our people. It would be unnatural for me not to make Jewish priorities my own: Israel, Soviet Jewry, Jews in Arab lands . . . But there are others as important to me. Apartheid[1] is, in my view, as abhorrent as anti-Semitism. To me, Andrei Sakharov's[2] isolation is as much of a disgrace as Josef Biegun's[3] imprisonment. As is the denial of Solidarity and its leader Lech Wałęsa's[4] right to dissent. And Nelson Mandela's[5] interminable imprisonment.

10   There is so much injustice and suffering crying out for our attention: victims of hunger, of racism, and political persecution, writers and poets, prisoners in so many lands governed by the Left and by the Right. Human rights are being violated on every continent. More people are oppressed than free. And then, too, there are the Palestinians[6] to whose plight I am sensitive but whose methods I deplore. Violence and terrorism are not the answer. Something must be done about their suffering, and soon. I trust Israel, for I have faith in the Jewish people. Let Israel be given a chance, let hatred and danger be removed from her horizons, and there will be peace in and around the Holy Land.

11   Yes, I have faith. Faith in God and even in His creation. Without it no action would be possible. And action is the only remedy to indifference: the most insidious danger of all. Isn't this the meaning of Alfred Nobel's legacy? Wasn't his fear of war a shield against war?

---

1. **Apartheid** *n.* social policy in South Africa from 1950 to 1994 that separated the country's white and nonwhite populations, creating discrimination against the nonwhites.
2. **Andrei Sakharov** (1921–1989) nuclear physicist and human-rights activist who was banished from the Soviet Union for criticizing the government.
3. **Josef Biegun** Jewish man who was imprisoned and murdered during the Holocaust.
4. **Lech Wałęsa** (b. 1943) labor activist who helped form and led Poland's first independent trade union, Solidarity, despite opposition from the Polish government.
5. **Nelson Mandela** (1918–2013) leader of the struggle to end apartheid in South Africa; he had been sentenced to life in prison at the time of this speech.
6. **Palestinians** reference to the violent conflict between Palestinian Arabs and Israeli Jews, who have been fighting to claim the same territory.

12   There is much to be done, there is much that can be done. One person—a Raoul Wallenberg,[7] an Albert Schweitzer,[8] one person of integrity—can make a difference, a difference of life and death. As long as one dissident[9] is in prison, our freedom will not be true. As long as one child is hungry, our lives will be filled with anguish and shame. What all these victims need above all is to know that they are not alone; that we are not forgetting them, that when their voices are stifled we shall lend them ours, that while their freedom depends on ours, the quality of our freedom depends on theirs.

13   This is what I say to the young Jewish boy wondering what I have done with his years. It is in his name that I speak to you and that I express to you my deepest gratitude. No one is as capable of gratitude as one who has emerged from the kingdom of night. We know that every moment is a moment of grace, every hour an offering; not to share them would mean to betray them. Our lives no longer belong to us alone; they belong to all those who need us desperately.

14   Thank you, Chairman Aarvik. Thank you, members of the Nobel Committee. Thank you, people of Norway, for declaring on this singular occasion that our survival has meaning for mankind. ❧

7. **Raoul Wallenberg** (1912–1947?) Swedish diplomat in Hungary who saved tens of thousands of Jews during the Holocaust by issuing passports and providing shelter.
8. **Albert Schweitzer** (1875–1965) Alsatian doctor known for his important contributions in many fields, such as philosophy, religion, music, and medicine.
9. **dissident** *n.* person who disagrees with an official religious or political system.

Comprehension Check

Complete the following items after you finish your first read. Review and clarify details with your group.

📓 **Notebook** Respond to the questions.

1. Upon accepting the honor of the Nobel Peace Prize, what two emotions does Elie Wiesel have?

2. According to Weisel, what is the biggest threat to freedom?

3. Confirm your understanding of the speech by writing a summary of the author's main points.

RESEARCH

Research to Explore Choose one historical figure mentioned in the speech whom you would like to know more about. Briefly research that person. How does knowing more about this person help you better understand the points Wiesel makes?

ACCEPTANCE SPEECH FOR
THE NOBEL PEACE PRIZE

© Pearson Education, Inc., or its affiliates. All rights reserved.

Close Read the Text

With your group, revisit sections of the text you marked during your first read. **Annotate** what you notice. What **questions** do you have? What can you **conclude**?

Close Read
ANNOTATE • QUESTION • CONCLUDE

Analyze the Text

CITE TEXTUAL EVIDENCE
to support your answers.

 Notebook Complete the activities.

1. **Review and Clarify** With your group, reread paragraphs 4–7 of the selection. Discuss the young Jewish boy to whom the author refers. Whom or what does this boy **symbolize,** or represent? Why might Wiesel have chosen to convey his point through symbolism?

2. **Present and Discuss** Now, work with your group to share the passages from the text that you found especially important. Take turns presenting your passages. Discuss what you noticed in the text, what questions you asked, and what conclusions you reached.

3. **Essential Question:** *How do we remember the past?* What has this speech taught you about how we remember the past? Discuss.

Concept Vocabulary

humiliation	persecution	traumatized

Why These Words? The concept vocabulary words from the text are related. With your group, determine what the words have in common. Write your ideas and add another word that fits the category.

Practice

 Notebook Confirm your understanding of the concept vocabulary words by correctly using each one in a sentence.

Word Study

Notebook **Word Families** The noun *trauma* is the base word for a word family, or group of related words, that includes the verb *traumatize,* the adjective *traumatic,* and the adverb *traumatically.* For each of the following words, identify at least two words that are part of its word family: *captive; humility; injure.*

Analyze Craft and Structure

Author's Purpose and Point of View An **author's purpose** is his or her reason for writing. In a broad sense, a writer's purpose may be to inform or explain, to persuade, or to entertain. Usually, an author's purpose is some mixture of all of those things. No matter what an author's purpose, his or her point of view will influence the writing.

An **author's point of view** is his or her perspective on a topic. It is shaped by the author's knowledge, beliefs, and experiences. Sometimes, an author states his or her point of view directly. Often, however, readers must use evidence in the text to make **inferences,** or educated guesses, to determine the author's point of view.

When you analyze author's purpose and point of view, focus on how the author acknowledges and responds to conflicting evidence or viewpoints. Doing so will reveal telling details about an author's position—how the author distinguishes his or her perspective from those who may disagree.

Practice

CITE TEXTUAL EVIDENCE
to support your answers.

Notebook Reread Elie Wiesel's Acceptance Speech for the Nobel Peace Prize. Work with your group to analyze the speech, and determine Wiesel's purposes and point of view. Use the chart to record your ideas. Then, answer the questions that follow.

PURPOSE AND POINT OF VIEW	EVIDENCE THAT SUPPORTS MY INFERENCE
Purpose #1:	
Purpose #2:	
Point of View:	

1. **(a)** In paragraph 7, Wiesel claims, "Because if we forget, we are guilty, we are accomplices." What do you think he means by this statement? **(b)** What does this statement reveal about his point of view?

2. What is Wiesel's point of view, or perspective, on the individual's responsibility to end human suffering? Identify a quotation from the text that supports your response.

3. Review paragraphs 9–11 of the speech. **(a)** How does Wiesel acknowledge and respond to other viewpoints on contemporary political conflicts? **(b)** What aspects of his unique point of view does he use to distinguish, or differentiate, his viewpoint from others?

Conventions

Perfect Tenses of Verbs The **tense** of a verb shows the time of an action or a condition. Each of the **perfect tenses** describes an action or a condition that was or will be completed before a certain time, or a past action or condition that continues into the present.

Perfect tenses are formed by adding a form of the verb *have* to the past participle of the main verb.

VERB TENSE	EXAMPLE
present perfect: action in the past that continues into the present	I have tried to call you five times.
past perfect: action in the past that ended before another past action	I had tried to text but got no reply.
future perfect: action in the future that will have ended before a certain point in time	If I call again, I will have tried to contact you six times.

Read It

Work with your group to identify examples of the use of the present perfect tense in Elie Wiesel's Nobel Peace Prize acceptance speech. Then, discuss as a group the significance of Wiesel's use of the present perfect tense.

EXAMPLE	SIGNIFICANCE

© Pearson Education, Inc., or its affiliates. All rights reserved.

Write It

📓 **Notebook** Write a paragraph about something that you have been doing for some time and continue to do. Use the present perfect tense at least twice in your paragraph, marking each use.

Speaking and Listening

Assignment

With your group, conduct a **discussion** on one of the following quotations from Elie Wiesel's speech.

☐ "We must always take sides. Neutrality helps the oppressor, never the victim. Silence encourages the tormentor, never the tormented. Sometimes we must interfere." *(paragraph 8)*

☐ "What all these victims need above all is to know that they are not alone; that we are not forgetting them, that when their voices are stifled we shall lend them ours, that while their freedom depends on ours, the quality of our freedom depends on theirs." *(paragraph 12)*

Prepare for the Discussion Prior to the discussion, review the speech individually and briefly respond to the following questions:

- What does the quotation mean? What larger idea is Wiesel trying to communicate?

- How does Wiesel develop and support the ideas expressed in the quotation throughout his speech?

Use your responses to these questions to guide your group discussion.

During the Discussion Before you begin your discussion, assign roles for each member of your group. Roles may include a group leader, who keeps the discussion on topic; a timekeeper, who makes sure the discussion stays within the timeframe designated by your teacher; and a note-taker to record the group's ideas. Use these guidelines to ensure a productive group discussion:

- Draw on the speech to explore and develop your ideas. Be sure to refer to specific passages to support your opinions.

- Take turns speaking, and listen attentively as other group members express their thoughts and opinions.

- Be respectful of others' ideas and opinions. If you disagree with a speaker, express your difference of opinion respectfully and politely.

✎ EVIDENCE LOG

Before moving on to a new selection, go to your Evidence Log and record what you learned from Elie Wiesel's Nobel Peace Prize acceptance speech.

☰ STANDARDS

Speaking and Listening
Engage effectively in a range of collaborative discussions with diverse partners on *grade 8 topics, texts, and issues,* building on others' ideas and expressing their own clearly.

a. Come to discussions prepared, having read or researched material under study; explicitly draw on that preparation by referring to evidence on the topic, text, or issue to probe and reflect on ideas under discussion.
b. Follow rules for collegial discussions and decision-making, track progress toward specific goals and deadlines, and define individual roles as needed.

About the Author

Art Spiegelman (b. 1948) is an American author and illustrator whose Holocaust narratives—*Maus* (1986) and *Maus II* (1991)—helped to establish the graphic novel as a sophisticated literary form. *Maus* was serialized from 1980 to 1991, and it depicts Spiegelman interviewing his father about his experiences as a Polish Jew and Holocaust survivor.

from Maus

Media Vocabulary

The following words will be useful to you as you analyze, discuss, and write about graphic novels.

panel: individual frame of a graphic novel depicting a single moment	• The panels work together to tell a story. • The panels cannot show everything that happens, so readers must use their imaginations to fill in the blanks.
encapsulation: choice of which scenes to capture, or display, in panels	• The layout and choice of the scenes drives the readers' interpretations. • Graphic novelists can use different sizes and shapes to give more or less weight to scenes.
speech balloon: display of what a character is speaking or thinking	• The size, shape, and color of the speech balloon can show the emotion of the speaker. • Speech balloons can also show emotion through the use of punctuation marks and musical symbols.

First Review MEDIA: GRAPHIC NOVEL

Apply these strategies as you conduct your first review. You will have an opportunity to a close review after your first review.

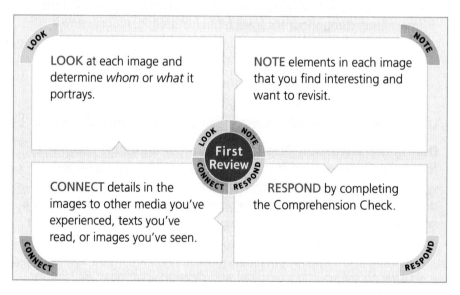

LOOK at each image and determine *whom* or *what* it portrays.

NOTE elements in each image that you find interesting and want to revisit.

CONNECT details in the images to other media you've experienced, texts you've read, or images you've seen.

RESPOND by completing the Comprehension Check.

☷ STANDARDS

Reading Literature
By the end of the year, read and comprehend literature, including stories, dramas, and poems, at the high end of grades 6–8 text complexity band independently and proficiently.

Language
Acquire and use accurately grade-appropriate general academic and domain-specific words and phrases; gather vocabulary knowledge when considering a word or phrase important to comprehension or expression.

BACKGROUND

In *Maus*, Art Spiegelman tells the story of his parents, Vladek and Anja Spiegelman, who survived the Holocaust. At the start of this excerpt, Vladek and Anja are living in hiding with Mrs. Motonowa, whose husband does not know she is hiding Jews. They arrange a meeting with smugglers at the house of a woman named Mrs. Kawka to discuss plans to be smuggled out of Poland.

SCAN FOR
MULTIMEDIA

from Maus **231**

WHEN I ARRIVED TO KAWKA, THE TWO SMUGGLERS WERE THERE TOGETHER SITTING IN THE KITCHEN..

Panel 1: PLEASE WAIT IN THE OTHER ROOM. THEY'LL SEE YOU SOON.

Panel 2: MR. MANDELBAUM!

VLADEK SPIEGELMAN!

MANDELBAUM, BEFORE THE WAR OWNED A SWEETS SHOP.

ANJA AND I BOUGHT ALWAYS PASTRIES THERE. HE USED TO BE A VERY RICH MAN IN SOSNOWIEC.

BACK WHEN IT WAS THE GHETTO, ABRAHAM WAS A BIG MEMBER OF THE JEWISH COUNCIL.

Panel 3: THIS IS MY WIFE...AND YOU KNOW MY NEPHEW..

HELLO, ABRAHAM. WHAT ARE YOU ALL DOING HERE?

Panel 4: WE'RE TRYING TO GET OUT OF POLAND—

—TO **HUNGARY**?! YES. ANJA AND I ARE TRYING TO ARRANGE THAT TOO!

THE SMUGGLERS PROPOSED US HOW THEY WOULD DO.

WE SPOKE YIDDISH SO THE POLES DON'T UNDERSTAND.

Panel 5: "...AND AT THE BORDER OUR PARTNERS WILL TAKE YOU THROUGH THE MOUNTAINS.

WHEW— IT'S RISKY AND VERY EXPENSIVE!

Panel 6: NIE, VAS DENKST DIE?

YECH KENN DIE FRAU KAWKA, UBER YECH BIN NISH ZICHER VEGEN DIE ZWEI.

So, what do you think?

I know Mrs. Kawka, but I'm not sure about these two.

Panel 7: HERR MECH TSE! YECH GEI KOIDEM MIT ZEI. AZ ALLES VET ZEIN BESEDER, YECH VIL SCHREIBEN TSE DEYER.

Listen! I'll go first. If everything is okay, I'll write back to you.

Panel 8: THE OTHERS WANT TO THINK ABOUT IT A LITTLE LONGER, BUT I'M READY TO GO NOW.

FINE, FINE.

I AGREED WITH MANDELBAUM TO MEET AGAIN HERE. IF IT CAME A GOOD LETTER, WE'LL GO.

BUT IF EVER I TALKED OF THIS PLAN TO ANJA...

NO, VLADEK! YOU'RE CRAZY! IT'S TOO DANGEROUS!

BUT IF WE HEAR FROM ABRAHAM—

WE'RE SAFE HERE—FORGET ABOUT HUNGARY!

BUT WHAT DO WE DO IF THE GESTAPO COMES TO SEARCH FOR ILLEGAL GOODS? ...WHAT IF A NEIGHBOR NOTICES US THROUGH THE KITCHEN WINDOW?...

I'M NOT GOING!

WHAT IF HER HUSBAND FINDS OUT ABOUT US? EVEN THE BOY COULD LET SOMETHING SLIP! ...THIS WAR COULD LAST ANOTHER 4 OR 5 YEARS. WHAT DO WE DO WHEN OUR MONEY RUNS OUT?

PLEASE!

IN HUNGARY WE COULD BE FREE TO WALK THE STREETS AGAIN, LIKE HUMAN BEINGS... I'VE ALWAYS TAKEN CARE OF YOU—TRUST ME.

I'M SO SCARED. >SOB<

DON'T DO IT, MR. SPIEGELMAN—IT'S JUST NOT SAFE! YOU DON'T KNOW ANYTHING ABOUT THESE SMUGGLERS.

SNF. IT'S LIKE TALKING TO A WALL.

WE WON'T GO UNLESS WE HEAR THAT OUR FRIEND GOT THROUGH.

I'VE HAD AWFUL NIGHTMARES ABOUT YOUR TRIP—PLEASE STAY WITH ME!

SNF

WAIT—NOW WHERE ARE YOU GOING?

—TO VISIT MY COUSIN AND SEE WHERE HE'S HIDING. IF WE DO GO TO HUNGARY, HE MAY BE BETTER OFF HERE WITH YOU!

MILOCH HELPED ME IN SRODULA. MAYBE NOW, IF HE NEEDED, I COULD HELP HIM.

from Maus 233

A FEW DAYS AFTER, I CAME AGAIN TO THE SMUGGLERS. AND MANDELBAUM WAS ALSO THERE.

LOOK, VLADEK—MY NEPHEW IS SAFE! THEY BROUGHT ME A LETTER FROM HIM.

IT WAS IN YIDDISH AND IT WAS SIGNED REALLY BY ABRAHAM. SO WE AGREED RIGHT AWAY TO GO AHEAD.

BUT ANJA JUST DIDN'T WANT WE WOULD GO...

PLEASE, VLADEK, CALL IT OFF!

BUT IT'S ALL ARRANGED. I'VE EVEN GIVEN THEM HALF THEIR MONEY!

NO! NO! NO! IT'S SOME KIND OF TRICK!

BE REASONABLE. I SAW ABRAHAM'S LETTER WITH MY OWN EYES!

WH-WHAT DID IT SAY?

"DEAR AUNT AND UNCLE, EVERYTHING IS WONDERFUL HERE. I ARRIVED SAFELY. I'M FREE AND HAPPY. DON'T LOSE A MINUTE. JOIN ME AS SOON AS YOU CAN. YOUR LOVING NEPHEW, ABRAHAM."

I-I DON'T KNOW...

WE LEAVE THE DAY AFTER TOMORROW FROM THE KATOWICE TRAIN STATION.

AND FINALLY I CONVINCED HER.

SO, I WENT ONE MORE TIME OVER TO MILOCH IN HIS GARBAGE BUNKER AND DIRECTED HIM HOW HE MUST GO TO SZOPIENICE AND HIDE...

AND, YOU KNOW, MILOCH AND HIS WIFE AND BOY, THEY ALL SURVIVED THEMSELVES THE WHOLE WAR... SITTING THERE ... WITH MOTONOWA...

BUT, FOR ANJA AND I, IT WAS FOR US WAITING ANOTHER DESTINY...

WE CAME WITH NO PROBLEM BY TROLLEY CAR TO OUR MEETING POINT WITH THE MANDELBAUMS AND THE SMUGGLERS.

EVERYTHING IS ARRANGED. HERE ARE YOUR TICKETS.

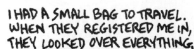
I HAD A SMALL BAG TO TRAVEL. WHEN THEY REGISTERED ME IN, THEY LOOKED OVER EVERYTHING.

38 WHAT'S THIS? SHOE POLISH??

YES. I LIKE TO KEEP MYSELF NEAT.

WITH A SPOON HE TOOK OUT, LITTLE BY LITTLE, ALL THE POLISH.

39 WELL, WELL... A GOLD WATCH. YOU JEWS *ALWAYS* HAVE GOLD!

WRAPPED IN FOIL, I KEPT IT HIDDEN THERE.... IT WAS MY LAST TREASURE.

40 IT WAS THIS WATCH I GOT FROM FATHER-IN-LAW WHEN FIRST I MARRIED TO ANJA.

41 WELL, NEVER MIND...THEY TOOK IT AND THREW ME WITH MANDELBAUM INTO A CELL...

42 WAIT A MINUTE! WHATEVER HAPPENED TO ABRAHAM?

WHO?

-BUT

43 AH, MANDELBAUM'S NEPHEW! YES. HE FINISHED THE SAME AS US TO CONCENTRATION CAMP.

44 YES. I'LL TELL YOU HOW IT WAS WITH HIM- BUT NOW I'M TELLING HERE IN THE PRISON...

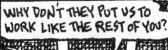
HERE WE GOT VERY LITTLE TO EAT—MAYBE SOUP ONE TIME A DAY—AND WE SAT WITH NOTHING TO DO.

45 WHY DON'T THEY PUT US TO WORK LIKE THE REST OF YOU?

IT MEANS YOU WON'T BE HERE VERY LONG...

46 ...EVERY WEEK OR SO A TRUCK TAKES SOME OF THE PRISONERS AWAY.

EXCUSE ME... DO ANY OF YOU KNOW GERMAN?

47 MY FAMILY JUST SENT ME A FOOD PARCEL. IF I WRITE BACK THEY'LL SEND ANOTHER, BUT WE'RE ONLY ALLOWED TO WRITE GERMAN.

I KNEW **WELL** TO WRITE GERMAN...SO I WROTE...

IN A SHORT TIME HE GOT AGAIN A PACKAGE...

48 YOU DID A GREAT JOB! TAKE ANYTHING YOU WANT FOR YOU AND YOUR FRIEND!

IT WAS EGGS THERE...IT WAS EVEN CHOCOLATES. ...I WAS VERY LUCKY TO GET SUCH GOODIES!

from Maus **237**

Comprehension Check

Complete the following items after you finish your first read. Review and clarify details with your group.

1. Why does Vladek Spiegelman want to go to Hungary?

2. What does Anja Spiegelman feel about the smuggling idea?

3. Once the Spiegelmans are on the train, whom do the smugglers say they're calling? Whom do they actually call?

4. Why does Vladek Spiegelman wear a pig mask in some of the panels of the graphic novel?

5. 🖃 **Notebook** Confirm your understanding of the excerpt by writing a summary..

- -

RESEARCH

Research to Clarify Choose at least one unfamiliar historical detail in the graphic novel. Briefly research that detail. In what way does the historical information shed light on the story?

Research to Explore The excerpt from the graphic novel may inspire you to learn more about the plight of European Jews under the Nazis. Formulate a research question about the subject, and briefly research it. Share your findings with your group.

from MAUS

Close Review

With your group, revisit sections of the graphic novel you marked during your first read. What do you notice? What **questions** do you have? What can you **conclude**?

Analyze the Media

> **CITE TEXTUAL EVIDENCE**
> to support your answers.

📓 **Notebook** Complete the activities.

1. **Review and Clarify** With your group, review the panels that focus on Miloch and his family. Where are they living? What are they doing there? How do the graphics help you understand their situation?

2. **Present and Discuss** Now, work with your group to share the panels that you found especially significant or moving. Take turns presenting your panels. Discuss what you noticed, what questions you asked, and what conclusions you reached.

3. **Essential Question:** *How do we remember the past?* What has this graphic novel taught you about how we remember the past? Discuss with your group.

LANGUAGE DEVELOPMENT

Media Vocabulary

panel	encapsulation	speech balloon

Use these vocabulary words in your responses to the following questions.

1. What technique does the author use to show that a character is speaking?

2. How does the author give special emphasis to important scenes, lines of dialogue, or exchanges between characters?

3. How does the author help readers interpret the story in a graphic novel?

🔧 **WORD NETWORK**

Add words related to the Holocaust from the text to your Word Network.

📋 **STANDARDS**

Speaking and Listening
Analyze the purpose of information presented in diverse media and formats and evaluate the motives behind its presentation.

Language
Acquire and use accurately grade-appropriate general academic and domain-specific words and phrases; gather vocabulary knowledge when considering a word or phrase important to comprehension or expression.

Research

> ### Assignment
> Work with your group to research Art Spiegelman, the author of *Maus*. Then, write a brief **informative report** in which you discuss the ways in which Spiegelman's personal experiences are reflected in his graphic novel.

Conduct Research Work with your group to find the information you will need to write your report. Consult multiple print and digital sources, and evaluate the credibility of each one. *Credibility* refers to the believability of a source. A credible source can be trusted to provide accurate, unbiased information. To evaluate the credibility of sources you might use, answer the following questions. If you check "no" for any source, do not plan to use it.

- **Does the information come from a reliable publication?** ☐ Yes ☐ No

  A reliable print publication may be a respected newspaper, a scholarly journal, or a textbook. A reliable web site may be managed by the government (.gov), a museum or other nonprofit (.org), or a college or university (.edu).

- **Does the author have a good reputation?** ☐ Yes ☐ No

  Find out if the author is connected to a university or other reliable institution. Consider what else the author has written.

- **Does the text show bias or prejudice?** ☐ Yes ☐ No

  Bias can sometimes be hidden. Be on the alert for statements that are not supported with evidence, or opinions masquerading as facts.

For each source you plan to use, collect the information you will need to create a **Works-Cited list,** or **bibliography**. To avoid plagiarism, or presenting someone else's ideas as your own, be sure to credit all the sources you use in your report.

Organize Your Ideas After you have finished your research, discuss how events and experiences in Spiegelman's life are reflected in the excerpt from *Maus*. With your group, determine two or three key points on which to focus in your report.

Clarify and Support Your Ideas As you draft, be sure to make clear connections that show how Spiegelman's events and experiences are reflected in *Maus*. Use details from the graphic novel and your research to support and elaborate on your main points.

Use Domain-Specific Vocabulary As you write your report, use specific vocabulary to relate the story and other information presented in *Maus*. Using the media vocabulary words provided and other media-specific words will help you describe your subject clearly and precisely. In your report, be sure to define or explain any terms with which your audience may be unfamiliar.

✒ EVIDENCE LOG

Before moving on to a new selection, go to your Evidence Log and record what you learned from the excerpt from *Maus*.

☰ STANDARDS

Writing
- Write informative/explanatory texts to examine a topic and convey ideas, concepts, and information through the selection, organization, and analysis of relevant content.

  a. Introduce a topic clearly, previewing what is to follow; organize ideas, concepts, and information into broader categories; include formatting, graphics, and multimedia when useful to aiding comprehension.
  b. Develop the topic with relevant, well-chosen facts, definitions, concrete details, quotations, or other information and examples.
  d. Use precise language and domain-specific vocabulary to inform about or explain the topic.

- Conduct short research projects to answer a question, drawing on several sources and generating additional related, focused questions that allow for multiple avenues of exploration.
- Gather relevant information from multiple print and digital sources, using search terms effectively; assess the credibility and accuracy of each source; and quote or paraphrase the data and conclusions of others while avoiding plagiarism and following a standard format for citation.

from Maus **241**

Deliver a Multimedia Presentation

Assignment

Create and present an **explanatory multimedia presentation** in response to the following prompt:

> How do the selections contribute to your understanding of the Holocaust and the ways in which we remember the past?

Plan With Your Group

Analyze the Texts With your group, analyze how each selection contributes to your understanding of the Holocaust. Use this chart to organize your ideas.

SELECTION	PLACES AND PEOPLE AFFECTED	HISTORICAL EVENTS	HOW REMEMBERED TODAY
from Anne Frank: The Diary of a Young Girl			
Acceptance Speech for the Nobel Peace Prize			
from Maus			

Gather Evidence and Media Examples Each group member should choose one selection on which to focus. Work individually to gather important details and information. Next, organize the ideas, and draft a brief explanatory essay for your section of the presentation. Then, conduct additional research to find relevant media to include in the presentation.

Organize Your Ideas As a group, organize the sections of the presentation, and decide how to transition smoothly from one section and speaker to the next. Be sure you tie all the ideas and information together at the end of your presentation.

Rehearse With Your Group

Practice With Your Group As you deliver your portion of the presentation, use this checklist to evaluate the effectiveness of your group's rehearsal. Then, use your evaluation and the instruction here to guide your revisions to the presentation.

CONTENT	USE OF MEDIA	PRESENTATION TECHNIQUES
☐ The presentation clearly responds to the prompt.	☐ The use of photographs, illustrations, and other still images supports the presentation.	☐ Each member uses a formal tone, appropriate eye contact, adequate volume, and clear pronunciation.
☐ The presentation includes information from the texts and from additional research that supports the main idea.	☐ Videos, recorded interviews, and other multimedia enhance and clarify the presentation.	☐ The pacing of the presentation is measured and helps the audience comprehend the information.
☐ The presentation includes a strong conclusion.		

Fine-Tune the Content Be sure you are clearly explaining the events of the Holocaust and the ways in which we remember the past. Use specific details from the text as well as outside research.

Improve Your Use of Media Check that images and multimedia are presented in context. Each piece of multimedia should relate directly to a key point and should help the audience better understand the information.

Brush-Up on Your Presentation Techniques As you rehearse, point out where group members should vary their pacing and tone to emphasize certain parts of the presentation. Be sure everyone uses formal English when speaking.

Present and Evaluate

Give members of your group and members of other groups your full support and attention when they are presenting. As you listen to other groups, consider their content, use of media, and presentation techniques. Think about the ways in which other groups' presentations deepened your understanding of the Holocaust and the ways in which we remember the past. Be ready to ask questions.

STANDARDS

Speaking and Listening
• Present claims and findings, emphasizing salient points in a focused, coherent manner with relevant evidence, sound valid reasoning, and well-chosen details; use appropriate eye contact, adequate volume, and clear pronunciation.
• Integrate multimedia and visual displays into presentations to clarify information, strengthen claims and evidence, and add interest.
• Adapt speech to a variety of contexts and tasks, demonstrating command of formal English when indicated or appropriate.

Performance Task: Deliver a Multimedia Presentation **243**

ESSENTIAL QUESTION:

How do we remember the past?

There are many ways to remember, and all of them can add to our understanding of the past. In this section, you will choose one additional selection about the Holocaust for your final reading experience in this unit. You'll then share what you learn with classmates. To choose a text, follow these steps.

Look Back Think about the selections you have already read. What more do you want to know about the Holocaust?

Look Ahead Preview the selections by reading the descriptions. Which one seems most interesting and appealing to you?

Look Inside Take a few minutes to scan through the text you chose. Make another selection if this text doesn't meet your needs.

Independent Learning Strategies

Throughout your life, in school, in your community, and in your career, you will need to rely on yourself to learn and work on your own. Review these strategies and the actions you can take to practice them during Independent Learning. Add ideas of your own for each category.

STRATEGY	ACTION PLAN
Apply strategies	• Understand your goals and deadlines. • Make a plan for what to do each day. •
Practice what you have learned	• Use first-read and close-read strategies to deepen your understanding. • After you read, evaluate the usefulness of the evidence to help you understand the topic. • Consider the quality and reliability of the source. •
Take notes	• Record important ideas and information. • Review your notes before preparing to share with a group. •

SCAN FOR MULTIMEDIA

CONTENTS

Choose one selection. Selections are available online only.

PERFORMANCE-BASED ASSESSMENT PREP

Review Evidence for an Explanatory Essay

Complete your Evidence Log for the unit by evaluating what you've learned and synthesizing the information you've recorded.

 SCAN FOR MULTIMEDIA

First-Read Guide

Use this page to record your first-read ideas.

Selection Title: _____

🔧 **Tool Kit**
First-Read Guide and
Model Annotation

NOTICE new information or ideas you learn about the unit topic as you first read this text.

NOTICE

ANNOTATE by marking vocabulary and key passages you want to revisit.

ANNOTATE

NOTICE ANNOTATE
First Read
CONNECT RESPOND

CONNECT ideas within the selection to other knowledge and the selections you have read.

CONNECT

RESPOND by writing a brief summary of the selection.

RESPOND

≣ **STANDARD**

Reading Read and comprehend complex literary and informational texts independently and proficiently.

Close-Read Guide

Use this page to record your close-read ideas.

Selection Title: _____

Close Read the Text

Revisit sections of the text you marked during your first read. Read these sections closely and **annotate** what you notice. Ask yourself **questions** about the text. What can you **conclude**? Write down your ideas.

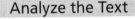

Analyze the Text

Think about the author's choices of patterns, structure, techniques, and ideas included in the text. Select one, and record your thoughts about what this choice conveys.

QuickWrite

Pick a paragraph from the text that grabbed your interest. Explain the power of this passage.

_____
_____
_____
_____
_____
_____
_____
_____
_____

STANDARD
Reading Read and comprehend complex literary and informational texts independently and proficiently.

Share Your Independent Learning

Prepare to Share

How do we remember the past?

Even when you read something independently, you can continue to grow by sharing what you have learned with others. Reflect on the text you explored independently, and write notes about its connection to the unit. In your notes, consider why this text belongs in this unit.

Learn from Your Classmates

Discuss It Share your ideas about the text you explored on your own. As you talk with others in your class, jot down ideas that you learn from them.

Reflect

Review your notes, and mark the most important insight you gained from these writing and discussion activities. Explain how this idea adds to your understanding of the Holocaust.

STANDARDS

Speaking and Listening
Engage effectively in a range of collaborative discussions with diverse partners on *grade 8 topics, texts, and issues*, building on others' ideas and expressing their own clearly.

Review Evidence for an Explanatory Essay

At the beginning of this unit, you took a position on the following statement:

> How can literature help us remember and honor the victims of the Holocaust?

✐ EVIDENCE LOG

Review your Evidence Log and your QuickWrite from the beginning of the unit. Did you learn anything new?

NOTES

Identify at least three pieces of evidence that suggest the role literature can play in honoring and remembering Holocaust victims.

1.

2.

3.

Identify one or two key quotations from the evidence you listed:

_____

_____

Develop your thoughts into a topic sentence for an explanatory essay. Clarify your thinking by completing these sentence starters:

In honoring and remembering victims of the Holocaust, we face these challenges:

_____

_____

Literature can help us overcome these challenges by

_____

_____

■ STANDARDS

Writing
Write informative/explanatory texts to examine a topic and convey ideas, concepts, and information through the selection, organization, and analysis of relevant content.

b. Develop the topic with relevant, well-chosen facts, definitions, concrete details, quotations, or other information and examples.

SOURCES

• WHOLE-CLASS SELECTIONS

• SMALL-GROUP SELECTIONS

• INDEPENDENT-LEARNING SELECTION

WORD NETWORK

As you write and revise your explanatory essay, use your Word Network to help vary your word choices.

PART 1
Writing to Sources: Explanatory Essay

In this unit, you have read a variety of selections that are related to the historical events known as the Holocaust. These selections are all examples of literature that addresses one of the most terrible periods in human history.

Assignment

Write an **explanatory essay** in response to the following question:

> How can literature help us remember and honor the victims of the Holocaust?

Use your analysis of the selections in this unit to enumerate the ways in which literature can help us remember and honor victims of the Holocaust. Consider how the various texts in the unit illuminate the experiences of different types of people in a wide variety of places. Support your explanation with relevant details, quotations, and examples from the texts.

Reread the Assignment Review the assignment to be sure you fully understand it. The assignment may reference some of the academic words presented at the beginning of the unit. Be sure you understand each of the words given below in order to complete the assignment correctly.

Academic Vocabulary

theorize	sustain	declaration
pronounce	enumerate	

Review the Elements of Effective Explanatory Essays Before you begin writing, read the Explanatory Essay Rubric. Once you have completed your first draft, check it against the rubric. If one or more of the elements is missing or not as strong as it could be, revise your essay to add or strengthen that component.

STANDARDS
Writing
• Write informative/explanatory texts to examine a topic and convey ideas, concepts, and information through the selection, organization, and analysis of relevant content.

• Write routinely over extended time frames and shorter time frames for a range of discipline-specific tasks, purposes, and audiences.

Explanatory Essay Rubric

	Focus and Organization	Evidence and Elaboration	Language Conventions
4	The introduction is clear and engaging and establishes the topic in a compelling way. Ideas are well organized and progress logically. A variety of transitions are included to create cohesion and show the relationships among ideas. The conclusion follows from and supports the information in the essay.	The topic is developed with relevant and well-chosen facts, definitions, details, quotations, and other examples. The tone of the essay is formal. The vocabulary is precise and relevant to the topic, audience, and purpose.	The essay intentionally uses standard English conventions of usage and mechanics.
3	The introduction is clear and engaging in a way that grabs readers' attention. Ideas are well organized. Transitions are included to show the relationships among ideas. The conclusion mostly follows from the information in the essay.	The topic is developed with some relevant facts, definitions, details, quotations, and other examples. The tone of the essay is mostly formal. The vocabulary is generally appropriate for the topic, audience, and purpose.	The essay demonstrates accuracy in standard English conventions of usage and mechanics.
2	The introduction establishes the topic. Ideas are somewhat organized. A few transitions are included that show the relationships among ideas. The conclusion is related to the topic of the essay.	The topic is developed with a few facts, definitions, details, quotations, or other examples. The tone of the essay is occasionally formal. The vocabulary is somewhat appropriate for the topic, audience, and purpose.	The essay demonstrates some accuracy in standard English conventions of usage and mechanics.
1	The topic is not clearly stated. Ideas are disorganized and do not follow a logical sequence. Transitions are not included. The conclusion is not related to the essay topic, or is nonexistent.	The topic is not developed with relevant evidence. The tone is informal. The vocabulary is limited or inappropriate.	The essay contains mistakes in standard English conventions of usage and mechanics.

PART 2
Speaking and Listening: Oral Presentation

Assignment
After completing the final draft of your essay, use it as the foundation for a brief **oral presentation**.

Do not simply read your essay aloud. Instead, take the following steps to make your presentation lively and engaging.

- Go back to your essay and annotate the most important ideas and supporting details from your introduction, body paragraphs, and conclusion.
- Refer to your annotated text to guide your presentation and keep it focused.
- Speak clearly and make eye contact with the audience.

Review the Rubric The criteria by which your oral presentation will be evaluated appears in the rubric. Review these criteria before presenting to ensure that you are prepared.

STANDARDS

Speaking and Listening
Present claims and findings, emphasizing salient points in a focused, coherent manner with relevant evidence, sound valid reasoning, and well-chosen details; use appropriate eye contact, adequate volume, and clear pronunciation.

	Content	Organization	Presentation Technique
3	The introduction is engaging and clearly establishes the topic in a compelling way. The speaker points to key details and evidence to support his or her ideas. The conclusion is clear and reflects the information presented.	The presentation uses time effectively, devoting the right amount of time to each idea. Ideas progress logically and are presented in a focused, coherent manner. Listeners can follow presentation.	The speaker speaks clearly and loudly enough for the audience to hear. The speaker maintains eye contact.
2	The introduction clearly establishes the topic. The speaker uses some evidence to support his or her ideas. The conclusion reflects the information presented.	The presentation mostly uses time effectively, but may spend too much or too little time on some parts. Ideas progress somewhat logically. Listeners can mostly follow presentation.	The speaker speaks clearly. The speaker makes some eye contact.
1	The introduction does not establish the topic. The speaker does not support his or her ideas with evidence. The conclusion is not related to the topic.	The presentation does not use time effectively. Ideas do not progress logically. Listeners have difficulty following presentation.	The speaker speaks too quickly or slowly or mumbles. The speaker does not make eye contact with the audience.

Reflect on the Unit

Now that you've completed the unit, take a few moments to reflect on your learning.

Reflect on the Unit Goals

Look back at the goals at the beginning of the unit. Use a different colored pen to rate yourself again. Then, think about readings and activities that contributed the most to the growth of your understanding. Record your thoughts.

Reflect on the Learning Strategies

💬 Discuss It Write a reflection on whether you were able to improve your learning based on your Action Plans. Think about what worked, what didn't, and what you might do to keep working on these strategies. Record your ideas before joining a class discussion.

Reflect on the Text

Choose a selection that you found challenging, and explain what made it difficult.

Describe something that surprised you about a text in the unit.

Which activity taught you the most about the Holocaust? What did you learn?

SCAN FOR
MULTIMEDIA

What Matters

Sometimes standing up means refusing to back down.

Philippe Petit

Discuss It Why is volunteering, engaging in sports and hobbies, and pursuing personal dreams so fulfilling?

Write your response before sharing your ideas.

SCAN FOR MULTIMEDIA

UNIT INTRODUCTION

ESSENTIAL QUESTION:

When is it right to take a stand?

LAUNCH TEXT
ARGUMENT MODEL
Freedom of the Press?

WHOLE-CLASS LEARNING

ANCHOR TEXT: MAGAZINE ARTICLE

Barrington Irving, Pilot and Educator
National Geographic

▸ MEDIA CONNECTION:
Barrington Irving: Got
30 Dollars in My Pocket

ANCHOR TEXT: OPINION PIECE

Three Cheers for the Nanny State
Sarah Conly

COMPARE

ANCHOR TEXTS: OPINION PIECES

Ban the Ban!
SidneyAnne Stone

Soda's a Problem but . . .
Karin Klein

SMALL-GROUP LEARNING

PERSUASIVE SPEECH

Words Do Not Pay
Chief Joseph

NONFICTION NARRATIVE

from **Follow the Rabbit-Proof Fence**
Doris Pilkington

MEDIA: VIDEO

The Moth Presents: Aleeza Kazmi

INDEPENDENT LEARNING

MEMOIR

from **Through My Eyes**
Ruby Bridges

POETRY

The Unknown Citizen
W. H. Auden

BIOGRAPHY

Harriet Tubman: Conductor on the Underground Railroad
Ann Petry

PERFORMANCE TASK

WRITING FOCUS:
Write an Argument

PERFORMANCE TASK

SPEAKING AND LISTENING FOCUS:
Deliver an Oral Presentation

PERFORMANCE-BASED ASSESSMENT PREP

Review Evidence for an Argument

PERFORMANCE-BASED ASSESSMENT

Argument: Essay and Oral Presentation

PROMPT:

Is it important for people to make their own choices in life?

Unit Goals

Throughout this unit, you will deepen your perspective about what it means to stand up for things that matter, by reading, writing, speaking, listening, and presenting. These goals will help you succeed on the Unit Performance-Based Assessment.

Rate how well you meet these goals right now. You will revisit your ratings later when you reflect on your growth during this unit.

1	2	3	4	5
NOT AT ALL WELL	NOT VERY WELL	SOMEWHAT WELL	VERY WELL	EXTREMELY WELL

READING GOALS

	1	2	3	4	5

- Evaluate written arguments by analyzing how authors state and support their claims.

- Expand your knowledge and use of academic and concept vocabulary.

WRITING AND RESEARCH GOALS

	1	2	3	4	5

- Write an argumentative essay in which you effectively incorporate the key elements of an argument.

- Conduct research projects of various lengths to explore a topic and clarify meaning.

LANGUAGE GOAL

	1	2	3	4	5

- Demonstrate command of the conventions of standard English grammar and usage, including correct usage of nouns, pronouns, adjectives, adverbs, clauses, and sentence structure.

SPEAKING AND LISTENING GOALS

	1	2	3	4	5

- Collaborate with your team to build on the ideas of others, develop consensus, and communicate.

- Integrate audio, visuals, and text in presentations.

≣ STANDARDS

Language
Acquire and use accurately grade-appropriate general academic and domain-specific words and phrases; gather vocabulary knowledge when considering a word or phrase important to comprehension or expression.

SCAN FOR MULTIMEDIA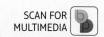

Academic Vocabulary: Argument

Academic terms appear in all subjects and can help you read, write, and discuss with more precision. Here are five academic words that will be useful to you in this unit as you analyze and write arguments.

Complete the chart.

1. Review each word, its root, and the mentor sentences.

2. Use the information and your own knowledge to predict the meaning of each word.

3. For each word, list at least two related words.

4. Refer to the dictionary or other resources if needed.

TIP

FOLLOW THROUGH
Study the words in this chart, and mark them or their forms wherever they appear in the unit.

WORD	MENTOR SENTENCES	PREDICT MEANING	RELATED WORDS
retort ROOT: **-tort-** "twist"	1. His grumpy *retort* made me sorry I had asked the question. 2. I fired off a *retort* so clever she couldn't think of anything to add.		contort; torture
candid ROOT: **-cand-** "shine"; "white"	1. Take a *candid* photo of us so that we look like we do in real life. 2. I wish she were more *candid* with me; I never know what she means.		
rectify ROOT: **-rect-** "straight"	1. I will try to *rectify* the situation, but I think things are beyond fixing. 2. Don't worry, I will *rectify* the problem as soon as I get to the office.		
speculate ROOT: **-spec-** "look"	1. The police did not want to *speculate* as to what motivated the crime. 2. When I'm reading a really good book, it is hard not to *speculate* on how it is going to end.		
verify ROOT: **-ver-** "truth"	1. Can you please *verify* that your name is correct on this form? 2. The claim isn't valid because no one can *verify* the source of the information on which it is based.		

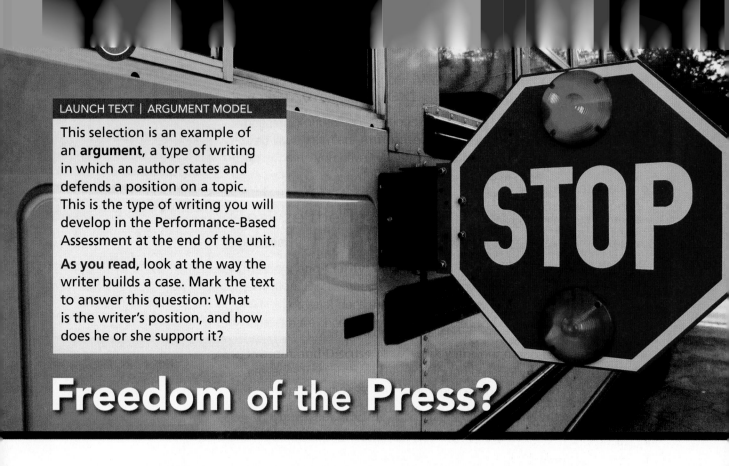

LAUNCH TEXT | ARGUMENT MODEL

This selection is an example of an **argument**, a type of writing in which an author states and defends a position on a topic. This is the type of writing you will develop in the Performance-Based Assessment at the end of the unit.

As you read, look at the way the writer builds a case. Mark the text to answer this question: What is the writer's position, and how does he or she support it?

Freedom of the Press?

NOTES

1   The First Amendment of the U.S. Constitution gives newspapers, magazines, and other publications the right to print whatever they see fit, without interference from the government. The framers of the Constitution felt that a free press is vital to a democratic society.

2   This important idea breaks down when schools are involved. As it turns out, there is a difference between "free press" and high school newspapers.

3   The difference is technical. The First Amendment prevents the government from censoring the press. However, private publishers can censor whatever they want. Since schools and school districts pay the student newspaper's publication costs, they are private publishers. This means that they can edit information as they see fit. They can even refuse to publish some articles.

4   This is a tough lesson for budding journalists, some of whom have challenged the restrictions. One case even made it to the Supreme Court, in *Hazelwood School District v. Kuhlmeier.*

5   Here are the facts. In 1983, students at Hazelwood High, a public high school near St. Louis, Missouri, saw two pages missing from their school newspaper, *The Spectrum.* They found out that the principal, Robert Reynolds, had removed two of the articles after finding them unfit for publication. One article, about teen pregnancy, contained interviews with pregnant students whose names were changed; the other article dealt with divorce.

6   Principal Reynolds said the pregnancy article was not appropriate for a high school audience. He was also concerned

SCAN FOR MULTIMEDIA

that the girls' identities would have been revealed eventually in such a small school. His problem with the divorce article was that it was not "fair and balanced." He felt it criticized parents without providing their side of the story.

7   Some students were outraged and sued the school. They argued that the issue was not the content of the articles, but whether or not the school had the right to suppress them.

8   In 1988, the Supreme Court ruled 5–3 in favor of the school. The ruling said that while students "do not shed their first amendment rights at the schoolhouse gate," no school should tolerate activities "inconsistent with its basic educational mission." In other words, when student expression is school-sponsored, it can be censored—as long as those doing the censoring have valid educational reasons. The law now varies from state to state. States that disagree with parts of the ruling have their own laws that govern students' freedom of expression.

9   We are now left with these critical questions: Is it fair for some students to have greater freedom of speech in their high school newspapers when others are subjected to censorship? What does this situation say about us as a society and a nation?

10   The framers of the Constitution believed that if governments could censor opinions they did not like, the public would be less educated. Given that schools are places of education, it seems counterproductive to limit students' free speech. The more opinions students are exposed to, the better equipped they will be to handle the issues they will face later in life. ❧

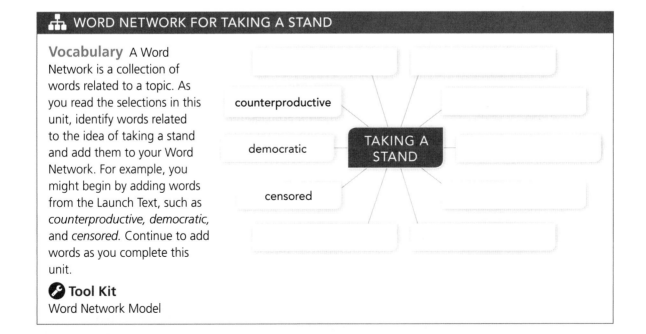

WORD NETWORK FOR TAKING A STAND

Vocabulary A Word Network is a collection of words related to a topic. As you read the selections in this unit, identify words related to the idea of taking a stand and add them to your Word Network. For example, you might begin by adding words from the Launch Text, such as *counterproductive, democratic,* and *censored.* Continue to add words as you complete this unit.

🔧 **Tool Kit**
Word Network Model

counterproductive

democratic

censored

TAKING A STAND

Summary

Write a summary of "Freedom of the Press?" A **summary** is a concise, complete, and accurate overview of a text. It should not include a statement of your opinion or an analysis.

Launch Activity

Class Statement Think about this question: How do people determine what matters to them and make their own choices in life? Consider your response by completing this statement:

Some things people should bear in mind when making important decisions are _____

_____

- On a sticky note, record a brief phrase to complete the statement.
- Place all sticky notes with suggestions on the board; and then read the suggestions aloud. Work together to group ideas that are related.
- As a class, decide which phrase or phrases best complete the statement. Students may vote for one, two, or three phrases.
- Place a tally mark on the notes that indicate your choices.
- Use the tally results to create and edit a class thesis statement.

QuickWrite

Consider class discussions, the video, and the Launch Text as you think about the prompt. Record your first thoughts here.

PROMPT: **Is it important for people to make their own choices in life?**

📝 EVIDENCE LOG FOR TAKING A STAND

Review your QuickWrite. Summarize your point of view in one sentence to record in your Evidence Log. Then, record evidence from "Freedom of the Press?" that supports your point of view.

Prepare for the Performance-Based Assessment at the end of the unit by completing the Evidence Log after each selection.

 Tool Kit
Evidence Log Model

Title of Text: _____ Date: _____

CONNECTION TO PROMPT	TEXT EVIDENCE/DETAILS	ADDITIONAL NOTES/IDEAS

How does this text change or add to my thinking? _____ Date: _____

 SCAN FOR MULTIMEDIA

ESSENTIAL QUESTION:

When is it right to take a stand?

What issues are worth defending? In today's complex world, it's important to get our priorities straight. Each of us must decide for ourselves what matters most—a principle, another human being, or the right to express ourselves. As you read, you will work with your whole class to explore some of the issues that have caused people to take a stand.

Whole-Class Learning Strategies

Throughout your life, in school, in your community, and in your career, you will continue to learn and work in large-group environments.

Review these strategies and the actions you can take to practice them as you work with your whole class. Add ideas of your own for each step. Get ready to use these strategies during Whole-Class Learning.

STRATEGY	ACTION PLAN
Listen actively	• Eliminate distractions. For example, put your cellphone away. • Keep your eyes on the speaker. •
Clarify by asking questions	• If you're confused, other people probably are, too. Ask a question to help your whole class. • If you see that you are guessing, ask a question instead. •
Monitor understanding	• Notice what information you already know and be ready to build on it. • Ask for help if you are struggling. •
Interact and share ideas	• Share your ideas and answer questions, even if you are unsure. • Build on the ideas of others by adding details or making a connection. •

SCAN FOR
MULTIMEDIA

CONTENTS

COMPARE

PERFORMANCE TASK

WRITING FOCUS

Write an Argument

The Whole-Class readings focus on people who have taken a stand for or against something they felt strongly about. After reading, you will write an essay in which you make an argument about a problem you think is worth solving and how to solve it.

About the Publication

National Geographic
(originally named *The National Geographic Magazine*) has been published continuously for more than 125 years. It is famous for its articles on history, geography, and culture around the world. Early in its life, the magazine became equally celebrated for the quality and content of its photography, which has remained a standard that many other publications try to match.

Barrington Irving, Pilot and Educator

Concept Vocabulary

As you conduct your first read of "Barrington Irving, Pilot and Educator," you will encounter these words. Before reading, note how familiar you are with each word. Then, rank the words in order from most familiar (1) to least familiar (6).

WORD	YOUR RANKING
determination	
achieve	
pursue	
tackling	
accomplish	
purposeful	

After completing your first read, review your original rankings. Mark changes to your original rankings as needed.

First Read NONFICTION

Apply these strategies as you conduct your first read. You will have an opportunity to complete the close-read notes after your first read.

🔧 Tool Kit

First-Read Guide and Model Annotation

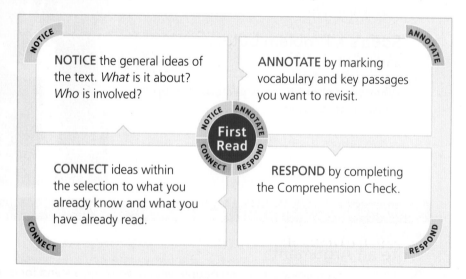

NOTICE the general ideas of the text. *What* is it about? *Who* is involved?

ANNOTATE by marking vocabulary and key passages you want to revisit.

First Read

CONNECT ideas within the selection to what you already know and what you have already read.

RESPOND by completing the Comprehension Check.

STANDARDS

Reading Informational Text
By the end of the year, read and comprehend literary nonfiction at the high end of the grades 6–8 text complexity band independently and proficiently.

Barrington Irving, **Pilot** and **Educator**

National Geographic

BACKGROUND

One way to travel around the world is to become a pilot. In order to get a professional pilot's license, a person must be at least eighteen years old, pass a written exam, and practice flying for more than 1,000 hours. Pilots need to be able to communicate clearly, solve problems, observe and react quickly, and know how to use aircraft computer and navigation systems.

SCAN FOR MULTIMEDIA

1   **B**arrington Irving is very good at rising above obstacles. Literally. Raised in Miami's inner city, surrounded by crime, poverty, and failing schools, he beat the odds to become the youngest person and only African American ever to fly solo around the world. He built a plane himself, made his historic flight, graduated magna cum laude[1] from an aeronautical science program, and founded a dynamic educational nonprofit. Then he turned 28.

NOTES

---

1. **magna cum laude** (MAG nuh kum LOW duh) with high honors, from Latin.

2   His message for kids: "The only thing that separates you from CEOs in corner offices or scientists in labs is **determination**, hard work, and a passion for what you want to **achieve**. The only person who can stop you from doing something great is you. Even if no one believes in your dream, you have to **pursue** it." The secret, he believes, is having a dream in the first place, and that starts with powerful learning experiences that inspire kids to pursue careers—particularly in science, technology, engineering, and math.

3   The moment of inspiration for Irving came at age 15 while he was working in his parents' bookstore. One of their customers, a Jamaican-born professional pilot, asked Irving if he'd ever thought about becoming a pilot. "I told him I didn't think I was smart enough; but the next day he gave me the chance to sit in the cockpit of the commercial airplane he flew, and just like that I was hooked. There are probably millions of kids out there like me who find science and exploration amazing, but lack the confidence or opportunity to take the next step."

4   To follow his dream, Irving turned down a full football scholarship to the University of Florida. He washed airplanes to earn money for flight school and increased his flying skills by practicing at home on a $40 flight simulator video game.

5   Then another dream took hold: flying solo around the world. He faced more than 50 rejections for sponsorship before convincing several manufacturers to donate individual aircraft components. He took off with no weather radar, no de-icing system, and just $30 in his pocket. "I like to do things people say I can't do."

"The only person who can stop you from doing something great is you."

6   After 97 days, 26 stops, and dozens of thunderstorms, monsoons, snowstorms, and sandstorms, he touched down to a roaring crowd in Miami. "Stepping from the plane, it wasn't all the fanfare that changed my life. It was seeing so many young people watching and listening. I had no money, but I was determined to give back with my time, knowledge, and experience." He's been doing it ever since.

7   Irving's nonprofit organization,[2] Experience Aviation, aims to boost the numbers of youth in aviation and other science- and math-related careers. Middle and high school students attend

2. **nonprofit organization** company formed to provide a benefit to the community rather than to make money for its own gain.

summer and after-school programs **tackling** hands-on robotics projects, flight simulator challenges, and field trips to major industries and corporations. In his Build and Soar program, 60 students from failing schools built an airplane from scratch in just ten weeks and then watched Irving pilot it into the clouds.

8   "We want to create a one-of-a-kind opportunity for students to take ownership and **accomplish** something amazing," he notes. "Meaningful, real-world learning experiences fire up the neurons in kids' minds. If you don't do that, you've lost them. **Purposeful**, inspiring activities increase the chance they'll stay on that learning and career path. We've had one young lady receive a full scholarship to Duke University as a math major, and several young men are now pilots, engineers, and aircraft mechanics."

9   "It's great to reach a few hundred kids every year," he says, "but I also wanted to find a way to inspire on a larger scale." How about millions of kids? Irving's next endeavor will transform a jet into a flying classroom that will circle the globe sharing science, technology, engineering, math, geography, culture, and history. "This isn't just an aircraft; it's an exploration vehicle for learning that will teach millions of kids in ways they've never been taught before—making them part of the expedition and research."

10   A web-based experience will make it easy for kids to participate at home and school, voting on everything from where Irving should make a fuel stop to what local food he should sample. He plans to call classrooms from the cockpit; broadcast live video from 45,000 feet; blog with students; collect atmospheric data; communicate with the International Space Station; and wear a NASA[3] body suit that transmits his heart rate, blood pressure, and other vital signs.

11   Along the way, kids will have a virtual window on about 75 ground expeditions, including Machu Picchu, the Galápagos Islands, the Pyramids, the Serengeti Plains, the Roman Coliseum, the Taj Mahal, and the Great Wall of China. Cameras will provide 360-degree panoramic views of destinations from ancient archeological sites to Hong Kong skyscrapers. Apps will track adventures such as shark tagging, giving students ongoing location and water temperature data.

12   A steady stream of challenges will let kids compete to solve problems ranging from evacuating populations after tsunamis to collecting trash in space. "We also want to create a forum where

---

3. **NASA** *abbr.* National Aeronautics and Space Administration.

NOTES

tackling (TAK lihng) *v.* dealing with or handling a problem or situation

accomplish (uh KOM plish) *v.* carry out; finish or complete

purposeful (PUR puhs fuhl) *adj.* having a clear aim or goal

CLOSE READ

ANNOTATE: Mark details in paragraph 11 that describe the "virtual window."

QUESTION: Why do you think the writer has listed so many details?

CONCLUDE: What do these details lead you to conclude about the scope of Irving's project?

kids, parents, and teachers can speak to astronauts, scientists, and other specialists."

13   This "Journey for Knowledge" flight is scheduled to depart in 2013 and will make Irving the youngest person ever to fly to all seven continents.

14   Perhaps Irving's most compelling educational tool is the example his own life provides. After landing his record-breaking flight at age 23, he smiled out at the airfield crowd and said, "Everyone told me what I couldn't do. They said I was too young, that I didn't have enough money, experience, strength, or knowledge. They told me it would take forever and I'd never come home. Well . . . guess what?" ❧

MEDIA CONNECTION

Barrington Irving: Got 30
Dollars in My Pocket

💬 **Discuss It** How does viewing this video add to your appreciation of Barrington Irving's personal accomplishments?

Write your response before sharing your ideas.

SCAN FOR
MULTIMEDIA

Comprehension Check

Complete the following items after you finish your first read.

1. Name two obstacles Barrington Irving had to overcome in order to achieve his dream.

2. What were two of Irving's first big dreams?

3. How did Irving increase his flying skills at home?

4. What is Experience Aviation?

5. 🗐 **Notebook** Write a timeline of events in the life of Barrington Irving.

- -

RESEARCH

Research to Clarify Choose at least one unfamiliar detail from the text. Briefly research that detail. In what way does the information you learned shed light on an aspect of the article?

Research to Explore Choose something that interested you from the text, and use it to formulate a research question.

Close Read the Text

1. The model, from paragraph 5, shows two sample annotations, along with questions and conclusions. Close read the passage, and find another detail to annotate. Then, write a question and your conclusion.

ANNOTATE: These details relate to Irving's pursuit of his next dream.

QUESTION: Why might the author have included these details?

CONCLUDE: These details show Irving's ambition, the obstacles he faced, and his attitude toward those obstacles.

ANNOTATE: The author includes details about what Irving *did not* have on his solo flight.

QUESTION: Why might the author have included these details?

CONCLUDE: These details show the challenges Irving faced and overcame.

Then another dream took hold: flying solo around the world. He faced more than 50 rejections for sponsorship before convincing several manufacturers to donate individual aircraft components. He took off with no weather radar, no de-icing system, and just $30 in his pocket. "I like to do things people say I can't do."

2. For more practice, go back into the text and complete the close-read notes.

3. Revisit a section of the text you found important during your first read. Read this section closely, and **annotate** what you notice. Ask yourself **questions** such as "Why did the author make this choice?" What can you **conclude**?

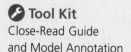

Tool Kit
Close-Read Guide
and Model Annotation

Analyze the Text

CITE TEXTUAL EVIDENCE
to support your answers.

Notebook Respond to these questions.

1. **Paraphrase** A **paraphrase** is a restatement of another person's ideas in your own words. Reread paragraph 3. Then, paraphrase how Barrington Irving discovered his life's calling.

2. **Make a Judgment** The author states that Irving's life is his "most compelling educational tool." Do you agree? Explain your thinking.

3. **Essential Question:** *When is it right to take a stand?* What have you learned about when and how to take action from reading this article?

Analyze Craft and Structure

Characterization in Nonfiction Nonfiction writers often adapt techniques typically used by fiction writers to vividly portray the real-life people who are the subjects of their works. Taken together, the techniques writers use to portray characters are called **characterization**. There are two types of characterization:

- With **direct characterization,** the author simply tells the reader what a person is like. For example, the author might say a person is *stubborn, generous, shy,* or *brave.*

- With **indirect characterization,** the author reveals a subject's personality by including his or her words and describing his or her actions, appearance, and behavior. The author may also show how other people feel about the person.

When an author uses indirect characterization, the reader must make **inferences,** or educated guesses, to determine what the person is like. To make inferences, connect details in the text to your own background knowledge. For example, if an author describes someone who arrives as arriving late and out of breath, you might infer that the person had been running. Practice making an inference by reading this passage and marking details about Irving. Then, note an inference you can make based on those details.

PASSAGE FROM THE TEXT	MY INFERENCE
A web-based experience will make it easy for kids to participate at home and school, voting on everything from where Irving should make a fuel stop to what local food he should sample. He plans to call classrooms from the cockpit; broadcast live video from 45,000 feet; blog with students; collect atmospheric data; communicate with the International Space Station; and wear a NASA3 body suit that transmits his heart rate, blood pressure, and other vital signs. (paragraph 10)	

CITE TEXTUAL EVIDENCE to support your answers.

Practice

🔲 **Notebook** **Respond to these questions.**

1. **(a)** Identify an example of direct characterization in paragraph 1. **(b)** What clues in the text indicate that this is direct characterization?

2. **(a)** Reread paragraph 6 of the article. What type of characterization does the author use in this paragraph? **(b)** What does the information in this paragraph reveal about Irving's character?

3. In paragraph 9, the author uses direct quotations, or Irving's exact words, to reveal Irving's goals for the future. What can you infer about Irving based on the quotations in this paragraph?

4. Reread paragraph 14. **(a)** How many examples of characterization appear in that passage? **(b)** Which detail do you find most revealing? Explain.

BARRINGTON IRVING, PILOT
AND EDUCATOR

Concept Vocabulary

determination	pursue	accomplish
achieve	tackling	purposeful

Why These Words? The concept vocabulary words all relate to the effort an individual puts forth in order to succeed. For example, according to Irving, *determination* is a key factor in a person's success.

1. How does the concept vocabulary help the reader understand the reasons for Barrington's Irving's success?

2. What other words in the selection relate to success?

Practice

Notebook Complete the following activities.

1. What goals do you have and what will you need to *achieve* them? Use concept vocabulary words in your response.

2. With a partner, take turns listing as many **synonyms,** or words with similar meanings, as you can for each concept vocabulary word.

Word Study

Old English Suffix: *-ful* The Old English suffix *-ful* means "full of" or "having qualities of." In the article, Irving says that he thinks *purposeful* activities, or activities that are goal-oriented, are most likely to inspire kids.

1. Irving says, "Meaningful, real-world learning experiences fire up the neurons in kids' minds." Based on this sentence and on what you know about the suffix *-ful*, define *meaningful.*

2. What other words containing the suffix *-ful* can you use to describe Barrington Irving?

▲ WORD NETWORK

Add words related to taking a stand from the text to your Word Network.

▤ STANDARDS

Language
• Demonstrate command of the conventions of standard English grammar and usage when writing or speaking.
• Demonstrate command of the conventions of standard English capitalization, punctuation, and spelling when writing.
   c. Spell correctly.
• Determine or clarify the meaning of unknown and multiple-meaning words or phrases based on *grade 8 reading and content,* choosing flexibly from a range of strategies.
• Demonstrate understanding of figurative language, word relationships, and nuances in word meanings.
   b. Use the relationship between particular words to better understand each of the words.

Conventions

Nouns and Pronouns Correct capitalization and spelling of nouns and pronouns are key to clear writing. A **noun** is used to name a person, place, or thing. A **pronoun** is used to replace a noun in a sentence. There are different kinds of nouns and pronouns, such as the ones listed here:

- **Proper nouns** name specific persons, places, or things, such as *Barrington Irving*. Proper nouns begin with capital letters.

- **Possessive nouns** such as *Miami's* show ownership.

- **Personal pronouns** such as *I, you,* and *they* refer to persons or things. The personal pronoun *I* is always capitalized.

- **Possessive pronouns** such as *my, your, its,* and *their* replace possessive nouns and also show ownership.

Be sure not to confuse possessive pronouns with words that sound the same: *Your* is a possessive pronoun, while *you're* is a contraction that stands for "you are." *Its* is a possessive pronoun, while *it's* is a contraction that stands for "it is." *Their* is a possessive pronoun, while *they're* is a contraction that stands for "they are."

 TIP

Pay attention to capitalization and spelling when you use nouns and pronouns. Remember, all proper nouns and the personal pronoun I are capitalized.

Read It

1. Identify the proper nouns, personal pronouns, possessive nouns, and possessive pronouns in the following sentences from the selection.

   a. To follow his dream, Irving turned down a full football scholarship to the University of Florida.

   b. Irving's nonprofit organization, Experience Aviation, aims to boost the numbers of youth in aviation and other science- and math-related careers.

2. Reread paragraph 10 of "Barrington Irving, Pilot and Educator." Mark and then label at least one example of each of the following: proper noun, personal pronoun, and possessive pronoun.

Write It

📓 **Notebook** Revise the paragraph below. Make sure that proper nouns and pronouns are capitalized correctly and that possessive pronouns are spelled correctly.

When barrington irving was a young man, no one encouraged him to pursue his dreams. In fact, he said, "Everyone told me what i couldn't do." Irving started a nonprofit organization. It's goal is to help kids achieve they're dreams in science and aviation.

BARRINGTON IRVING, PILOT
AND EDUCATOR

Writing to Sources

In an argumentative essay, a writer states a claim, or position, on a subject. He or she then explains reasons for that position, and uses evidence to show why the reasons makes sense.

Assignment

Write an **argumentative essay** in which you state a claim in response to the following statement:

> Having passion for a subject is more important than having knowledge about it.

Be sure each piece of evidence you use to support your claim clearly relates to the reasons you provide. Begin your essay with a clear introduction in which you state your claim. Then, explain your reasons and give evidence that supports them. Finally, end with a conclusion that states your claim in a different way. Try to make that conclusion memorable for readers.

Vocabulary and Conventions Connection Consider including several of the concept vocabulary words in your essay. Also, remember to proofread your draft to correct any errors in the spelling and capitalization of nouns and pronouns.

| determination | achieve | pursue |
| tackling | accomplish | purposeful |

- -

Reflect on Your Writing

After you have written your argument, answer the following questions.

1. How do you think your evidence helps support your claim?

2. How might you revise the way you present your evidence so that it supports the claim more persuasively?

3. Why These Words? The words you choose make a difference in your writing. Which words did you specifically choose to clearly convey your ideas?

STANDARDS

Writing
• Write arguments to support claims with clear reasons and relevant evidence.
    a. Introduce claim(s), acknowledge and distinguish the claim(s) from alternate or opposing claims, and organize the reasons and evidence logically.
    b. Support claim(s) with logical reasoning and relevant evidence, using accurate, credible sources and demonstrating an understanding of the topic or text.
    e. Provide a concluding statement or section that follows from and supports the argument presented.
• Conduct short research projects to answer a question, drawing on several sources and generating additional related, focused questions that allow for multiple avenues of exploration.

Speaking and Listening
• Delineate a speaker's argument and specific claims, evaluating the soundness of the reasoning and relevance and sufficiency of the evidence and identifying when irrelevant evidence is introduced.
• Present claims and findings, emphasizing salient points in a focused, coherent manner with relevant evidence, sound valid reasoning, and well-chosen details; use appropriate eye contact, adequate volume, and clear pronunciation.

Speaking and Listening

Assignment

Work with a partner to conduct research on one of the educational nonprofit organizations or programs mentioned in the article. Use the information you gather to develop and deliver a **persuasive presentation** that highlights the benefits of the organization or program. Show why the organization deserves support, or why its programs provide valuable experiences.

1. **Evaluate Your Evidence** As you prepare your presentation, make sure you have supported your claims about the program or organization. Answer the following questions to determine whether you need more supporting evidence:

   - Have you described the features of the organization or program clearly and accurately?

   - Do you explain why each feature is beneficial or exciting?

   - Did you include evidence to show the organization or program and its features are successful?

2. **Prepare Your Presentation** Practice your presentation before you deliver it to the class. Use the following techniques in your delivery:

   - Speak loudly enough to be heard by the entire class.

   - Maintain eye contact with your audience as you present.

3. **Evaluate Presentations** As your classmates deliver their presentations, listen attentively. Then, evaluate the presentations to decide which one you felt was most convincing. Consider the reasoning and evidence and the speakers' presentation skills. Use a presentation evaluation guide like the one shown to analyze classmates' presentations.

EVIDENCE LOG

Before moving on to a new selection, go to your Evidence Log and record what you learned from "Barrington Irving, Pilot and Educator."

EVALUATION GUIDE

Rate each statement on a scale of 1 (not demonstrated) to 5 (demonstrated).

☐ The presentation was persuasive and supported by relevant evidence.

☐ The speaker clearly explained his or her reasons.

☐ The speaker spoke at an appropriate volume and maintained eye contact.

THREE CHEERS FOR THE NANNY STATE

Comparing Texts

In this lesson, you will read and compare two selections that present different arguments about the same issue. First, you will complete the first read and close read activities for "Three Cheers for the Nanny State."

• BAN THE BAN!
• SODA'S A PROBLEM BUT...

About the Author

Sarah Conly holds the title of Associate Professor of Philosphy at Bowdoin College in Brunswick, Maine. She is the author of numerous essays, journal articles, and opinion pieces focusing on issues of personal choice and public policy.

🔧 **Tool Kit**
First-Read Guide and Model Annotation

Three Cheers for the Nanny State

Concept Vocabulary

As you conduct your first read of "Three Cheers for the Nanny State," you will encounter these words. Before you read, rate how familiar you are with each word. Then, rank the words in order from most familiar (1) to least familiar (5).

WORD	YOUR RANKING
impose	
rational	
justifiable	
principle	
status quo	

After completing your first read, come back to the selection vocabulary and review your ratings. Mark changes to your original rankings as needed.

First Read NONFICTION

Apply these strategies as you conduct your first read. You will have an opportunity to complete a close read after your first read.

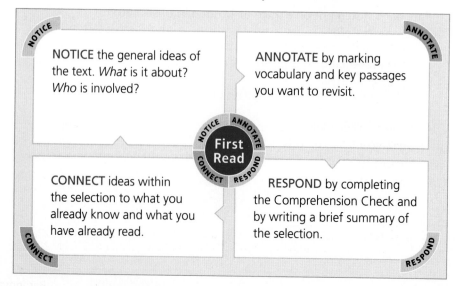

NOTICE the general ideas of the text. *What* is it about? *Who* is involved?

ANNOTATE by marking vocabulary and key passages you want to revisit.

CONNECT ideas within the selection to what you already know and what you have already read.

RESPOND by completing the Comprehension Check and by writing a brief summary of the selection.

First Read

NOTICE ANNOTATE CONNECT RESPOND

📋 **STANDARDS**
Reading Informational Text
By the end of the year, read and comprehend literary nonfiction at the high end of the grades 6–8 text complexity band independently and proficiently.

Three Cheers for the Nanny State
Sarah Conly

BACKGROUND

The term "nanny state" is a negative nickname for a welfare state, which is a model of government that takes direct responsibility for the protection and well-being of its citizens. Welfare states offer basic social support, such as free health care or low-income housing, but also create laws and policies that attempt to control or influence how people behave.

SCAN FOR MULTIMEDIA

1 Why has there been so much fuss about New York City's attempt to **impose** a soda ban,[1] or more precisely, a ban on large-size "sugary drinks"? After all, people can still get as much soda as they want. This isn't Prohibition. It's just that getting it would take slightly more effort. So, why is this such a big deal?

2 Obviously, it's not about soda. It's because such a ban suggests that sometimes we need to be stopped from doing foolish stuff, and this has become, in contemporary American politics, highly controversial, no matter how trivial the particular issue. (Large cups of soda as symbols of human dignity? Really?)

3 Americans, even those who generally support government intervention in our daily lives, have a reflexive response to being told what to do, and it's not a positive one. It's this common desire to be left alone that prompted the Mississippi Legislature earlier this month to pass a ban on bans—a law that forbids municipalities to place local restrictions on food or drink.

---

1. **soda ban** In 2013, New York City passed a law prohibiting soda containers larger than 16 ounces in volume. The New York State Court of Appeals later overturned the law.

NOTES

impose (im POHZ) *v.* force a law, idea, or belief on someone by using authority

CLOSE READ

ANNOTATE: In paragraph 1, mark the questions that the author does not answer.

QUESTION: Why might the author have begun the article with several unanswered questions?

CONCLUDE: What effect do these questions have on the reader?

NOTES

rational (RASH uh nuhl) *adj.* able to make decisions based on reason rather than emotion; sensible

justifiable (juhs tuh FY uh buhl) *adj.* able to be defended as correct; reasonable and logical

principle (PRIHN suh puhl) *n.* moral rule or set of ideas about right or wrong that influences individuals to behave in a certain way

CLOSE READ

ANNOTATE: In paragraphs 8–10, mark the types of **bias**, or judgments and prejudices, the author describes.

QUESTION: Why does the author include these explanations of different biases?

CONCLUDE: How does this information affect the persuasiveness of her argument?

status quo (STAT uhs kwoh) *n.* existing state or condition at a particular time

4   We have a vision of ourselves as free, **rational** beings who are totally capable of making all the decisions we need to in order to create a good life. Give us complete liberty, and, barring natural disasters, we'll end up where we want to be. It's a nice vision, one that makes us feel proud of ourselves. But it's false.

5   John Stuart Mill[2] wrote in 1859 that the only **justifiable** reason for interfering in someone's freedom of action was to prevent harm to others. According to Mill's "harm **principle**," we should almost never stop people from behavior that affects only themselves, because people know best what they themselves want.

6   That "almost," though, is important. It's fair to stop us, Mill argued, when we are acting out of ignorance and doing something we'll pretty definitely regret. You can stop someone from crossing a bridge that is broken, he said, because you can be sure no one wants to plummet into the river. Mill just didn't think this would happen very often.

7   Mill was wrong about that, though. A lot of times we have a good idea of where we want to go, but a really terrible idea of how to get there. It's well established by now that we often don't think very clearly when it comes to choosing the best means to attain our ends. We make errors. This has been the object of an enormous amount of study over the past few decades, and what has been discovered is that we are all prone to identifiable and predictable miscalculations.

8   Research by psychologists and behavioral economists, including the Nobel Prize-winner Daniel Kahneman and his research partner Amos Tversky, identified a number of areas in which we fairly dependably fail. They call such a tendency a "cognitive[3] bias," and there are many of them—a lot of ways in which our own minds trip us up.

9   For example, we suffer from an optimism bias, that is we tend to think that however likely a bad thing is to happen to most people in our situation, it's less likely to happen to us—not for any particular reason, but because we're irrationally optimistic. Because of our "present bias," when we need to take a small, easy step to bring about some future good, we fail to do it, not because we've decided it's a bad idea, but because we procrastinate.

10 We also suffer from a **status quo** bias, which makes us value what we've already got over the alternatives, just because we've already got it—which might, of course, make us react badly to

---

2. **John Stuart Mill** (1806–1873) British philosopher.
3. **cognitive** (KOG nih tihv) *adj.* related to thinking.

new laws, even when they are really an improvement over what we've got. And there are more.

11   The crucial point is that in some situations it's just difficult for us to take in the relevant information and choose accordingly. It's not quite the simple ignorance Mill was talking about, but it turns out that our minds are more complicated than Mill imagined. Like the guy about to step through the hole in the bridge, we need help.

12   Is it always a mistake when someone does something imprudent, when, in this case, a person chooses to chug 32 ounces of soda? No. For some people, that's the right choice. They don't care that much about their health, or they won't drink too many big sodas, or they just really love having a lot of soda at once.

13   But laws have to be sensitive to the needs of the majority. That doesn't mean laws should trample the rights of the minority, but that public benefit is a legitimate concern, even when that may inconvenience some.

14   So do these laws mean that some people will be kept from doing what they really want to do? Probably—and yes, in many ways it hurts to be part of a society governed by laws, given that laws aren't designed for each one of us individually. Some of us can drive safely at 90 miles per hour, but we're bound by the same laws as the people who can't, because individual speeding laws aren't practical. Giving up a little liberty is something we agree to when we agree to live in a democratic society that is governed by laws.

15   The freedom to buy a really large soda, all in one cup, is something we stand to lose here. For most people, given their desire for health, that results in a net gain. For some people, yes, it's an absolute loss. It's just not much of a loss.

16   Of course, what people fear is that this is just the beginning: today it's soda, tomorrow it's the guy standing behind you making you eat your broccoli, floss your teeth, and watch *PBS NewsHour*[4] every day. What this ignores is that successful paternalistic[5] laws are done on the basis of a cost-benefit analysis: if it's too painful, it's not a good law. Making these analyses is something the government has the resources to do, just as now it sets automobile construction standards while considering both the need for affordability and the desire for safety.

17   Do we care so much about our health that we want to be forced to go to aerobics every day and give up all meat, sugar and salt?

NOTES

CLOSE READ

ANNOTATE: In paragraph 14, mark the example the author uses to support her claim.

QUESTION: Why might the author have chosen this specific example as support?

CONCLUDE: How does the inclusion of this example affect the author's argument?

---

4. *PBS NewsHour* television news program in the United States.
5. **paternalistic** (puh tuhr nuh LIHS tihk) *adj.* protective, but controlling; in the manner of a parent.

No. But in this case, it's some extra soda. Banning a law on the grounds that it might lead to worse laws would mean we could have no laws whatsoever.

18   In the old days we used to blame people for acting imprudently, and say that since their bad choices were their own fault, they deserved to suffer the consequences. Now we see that these errors aren't a function of bad character, but of our shared cognitive inheritance. The proper reaction is not blame, but an impulse to help one another.

19   That's what the government is supposed to do, help us get where we want to go. It's not always worth it to intervene, but sometimes, where the costs are small and the benefit is large, it is. That's why we have prescriptions for medicine. And that's why, as irritating as it may initially feel, the soda regulation is a good idea. It's hard to give up the idea of ourselves as completely rational. We feel as if we lose some dignity. But that's the way it is, and there's no dignity in clinging to an illusion. ❧

Comprehension Check

Complete the following items after you finish your first read.

1. What new law was proposed in New York City?

2. What is a "cognitive bias"?

3. According to the author, what do people fear they will lose as a result of the new law?

4. According to the author, what will most people gain from the soda ban?

5. 📓 **Notebook** Write a summary of "Three Cheers for the Nanny State."

- -

RESEARCH

Research to Clarify Choose at least one unfamiliar detail from the text. Briefly research that detail. In what way does the information you learned shed light on an aspect of the text?

Research to Explore Write a research question that you might use to find out more about the concept of the "nanny state."

THREE CHEERS FOR THE
NANNY STATE

Close Read the Text

1. The model, from paragraph 16, shows two sample annotations, along with questions and conclusions. Close read the passage, and find another detail to annotate. Then, write a question and your conclusion.

ANNOTATE: The author begins the paragraph with the transition phrase *Of course*.

QUESTION: Why might the author have chosen this specific transition?

CONCLUDE: The author uses this phrase to show that she recognizes and, to some degree, understands opposing views.

ANNOTATE: The author lists activities.

QUESTION: Why does the author list these activities?

CONCLUDE: Each activity is considered "good" for people, and is something we usually do at home. The list exaggerates the idea of government control of our behavior.

> Of course, what people fear is that this is just the beginning: today it's soda, tomorrow it's the guy standing behind you making you eat your broccoli, floss your teeth, and watch *PBS NewsHour* every day.

🔧 **Tool Kit**
Close-Read Guide
and Model Annotation

2. For more practice, go back into the text and complete the close-read notes.

3. Revisit a section of the text you found important during your first read. Read this section closely, and **annotate** what you notice. Ask yourself **questions** such as "Why did the author make this choice?" What can you **conclude**?

Analyze the Text

CITE TEXTUAL EVIDENCE
to support your answers.

📓 **Notebook** Respond to these questions.

1. (a) **Distinguish** What is the author's **tone**, or attitude toward her subject and audience? (b) **Support** What words and phrases does the author use that create that tone?

2. (a) **Deduce** What is the larger issue that the author is addressing in this opinion piece? (b) **Interpret** Why do you think the author uses the soda-ban debate as a catalyst, or motivating force, for addressing this issue?

3. **Essential Question:** *When is it right to take a stand?* What have you learned from this text about when it is right to take a stand?

📋 STANDARDS
Reading Informational Text
• Determine an author's point of view or purpose in a text and analyze how the author acknowledges and responds to conflicting evidence or viewpoints.
• Delineate and evaluate the argument and specific claims in a text, assessing whether the reasoning is sound and the evidence is relevant and sufficient; recognize when irrelevant evidence is introduced.

Analyze Craft and Structure

Author's Argument An **author's argument** is his or her position on a controversial or debatable topic or issue. In an argument, the author makes a **claim,** or statement of a specific position. The author's reason for writing is to convince readers to share that position. To do so, the author gives reasons for taking the position, and provides supporting evidence that is **relevant**, or related, to it. The most basic forms of evidence are facts and opinions:

- A **fact** is something that can be proved.

- An **opinion** is a person's judgment or belief. It may be supported by facts, but it cannot be proved.

A successful persuasive argument relies on factual evidence. It also uses **logical reasoning,** or clear thinking, that shows how an author has arrived at his or her position.

An author's argument and choices of supporting evidence can be influenced by various factors, including his or her perspective. An **author's perspective,** which can also be called **point of view,** includes his or her attitudes, beliefs, and feelings. If an author's personal beliefs, attitudes, or feelings are too prominent, an argument may seem less convincing. In extreme cases, it may even be read as **bias,** which is an unfair preference either for or against an idea, person, or group.

Practice

CITE TEXTUAL EVIDENCE
to support your answers.

📓 **Notebook** Use the chart to identify at least four facts the author uses to support her argument. Then, answer the questions that follow.

FACTS	HOW THEY SUPPORT THE ARGUMENT

1. **(a)** What **generalizations,** or broad statements, does the author make about Americans? **(b)** What reasons does the author give for these generalizations? **(c)** Are the reasons based on facts or opinions?

2. **(a)** Do you think the author's argument will benefit the health of most people? Why or why not? **(b)** What evidence from the text supports your opinion?

3. Based on your evaluation, did you find the author's argument convincing and persuasive? Why or why not?

THREE CHEERS FOR THE
NANNY STATE

Concept Vocabulary

impose	justifiable	status quo
rational	principle	

Why These Words? These concept words help the author discuss rules and laws. For example, part of deciding whether a law is *justifiable*, or defensible, is to see if it is *rational*, or reasonable. Rules are often based on a *principle*, or idea, about cooperation or safety.

1. How is each concept vocabulary word related to the author's argument about the new law in New York?

2. What other words in the selection connect to rules or laws?

Practice

⊖ Notebook The concept vocabulary words appear in "Three Cheers for the Nanny State." First, use each concept vocabulary word in a sentence that shows your understanding of the word's meaning. Then, find a **synonym**, or word with a similar meaning, for each vocabulary word. Confirm your understanding of each synonym by checking the meanings in a dictionary.

Word Study

Latin Root: -*just*- The Latin root -*just*- means "law" or "fair and right." In "Three Cheers for the Nanny State," the author refers to John Stuart Mill's idea that preventing harm to others is the only *justifiable* reason for interfering with a person's freedom. Mill felt that this was the only "fair and right" reason to interfere.

1. Think about how the root -*just*- contributes to the meaning of the concept vocabulary word *justifiable*. Then, write a sentence in which you correctly use *justifiable*. Remember to include context clues that show the relationship between the root -*just*- and the word's meaning.

2. Using your knowledge of the Latin root -*just*-, explain how the root contributes to the meaning of the following words: *adjust, justice, justification*.

WORD NETWORK

Add words related to taking a stand from the text to your Word Network.

⊞ STANDARDS

Language
• Demonstrate command of the conventions of standard English grammar and usage when writing or speaking.

• Demonstrate command of the conventions of standard English capitalization, punctuation, and spelling when writing.

• Determine or clarify the meaning of unknown and multiple-meaning words or phrases based on *grade 8 reading and content*, choosing flexibly from a range of strategies.

  b. Use common, grade-appropriate Greek or Latin affixes and roots as clues to the meaning of a word.
  d. Verify the preliminary determination of the meaning of a word or phrase.

• Demonstrate understanding of figurative language, word relationships, and nuances in word meanings.

  b. Use the relationship between particular words to better understand each of the words.

Conventions

Clauses A **clause** is a group of words that has both a subject and a verb. An **independent clause** has a subject and a verb, and it can stand by itself as a sentence. A **dependent**, or **subordinate**, **clause** has a subject and a verb, but it cannot stand alone as a complete sentence.

Subordinate clauses are classified according to their function in a sentence. The three kinds are **adverb clauses, relative clauses** (also called **adjective clauses**), and **noun clauses.**

CLAUSE	DESCRIPTION	EXAMPLE
Independent clause	• Can stand by itself as a sentence	Although many people oppose the new law, <u>the author supports it.</u>
Adverb clause	• Acts as an adverb • Begins with a subordinating conjunction such as *if, although, when,* or *because*	<u>Although many people oppose the new law,</u> the author supports it.
Relative clause	• Acts as an adjective • Usually begins with a relative pronoun: *who, whom, whose, which,* or *that*	The author supports a law <u>that bans large-size sugary drinks.</u>
Noun clause	• Acts as a noun • Begins with a word such as *what, whatever, when, where, why,* or *how*	The author explains <u>how the new law will work.</u>

In a sentence with two or more clauses, you may need a comma between the clauses. For example, you usually need a comma between an adverb clause and an independent clause.

Read It

1. Identify whether each clause is an independent clause or a dependent clause. If it is a dependent clause, tell which kind.

   a. People suffer from "cognitive bias"

   b. Which makes us value what we already have

   c. Because we procrastinate

   d. Some new laws are really an improvement

2. Reread paragraph 5 of "Three Cheers for the Nanny State." Mark and then label one example of an independent clause and one example of a dependent clause.

Write It

📝 **Notebook** Write a brief paragraph about the goals of the new law in New York. Make sure to use at least two independent clauses and two dependent clauses in your paragraph. Then, identify each type of clause in your writing.

📝 **EVIDENCE LOG**

Before moving on to a new selection, go to your Evidence Log and record what you have learned from "Three Cheers for the Nanny State."

Three Cheers for the Nanny State **285**

THREE CHEERS FOR THE
NANNY STATE

Comparing Texts

You will now read "Ban the Ban!" and "Soda's
a Problem but. . . ." First, complete the first-
read and close-read activities. Then, compare
the arguments in these opinion pieces with the
argument in "Three Cheers for the Nanny State."

- BAN THE BAN!
- SODA'S A PROBLEM BUT...

About the Authors
SidneyAnne Stone
is a freelance writer,
entrepreneur, marathoner,
breast cancer survivor, and
activist. She is currently
working on her first novel
and documentary.

Karin Klein has won
awards for her editorial
and environmental writing.
She attended Wellesley
College and the University
of California—Berkeley,
and she is now an adjunct
professor at Chapman
University in Orange,
California.

🔧 **Tool Kit**
First-Read Guide
and Model Annotation

Ban the Ban!
Soda's a Problem but...

Concept Vocabulary

You will encounter these words as you read. Before reading, note how
familiar you are with each word. Then, rank the words from most familiar
(1) to least familiar (6).

WORD	YOUR RANKING
implemented	
mandates	
intervene	
intentions	
dictate	
exemption	

After completing the first read, come back to the concept vocabulary and
review your rankings. Mark changes to your original rankings as needed.

First Read NONFICTION

Apply these strategies as you conduct your first read. You will have an
opportunity to complete the close-read notes after your first read.

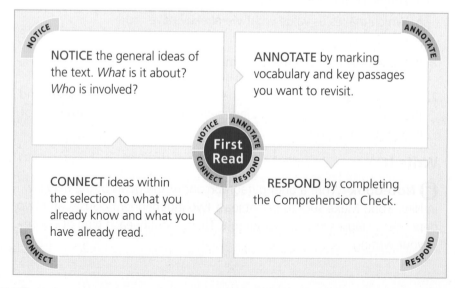

NOTICE the general ideas of
the text. *What* is it about?
Who is involved?

ANNOTATE by marking
vocabulary and key passages
you want to revisit.

CONNECT ideas within
the selection to what you
already know and what you
have already read.

RESPOND by completing
the Comprehension Check.

NOTICE ANNOTATE
First Read
CONNECT RESPOND

Ban the Ban! SidneyAnne Stone

Soda's a Problem but . . .
Karin Klein

BACKGROUND In 2012, New York City's Mayor Bloomberg pushed for a law limiting soft-drink sizes as part of his focus on public health. The law won the approval of the city's Board of Health, but industry groups claimed it was illegal because it interfered with consumers' choices. A judge ruled against the law because it excluded certain businesses and did not apply to all beverages.

SCAN FOR MULTIMEDIA

Ban the Ban!

1   When Mayor Bloomberg **implemented** laws banning smoking in bars, parks and restaurants, that made sense. Whether or not I agreed, I understood the rationale because other people's health would inadvertently be impacted by the smoke. When he insisted on calorie counts being posted, I think many of us cringed but, again, it made sense. If you want to know how many calories something is before you indulge, it is now spelled out for you. On days when you feel like being especially naughty, you just don't look and order it anyway! That's what life is all about, isn't it? Choices. Informed decisions. I respect being given information that enables me to make an informed decision. What I do not respect is having my civil liberties stripped away.

2   When you take away the option to order a soda over a certain size, you have now removed my options. I no longer have a choice. That is not what this country is all about. I agree wholeheartedly that obesity is an issue that needs to be addressed. It is one that needs to be addressed with education, compassion and support, not government **mandates**. If, despite all those efforts, someone chooses to have a sugary drink anyway, that is their choice and their right. If they know all the facts and they do it anyway, that is a personal choice. It is not the place of our elected officials to **intervene**.

3   We cannot allow our government to make these kinds of decisions for us. I have said it before and I will say it again, once you allow the government to make choices on your behalf, it becomes a very slippery slope. I, personally, feel that it goes against everything this country stands for—we are a country built on freedom. That includes basic freedoms like what you are going to drink while watching a movie, and eating what will soon be un-buttered and un-salted popcorn, according to Mayor Bloomberg. Remember the days when New York was a really cool and fun place

NOTES

implemented (IHM pluh mehnt ihd) *v.* carried out; put into effect

mandates (MAN dayts) *n.* orders or commands

intervene (ihn tuhr VEEN) *v.* interfere with; take action to try to stop a dispute or conflict

CLOSE READ

ANNOTATE: Mark the term in the fourth sentence of paragraph 4 that the author repeats.

QUESTION: Why do you think the author repeats this term?

CONCLUDE: What effect does this repetition have on the reader?

intentions (ihn TEHN shuhnz) *n.* purposes for or goals of one's actions

dictate (DIHK tayt) *v.* give orders to control or influence something

exemption (ehg ZEHMP shuhn) *n.* permission not to do or pay for something that others are required to do or pay

to live? Me too. Now a simple thing like going to the movies has even lost its "flavor."

4   The people of New York need to show our mayor that money can't buy him everything. He says he's going to "fight back" to get this pushed through. Well, it is our responsibility to fight back too. People might think it is not important because it is just soda but it is so much more than that—it is about freedom and the freedom to make your own decisions about what you do and what you put into your bodies. It started with soda and he has already moved on to salt. What is going to be next? If you're reading this and you are not a New Yorker, don't think you are not going to be affected. You will! It starts here and it will spread throughout the nation. I hope you will all start to speak up about this issue or, before you know it, it won't be the "land of the free and home of the brave" anymore. One day in the not too distant future we are all going to wake up in the land of "Big Brother"[1] with a list of things we can and cannot do, eat, drink, say, and so on, and we'll be wondering how we got there. Well, this is how. 🥄

Soda's a Problem but . . .

1   The **intentions** of New York Mayor Michael R. Bloomberg may be laudable, but it's wrong for one man, even an elected official and even a well-meaning one at that, to **dictate** to people how big a cup of sugary soda they're allowed.

2   Not that I have tremendous regard for soda. It's bad for you, especially in large quantities. The evidence against it mounts on a semi-regular basis. But the mayor's initiative goes further than something like a soda tax, which might aim to discourage people from purchasing something by making it cost a bit more but leaves the decision in their hands. Bloomberg is playing nanny in the worst sort of way by interfering in a basic, private transaction involving a perfectly legal substance. In restaurants and other establishments overseen by the city's health inspectors, it would have been illegal to sell a serving of most sugary drinks (except fruit juice; I always wonder about that **exemption**, considering the sugar calories in apple juice) that's more than 16 ounces.

3   Convenience stores such as 7-Eleven are overseen by the state and would be exempt, but a Burger King across the street would be restricted. A pizza restaurant would not be able to sell a 2-liter bottle of soda that would be shared out among the children at a birthday party. But they could all have a 16-ounce cup. The inherent contradictions that make it easy to sneer at such rules have been well-reported and were a good part of why earlier this week a judge stopped the new rules from being implemented. But he also pointed out a deeper problem: Bloomberg essentially made this decision himself. It was approved by the Board of Health, but that's a board of the administration, appointed by the mayor. That was

---

1. **the land of "Big Brother"** place in which the government or another organization exercises total control over people's lives; the term *Big Brother* was coined by George Orwell in his famous dystopian novel, *1984*.

an overreach that thwarted the system of checks and balances, according to the judge: The separately elected City Council would have to approve the law.

4   That still leaves the question of whether governments or their leaders can begin dictating the look of an individual's meal, the portion sizes for each aspect. There are times when government has to step in on obviously dangerous situations—especially those, such as smoking, that affect people other than the person whose behavior would be curbed—but it's my belief that we want to scrutinize them carefully and keep them to a minimum. For that matter, it's not as though the mayor is moving to limit sales of tobacco to two cigarettes per transaction.

5   Not that government has to aid and abet the situation. Schools don't have to sell junk foods, and, thankfully, after years of sacrificing their students' health to their desire to raise more money, most of them have stopped allowing vending machines stocked with sodas. Governments are under no obligation to sell such stuff in park or pool vending machines or in their offices. In such cases, government is simply the vendor making a decision about what it wants to sell.

6   I don't buy the argument that people are helpless in the face of sugar and that it's better to have the government rather than the corporations dictate their behaviors. If people are so helpless against soda, the mayor's edict would be even more meaningless because people would simply buy two 16-ounce cups. But people are not helpless, and it's worrisome to promote a philosophy that infantilizes the individual. The public is simply ill-informed. It takes a while for people to become aware, but they do and they react. Soda consumption already is slipping nationwide.

7   Let's not forget that scientists and even governments have at times pushed people—with better intentions than food corporations, certainly—into eating high levels of refined carbohydrates and sugars by sending out word that the only thing that really matters when it comes to obesity is to eat a very low-fat diet. ❧

NOTES

CLOSE READ
ANNOTATE: Mark the text in paragraph 4 in which the author makes exceptions to her claims.

QUESTION: Why might the author have chosen to include this information, which does not support her argument?

CONCLUDE: What effect does the author's inclusion of this information have on the reader?

Comprehension Check

Complete the following items after you finish your first review.

1. Who is Michael Bloomberg?

2. According to the author of "Ban the Ban!," what is "life all about"?

3. What does the author of "Soda's a Problem but..." think of the argument that "people are helpless in the face of sugar"?

RESEARCH

Research to Explore
Formulate a research question that you might use to find out more about other issues that relate to the concept of the "nanny state."

Close Read the Text

1. This model from paragraph 6 of "Soda's a Problem but..." shows two sample annotations along with questions and conclusions. Close read the passage, and find another detail to annotate. Then, write a question and your conclusion.

Close Read
ANNOTATE · QUESTION · CONCLUDE

ANNOTATE: The author repeats the word *helpless*. She also uses a negative word that suggests people are being treated like babies (infants).

QUESTION: Why does the author stress the idea of helplessness?

CONCLUDE: She stresses this idea to engage readers' emotions. Adults do not want to be treated like helpless infants.

ANNOTATE: The author considers a premise, but then rejects it.

QUESTION: Why does the author structure her idea in this way?

CONCLUDE: This structure shows that the author considered another point of view, but found it unconvincing.

> If people are so helpless against soda, the mayor's edict would be even more meaningless because people would simply buy two 16-ounce cups. But people are not helpless, and it's worrisome to promote a philosophy that infantilizes the individual.

2. For more practice, go back into the text, and complete the close-read notes.

3. Revisit a section of the text you found important during your first read. Read this section closely, and **annotate** what you notice. Ask yourself **questions** such as "Why did the author make this choice?" What can you **conclude**?

🔧 Tool Kit
Close-Read Guide and
Model Annotation

Analyze the Text

CITE TEXTUAL EVIDENCE
to support your answers.

📓 **Notebook** Respond to these questions.

1. (a) **Make Inferences** In paragraph 3 of "Ban the Ban!," what does the author mean by the phrase "a very slippery slope"?
   (b) **Support** Which details in the text support your thinking?

2. (a) According to the author of "Soda's a Problem but...," why did the judge stop the soda ban from being put into effect?
   (b) **Connect** What "inherent contradictions" in the soda ban does the author believe the judge's opinion reflects?

3. (a) How does the author of "Soda's a Problem but..." view the public?
   (b) **Make a Judgment** Do you agree with her assessment of "the public"? Why or why not?

4. **Essential Question: *When is it right to take a stand?*** What have you learned about taking a stand from reading these opinion pieces?

STANDARDS
Reading Informational Text
• Cite the textual evidence that most strongly supports an analysis of what the text says explicitly as well as inferences drawn from the text.
• Delineate and evaluate the argument and specific claims in a text, assessing whether the reasoning is sound and the evidence is relevant and sufficient; recognize when irrelevant evidence is introduced.
• Analyze a case in which two or more texts provide conflicting information on the same topic and identify where the texts disagree on matters of fact or interpretation.

Analyze Craft and Structure

Conflicting Arguments In an **argument,** an author presents a **claim,** or position, about a debatable topic. He or she then explains reasons for taking that position, and uses evidence to show why the reasons are sound. Strong arguments rely on facts. Weak arguments may express the author's opinions but not use facts to support them. Weak arguments may also have poor reasoning or rely too heavily on exciting readers' emotions. Some types of poor reasoning or over-reliance on emotions are called **logical fallacies.** Common logical fallacies include the following:

- An **overgeneralization** is a conclusion that overstates the facts. A statement that includes words such as *always, never, everything,* or *only* may be an overgeneralization.

- A **slippery slope** assumes that if A happens then B, C, D,…X, Y, Z are inevitable. This fallacy says that event A, which might be minor, is the same as event Z, which might be terrible. If you do not want Z to occur, you must prevent A from occurring, too. The idea that such a chain of events will definitely happen may simply be untrue.

Although two authors might express the same position, they may not present it in the same way. Authors arguing similar positions may offer different reasons and evidence. One may use facts and sound reasoning, whereas another may use few or no facts and logical fallacies.

Practice

CITE TEXTUAL EVIDENCE to support your answers.

📓 **Notebook** Answer the following questions.

1. What position on the question of the soda ban do both authors express?

2. (a) Identify one fact about Mayor Bloomberg and the soda ban that both authors cite. (b) Note one fact that appears in one piece, but not in the other.

3. Consider this statement from paragraph 3 of "Ban the Ban!": "Remember the days when New York was a really cool and fun place to live? Me too. Now a simple thing like going to the movies has even lost its 'flavor.'" In what ways is this statement an example of overgeneralization?

4. In the last paragraph of "Ban the Ban!" explain how the sentence "What is going to be next?" introduces the logical fallacy of slippery slope.

5. Which author presents a more convincing argument? Explain your thinking.

Concept Vocabulary

implemented	mandates	intervene
intentions	dictate	exemption

Why These Words? The concept vocabulary words help the authors discuss the rules, laws, and regulations involved in the soda-ban debate. In "Ban the Ban!," the author feels that it is not the government's place to *intervene* with an individual's personal choice. In other words, she feels that elected officials should not make laws that interfere with an individual's right to make his or her own decisions.

1. How does the concept vocabulary clarify your understanding of the issues presented in the opinion pieces?

2. What other words in the opinion pieces connect to the concept of rules, laws, and regulations?

Practice

Correctly complete the following sentences using a concept vocabulary word.

1. Roberto's repeated efforts to help shows that he has good _____.

2. My school _____ a new dress code this year that requires all students to wear uniforms.

3. Some large companies receive a tax _____ when they move to a rural area in the hope that they will improve the local economy.

4. New local _____ require that all dogs be on leashes in public places.

5. The doctor felt it was necessary to _____ when he saw a patient being given the wrong treatment.

6. The new community council will _____ the terms and conditions of the new development.

Word Study

Notebook Latin Prefix: ex- The Latin prefix *ex-* means "out" or "out from within." In "Soda's a Problem but...," the author is curious about the reasons sales of fruit juices are given an *exemption* from the 16-ounce cap on soda sizes. Sellers of juice receive an *exemption* because the new rules do not apply to them—they are left "out" of the new laws. Explain how the prefix *ex-* contributes to the meaning of each of the following words: *exhale, explore, exceptional, excommunicate.*

STANDARDS

Language
• Demonstrate command of the conventions of standard English capitalization, punctuation, and spelling when writing.
• Use knowledge of language and its conventions when writing, speaking, reading, or listening.
• Determine or clarify the meaning of unknown and multiple-meaning words or phrases based on *grade 8 reading and content,* choosing flexibly from a range of strategies.
  b. Use common, grade-appropriate Greek or Latin affixes and roots as clues to the meaning of a word.
• Demonstrate understanding of figurative language, word relationships, and nuances in word meanings.
  b. Use the relationship between particular words to better understand each of the words.

Conventions

Basic Sentence Structures Good writers use a variety of sentence structures to make their writing smoother and more interesting to the reader. **Sentence structure** is defined by the types of **clauses** in a sentence. An **independent clause** forms a complete thought or a stand-alone sentence. A **dependent clause** is an incomplete thought. The four basic sentence structures are shown in the chart. Independent clauses are shown in bold. Dependent clauses are underlined.

SENTENCE STRUCTURE	EXAMPLE
A **simple sentence** has a single independent clause with at least one subject and verb.	**The author opposes the new law.**
A **compound sentence** consists of two or more independent clauses joined either by a comma and a conjunction or by a semicolon.	**The author opposes the new law,** but **many people support it.**
A **complex sentence** consists of an independent clause and one or more dependent clauses.	**The author opposes the new law,** <u>which bans sales of large-size sweet drinks</u>.
A **compound-complex sentence** consists of two or more independent clauses and one or more dependent clauses.	**The author opposes the new law,** <u>which bans sales of large-size sweet drinks</u>, but **many people support it.**

Read It

1. Identify the type of sentence represented in each lettered item.

   a. If you want to know how many calories something is before you indulge, it is now spelled out for you.

   b. Soda consumption already is slipping nationwide.

   c. It takes a while for people to become aware, but they do and they react.

2. Reread the first four sentences in paragraph 1 of "Ban the Ban!" Identify the type of sentence each one represents.

Write It

🗐 **Notebook** Add one or more clauses to this simple sentence to form the type of sentence indicated in each numbered item: *Sugary drinks are unhealthy.*

1. Compound sentence

2. Complex sentence

3. Compound-complex sentence

THREE CHEERS FOR THE
NANNY STATE

BAN THE BAN! | SODA'S A
PROBLEM BUT . . .

Writing to Compare

You have studied opinion pieces that present arguments on the same topic—the soda ban in New York City and the larger question of how much the government should be involved in personal decisions. Deepen your analysis by comparing and contrasting the arguments presented in the pro-soda ban opinion piece, "Three Cheers for the Nanny State," and the anti-soda ban opinion pieces, "Ban the Ban!" and "Soda's a Problem but. . . ."

Assignment

Write an **argumentative essay** in which you state a claim about which of the three arguments you found most convincing. To support your claim, analyze the facts and other information the three authors include. Consider these questions:

- What facts do all three authors include?
- Do they use any conflicting information—facts that are not the same? If so, what are they and why are they conflicting?
- Is one author's conclusion or interpretation of the facts more convincing than the others? If so, why?

Include evidence from all three opinion pieces to support your ideas.

STANDARDS

Reading Informational Text
Analyze a case in which two or more texts provide conflicting information on the same topic and identify where the texts disagree on matters of fact or interpretation.

Writing
Draw evidence from literary or informational texts to support analysis, reflection, and research.

b. Apply *grade 8 Reading standards* to literary nonfiction.

Planning and Prewriting

Analyzing the Texts Review the texts and identify facts each author uses, conclusions each author draws, and personal opinions each author expresses. Use the chart to capture your observations.

	THREE CHEERS FOR THE NANNY STATE	BAN THE BAN!		SODA'S A PROBLEM BUT...
facts included			
conclusion or interpretation based on facts			
author's personal opinions (if any)			

📓 **Notebook** **Respond to these questions.**

1. Do the authors disagree on the facts or is it just their interpretation of those facts that differs?
2. Are there any weaknesses in any author's reasoning? Explain.
3. Which argument is strongest? Explain your thinking.

Drafting

Write a Strong Claim A strong, specific claim is the basis for a strong argument. A narrower claim is usually more effective because it focuses your argument and makes it more manageable. Consider using words and phrases that limit the scope of your claim. These types of words and phrases include *generally, for the most part,* and *on average.* Consider the following examples:

> **Broad Claim:** Laws governing food safety do a good job of protecting public health.
>
> **Narrower Claim:** In general, laws governing food safety do a reasonably good job of protecting public health.

Use the space to write a working claim. As you draft your essay, you may refocus your claim as necessary.

_____

_____

_____

Review, Revise, and Edit

Revising for Clarity and Cohesion Precise word choices can clarify and strengthen your argument. Review your draft, and look for places in which you have not clearly connected your claim, reasons, and evidence. Ask yourself questions such as: *How does this fact support my reasoning? How does the fact in combination with my reasons support my claim?* Consider the following examples:

> **Unclear Connection:** Our town should invest in computers. Libraries that have computers are more useful.
>
> **Clear Connection:** There are many reasons why our town should invest in computers for the library. First, libraries that have computers provide a wider range of service. Second, libraries with computers are used more often by the community.

In the first example, the relationship between the ideas is not clear or specific. In the second example, the relationship is clear. "Many reasons" is followed by two specific examples that are set up in order of importance.

Edit for Word Choice and Conventions Reread your essay to identify any words that are vague or do not mean exactly what you want to say. If necessary, consult a thesaurus or other resource to find other words that are more accurate. Make sure you are sure of a word's meaning before you use it. Then, reread your essay again, identifying errors in grammar, spelling, or punctuation. Fix any errors you find.

✒ EVIDENCE LOG

Before moving on to a new selection, go to your Evidence Log and record what you learned from "Ban the Ban!," and "Soda's a Problem but...."

☰ STANDARDS

Writing
• Write arguments to support claims with clear reasons and relevant evidence.

  b. Support claim(s) with logical reasoning and relevant evidence, using accurate, credible sources and demonstrating an understanding of the topic or text.
  c. Use words, phrases, and clauses to create cohesion and clarify the relationships among claim(s), counterclaims, reasons, and evidence.

• Produce clear and coherent writing in which the development, organization, and style are appropriate to task, purpose, and audience.

Write an Argument

The texts in Whole-Class reading focus on problems and solutions. For example, Barrington Irving found solutions to the obstacles he faced as he pursued his dream of becoming a pilot. In the opinion pieces about the New York City soda ban, authors discuss their responses to a proposed solution for a public health problem. Now you will have a chance to write about a problem you think is important and propose a solution you think will help.

> ### Assignment
>
> Write a **problem-and-solution essay** on these questions:
>
> > What is a problem you think needs to be solved?
> > How would you solve it?
>
> Base your essay on your own observations and experiences, and conduct research as needed. In your essay, define the problem, explain the importance of solving it, and propose a specific solution in a persuasive way.

🔧 Tool Kit

Student Model of an Argument

ACADEMIC VOCABULARY

As you craft your argument, consider using some of the academic vocabulary you learned in the beginning of the unit.

retort
candid
rectify
speculate
verify

Elements of an Argument

A **problem-and-solution essay** is a type of argument in which a writer identifies a problem and proposes at least one way to solve it. Both elements—the problem and the solution— require the building of an argument. The writer must convince readers that a situation is actually a problem, and that a proposed solution will make things better. An effective problem-and-solution essay contains these elements:

- a central claim about the importance of a problem and the effectiveness of a particular solution

- reasons, evidence, and examples that support the claim

- a clear and logical organization

- consideration of opposing positions, or counterclaims

- a formal style that conveys ideas in a serious way

- a conclusion that follows from and supports the claim

Model Argument For a model of a well-crafted argument, see the Launch Text, "Freedom of the Press?"

Challenge yourself to find all of the elements of an effective argument in the text. You will have an opportunity to review these elements as you prepare to write your own argument.

LAUNCH TEXT

Freedom of the Press?

☰ STANDARDS

Writing
Write arguments to support claims with clear reasons and relevant evidence.

Prewriting / Planning

Choose a Focus Reread the prompt. Then, decide what problem you will explain and what solution you can offer. This will be the starting point for your claim. Write your ideas here: State your claim in a sentence:

Problem: An important problem that demands a solution is _____

_____

Solution: The most effective solution to this problem would be _____

_____

Consider Possible Counterclaims A strong argument does not just present a claim. It also considers opposing positions, or counterclaims. Think about reasons people might *not* agree that the situation you describe is a problem, or that your proposed solution will be effective. List possible counterclaims in the chart. Then, decide how you will address and refute, or disprove, each one. Will be you able to provide specific details or examples? Will you need to do some research?

COUNTERCLAIM	STRATEGY ADDRESS IT

Gather Evidence From Sources While some of your evidence can come from your own experience and knowledge, you will probably need to do some research to find specific information that supports your position. Consult a variety of reliable sources—both print and digital—to find facts, data, or expert opinions.

Reliable sources are up-to-date and free from bias. The information provided in a reliable source can be confirmed in other sources. If you see a ".gov" or a ".edu" on the end of a Web address, that means the information comes from a governmental or educational institution. These types of web sites are often more trustworthy than those managed by private individuals or businesses.

Using evidence from a variety of sources can make your argument stronger. Study the Launch Text to identify the different types of evidence the author uses to develop the argument.

Connect Across Texts To see how a problem can be identified and solved creatively, consider how Barrington Irving devised ways to help young people learn about aviation, the larger world, and their own futures.

To consider how to deal effectively with counterclaims, review the articles on New York City's soda ban. For example, you might consider how the authors of "Ban the Ban!" and "Soda's a Problem but. . ." answer the counterclaim that there are already widely accepted bans in place for other unhealthy activities, such as smoking. The authors simply point out how cigarettes are different from soda. The harmful effects of smoking are not limited to the smoker—other people are affected. By contrast, the drinking of large amounts of soda affects only the health of the drinker.

✎ EVIDENCE LOG

Review your Evidence Log and identify key details you may want to cite in your argument.

▤ STANDARDS

Writing
Write arguments to support claims with clear reasons and relevant evidence.
  a. Introduce claim(s), acknowledge and distinguish the claim(s) from alternate or opposing claims, and organize the reasons and evidence logically.
  b. Support claim(s) with logical reasoning and relevant evidence, using accurate, credible sources and demonstrating an understanding of the topic or text.

STANDARDS

Writing
Write arguments to support claims with clear reasons and relevant evidence

a. Introduce claim(s), acknowledge and distinguish the claim(s) from alternate or opposing claims, and organize the reasons and evidence logically.
c. Use words, phrases, and clauses to create cohesion and clarify the relationships among claim(s), counterclaims, reasons, and evidence.
e. Provide a concluding statement or section that follows from and supports the argument presented.

Drafting

Organize Ideas and Evidence A logical organization can make your ideas easier for readers to follow. Some arguments present the strongest ideas and supporting evidence first. Others go from weakest to strongest. Create an outline to plan a sequence for your ideas and supporting evidence.

- Start by introducing your problem and solution.
- Add supporting reasons and evidence in a logical order.
- Use transitional words and phrases such as *furthermore, additionally,* and *on the other hand,* to make clear connections from your claim, to your reasons, to the evidence. Work to guide your readers through your ideas.
- Finish with a conclusion that restates your claim.

The outline here shows how the Launch Text is organized.

LAUNCH TEXT

Model: "Freedom of the Press?" Argument Outline

INTRODUCTION
The claim is introduced: *Freedom of the press does not apply to school newspapers.*

BODY
- High-school journalists have challenged efforts to limit their freedom of expression.
- Counterclaim: The Supreme Court ruled in the school's favor, because the censorship was for "valid educational reasons."
- "Valid educational reasons" is not a clear standard.
- Freedom of expression is an important part of becoming educated.

CONCLUSION
Schools should not limit students' free speech.

Argument Outline

INTRODUCTION

BODY
-
-
-
-

CONCLUSION

Write a First Draft Follow the order of ideas and evidence you planned in your outline. As you write, you may see a better way to sequence your ideas. Allow yourself to make adjustments that will improve the flow of your essay.

As you write, use a formal, academic style. Avoid slang or expressions that sound as though you are simply talking to someone. Instead, choose words that convey your ideas accurately. Define terms and explain situations that may be unfamiliar to your audience. Make sure to include transitional words and phrases that show how your ideas and evidence connect.

LANGUAGE DEVELOPMENT: CONVENTIONS

Revising for Pronoun-Antecedent Agreement

A **pronoun** is a word that takes the place of a noun or another pronoun. An **antecedent** is the word or group of words to which a pronoun refers. Pronouns should agree with their antecedents in number and person. *Number* refers to whether a pronoun is singular or plural. *Person* tells to whom a pronoun refers—the one(s) speaking, the one(s) spoken to, or the one(s) spoken about.

Read It

These Launch Text sentences contain pronouns and their antecedents.

- *His problem with **the divorce article** was that **it** was not "fair and balanced."* **(third person singular)**
- *He felt it criticized **parents** without providing **their** side of the story.* **(third person plural)**

Write It

As you draft your problem-and-solution essay, make sure your pronouns agree with their antecedents in person and number. This chart may help you.

PERSON	NUMBER	PRONOUNS
First—the one speaking	Singular	*I, me, my, mine*
First—the ones speaking	Plural	*we, us, our, ours*
Second—the one spoken to	Singular	*you, your, yours*
Second—the ones spoken to	Plural	*you, your, yours*
Third—the one spoken about	Singular	*he, she, it, his, her, hers, its*
Third—the ones spoken about	Plural	*they, them, their, theirs*

Some **indefinite** pronouns—words that take the place of non-specific nouns or pronouns—can cause agreement problems.

- If the antecedent is a singular indefinite pronoun, use a singular personal pronoun to refer back to it. These indefinite pronouns are always singular: *another, anyone, anything, each, everybody, everything, little, much, nobody, nothing, one, other, someone, something*.

- If the antecedent is a plural indefinite pronoun, use a plural personal pronoun to refer back to it. These indefinite pronouns are always plural: *both, few, many, others, several*.

- If the antecedent can be either singular or plural, match the antecedent of the indefinite pronoun. These indefinite pronouns can be either singular or plural: *all, any, most, none, some*.

TIP

SPELLING

Make sure to spell pronouns correctly. Some are easily confused with other words or forms.

- *Your* refers to something that belongs to you. *You're* is a contraction for "you are."

- *Their* refers to something that belongs to them. *There* refers to a place.

- *Its* refers to something that belongs to it. *It's* is a contraction for "it is." There is no correct use of *its'*.

≡ STANDARDS

Language
- Demonstrate command of the conventions of standard English grammar and usage when writing or speaking.
- Demonstrate command of the conventions of standard English capitalization, punctuation, and spelling when writing.

c. Spell correctly.

Revising

Evaluating Your Draft

Use the following checklist to evaluate the effectiveness of your first draft. Then, use your evaluation and the instruction on this page to guide your revision.

FOCUS AND ORGANIZATION	EVIDENCE AND ELABORATION	CONVENTIONS
☐ Presents a clearly stated claim about a problem and proposed solution.	☐ Uses relevant, logical evidence and reasons to support the main claim.	☐ Attends to the norms and conventions of the discipline, especially correct pronoun-antecedent agreement.
☐ Organizes supporting reasons, evidence, and examples in a logical way.	☐ Addresses and refutes possible counterclaims.	
☐ Presents ideas in a clear and formal style.	☐ Includes language that clarifies how claims, counterclaims, and supporting details are related.	
☐ Includes a conclusion that supports the main argument.		

Revising for Focus and Organization

Maintain Formal Style Writers that propose solutions to important problems make sure that their **tone**—their attitude toward their subject—is earnest and serious. Their goal is to persuade readers that theirs is the best solution. Review your essay, and make sure your style and tone are formal and serious.

- Avoid informal expressions and slang words.
- Use precise words to help your readers grasp your ideas easily.
- Use humor sparingly. Overall, your style and tone should be serious.

Revising for Evidence and Elaboration

Use Relevant, Logical Evidence Make sure all of your reasons and evidence directly support your main claim.

To do so, review your essay and mark your claim. Then, mark each supporting reason for your claim. Finally, mark each piece of evidence that supports your reasons. Look at your marked-up essay to determine if some points need additional support. Consider eliminating any details that do not support your main claim or reasons.

WORD NETWORK

Include words from your Word Network in your argument.

STANDARDS

Writing
Write arguments to support claims with clear reasons and relevant evidence.

b. Support claim(s) with logical reasoning and relevant evidence, using accurate, credible sources and demonstrating an understanding of the topic or text.
d. Establish and maintain a formal style.

PEER REVIEW

Exchange essays with a classmate. Use the checklist to evaluate your classmate's problem-and-solution essays and provide supportive feedback.

1. Is the claim clearly stated, and does it propose a solution to a problem?

☐ yes ☐ no   If no, suggest how the writer might improve it.

2. Are the reasons and evidence logical and relevant?

☐ yes ☐ no   If no, explain what the author might add or remove.

3. Does the argument address counterclaims?

☐ yes ☐ no   If no, tell what you think might be missing.

4. What is the strongest part of your classmate's essay? Why?

Editing and Proofreading

Edit for Conventions Reread your draft for accuracy and consistency. Correct errors in grammar and word usage. Make sure all the pronouns you use agree in person and number with their antecedents.

Proofread for Accuracy Read your draft carefully, looking for errors in spelling and punctuation. As you proofread, watch out for **homophones**. A homophone is a word that sounds the same as another word but is spelled differently, such as *your* and *you're*, *there* and *their*, and *its* and *it's*.

Publishing and Presenting

Create a final version of your essay. Consider one of the following ways to share your essay:

- Post your essay online or on a bulletin board, along with the essays written by other class members. Read and comment on the essays of other class members, and respond to comments on your own essay.

- Ask your city, your school, or another local organization to help implement the solution to the problem suggested in your essay. Note any action taken and how well it worked.

Reflecting

Reflect on what you learned as you wrote your argument. What was the most challenging aspect of composing your argument? What did you learn from reviewing the work of others and discussing your argument with your classmates that might inform your writing process in the future?

☰ STANDARDS

Writing
- Produce clear and coherent writing in which the development, organization, and style are appropriate to task, purpose, and audience.
- With some guidance and support from peers and adults, develop and strengthen writing as needed by planning, revising, editing, rewriting, or trying a new approach, focusing on how well purpose and audience have been addressed.
- Use technology, including the Internet, to produce and publish writing and present the relationships between information and ideas efficiently as well as to interact and collaborate with others.

Language
Demonstrate command of the conventions of standard English capitalization, punctuation, and spelling when writing.
  c. Spell correctly.

ESSENTIAL QUESTION:

When is it right to take a stand?

What issues matter to you? Maybe they matter to other people, too. When you stand up for what you believe in, you may find that your action inspires others to act as well. In this section, you will work with your group to learn about individuals who took a stand in an effort to promote the greater good.

Small-Group Learning Strategies

Throughout your life, in school, in your community, and in your career, you will continue to learn and work with others.

Review these strategies and the actions you can take to practice them as you work in teams. Add ideas of your own for each step. Use these strategies during Small-Group Learning.

STRATEGY	ACTION PLAN
Prepare	• Complete your assignments so that you are prepared for group work. • Organize your thinking so you can contribute to your group's discussion. •
Participate fully	• Make eye contact to signal that you are listening and taking in what is being said. • Use text evidence when making a point. •
Support others	• Build on ideas from others in your group. • Invite others who have not yet spoken to do so. •
Clarify	• Paraphrase the ideas of others to ensure that your understanding is correct. • Ask follow-up questions. •

SCAN FOR
MULTIMEDIA

CONTENTS

Working as a Team

1. **Take a Position** In your group, discuss the following question:

   What are some character traits of people who stand up for their beliefs?

   As you take turns sharing your thoughts, be sure to provide examples. After all group members have shared, discuss the ways in which these character traits are demonstrated in the actions of those who stand up for their beliefs.

2. **List Your Rules** As a group, decide on the rules that you will follow as you work together. Two samples are provided; add two more of your own. You may add or revise rules based on your experience together.

   - Everyone should participate in group discussions.
   - People should not interrupt.

   - _____

     _____

   - _____

     _____

3. **Apply the Rules** Share what you have learned about taking a stand. Make sure each person in the group contributes. Take notes and be prepared to share with the class one thing that you heard from another member of your group.

4. **Name Your Group** Choose a name that reflects the unit topic.

   Our group's name: _____

5. **Create a Communication Plan** Decide how you want to communicate with one another. For example, you might use online collaboration tools, email, or instant messaging.

   Our group's decision: _____

   _____

Making a Schedule

First, find out the due dates for the small-group activities. Then, preview the texts and activities with your group and make a schedule for completing the tasks.

SELECTION	ACTIVITIES	DUE DATE
Words Do Not Pay		
from Follow the Rabbit-Proof Fence		
The Moth Presents: Aleeza Kazmi		

Working on Group Projects

As your group works together, you'll find it more effective if each person has a specific role. Different projects require different roles. Before beginning a project, discuss the necessary roles and choose one for each group member. Here are some possible roles; add your own ideas.

Project Manager: monitors the schedule and keeps everyone on task

Researcher: organizes research activities

Recorder: takes notes during group meetings

_____

_____

_____

_____

_____

_____

SCAN FOR
MULTIMEDIA

Chief Joseph was a famous leader of the Nez Percé tribe. He was known by his people as Hin-mah-too-yah-lat-kekt, or Thunder Rolling Down the Mountain. He was born in Wallowa Valley in 1840, in what is now Oregon. In 1877, when the U.S. government threatened to forcefully move the Nez Percé to a reservation, Chief Joseph refused, choosing instead to lead leading his people north toward Canada. Chief Joseph died in 1904, never having returned to the land he had fought so hard to keep for his tribe. His doctor said he died "of a broken heart."

Words Do Not Pay
Concept Vocabulary

You will encounter the following words as you read "Words Do Not Pay."

> misrepresentations   misunderstandings

Context Clues To find the meaning of an unfamiliar word, look for clues in the context, which consists of the other words that surround the unknown word in a text. If you are still unsure of the meaning, look up the word in a dictionary. Consider this example of how to apply the strategy.

> **Example:** Good words will neither return our land nor **restore** our way of life.
>
> **Analysis of Clues in the Text:** Good words will not return or *restore* something that has been taken.
>
> **Possible Meaning:** *Restore* means "to return or give back."

Apply your knowledge of context clues and other vocabulary strategies to determine the meanings of unfamiliar words you encounter during your first read of "Words Do Not Pay."

First Read NONFICTION

Apply these strategies as you conduct your first read. You will have an opportunity to complete a close read after your first read.

NOTICE the general idea of the speech. *What* is it about? *Who* is involved?

ANNOTATE by marking vocabulary and key passages you want to revisit.

First Read

CONNECT ideas within the selection to what you already know and what you have already read.

RESPOND by completing the Comprehension Check and by writing a brief summary of the speech.

Words Do Not Pay

Chief Joseph

SCAN FOR
MULTIMEDIA

BACKGROUND

In 1863, the Nez Percé tribe refused to sign a treaty that would make them move from their ancestral land in Oregon to a much smaller reservation in Idaho. Despite the refusal, the United States government sent in federal troops to force the Nez Percé off their land. In response, Chief Joseph led his people toward Canada in a three-month, 1600-mile flight across the Rocky Mountains. He eventually surrendered to General Miles in 1877, under the terms that his tribe could return to their homeland. Instead, the Nez Percé were sent to Oklahoma, and half of them died during the trip. In one of many appeals to Congress on behalf of his people, Chief Joseph made this speech in 1879 in Washington D.C.

1   I do not understand why nothing is done for my people. I have heard talk and talk, but nothing is done. Good words do not last long unless they amount to something. Words do not pay for my dead people. They

Mark context clues or indicate another strategy that helped you determine meaning.

misrepresentations (mihs rehp rih zehn TAY shuhnz) *n.*

MEANING:

misunderstandings (mihs uhn duhr STAND ihngz) *n.*

MEANING:

do not pay for my country, now overrun by white men. They do not protect my father's grave. They do not pay for all my horses and cattle. Good words will not give me back my children. Good words will not make good the promise of your war chief General Miles. Good words will not give my people good health and stop them from dying. Good words will not get my people a home where they can live in peace and take care of themselves. I am tired of talk that comes to nothing. It makes my heart sick when I remember all the good words and all the broken promises. There has been too much talking by men who had no right to talk. Too many **misrepresentations** have been made, too many **misunderstandings** have come up between the white men about the Indians. If the white man wants to live in peace with the Indian he can live in peace. There need be no trouble. Treat all men alike. Give them all the same law. Give them all an even chance to live and grow. All men were made by the same Great Spirit Chief. They are all brothers. The earth is the mother of all people, and all people should have equal rights upon it. You might as well expect the rivers to run backward as that any man who was born a free man should be contented when penned up and denied liberty to go where he pleases. . . .

2 Let me be a free man—free to travel, free to stop, free to work, free to trade where I choose, free to choose my own teachers, free to follow the religion of my fathers, free to think and talk and act for myself—and I will obey every law, or submit to the penalty. ❧

Comprehension Check

Complete these items after you finish your first read. Review and clarify details with your group.

1. What is one problem that Chief Joseph has with the "good words" of others?

2. According to Chief Joseph, what is one thing the white man needs to do to live in peace with the Indian?

3. According to Chief Joseph, what is one thing all men have in common?

4. What activities does Chief Joseph associate with being a "free man"?

5. 📒 **Notebook** Confirm your understanding of the speech by writing a summary.

- -

RESEARCH

Research to Clarify Choose at least one unfamiliar detail from the speech. Briefly research that detail. In what way does the information you learned shed light on an aspect of the speech?

Close Read the Text

With your group, revisit sections of the text you marked during your first read. **Annotate** details that you notice. What **questions** do you have? What can you **conclude**?

Analyze the Text

CITE TEXTUAL EVIDENCE
to support your answers.

⊟ Notebook **Complete the activities.**

1. **Review and Clarify** With your group, reread the speech. What do you think the author means when he claims that "words do not pay"? How does he use examples to support his claim?

2. **Present and Discuss** Share the passages from the text that you found important. Discuss what you noticed in the text, what questions you asked, and what conclusions you reached.

3. **Essential Question: *When is it right to take a stand?*** How is Chief Joseph taking a stand? Do you think his reasons for doing so are legitimate? Discuss with your group.

TIP

GROUP DISCUSSION

As you discuss the speech, make sure that everyone listens respectfully to each other's ideas.

⊞ WORD NETWORK

Add words related to taking a stand from the text to your Word Network.

LANGUAGE DEVELOPMENT

Concept Vocabulary

> misrepresentations   misunderstandings

Why These Words? The two concept vocabulary words from the text are related. With your group, discuss the words and identify a concept they have in common. How do these words enhance the impact of the text?

Practice

⊟ Notebook Confirm your understanding of the concept vocabulary words by using each one in a sentence.

Word Study

⊟ Notebook **Old English Prefix: *mis-*** The Old English prefix *mis-* means "opposite," "badly," or "wrongly." When added to a word, it creates an opposing or contrasting meaning. In his speech, Chief Joseph refers to "misrepresentations," or wrong representations, of Indians. Using your knowledge of the prefix *mis-*, answer the following questions.

- What might happen if you have a *miscommunication* as to the time you are meeting a friend?
- What can happen if you *misread* the instructions for a recipe?

☰ STANDARDS

Reading Informational Text
Determine the meaning of words and phrases as they are used in a text, including figurative, connotative, and technical meanings; analyze the impact of specific word choices on meaning and tone, including analogies or allusions to other texts.

Language
• Determine or clarify the meaning of unknown and multiple-meaning words or phrases based on *grade 8 reading and content*, choosing flexibly from a range of strategies.
• Demonstrate understanding of figurative language, word relationships, and nuances in word meanings.
  c. Distinguish among the connotations of words with similar denotations.

Analyze Craft and Structure

Persuasive Techniques and Word Choice Writers use persuasive techniques in an argument to lead an audience to agree with them. These are some of the persuasive techniques that writers use:

- **Repetition** consists of saying something repeatedly for effect.
- **Appeals to reason** invite the audience to use logic as they draw conclusions from the evidence presented by the writer.
- **Appeals to emotions** attempt to persuade readers by triggering their feelings about a subject.
- **Appeals to authority** are references to expert opinions.

A writer's **word choice** includes not only individual words but also the phrases and expressions the writer uses. Word choice can convey **tone**— the writer's attitude toward the topic or audience. These factors influence word choice:

- the writer's intended audience and purpose
- the **denotations** of words, or their dictionary definitions
- the **connotations** of words, or their negative or positive associations (For example, *assertive* and *pushy* have similar denotations but different connotations.)

A writer's word choice and tone can contribute to the power of the argument he or she presents. The denotations and connotations of the words a writer chooses as well as the phrases and expressions he or she includes in an argument can impact the effectiveness of persuasive techniques. For example, a writer may choose to create repetition in an argument using words with specific connotations in order to appeal to a specific audience.

TIP

CLARIFICATION
Consulting a dictionary for a word's denotation will help you grasp the difference between a word's precise meaning and the meaning suggested by its connotations.

Practice

CITE TEXTUAL EVIDENCE to support your answers.

🗐 **Notebook** Use a chart like this one to analyze Chief Joseph's persuasive techniques. Then, share your chart with your group, and discuss any different examples you have noted.

WORDS DO NOT PAY	
PERSUASIVE TECHNIQUE	EXAMPLES
repetition	
appeal to reason	
appeal to emotion	
appeal to authority	

Now, work as a group to identify words, phrases, and expressions in the examples that contribute to Chief Joseph's word choice and convey his tone. Then, discuss whether Chief Joseph's word choice and tone are effective and persuasive.

WORDS DO NOT PAY

© Pearson Education, Inc., or its affiliates. All rights reserved.

Author's Style

Rhetorical Devices Parallelism is the use of similar grammatical forms or patterns to express similar ideas within a sentence. Parallelism adds rhythm and balance to writing and strengthens the connections among an author's ideas.

Writing without parallelism produces awkward, distracting shifts for readers. By contrast, parallel constructions place ideas of equal weight in words, phrases, or clauses of similar types.

> **Nonparallel:** Dress codes are less restrictive, less costly, and are not a controversial system.

> **Parallel:** Dress codes are less restrictive, less costly, and less controversial.

SAMPLE PARALLEL FORMS	
modified nouns	bright eyes, large hands, strong fingers
verb forms	to ask, to learn, to share
phrases	under a gray sky, near an icy river
adverb clauses	when I am happy, when I am peaceful
adjective clauses	who read with care, who act with concern

Read It

Work with your group to identify examples of parallelism in Chief Joseph's speech "Words Do Not Pay." Underline the parallel constructions of words, phrases, and clauses throughout the speech. Then, discuss with your group the ways in which Chief Joseph's use of parallelism creates rhythm and balance in the speech. How do his parallel constructions strengthen the connections between his ideas? Does the use of parallelism make his argument stronger and more persuasive?

Write It

Write three sentences about the speech in which you correctly use parallelism.

STANDARDS

Writing
• Write informative/explanatory texts to examine a topic and convey ideas, concepts, and information through the selection, organization, and analysis of relevant content.
  a. Introduce a topic clearly, previewing what is to follow; organize ideas, concepts, and information into broader categories; include formatting, graphics, and multimedia when useful to aiding comprehension.
  b. Develop the topic with relevant, well-chosen facts, definitions, concrete details, quotations, or other information and examples.
  f. Provide a concluding statement or section that follows from and supports the information or explanation presented.
• Conduct short research projects to answer a question, drawing on several sources and generating additional related, focused questions that allow for multiple avenues of exploration.
• Gather relevant information from multiple print and digital sources, using search terms effectively; assess the credibility and accuracy of each source; and quote or paraphrase the data and conclusions of others while avoiding plagiarism and following a standard format for citation.

Language
• Demonstrate command of the conventions of standard English grammar and usage when writing or speaking.
• Use knowledge of language and its conventions when writing, speaking, reading, or listening.

Research

> ## Assignment
>
> Work with your group to create a **research report** about Chief Joseph or the Nez Percé people. In your report, analyze the ways in which the topic your group chooses contributes to your understanding of Chief Joseph's argument. Choose one of the following topics:
>
> ☐ a **historical report** on the history of the Nez Percé tribe, including information about their beliefs and culture
>
> ☐ a **biographical report** on the life of Chief Joseph, including his upbringing and influences

Assign Tasks Use the chart to assign tasks for each group member.

TASK	GROUP MEMBER(S)	COMPLETED
Search for and take notes on reliable sources.		
Organize the information.		
Write the report.		
Proofread and edit the report.		

Conduct Research As you conduct research, follow these guidelines:

- When researching online, choose search terms that are specific and unique to your topic. General terms may have more than one meaning, and therefore may produce unhelpful results.

- Make sure the sources you find are relevant and reliable, and take detailed notes to use in your bibliography or Works Cited page.

- Include information from several different sources. Do not rely solely on one source, even if it is a credible one.

- **Paraphrase,** or restate, information from sources, and note **direct quotations,** that are particularly powerful. Remember to put direct quotations in quotation marks to indicate that they are the exact words of another writer.

Organize Your Report Organize the information from your research logically. For example, in a historical or biographical report, you may choose to present information about events and experiences in **chronological order**, or the order in which the events happened. Conclude your report by reflecting on the ways in which the knowledge you gained from your research helped you to better understand the Chief Joseph's speech.

 EVIDENCE LOG

Before moving on to a new selection, go to your Evidence Log, and record what you learned from "Words Do Not Pay."

About the Author

Doris Pilkington (1937–2014) was an Aboriginal author best known for her nonfiction narrative *Follow the Rabbit-Proof Fence*, based on her mother's 1931 escape from the Moore River Mission. Under the Aborigines Act (1906–1954), approximately 100,000 children were removed from their tribal lands and placed in the care of the state. In 1940, when she was three-and-a-half years old, Doris became one of these children.

from Follow the Rabbit-Proof Fence

Concept Vocabulary

As you conduct your first read of the excerpt from *Follow the Rabbit-Proof Fence,* you will encounter these words.

urgently	nervously	confidently	cautiously

Using a Dictionary and Thesaurus If a word is unfamiliar to you and you cannot understand the meaning from the context, look up the word in a dictionary or thesaurus. Most **dictionaries**, whether print or online, will provide the meaning of the word, its part of speech, its pronunciation, and its etymology. A **thesaurus**, on the other hand, will not provide definitions but will include synonyms of the word, or words with similar meanings. For instance, compare these two entries for the word *crimson*.

Dictionary

crim•son (KRIHM zuhn) *adj.* red in color

Thesaurus

crimson *adj.* dark red, bloody, cherry, scarlet, rosy, cardinal, ruby

Apply your knowledge of using a dictionary and thesaurus as well as other vocabulary strategies to determine the meanings of unfamiliar words you encounter during your first read.

First Read NONFICTION

Apply these strategies as you conduct your first read. You will have an opportunity to complete a close read after your first read.

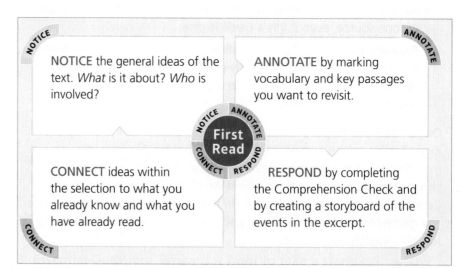

NOTICE the general ideas of the text. *What* is it about? *Who* is involved?

ANNOTATE by marking vocabulary and key passages you want to revisit.

CONNECT ideas within the selection to what you already know and what you have already read.

RESPOND by completing the Comprehension Check and by creating a storyboard of the events in the excerpt.

STANDARDS

Reading Informational Text
By the end of the year, read and comprehend literary nonfiction at the high end of the grades 6–8 text complexity band independently and proficiently.

Language
Determine or clarify the meaning of unknown and multiple-meaning words or phrases based on *grade 8 reading and content,* choosing flexibly from a range of strategies.

c. Consult general and specialized reference materials, both print and digital, to find the pronunciation of a word or determine or clarify its precise meaning or its part of speech.

from Follow the Rabbit-Proof Fence

Doris Pilkington

BACKGROUND

Aboriginal Australians are the native people of the Australian continent. From 1910 to 1970, many children of mixed Aboriginal and white descent were taken from their families by the government in an effort to train them to fit into white Australian culture. *Follow the Rabbit-Proof Fence* is a nonfiction narrative account of three Mardu Aboriginal girls who escaped a government settlement in 1931 to return home. The Mardu are the indigenous, or native, people of the Australian desert.

SCAN FOR MULTIMEDIA

1   The other girls were now getting ready for school, and the three watched quietly amidst all the activity. Bossing and bullying was everywhere around them and there were cries and squeals of, "Don't, you're hurting my head," as the tangled knots were combed out with tiny, fragile combs.

2   "Oh, Mummy, Daddy, Mummy, Daddy, my head," yelled a young girl, who stamped her feet and tried to pull away from her torturer, an older, well-built girl who seemed to have adopted the girl as her baby sister. They performed this ritual together every morning before school.

3   "Come on, you girls," ordered Martha Jones as she passed by their bed. "The school bell's gone. Don't be late on your first day."

4   "Alright, we're coming as soon as we empty the toilet bucket," answered Molly softly.

5   "I'll wait for you then," said Martha.

6   "No, don't wait we'll follow you, we know where the school is."

7   "Alright then, we'll go along. Come on, Rosie," she said as she rushed out of the door into the cold, drizzly morning.

8   As soon as the other girls left the dormitory, Molly beckoned her two sisters to come closer to her, then she whispered **urgently**, "We're not going to school, so grab your bags. We're not staying here." Daisy and Gracie were stunned and stood staring at her.

9   "What did you say?" asked Gracie.

10   "I said, we're not staying here at the settlement, because we're going home to Jigalong."[1]

NOTES

Use a dictionary or a thesaurus or indicate another strategy you used to help you determine meaning.

urgently (UR juhnt lee) *adv.*

MEANING:

---

1. **Jigalong** *n.* region in Western Australia where the Mardu Aboriginal people live.

Use a dictionary or a thesaurus or indicate another strategy you used to help you determine meaning.

nervously (NUR vuhs lee) *adv.*

MEANING:

confidently (KON fuh dehnt lee) *adv.*

MEANING:

11 Gracie and Daisy weren't sure whether they were hearing correctly or not.

12 "Move quickly," Molly ordered her sisters. She wanted to be miles away before their absence was discovered. Time was of the essence.

13 Her two young sisters faced each other, both looking very scared and confused. Daisy turned to Molly and said **nervously**, "We're frightened, Dgudu.[2] How are we going to find our way back home to Jigalong? It's a long way from home."

14 Molly leaned against the wall and said **confidently**, "I know it's a long way to go but it's easy. We'll find the rabbit-proof fence[3] and follow that all the way home."

15 "We gunna walk all the way?" asked Daisy.

16 "Yeah," replied Molly, getting really impatient now. "So don't waste time."

17 The task of finding the rabbit-proof fence seemed like a simple solution for a teenager whose father was an inspector who traveled up and down the fences, and whose grandfather had worked with him. Thomas Craig told her often enough that the fence stretched from coast to coast, south to north across the country. It was just a matter of locating a stretch of it then following it to Jigalong. The two youngsters trusted their big sister because she was not only the eldest but she had always been the bossy one who made all the decisions at home. So they did the normal thing and said, "Alright, Dgudu, we'll run away with you."

18 They snatched up their meager possessions and put them into calico bags and pulled the long drawstrings and slung them around their necks. Each one put on two dresses, two pairs of calico bloomers, and a coat.

19 Gracie and Daisy were about to leave when Molly told them to, "Wait. Take those coats off. Leave them here."

20 "Why?" asked Gracie.

21 "Because they're too heavy to carry."

22 The three sisters checked to make sure they hadn't missed anything then, when they were absolutely satisfied, Molly grabbed the galvanized bucket and ordered Gracie to get hold of the other side and walk quickly trying not to spill the contents as they made their way to the lavatories. Daisy waited under the large pine tree near the stables. She reached up and broke a small twig that was hanging down low and was examining it closely when the other two joined her.

---

2. **Dgudu** older sister in Mardudjara, the Mardu Aborigines' native language.
3. **the rabbit-proof fence** fence that ran from the north coast of Australia to the south coast to deter pests such as rabbits.

23   "Look, Dgudu, like grass indi?[4]" asked Daisy, passing the twig to Molly to feel.

24   "Youay,"[5] she said, as she gave it to Gracie who crushed the green pine needles into her small hands and sniffed them. She liked the smell and was about to give her opinion when Molly reminded them that they didn't have time to stand around examining pine needles.

25   "Come on, run, you two," she said sharply as she started to run towards the river.

26   Many young people had stood under the same big pine tree and waited while someone went into the stable or the garage to distract Maitland, the caretaker and stableman. Then they would give the signal that the coast was clear and everyone would dash into the grainary and fill their empty fruit tins with wheat from one of the opened bags at the back of the shed. Some of it was roasted on flat tins over the hot coals, the rest was saved to fill initials that had been dug into the sloping embankment of firm yellow sand along the cliffs. These were left until the first rain came, then all the inmates would rush down to inspect the cliffs. This grass graffiti revealed the new summer romances between the older boys and girls. But these three girls from the East Pilbara had no intention of participating, they had a more important task ahead of them.

27   On they went, dashing down the sandy slope of the cliffs, dodging the small shrubs on the way and following the narrow path to the flooded river. They slowed down only when they reached the bottom. Molly paused briefly, glancing at the pumping shed on their right where they had been the day before. Turning towards it she said to Gracie and Daisy, "This way." She ran for about 25 meters, crashing into the thick paperbark trees and the branches of the river gums that blocked their path.

28   Molly strode on as best as she could along the muddy banks, pausing only to urge her young sisters to hurry up and try to keep up with her. She kept up that pace until she saw what she thought to be a likely spot to cross the swift flowing river.

29   The three girls watched the swirling currents and the white and brown frothy foam that clung to the trunks of the young river gums and clumps of tea-trees. They didn't know that this became one of the most popular spots during the hot summer days. This was the local swimming pool that would be filled with naked or semi-naked brown bodies, laughing, splashing, swimming and diving into the cool brown water during the long summer afternoons. Every now and then, the swimmers would sit on the coarse river sand and yank ugly, brown, slimy leeches off

4. **indi?** "isn't it?" (Mardudjara).
5. **Youay** "Yes" (Mardudjara).

their bodies and impale them on sticks and turn them inside out and plunge them into the hot burning mud. The next day the swimmers would pull the sticks out of the sand and gloat at the shriveled dry skins that once were horrible little creatures, ready to suck all the blood from their bodies—or so the young people were led to believe.

30   "The river is too deep and fast here, let's try up further," Molly said, leading the way through the thick young suckers and washed-up logs. They continued along the bank making slow progress through the obstacles that nature had left in their path. At last they came to a section in the river that seemed narrow enough to cross.

31   "We'll try here," said Molly as she bent down to pick up a long stick. She slid down the bank into the river and began measuring its depth just as she had seen Edna Green do the previous afternoon, while Daisy and Gracie watched patiently on the bank.

32   "Nah, too deep," Molly said in disgust. "Not here."

33   "Gulu,[6] Dgudu," cried the youngsters as they ran to follow her through the wet foliage.

34   The three girls walked along the muddy banks for another 25 meters when they came to a clearing, devoid of any shrubs or young suckers, where the floods had receded.

35   In a couple of weeks' time, this place would become a muddy skating rink where the girls of the settlement would spend hours having fun skating up and down the slippery mud. The idea was to skate by placing one foot in front of the other and maintain your balance for a couple of meters at least. The boys had their own skating area further up in a more secluded place amongst the thick tea-tree shrub. Peeping toms never existed in those days. Each group respected each other's privacy. Nearby, a huge fire would be lit and kept stoked. When everyone had finished skating in the slippery mud they would dive into the icy cold river to wash off the mud, then dry themselves by the roaring fire, dress, and return to the compound.

36   Molly decided to follow the paths made by the cattle. Another attempt was made to cross the river but once again proved unsuccessful. She walked on angrily, pushing the thick growth of eucalyptus suckers roughly aside, at the same time urging Daisy and Gracie to walk faster. But they decided that it was much safer at a distance and they followed her muddy footprints in silence without any questions, trusting her leadership totally.

37   They were still fighting their way through the tea-trees for almost an hour when they heard Molly call out to them somewhere down the track. "Yardini! Bukala! Bukala!"[7]

---

6. **Gulu** "wait" (Mardudjara).
7. **Yardini! Bukala! Bukala!** "Come here! Hurry! Hurry!" (Mardudjara).

38   Daisy and Gracie ran as fast as they could along the muddy path until they reached her. Molly was standing near a large river gum. As they stood gasping for wind she said, "We gunna cross here."

39   As three pairs of eager eyes examined it closely, they knew that they had found the perfect place to cross the flooded river. A tree leaned over the water creating a natural bridge for them to cross safely to the other side.

40   The girls scraped mud from their feet then climbed onto the trunk and walked **cautiously** to the end then swung down off the limb onto the slippery, muddy bank on the other side. They sloshed through the wet, chocolate-colored banks for at least another two hours, then decided to rest amongst the thick reeds behind the tall river gums.

41   A few minutes later, Molly stood up and told her young sisters to get up. "We go kyalie[8] now all the way." They obeyed without any protests. Ducking under the hanging branches of the paperbark trees they hurried as best they could, stomping on the reeds and bull rushes that covered the banks of the fast flowing river. The only sounds that could be heard were the startled birds fluttering above as they left their nests in fright, and the *slish, slosh* of the girls' feet as they trampled over the bull rushes. ❧

8. **kyalie** "north" (Mardudjara).

NOTES

Use a dictionary or a thesaurus or indicate another strategy you used to help you determine meaning.

cautiously (KAW shuhs lee) *adv.*

MEANING:

Comprehension Check

Complete the following items after you finish your first read. Review and clarify details with your group.

1. At the beginning of the excerpt, where are the three sisters living?

2. Where does Molly want to go?

3. How does Molly know about the rabbit-proof fence?

4. What does Molly try to avoid when looking for a place to cross the river?

5. 🗐 **Notebook** Confirm your understanding of the excerpt by creating a storyboard of events.

RESEARCH

Research to Clarify Choose at least one unfamiliar detail in the text. Briefly research that detail. In what way does the information you learned shed light on an aspect of the narrative?

Close Read the Text

With your group, revisit sections of the text you marked during your first read. **Annotate** details that you noticed. What **questions** do you have? What can you **conclude**?

Analyze the Text

CITE TEXTUAL EVIDENCE
to support your answers.

📓 **Notebook** Complete the activities.

1. **Review and Clarify** With your group, reread paragraph 17 of the selection. What important information about the three girls is conveyed? What is the author saying about the way the girls relate to one another?

2. **Present and Discuss** Now, work with your group to share the passages from the text that you found especially important. Take turns presenting your passages. Discuss what you noticed in the text, what questions you asked, and what conclusions you reached.

TIP

GROUP DISCUSSION

As you discuss the nonfiction narrative, ask questions that help other group members elaborate on their ideas.

🔗 **WORD NETWORK**

Add words related to taking a stand from the text to your Word Network.

☰ **STANDARDS**

Reading Informational Text
• Determine the meaning of words and phrases as they are used in a text, including figurative, connotative, and technical meanings; analyze the impact of specific word choices on meaning and tone, including analogies or allusions to other texts.
• Analyze in detail the structure of a specific paragraph in a text, including the role of particular sentences in developing and refining a key concept.
• Determine an author's point of view or purpose in a text and analyze how the author acknowledges and responds to conflicting evidence or viewpoints.

Language
Demonstrate understanding of figurative language, word relationships, and nuances in word meanings.

LANGUAGE DEVELOPMENT

Concept Vocabulary

| urgently | nervously | confidently | cautiously |

Why These Words? The concept vocabulary words from the text are related. With your group, determine what the words have in common. How do these words enhance the impact of the text?

Practice

📓 **Notebook** Confirm your understanding of the vocabulary words by using them in sentences.

Word Study

Old English Suffix: -ly The Old English suffix *-ly* is often used to make an adjective into an **adverb,** or a word that describes how, when, or how often something is done. For example, adding the suffix *-ly* to the adjective *urgent* creates the adverb *urgently*. In the excerpt, Molly whispers *urgently* to the other girls because the situation requires immediate action. Use a dictionary to find the precise meanings of the other three concept vocabulary words, which all end with the suffix *-ly*. Then, write a sentence or two explaining how the suffix *-ly* contributes to the meaning of each vocabulary word.

Analyze Craft and Structure

Descriptive Writing A **description** is a portrait in words of a person, place, or thing. Descriptive writing uses **sensory details,** or language that appeals to the senses: sight, hearing, taste, smell, and touch. Effective description helps readers visualize settings, events, and characters clearly. It also helps convey emotions and ideas. Authors use description to emphasize a point of view and to create mood in a literary work.

TIP

CLARIFICATION
As you analyze descriptive writing, consider the ways in which an author's descriptions contribute to the development of his or her ideas.

- An author's **point of view** is his or her perspective or unique way of viewing a topic. Point of view is shaped by the author's knowledge, beliefs, and experiences. Description helps to convey that point of view because it shows more than just what a subject looks like. It reveals *how* the author sees the subject.
- **Mood** is the overall feeling created in a reader by a literary work. The mood of a work can typically be described using emotion words, such as *joyous, gloomy, peaceful,* or *frightening*. Some literary works convey a single mood. In other works, the mood changes within the selection.

Practice

CITE TEXTUAL EVIDENCE
to support your answers.

Analyze how the author's use of description reveals his or her point of view and creates a specific mood, or emotional atmosphere, in the excerpt. Note words and phrases from the text that support your analysis. Use the chart to capture your observations.

PASSAGE	POINT OF VIEW	MOOD

from Follow the Rabbit-Proof Fence **321**

from FOLLOW THE
RABBIT-PROOF FENCE

Conventions

Adjectives and Adverbs Authors use **adjectives** and **adverbs** to tell more about the nouns and verbs in their sentences. An adjective modifies, or adds meaning to, a noun or a pronoun. An adverb modifies a verb, an adjective, or another adverb.

An adjective gives more information about a noun. For example, in the sentence *It's a long way from home*, the adjective *long* modifies the noun *way*. It answers the question *What kind (of way)?* Look at the chart to see examples of questions that adjectives answer.

What kind?	cold, long, easy, muddy, simple
Which one?	that, this, those
How many?	two, many, three
How much?	most, some, meager, huge
Whose?	her, their, my, your

An adverb gives more information about a verb, adjective, or another adverb. For example, in the sentence *She whispered urgently,* the adverb *urgently* modifies the verb *whispered*, answering the question *In what manner (did she whisper)?* Look at the chart to see examples of questions that adverbs answer. Note that adverbs often end in the suffix *-ly*.

When?	now, before, yesterday
Where?	everywhere, here, ahead
In what manner?	quietly, playfully, correctly, well
To what extent?	too, absolutely, totally

Be careful not to use adjectives in place of adverbs, as shown in this example: **Incorrect:** Move quick. **Correct:** Move quickly.

Read It

1. Work individually. Underline the adjective in each sentence.
   a. They did the normal thing.

   b. They dashed down the sandy slopes.

2. Correct each sentence by replacing the adjective with an adverb.
   a. Molly spoke soft.

   b. Daisy tried to walk careful.

Write It

🖥 **Notebook** Write a short paragraph about the excerpt. Use at least two adjectives and two adverbs in your paragraph.

STANDARDS
Language
Demonstrate command of the conventions of standard English grammar and usage when writing or speaking.

Writing to Sources

Assignment

Work individually to write a **fictional retelling** of the excerpt from *Follow the Rabbit-Proof Fence* from the perspective of Molly, Daisy, or Gracie. If needed, conduct research to find out more information to help you create a vivid picture for your readers. Choose from the following topics:

- [ ] Write a **journal entry** from the perspective of the character you chose. Include the events and experiences detailed in the excerpt as well as your reflections on these events and experiences—were you afraid? frustrated? sad?

- [ ] Write a **letter** to one of the girls still living at the government settlement. Use details from the excerpt to describe how you escaped, the challenges of doing so, and the obstacles you encountered on your journey. Also, include your reflections on these events and experiences—were you nervous? confident? happy?

Establish Your Point of View Decide from which character's point of view you will write. Then, use the **first-person point of view** to retell the story. This means that your character participates in the story, relates events from her perspective, and uses the first-person pronouns *I, me, us,* and *we.* Draw on details from the text to represent your narrator vividly and accurately.

Conduct Additional Research To make the events and experiences in your retelling come alive for readers, briefly research topics that will help you better understand the setting and characters. For example, conduct research on life in the Australian Outback, the natural environment and wildlife of Australia, and techniques people use to survive in the wilderness.

Compare Your Retellings Once you have completed drafting, share your retelling with your group. Compare the ways in which your retellings are similar and different. Are you surprised at the way other members portrayed certain characters? Comment on each other's retellings, and offer ideas that will help others to improve their narratives:

- Did the character's actions and reactions make sense to you based on the details in the excerpt?
- Are there things that you found confusing or that did not align with your understanding of the excerpt?

Use the feedback from your group members to revise your retelling before handing it in to your teacher.

✍ EVIDENCE LOG

Before moving on to a new selection, go to your Evidence Log, and record what you learned from *Follow the Rabbit-Proof Fence.*

☰ STANDARDS

Writing

• Write narratives to develop real or imagined experiences or events using effective techniques, relevant descriptive details, and well-structured event sequences.

  a. Engage and orient the reader by establishing a context and point of view and introducing a narrator and/or characters; organize an event sequence that unfolds naturally and logically.

  b. Use narrative techniques, such as dialogue, pacing, description, and reflection, to develop experiences, events, and/or characters.

  d. Use precise words and phrases, relevant descriptive details, and sensory language to capture the action and convey experiences and events.

• With some guidance and support from peers and adults, develop and strengthen writing as needed by planning, revising, editing, rewriting, or trying a new approach, focusing on how well purpose and audience have been addressed.

• Conduct short research projects to answer a question, drawing on several sources and generating additional related, focused questions that allow for multiple avenues of exploration.

About the Speaker

Aleeza Kazmi is a student who attended the Beacon School in New York City. She intends to major in Journalism and Political Science. In her spare time, Aleeza can be found with her friends or in her backyard with her dogs.

The Moth Presents: Aleeza Kazmi

Media Vocabulary

These words will be useful to you as you analyze, discuss, and write about the video.

performance: entertainment presented before an audience, such as music or a drama	• Storytelling is the oldest form of performance art. • A storyteller can perform live or on a recording, from notes or without notes. • Stories can be rehearsed or improvised.
personal account: account of a personal experience, told from the first-person point of view	• A personal account can be written, performed live, or recorded. • When telling about a personal experience in front of a live audience, the storyteller (and audience) can get caught up in emotion.
volume and pacing: softness or loudness of one's voice and the rate at which one speaks (e.g., quickly or slowly)	• A speaker may vary the volume of his or her voice to convey emotion and to keep the audience's attention. • During a performance, a speaker may change his or her pacing by pausing, speeding up, or slowing down to emphasize ideas or express emotion.

First Review MEDIA: VIDEO

Apply these strategies as you conduct your first review. You will have an opportunity to complete a close review after your first review.

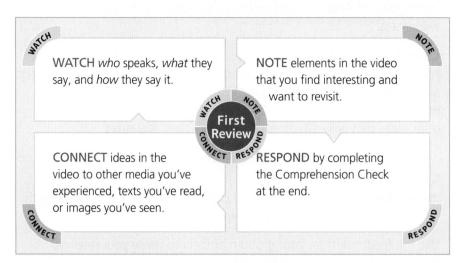

WATCH *who* speaks, *what* they say, and *how* they say it.

NOTE elements in the video that you find interesting and want to revisit.

CONNECT ideas in the video to other media you've experienced, texts you've read, or images you've seen.

RESPOND by completing the Comprehension Check at the end.

☷ STANDARDS

Reading Informational Text
By the end of the year, read and comprehend literary nonfiction at the high end of the grades 6–8 text complexity band independently and proficiently.

Language
Acquire and use accurately grade-appropriate general academic and domain-specific words and phrases; gather vocabulary knowledge when considering a word or phrase important to comprehension or expression.

The Moth Presents: Aleeza Kazmi

BACKGROUND

The Moth is a nonprofit organization devoted to the art and craft of storytelling. Established in 1997, The Moth has featured thousands of stories that showcase a wide range of human experiences. The Moth's storytellers present their narratives live and without notes to standing-room-only crowds throughout the world. Each of The Moth's shows centers around a different theme, which the featured storytellers explore in distinct, and often unexpected, ways. Some of the storytellers are experienced in the art and craft of narration, whereas others have never told a story in performance before. The stories featured in The Moth's shows are recorded for broadcast and can be heard on many National Public Radio radio stations.

SCAN FOR
MULTIMEDIA

NOTES

Comprehension Check

Complete the following items after you finish your first review. Review and clarify details with your group.

1. Why was Aleeza excited about the self-portrait project?

2. Why did she think peach was a good color to use?

3. What did Miss Harrington do that upset Aleeza?

4. How does Aleeza finally take a stand?

MEDIA VOCABULARY

Use these words as you discuss and write about the video.

performance
personal account
volume and pacing

WORD NETWORK

Add interesting words related to taking a stand from the text to your Word Network.

STANDARDS
Speaking and Listening
Analyze the purpose of information presented in diverse media and formats and evaluate the motives behind its presentation.

Close Review

Watch the video, or parts of it, again. Write down any new observations that seem important. What **questions** do you have? What can you **conclude**?

Analyze the Media

📄 **Notebook** Complete the activities.

1. **Present and Discuss** Choose the section of the video you found most interesting or powerful. Explain what you noticed in the section, what questions it raised for you, and what conclusions you reached about it.

2. **Review and Synthesize** With your group, review the video. What do you think Aleeza's purpose was in telling her story? How does Aleeza's sincerity in her storytelling help viewers understand her perspective and her experience?

3. **Essential Question:** *When is it right to take a stand?* What has this video taught you about taking a stand? Discuss with your group.

Speaking and Listening

THE MOTH PRESENTS:
ALEEZA KAZMI

Assignment

Take part in a **group discussion** about Aleeza Kazmi's story. Choose from the following topics:

☐ How does Kazmi's story support the idea that it is important to stand up for yourself and your beliefs?

☐ How does Kazmi's story support the idea that each person should be able to determine her or his own identity?

Prepare for the Discussion To prepare for the discussion, review the video and take notes on the following aspects:

- sections of the video in which Kazmi discusses specific central ideas that are relevant to your discussion topic
- ideas that Kazmi **implies**, or suggests, but does not state directly
- descriptive details that Kazmi uses to develop her story and capture her audience's attention
- **direct quotations**, or Kazmi's exact words, that are related to your discussion topic
- the ways in which Kazmi delivers her story—changes in her tone that indicate emotion, emphasis she places on specific words or phrases, key points she repeats for emphasis

Review your notes and consider the ways in which Kazmi deals will both the internal and external conflicts created by her experience. An **internal conflict** takes place in a person's mind, as when he or she is struggling with opposing feelings. An **external conflict** takes place between a person and an outside force, such as another person or the environment with which they are surrounded. Consider how Kazmi's conflicts and the ways in which she resolves them relate to your discussion topic.

During the Discussion Listen to the ideas of other members of your group and consider the ways in which they are similar to and different from your own. To connect your own ideas with the ideas of other group members, ask questions that help to clarify the relationship between the different ideas expressed. Use your notes to support your ideas when responding to questions from other group members. Don't be afraid to change your ideas or views if another group member offers new thoughts or information that you agree with, provided that the ideas are well supported with evidence.

✒ EVIDENCE LOG

Before moving on to a new selection, go to your Evidence Log, and record what you learned from "The Moth Presents: Aleeza Kazmi."

▦ STANDARDS

Speaking and Listening
- Engage effectively in a range of collaborative discussions with diverse partners on *grade 8 topics, texts, and issues*, building on others' ideas and expressing their own clearly.

   a. Come to discussions prepared, having read or researched material under study; explicitly draw on that preparation by referring to evidence on the topic, text, or issue to probe and reflect on ideas under discussion.
   c. Pose questions that connect the ideas of several speakers and respond to others' questions and comments with relevant evidence, observations, and ideas.
   d. Acknowledge new information expressed by others, and, when warranted, qualify or justify their own views in light of the evidence presented.

- Analyze the purpose of information presented in diverse media and formats and evaluate the motives behind its presentation.

SOURCES

• WORDS DO NOT PAY

• *from* FOLLOW THE RABBIT-PROOF FENCE

• THE MOTH PRESENTS: ALEEZA KAZMI

Deliver an Oral Presentation

Assignment

The selections in this section present people who took a stand, often against hopeless odds. Each one demonstrates courage and determination. Their efforts, however, are not always successful. They raise questions about ideas of winning and losing when one acts on principle. Work with your group to prepare and deliver an **oral presentation** in response to this question:

When you take a stand, how much does winning matter?

STANDARDS

Speaking and Listening
Engage effectively in a range of collaborative discussions with diverse partners on *grade 8 topics, texts, and issues,* building on others' ideas and expressing their own clearly.
a. Come to discussions prepared, having read or researched material under study; explicitly draw on that preparation by referring to evidence on the topic, text, or issue to probe and reflect on ideas under discussion.

Plan With Your Group

Analyze the Texts All of the people featured in the Small-Group readings took a stand in words, actions, or both. In each case, the people or group they opposed were powerful, and the odds of success in opposing them were low. Review the texts and think about what was at stake for Chief Joseph, the three Mardu sisters, and Aleeza Kami. Consider how these people or groups probably viewed their chances of success and why they chose to take a stand. With your group, discuss your observations and ideas, and note them in the chart.

TITLE	WHOM/WHAT THEY OPPOSED AND CHANCES OF SUCCESS
Words Do Not Pay	
from Follow the Rabbit-Proof Fence	
The Moth Presents: Aleeza Kazmi	

Determine Your Position and Gather Evidence As you discuss the texts, work toward a consensus about the position you will present. Will you argue that taking a stand is valuable, even if the result is failure? Or will you argue that people should measure the possibility of success before taking a stand against something? Use evidence from the texts to support your claims. Identify passages to quote directly, details to paraphrase, and situations to summarize and use as examples.

Organize Your Ideas. As a group, organize the script for your skit. Each member of the group should play a character who expresses his or her ideas in response to the question "What can you learn from people who have chosen to take a stand?" Each character should present evidence from the text to support his or her points.

TASK	ASSIGNED TO

Rehearse With Your Group

Practice With Your Group Practice delivering your oral presentation. Then, use this checklist to evaluate the effectiveness of your first run-through. If you need to improve the content, rewrite or reorganize the material. If you need to improve the delivery, practice again, speaking clearly and with energy and expression.

CONTENT	PRESENTATION TECHNIQUES
☐ Claims and evidence are presented clearly and in a logical order.	☐ Each speaker presents with energy, enthusiasm, and expression.
☐ Claims and reasons are effectively supported with textual evidence.	☐ Speakers do not rush through the presentation, nor do they speak too slowly.
☐ The content engages viewers' interest from start to finish.	☐ Speakers behave with an appropriate level of formality.
☐ Transitions from section to section are smooth.	

Fine-Tune the Content To make your oral presentation stronger, you may need to reorder ideas, add or change supporting reasons, or replace evidence. Review the presentation, adding material or finding better ways to phrase your ideas.

Improve Use of Media If you have included images or other media, make sure they are necessary and effective. If any media choices are not directly related to your claims and evidence, or are simply distracting, take them out of the presentation.

Brush Up on Your Presentation Techniques Practice your oral presentation before you present it to the class. Pay attention to all aspects of your delivery, including how you use your voice and how you conduct yourself in front of the class.

Present and Evaluate

When you deliver your oral presentation, make sure that all of you have considered each of the checklist items. As you listen to other groups' presentations, consider their claims and reasoning as you evaluate how well they meet the requirements.

STANDARDS
Speaking and Listening
Present claims and findings, emphasizing salient points in a focused, coherent manner with relevant evidence, sound valid reasoning, and well-chosen details; use appropriate eye contact, adequate volume, and clear pronunciation.

ESSENTIAL QUESTION:

When is it right to take a stand?

As you have learned from the selections you have read so far, "taking a stand" can be defined in many ways—it can be small or large, personal or political, for the benefit of an individual or an entire community. In this section, you will choose one additional selection about this topic for your final reading experience in this unit. Follow these steps to help you choose.

Look Back Think about the selections you have already read. What more do you want to know about taking a stand?

Look Ahead Preview the selections by reading the descriptions. Which one seems most interesting and appealing to you?

Look Inside Take a few minutes to scan through the text you chose. Choose a different one if this text doesn't meet your needs.

Independent Learning Strategies

Throughout your life, in school, in your community, and in your career, you will need to rely on yourself to learn and work on your own. Review these strategies and the actions you can take to practice them during Independent Learning. Add ideas of your own for each category.

STRATEGY	ACTION PLAN
Create a schedule	• Understand your goals and deadlines. • Make a plan for what to do each day. •
Practice what you have learned	• Use first-read and close-read strategies to deepen your understanding. • After you read, evaluate usefulness of the evidence to help you understand the topic. • Consider the quality and reliability of the source. •
Take notes	• Record important ideas and information. • Review your notes before sharing with the group. •

SCAN FOR
MULTIMEDIA

CONTENTS

Choose one selection. Selections are available online only.

PERFORMANCE-BASED ASSESSMENT PREP

Review Evidence for an Argument

Complete your Evidence Log for the unit by evaluating what you have learned and synthesizing the information you have recorded.

SCAN FOR MULTIMEDIA

First-Read Guide

Use this page to record your first-read ideas.

Tool Kit
First-Read Guide and
Model Annotation

Selection Title: _____

NOTICE

NOTICE new information or ideas you learn about the unit topic as you first read this text.

ANNOTATE

ANNOTATE by marking vocabulary and key passages you want to revisit.

First Read
NOTICE · ANNOTATE · CONNECT · RESPOND

CONNECT

CONNECT ideas within the selection to other knowledge and the selections you have read.

RESPOND

RESPOND by writing a brief summary of the selection.

≣ STANDARD

Reading Read and comprehend complex literary and informational texts independently and proficiently.

Close-Read Guide

Use this page to record your close-read ideas.

Selection Title: _____

Close Read the Text

Revisit sections of the text you marked during your first read. Read these sections closely and **annotate** what you notice. Ask yourself **questions** about the text. What can you **conclude**? Write down your ideas.

ANNOTATE · QUESTION · **Close Read** · CONCLUDE

Analyze the Text

Think about the author's choices of patterns, structure, techniques, and ideas included in the text. Select one, and record your thoughts about what this choice conveys.

QuickWrite

Pick a paragraph from the text that grabbed your interest. Explain the power of this passage.

▤ STANDARD
Reading Read and comprehend complex literary and informational texts independently and proficiently.

Share Your Independent Learning

Prepare to Share

When is it right to take a stand?

Even when you read something independently, you can continue to grow by sharing what you have learned with others. Reflect on the text you explored independently, and take notes about its connection to the unit. As you take notes, consider why this text belongs in this unit.

Learn From Your Classmates

Discuss It Share your ideas about the text you explored on your own. As you talk with your classmates, jot down ideas that you learn from them.

Reflect

Mark the most important insight you gained from these writing and discussion activities. Explain how this idea adds to your understanding of the topic.

STANDARDS

Speaking and Listening
Engage effectively in a range of collaborative discussions with diverse partners on *grade 8 topics, texts, and issues*, building on others' ideas and expressing their own clearly.

Review Evidence for an Argument

At the beginning of this unit you took a position on the following question:

Is it important for people to make their own choices in life?

✐ EVIDENCE LOG

Review your Evidence Log and your QuickWrite from the beginning of the unit. Has your position changed?

☐ YES	☐ NO
Identify at least three pieces of evidence that convinced you to change your mind.	Identify at least three new pieces of evidence that reinforced your initial position.
1.	1.
2.	2.
3.	3.

State your position: _____

_____

_____

Identify a possible counterclaim, or opposing position: _____

_____

_____

Evaluate the Strength of Your Evidence Consider your argument. Do you have enough evidence to support your claim? Do you have enough evidence to refute a counterclaim? If not, make a plan.

☐ Do more research   ☐ Talk with my classmates

☐ Reread a selection   ☐ Ask an expert

☐ Other: _____

☰ STANDARDS

Writing
Write arguments to support claims with clear reasons and relevant evidence.
a. Introduce claim(s), acknowledge and distinguish the claim(s) from alternate or opposing claims, and organize the reasons and evidence logically.
b. Support claim(s) with logical reasoning and relevant evidence, using accurate, credible sources and demonstrating an understanding of the topic or text.

SOURCES

• WHOLE-CLASS SELECTIONS

• SMALL-GROUP SELECTIONS

• INDEPENDENT-LEARNING SELECTION

PART 1

Writing to Sources: Argument

In this unit, you read about various people who take a stand for what matters. In some cases, they are the authors themselves, writing to convince others to adopt their point of view. In others, the authors or their subjects are discovering what matters to them.

> **Assignment**
>
> Write an **argument** in which you state and defend a claim in response to the following question:
>
> ## Is it important for people to make their own choices in life?
>
> Use examples from the selections you read, viewed, and researched in this unit to support and verify your claim. Organize your ideas so that they flow logically and are easy for readers to follow. Use a formal style and tone.

Reread the Assignment Review the assignment to be sure you fully understand it. The task may reference some of the academic words presented at the beginning of the unit. Be sure you understand each of the words in order to complete the assignment correctly. Also, consider using the academic vocabulary words in your argument. These words may help you to clarify your claims.

Academic Vocabulary

verify	speculate	rectify
candid	retort	

Review the Elements of Effective Argument Before you begin writing, read the Argument Rubric. Once you have completed your first draft, check it against the rubric. If one or more of the elements is missing or not as strong as it could be, revise your argument to add or strengthen that component.

WORD NETWORK

As you write and revise your argument, use your Word Network to help vary your word choices.

STANDARDS

Writing
• Write arguments to support claims with clear reasons and relevant evidence.
• Draw evidence from literary or informational texts to support analysis, reflection, and research.
• Write routinely over extended time frames and shorter time frames for a range of discipline-specific tasks, purposes, and audiences.

Argument Rubric

	Focus and Organization	Evidence and Elaboration	Language Conventions
4	The introduction engages the reader and establishes the claim in a compelling way. The claim is supported by logical reasons and relevant evidence, and opposing claims are addressed. The reasons and evidence are organized logically so that the argument is easy to follow. Clearly shows the relationships among claims, counterclaims, reasoning, and relevant evidence. The conclusion supports the argument presented and provides a new insight that follows from the information in the argument.	The sources of evidence are relevant and credible. Logical reasoning is used to connect specific supporting evidence to specific claims. The tone and style of the argument is formal and objective. Words are carefully chosen and suited to the audience and purpose.	The argument intentionally uses standard English conventions of usage and mechanics. The argument intentionally uses transitions to create cohesion.
3	The introduction is somewhat engaging and states the claim clearly. The claim is supported by reasons and evidence, and opposing claims are acknowledged. Reasons and evidence are organized so that the argument can be followed. Shows the relationships among claims, counterclaims, reasoning, and relevant evidence. The conclusion restates the claim and supports the argument.	The sources are relevant. Logical reasoning is used to connect supporting evidence to claims. The tone and style of the argument is mostly formal and objective. Words are generally suited to the audience and purpose.	The argument demonstrates general accuracy in standard English conventions of usage and mechanics. The argument uses transitions to create cohesion.
2	The introduction states the claim. The claim is supported by some reasons and evidence, and opposing claims may be briefly acknowledged. Reasons and evidence are organized somewhat logically. The conclusion relates to the claim.	Some sources are relevant. Logical reasoning is sometimes used to connect supporting evidence to claims. The tone and style of the argument is occasionally formal and objective. Words are somewhat suited to the audience and purpose.	The argument demonstrates some accuracy as well as minor mistakes in standard English conventions of usage and mechanics. The argument sometimes uses transitions to create cohesion.
1	The claim is not clearly stated. The claim is not supported by reasons and evidence, and opposing claims are not addressed. Reasons and evidence are disorganized and the argument is difficult to follow. The conclusion does not relate to the argument presented.	Reliable and relevant evidence is not included. The tone and style of the argument is informal. Vague words are used and word choices are not appropriate to the audience or purpose.	The argument contains many mistakes in standard English conventions of usage and mechanics. The argument does not use transitions to create cohesion.

PART 2

Speaking and Listening: Oral Presentation

Assignment

After completing the final draft of your argument, use it as the foundation for a short **oral presentation**.

Instead of reading your argument aloud, take the following steps to make your oral presentation lively and engaging.

- In your argument, annotate the most important claims and supporting details from the introduction, body paragraphs, and conclusion.
- Include visuals or other media that add interest to your presentation.
- Refer to your annotated text to keep your presentation focused.
- Deliver your argument with confidence. Look up from your annotated text frequently, and make eye contact with listeners.

Review the Oral Presentation Rubric Before you deliver your presentation, check your plans against this rubric. If elements are missing or not as strong as they could be, revise your presentation.

■ STANDARDS

Speaking and Listening
• Present claims and findings, emphasizing salient points in a focused, coherent manner with relevant evidence, sound valid reasoning, and well-chosen details; use appropriate eye contact, adequate volume, and clear pronunciation.
• Integrate multimedia and visual displays into presentations to clarify information, strengthen claims and evidence, and add interest.

	Content	Organization	Presentation Techniques
3	The introduction engages the reader and establishes a claim in a compelling way.	The speaker uses a variety of media effectively to support the claim.	The speaker maintains appropriate eye contact and speaks clearly and with adequate volume.
	The presentation has valid reasons and evidence for support and answers counterclaims.	Ideas progress logically, with clear transitions so that listeners can easily follow the argument.	The speaker presents with strong confidence and energy.
	The conclusion offers fresh insight into the claim.	The speaker uses time effectively by spending the right amount of time on each part.	
2	The introduction establishes the claim.	The speaker uses some media to support the claim.	The speaker sometimes maintains appropriate eye contact and speaks somewhat clearly and with adequate volume.
	The presentation includes some valid reasons and evidence to support the claim and acknowledges counterclaims.	Ideas progress somewhat logically, with transitions among ideas so that listeners can follow the argument.	The speaker presents with some confidence and energy.
	The conclusion offers some insight into the claim and restates important information.	The speaker mostly uses time effectively by spending almost the right amount of time on each part.	
1	The introduction does not clearly state the claim.	The speaker doesn't use media to support the claim.	The speaker does not maintain appropriate eye contact or speak clearly with adequate volume.
	The presentation does not include reasons or evidence to support the claim or acknowledge counterclaims.	Ideas do not progress logically. Listeners have difficulty following.	The speaker presents without confidence or energy.
	The conclusion does not restate information about the claim.	The speaker does not use time effectively, spending too much time on some parts of the presentation, and too little on others.	

Reflect on the Unit

Now that you've completed the unit, take a few moments to reflect on your learning.

Reflect on the Unit Goals

Look back at the goals at the beginning of the unit. Use a different colored pen to rate yourself again. Then, think about readings and activities that contributed the most to the growth of your understanding. Record your thoughts.

Reflect on the Learning Strategies

💬 **Discuss It** Write a reflection on whether you were able to improve your learning based on your Action Plans. Think about what worked, what didn't, and what you might do to keep working on these strategies. Record your ideas before joining a class discussion.

Reflect on the Text

Choose a selection that you found challenging and explain what made it difficult.

Explain something that surprised you about a text in the unit.

Which activity taught you the most about standing up for what matters? What did you learn?

🄑 SCAN FOR
MULTIMEDIA

Human Intelligence

There are an infinite number of ways in which humans express intelligence.

Amazing Man Draws NYC
From Memory

Discuss It What limits might there be on the capacity of human memory?

Write your response before sharing your ideas.

SCAN FOR
MULTIMEDIA

UNIT 4

ESSENTIAL QUESTION: **In what different ways can people be intelligent?**

LAUNCH TEXT
INFORMATIVE MODEL
The Human Brain

WHOLE-CLASS LEARNING

COMPARE

ANCHOR TEXT: SHORT STORY

Flowers for Algernon
Daniel Keyes

SCRIPT

from Flowers for Algernon
David Rogers

SMALL-GROUP LEARNING

MEMOIR

from Blue Nines and Red Words
from Born on a Blue Day
Daniel Tammet

MEDIA: INFOGRAPHIC

The Theory of Multiple Intelligences Infographic
Howard Gardner

POETRY COLLECTION

Retort
Paul Laurence Dunbar

from The People, Yes
Carl Sandburg

INDEPENDENT LEARNING

ARGUMENT

Is Personal Intelligence Important?
John D. Mayer, Ph.D.

BLOG POST

Why Is Emotional Intelligence Important for Teens?
Divya Parekh

EXPLANATORY ESSAY

The More You Know, the Smarter You Are?
Jim Vega

EXPOSITORY NONFICTION

from The Future of the Mind
Michio Kaku

PERFORMANCE TASK

WRITING FOCUS:
Write an Informative Speech

PERFORMANCE TASK

SPEAKING AND LISTENING FOCUS:
Deliver a Multimedia Presentation

PERFORMANCE-BASED ASSESSMENT PREP

Review Evidence for an Informative Essay

PERFORMANCE-BASED ASSESSMENT

Informative Text: Essay and Speech

PROMPT:
In what different ways can people be intelligent?

Unit Goals

Throughout this unit, you will deepen your perspective about human intelligence by reading, writing, speaking, listening, and presenting. These goals will help you succeed on the Unit Performance-Based Assessment.

Rate how well you meet these goals right now. You will revisit your ratings later when you reflect on your growth during this unit.

SCALE	1	2	3	4	5
	NOT AT ALL WELL	NOT VERY WELL	SOMEWHAT WELL	VERY WELL	EXTREMELY WELL

READING GOALS

	1	2	3	4	5
• Gather information and ideas from a variety of texts.	○	○	○	○	○
• Expand your knowledge and use of academic and concept vocabulary.	○	○	○		○

WRITING AND RESEARCH GOALS

	1	2	3	4	5
• Write an informative essay in which you examine a topic and convey ideas, concepts, and information.	○	○	○	○	○
• Conduct research projects of various lengths to explore a topic and clarify meaning.	○	○	○	○	○

LANGUAGE GOALS

	1	2	3	4	5
• Demonstrate command of the conventions of standard English grammar and usage, including correct agreement of nouns and verbs.	○	○	○	○	○

SPEAKING AND LISTENING GOALS

	1	2	3	4	5
• Collaborate with your team to build on the ideas of others, develop consensus, and communicate.	○	○	○	○	○
• Integrate audio, visuals, and text in presentations.	○	○	○	○	○

☰ STANDARDS

Language
Acquire and use accurately grade-appropriate general academic and domain-specific words and phrases; gather vocabulary knowledge when considering a word or phrase important to comprehension or expression.

SCAN FOR MULTIMEDIA

Academic Vocabulary: Informative Texts

Academic terms appear in all subjects and can help you read, write, and discuss with more precision. Informative writing relies on facts to inform or explain. Here are five academic words that will be useful to you in this unit as you analyze and write informative texts.

Complete the chart.

1. Review each word, its root, and the mentor sentences.

2. Use the information and your own knowledge to predict the meaning of each word.

3. For each word, list at least two related words.

4. Refer to the dictionary or other resources if needed.

TIP

FOLLOW THROUGH
Study the words in this chart, and mark them or their forms wherever they appear in the unit.

WORD	MENTOR SENTENCES	PREDICT MEANING	RELATED WORDS
assimilate ROOT: **-sim-** "like"	**1.** Once I *assimilate* all the information, I will start the project. **2.** The body can *assimilate* nutrients and use them for energy.		similar; simile
tendency ROOT: **-ten-** "stretch"	**1.** People have a *tendency* to believe good things about friends. **2.** My *tendency* is to avoid trouble rather than risk a fight.		
integrate ROOT: **-teg-** "touch"	**1.** We will *integrate* this new activity into the lesson. **2.** The new student should *integrate* into our school very quickly.		
observation ROOT: **-serv-** "watch over"	**1.** My findings are based on close *observation* over many weeks. **2.** Ed went to the hospital for *observation* after he fainted.		
documentation ROOT: **-doc-** "show"	**1.** The *documentation* explains how to use the software. **2.** They found *documentation* from the 1800s that proved the family owned the land.		

The Human Brain

LAUNCH TEXT | INFORMATIVE MODEL

This selection is an example of an **informative text**, a type of writing in which an author presents facts and details. This is the type of writing you will develop in the Performance-Based Assessment at the end of the unit.

As you read, look at the way the ideas are introduced and facts and details are presented. Mark the text to help you determine key ideas and details.

NOTES

1 The famous scientist James Watson summarized it this way: The brain boggles the mind! The human brain is truly impressive: It weighs only about three pounds but controls everything a person does, ever has done, and ever will do—physically, intellectually, and emotionally. No computer even comes close to having the brain's abilities. The brain controls a person's actions, reactions, and survival functions, such as breathing. It also has the ability to think, remember, process information, and learn new things.

2 The brain is one part of the central nervous system—the system that controls all of the body's activities. The central nervous system is made up of the brain and the spinal cord. The brain is protected by the skull, and the spinal cord runs through vertebrae of the back—the bones that make up the spine. The spinal cord transmits messages between the brain and other parts of the body through nerve cells called neurons. If a person decides to pick up a book from the shelf—a voluntary action—the brain sends that message to the arm and hand through the spinal cord. And if a person touches a hot surface and burns his or her hand— an involuntary action—the nerve cells in the hand send a pain message to the brain through the spinal cord.

SCAN FOR MULTIMEDIA

NOTES

3   A constant stream of messages travels through the neurons in the spinal cord, at speeds of more than 150 miles per hour. The human brain never stops working, even when a person is asleep. As well as transmitting messages through the spinal cord, neurons transmit messages from one part of the brain to another. There are approximately 85 billion of these cells in the brain alone. Neurons send messages through tiny branch-like structures that connect to other neurons in different parts of the brain, as well as other parts of the body. The points where neurons meet and transmit information to each other are called synapses. Each neuron may be connected to as many as 10,000 other neurons, resulting in more than 100 trillion synapses in a single brain.

4   Although a person cannot increase the amount of neurons in his or her brain, learning new things increases the number of synapse connections between them. Learning and education actually change the structure of the human brain. That structure changes every time a person learns, and every time that person has a new thought or memory. The more a person learns the more there is to think about. And the more there is to think about, the more there is to remember. As a result, the connections between neurons get stronger, and the brain is able to function more effectively. It processes, thinks, analyzes, and stores information more quickly and productively than it did before these connections were made. Neurons are just cells, and everything a person knows is the result of the connections between them.

5   Scientists have gained a wealth of knowledge about the human brain, but there is a lot they do not yet understand. The neurologist Santiago Ramón y Cajal, for example, compares the brain to a world of unexplored continents with great stretches of unknown territory. Even so, new discoveries continually increase our knowledge of how the brain functions and how people learn. ❧

⬚ WORD NETWORK FOR HUMAN INTELLIGENCE

Vocabulary A Word Network is a collection of words related to a topic. As you read the selections in this unit, identify interesting words related to human intelligence, and add them to your Word Network. For example, you might begin by adding words from the Launch Text, such as *spinal cord*, *neuron*, and *synapse*.

🔧 **Tool Kit**
Word Network Model

spinal cord

neuron

synapse

HUMAN INTELLIGENCE

The Human Brain **345**

Summary

Write a summary of "The Human Brain." A **summary** is a concise, complete, and accurate overview of a text. It should not include a statement of your opinion or an analysis.

Launch Activity

Draft a Research Plan Think about this question: **In what different ways can people be intelligent?** Consider your response by completing this statement: *I can find more information about human intelligence by . . .*

- On a sticky note, record a brief phrase to complete the statement.

- Place all sticky notes on the board, and then read the suggestions aloud. Work together to group ideas that are the same or closely related.

- As a class, decide on the order in which the suggested research strategies should be pursued. Vote on which suggestion should be done first.

- Place a tally mark on the note or notes that list your choice or choices.

- Use the tally results to create a class research plan.

QuickWrite

Consider class discussions, the video, and the Launch Text as you think about the prompt. Record your first thoughts here.

PROMPT: **In what different ways can people be intelligent?**

EVIDENCE LOG FOR HUMAN INTELLIGENCE

Review your QuickWrite. Summarize your point of view in one sentence to record in your Evidence Log. Then, record evidence from "The Human Brain" that supports your point of view.

After each selection, you will continue to use your Evidence Log to record the evidence you gather and the connections you make. This graphic shows what your Evidence Log looks like.

 Tool Kit
Evidence Log Model

Title of Text: _____   Date: _____

CONNECTION TO PROMPT	TEXT EVIDENCE/DETAILS	ADDITIONAL NOTES/IDEAS

How does this text change or add to my thinking?   Date: _____

 SCAN FOR MULTIMEDIA

ESSENTIAL QUESTION:

In what different ways can people be intelligent?

Intelligence shows itself in many ways—sometimes in ways that do not overlap. A master painter may be terrible at mathematics; a bestselling author may have no sense of direction. Where one person excels, another may fail—and it's often impossible to make a judgment about which of the two people is smarter. As you read, you will work with your whole class to explore some of the ways in which people are intelligent.

Whole-Class Learning Strategies

Throughout your life, in school, in your community, and in your career, you'll continue to learn in large-group environments.

Review these strategies and the actions you can take to practice them as you work with your whole class. Add ideas of your own for each step. Get ready to use these strategies during Whole-Class Learning.

STRATEGY	ACTION PLAN
Listen actively	• Eliminate distractions. For example, put your cellphone away. • Keep your eyes on the speaker. •
Clarify by asking questions	• If you're confused, other people probably are, too. Ask a question to help your whole class. • If you see that you are guessing, ask a question instead. •
Monitor understanding	• Notice what information you already know, and be ready to build on it. • Ask for help if you are struggling. •
Interact and share ideas	• Share your ideas and answer questions, even if you are unsure. • Build on the ideas of others by adding details or making a connection. •

SCAN FOR MULTIMEDIA

CONTENTS

PERFORMANCE TASK

WRITING FOCUS
Write an Informative Speech

The Whole-Class selections focus on a fictional story about a character named Charlie whose level of intelligence is transformed dramatically by an experimental treatment. After reading the texts, you will write an informative speech from Charlie's point of view.

FLOWERS FOR ALGERNON
(short story)

Comparing Texts

In this lesson, you will read the short story "Flowers for Algernon." You will then read an excerpt from the script for a film adaptation of the story. Finally, you will compare the short story and the script.

from FLOWERS FOR ALGERNON (script)

About the Author

Raised in Brooklyn, New York, writer and teacher **Daniel Keyes** (1927–2014) was also a photographer, a merchant seaman, and an editor. Keyes was fascinated by unusual psychological conditions. A meeting with a man with a mental disability gave Keyes the idea for "Flowers for Algernon." After winning the Hugo Award for the story in 1959, Keyes expanded "Flowers for Algernon" into a novel. The story also inspired the award-winning movie adaptation *Charly,* released in 1968.

🔧 **Tool Kit**
First-Read Guide and Model Annotation

Flowers for Algernon

Concept Vocabulary

As you conduct your first read of "Flowers for Algernon," you will encounter these words. Before reading, note how familiar you are with each word. Then, rank the words in order from most familiar (1) to least familiar (6).

WORD	YOUR RANKING
subconscious	
suspicion	
despised	
deterioration	
introspective	
regression	

First Read FICTION

Apply these strategies as you conduct your first read. You will have an opportunity to complete the close-read notes after your first read.

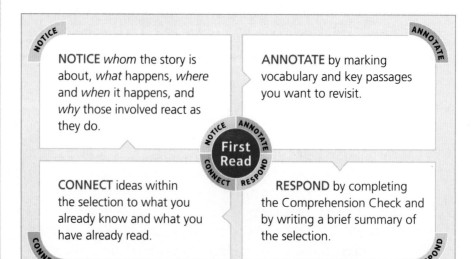

NOTICE *whom* the story is about, *what* happens, *where* and *when* it happens, and *why* those involved react as they do.

ANNOTATE by marking vocabulary and key passages you want to revisit.

First Read

CONNECT ideas within the selection to what you already know and what you have already read.

RESPOND by completing the Comprehension Check and by writing a brief summary of the selection.

☰ STANDARDS

Reading Literature
By the end of the year, read and comprehend literature, including stories, dramas, and poems, at the high end of grades 6–8 text complexity band independently and proficiently.

Flowers for Algernon

Daniel Keyes

SCAN FOR
MULTIMEDIA

BACKGROUND

Charlie Gordon, the main character in "Flowers for Algernon," undergoes surgery to increase his intelligence. In the story, doctors measure his progress with IQ, or intelligence quotient, tests. These tests were once widely used to measure intelligence and learning ability. Researchers now recognize that one test cannot accurately measure the wide range of intellectual abilities.

NOTES

progris riport 1—martch 5 1965

1   Dr. Strauss says I shud rite down what I think and evrey thing that happins to me from now on. I dont know why but he says its importint so they will see if they will use me. I hope they use me. Miss Kinnian says maybe they can make me smart. I want to be smart. My name is Charlie Gordon. I am 37 years old and 2 weeks ago was my brithday. I have nuthing more to rite now so I will close for today.

progris riport 2—martch 6

2   I had a test today. I think I faled it. and I think that maybe now they wont use me. What happind is a nice young man was in the room and he had some white cards with ink spilled all over them. He sed Charlie what do you see on this card. I was very skared even tho I had my rabits foot in my pockit because when I was a kid I always faled tests in school and I spillled ink to.

3   I told him I saw a inkblot. He said yes and it made me feel good. I thot that was all but when I got up to go he stopped me.

He said now sit down Charlie we are not thru yet. Then I dont remember so good but he wantid me to say what was in the ink. I dint see nuthing in the ink but he said there was picturs there other pepul saw some picturs. I coudnt see any picturs. I reely tryed to see. I held the card close up and then far away. Then I said if I had my glases I coud see better I usally only ware my glases in the movies or TV but I said they are in the closit in the hall. I got them. Then I said let me see that card agen I bet Ill find it now.

4   I tryed hard but I still coudnt find the picturs I only saw the ink. I told him maybe I need new glases. He rote something down on a paper and I got skared of faling the test. I told him it was a very nice inkblot with littel points all around the eges. He looked very sad so that wasnt it. I said please let me try agen. Ill get it in a few minits becaus Im not so fast somtimes. Im a slow reeder too in Miss Kinnians class for slow adults but I'm trying very hard.

5   He gave me a chance with another card that had 2 kinds of ink spilled on it red and blue.

6   He was very nice and talked slow like Miss Kinnian does and he explaned it to me that it was a *raw shok*.[1] He said pepul see things in the ink. I said show me where. He said think. I told him I think a inkblot but that wasnt rite eather. He said what does it remind you—pretend somthing. I closd my eyes for a long time to pretend. I told him I pretned a fowntan pen with ink leeking all over a table cloth. Then he got up and went out.

7   I dont think I passd the *raw shok* test.

progris riport 3—martch 7

8   Dr Strauss and Dr Nemur say it dont matter about the inkblots. I told them I dint spill the ink on the cards and I coudnt see anything in the ink. They said that maybe they will still use me. I said Miss Kinnian never gave me tests like that one only spelling and reading. They said Miss Kinnian told that I was her bestist pupil in the adult nite scool because I tryed the hardist and I reely wantid to lern. They said how come you went to the adult nite scool all by yourself Charlie. How did you find it. I said I askd pepul and sumbody told me where I shud go to lern to read and spell good. They said why did you want to. I told them becaus all my life I wantid to be smart and not dumb. But its very hard to be smart. They said you know it will probly be tempirery. I said yes. Miss Kinnian told me. I dont care if it herts.

9   Later I had more crazy tests today. The nice lady who gave it me told me the name and I asked her how do you spellit so I can rite it in my progris riport. THEMATIC APPERCEPTION TEST.[2]

© Pearson Education, Inc., or its affiliates. All rights reserved.

---

1. *raw shok* misspelling of Rorschach (RAWR shok) test, a psychological test that requires a subject to describe the images suggested by inkblots.
2. **THEMATIC** (thee MAT ihk) **APPERCEPTION** (ap uhr SEHP shuhn) **TEST** personality test in which the subject makes up stories about a series of pictures.

CLOSE READ

ANNOTATE: In paragraph 8, mark every misspelled word you see.

QUESTION: Looking over the marked words, would you describe the number of spelling errors as a few, some, or many?

CONCLUDE: What does the number of spelling errors suggest about the person writing these diary entries?

I dont know the frist 2 words but I know what *test* means. You got to pass it or you get bad marks. This test lookd easy becaus I coud see the picturs. Only this time she dint want me to tell her the picturs. That mixd me up. I said the man yesterday said I shoud tell him what I saw in the ink she said that dont make no difrence. She said make up storys about the pepul in the picturs.

10   I told her how can you tell storys about pepul you never met. I said why shud I make up lies. I never tell lies any more becaus I always get caut.

11   She told me this test and the other one the raw-shok was for getting personalty. I laffed so hard. I said how can you get that thing from inkblots and fotos. She got sore and put her picturs away. I dont care. It was sily. I gess I faled that test too.

12   Later some men in white coats took me to a difernt part of the hospitil and gave me a game to play. It was like a race with a white mouse. They called the mouse Algernon. Algernon was in a box with a lot of twists and turns like all kinds of walls and they gave me a pencil and a paper with lines and lots of boxes. On one side it said START and on the other end it said FINISH. They said it was *amazed*[3] and that Algernon and me had the same *amazed* to do. I dint see how we could have the same *amazed* if Algernon had a box and I had a paper but I dint say nothing. Anyway there wasnt time because the race started.

13   One of the men had a watch he was trying to hide so I woudnt see it so I tryed not to look and that made me nervus.

14   Anyway that test made me feel worser than all the others because they did it over 10 times with difernt *amazeds* and Algernon won every time. I dint know that mice were so smart. Maybe thats because Algernon is a white mouse. Maybe white mice are smarter than other mice.

progris riport 4—Mar 8

15   Their going to use me! Im so exited I can hardly write. Dr Nemur and Dr Strauss had a argament about it first. Dr Nemur was in the office when Dr Strauss brot me in. Dr Nemur was worryed about using me but Dr Strauss told him Miss Kinnian rekemmended me the best from all the pepul who she was teaching. I like Miss Kinnian becaus shes a very smart teacher. And she said Charlie your going to have a second chance. If you volenteer for this experament you mite get smart. They dont know if it will be perminint but theirs a chance. Thats why I said ok even when I was scared because she said it was an operashun. She said dont be scared Charlie you done so much with so little I think you deserv it most of all.

---

3. **amazed** Charlie means "a maze," or a confusing series of paths. Often, the intelligence of animals is assessed by how fast they go through a maze.

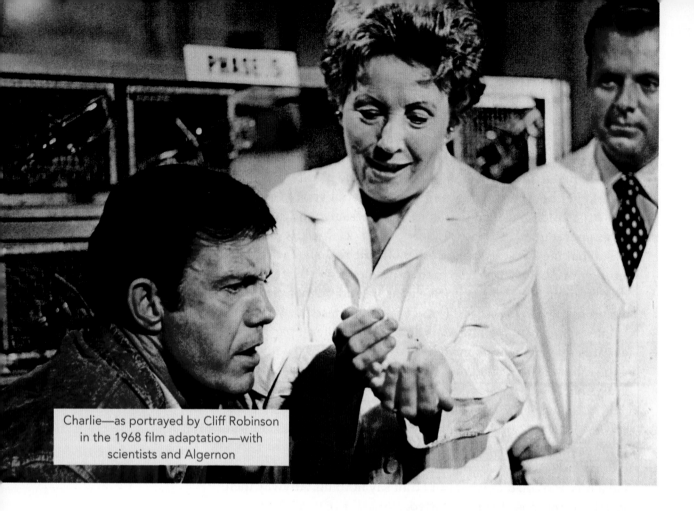

Charlie—as portrayed by Cliff Robinson in the 1968 film adaptation—with scientists and Algernon

NOTES

16   So I got scaird when Dr Nemur and Dr Strauss argud about it. Dr Strauss said I had something that was very good. He said I had a good *motor-vation*.[4] I never even knew I had that. I felt proud when he said that not every body with an eye-q[5] of 68 had that thing. I dont know what it is or where I got it but he said Algernon had it too. Algernons *motor-vation* is the cheese they put in his box. But it cant be that because I didnt eat any cheese this week.

17   Then he told Dr Nemur something I dint understand so while they were talking I wrote down some of the words.

18   He said Dr Nemur I know Charlie is not what you had in mind as the first of your new brede of intelek** (coudnt get the word) superman. But most people of his low ment** are host** and uncoop** they are usualy dull apath** and hard to reach. He has a good natcher hes intristed and eager to please.

19   Dr Nemur said remember he will be the first human beeng ever to have his intelijence trippled by surgicle meens.

20   Dr Strauss said exakly. Look at how well hes lerned to read and write for his low mentel age its as grate an acheve** as you and I lerning einstines therey of **vity without help. That shows the intenss motor-vation. Its comparat** a tremen** achev** I say we use Charlie.

---

4. *motor-vation* motivation, or desire to work hard and achieve a goal.
5. *eye-q* IQ, or intelligence quotient—a way of measuring human intelligence.

21   I dint get all the words and they were talking to fast but it sounded like Dr Strauss was on my side and like the other one wasnt.

22   Then Dr Nemur nodded he said all right maybe your right. We will use Charlie. When he said that I got so exited I jumped up and shook his hand for being so good to me. I told him thank you doc you wont be sorry for giving me a second chance. And I mean it like I told him. After the operashun Im gonna try to be smart. Im gonna try awful hard.

progris ript 5—Mar 10

23   Im skared. Lots of people who work here and the nurses and the people who gave me the tests came to bring me candy and wish me luck. I hope I have luck. I got my rabits foot and my lucky penny and my horse shoe. Only a black cat crossed me when I was comming to the hospitil. Dr Strauss says don't be supersitis Charlie this is sience. Anyway Im keeping my rabits foot with me.

24   I asked Dr Strauss if Ill beat Algernon in the race after the operashun and he said maybe. If the operashun works Ill show that mouse I can be as smart as he is. Maybe smarter. Then Ill be abel to read better and spell the words good and know lots of things and be like other people. I want to be smart like other people. If it works perminint they will make everybody smart all over the wurld.

25   They dint give me anything to eat this morning. I dont know what that eating has to do with getting smart. Im very hungry and Dr Nemur took away my box of candy. That Dr Nemur is a grouch. Dr Strauss says I can have it back after the operashun. You cant eat befor a operashun . . .

Progress Report 6—Mar 15

26   The operashun dint hurt. He did it while I was sleeping. They took off the bandijis from my eyes and my head today so I can make a PROGRESS REPORT. Dr Nemur who looked at some of my other ones says I spell PROGRESS wrong and he told me how to spell it and REPORT too. I got to try and remember that.

27   I have a very bad memary for spelling. Dr Strauss says its ok to tell about all the things that happin to me but he says I shoud tell more about what I feel and what I think. When I told him I dont know how to think he said try. All the time when the bandijis were on my eyes I tryed to think. Nothing happened. I dont know what to think about. Maybe if I ask him he will tell me how I can think now that Im suppose to get smart. What do smart people think about. Fancy things I suppose. I wish I knew some fancy things alredy.

NOTES

CLOSE READ

ANNOTATE: Mark the sentences in the March 10 entry that set out Charlie's goals.

QUESTION: What do you notice about these goals and the way that Charlie writes about them?

CONCLUDE: How do Charlie's goals and the way he states them make you feel sympathetic toward him?

Progress Report 7—Mar 19

28   Nothing is happining. I had lots of tests and different kinds of races with Algernon. I hate that mouse. He always beats me. Dr Strauss said I got to play those games. And he said some time I got to take those tests over again. Thse inkblots are stupid. And those pictures are stupid too. I like to draw a picture of a man and a woman but I wont make up lies about people.

29   I got a headache from trying to think so much. I thot Dr Strauss was my frend but he dont help me. He dont tell me what to think or when Ill get smart. Miss Kinnian dint come to see me. I think writing these progress reports are stupid too.

Progress Report 8—Mar 23

30   Im going back to work at the factery. They said it was better I shud go back to work but I cant tell anyone what the operashun was for and I have to come to the hospitil for an hour evry night after work. They are gonna pay me mony every month for lerning to be smart.

31   Im glad Im going back to work because I miss my job and all my frends and all the fun we have there.

32   Dr Strauss says I shud keep writing things down but I don't have to do it every day just when I think of something or something speshul happins. He says dont get discoridged because it takes time and it happins slow. He says it took a long time with Algernon before he got 3 times smarter then he was before. Thats why Algernon beats me all the time because he had that operashun too. That makes me feel better. I coud probly do that *amazed* faster than a reglar mouse. Maybe some day Ill beat Algernon. Boy that would be something. So far Algernon looks like he mite be smart perminent.

Mar 25

33   (I dont have to write PROGRESS REPORT on top any more just when I hand it in once a week for Dr Nemur to read. I just have to put the date on. That saves time)

34   We had a lot of fun at the factery today. Joe Carp said hey look where Charlie had his operashun what did they do Charlie put some brains in. I was going to tell him but I remembered Dr Strauss said no. Then Frank Reilly said what did you do Charlie forget your key and open your door the hard way. That made me laff. Their really my friends and they like me.

35   Sometimes somebody will say hey look at Joe or Frank or George he really pulled a Charlie Gordon. I dont know why they say that but they always laff. This morning Amos Borg who is the 4 man at Donnegans used my name when he shouted at Ernie the

office boy. Ernie lost a packige. He said Ernie what are you trying to be a Charlie Gordon. I don't understand why he said that. I never lost any packiges.

Mar 28

36   Dr Straus came to my room tonight to see why I dint come in like I was suppose to. I told him I dont like to race with Algernon any more. He said I dont have to for a while but I shud come in. He had a present for me only it wasnt a present but just for lend. I thot it was a little television but it wasnt. He said I got to turn it on when I go to sleep. I said your kidding why shud I turn it on when Im going to sleep. Who ever herd of a thing like that. But he said if I want to get smart I got to do what he says. I told him I dint think I was going to get smart and he put his hand on my sholder and said Charlie you dont know it yet but your getting smarter all the time. You wont notice for a while. I think he was just being nice to make me feel good because I don't look any smarter.

37   Oh yes I almost forgot. I asked him when I can go back to the class at Miss Kinnians school. He said I wont go their. He said that soon Miss Kinnian will come to the hospital to start and teach me speshul. I was mad at her for not comming to see me when I got the operashun but I like her so maybe we will be frends again.

Mar 29

38   That crazy TV kept me up all night. How can I sleep with something yelling crazy things all night in my ears. And the nutty pictures. Wow. I dont know what it says when Im up so how am I going to know when Im sleeping.

39   Dr Strauss says its ok. He says my brains are lerning when I sleep and that will help me when Miss Kinnian starts my lessons in the hospitl (only I found out it isnt a hospitil its a labatory. I think its all crazy. If you can get smart when your sleeping why do people go to school. That thing I dont think will work. I use to watch the late show and the late late show on TV all the time and it never made me smart. Maybe you have to sleep while you watch it.

Progress Report 9—APRIL 3

40   Dr Strauss showed me how to keep the TV turned low so now I can sleep. I don't hear a thing. And I still dont understand what it says. A few times I play it over in the morning to find out what I lerned when I was sleeping and I dont think so. Miss Kinnian says Maybe its another langwidge or something. But most times it sounds american. It talks so fast faster then even Miss Gold who was my teacher in 6 grade and I remember she talked so fast I coudnt understand her.

41 I told Dr Strauss what good is it to get smart in my sleep. I want to be smart when Im awake. He says its the same thing and I have two minds. Theres the *subconscious* and the *conscious* (thats how you spell it). And one dont tell the other one what its doing. They dont even talk to each other. Thats why I dream. And boy have I been having crazy dreams. Wow. Ever since that night TV. The late late late late late show.

42 I forgot to ask him if it was only me or if everybody had those two minds.

43 (I just looked up the word in the dictionary Dr Strauss gave me. The word is *subconscious.* adj. *Of the nature of mental operations yet not present in consciousness; as, subconscious conflict of desires.*) There's more but I still dont know what it means. This isnt a very good dictionary for dumb people like me.

44 Anyway the headache is from the party. My frends from the factery Joe Carp and Frank Reilly invited me to go with them to Muggsys Saloon for some drinks. I dont like to drink but they said we will have lots of fun. I had a good time.

45 Joe Carp said I shoud show the girls how I mop out the toilet in the factory and he got me a mop. I showed them and everyone laffed when I told that Mr Donnegan said I was the best janiter he ever had because I like my job and do it good and never come late or miss a day except for my operashun.

46 I said Miss Kinnian always said Charlie be proud of your job because you do it good.

47 Everybody laffed and we had a good time and they gave me lots of drinks and Joe said Charlie is a card when hes potted. I dont know what that means but everybody likes me and we have fun. I cant wait to be smart like my best frends Joe Carp and Frank Reilly.

48 I dont remember how the party was over but I think I went out to buy a newspaper and coffe for Joe and Frank and when I came back there was no one their. I looked for them all over till late. Then I dont remember so good but I think I got sleepy or sick. A nice cop brot me back home. Thats what my landlady Mrs Flynn says.

49 But I got a headache and a big lump on my head and black and blue all over. I think maybe I fell. Anyway I got a bad headache and Im sick and hurt all over. I dont think Ill drink anymore.

April 6

50 I beat Algernon! I dint even know I beat him until Burt the tester told me. Then the second time I lost because I got so exited I fell off the chair before I finished. But after that I beat him 8 more times. I must be getting smart to beat a smart mouse like Algernon. But I dont *feel* smarter.

Charlie with Miss Kinnian—as portrayed by Claire Bloom

51   I wanted to race Algernon some more but Burt said that's enough for one day. They let me hold him for a minit. Hes not so bad. Hes soft like a ball of cotton. He blinks and when he opens his eyes their black and pink on the eges.

52   I said can I feed him because I felt bad to beat him and I wanted to be nice and make frends. Burt said no Algernon is a very specshul mouse with an operashun like mine, and he was the first of all the animals to stay smart so long. He told me Algernon is so smart that every day he has to solve a test to get his food. Its a thing like a lock on a door that changes every time Algernon goes in to eat so he has to lern something new to get his food. That made me sad because if he coudnt lern he woud be hungry.

53   I dont think its right to make you pass a test to eat. How woud Dr Nemur like it to have to pass a test every time he wants to eat. I think Ill be frends with Algernon.

April 9

54   Tonight after work Miss Kinnian was at the laboratory. She looked like she was glad to see me but scared. I told her dont worry Miss Kinnian Im not smart yet and she laffed. She said I have confidence in you Charlie the way you struggled so hard to read and right better than all the others. At werst you will have it for a littel wile and your doing something for sience.

55   We are reading a very hard book. I never read such a hard book before. Its called *Robinson Crusoe*[6] about a man who gets merooned on a dessert Iland. Hes smart and figers out all kinds of things so

6. ***Robinson Crusoe*** (KROO soh) 1719 novel written by Daniel Defoe, a British author.

he can have a house and food and hes a good swimmer. Only I feel sorry because hes all alone and has no frends. But I think their must be somebody else on the iland because theres a picture with his funny umbrella looking at footprints. I hope he gets a frend and not be lonly.

April 10

56   Miss Kinnian teaches me to spell better. She says look at a word and close your eyes and say it over and over until you remember. I have lots of truble with *through* that you say *threw* and *enough* and *tough* that you dont say *enew* and *tew*. You got to say *enuff* and *tuff*. Thats how I use to write it before I started to get smart. Im confused but Miss Kinnian says theres no reason in spelling.

April 14

57   Finished Robinson Crusoe. I want to find out more about what happens to him but Miss Kinnian says thats all there is. *Why*

April 15

CLOSE READ

ANNOTATE: Mark the spelling errors you find in Charlie's April 15 entry.

QUESTION: What do you notice about the number of errors, as compared to the total you marked in the March 7 entry?

QUESTION: What does this reveal about the effect of the operation on Charlie's ability to think and write?

58   Miss Kinnian says Im lerning fast. She read some of the Progress Reports and she looked at me kind of funny. She says Im a fine person and Ill show them all. I asked her why. She said never mind but I shoudnt feel bad if I find out that everybody isnt nice like I think. She said for a person who god gave so little to you done more then a lot of people with brains they never even used. I said all my frends are smart people but there good. They like me and they never did anything that wasnt nice. Then she got something in her eye and she had to run out to the ladys room.

April 16

59   Today, I lerned, the comma, this is a comma (,) a period, with a tail, Miss Kinnian, says its importent, because, it makes writing, better, she said, somebody, coud lose, a lot of money, if a comma, isnt, in the, right place, I dont have, any money, and I dont see, how a comma, keeps you, from losing it,

60   But she says, everybody, uses commas, so Ill use, them too,

April 17

61   I used the comma wrong. Its punctuation. Miss Kinnian told me to look up long words in the dictionary to lern to spell them. I said whats the difference if you can read it anyway. She said its part of your education so now on Ill look up all the words Im not sure how to spell. It takes a long time to write that way but I think Im remembering. I only have to look up once and after that I get it right. Anyway thats how come I got the word *punctuation* right. (Its that way in the dictionary). Miss Kinnian says a period is punctuation too, and there are lots of other marks to lern. I told her I thot all the periods had to have tails but she said no.

62   You got to mix them up, she showed? me" how. to mix! them(up,. and now; I can! mix up all kinds" of punctuation, in! my writing? There, are lots! of rules? to lern; but Im gettin'g them in my head.

63   One thing I? like about, Dear Miss Kinnian: (thats the way it goes in a business letter if I ever go into business) is she, always gives me' a reason" when—I ask. She's a gen'ius! I wish! I cou'd be smart" like, her;

64   (Punctuation, is; fun!)

April 18

65   What a dope I am! I didn't even understand what she was talking about. I read the grammar book last night and it explanes the whole thing. Then I saw it was the same way as Miss Kinnian was trying to tell me, but I didn't get it. I got up in the middle of the night, and the whole thing straightened out in my mind.

66   Miss Kinnian said that the TV working in my sleep helped out. She said I reached a plateau. Thats like the flat top of a hill.

67   After I figgered out how punctuation worked, I read over all my old Progress Reports from the beginning. Boy, did I have crazy spelling and punctuation! I told Miss Kinnian I ought to go over the pages and fix all the mistakes but she said, "No. Charlie, Dr. Nemur wants them just as they are. That's why he let you keep them after they were photostated, to see your own progress. You're coming along fast, Charlie."

68   That made me feel good. After the lesson I went down and played with Algernon. We don't race any more.

April 20

69   I feel sick inside. Not sick like for a doctor, but inside my chest it feels empty like getting punched and a heartburn at the same time.

70   I wasn't going to write about it, but I guess I got to, because its important. Today was the first time I ever stayed home from work.

71   Last night Joe Carp and Frank Reilly invited me to a party. There were lots of girls and some men from the factory. I remembered how sick I got last time I drank too much, so I told Joe I didn't want anything to drink. He gave me a plain coke instead. It tasted funny, but I thought it was just a bad taste in my mouth.

72   We had a lot of fun for a while. Joe said I should dance with Ellen and she would teach me the steps. I fell a few times and I couldn't understand why because no one else was dancing besides Ellen and me. And all the time I was tripping because somebody's foot was always sticking out.

73   Then when I got up I saw the look on Joe's face and it gave me a funny feeling in my stomack. "He's a scream," one of the girls said. Everybody was laughing.

74   Frank said, "I ain't laughed so much since we sent him off for the newspaper that night at Muggsy's and ditched him."

75   "Look at him. His face is red."

76   "He's blushing. Charlie is blushing."

77   "Hey, Ellen, what'd you do to Charlie? I never saw him act like that before."

78   I didn't know what to do or where to turn. Everyone was looking at me and laughing and I felt naked. I wanted to hide myself. I ran out into the street and I threw up. Then I walked home. It's a funny thing I never knew that Joe and Frank and the others liked to have me around all the time to make fun of me.

79   Now I know what it means when they say "to pull a Charlie Gordon."

80   I'm ashamed.

Progress Report 11—April 21

81   Still didn't go into the factory. I told Mrs. Flynn my landlady to call and tell Mr. Donnegan I was sick. Mrs. Flynn looks at me very funny lately like she's scared of me.

> I didn't know what to do or where to turn. Everyone was looking at me and laughing and I felt naked.

82   I think it's a good thing about finding out how everybody laughs at me. I thought about it a lot. It's because I'm so dumb and I don't even know when I'm doing something dumb. People think it's funny when a dumb person can't do things the same way they can.

83   Anyway, now I know I'm getting smarter every day. I know punctuation and I can spell good. I like to look up all the hard words in the dictionary and I remember them. I'm reading a lot now, and Miss Kinnian says I read very fast. Sometimes I even understand what I'm reading about, and it stays in my mind. There are times when I can close my eyes and think of a page and it all comes back like a picture.

84   Besides history, geography and arithmetic, Miss Kinnian said I should start to learn a few foreign languages. Dr. Strauss gave me some more tapes to play while I sleep. I still don't understand how that conscious and unconscious mind works, but Dr. Strauss says not to worry yet. He asked me to promise that when I start learning college subjects next week I wouldn't read any books on psychology—that is, until he gives me permission.

85   I feel a lot better today, but I guess I'm still a little angry that all the time people were laughing and making fun of me because I wasn't so smart. When I become intelligent like Dr. Strauss says, with three times my I.Q. of 68, then maybe I'll be like everyone else and people will like me and be friendly.

86   I'm not sure what an I.Q. is. Dr. Nemur said it was something that measured how intelligent you were—like a scale in the drugstore weighs pounds. But Dr. Strauss had a big arguement with him and said an I.Q. didn't weigh intelligence at all. He said an I.Q. showed how much intelligence you could get, like the numbers on the outside of a measuring cup. You still had to fill the cup up with stuff.

87   Then when I asked Burt, who gives me my intelligence tests and works with Algernon, he said that both of them were wrong (only I had to promise not to tell them he said so). Burt says that the I.Q. measures a lot of different things including some of the things you learned already, and it really isn't any good at all.

88   So I still don't know what I.Q. is except that mine is going to be over 200 soon. I didn't want to say anything, but I don't see how if they don't know *what* it is, or *where* it is—I don't see how they know *how much* of it you've got.

89   Dr. Nemur says I have to take a *Rorshach Test* tomorrow. I wonder what *that* is.

April 22

90   I found out what a *Rorshach* is. It's the test I took before the operation—the one with the inkblots on the pieces of cardboard. The man who gave me the test was the same one.

91   I was scared to death of those inkblots. I knew he was going to ask me to find the pictures and I knew I wouldn't be able to. I was thinking to myself, if only there was some way of knowing what kind of pictures were hidden there. Maybe there weren't any pictures at all. Maybe it was just a trick to see if I was dumb enough too look for something that wasn't there. Just thinking about that made me sore at him.

92   "All right, Charlie," he said, "you've seen these cards before, remember?"

93   "Of course I remember."

94   The way I said it, he knew I was angry, and he looked surprised. "Yes, of course. Now I want you to look at this one. What might this be? What do you see on this card? People see all sorts of things in these inkblots. Tell me what it might be for you— what it makes you think of."

95   I was shocked. That wasn't what I had expected him to say at all. "You mean there are no pictures hidden in those inkblots?"

96   He frowned and took off his glasses. "What?"

97   "Pictures. Hidden in the inkblots. Last time you told me that everyone could see them and you wanted me to find them too."

98   He explained to me that the last time he had used almost the exact same words he was using now. I didn't believe it, and I still have the **suspicion** that he misled me at the time just for the

NOTES

CLOSE READ
ANNOTATE: Mark the sentences in paragraph 91 that begin in similar ways.

QUESTION: What emotions are emphasized by the repetition?

CONCLUDE: What is the author showing about Charlie's state of mind by writing the paragraph in this way?

suspicion (suh SPIHSH uhn)
n. feeling of doubt or mistrust

fun of it. Unless—I don't know any more—could I have been *that* feeble-minded?

99   We went through the cards slowly. One of them looked like a pair of bats tugging at some thing. Another one looked like two men fencing with swords. I imagined all sorts of things. I guess I got carried away. But I didn't trust him any more, and I kept turning them around and even looking on the back to see if there was anything there I was supposed to catch. While he was making his notes, I peeked out of the corner of my eye to read it. But it was all in code that looked like this:

$$WF + A\ DdF\text{-}Ad\ orig.\ WF\text{-}A$$
$$SF + obj$$

100   The test still doesn't make sense to me. It seems to me that anyone could make up lies about things that they didn't really see. How could he know I wasn't making a fool of him by mentioning things that I didn't really imagine? Maybe I'll understand it when Dr. Strauss lets me read up on psychology.

April 25

101   I figured out a new way to line up the machines in the factory, and Mr. Donnegan says it will save him ten thousand dollars a year in labor and increased production. He gave me a $25 bonus.

102   I wanted to take Joe Carp and Frank Reilly out to lunch to celebrate, but Joe said he had to buy some things for his wife, and Frank said he was meeting his cousin for lunch. I guess it'll take a little time for them to get used to the changes in me. Everybody seems to be frightened of me. When I went over to Amos Borg and tapped him on the shoulder, he jumped up in the air.

103   People don't talk to me much any more or kid around the way they used to. It makes the job kind of lonely.

April 27

104   I got up the nerve today to ask Miss Kinnian to have dinner with me tomorrow night to celebrate my bonus.

105   At first she wasn't sure it was right, but I asked Dr. Strauss and he said it was okay. Dr. Strauss and Dr. Nemur don't seem to be getting along so well. They're arguing all the time. This evening when I came in to ask Dr. Strauss about having dinner with Miss Kinnian, I heard them shouting. Dr. Nemur was saying that it was *his* experiment and *his* research, and Dr. Strauss was shouting back that he contributed just as much, because he found me through Miss Kinnian and he performed the operation. Dr. Strauss said that someday thousands of neurosurgeons[7] might be using his technique all over the world.

---

7. **neurosurgeons** (NUR oh sur juhnz) *n.* doctors who operate on the nervous system, including the brain and spine.

106   Dr. Nemur wanted to publish the results of the experiment at the end of this month. Dr. Strauss wanted to wait a while longer to be sure. Dr. Strauss said that Dr. Nemur was more interested in the Chair[8] of Psychology at Princeton than he was in the experiment. Dr. Nemur said that Dr. Strauss was nothing but an opportunist who was trying to ride to glory on *his* coattails.

107   When I left afterwards, I found myself trembling. I don't know why for sure, but it was as if I'd seen both men clearly for the first time. I remember hearing Burt say that Dr. Nemur had a shrew of a wife who was pushing him all the time to get things published so that he could become famous. Burt said that the dream of her life was to have a big shot husband.

108   Was Dr. Strauss really trying to ride on his coattails?

April 28

109   I don't understand why I never noticed how beautiful Miss Kinnian really is. She has brown eyes and feathery brown hair that comes to the top of her neck. She's only thirty-four!

110   I think from the beginning I had the feeling that she was an unreachable genius—and very, very old. Now, every time I see her she grows younger and more lovely.

111   We had dinner and a long talk. When she said that I was coming along so fast that soon I'd be leaving her behind, I laughed.

112   "It's true, Charlie. You're already a better reader than I am. You can read a whole page at a glance while I can take in only a few lines at a time. And you remember every single thing you read. I'm lucky if I can recall the main thoughts and the general meaning."

113   "I don't feel intelligent. There are so many things I don't understand."

114   "You've got to be a *little* patient. You're accomplishing in days and weeks what it takes normal people to do in half a lifetime. That's what makes it so amazing. You're like a giant sponge now, soaking things in. Facts, figures, general knowledge. And soon you'll begin to connect them, too. You'll see how the different branches of learning are related. There are many levels, Charlie, like steps on a giant ladder that take you up higher and higher to see more and more of the world around you.

115   "I can see only a little bit of that, Charlie, and I won't go much higher than I am now, but you'll keep climbing up and up, and see more and more, and each step will open new worlds that you never even knew existed." She frowned. "I hope . . . I just hope to God—"

116   "What?"

---

8. **Chair** *n.* professorship.

Charlie and Miss Kinnian walking in the park

NOTES

117   "Never mind, Charles. I just hope I wasn't wrong to advise you to go into this in the first place."

118   I laughed. "How could that be? It worked, didn't it? Even Algernon is still smart."

119   We sat there silently for a while and I knew what she was thinking about as she watched me toying with the chain of my rabbit's foot and my keys. I didn't want to think of that possibility any more than elderly people want to think of death. I *knew* that this was only the beginning. I knew what she meant about levels because I'd seen some of them already. The thought of leaving her behind made me sad.

120   I'm in love with Miss Kinnian.

Progress Report 12—April 30

121   I've quit my job with Donnegan's Plastic Box Company. Mr. Donnegan insisted that it would be better for all concerned if I left. What did I do to make them hate me so?

122   The first I knew of it was when Mr. Donnegan showed me the petition. Eight hundred and forty names, everyone connected with the factory, except Fanny Girden. Scanning the list quickly, I saw at once that hers was the only missing name. All the rest demanded that I be fired.

123   Joe Carp and Frank Reilly wouldn't talk to me about it. No one else would either, except Fanny. She was one of the few people I'd known who set her mind to something and believed it no matter

what the rest of the world proved, said or did—and Fanny did not believe that I should have been fired. She had been against the petition on principle and despite the pressure and threats she'd held out.

124   "Which don't mean to say," she remarked, "that I don't think there's something mighty strange about you. Charlie. Them changes. I don't know. You used to be a good, dependable, ordinary man—not too bright maybe, but honest. Who knows what you done to yourself to get so smart all of a sudden. Like everybody around here's been saying, Charlie, it's not right."

125   "But how can you say that, Fanny? What's wrong with a man becoming intelligent and wanting to acquire knowledge and understanding of the world around him?"

126   She stared down at her work, and I turned to leave. Without looking at me, she said: "It was evil when Eve listened to the snake and ate from the tree of knowledge. It was evil when she saw that she was naked. If not for that none of us would ever have to grow old and sick, and die."

127   Once again now I have the feeling of shame burning inside me. This intelligence has driven a wedge between me and all the people I once knew and loved. Before, they laughed at me and **despised** me for my ignorance and dullness; now, they hate me for my knowledge and understanding. What do they want of me?

128   They've driven me out of the factory. Now I'm more alone than ever before . . .

May 15

129   Dr. Strauss is very angry at me for not having written any progress reports in two weeks. He's justified because the lab is now paying me a regular salary. I told him I was too busy thinking and reading. When I pointed out that writing was such a slow process that it made me impatient with my poor handwriting, he suggested that I learn to type. It's much easier to write now because I can type nearly seventy-five words a minute. Dr. Strauss continually reminds me of the need to speak and write simply so that people will be able to understand me.

130   I'll try to review all the things that happened to me during the last two weeks. Algernon and I were presented to the American Psychological Association sitting in convention with the World Psychological Association last Tuesday. We created quite a sensation. Dr. Nemur and Dr. Strauss were proud of us.

131   I suspect that Dr. Nemur, who is sixty—ten years older than Dr. Strauss—finds it necessary to see tangible[9] results of his work. Undoubtedly the result of pressure by Mrs. Nemur.

despised (dih SPYZD) v. hated; scorned

---

9. **tangible** (TAN juh buhl) adj. able to be felt or perceived; substantial.

CLOSE READ

ANNOTATE: Mark the specialized academic terms that Charlie uses in paragraphs 134–138.

QUESTION: From the use of this language, what is apparent about Charlie's level of intelligence compared to that of the people around him?

CONCLUDE: What potential problems could result from Charlie's use of language such as this?

132   Contrary to my earlier impressions of him, I realize that Dr. Nemur is not at all a genius. He has a very good mind, but it struggles under the specter of self-doubt. He wants people to take him for a genius. Therefore, it is important for him to feel that his work is accepted by the world. I believe that Dr. Nemur was afraid of further delay because he worried that someone else might make a discovery along these lines and take the credit from him.

133   Dr. Strauss on the other hand might be called a genius, although I feel that his areas of knowledge are too limited. He was educated in the tradition of narrow specialization; the broader aspects of background were neglected far more than necessary—even for a neurosurgeon.

134   I was shocked to learn that the only ancient languages he could read were Latin, Greek and Hebrew, and that he knows almost nothing of mathematics beyond the elementary levels of the calculus of variations. When he admitted this to me, I found myself almost annoyed. It was as if he'd hidden this part of himself in order to deceive me, pretending—as do many people I've discovered—to be what he is not. No one I've ever known is what he appears to be on the surface.

135   Dr. Nemur appears to be uncomfortable around me. Sometimes when I try to talk to him, he just looks at me strangely and turns away. I was angry at first when Dr. Strauss told me I was giving Dr. Nemur an inferiority complex. I thought he was mocking me and I'm oversensitive at being made fun of.

136   How was I to know that a highly respected psycho-experimentalist like Nemur was unacquainted with Hindustani[10] and Chinese? It's absurd when you consider the work that is being done in India and China today in the very field of his study.

137   I asked Dr. Strauss how Nemur could refute Rahajamati's attack on his method and results if Nemur couldn't even read them in the first place. That strange look on Dr. Strauss' face can mean only one of two things. Either he doesn't want to tell Nemur what they're saying in India, or else—and this worries me—Dr. Strauss doesn't know either. I must be careful to speak and write clearly and simply so that people won't laugh.

May 18

138   I am very disturbed. I saw Miss Kinnian last night for the first time in over a week. I tried to avoid all discussions of intellectual concepts and to keep the conversation on a simple, everyday level, but she just stared at me blankly and asked me what I meant about the mathematical variance equivalent in Dorbermann's *Fifth Concerto*.

10. **Hindustani** (hihn du STAH nee) *n.* a language of northern India.

139 When I tried to explain she stopped me and laughed. I guess I got angry, but I suspect I'm approaching her on the wrong level. No matter what I try to discuss with her, I am unable to communicate. I must review Vrostadt's equations on *Levels of Semantic Progression*. I find that I don't communicate with people much any more. Thank God for books and music and things I can think about. I am alone in my apartment at Mrs. Flynn's boarding house most of the time and seldom speak to anyone.

May 20

140 I would not have noticed the new dishwasher, a boy of about sixteen, at the corner diner where I take my evening meals if not for the incident of the broken dishes.

141 They crashed to the floor, shattering and sending bits of white china under the tables. The boy stood there, dazed and frightened, holding the empty tray in his hand. The whistles and catcalls from the customers (the cries of "hey, there go the profits!" . . . "*Mazeltov!*" . . . and "well, he didn't work here very long . . . " which invariably seems to follow the breaking of glass or dishware in a public restaurant) all seemed to confuse him.

142 When the owner came to see what the excitement was about, the boy cowered as if he expected to be struck and threw up his arms as if to ward off the blow.

143 "All right! All right, you dope," shouted the owner, "don't just stand there! Get the broom and sweep that mess up. A broom . . . a broom, you idiot! It's in the kitchen. Sweep up all the pieces."

144 The boy saw that he was not going to be punished. His frightened expression disappeared and he smiled and hummed as he came back with the broom to sweep the floor. A few of the rowdier customers kept up the remarks, amusing themselves at his expense.

145 "Here, sonny, over here there's a nice piece behind you . . ."

146 "C'mon, do it again . . ."

147 "He's not so dumb. It's easier to break 'em than to wash 'em . . ."

> . . . he slowly mirrored their smiles and finally broke into an uncertain grin at the joke which he obviously did not understand.

148 As his vacant eyes moved across the crowd of amused onlookers, he slowly mirrored their smiles and finally broke into an uncertain grin at the joke which he obviously did not understand.

149 I felt sick inside as I looked at his dull, vacuous smile, the wide, bright eyes of a child, uncertain but eager to please. They were laughing at him because he was mentally retarded.

150 And I had been laughing at him too.

151 Suddenly, I was furious at myself and all those who were smirking at him. I jumped up and shouted, "Shut up! Leave him

alone! It's not his fault he can't understand! He can't help what he is! But . . . he's still a human being!"

152   The room grew silent. I cursed myself for losing control and creating a scene. I tried not to look at the boy as I paid my check and walked out without touching my food. I felt ashamed for both of us.

153   How strange it is that people of honest feelings and sensibility, who would not take advantage of a man born without arms or legs or eyes—how such people think nothing of abusing a man born with low intelligence. It infuriated me to think that not too long ago I, like this boy, had foolishly played the clown.

154   And I had almost forgotten.

155   I'd hidden the picture of the old Charlie Gordon from myself because now that I was intelligent it was something that had to be pushed out of my mind. But today in looking at that boy, for the first time I saw what I had been. *I was just like him!*

156   Only a short time ago, I learned that people laughed at me. Now I can see that unknowingly l joined with them in laughing at myself. That hurts most of all.

157   I have often reread my progress reports and seen the illiteracy, the childish naivete, the mind of low intelligence peering from a dark room, through the keyhole, at the dazzling light outside. I see that even in my dullness I knew that I was inferior, and that other people had something I lacked—something denied me. In my mental blindness, I thought that it was somehow connected with the ability to read and write, and I was sure that if I could get those skills I would automatically have intelligence too.

158   Even a feeble-minded man wants to be like other men.

159   A child may not know how to feed itself, or what to eat, yet it knows of hunger.

160   This then is what I was like. I never knew. Even with my gift of intellectual awareness, I never really knew.

161   This day was good for me. Seeing the past more clearly, I have decided to use my knowledge and skills to work in the field of increasing human intelligence levels. Who is better equipped for this work? Who else has lived in both worlds? These are my people. Let me use my gift to do something for them.

162   Tomorrow, I will discuss with Dr. Strauss the manner in which I can work in this area. I may be able to help him work out the problems of widespread use of the technique which was used on me. I have several good ideas of my own.

163   There is so much that might be done with this technique. If I could be made into a genius, what about thousands of others like myself? What fantastic levels might be achieved by using this technique on normal people? On *geniuses*?

164   There are so many doors to open. I am impatient to begin.

PROGRESS REPORT 13—May 23

165   It happened today. Algernon bit me. I visited the lab to see him as I do occasionally, and when I took him out of his cage, he snapped at my hand. I put him back and watched him for a while. He was unusually disturbed and vicious.

May 24

166   Burt, who is in charge of the experimental animals, tells me that Algernon is changing. He is less cooperative; he refuses to run the maze any more; general motivation has decreased. And he hasn't been eating. Everyone is upset about what this may mean.

May 25

167   They've been feeding Algernon, who now refuses to work the shifting-lock problem. Everyone identifies me with Algernon. In a way we're both the first of our kind. They're all pretending that Algernon's behavior is not necessarily significant for me. But it's hard to hide the fact that some of the other animals who were used in this experiment are showing strange behavior.

168   Dr. Strauss and Dr. Nemur have asked me not to come to the lab any more. I know what they're thinking but I can't accept it. I am going ahead with my plans to carry their research forward. With all due respect to both of these fine scientists, I am well aware of their limitations. If there is an answer, I'll have to find it out for myself. Suddenly, time has become very important to me.

May 29

169   I have been given a lab of my own and permission to go ahead with the research. I'm on to something. Working day and night. I've had a cot moved into the lab. Most of my writing time is spent on the notes which I keep in a separate folder, but from time to time I feel it necessary to put down my moods and my thoughts out of sheer habit.

170   I find the *calculus of intelligence* to be a fascinating study. Here is the place for the application of all the knowledge I have acquired. In a sense it's the problem I've been concerned with all my life.

May 31

171   Dr. Strauss thinks I'm working too hard. Dr. Nemur says I'm trying to cram a lifetime of research and thought into a few weeks. I know I should rest, but I'm driven on by something inside that won't let me stop. I've got to find the reason for the sharp **regression** in Algernon. I've got to know *if* and *when* it will happen to me.

NOTES

CLOSE READ

ANNOTATE: In paragraph 169, mark the two shortest sentences.

QUESTION: What can you tell about Charlie's state of mind from the short sentences?

CONCLUDE: Why has the author made this choice?

regression (ri GREHSH uhn) *n.* return to a previous, less advanced state

June 4

172 Letter to Dr. Strauss (copy)

173 Dear Dr. Strauss:

174 Under separate cover I am sending you a copy of my report entitled, "The Algernon-Gordon Effect: A Study of Structure and Function of Increased Intelligence," which I would like to have you read and have published.

175   As you see, my experiments are completed. I have included in my report all of my formulae, as well as mathematical analysis in the appendix. Of course, these should be verified.

176   Because of its importance to both you and Dr. Nemur (and need I say to myself, too?) I have checked and rechecked my results a dozen times in the hope of finding an error. I am sorry to say the results must stand. Yet for the sake of science, I am grateful for the little bit that I here add to the knowledge of the function of the human mind and of the laws governing the artificial increase of human intelligence.

177   I recall your once saying to me that an experimental *failure* or the *disproving* of a theory was as important to the advancement of learning as a success would be. I know now that this is true. I am sorry, however, that my own contribution to the field must rest upon the ashes of the work of two men I regard so highly.

178   Yours Truly,
                    Charles Gordon

179 encl.: rept.

June 5

180   I must not become emotional. The facts and the results of my experiments are clear, and the more sensational aspects of my own rapid climb cannot obscure the fact that the tripling of intelligence by the surgical technique developed by Drs. Strauss and Nemur must be viewed as having little or no practical applicability (at the present time) to the increase of human intelligence.

181   As I review the records and data on Algernon, I see that although he is still in his physical infancy, he has regressed mentally. Motor activity[11] is impaired; there is a general reduction of glandular activity; there is an accelerated loss of coordination.

182   There are also strong indications of progressive amnesia.

183   As will be seen by my report, these and other physical and mental **deterioration** syndromes[12] can be predicted with statistically significant results by the application of my formula.

184   The surgical stimulus to which we were both subjected has resulted in an intensification and acceleration of all mental processes. The unforeseen development, which I have taken the

deterioration (dih tihr ee uh RAY shuhn) *n.* process of becoming worse

---

11. **Motor activity** movement; physical coordination.
12. **syndromes** (SIHN drohmz) *n.* a number of symptoms occurring together and characterizing a specific disease or condition.

Charlie, months into the experiment

liberty of calling the "Algernon-Gordon Effect," is the logical extension of the entire intelligence speedup. The hypothesis here proven may be described simply in the following terms: Artificially increased intelligence deteriorates at a rate of time directly proportional to the quantity of the increase.

185   I feel that this, in itself, is an important discovery.

186   As long as I am able to write, I will continue to record my thoughts in these progress reports. It is one of my few pleasures. However, by all indications, my own mental deterioration will be very rapid.

187   I have already begun to notice signs of emotional instability and forgetfulness, the first symptoms of the burnout.

June 10

188   Deterioration progressing. I have become absent-minded. Algernon died two days ago. Dissection shows my predictions were right. His brain had decreased in weight and there was a general smoothing out of cerebral convolutions as well as a deepening and broadening of brain fissures.

189   I guess the same thing is or will soon be happening to me. Now that it's definite, I don't want it to happen.

CLOSE READ

ANNOTATE: Mark the choppy sentences that appear at the beginning of paragraph 188.

QUESTION: What does this change in writing style suggest?

CONCLUDE: What effect does knowing what is happening to Charlie have on the reader?

190   I put Algernon's body in a cheese box and buried him in the back yard. I cried.

June 15

191   Dr. Strauss came to see me again. I wouldn't open the door and I told him to go away. I want to be left to myself. I have become touchy and irritable. I feel the darkness closing in. I keep telling myself how important this **introspective** journal will be.

introspective (ihn truh SPEHK tihv) *adj.* thoughtful; inward-looking

192   It's a strange sensation to pick up a book that you've read and enjoyed just a few months ago and discover that you don't remember it. I remembered how great I thought John Milton[13] was, but when I picked up *Paradise Lost* I couldn't understand it at all. I got so angry I threw the book across the room.

193   I've got to try to hold on to some of it. Some of the things I've learned. Oh, God, please don't take it all away.

June 19

194   Sometimes, at night, I go out for a walk. Last night I couldn't remember where I lived. A policeman took me home. I have the strange feeling that this has all happened to me before—a long time ago. I keep telling myself I'm the only person in the world who can describe what's happening to me.

June 21

195   Why can't I remember? I've got to fight. I lie in bed for days and I don't know who or where I am. Then it all comes back to me in a flash. Fugues of amnesia.[14] Symptoms of senility—second childhood. I can watch them coming on. It's so cruelly logical. I learned so much and so fast. Now my mind is deteriorating rapidly. I won't let it happen. I'll fight it. I can't help thinking of the boy in the restaurant, the blank expression, the silly smile, the people laughing at him. No—please—not that again . . .

June 22

196   I'm forgetting things that I learned recently. It seems to be following the classic pattern—the last things learned are the first things forgotten. Or is that the pattern? I'd better look it up again . . .

197   I reread my paper on the "Algernon-Gordon Effect" and I get the strange feeling that it was written by someone else. There are parts I don't even understand.

198   Motor activity impaired. I keep tripping over things, and it becomes increasingly difficult to type.

June 23

199   I've given up using the typewriter completely. My coordination is bad. I feel that I'm moving slower and slower. Had a terrible

13. **John Milton** British poet (1608–1674) who wrote *Paradise Lost.*
14. **Fugues** (fyoogz) **of amnesia** (am NEE zhuh) periods of memory loss.

shock today. I picked up a copy of an article I used in my research, Krueger's "Uber psychische Ganzheit," to see if it would help me understand what I had done. First I thought there was something wrong with my eyes. Then I realized I could no longer read German. I tested myself in other languages. All gone.

June 30

200   A week since I dared to write again. It's slipping away like sand through my fingers. Most of the books I have are too hard for me now. I get angry with them because I know that I read and understood them just a few weeks ago.

201   I keep telling myself I must keep writing these reports so that somebody will know what is happening to me. But it gets harder to form the words and remember spellings. I have to look up even simple words in the dictionary now and it makes me impatient with myself.

202   Dr. Strauss comes around almost every day, but I told him I wouldn't see or speak to anybody. He feels guilty. They all do. But I don't blame anyone. I knew what might happen. But how it hurts.

July 7

203   I don't know where the week went. Todays Sunday I know because I can see through my window people going to church. I think I stayed in bed all week but I remember Mrs. Flynn bringing food to me a few times. I keep saying over and over Ive got to do something but then I forget or maybe its just easier not to do what I say Im going to do.

204   I think of my mother and father a lot these days. I found a picture of them with me taken at a beach. My father has a big ball under his arm and my mother is holding me by the hand. I dont remember them the way they are in the picture. All I remember is my father arguing with mom about money.

205   He never shaved much and he used to scratch my face when he hugged me. He said he was going to take me to see cows on a farm once but he never did. He never kept his promises . . .

July 10

206   My landlady Mrs Flynn is very worried about me. She said she doesnt like loafers. If Im sick its one thing, but if Im a loafer thats another thing and she wont have it. I told her I think Im sick.

207   I try to read a little bit every day, mostly stories, but sometimes I have to read the same thing over and over again because I dont know what it means. And its hard to write. I know I should look up all the words in the dictionary but its so hard and Im so tired all the time.

NOTES

CLOSE READ

ANNOTATE: In paragraph 203, mark errors in Charlie's punctuation.

QUESTION: Why are these errors both familiar and alarming?

CONCLUDE: What effect do these errors have on the reader?

208   Then I got the idea that I would only use the easy words instead of the long hard ones. That saves time. I put flowers on Algernon s grave about once a week. Mrs. Flynn thinks Im crazy to put flowers on a mouses grave but I told her that Algernon was special.

July 14

209   Its sunday again. I dont have anything to do to keep me busy now because my television set is broke and I dont have any money to get it fixed. (I think I lost this months check from the lab. I dont remember)

210   I get awful headaches and asperin doesnt help me much. Mrs. Flynn knows Im really sick and she feels very sorry for me. Shes a wonderful woman whenever someone is sick.

July 22

211   Mrs. Flynn called a strange doctor to see me. She was afraid I was going to die. I told the doctor I wasnt too sick and that I only forget sometimes. He asked me did I have any friends or relatives and I said no I dont have any. I told him I had a friend called Algernon once but he was a mouse and we used to run races together. He looked at me kind of funny like he thought I was crazy.

212   He smiled when I told him I used to be a genius. He talked to me like I was a baby and he winked at Mrs Flynn. I got mad and chased him out because he was making fun of me the way they all used to.

July 24

213   I have no more money and Mrs Flynn says I got to go to work somewhere and pay the rent because I havent paid for over two months. I dont know any work but the job I used to have at Donnegans Plastic Box Company. I dont want to go back there because they all knew me when I was smart and maybe they'll laugh at me. But I dont know what else to do to get money.

July 25

214   I was looking at some of my old progress reports and its very funny but I cant read what I wrote. I can make out some of the words but they dont make sense.

215   Miss Kinnian came to the door but I said go away I dont want to see you. She cried and I cried too but I wouldnt let her in because I didnt want her to laugh at me. I told her I didn't like her any more. I told her I didn't want to be smart any more. Thats not true. I still love her and I still want to be smart but I had to say that so shed go away. She gave Mrs. Flynn money to pay the rent. I dont want that. I got to get a job.

216   Please . . . please let me not forget how to read and write . . .

July 27

217   Mr. Donnegan was very nice when I came back and asked him for my old job of janitor. First he was very suspicious but I told him what happened to me then he looked very sad and put his hand on my shoulder and said Charlie Gordon you got guts.

218   Everybody looked at me when I came downstairs and started working in the toilet sweeping it out like I used to. I told myself Charlie if they make fun of you dont get sore because you remember their not so smart as you once thot they were. And besides they were once your friends and if they laughed at you that doesnt mean anything because they liked you too.

219   One of the new men who came to work there after I went away made a nasty crack he said hey Charlie I hear you're a very smart fella a real quiz kid. Say something intelligent. I felt bad but Joe Carp came over and grabbed him by the shirt and said leave him alone or Ill break your neck. I didn't expect Joe to take my part so I guess hes really my friend.

220   Later Frank Reilly came over and said Charlie if anybody bothers you or trys to take advantage you call me or Joe and we will set em straight. I said thanks Frank and I got choked up so I had to turn around and go into the supply room so he wouldnt see me cry. Its good to have friends.

CLOSE READ

ANNOTATE: In paragraph 219, mark the conclusion that Charlie reaches about Joe Carp.

QUESTION: How is the situation not really as simple as Charlie describes?

CONCLUDE: What does the inclusion of this dialogue help the author show about Charlie?

July 28

221   I did a dumb thing today I forgot I wasnt in Miss Kinnians class at the adult center any more like I use to be. I went in and sat down in my old seat in the back of the room and she looked at me funny and she said Charles. I dint remember she ever called me that before only Charlie so I said hello Miss Kinnian Im ready for my lesin today only I lost my reader that we was using. She startid to cry and run out of the room and everybody looked at me and I saw they wasnt the same pepul who use to be in my class.

222   Then all of a suddin I rememberd some things about the operashun and me getting smart and I said holy smoke I reely pulled a Charlie Gordon that time. I went away before she come back to the room.

223   Thats why Im going away from New York for good. I don't want to do nothing like that agen. I dont want Miss Kinnian to feel sorry for me. Evry body feels sorry at the factery and I dont want that eather so Im going someplace where nobody knows that Charlie Gordon was once a genus and now he cant even reed a book or rite good.

> . . . Im going someplace where nobody knows that Charlie Gordon was once a genus and now he cant even reed a book or rite good.

224   Im taking a cuple of books along and even if I cant reed them Ill practise hard and maybe I wont forget every thing I lerned. If I try reel hard maybe Ill be a littel bit smarter then I was before the operashun. I got my rabits foot and my luky penny and maybe they will help me.

225   If you ever reed this Miss Kinnian dont be sorry for me Im glad I got a second chanse to be smart becaus I lerned a lot of things that I never even new were in this world and Im grateful that I saw it all for a littel bit. l dont know why Im dumb agen or what I did wrong maybe its becaus I dint try hard enuff. But if I try and practis very hard maybe Ill get a littl smarter and kow what all the words are. I remember a littel bit how nice I had a feeling with the blue book that has the torn cover when I reit. Thats why Im gonna keep trying to get smart so I can have that feeling agen. Its a good feeling to know things and be smart. I wish I had it rite now if I did I woud sit down and reed all the time. Anyway I bet Im the first dumb person in the world who ever found out something importent for sience. I remember I did somthing but I don't remember what. So I gess its like I did it for all the dumb pepul like me.

226   Goodbye Miss Kinnian and Dr Strauss and evreybody. And P.S. please tell Dr Nemur not to be such a grouch when pepul laff at him and he woud have more frends. Its easy to make frends if you let pepul laff at you. Im going to have lots of frends where I go.

227   P.P.S. Please if you get a chanse put some flowrs on Algernons grave in the bak yard . . . 🙖

Comprehension Check

Complete the following items after you finish your first read.

1. Who is Algernon, and why is he important?

2. What is the goal of the operation Dr. Strauss performs on Charlie?

3. What are three ways the operation changes Charlie's life?

4. What happens to Algernon in May and June?

5. What happens to Charlie at the end of the story?

6. 🗐 **Notebook** Write a summary of "Flowers for Algernon."

- -

RESEARCH

Research to Clarify Choose at least one unfamiliar detail from the text. Briefly research that detail. In what way does the information you learned shed light on an aspect of the story?

Research to Explore Choose something that interested you from the text, and formulate a research question.

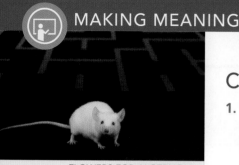

FLOWERS FOR ALGERNON

Close Read the Text

1. This model, from paragraphs 149–150 of the text, shows two sample annotations, along with questions and conclusions. Close read the passage, and find another detail to annotate. Then, write a question and a conclusion.

Close Read
ANNOTATE · QUESTION · CONCLUDE

ANNOTATE: This sentence contains many descriptive adjectives.

QUESTION: What purpose do these adjectives serve?

CONCLUDE: The author is showing that Charlie has become quite perceptive about human behavior.

ANNOTATE: This paragraph consists of a single sentence.

QUESTION: What is the purpose of a single-sentence paragraph?

CONCLUDE: The author is showing that this idea is important enough to stand alone.

> I felt sick inside as I looked at his dull, vacuous smile, the wide, bright eyes of a child, uncertain but eager to please. They were laughing at him because he was mentally retarded.
> And I had been laughing at him too.

Tool Kit
Close-Read Guide and Model Annotation

2. For more practice, go back into the text, and complete the close-read notes.

3. Revisit a section of the text you found important during your first read. Read this section closely, and **annotate** what you notice. Ask yourself **questions** such as "Why did the author make this choice?" What can you **conclude**?

Analyze the Text

CITE TEXTUAL EVIDENCE
to support your answers.

Notebook Respond to these questions.

1. **Compare and Contrast** In what sense is Charlie the same at the end of the story as he is at the beginning? In what sense is he different?

2. **Analyze** How does Charlie's diary reveal his changing mental state?

3. **Draw Conclusions** Review the journal entry for July 28. What has Charlie gained through his experience?

4. **Analyze** In what ways does Charlie's operation affect his relationships with the people around him?

5. **Essential Question: *In what different ways can people be intelligent?*** What have you learned about human intelligence from reading this story?

Analyze Craft and Structure

Development of Theme The **theme** of a literary work is the central message about life that it conveys. In some works, the author expresses the theme by stating it directly. More often, however, the author implies or suggests the theme. To identify an implied theme, the reader analyzes the elements of the story, such as the setting, characters, and plot. The reader also considers the author's choices about how to structure the story and how to present details.

The **point of view,** or perspective from which a story is told, can provide clues to the theme.

- In **first-person point of view,** the narrator is a participant in the events of the story and uses first-person pronouns, such as *I, me,* and *my.* The narrator can tell only what he or she sees, knows, thinks, and feels. In **first-person naive point of view,** the narrator does not fully understand what is happening—for example, because he or she is a child or is traveling in an unfamiliar place.

- In **third-person point of view,** the narrator is not part of the story's events. Such a narrator uses only third-person pronouns, such as *he, she,* and *they.*

Authors may also provide clues to the theme by using allusions. An **allusion** is an unexplained reference to a well-known person, place, event, literary work, or work of art. For instance, an author may make an allusion to Greek or Roman mythology or to the Bible.

Practice

CITE TEXTUAL EVIDENCE to support your answers.

Notebook Answer the following questions.

1. (a) Who is the narrator of this story? (b) What point of view does this narrator use? Explain.

2. (a) At the beginning of the story, what does Charlie know and not know about himself and others? (b) How does his understanding change as the story progresses?

3. Cite specific ways in which the narrative point of view affects what readers learn about all the characters, especially their feelings and thoughts. Explain.

4. (a) Is Charlie's life better or worse at the end of the story than it was at the beginning? (b) What possible theme is suggested by Charlie's experience?

5. In paragraph 126, Fanny makes an allusion to a biblical story. If this story is unfamiliar to you, briefly research it. (a) How does this story relate to Charlie's experiences? (b) What theme does the author's use of this allusion help him develop? (c) In what ways is Charlie's experience different—a fresh take on the biblical story?

FLOWERS FOR ALGERNON

Concept Vocabulary

subconscious	despised	introspective
suspicion	deterioration	regression

Why These Words? These concept vocabulary words are related to emotional and psychological states. Charlie experiences a range of these states. For example, the experiment makes him aware that his co-workers laughed at him and *despised* him. The experiment also changes Charlie's personality as his *suspicion* of everyone grows and he becomes more *introspective*.

1. How does the concept vocabulary sharpen the reader's understanding of the experiment Charlie undergoes?

2. What other words in the story connect to Charlie's experience?

Practice

Notebook The concept vocabulary words appear in "Flowers for Algernon."

1. Suppose you were a psychology researcher. Write a paragraph about an experiment you would like to design. Use at least four of the concept vocabulary words in your paragraph.

2. With a partner, see if you can match each concept word to a related word in the same word family.

Word Study

Latin Prefix: *sub-* You can use the Latin prefix *sub-*, which means "under" or "beneath," to help you determine the meaning of an unfamiliar word. In "Flowers for Algernon," Charlie learns that his *subconscious* is responsible for producing dreams and helping him learn. His subconscious thoughts, or the ones of which he is unaware, sit below his conscious thoughts, or the ones he knows he is having.

1. Which would you expect to be a more important part of an outline, a *topic* or a *subtopic*? Why?

2. How does the definition of *sub-* help you determine where you might find a *submarine*?

WORD NETWORK

Add words related to human intelligence from the text to your Word Network.

STANDARDS

Language
• Demonstrate command of the conventions of standard English grammar and usage when writing or speaking.
• Use common, grade-appropriate Greek or Latin affixes and roots as clues to the meaning of a word.
• Demonstrate understanding of figurative language, word relationships, and nuances in word meanings.
• Acquire and use accurately grade-appropriate general academic and domain-specific words and phrases; gather vocabulary knowledge when considering a word or phrase important to comprehension or expression.

Conventions

Direct and Indirect Objects Writers use objects to show whom or what is affected by a verb's action. A **direct object** is a noun or pronoun that receives the action of the verb. A direct object answers the question *Whom?* or *What?* after an action verb.

An **indirect object** is a noun or pronoun that comes after an action verb and names the person or thing to which or for which something is done. To find the indirect object, first find the direct object of the verb. Then, ask: *To whom? For whom? To what?* or *For what?* The indirect object will almost always come between the verb and the direct object.

DIRECT OBJECT	INDIRECT OBJECT
S V DO	S V IO DO
Sentence: Bill baked some cookies.	**Sentence:** Bill baked Marissa some cookies.
Baked what? cookies	**Baked for whom?** Marissa

Read It

1. In each sentence, identify the subject, the verb, the direct object, and the indirect object. Some sentences do not include indirect objects.

   a. In their first race, Algernon beats Charlie.

   b. Miss Kinnian teaches Charlie reading and writing.

   c. Charlie trusts the doctors.

2. Reread the first clause of paragraph 174 of "Flowers for Algernon." Mark the subject, the verb, the direct object, and the indirect object.

Write It

🗐 **Notebook** In each sentence, identify the subject, the verb, the direct object, and the indirect object (if there is one). Then, rewrite the sentence with a different direct or indirect object. Your revisions do not have to stay true to the events of the story.

> EXAMPLE
> In his progress reports, Charlie expresses his feelings.
>
>   S   V   DO
> *In his progress reports, Charlie expresses his thoughts and ideas.*

1. The doctors give Charlie many tests.

2. Charlie's co-workers often trick him.

3. Charlie greatly admires Miss Kinnian.

4. Charlie brings Algernon flowers.

FLOWERS FOR ALGERNON
(short story)

Comparing Texts

The script you are about to read is based on the novel version of *Flowers for Algernon*. After you read the script, you will perform the scene with a group and then analyze your classmates' performances. The work you do will help prepare you for the final comparing task.

from FLOWERS FOR ALGERNON (script)

About the Playwright

David Rogers (1927–2013) was an author, playwright, and actor. He was born in New York City and fell in love with the theater at an early age. In time, he became an actor himself, appearing on Broadway in a production of William Shakespeare's *As You Like It*. During his remarkable career, Rogers was a writer for the *Jackie Gleason Show* and the *Carol Burnett Show*; he also wrote an award-winning opera for New York City's Lincoln Center and numerous adaptations of literary works for the stage.

from Flowers for Algernon

Concept Vocabulary

You will encounter the following words as you read the excerpt from the script for *Flowers for Algernon*. Before reading, note how familiar you are with each word. Then, rank the words in order from most familiar (1) to least familiar (3).

WORD	YOUR RANKING
clarity	
peak	
unleashed	

After completing the first read, come back to the concept vocabulary and review your rankings. Mark changes to your original rankings as needed.

First Read DRAMA

Apply these strategies as you conduct your first read. You will have an opportunity to complete a close read after your first read.

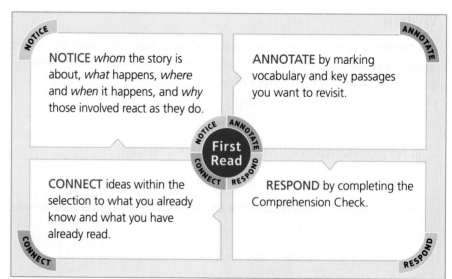

NOTICE *whom* the story is about, *what* happens, *where* and *when* it happens, and *why* those involved react as they do.

ANNOTATE by marking vocabulary and key passages you want to revisit.

CONNECT ideas within the selection to what you already know and what you have already read.

RESPOND by completing the Comprehension Check.

First Read

STANDARDS

Reading
By the end of the year, read and comprehend literature, including stories, dramas, and poems, at the high end of the grades 6–8 text complexity band independently and proficiently.

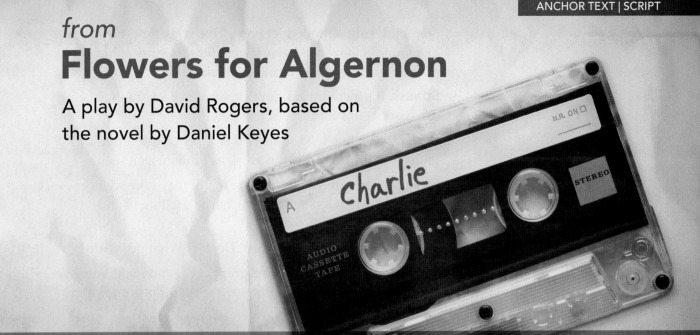

from
Flowers for Algernon

A play by David Rogers, based on the novel by Daniel Keyes

BACKGROUND

This script is based on Daniel Keyes's novel *Flowers for Algernon,* an expanded version of the short story you've just read. This particular scene is a dramatic expansion of the progress report dated May 31. The characters Doctor Strauss, Burt, and Charlie—or at least his voice—from the short story are present in this scene.

SCAN FOR MULTIMEDIA

1   [*Lights come up on* Strauss *in his office.* Burt *is just entering, carrying a huge pile of typed sheets which he puts on* Strauss' *desk.*]

2   **Strauss.** What's that?

3   **Burt.** More of Charlie's notes.

4   **Strauss.** How many days' work is that?

5   **Burt.** Two.

6   **Strauss.** Dear heaven.

7   **Burt.** I've got three stenographers[1] working. I had to call in extra help.

8   **Strauss.** Don't tell me. I'm here every night till one listening to his tapes. [*He pushes the play button of his tape recorder and they listen to:*]

9   **Charlie's Voice.** July eighteenth. They all think I'm killing myself at this pace. But they don't understand I'm living at a **peak** of **clarity** and beauty I never knew existed. It's as if all the knowledge I've soaked in during the past months has lifted me to a peak of light and understanding. This is beauty,

NOTES

peak (peek) *n.* highest level
clarity (KLAR uh tee) *n.* state of thinking clearly

---

1. **stenographers (stuh NOG ruh fuhrz)** *n.* office workers who transcribe speech into typed notes.

love, and truth all rolled into one. This is joy. And now that I've found it, how can I give it up? [Strauss *snaps off the machine and inserts new tape as he speaks.*]

10 **Strauss.** It's incredible. I can't even believe any human being can work at this level . . . at this pace.

11 **Burt.** Doctor. I've read some of this . . . of course, I don't understand it, but . . . is this work as brilliant as it seems?

12 **Strauss.** What are you asking me for? It may take science forty years to understand what Charlie's telling us this month.

13 **Burt.** What have we **unleashed**, Doctor? What do we do?

14 **Strauss.** We hire another stenographer . . . and make sure she gets it all down correctly. [Burt *exits right.* Strauss *pushes the play button.*]

15 **Charlie's Voice.** July twenty-fifth. Algernon became lost in the maze today. He threw himself against the walls . . .

unleashed (uhn LEESHD) *v.* released; set loose on the world

CITE TEXTUAL EVIDENCE
to support your answers.

Comprehension Check

Complete the following items after you finish your first read.

1. What phase of the experiment does this scene depict? How can you tell?

2. Why are Dr. Strauss and Burt reacting to Charlie in this way?

3. How has the position of the other men changed in reference to Charlie?

4. What important information does Charlie reveal about Algernon?

Close Read the Text

Reread the script. As you read, imagine how each line would be delivered on stage. What tones of voice would convey the amazement the characters feel about Charlie's progress?

Close Read
ANNOTATE · QUESTION · CONCLUDE

from FLOWERS FOR ALGERNON (script)

Analyze the Text

CITE TEXTUAL EVIDENCE
to support your answers.

Complete the activities.

1. **Prepare the Scene** Form groups of three. With your group, prepare to perform the scene in front of the class. First, reread the script. Next, discuss how you want to portray each character—his movements, gestures, voice inflections, and so on. Then, rehearse the scene several times. After each run-through, discuss ways to improve your performance. You may even consider changing the exact words of the script to better reflect your own interpretations of the story. Finally, when your group is ready to perform, rejoin the whole class.

2. **Perform the Scene** As a class, decide the order in which the groups will present their scenes. When it is your group's turn, perform the scene for the class. As other groups perform, take notes about the choices they have made. If they have decided to depart from the exact words of the script, jot down your ideas about the effectiveness of their choices.

3. **Analyze the Scene** As a class, analyze each group's performance. First, discuss the choices the actors made about how to portray the characters. Then, identify the extent to which they chose to depart from the exact words of the script. Cite specific examples. Finally, evaluate the effects and effectiveness of those choices.

🔲 **WORD NETWORK**

Add words related to human intelligence from the text to your Word Network.

LANGUAGE DEVELOPMENT

Concept Vocabulary

| peak | clarity | unleashed |

Why These Words? The three concept vocabulary words are used to describe someone who is performing at the highest level—in this case, Charlie. For example, the experiment has *unleashed* his full potential. Identify two other words from the selection that relate to great intelligence or emotion.

Practice

📓 **Notebook** Write a paragraph from the perspective of a high-performing athlete who is competing against other high-performing athletes. Use each of the vocabulary words correctly in the paragraph.

📋 **STANDARDS**

Reading Literature
Analyze the extent to which a filmed or live production of a story or drama stays faithful to or departs from the text or script, evaluating the choices made by the director or actors.

FLOWERS FOR ALGERNON
(short story)

from FLOWERS FOR ALGERNON
(script)

Writing to Compare

Daniel Keyes, the author of the short story "Flowers for Algernon," and David Rogers, the playwright behind the dramatic adaptation, use different techniques to tell the same story. The specific features of a writing form have a strong influence on a writer's choices. Now, deepen your understanding of those choices by comparing and contrasting them.

> **Assignment**
>
> Using information from class discussion, as well as details from the selections, write an explanatory **comparison-and-contrast essay** in which you identify the unique characteristics of a short story and a script and explain how those characteristics influence the ways in which a writer tells a story.

Planning and Prewriting

Compare Techniques Discuss the techniques used by the writers of the short story and the script to present the same topic. Use the chart below to note advantages and disadvantages of each medium.

	SHORT STORY	SCRIPT
Point of View From what point of view, or perspective, is the story told?		
Characterization How do readers find out what characters are like?		
Conflict How does the writer depict the conflicts characters face?		

🔲 **Notebook** **Respond to these questions.**

1. Visualization, or forming an image in your mind, can help you read both a short story and a script. Is visualization more important when reading one of these forms than when reading the other? Why or why not?

2. A story and a script usually reflect one point of view, or perspective, on events. Is one point of view more objective or reliable? Does one point of view force readers to make more inferences about what is *really* happening? Explain.

≔ STANDARDS

Reading Literature
Compare and contrast the structure of two or more texts and analyze how the differing structure of each text contributes to its meaning and style.

Writing
• Write informative/explanatory texts to examine a topic and convey ideas, concepts, and information through the selection, organization, and analysis of relevant content.
   a. Introduce a topic clearly, previewing what is to follow; organize ideas, concepts, and information into broader categories; include formatting, graphics, and multimedia when useful to aiding comprehension.
   b. Develop the topic with relevant, well-chosen facts, definitions, concrete details, quotations, or other information and examples.
   f. Provide a concluding statement or section that follows from and supports the information or explanation presented.
• Apply *grade 8 Reading standards* to literature.

Drafting

Outline Decide the order in which you will present details in your essay. If you use block organization, you will explain all of the techniques used in one form and then discuss all of the techniques used in the other. If you use point-by-point organization, you will choose important topics, or points, and explain the techniques used in both forms to present one topic, then another topic, and so on. Use the models below to help you complete an outline for your essay.

Block Organization	Point-by-Point Organization
I. Introduction	I. Introduction
II. Short Story	II. Point of View
A. Point of View	A. Short Story
B. Characterization	B. Script
C. Conflict	III. Characterization
III. Script	A. Short Story
A. Point of View	B. Script
B. Characterization	IV. Conflict
C. Conflict	A. Short Story
IV. Conclusion	B. Script
	V. Conclusion

✎ EVIDENCE LOG

Before moving on to a new selection, go to your Evidence Log and record what you learned from the short story "Flowers for Algernon" and the scene from the script of the dramatic adaptation.

Draft a Strong Introduction and Conclusion Planning your introduction and conclusion before you draft can help you write a satisfying essay. Follow these planning steps:

- **Write an introduction.** Begin with an introductory thesis statement that clearly identifies the forms you will be comparing and summarizes your main findings. Identify and mark key words in the assignment prompt, and consider using those words or synonyms in your introduction.

  Thesis Statement: _____

  _____

- **Write a concluding thought.** After presenting evidence in the body of your essay, your conclusion will restate your main points. End with a final statement that leaves readers with an interesting or challenging idea about the two forms you compared.

  Concluding Thought: _____

  _____

Reviewing, Revising, and Editing

After drafting your essay, review the assignment to make sure your writing fulfills your goals. Ask yourself:

- Have I compared and contrasted techniques used in both forms?
- Does the information provided follow a clear and logical organization?
- Are the introduction and conclusion effective?
- Is my essay free from errors in spelling, punctuation, and grammar?

WRITING TO SOURCES

• FLOWERS FOR ALGERNON (short story)

• *from* FLOWERS FOR ALGERNON (script)

Write an Informative Speech

You have just read a short story and an excerpt from a script about a character whose intelligence transforms dramatically. Now, you will use your knowledge of these texts to write an informative speech from Charlie's point of view. Your speech should authentically portray Charlie's character, as well as his knowledge and ideas, based on details from the short story and script.

Assignment

You have read about Charlie's intellectual transformation, the research he is a part of, and the knowledge he gains from his experience. Imagine yourself as Charlie at the beginning of June, ten weeks after the experimental surgery. Write an **informative speech** on this question:

> What has happened to you so far as a result of the experiment, and what do you predict will happen to you as time progresses?

🔧 **Tool Kit**
Student Model of an Informative Text

Elements of an Informative Speech

An informative text or speech provides facts and details about a topic. Your assignment—writing as Charlie—is to recount the results of the experiment you have undergone and predict what will happen to you as time progresses.

ACADEMIC VOCABULARY

As you craft your essay, consider using some of the academic vocabulary you learned in the beginning of the unit.

assimilate
tendency
integrate
observation
documentation

An effective informative text or speech does the following:

- introduces the topic clearly and organizes it in a way that an audience can easily understand
- uses headings, charts, tables, other graphics, or multimedia elements to help illustrate ideas related to the topic
- develops the topic with facts, definitions, concrete details, and quotations as needed
- uses a variety of transitions to make relationships among ideas clear
- demonstrates a formal style and precise word choices
- provides a concluding statement or section that supports or extends the information provided

STANDARDS
Writing
• Write informative/explanatory texts to examine a topic and convey ideas, concepts, and information through the selection, organization, and analysis of relevant content.
• Write routinely over extended time frames and shorter time frames for a range of discipline-specific tasks, purposes, and audiences.

Model Informative Text For a model of a well-crafted informative text, see the Launch Text, "The Human Brain."

Challenge yourself to find all of the elements of an effective informative text. You will have an opportunity to review these elements as you prepare to write your own informative speech.

Prewriting / Planning

Focus on Giving Information Reread the assignment. Remember, an informative speech focuses on giving information about a topic, rather than simply telling a story. State your topic in a sentence:

This speech is meant to give information about _____ .

Consider Central Ideas An informative speech presents details about key ideas on the topic. Determining your central ideas will keep your speech focused. What three ideas do you want your audience to walk away with?

1. _____

2. _____

3. _____

Gather Evidence To develop your topic, you will need to add relevant facts, details, and definitions. Start with information from the short story. You may wish to research information on related topics. Because the story and experiment are fictional, you may also invent details. Make sure, however, that the details are believable, based on information in the story, and that they make sense in the context of the story. Explain why or how each piece of evidence relates to your topic. Study the Launch Text to see how the writer uses different types of evidence to develop a topic.

✐ EVIDENCE LOG

Review your Evidence Log and identify key details you may want to cite in your informative speech.

EVIDENCE	SOURCE	WHY OR HOW EVIDENCE IS IMPORTANT

Connect Across Texts To connect your speech with the Anchor Texts, look for details that show the moment Charlie knows his intelligence has increased. How can you show this realization in your speech? In addition, consider how the script and the short story show Charlie's personality. Use this information to help write a speech in the character's voice.

▤ STANDARDS

Writing
Write informative/explanatory texts to examine a topic and convey ideas, concepts, and information through the selection, organization, and analysis of relevant content.
  a. Introduce a topic clearly, previewing what is to follow; organize ideas, concepts, and information into broader categories; include formatting, graphics, and multimedia when useful to aiding comprehension.
  b. Develop the topic with relevant, well-chosen facts, definitions, concrete details, quotations, or other information and examples.

Drafting

Choose an Effective Organization Keep in mind that the purpose of your informative speech is to help your audience understand the intellectual transformation Charlie undergoes. Put your details in an order that walks the audience through the experiment, the changes it causes, and Charlie's predictions of what will happen to him later. Consider organizing your speech in one of these ways:

- In **cause-and-effect organization,** you examine the relationships between or among events, explaining how one event or situation (the cause) leads to a certain effect, result, or outcome. For instance, the experiment can be the cause, and the effects can be the changes Charlie experiences.

- In **comparison-and-contrast organization,** you analyze the similarities and differences between or among two or more things. For example, you can explain the process by comparing and contrasting Charlie at various points in time.

- In **problem-and-solution organization,** you describe a problem, offer at least one solution, and lay out steps to achieve this solution. Similar to cause-and-effect organization, this organization presents the cause as the problem. Remember that you are writing from Charlie's point of view. What would Charlie describe as the problem—his intellect or the experiment? What would he list as possible solutions?

No matter which structure you choose, your informative speech should feature a clear introduction, body, and conclusion, and include supporting information and examples. The graphic organizer here shows how the Launch Text is organized.

STANDARDS

Writing
Write informative/explanatory texts to examine a topic and convey ideas, concepts, and information through the selection, organization, and analysis of relevant content.
  a. Introduce a topic clearly, previewing what is to follow; organize ideas, concepts, and information into broader categories; include formatting, graphics, and multimedia when useful to aiding comprehension.

LAUNCH TEXT

MODEL: "The Human Brain"

INTRODUCTION
The human brain can do amazing things.

BODY ORGANIZATION
The author mostly uses cause-and-effect organization in describing how the brain works.

CONCLUSION
Scientists are still learning more about the human brain.

Charlie's Informative Speech

INTRODUCTION

BODY ORGANIZATION

CONCLUSION

Write a First Draft Use the information in your graphic organizer and the text structure you have chosen to write a first draft of your speech. Remember to use supporting evidence and examples to clarify your ideas.

LANGUAGE DEVELOPMENT: CONVENTIONS

Subject-Verb Agreement

A verb must agree with its subject in number. The number of a noun or pronoun may be **singular** (indicating *one*) or **plural** (indicating *more than one*).

- Here are examples of nouns and pronouns used as singular subjects: *bus, goose, I, you, Seth or Mia*
- Here are examples of nouns and pronouns used as plural subjects: *buses, geese, we, you, Seth and Mia*

Most verbs have the same singular and plural form, except that in the present tense they add -*s* or -*es* for the third-person singular form. For example, <u>Sam</u> *runs;* <u>Trudy</u> *goes.*

Like all verbs, the verb *be* must agree with its subject in person and number. It takes the form *am* or *was* with the subject *I, is* or *was* with third-person singular subjects (such as *she* or *Alex*), and *are* or *were* with the subject *you* and all third-person plural subjects (such as *they* or *children*).

Read It

These sentences from the Launch Text show subject-verb agreement.

- ***The brain*** <u>***controls***</u> *a person's actions, reactions, and survival functions, such as breathing.* **(singular)**
- ***Neurons*** <u>***send***</u> *messages through tiny branch-like structures that connect to other neurons in different parts of the brain, as well as other parts of the body.* **(plural)**

Write It

As you draft your speech, make sure your subjects and verbs agree. This chart may help you.

SUBJECT-VERB AGREEMENT	
SINGULAR	PLURAL
<u>I</u> *am* busy.	<u>We</u> *are* busy.
<u>He</u> *runs.*	<u>They</u> *run.*
The <u>child</u> *goes* to sleep.	The <u>children</u> *go* to sleep.
<u>Seth</u> *agrees.*	<u>Seth and Mia</u> *agree.*

TIP

CLARIFICATION

Make sure that every verb you use, whether in the **active voice** or the **passive voice,** agrees with its subject.

- In the **active voice**, a verb's subject performs the action—for example, *Amanda* <u>*wrote*</u> *the speech.*
- In the **passive voice**, the verb's subject receives the action—for example, *The* <u>*speech*</u> *was written by Amanda.*

Use mainly active verbs in your writing to emphasize the actor, not the action, of a sentence. Active voice makes writing livelier, more precise, and more dynamic.

▦ STANDARDS

Language
Demonstrate command of the conventions of standard English grammar and usage when writing or speaking.
  b. Form and use verbs in the active and passive voice.

Revising

Evaluating Your Draft

Use the following checklist to evaluate the effectiveness of your first draft. Then, use your evaluation and the instruction on this page to guide your revision.

FOCUS AND ORGANIZATION	EVIDENCE AND ELABORATION	CONVENTIONS
☐ Introduces the topic clearly.	☐ Uses facts, definitions, concrete details, and quotations to develop the topic.	☐ Attends to the norms and conventions of the discipline, especially correct subject-verb agreement.
☐ Organizes supporting information and explanations in a way that is easy to understand, possibly including graphical or multimedia elements.	☐ Uses transitions to make relationships between ideas clear.	
☐ Presents ideas in a formal style using precise words.		
☐ Provides a conclusion that supports the information provided.		

WORD NETWORK

You may want to include interesting words from your Word Network in your informative speech.

STANDARDS

Writing
Write informative/explanatory texts to examine a topic and convey ideas, concepts, and information through the selection, organization, and analysis of relevant content.
a. Introduce a topic clearly, previewing what is to follow; organize ideas, concepts, and information into broader categories; include formatting, graphics, and multimedia when useful to aiding comprehension.
c. Use appropriate and varied transitions to create cohesion and clarify the relationships among ideas and concepts.
d. Use precise language and domain-specific vocabulary to inform about or explain the topic.
e. Establish and maintain a formal style.

Revising for Focus and Organization

Choose Precise, Formal Words Choose words that capture your meaning precisely. For example, the term *IQ* might express your meaning more clearly than *smarts*. Since this is a speech about a scientific experiment, some technical language is appropriate. Avoid slang terms. Using words correctly will reflect Charlie's extended vocabulary at this point in the story. Remember to use complete sentences, correct grammar, and clear language to explain information.

Provide a Strong Introductory Statement

Strong informative speeches grab the audience's attention right away and hold it throughout the speech.

In your introduction, present your topic in a way that emphasizes its importance. Consider using a quotation from one of the texts, a personal anecdote, or another memorable statement to begin your speech. Remember that you are writing in Charlie's voice. Make sure that you choose details that Charlie might have chosen at the beginning of June.

Revising for Evidence and Elaboration

Use Transitions Transitions are words and phrases that connect and show relationships among ideas. In an informative text, transitions show readers or listeners how ideas or pieces of information are related.

- Words such as *likewise, similarly,* and *conversely* indicate a comparison or contrast.
- Words such as *first, next,* and *later* tell the order in which events occurred.
- Words such as *thus* and *consequently* signal causes and effects.

PEER REVIEW

Exchange speeches with a classmate. Use the checklist to evaluate your classmate's informative speech and provide supportive feedback.

1. Is the topic clearly introduced and organized in a way that is easy to understand?

☐ yes ☐ no   If no, suggest how the writer might improve it.

2. Is the topic developed with facts, definitions, concrete details, and quotations as needed?

☐ yes ☐ no   If no, explain what the author might add or remove.

3. Does the speech use formal, precise language?

☐ yes ☐ no   If no, tell what you think might be missing.

4. What is the strongest part of your classmate's speech? Explain.

Editing and Proofreading

Edit for Conventions Reread your draft for accuracy and consistency. Correct errors in grammar and word usage. Make sure all your subjects and verbs agree in number.

Proofread for Accuracy Read your draft carefully, looking for errors in spelling and punctuation. Use a dictionary to check the spelling of all key terms. In addition, check your spelling of commonly confused words, such as *affect* (usually a verb) and *effect* (usually a noun). Finally, check your spelling of homonyms—words that sound the same but have different meanings and usually spellings, such as *their, they're,* and *there.*

Publishing and Presenting

Create a final version of your speech. Hold a class conference in which you present your speech to a small panel of your classmates. Discuss ways in which your speeches are similar and different. Did you include any of the same information? Did you connect your information in the same ways? Is the content similar but the style different? Share your thoughts with the class. Discuss what comparing the speeches taught you about developing a topic.

Reflecting

Reflect on what you learned as you wrote your informative speech. What did you learn about different ways to be intelligent? What was the most challenging aspect of writing your informative speech? Did you learn something from the review process that might inform your writing process in the future?

⊞ STANDARDS

Writing
• Produce clear and coherent writing in which the development, organization, and style are appropriate to task, purpose, and audience.
• With some guidance and support from peers and adults, develop and strengthen writing as needed by planning, revising, editing, rewriting, or trying a new approach, focusing on how well purpose and audience have been addressed.

ESSENTIAL QUESTION:

In what different ways can people be intelligent?

Throughout history, the topic of human intelligence has been a subject of much debate. Scientists, writers, artists, and scholars have all reflected on the concept of human intelligence and the factors that define it. Work with your group to explore the ideas about different types of intelligence that are presented in the selections in this section.

Small-Group Learning Strategies

Throughout your life, in school, in your community, and in your career, you will continue to learn and work with others.

Review these strategies and the actions you can take to practice them as you work in teams. Add ideas of your own for each step. Use these strategies during Small-Group Learning.

STRATEGY	ACTION PLAN
Prepare	• Complete your assignments so that you are prepared for group work. • Organize your thinking so you can contribute to your group's discussion. •
Participate fully	• Make eye contact to signal that you are listening and taking in what is being said. • Use text evidence when making a point. •
Support others	• Build on ideas from others in your group. • Invite others who have not yet spoken to do so. •
Clarify	• Paraphrase the ideas of others to ensure that your understanding is correct. • Ask follow-up questions. •

SCAN FOR
MULTIMEDIA

CONTENTS

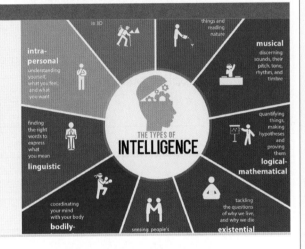

Working as a Team

1. **Discuss the Topic** In your group, discuss the following question:

   What are some ways in which intelligence can be obvious yet unconventional?

   As you take turns sharing your thoughts, be sure to provide examples and reasons for your responses. After all group members have shared, discuss some of the character traits associated with the ways of being intelligent that you identified.

2. **List Your Rules** As a group, decide on the rules that you will follow as you work together. Two samples are provided; add two more of your own. You may add or revise rules based on your experience together.

   • Everyone should participate in group discussions.

   • People should not interrupt.

   • _____

     _____

   • _____

     _____

3. **Apply the Rules** Share what you have learned about intelligence. Make sure each person in the group contributes. Take notes and be prepared to share with the class one thing that you heard from another member of your group.

4. **Name Your Group** Choose a name that reflects the unit topic.

   Our group's name: _____

5. **Create a Communication Plan** Decide how you want to communicate with one another. For example, you might use online collaboration tools, email, or instant messaging.

   Our group's decision: _____

   _____

Making a Schedule

First, find out the due dates for the small-group activities. Then, preview the texts and activities with your group and make a schedule for completing the tasks.

SELECTION	ACTIVITIES	DUE DATE
from Blue Nines and Red Words		
The Theory of Multiple Intelligences Infographic		
Retort *from* The People, Yes		

Working on Group Projects

As your group works together, you'll find it more effective if each person has a specific role. Different projects require different roles. Before beginning a project, discuss the necessary roles, and choose one for each group member. Here are some possible roles; add your own ideas to the list.

Project Manager: monitors the schedule and keeps everyone on task

Researcher: organizes research activities

Recorder: takes notes during group meetings

_____

_____

_____

_____

_____

SCAN FOR MULTIMEDIA

About the Author

Daniel Tammet (b. 1979) grew up in a working-class suburb of London, England, and is the eldest of nine children. In 2004, when he was 25, Tammet was diagnosed with "high-functioning autistic savant syndrome," a form of autism. In 2005, he was the subject of a documentary film entitled *Extraordinary People: The Boy With the Incredible Brain*, first broadcast on British television. Tammet's four books, the last of which was published in 2016, have been translated into 20 languages.

☰ STANDARDS

Reading Informational Text
By the end of the year, read and comprehend literary nonfiction at the high end of the grades 6–8 text complexity band independently and proficiently.

Language
Determine or clarify the meaning of unknown and multiple-meaning words or phrases based on *grade 8 reading and content,* choosing flexibly from a range of strategies.

from Blue Nines and Red Words

Concept Vocabulary

As you perform your first read of the excerpt from "Blue Nines and Red Words," you will encounter the following words.

symmetrical	spiral	aesthetic

Base Words If these words are unfamilar to you, analyze each one to see whether it contains a base word you know. Then, use your knowledge of the base word, or "inside" word, along with context, to determine the meaning of the concept word. Here is an example of how to apply the strategy.

> **Unfamiliar Word:** *skillful*
>
> **Familiar "Inside" Word:** *skill*, with meanings including "expertise" and "learned power"
>
> **Context:** I was astonished at the professor's *skillful* ability to pass along complicated information.
>
> **Conclusion:** The narrator is impressed with someone's ability, so *skillful* might mean "with skill," or "showing expertise."

Apply your knowledge of base words and other vocabulary strategies to determine the meanings of unfamiliar words you encounter during your first read.

First Read NONFICTION

Apply these strategies as you conduct your first read. You will have an opportunity to complete a close read after your first read.

NOTICE the general ideas of the text. *What* is it about? *Who* is involved?

ANNOTATE by marking vocabulary and key passages you want to revisit.

First Read

CONNECT ideas within the selection to what you already know and what you have already read.

RESPOND by completing the Comprehension Check and by writing a brief summary of the selection.

from

Blue Nines and Red Words

from Born on a Blue Day

Daniel Tammet

BACKGROUND

Although *synesthesia*, the topic of this memoir excerpt, is a neurological condition, it also refers to a figure of speech. In synesthesia, one sense is described using terms typically used to describe another. Many common idioms are examples of synesthesia, such as "I smell trouble" and "The air was so thick you could cut it with a knife."

SCAN FOR MULTIMEDIA

NOTES

1   I was born on January 31, 1979—a Wednesday. I know it was a Wednesday, because the date is blue in my mind and Wednesdays are always blue, like the number 9 or the sound of loud voices arguing. I like my birth date, because of the way I'm able to visualize most of the numbers in it as smooth and round shapes, similar to pebbles on a beach. That's because they are prime numbers: 31, 19, 197, 97, 79, and 1979 are all divisible only by themselves and 1. I can recognize every prime up to 9,973 by their "pebble-like" quality. It's just the way my brain works.

2   I have a rare condition known as savant syndrome, little known before its portrayal by actor Dustin Hoffman in the Oscar-winning 1988 film *Rain Man*. Like Hoffman's character, Raymond Babbitt, I have an almost obsessive need for order and routine which affects virtually every aspect of my life. For example, I eat exactly 45 grams of porridge for breakfast each morning: I weigh the bowl with an electronic scale to make sure. Then I count the number of items of clothing I'm wearing before I leave my house. I get anxious if I can't drink my cups of tea at the same time each day. Whenever I become too stressed and I can't breathe properly,

I close my eyes and count. Thinking of numbers helps me to become calm again.

3   Numbers are my friends, and they are always around me. Each one is unique and has its own personality. The number 11 is friendly and 5 is loud, whereas 4 is both shy and quiet—it's my favorite number, perhaps because it reminds me of myself. Some are big—23, 667, 1,179—while others are small: 6, 13, 581. Some are beautiful, like 333, and some are ugly, like 289. To me, every number is special.

4   No matter where I go or what I'm doing, numbers are never far from my thoughts. In an interview with talk-show host David Letterman in New York, I told David he looked like the number 117—tall and lanky. Later outside, in the appropriately numerically named Times Square, I gazed up at the towering skyscrapers and felt surrounded by 9s—the number I most associate with feelings of immensity.

5   Scientists call my visual, emotional experience of numbers *synesthesia*, a rare neurological[1] mixing of the senses, which most commonly results in the ability to see alphabetical letters and/ or numbers in color. Mine is an unusual and complex type, through which I see numbers as shapes, colors, textures, and motions. The number 1, for example, is a brilliant and bright white, like someone shining a flashlight into my eyes. Five is a clap of thunder or the sound of waves crashing against rocks. Thirty-seven is lumpy like porridge, while 89 reminds me of falling snow.

6   Probably the most famous case of synesthesia was the one written up over a period of thirty years from the 1920s by the Russian psychologist A. R. Luria of a journalist called Shereshevsky with a prodigious memory. "S," as Luria called him in his notes for the book *The Mind of a Mnemonist*, had a highly visual memory which allowed him to "see" words and numbers as different shapes and colors. "S" was able to remember a matrix of 50 digits after studying it for three minutes, both immediately afterwards and many years later. Luria credited Shereshevsky's synesthetic experiences as the basis for his remarkable short- and long-term memory.

7   Using my own synesthetic experiences since early childhood, I have grown up with the ability to handle and calculate huge numbers in my head without any conscious effort, just like the Raymond Babbitt character. In fact, this is a talent common to

---

1. **neurological** (nur uh LOJ uh kuhl) *adj.* occurring in the brain.

several other real-life savants (sometimes referred to as "lightning calculators"). Dr. Darold Treffert, a Wisconsin physician and the leading researcher in the study of savant syndrome, gives one example, of a blind man with "a faculty of calculating to a degree little short of marvelous" in his book *Extraordinary People*:

8   When he was asked how many grains of corn there would be in any one of 64 boxes, with 1 in the first, 2 in the second, 4 in the third, 8 in the fourth, and so on, he gave answers for the fourteenth (8,192), for the eighteenth (131,072) and the twenty-fourth (8,388,608) instantaneously, and he gave the figures for the forty-eighth box (140,737,488,355,328) in six seconds. He also gave the total in all 64 boxes correctly (18,446,744,073,709,551,616) in forty-five seconds.

9   My favorite kind of calculation is power multiplication, which means multiplying a number by itself a specified number of times. Multiplying a number by itself is called squaring; for example, the square of 72 is $72 \times 72 = 5{,}184$. Squares are always **symmetrical** shapes in my mind, which makes them especially beautiful to me. Multiplying the same number three times over is called cubing or "raising" to the third power. The cube, or third power, of 51 is equivalent to $51 \times 51 \times 51 = 132{,}651$. I see each result of a power multiplication as a distinctive visual pattern in my head. As the sums and their results grow, so the mental shapes and colors I experience become increasingly more complex. I see 37's fifth power—$37 \times 37 \times 37 \times 37 \times 37 = 69{,}343{,}957$—as a large circle composed of smaller circles running clockwise from the top around.

10   When I divide one number by another, in my head I see a **spiral** rotating downwards in larger and larger loops, which seem to warp and curve. Different divisions produce different sizes of spirals with varying curves. From my mental imagery I'm able to calculate a sum like $13 \div 97$ (0.1340206 . . .) to almost a hundred decimal places.

11   I never write anything down when I'm calculating, because I've always been able to do the sums in my head, and it's much easier for me to visualize the answer using my synesthetic shapes than to try to follow the "carry the one" techniques taught in the textbooks we are given at school. When multiplying, I see the two numbers as distinct shapes. The image changes and a third shape emerges—the correct answer. The process takes a matter of seconds and happens spontaneously. It's like doing math without having to think.

NOTES

Mark base words or indicate another strategy you used to help you determine meaning.

symmetrical (sih MEH trih kuhl) *adj.*

MEANING:

spiral (SPY ruhl) *n.*

MEANING:

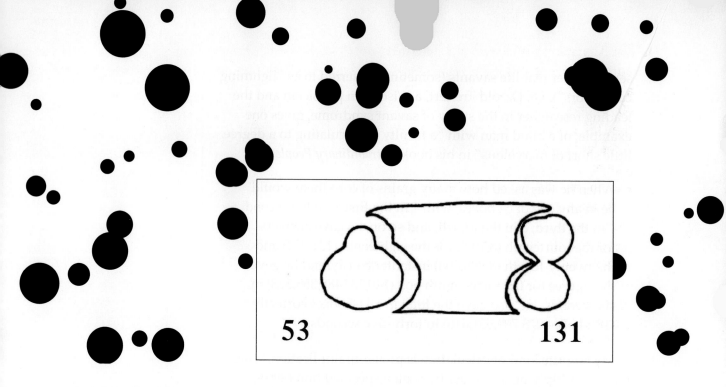

NOTES

Mark base words or indicate another strategy you used to help you determine meaning.

aesthetic (ehs THEHT ihk) *adj.*

MEANING:

12 In the illustration above I'm multiplying 53 by 131. I see both numbers as a unique shape and locate each spatially opposite the other. The space created between the two shapes creates a third, which I perceive as a new number: 6,943, the solution to the sum.

13 Different tasks involve different shapes, and I also have various sensations or emotions for certain numbers. Whenever I multiply with 11 I always experience a feeling of the digits tumbling downwards in my head. I find 6s hardest to remember of all the numbers, because I experience them as tiny black dots, without any distinctive shape or texture. I would describe them as like little gaps or holes. I have visual and sometimes emotional responses to every number up to 10,000, like having my own visual, numerical vocabulary. And just like a poet's choice of words, I find some combinations of numbers more beautiful than others: ones go well with darker numbers like 8s and 9s, but not so well with 6s. A telephone number with the sequence 189 is much more beautiful to me than one with a sequence like 116.

14 This **aesthetic** dimension to my synesthesia is something that has its ups and downs. If I see a number I experience as particularly beautiful on a shop sign or a car license plate, there's a shiver of excitement and pleasure. On the other hand, if the numbers don't match my experience of them—if, for example, a shop sign's price has "99 pence" in red or green (instead of blue)—then I find that uncomfortable and irritating.

15 It is not known how many savants have synesthetic experiences to help them in the areas they excel in. One reason for this is that, like Raymond Babbitt, many suffer profound disability, preventing them from explaining to others how they do the things that they do. I am fortunate not to suffer from any of the most severe impairments that often come with abilities such as mine.

16   Like most individuals with savant syndrome, I am also on the autistic spectrum. I have Asperger's syndrome, a relatively mild and high-functioning form of autism that affects around 1 in every 300 people in the United Kingdom. According to a 2001 study by the U.K.'s National Autistic Society, nearly half of all adults with Asperger's syndrome are not diagnosed until after the age of sixteen. I was finally diagnosed at age twenty-five following tests and an interview at the Autism Research Centre in Cambridge.

17   Autism, including Asperger's syndrome, is defined by the presence of impairments affecting social interaction, communication, and imagination (problems with abstract or flexible thought and empathy, for example). Diagnosis is not easy and cannot be made by a blood test or brain scan; doctors have to observe behavior and study the individual's developmental history from infancy.

18   People with Asperger's often have good language skills and are able to lead relatively normal lives. Many have above-average IQs and excel in areas that involve logical or visual thinking. Like other forms of autism, Asperger's is a condition affecting many more men than women (around 80 percent of autistics and 90 percent of those diagnosed with Asperger's are men). Single-mindedness is a defining characteristic, as is a strong drive to analyze detail and identify rules and patterns in systems. Specialized skills involving memory, numbers, and mathematics are common. It is not known for certain what causes someone to have Asperger's, though it is something you are born with.

19   For as long as I can remember, I have experienced numbers in the visual, synesthetic way that I do. Numbers are my first language, one I often think and feel in. Emotions can be hard for me to understand or know how to react to, so I often use numbers to help me. If a friend says they feel sad or depressed, I picture myself sitting in the dark hollowness of number 6 to help me experience the same sort of feeling and understand it. If I read in an article that a person felt intimidated by something, I imagine myself standing next to the number 9. Whenever someone describes visiting a beautiful place, I recall my numerical landscapes and how happy they make me feel inside. By doing this, numbers actually help me get closer to understanding other people.

20   Sometimes people I meet for the first time remind me of a particular number and this helps me to be comfortable around them. They might be very tall and remind me of the number 9, or round and remind me of the number 3. If I feel unhappy or anxious or in a situation I have no previous experience of (when I'm much more likely to feel stressed and uncomfortable), I count to myself. When I count, the numbers form pictures and patterns in my mind that are consistent and reassuring to me. Then I can relax and interact with whatever situation I'm in.

from Blue Nines and Red Words **405**

21   Thinking of calendars always makes me feel good, all those numbers and patterns in one place. Different days of the week elicit different colors and emotions in my head: Tuesdays are a warm color while Thursdays are fuzzy. Calendrical calculation—the ability to tell what day of the week a particular date fell or will fall on—is common to many savants. I think this is probably due to the fact that the numbers in calendars are predictable and form patterns between the different days and months. For example, the thirteenth day in a month is always two days before whatever day the first falls on, excepting leap years, while several of the months mimic the behavior of others, like January and October, September and December, and February and March (the first day of February is the same as the first day of March). So if the first of February is a fuzzy texture in my mind (Thursday) for a given year, the thirteenth of March will be a warm color (Tuesday).

22   In his book *The Man Who Mistook His Wife for a Hat*, writer and neurologist Oliver Sacks mentions the case of severely autistic twins John and Michael as an example of how far some savants are able to take calendrical calculations. Though unable to care for themselves (they had been in various institutions since the age of seven), the twins were capable of calculating the day of the week for any date over a 40,000-year span.

23   Sacks also describes John and Michael as playing a game that involved swapping prime numbers with each other for hours at a time. Like the twins, I have always been fascinated by prime numbers. I see each prime as a smooth-textured shape, distinct from composite numbers (non-primes) that are grittier and less distinctive. Whenever I identify a number as prime, I get a rush of feeling in my head (in the front center) which is hard to put into words. It's a special feeling, like the sudden sensation of pins and needles.

24   Sometimes I close my eyes and imagine the first thirty, fifty, hundred numbers as I experience them spatially, synesthetically. Then I can see in my mind's eye just how beautiful and special the primes are by the way they stand out so sharply from the other number shapes. It's exactly for this reason that I look and look and look at them; each one is so different from the one before and the one after. Their loneliness among the other numbers makes them so conspicuous and interesting to me.

25   There are moments, as I'm falling into sleep at night, that my mind fills suddenly with bright light and all I can see are numbers—hundreds, thousands of them—swimming rapidly over my eyes. The experience is beautiful and soothing to me. Some nights, when I'm having difficulty falling asleep, I imagine myself walking around my numerical landscapes. Then I feel safe and happy. I never feel lost, because the prime number shapes act as signposts. ❧

Comprehension Check

Complete the following items after you finish your first read. Review and clarify details with your group.

1. Why does Tammet call his birth date blue?

2. What is one way in which the author says he demonstrates savant syndrome?

3. How does the author compare his experience with numbers to a poet's choice of words?

4. What is the author's favorite type of calculation?

5. 🗒 **Notebook** Confirm your understanding of the text by writing a short summary.

RESEARCH

Research to Clarify Choose at least one unfamiliar point that Daniel Tammet makes about intelligence. Briefly research that detail. In what way does the information you learned shed light on an aspect of the memoir?

from BLUE NINES AND
RED WORDS

Close Read the Text

With your group, revisit sections of the text you marked during your first read. **Annotate** what you notice. What **questions** do you have? What can you **conclude**?

- -

Analyze the Text

CITE TEXTUAL EVIDENCE
to support your answers.

📓 **Notebook** **Complete the activities.**

1. **Review and Clarify** With your group, reread paragraphs 9–12. Discuss the author's descriptions of his experiences with numbers. How are his experiences of numbers an example of a kind of intelligence?

2. **Present and Discuss** Now, work with your group to share the passages from the text that you found especially important. Take turns presenting your passages. Discuss what you noticed in the text, what questions you asked, and what conclusions you reached.

3. **Essential Question:** *In what different ways can people be intelligent?* What has this memoir taught you about the different ways people can be intelligent? Discuss with your group.

⬚ WORD NETWORK

Add words related to human intelligence from the text to your Word Network.

LANGUAGE DEVELOPMENT

Concept Vocabulary

symmetrical	spiral	aesthetic

Why These Words? The concept vocabulary words from the text are related. With your group, determine what the words have in common. Write your ideas, and add another word that fits the category.

Practice

📓 **Notebook** Confirm your understanding of the concept vocabulary words by using each one in a sentence. In each sentence, provide context clues for the vocabulary word to demonstrate your understanding of the word's meaning.

Word Study

Latin Suffix: *-ical* In "Blue Nines and Red Words," Daniel Tammet uses the word *symmetrical* to describe how he envisions squared numbers. The word *symmetrical* ends with the Latin suffix *-ical*, which means "having to do with," "made of," or "characterized by." Find other words in the selection that have this suffix. Use a dictionary to verify the precise meanings of these words.

Analyze Craft and Structure

Memoir and Reflective Writing An **autobiography** is a true account of events and experiences written by the person who directly experienced them. A **memoir** is a type of autobiography that focuses on a specific period in the author's life or an experience that holds particular significance for the author. For example, in the excerpt from "Blue Nines and Red Words," Daniel Tammet explores his experience with savant syndrome.

In a memoir, an author will often use **reflective writing** to communicate his or her thoughts and feelings—or reflections—about an event, experience, or idea. The purpose of reflective writing is to communicate these reflections in a way that inspires readers to respond with their own reflections. Reflective writing can reveal a variety of insights:

- what the author learned from the event or experience
- what the experience revealed about the author's personality
- how the author feels about other people in his or her life
- how the author relates to his or her environment and the world
- how the author responds to the conflicts, or struggles, with which he or she is faced

These insights help develop and reveal the author's **central ideas,** or main points, in a memoir. The ways in which the author structures and connects his or her experiences and insights in a reflective piece enable the author to achieve his or her purpose, or reason for writing.

TIP

CLARIFICATION

As you read a reflective piece, pay attention to the comparisons and contrasts an author makes to connect people, ideas, and events.

Practice

CITE TEXTUAL EVIDENCE to support your answers.

Notebook Work individually to analyze Tammet's use of reflective writing in "Blue Nines and Red Words," using a chart like the one shown. After you have completed the chart, compare charts with your group members. Then, as a group, determine the central ideas that are revealed through your analysis.

TAMMET'S EXPERIENCES	TAMMET'S REFLECTIONS	CLUES ABOUT CENTRAL IDEA

from BLUE NINES AND
RED WORDS

Conventions

Pronoun Case English has three **cases,** or forms, of pronouns. Writers use pronoun cases according to a pronoun's function in a sentence.

- **nominative case:** used for the subjects of verbs and for predicate pronouns; also known as the **subjective case**
- **objective case:** used for direct and indirect objects and for objects of prepositions
- **possessive case:** used to show ownership

The chart below shows the three categories for personal pronouns.

CASE	PRONOUNS	FUNCTION IN A SENTENCE
nominative (subject)	I, we, you, he, she, it, they	subject of a verb ("*She* read the book.")
		predicate pronoun ("The book reader was *she*.")
objective (object)	me, us, you, him, her, it, them	direct object ("Daniel said *it* to Mia.")
		indirect object ("Daniel told *her* his idea.")
		object of a preposition ("Daniel told the idea to *her*.")
possessive	my, mine, our, ours, your, yours, his, her, hers, its, their, theirs	to show ownership ("Daniel told *his* idea to Mia.")

TIP

COLLABORATION

Discuss the definitions and examples of these pronoun cases as a group. If you have a good grasp of the concepts, explain them to others. If your group is still having difficulty, consult with your teacher.

Read It

Work individually to choose the correct pronouns and give their cases.

1. When Daniel Tammet thinks of numbers, (he/his) sees colors.

2. Prime numbers look like pebbles, and Daniel likes (they/them).

3. When (he/him) adds or multiplies numbers, Daniel does not write (they/them) down.

4. Daniel Tammet sees (he/his) own birthday as blue.

Write It

Notebook Write three sentences about the selection. Use all three pronoun cases at least once.

STANDARDS

Language
Demonstrate command of the conventions of standard English grammar and usage when writing or speaking.

Research

Assignment

With your group, write a brief **informational report.** Choose from the following options:

☐ Conduct research to learn more about the condition known as *synesthesia.* Then, write a report in which you explain the ways in which Daniel Tammet's experience serves as an example of this condition.

☐ Conduct research to learn more about a well-known savant in a specific field, such as mathematics, music, language, or memory. Then, write a report in which you compare the experience of the savant you chose to Tammet's experience.

Gather Evidence Gather a variety of evidence from relevant, reliable sources. Use the chart to guide your research and note important information.

QUESTION	EVIDENCE
What is the condition or ability, and what makes it extraordinary?	
How has the condition or ability shaped the person's life?	
In what ways does Tammet's experience reflect the condition or ability?	

Explain Technical Vocabulary In "Blue Nines and Red Words," you may have noticed scientific terms such as *autistic spectrum* and *Asperger's syndrome.* As you conduct research, you will encounter various other technical terms. It is important to understand what these words mean so that you can use and explain them in your report. The following strategies will help you clarify technical terms for readers who might not be familiar with them:

- Summarize or paraphrase the term's meaning by putting it into your own words.
- Provide examples of a complicated idea or process so readers can connect it with something familiar.

✎ EVIDENCE LOG

Before moving on to a new selection, go to your Evidence Log, and record what you learned from the excerpt from "Blue Nines and Red Words."

⋮☰ STANDARDS

Writing
- Write informative/explanatory texts to examine a topic and convey ideas, concepts, and information through the selection, organization, and analysis of relevant content.

  b. Develop the topic with relevant, well-chosen facts, definitions, concrete details, quotations, or other information and examples.
  d. Use precise language and domain-specific vocabulary to inform about or explain the topic.

- Conduct short research projects to answer a question, drawing on several sources and generating additional related, focused questions that allow for multiple avenues of exploration.
- Gather relevant information from multiple print and digital sources, using search terms effectively; assess the credibility and accuracy of each source; and quote or paraphrase the data and conclusions of others while avoiding plagiarism and following a standard format for citation.

About the Theorist

Howard Gardner (b. 1943) is an American psychologist and a professor at the Harvard Graduate School of Education. The child of Jewish parents who fled Germany before World War II, Gardner has been called "one of the 100 most influential public intellectuals in the world." Although he has published dozens of books and research articles, he remains best known for his theory of multiple intelligences, which he outlined in his book *Frames of Mind: The Theory of Multiple Intelligences*.

The Theory of Multiple Intelligences Infographic

Media Vocabulary

The following words or concepts will be useful to you as you analyze, discuss, and write about infographics.

infographic: image used to present information, data, or knowledge quickly and clearly	• An infographic can help simplify a complicated subject and present it in an engaging way. • Infographics are structured to encourage readers to compare different ideas and information.
icons: symbols or graphic representations, often used in charts and on digital screens	• Icons are design to be simple, functional, and easily recognizable. • On digital screens, icons allow the user to easily identify and access files, programs, and applications.
labels and captions: short descriptive words or phrases that provide information	• Captions are used to briefly explain the content of an image. • Labels are often formatted to draw attention to specific content.

First Review MEDIA: INFOGRAPHIC

Apply these strategies as you conduct your first review. You will have an opportunity to complete a close review after your first review.

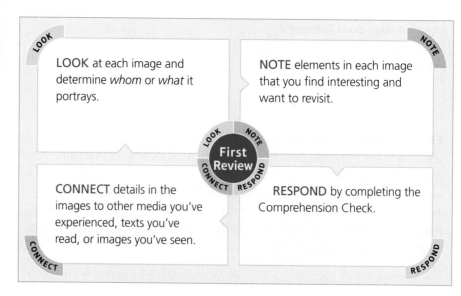

LOOK at each image and determine *whom* or *what* it portrays.

NOTE elements in each image that you find interesting and want to revisit.

CONNECT details in the images to other media you've experienced, texts you've read, or images you've seen.

RESPOND by completing the Comprehension Check.

⠿ STANDARDS

Reading Informational Text
By the end of the year, read and comprehend literary nonfiction at the high end of the grades 6–8 text complexity band independently and proficiently.

Language
Acquire and use accurately grade-appropriate general academic and domain-specific words and phrases; gather vocabulary knowledge when considering a word or phrase important to comprehension or expression.

The Theory of Multiple Intelligences Infographic

Howard Gardner

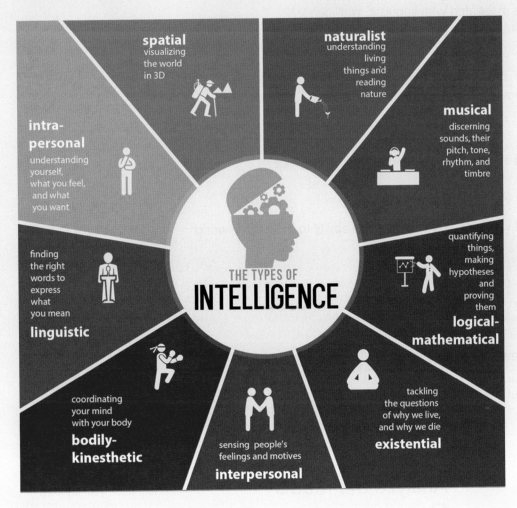

BACKGROUND

When Howard Gardner first developed his theory of multiple intelligences in 1983, he identified seven different ways that people can be intelligent. He added the naturalist and existential intelligences to his theory about a decade later. According to his theory, intelligence is not defined by a single ability, but by different types of related abilities. Gardner's theory claims that most people have a combination of these types of intelligences, but they will often display some types more strongly than others.

SCAN FOR MULTIMEDIA

NOTES

Comprehension Check

Complete the following items after you finish your first review. Review and clarify details with your group.

1. What ability is associated with linguistic intelligence?

2. Which type of intelligence is characterized by the ability to understand yourself and your feelings?

3. What ability is associated with interpersonal intelligence?

4. Which type of intelligence is shown by the ability to picture the world in 3D?

MEDIA VOCABULARY

Use these words as you discuss and write about the infographic.

infographic

icons

labels and captions

🔀 WORD NETWORK

Add words related to human intelligence from the text to your Word Network.

☰ STANDARDS

Reading Informational Text
Evaluate the advantages and disadvantages of using different mediums to present a particular topic or idea.

Close Review

With your group, review the infographic and your first-review notes. What **questions** do you have? What can you **conclude**?

Analyze the Media

CITE TEXTUAL EVIDENCE to support your answers.

🗐 **Notebook** Complete the activities.

1. **Analyze and Discuss** How do the captions and labels in the infographic enhance your understanding of the different ways in which people can be intelligent? Provide specific examples to support your response.

2. **Review and Synthesize** Review the infographic with your group. What are the advantages of presenting the information about multiple intelligences in an infographic? In what ways might presenting the information this way be disadvantageous?

3. **Essential Question:** *In what different ways can people be intelligent?* What has this infographic taught you about the different ways people can be intelligent? Discuss with your group.

Speaking and Listening

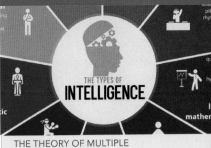

THE THEORY OF MULTIPLE INTELLIGENCES INFOGRAPHIC

Assignment

Take part in a **group discussion** about the different types of intelligence shown on the infographic. Choose from the following topics:

☐ With your group, engage in a collaborative discussion in which you analyze the nine types of intelligence. Then, pick three or four types on which to focus. For each type of intelligence, identify a well-known person, from the past or present, who has demonstrated that type of intelligence in a particularly strong way. For example, Dr. Martin Luther King, Jr., is a good example of a person with substantial linguistic intelligence. Finally, write a sentence or two about each person you have identified, in which you explain how he or she has demonstrated that type of intelligence.

☐ With your group, engage in a collaborative discussion in which you analyze the nine types of intelligence. Then, pick three or four types on which to focus. For each type of intelligence, identify a fictional character from literature who demonstrates that type of intelligence in a particularly strong way. For example, Sherlock Holmes might be a good example of a character who demonstrates great logical-mathematical intelligence. Finally, write a sentence or two about each character, in which you explain how he or she demonstrates that type of intelligence.

Notebook Record notes from your discussion in the chart.

PERSON/CHARACTER	TYPE OF INTELLIGENCE	WHY

Holding the Discussion Be sure to come to the discussion prepared with ideas that are supported with evidence from the infographic. If you disagree with someone else's ideas or views, express your disagreement respectfully. Pose questions that connect the ideas of other speakers, and respond to questions from other group members with relevant observations supported by details from the text. When another group member provides information that is new to you, reflect on your own ideas, and decide whether the new information has changed your ideas about the subject matter.

✎ EVIDENCE LOG

Before moving on to a new selection, go to your Evidence Log, and record what you learned from the infographic.

☷ STANDARDS

Speaking and Listening
Engage effectively in a range of collaborative discussions with diverse partners on *grade 8 topics, texts, and issues,* building on others' ideas and expressing their own clearly.

a. Come to discussions prepared, having read or researched material under study; explicitly draw on that preparation by referring to evidence on the topic, text, or issue to probe and reflect on ideas under discussion.
b. Follow rules for collegial discussions and decision-making, track progress toward specific goals and deadlines, and define individual roles as needed.
c. Pose questions that connect the ideas of several speakers and respond to others' questions and comments with relevant evidence, observations, and ideas.
d. Acknowledge new information expressed by others, and, when warranted, qualify or justify their own views in light of the evidence presented.

Retort

from The People, Yes

Archaic Vocabulary

Just as the way we live changes over time, so, too, does the way we speak and use language. The vocabulary words are "archaic" words because, though once in common usage, they are no longer used regularly today, or the way in which they are used has changed. As you conduct your first read of these poems, you will encounter these words.

art	tress	fair

Context Clues To find the meaning of an unfamiliar word, look for clues in the context—words and phrases that appear in nearby text.

> **Example from "Life's Tragedy," by Paul Laurence Dunbar:**
> It may be misery never to be loved, / But deeper <u>griefs</u> than these **beset** <u>the way</u>.
>
> **Possible Meaning:** Because of the context clues "griefs" and "the way," I can infer that *beset* may mean "pose obstacles."

Apply your knowledge of context clues and other vocabulary strategies to determine the meanings of unfamiliar words you encounter during your first read.

First Read POETRY

Apply these strategies as you conduct your first read. You will have an opportunity to complete a close read after your first read.

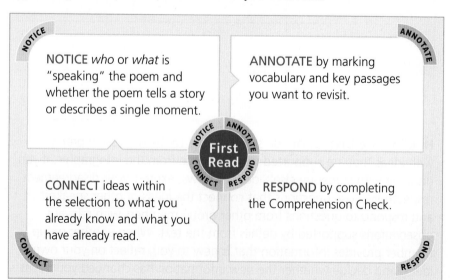

NOTICE *who* or *what* is "speaking" the poem and whether the poem tells a story or describes a single moment.

ANNOTATE by marking vocabulary and key passages you want to revisit.

First Read

CONNECT ideas within the selection to what you already know and what you have already read.

RESPOND by completing the Comprehension Check.

STANDARDS

Reading Literature
By the end of the year, read and comprehend literature, including stories, dramas, and poems, at the high end of grades 6–8 text complexity band independently and proficiently.

Language
Determine or clarify the meaning of unknown and multiple-meaning words or phrases based on *grade 8 reading and content,* choosing flexibly from a range of strategies.

a. Use context as a clue to the meaning of a word or phrase.

About the Poets

Paul Laurence Dunbar (1872–1906) was one of the first African American poets to achieve national prominence. The child of freed slaves from Kentucky, Dunbar often wrote stories and poems about plantation life, many of which were written in dialect. Despite being a fine student, Dunbar could not afford to pay for college, so he took a job as an elevator operator. In 1893, Dunbar self-published a collection of poems called *Oak and Ivy*. To help pay the publishing costs and gain an audience for his poetry, he sold the book for a dollar to people riding in his elevator.

Carl Sandburg (1878–1967) was a Pulitzer Prize–winning American poet, historian, and novelist. Born in Galesburg, Illinois, to Swedish immigrant parents, Sandburg decided at age six that he would be a writer. Although he had to quit school after eighth grade to go to work so he could help support his family, Sandburg continued to write. As he pursued writing, Sandburg worked in a variety of positions, from factory worker to newspaperman. He also became a well-known musician and political activist. The variety of Sandburg's experiences informed his writing, and Sandburg eventually gained recognition as an iconic American writer.

Backgrounds

Retort

In Greek mythology, the Muses were a group of goddesses who represented the arts and sciences. Currently, a muse can refer to any person who inspires an artist, writer, or musician and who may be a reoccurring focus of or subject in their work. Paul Laurence Dunbar addresses a woman named Phyllis, a possible muse, in this poem, as well as in several other poems, including "Phyllis" and "Response."

from The People, Yes

The excerpt in this section is part of a longer epic poem entitled *The People, Yes*. Carl Sandburg wrote this 300-page poem in the 1930s during the height of the Great Depression, a period when many people could not find work and lived in poverty. As a whole, the epic poem praises the perseverance and triumphs of the American people.

Retort

Paul Laurence Dunbar

"Thou **art** a fool," said my head to my heart,
"Indeed, the greatest of fools thou art,
　　To be led astray by the trick of a **tress**,
By a smiling face or a ribbon smart;"
5　　　And my heart was in sore distress.

Then Phyllis came by, and her face was **fair**,
The light gleamed soft on her raven hair;
　　And her lips were blooming a rosy red.
Then my heart spoke out with a right bold air:
10　　　"Thou art worse than a fool, O head!"

NOTES

Mark context clues or indicate another strategy you used that helped you determine meaning.

art (ahrt) *v.*
MEANING:

tress (trehs) *n.*
MEANING:

fair (fair) *adj.*
MEANING:

SCAN FOR
MULTIMEDIA

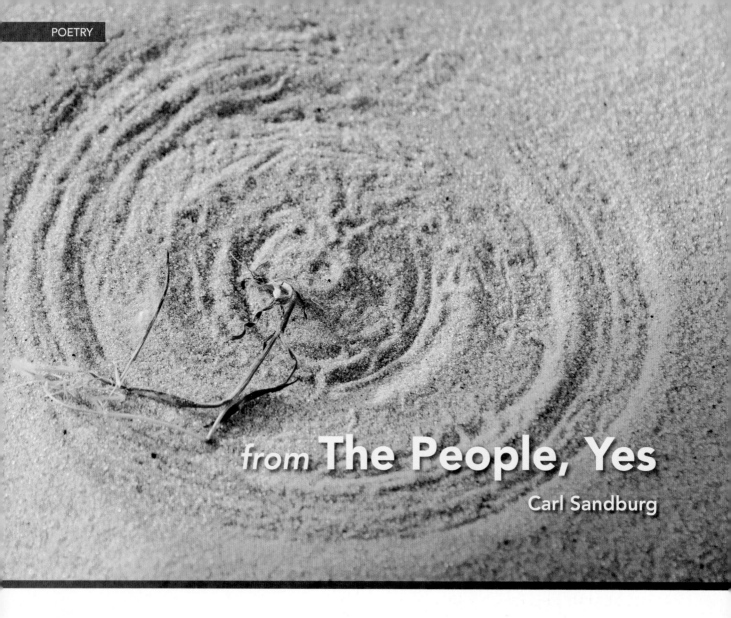

from The People, Yes

Carl Sandburg

SCAN FOR
MULTIMEDIA

NOTES

The white man drew a small circle in the sand
and told the red man, "This is what the Indian
knows," and drawing a big circle around the
small one, "This is what the white man knows."
5 The Indian took the stick and swept an immense
ring around both circles: "This is where the
white man and the red man know nothing."

Comprehension Check

Complete the following items after you finish your first read. Review and clarify
details with your group.

RETORT

1. In the first stanza of the poem, how does the speaker's heart feel?

2. How does the speaker describe Phyllis's face?

3. What kind of "air" does the speaker's heart speak with?

from THE PEOPLE, YES

Draw the figure created by the circles described in the poem. Label each circle
according to the details the speaker provides.

- -

RESEARCH

Research to Clarify Choose at least one unfamiliar detail from one of the poems.
Briefly research that detail. In what way does the information you learned shed light on
an aspect of the poem?

GROUP DISCUSSION

Make sure that everyone in the group has the opportunity to speak. Encourage quiet members to join the discussion.

🔗 WORD NETWORK

Add words related to human intelligence from the text to your Word Network.

☷ STANDARDS

Reading Literature
• Determine the meaning of words and phrases as they are used in a text, including figurative and connotative meanings; analyze the impact of specific word choices on meaning and tone, including analogies or allusions to other texts.

• Compare and contrast the structure of two or more texts and analyze how the differing structure of each text contributes to its meaning and style.

Language
• Determine or clarify the meaning of unknown and multiple-meaning words or phrases based on *grade 8 reading and content,* choosing flexibly from a range of strategies.
  c. Consult general and specialized reference materials, both print and digital, to find the pronunciation of a word or determine or clarify its precise meaning or its part of speech.

• Demonstrate understanding of figurative language, word relationships, and nuances in word meanings.
  b. Use the relationship between particular words to better understand each of the words.

Close Read the Text

With your group, revisit sections of the text you marked during your first read. **Annotate** what you notice. What **questions** do you have? What can you **conclude**?

Analyze the Text

CITE TEXTUAL EVIDENCE
to support your answers.

📓 Notebook **Complete the activities.**

1. **Review and Clarify** With your group, reread "Retort." Who are the two fools in the poem? Why are they both fools? How does Dunbar's poem connect to the idea of different types of intelligence?

2. **Present and Discuss** Now, work with your group to share lines from the poems that you found especially important. Take turns presenting your lines. Discuss what you noticed in the text, what questions you asked, and what conclusions you reached.

3. **Essential Question:** *In what different ways can people be intelligent?* What have these poems taught you about the different ways people can be intelligent? Discuss with your group.

LANGUAGE DEVELOPMENT

Archaic Vocabulary

| art | tress | fair |

Why These Words? The vocabulary words for these poems are all archaic words. Find at least one additional archaic word in the poems. Determine if the word you identified is no longer used in everyday English, or if it is used but its meaning has changed.

Practice

📓 Notebook Confirm your understanding of these words from the text by using each in a sentence. Provide context clues for each vocabulary word to demonstrate your understanding.

Word Study

📓 Notebook **Multiple-Meaning Words** In "Retort," the speaker describes Phyllis's face using the word *fair*—a word with multiple possible meanings. Write the meaning of the word as the speaker uses it. Then, write three other meanings of the word. If you have trouble thinking of three, use a dictionary to help you.

Analyze Craft and Structure

Author's Choices: Poetic Structures A **poetic form** is a set arrangement of poetic elements. A form may have a certain number of stanzas, lines, or both. It may require a pattern of rhyme, called a **rhyme scheme.** It may also use a certain meter, or pattern of stressed and unstressed syllables. Some forms of poetry have rules for all of these elements. This type of poetry is seen as having a formal structure. By contrast, **free verse** poetry does not follow any set pattern. A free verse poem may have rhyme or meter, but those elements will vary throughout the poem. Most poems—whether formal or free verse—include **sound devices.** These are combinations of words that emphasize the musical qualities of language. Common sound devices include the following types:

- **Alliteration:** repetition of consonant sounds at the beginnings of syllables, especially stressed syllables

  EXAMPLE: O <u>w</u>ild <u>W</u>est <u>W</u>ind

- **Consonance:** repetition of consonant sounds at the ends of syllables with different vowel sounds

  EXAMPLE: a quie<u>t</u> ligh<u>t</u>, and then no<u>t</u> even tha<u>t</u>

- **Assonance:** repetition of vowel sounds in stressed syllables that end with different consonant sounds

  EXAMPLE: p<u>e</u>bbles r<u>e</u>sting in w<u>e</u>t sand

Practice

> **CITE TEXTUAL EVIDENCE**
> to support your answers.

📓 **Notebook** Work with your group to analyze the poems in this collection. Use a chart like this one to record your ideas. Then, answer the questions that follow.

	RETORT	*from* THE PEOPLE, YES
Is the poem free verse or formal verse? How do you know?		
What kind of sound devices are used? Identify the line(s) in which the sound devices appear.		

1. (a) A *retort* is a quick, sharp reply, especially one that turns the words of the previous speaker back upon that speaker. Reread "Retort," and identify the central idea of each stanza. (b) How does the structure of the poem reflect its title?

2. (a) In the excerpt from *The People, Yes*, what effect is created by the use of repetition? (b) How does use of sound devices enhance this poem's meaning?

POETRY COLLECTION

Conventions

Participial and Infinitive Phrases Participles and infinitives and the phrases they form can make writing more concise or add important information to sentences.

A **participle** is a verb form that acts as an adjective. A **participial phrase** is made up of a participle with its modifiers, such as adverbs, and complements, such as objects. These all act together as an adjective, modifying a noun or pronoun. Present participles end in *-ing,* and past participles of regular verbs end in *-ed*. Past participles of irregular verbs have a variety of endings, such as *-en* or *-t*.

An **infinitive** is a verb form that acts as a noun, an adjective, or an adverb. Infinitives usually begin with the word *to*. An **infinitive phrase** is made up of an infinitive with modifiers or complements, all acting together as a single part of speech.

The chart below shows examples of participial phrases and infinitive phrases. In the chart, participles and infinitives are underlined, and phrases are in boldface.

PARTICIPIAL PHRASES AND THE WORDS THEY MODIFY	INFINITIVE PHRASES AND THEIR FUNCTIONS
Moving quickly, he picked up a stick. (modifies the subject, *he*)	**To prove how much he knew** was the man's main goal. (functions as a noun)
The man, **bothered by his thoughts**, tried to clear his head. (modifies the subject, *man*)	He agreed with the request **to listen to his heart**. (functions as an adjective modifying *request*)
The poem is about people **fooling themselves**. (modifies the object of a preposition, *people*)	They practice **to improve their skills.** (functions as an adverb modifying *practice*)

Read It

1. Mark the participial phrase in each sentence, and identify the word it modifies.

   a. One man, having made his point, walked away happy.

   b. He saw the woman thinking very hard.

2. Mark the infinitive phrase in each sentence, and identify its function.

   a. To teach the man a lesson, he drew a larger circle.

   b. The professor agreed to reward his students.

Write It

Choose one of the poems, and write two sentences about it. Use a participial phrase in one and an infinitive phrase in the other.

STANDARDS

Language
Demonstrate command of the conventions of standard English grammar and usage when writing or speaking.

a. Explain the function of verbals in general and their function in particular sentences.

Speaking and Listening

Assignment

With your group, develop a **multimedia presentation** of one of the poems from this collection. Make sure to come to your group's discussion prepared with ideas, and follow the rules for a friendly, productive discussion. Choose from the following options:

☐ With your group, identify a poem for a **dramatic reading**. Then, develop a plan for your presentation. Decide who will read each line, and determine how to read it. Which words should be emphasized? Should the line be read quickly or slowly? Softly or loudly? What type of emotions should the speaker show as he or she is reading the line? Remember to include multimedia elements, such as background music, props, and costumes.

☐ With your group, identify a poem for a **nonverbal multimedia presentation**. Then, discuss the poem, and develop a plan for your presentation in which you present the poem without words. Instead, convey the meaning of the poem by carefully arranging multimedia elements, such as music, video, dance, photos, original artwork, and mime.

Project Plan With your group, decide which members will carry out each task. Also, decide on the order of speakers or sequence of multimedia elements. You may wish to annotate a copy of the poem you chose in order to indicate what happens and when in the presentation it should occur. Use the chart to organize your presentation.

POEM LINE/STANZA	READER/ PERFORMER	MUSIC/SOUND	PROPS, COSTUMES, VISUALS	NOTES

EVIDENCE LOG

Before moving on to a new selection, go to your Evidence Log, and record what you learned from "Retort" and the excerpt from *The People, Yes*.

STANDARDS

Speaking and Listening
Engage effectively in a range of collaborative discussions with diverse partners on *grade 8 topics, texts, and issues,* building on others' ideas and expressing their own clearly.
  a. Come to discussions prepared, having read or researched material under study; explicitly draw on that preparation by referring to evidence on the topic, text, or issue to probe and reflect on ideas under discussion.

• Integrate multimedia and visual displays into presentations to clarify information, strengthen claims and evidence, and add interest.

Deliver a Multimedia Presentation

Assignment

In this section, you have analyzed various selections that explore the different ways people can be intelligent. Work with your group to develop a **multimedia presentation** that addresses this question:

> How does each selection highlight a different way to be intelligent?

Plan With Your Group

Analyze the Text With your group, discuss the ways in which the texts in this section explore different types of intelligence. Use the chart to list your ideas. For each selection, identify the type of intelligence featured. Note that in some selections more than one type of intelligence may be covered. Then, ask other group members questions you have about intelligence, and answer questions they may have. Work together to determine what each selection reveals about human intelligence.

SELECTION	TYPES OF INTELLIGENCE FEATURED
from Blue Nines and Red Words	
The Theory of Multiple Intelligences Infographic	
Retort	
from The People, Yes	

Gather Evidence and Media Examples Identify specific examples from the selections to support your group's ideas. Then, brainstorm about the types of multimedia you can use to clarify your ideas and emphasize key points. These may include charts, graphs, photos, video, or other visuals. Also, consider including audio elements, such as music. Allow each group member to make suggestions as to what multimedia content should be included, as well as how to sequence multimedia to engage your audience.

STANDARDS

Speaking and Listening
• Engage effectively in a range of collaborative discussions with diverse partners on *grade 8 topics, texts, and issues,* building on others' ideas and expressing their own clearly.

  a. Come to discussions prepared, having read or researched material under study; explicitly draw on that preparation by referring to evidence on the topic, text, or issue to probe and reflect on ideas under discussion.
  b. Follow rules for collegial discussions and decision-making, track progress toward specific goals and deadlines, and define individual roles as needed.
  c. Pose questions that connect the ideas of several speakers and respond to others' questions and comments with relevant evidence, observations, and ideas.

• Integrate multimedia and visual displays into presentations to clarify information, strengthen claims and evidence, and add interest.

Organize Your Ideas As a group, decide who is responsible for each part of the presentation. Decide when each part of the presentation will begin, and record what the presenter will say. Use a chart like this one to organize your script.

MULTIMEDIA PRESENTATION SCRIPT		
	Media Cues	Script
Presenter 1		
Presenter 2		
Presenter 3		

Rehearse With Your Group

Practice With Your Group As you work through the script for your presentation, use this checklist to evaluate the effectiveness of your group's first rehearsal. Then, use your evaluation and the instruction here to guide revisions to your presentation.

CONTENT	USE OF MEDIA	PRESENTATION TECHNIQUES
☐ The presentation clearly addresses the prompt. ☐ Main ideas are supported with evidence from the texts.	☐ Media clarify and emphasize important points in the presentation. ☐ Media are sequenced to engage the audience and add interest to the presentation.	☐ Speakers use adequate volume and maintain eye contact. ☐ Speakers use formal English and have an objective tone.

Fine-Tune the Content To make your presentation stronger, review your evidence to be sure you fully support your main points.

Improve Your Use of Media Review each piece of media to make sure it clarifies information effectively and adds interest to the presentation.

Brush Up on Your Presentation Techniques Make sure that your script includes only formal English, such as academic vocabulary and complete sentences. Avoid slang, idioms, contractions, run-on sentences, and sentence fragments. Practice delivering your presentation using a formal tone and proper English.

Present and Evaluate

Evaluate how well other presentations met the checklist criteria. Did other groups explore ideas you had not thought to include? After hearing the presentations of others, are there things you would do differently in your next presentation? In what ways? For what purpose?

STANDARDS

Speaking and Listening
- Engage effectively in a range of collaborative discussions with diverse partners on *grade 8 topics, texts, and issues,* building on others' ideas and expressing their own clearly.
   d. Acknowledge new information expressed by others, and, when warranted, qualify or justify their own views in light of the evidence presented.
- Present claims and findings, emphasizing salient points in a focused, coherent manner with relevant evidence, sound valid reasoning, and well-chosen details; use appropriate eye contact, adequate volume, and clear pronunciation.
- Integrate multimedia and visual displays into presentations to clarify information, strengthen claims and evidence, and add interest.
- Adapt speech to a variety of contexts and tasks, demonstrating command of formal English when indicated or appropriate.

ESSENTIAL QUESTION:

In what different ways can people be intelligent?

Human intelligence can be shown in small ways or in astonishing displays. In this section, you will complete your study of human intelligence by exploring an additional selection related to the topic. You'll then share what you learn with classmates. To choose a text, follow these steps.

Look Back Think about the selections you have already studied. What more do you want to know about human intelligence?

Look Ahead Preview the selections by reading the descriptions. Which one seems most interesting and appealing to you?

Look Inside Take a few minutes to scan through the text you chose. Choose a different one if this text doesn't meet your needs.

Independent Learning Strategies

Throughout your life, in school, in your community, and in your career, you will need to rely on yourself to learn and work on your own. Review these strategies and the actions you can take to practice them during Independent Learning. Add ideas of your own for each category.

STRATEGY	ACTION PLAN
Create a schedule	• Understand your goals and deadlines. • Make a plan for what to do each day. •
Practice what you have learned	• Use first-read and close-read strategies to deepen your understanding. • After you read, evaluate the usefulness of the evidence to help you understand the topic. • Consider the quality and reliability of the source. •
Take notes	• Record important ideas and information. • Review your notes before preparing to share with a group. •

SCAN FOR MULTIMEDIA

CONTENTS

Choose one selection. Selections are available online only.

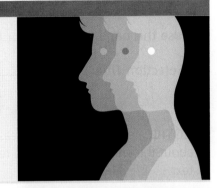

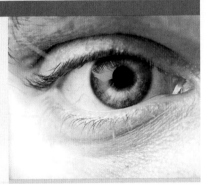

SCAN FOR MULTIMEDIA

First-Read Guide

Use this page to record your first-read ideas.

Selection Title: _____

Tool Kit
First-Read Guide and
Model Annotation

NOTICE new information or ideas you learn about the unit topic as you first read this text.

ANNOTATE by marking vocabulary and key passages you want to revisit.

CONNECT ideas within the selection to other knowledge and the selections you have read.

RESPOND by writing a brief summary of the selection.

▤ STANDARD
Reading Read and comprehend complex literary and informational texts independently and proficiently.

Close-Read Guide

Use this page to record your close-read ideas.

Selection Title: _____

Close Read the Text

Revisit sections of the text you marked during your first read. Read these sections closely and **annotate** what you notice. Ask yourself **questions** about the text. What can you **conclude**? Write down your ideas.

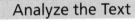

Analyze the Text

Think about the author's choices of patterns, structure, techniques, and ideas included in the text. Select one, and record your thoughts about what this choice conveys.

QuickWrite

Pick a paragraph from the text that grabbed your interest. Explain the power of this passage.

▦ STANDARD
Reading Read and comprehend complex literary and informational texts independently and proficiently.

Share Your Independent Learning

Prepare to Share

In what different ways can people be intelligent?

Even when you read something independently, you can continue to grow by sharing what you have learned with others. Reflect on the text you explored independently, and write notes about its connection to the unit. In your notes, consider why this text belongs in this unit.

Learn From Your Classmates

💬 **Discuss It** Share your ideas about the text you explored on your own. As you talk with your classmates, jot down ideas that you learn from them.

Reflect

Review your notes, and mark the most important insight you gained from these writing and discussion activities. Explain how this idea adds to your understanding of the different ways in which people can be intelligent.

☰ STANDARDS

Speaking and Listening
Engage effectively in a range of collaborative discussions with diverse partners on *grade 8 topics, texts, and issues*, building on others' ideas and expressing their own clearly.

Review Evidence for an Informative Essay

At the beginning of this unit, you responded to the following question:

In what different ways can people be intelligent?

✐ EVIDENCE LOG

Review your Evidence Log and your QuickWrite from the beginning of the unit. Have your ideas changed?

NOTES

Identify at least three pieces of evidence that interested you about the ways in which people demonstrate intelligence.

1.

2.

3.

Identify the way of demonstrating intelligence that made the strongest impression on you:

_____

_____

Develop your thoughts into a topic sentence for an informative essay. Complete this sentence starter:

One of the most unexpected ways in which people can show intelligence is _____

_____

_____

Evaluate Your Evidence Consider your ideas about intelligence prior to reading the texts in this unit. How did the texts you studied influence your ideas about intelligence? Note specific examples and key passages that piqued your curiosity.

▤ STANDARDS

Writing
Write informative/explanatory texts, to examine a topic and convey ideas, concepts, and information through the selection, organization, and analysis of relevant content.

b. Develop the topic with relevant, well-chosen facts, definitions, concrete details, quotations, or other information and examples.

SOURCES

- WHOLE CLASS SELECTIONS
- SMALL GROUP SELECTIONS
- INDEPENDENT-LEARNING SELECTION

 WORD NETWORK

As you write and revise your informative essay, use your Word Network to help vary your word choices.

PART 1
Writing to Sources: Informative Essay

In this unit, you have read a variety of perspectives on human intelligence. Both fiction and nonfiction texts have offered new ideas and explanations about the ways we think about and define human intelligence.

> **Assignment**
>
> Write an **informative essay** in which you address the Essential Question:
>
> > In what different ways can people be intelligent?
>
> Consider how each selection you read reveals a different perspective on what *intelligence* means. Make sure that you integrate relevant quotations, facts, and examples to support your ideas. Use a formal style and tone in your writing.

Reread the Assignment Review the assignment to be sure you fully understand it. The assignment may reference some of the academic words presented at the beginning of the unit. Be sure you understand each of the words given below in order to complete the assignment correctly. You may want to integrate some of the words into your essay.

Academic Vocabulary

assimilate	tendency	integrate
observation	documentation	

Review the Elements of an Effective Informative Essay Before you begin writing, read the Informative Essay Rubric. Once you have completed your first draft, check it against the rubric. If one or more of the elements is missing or not as strong as it could be, revise your essay to add or strengthen that component.

STANDARDS

Writing
- Write informative/explanatory texts to examine a topic and convey ideas, concepts, and information through the selection, organization, and analysis of relevant content.
- Draw evidence from literary or informational texts to support analysis, reflection, and research.
- Write routinely over extended time frames and shorter time frames for a range of discipline-specific tasks, purposes, and audiences.

Informative Essay Rubric

	Focus and Organization	Evidence and Elaboration	Conventions
4	The introduction engages the reader and states the topic in a compelling way. The essay is organized, and ideas progress logically. Transitions clearly show the relationships among ideas. The conclusion follows from the information in the essay and offers fresh insight into the topic.	The topic is developed with relevant facts, definitions, examples, and quotations. The style and tone of the essay are formal. The vocabulary is precise and suited to the topic, audience, and purpose.	The essay demonstrates mastery of standard English conventions of usage and mechanics.
3	The introduction is somewhat engaging and states the topic clearly. The essay is organized, and ideas progress somewhat logically. Some transitions are included to show the relationships among ideas. The conclusion follows from the information in the essay.	The topic is developed with facts, definitions, examples, and quotations. The style and tone of the essay are mostly formal. Vocabulary is generally suited to the topic, audience, and purpose.	The essay demonstrates accuracy in standard English conventions of usage and mechanics.
2	The introduction states the topic. The essay is somewhat organized, but not all ideas flow logically. A few transitions are included that show the relationship among ideas. The conclusion is somewhat related to the information in the essay.	The topic is developed with some facts, definitions, and quotations. The style and tone of the essay are occasionally formal. Vocabulary is somewhat suited to the topic, audience, and purpose.	The essay demonstrates some accuracy in standard English conventions of usage and mechanics.
1	The topic is not clearly stated. The essay is disorganized. Transitions are not included. The conclusion does not contain information that is related to the essay or is nonexistent.	Evidence is not used to develop the topic. The style and tone of the essay are informal. The vocabulary is not suited to the topic, audience, or purpose.	The essay contains mistakes in standard English conventions of usage and mechanics.

PART 2
Speaking and Listening: Speech

Assignment
After completing the final draft of your informative essay, use it as the foundation for a short **speech.**

Do not simply read your essay aloud. Instead, take the following steps to make your speech lively and engaging.

- Go back to your essay, and annotate its most important ideas and supporting details. Add details where needed to suit a listening audience.
- Refer to your annotated text to guide your presentation and keep it focused.
- Speak clearly and make eye contact with your audience.

Review the Rubric Before you deliver your presentation, check your plans against this rubric. If one or more of the elements is missing or not as strong as it could be, revise your presentation to improve it.

STANDARDS

Speaking and Listening
Present claims and findings, emphasizing salient points in a focused, coherent manner with relevant evidence, sound valid reasoning, and well-chosen details; use appropriate eye contact, adequate volume, and clear pronunciation.

	Content	Organization	Presentation Techniques
3	The introduction is engaging and establishes the topic in a compelling way. Ideas are clearly supported with relevant evidence. The conclusion offers fresh insight and follows from the rest of the presentation.	Ideas are organized and progress logically. Listeners can easily follow the presentation.	The speaker maintains effective eye contact. The speaker speaks clearly and with adequate volume.
2	The introduction establishes the topic. Ideas are usually supported with relevant evidence. The conclusion follows from the information in the presentation.	Ideas are organized. Listeners can mostly follow the presentation.	The speaker sometimes maintains eye contact. The speaker speaks somewhat clearly and usually with adequate volume.
1	The introduction does not clearly establish the topic. Ideas are not supported with relevant evidence. The information in the conclusion is not related to the presentation.	Ideas are disorganized. Listeners have difficulty following the presentation.	The speaker does not maintain eye contact. The speaker does not speak clearly or with adequate volume.

Reflect on the Unit

Now that you've completed the unit, take a few moments to reflect on your learning.

Reflect on the Unit Goals

Look back at the goals at the beginning of the unit. Use a different colored pen to rate yourself again. Then, think about readings and activities that contributed the most to the growth of your understanding. Record your thoughts.

Reflect on the Learning Strategies

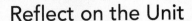 **Discuss It** Write a reflection on whether you were able to improve your learning based on your Action Plans. Think about what worked, what didn't, and what you might do to keep working on these strategies. Record your ideas before joining a class discussion.

Reflect on the Text

Choose a selection that you found challenging, and explain what made it difficult.

Describe something that surprised you about a text in the unit.

Which activity taught you the most about human intelligence? What did you learn?

 SCAN FOR MULTIMEDIA

Invention

Building something out of nothing is hard work.

💬 Discuss It What are some ways in which this invention might have failed?

Write your response before sharing your ideas.

Amazing Technology Invented By MIT - Tangible Media

SCAN FOR MULTIMEDIA

UNIT 5

UNIT INTRODUCTION

ESSENTIAL QUESTION: Are inventions realized through inspiration or perspiration?

LAUNCH TEXT
ARGUMENT MODEL
Inspiration Is
Overrated!

🖥 WHOLE-CLASS LEARNING

ANCHOR TEXT: NOVEL EXCERPT

Uncle Marcos
from **The House of the Spirits**
Isabel Allende, translated by Magda Bogin

ANCHOR TEXT: ESSAY

To Fly
from **Space Chronicles**
Neil deGrasse Tyson

▶ MEDIA CONNECTION:
When I Look Up

👥 SMALL-GROUP LEARNING

COMPARE

BIOGRAPHY

Nikola Tesla:
The Greatest
Inventor of All?
Vicky Baez

NOVEL EXCERPT

from **The Invention of Everything Else**
Samatha Hunt

SCIENCE ARTICLE

25 Years Later,
Hubble Sees Beyond
Troubled Start
Dennis Overbye

MEDIA: VIDEO

Sounds of a Glass
Armonica

👤 INDEPENDENT LEARNING

WEB ARTICLE

Ada Lovelace:
A Science Legend
James Essinger

WEB ARTICLE

Fermented Cow Dung
Air Freshener Wins
Two Students Top
Science Prize
Kimberley Mok

NEWS ARTICLE

Scientists Build Robot
That Runs, Call It
"Cheetah"
Rodrique Ngowi

NOVEL EXCERPT

from **The Time Machine**
H. G. Wells

MYTH

Icarus and Daedalus
retold by Josephine Preston Peabody

PERFORMANCE TASK

WRITING FOCUS:
Write an Argument

PERFORMANCE TASK

SPEAKING AND LISTENING FOCUS:
Conduct a Debate

PERFORMANCE-BASED ASSESSMENT PREP

Review Evidence for an Argument

PERFORMANCE-BASED ASSESSMENT

Argument: Essay and Speech

PROMPT:

Which invention described in this unit has had the biggest impact on humanity?

Unit Goals

Throughout this unit, you will deepen your perspective about creativity and invention by reading, writing, speaking, listening, and presenting. These goals will help you succeed on the Unit Performance-Based Assessment.

Rate how well you meet these goals right now. You will revisit your ratings later when you reflect on your growth during this unit.

SCALE	1	2	3	4	5
	NOT AT ALL WELL	NOT VERY WELL	SOMEWHAT WELL	VERY WELL	EXTREMELY WELL

READING GOALS

	1	2	3	4	5
• Read a variety of texts to gain the knowledge and insight needed to write about inspiration and invention.	○	○	○	○	○
• Expand your knowledge and use of academic and concept vocabulary.	○	○	○	○	○

WRITING AND RESEARCH GOALS

	1	2	3	4	5
• Write an argumentative essay in which you effectively incorporate the key elements of an argument.	○	○	○	○	○
• Conduct research projects of various lengths to explore a topic and clarify meaning.	○	○	○	○	○

LANGUAGE GOAL

	1	2	3	4	5
• Improve your writing by using gerund phrases and participial phrases to combine short, choppy sentences.	○	○	○	○	○

SPEAKING AND LISTENING GOALS

	1	2	3	4	5
• Collaborate with your team to build on the ideas of others, develop consensus, and communicate.	○	○	○	○	○
• Integrate audio, visuals, and text in presentations.	○	○	○	○	○

STANDARDS

Language
Acquire and use accurately grade-appropriate general academic and domain-specific words and phrases; gather vocabulary knowledge when considering a word or phrase important to comprehension or expression.

SCAN FOR MULTIMEDIA

Academic Vocabulary: Argument

Understanding and using academic terms can help you read, write, and speak with precision and clarity. Here are five academic words that will be useful in this unit as you analyze and write arguments.

Complete the chart.

1. Review each word, its root, and the mentor sentences.

2. Use the information and your own knowledge to predict the meaning of each word.

3. For each word, list at least two related words.

4. Refer to the dictionary or other resources if needed.

TIP

FOLLOW THROUGH
Study the words in this chart, and mark them or their forms wherever they appear in the unit.

WORD	MENTOR SENTENCES	PREDICT MEANING	RELATED WORDS
opponent ROOT: **-pon-** "place"; "put"	1. He managed to win the game against a strong *opponent*. 2. I respect her even though she is my *opponent*.		postpone; component
position ROOT: **-pos-** "place"; "put"	1. His *position* that everyone receive a different amount angered the other children. 2. Our debate team took the *position* that cellphone use should be banned from classrooms.		
contradict ROOT: **-dic-** "speak"; "assert"	1. Even though Abby knew Kyle was wrong, she did not *contradict* him. 2. The results of this study *contradict* the findings from earlier studies.		
legitimate ROOT: **-leg-** "law"	1. It's a *legitimate* argument, but they pretended not to hear it. 2. The judge determined that the oldest son was the *legitimate* heir to the fortune.		
dissent ROOT: **-sent-** "feel"	1. The proposal caused *dissent* because the members were against it. 2. The whole family wanted to go to the beach, so there was no *dissent* this time.		

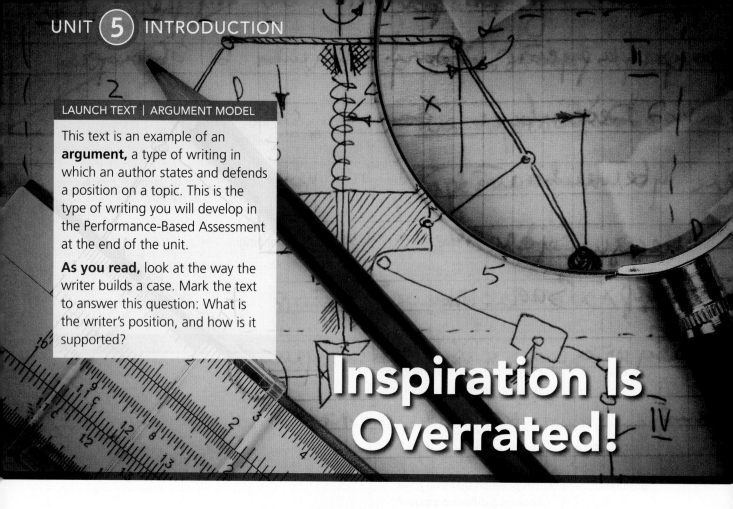

This text is an example of an **argument,** a type of writing in which an author states and defends a position on a topic. This is the type of writing you will develop in the Performance-Based Assessment at the end of the unit.

As you read, look at the way the writer builds a case. Mark the text to answer this question: What is the writer's position, and how is it supported?

Inspiration Is Overrated!

NOTES

1   Here's something that isn't on everyone's shopping list: a coffee mug that irons clothes. It's just one of a multitude of inventions that most of us have never heard of. Each of those forgotten contraptions was probably someone's bright idea—a flash of inspiration experienced while walking in the woods, an idea guaranteed to change the world. So what went wrong?

2   Some inventions are so much a part of everyday life we forget that they started off as someone's bright idea. Others are long forgotten or remembered only as being colossal duds.

3   For every invention that actually makes it to production, there are thousands that don't. The line between the bizarre and the ingenious is often very thin. History is filled with examples of new inventions that supporters thought would be transformational but turned out to be just minor fads.

4   Experts say that the odds are stacked astronomically against inventors, and that no amount of marketing can turn a situation around. The number of failed inventions reinforces how hard it is for inventors to make the leap from idea to marketable product.

5   Let's look at some figures. According to the U.S. Patent and Trademark Office, there are about 1.5 million products that have patents. Perhaps 3,000 of those make money. A noted business magazine states that only one in 5,000 inventions succeeds in the marketplace. This estimate is ten times lower than the one from the Trademark Office!

SCAN FOR
MULTIMEDIA

6   What explains the high rate of failure? Is there something the inventors failed to see? The answer is *yes*: They failed to see how much work is involved in getting a product off the ground. Someone once said that genius is one percent inspiration and ninety-nine percent perspiration. That is true for invention, too. Hard work is more important than a good idea.

7   Developing something new that actually works—and that people want—can take years. After an inventor has a brilliant idea, the hard part begins. A working model must be developed and tested. If the results are poor or inconsistent, the project may have to be rethought—or even scrapped. A good idea is necessary, but what comes after is more important.

8   When a working model is finally developed, the inventor must conduct what is called a "search for prior art." That means checking to make sure that there isn't a similar or even identical invention around. Sometimes it seems as if all the good ideas have been taken! That means more work.

9   When everything is ready to go, the inventor has to apply for a patent—a legal right to ownership of the invention. It's like a contract, and every single word has legal consequences. Many inventors hire patent lawyers to make sure their interests are protected. That means more work.

10   It's a common mistake to think that you can sell an idea. You can't. You can only sell an invention. Turning an idea into a viable invention takes work—time-consuming, tedious, and sometimes frustrating work!

11   If invention is one percent inspiration and ninety-nine percent perspiration, I'm putting my money on the ninety-nine percent. 🐝

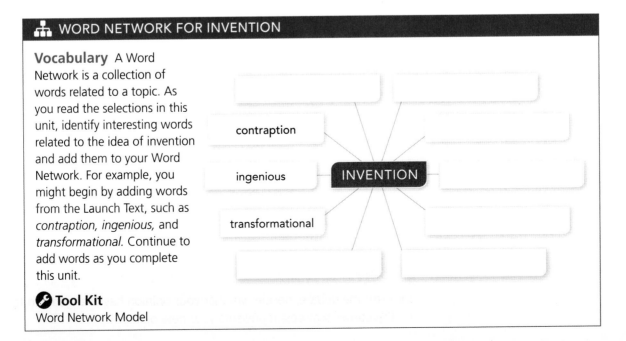

WORD NETWORK FOR INVENTION

Vocabulary A Word Network is a collection of words related to a topic. As you read the selections in this unit, identify interesting words related to the idea of invention and add them to your Word Network. For example, you might begin by adding words from the Launch Text, such as *contraption, ingenious,* and *transformational.* Continue to add words as you complete this unit.

contraption

ingenious

INVENTION

transformational

🔧 **Tool Kit**
Word Network Model

Summary

Write a summary of "Inspiration Is Overrated!" A **summary** is a concise, complete, and accurate overview of a text. It should not include a statement of your opinion or an analysis.

Launch Activity

Conduct a Four-Corner Debate Consider this statement: **Inventing takes one percent inspiration and ninety-nine percent perspiration.** Choose a position and explain why you feel this way.

☐ Strongly Agree ☐ Agree ☐ Disagree ☐ Strongly Disagree

_____

_____

- Join your classmates who chose the same response in one corner of the room. Together, formulate arguments for the class discussion.

- Share your group's ideas with your classmates. Then, ask questions or make comments. Remember to express your own point of view in a considerate, respectful way.

- After the debate, decide whether your opinion has changed. Go to the corner that best represents your new opinion.

QuickWrite

Consider class discussions, the video, and the Launch Text as you think about the prompt. Record your first thoughts here.

PROMPT: **Which invention has had the biggest impact on humanity?**

EVIDENCE LOG FOR INVENTION

Review your QuickWrite. Summarize your point of view in one sentence to record in your Evidence Log. Then, record evidence from "Inspiration Is Overrated!" that supports your point of view.

Prepare for the Performance-Based Assessment at the end of the unit by completing the Evidence Log after each selection.

 Tool Kit
Evidence Log Model

Title of Text: _____   Date: _____

CONNECTION TO PROMPT	TEXT EVIDENCE/DETAILS	ADDITIONAL NOTES/IDEAS

How does this text change or add to my thinking?   Date: _____

 SCAN FOR MULTIMEDIA

ESSENTIAL QUESTION:

Are inventions realized through inspiration or perspiration?

How do people invent? Does an idea simply come in a flash, or is there a long struggle to find a solution to a particular problem? You will work with your whole class to explore the concept of invention. The selections you are going to read present insights into some aspects of the topic.

Whole-Class Learning Strategies

Throughout your life, in school, in your community, and in your career, you will continue to learn and work in large-group environments.

Review these strategies and the actions you can take to practice them as you work with your whole class. Add ideas of your own for each step. Get ready to use these strategies during Whole-Class Learning.

STRATEGY	ACTION PLAN
Listen actively	• Eliminate distractions. For example, put your cellphone away. • Keep your eyes on the speaker. •
Clarify by asking questions	• If you're confused, other people probably are, too. Ask a question to help your whole class. • If you see that you are guessing, ask a question instead. •
Monitor understanding	• Notice what information you already know and be ready to build on it. • Ask for help if you are struggling. •
Interact and share ideas	• Share your ideas and answer questions, even if you are unsure. • Build on the ideas of others by adding details or making a connection. •

SCAN FOR
MULTIMEDIA

CONTENTS

PERFORMANCE TASK

WRITING FOCUS

Write an Argument

The Whole-Class readings focus on human flight—as realized by both real and fictitious inventors. After reading, you will write an essay in which you express your position about which text best captures the power of human inventiveness.

About the Author

Isabel Allende (b. 1942) is a Chilean American novelist, essayist, and lecturer who has been called the world's most widely read Spanish-language author. Allende's novels combine elements of myth and realism ("magical realism") and are often based on her personal experiences. In 1992, after the tragic death of her daughter, she established a foundation dedicated to the protection and empowerment of women and children worldwide. Allende became a U.S. citizen in 1993 and, in 2014, was awarded the Presidential Medal of Freedom by President Barack Obama.

⚙ **Tool Kit**
First-Read Guide and Model Annotation

⬛ STANDARDS

Reading Literature
By the end of the year, read and comprehend literature, including stories, dramas, and poems, at the high end of grades 6–8 text complexity band independently and proficiently.

Uncle Marcos

Concept Vocabulary

As you conduct your first read of "Uncle Marcos," you will encounter these words. Before reading, note how familiar you are with each word. Then, rank the words in order from most familiar (1) to least familiar (6).

WORD	YOUR RANKING
decipher	
invincible	
contraption	
newfangled	
ingenuity	
improvisations	

After completing the first read, come back to the concept vocabulary and review your rankings. Mark changes to your original rankings as needed.

First Read FICTION

Apply these strategies as you conduct your first read. You will have an opportunity to complete the close-read notes after your first read.

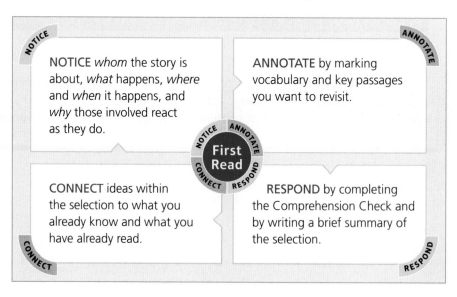

NOTICE *whom* the story is about, *what* happens, *where* and *when* it happens, and *why* those involved react as they do.

ANNOTATE by marking vocabulary and key passages you want to revisit.

CONNECT ideas within the selection to what you already know and what you have already read.

RESPOND by completing the Comprehension Check and by writing a brief summary of the selection.

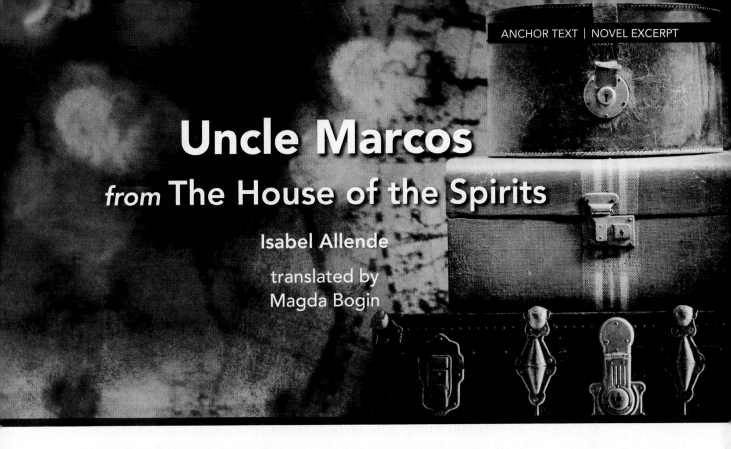

Uncle Marcos

from The House of the Spirits

Isabel Allende

translated by
Magda Bogin

BACKGROUND

"Uncle Marcos" is from Isabel Allende's first novel, which began as a letter to her 100-year-old grandfather. This excerpt draws on the Greek myth of Icarus and Daedalus. In the myth, Daedalus invents a pair of wings and teaches his son how to use them, but warns him not to fly too close to the sun because the wax in the wings would melt. Icarus is too excited to listen, and he drowns in the ocean after his wings melt.

SCAN FOR
MULTIMEDIA

1 It had been two years since Clara had last seen her Uncle Marcos, but she remembered him very well. His was the only perfectly clear image she retained from her whole childhood, and in order to describe him she did not need to consult the daguerreotype[1] in the drawing room that showed him dressed as an explorer leaning on an old-fashioned double-barreled rifle with his right foot on the neck of a Malaysian tiger, the same triumphant position in which she had seen the Virgin standing between plaster clouds and pallid angels at the main altar, one foot on the vanquished devil. All Clara had to do to see her uncle was close her eyes and there he was, weather-beaten and thin, with a pirate's mustache through which his strange, sharklike smile peered out at her. It seemed impossible that he could be inside that long black box that was lying in the middle of the courtyard.

2 Each time Uncle Marcos had visited his sister Nívea's home, he had stayed for several months, to the immense joy of his nieces and nephews, particularly Clara, causing a storm in which the

NOTES

CLOSE READ

ANNOTATE: In paragraph 1, mark details that show how Clara pictures her uncle, particularly his mustache and smile.

QUESTION: Why does the author use these descriptive details?

CONCLUDE: What is the effect of these details?

---

1. **daguerreotype** (duh GEHR oh typ) *n.* early type of photograph.

sharp lines of domestic order blurred. The house became a clutter of trunks, of animals in jars of formaldehyde,[2] of Indian lances and sailor's bundles. In every part of the house people kept tripping over his equipment, and all sorts of unfamiliar animals appeared that had traveled from remote lands only to meet their death beneath Nana's irate broom in the farthest corners of the house. Uncle Marcos's manners were those of a cannibal, as Severo put it. He spent the whole night making incomprehensible movements in the drawing room; later they turned out to be exercises designed to perfect the mind's control over the body and to improve digestion. He performed alchemy[3] experiments in the kitchen, filling the house with fetid smoke and ruining pots and pans with solid substances that stuck to their bottoms and were impossible to remove. While the rest of the household tried to sleep, he dragged his suitcases up and down the halls, practiced making strange, high-pitched sounds on savage instruments, and taught Spanish to a parrot whose native language was an Amazonic dialect. During the day, he slept in a hammock that he had strung between two columns in the hall, wearing only a loincloth that put Severo in a terrible mood but that Nívea forgave because Marcos had convinced her that it was the same costume in which Jesus of Nazareth had preached. Clara remembered perfectly, even though she had been only a tiny child, the first time her Uncle Marcos came to the house after one of his voyages. He settled in as if he planned to stay forever. After a short time, bored with having to appear at ladies' gatherings where the mistress of the house played the piano, with playing cards, and with dodging all his relatives' pressures to pull himself together and take a job as a clerk in Severo del Valle's law practice, he bought a barrel organ and took to the streets with the hope of seducing his Cousin Antonieta and entertaining the public in the bargain. The machine was just a rusty box with wheels, but he painted it with seafaring designs and gave it a fake ship's smokestack. It ended up looking like a coal stove. The organ played either a military march or a waltz, and in between turns of the handle the parrot, who had managed to learn Spanish although he had not lost his foreign accent, would draw a crowd with his piercing shrieks. He also plucked slips of paper from a box with his beak, by way of selling fortunes to the curious. The little pink, green, and blue papers were so clever that they always divulged the exact secret wishes of the customers. Besides fortunes there were little balls of sawdust to amuse the children. The idea of the organ was a last desperate attempt to win the hand of Cousin Antonieta after more conventional means of courting her had failed. Marcos thought

---

2. **formaldehyde** (fawr MAL duh hyd) *n.* solution used as a preservative.
3. **alchemy** (AL kuh mee) *n.* early form of chemistry, with philosophical and magical associations.

no woman in her right mind could remain impassive before a barrel-organ serenade. He stood beneath her window one evening and played his military march and his waltz just as she was taking tea with a group of female friends. Antonieta did not realize the music was meant for her until the parrot called her by her full name, at which point she appeared in the window. Her reaction was not what her suitor had hoped for. Her friends offered to spread the news to every salon[4] in the city, and the next day people thronged the downtown streets hoping to see Severo del Valle's brother-in-law playing the organ and selling little sawdust balls with a moth-eaten parrot, for the sheer pleasure of proving that even in the best of families there could be good reason for embarrassment. In the face of this stain to the family reputation, Marcos was forced to give up organ-grinding and resort to less conspicuous ways of winning over his Cousin Antonieta, but he did not renounce his goal. In any case, he did not succeed, because from one day to the next the young lady married a diplomat who was twenty years her senior; he took her to live in a tropical country whose name no one could recall, except that it suggested negritude,[5] bananas, and palm trees, where she managed to recover from the memory of that suitor who had ruined her seventeenth year with his military march and his waltz. Marcos sank into a deep depression that lasted two or three days, at the end of which he announced that he would never marry and that he was embarking on a trip around the world. He sold his organ to a blind man and left the parrot to Clara, but Nana secretly poisoned it with an overdose of cod-liver oil, because no one could stand its lusty glance, its fleas, and its harsh, tuneless hawking of paper fortunes and sawdust balls.

3   That was Marcos's longest trip. He returned with a shipment of enormous boxes that were piled in the far courtyard, between the chicken coop and the woodshed, until the winter was over. At the first signs of spring he had them transferred to the parade grounds, a huge park where people would gather to watch the soldiers file by on Independence Day, with the goosestep they had learned from the Prussians. When the crates were opened, they were found to contain loose bits of wood, metal, and painted cloth. Marcos spent two weeks assembling the contents according to an instruction manual written in English, which he was able to **decipher** thanks to his **invincible** imagination and a small dictionary. When the job was finished, it turned out to be a bird of prehistoric dimensions, with the face of a furious eagle, wings that moved, and a propeller on its back. It caused an uproar. The families of the oligarchy[6] forgot all about the barrel organ, and Marcos became the star attraction of the season.

---

4. **salon** (suh LON) *n.* regular gathering of distinguished guests that meets in a private home.
5. **negritude** (NEHG ruh tood) *n.* black people and their cultural heritage.
6. **oligarchy** (OL ih gahr kee) *n.* government ruled by only a few people.

NOTES

CLOSE READ
ANNOTATE: Mark the sentence in the latter part of paragraph 2 that suggests how Antonieta reacts to Marcos's barrel-organ music.

QUESTION: Why does the author provide so little description of her reaction?

CONCLUDE: What is the effect of this choice to suggest but not describe Antonieta's reaction?

decipher (dih SY fuhr) *v.* succeed in interpreting or understanding something

invincible (ihn VIHN suh buhl) *adj.* impossible to defeat

contraption (kuhn TRAP shuhn) *n.* machine that seems strange or unnecessarily complicated

newfangled (NOO fang uhld) *adj.* invented only recently and, therefore, strange-seeming

People took Sunday outings to see the bird; souvenir vendors and strolling photographers made a fortune. Nonetheless, the public's interest quickly waned. But then Marcos announced that as soon as the weather cleared he planned to take off in his bird and cross the mountain range. The news spread, making this the most talked-about event of the year. The **contraption** lay with its stomach on terra firma,[7] heavy and sluggish and looking more like a wounded duck than like one of those **newfangled** airplanes they were starting to produce in the United States. There was nothing in its appearance to suggest that it could move, much less take flight across the snowy peaks. Journalists and the curious flocked to see it. Marcos smiled his immutable[8] smile before the avalanche of questions and posed for photographers without offering the least technical or scientific explanation of how he hoped to carry out his plan. People came from the provinces to see the sight. Forty years later his great-nephew Nicolás, whom Marcos did not live to see, unearthed the desire to fly that had always existed in the men of his lineage. Nicolás was interested in doing it for commercial reasons, in a gigantic hot-air sausage on which would be printed an advertisement for carbonated drinks. But when Marcos announced his plane trip, no one believed that his contraption could be put to any practical use. The appointed day dawned full of clouds, but so many people had turned out that Marcos did not want to disappoint them. He showed up punctually at the appointed spot and did not once look up at the sky, which was growing darker and darker with thick gray clouds. The astonished crowd filled all the nearby streets, perching on rooftops and the balconies of the nearest houses and squeezing into the park. No political gathering managed to attract so many people until half a century later, when the first Marxist candidate attempted, through strictly democratic channels, to become President. Clara would remember this holiday as long as she lived. People dressed in their spring best, thereby getting a step ahead of the official opening of the season, the men in white linen suits and the ladies in Italian straw hats that were all the rage that year. Groups of elementary-school children paraded with their teachers, clutching flowers for the hero. Marcos accepted their bouquets and joked that they might as well hold on to them and wait for him to crash, so they could take them directly to his funeral. The bishop himself, accompanied by two incense bearers, appeared to bless the bird without having been asked, and the police band played happy, unpretentious music that pleased everyone. The police, on horseback and carrying lances, had trouble keeping the crowds far enough away from the center of

---

7. **terra firma** (TEHR uh FUR muh) *n.* firm earth; solid ground (from Latin).
8. **immutable** (ih MYOOT uh buhl) *adj.* never changing.

the park, where Marcos waited dressed in mechanic's overalls, with huge racer's goggles and an explorer's helmet. He was also equipped with a compass, a telescope, and several strange maps that he had traced himself based on various theories of Leonardo da Vinci and on the polar knowledge of the Incas.[9] Against all logic, on the second try the bird lifted off without mishap and with a certain elegance, accompanied by the creaking of its skeleton and the roar of its motor. It rose flapping its wings and disappeared into the clouds, to a send-off of applause, whistlings, handkerchiefs, drumrolls, and the sprinkling of holy water. All that remained on earth were the comments of the amazed crowd below and a multitude of experts, who attempted to provide a reasonable explanation of the miracle. Clara continued to stare at the sky long after her uncle had become invisible. She thought she saw him ten minutes later, but it was only a migrating sparrow. After three days the initial euphoria that had accompanied the first airplane flight in the country died down and no one gave the episode another thought, except for Clara, who continued to peer at the horizon.

4   After a week with no word from the flying uncle, people began to speculate that he had gone so high that he had disappeared into outer space, and the ignorant suggested he would reach the moon. With a mixture of sadness and relief, Severo decided that his brother-in-law and his machine must have fallen into some hidden crevice of the *cordillera*,[10] where they would never be found. Nívea wept disconsolately and lit candles to San Antonio, patron of lost objects. Severo opposed the idea of having masses said, because he did not believe in them as a way of getting into heaven, much less of returning to earth, and he maintained that masses and religious vows, like the selling of indulgences, images, and scapulars,[11] were a dishonest business. Because of his attitude, Nívea and Nana had the children say the rosary[12] behind their father's back for nine days. Meanwhile, groups of volunteer explorers and mountain climbers tirelessly searched peaks and passes, combing every accessible stretch of land until they finally returned in triumph to hand the family the mortal remains of the deceased in a sealed black coffin. The intrepid traveler was laid to rest in a grandiose funeral. His death made him a hero and his name was on the front page of all the papers for several days. The same multitude that had gathered to see him off the day he flew away in his

---

9. **Leonardo da Vinci . . . Incas** Leonardo da Vinci (1452–1519) was an Italian painter, sculptor, architect, and scientist. The Incas were Native Americans who dominated ancient Peru until Spanish conquest.

10. *cordillera* (kawr dihl YAIR uh) *n.* system or chain of mountains.

11. **indulgences, images, and scapulars** Indulgences are pardons for sins. Images are pictures or sculptures of religious figures. Scapulars are garments worn by Roman Catholics as tokens of religious devotion.

12. **say the rosary** use a set of beads to say prayers.

NOTES

CLOSE READ

ANNOTATE: Toward the end of paragraph 3, mark details that describe how Marcos is dressed as he waits to begin his flight.

QUESTION: Why does the author mention these details?

CONCLUDE: What do these details show about Marcos's knowledge and experience?

ingenuity (ihn juh NOO uh tee) *n.* quality of being original and clever

bird paraded past his coffin. The entire family wept as befit the occasion, except for Clara, who continued to watch the sky with the patience of an astronomer. One week after he had been buried, Uncle Marcos, a bright smile playing behind his pirate's mustache, appeared in person in the doorway of Nívea and Severo del Valle's house. Thanks to the surreptitious[13] prayers of the women and children, as he himself admitted, he was alive and well and in full possession of his faculties, including his sense of humor. Despite the noble lineage of his aerial maps, the flight had been a failure. He had lost his airplane and had to return on foot, but he had not broken any bones and his adventurous spirit was intact. This confirmed the family's eternal devotion to San Antonio, but was not taken as a warning by future generations, who also tried to fly, although by different means. Legally, however, Marcos was a corpse. Severo del Valle was obliged to use all his legal ingenuity to bring his brother-in-law back to life and the full rights of citizenship. When the coffin was pried open in the presence of the appropriate authorities, it was found to contain a bag of sand. This discovery ruined the reputation, up till then untarnished, of the volunteer explorers and mountain climbers, who from that day on were considered little better than a pack of bandits.

5   Marcos's heroic resurrection made everyone forget about his barrel-organ phase. Once again he was a sought-after guest in all the city's salons and, at least for a while, his name was cleared. Marcos stayed in his sister's house for several months. One night he left without saying goodbye, leaving behind his trunks, his books, his weapons, his boots, and all his belongings. Severo, and even Nívea herself, breathed a sigh of relief. His visit had gone on too long. But Clara was so upset that she spent a week walking in her sleep and sucking her thumb. The little girl, who was only seven at the time, had learned to read from her uncle's storybooks and been closer to him than any other member of the family because of her prophesying powers. Marcos maintained that his niece's gift could be a source of income and a good opportunity for him to cultivate his own clairvoyance. He believed that all human beings possessed this ability, particularly his own family, and that if it did not function well it was simply due to a lack of training. He bought a crystal ball in the Persian bazaar, insisting that it had magic powers and was from the East (although it was later found to be part of a buoy from a fishing boat), set it down on a background of black velvet, and announced that he could tell people's fortunes, cure the evil eye, and improve the quality of dreams, all for the modest sum of five centavos. His first customers were the maids from around the neighborhood. One of them had been accused of stealing, because her employer had misplaced a valuable ring. The crystal ball revealed the

13. **surreptitious** (sur uhp TIHSH uhs) *adj.* secretive.

exact location of the object in question: it had rolled beneath a wardrobe. The next day there was a line outside the front door of the house. There were coachmen, storekeepers, and milkmen; later a few municipal employees and distinguished ladies made a discreet appearance, slinking along the side walls of the house to keep from being recognized. The customers were received by Nana, who ushered them into the waiting room and collected their fees. This task kept her busy throughout the day and demanded so much of her time that the family began to complain that all there ever was for dinner was old string beans and jellied quince. Marcos decorated the carriage house with some frayed curtains that had once belonged in the drawing room but that neglect and age had turned to dusty rags. There he and Clara received the customers. The two divines wore tunics "the color of the men of light," as Marcos called the color yellow. Nana had dyed them with saffron powder, boiling them in pots usually reserved for rice and pasta. In addition to his tunic, Marcos wore a turban around his head and an Egyptian amulet around his neck. He had grown a beard and let his hair grow long and he was thinner than ever before. Marcos and Clara were utterly convincing, especially because the child had no need to look into the crystal ball to guess what her clients wanted to hear. She would whisper in her Uncle Marcos's ear, and he in turn would transmit the message to the client, along with any **improvisations** of his own that he thought pertinent. Thus their fame spread, because all those who arrived sad and bedraggled at the consulting room left filled with hope. Unrequited lovers were told how to win over indifferent hearts, and the poor left with foolproof tips on how to place their money at the dog track. Business grew so prosperous that the waiting room was always packed with people, and Nana began to suffer dizzy spells from being on her feet so many hours a day. This time Severo had no need to intervene to put a stop to his brother-in-law's venture, for both Marcos and Clara, realizing

improvisations (ihm pruh vy ZAY shuhnz) *n.* things that are created without any preparation

ANNOTATE: In the description of Marcos's stories in paragraph 6, mark details that relate to the senses of touch, sight, and hearing.

QUESTION: Why does the author include these sensory details?

CONCLUDE: What is the effect of these details?

that their unerring guesses could alter the fate of their clients, who always followed their advice to the letter, became frightened and decided that this was a job for swindlers. They abandoned their carriage-house oracle and split the profits, even though the only one who had cared about the material side of things had been Nana.

6   Of all the del Valle children, Clara was the one with the greatest interest in and stamina for her uncle's stories. She could repeat each and every one of them. She knew by heart words from several dialects of the Indians, was acquainted with their customs, and could describe the exact way in which they pierced their lips and earlobes with wooden shafts, their initiation rites, the names of the most poisonous snakes, and the appropriate antidotes for each. Her uncle was so eloquent that the child could feel in her own skin the burning sting of snakebites, see reptiles slide across the carpet between the legs of the jacaranda room divider, and hear the shrieks of macaws behind the drawing-room drapes. She did not hesitate as she recalled Lope de Aguirre's search for El Dorado[14], or the unpronounceable names of the flora and fauna her extraordinary uncle had seen; she knew about the lamas who take salt tea with yak lard and she could give detailed descriptions of the opulent women of Tahiti, the rice fields of China, or the white prairies of the North, where the eternal ice kills animals and men who lose their way, turning them to stone in seconds. Marcos had various travel journals in which he recorded his excursions and impressions, as well as a collection of maps and books of stories and fairy tales that he kept in the trunks he stored in the junk room at the far end of the third courtyard. From there they were hauled out to inhabit the dreams of his descendants, until they were mistakenly burned half a century later on an infamous pyre.

7   Now Marcos had returned from his last journey in a coffin. He had died of a mysterious African plague that had turned him as yellow and wrinkled as a piece of parchment. When he realized he was ill, he set out for home with the hope that his sister's ministrations and Dr. Cuevas's knowledge would restore his health and youth, but he was unable to withstand the sixty days on ship and died at the latitude of Guayaquil, ravaged by fever and hallucinating about musky women and hidden treasure. The captain of the ship, an Englishman by the name of Longfellow, was about to throw him overboard wrapped in a flag, but Marcos, despite his savage appearance and his delirium, had made so many friends on board and seduced so many women that the

14. **Lope de Aguirre's...El Dorado** Lope de Aguirre (LOH pay day ah GEER ray) was a Spanish adventurer (1510–1561) who journeyed through South America in search of the legendary city of El Dorado, which was supposedly rich in gold.

passengers prevented him from doing so, and Longfellow was obliged to store the body side by side with the vegetables of the Chinese cook, to preserve it from the heat and mosquitoes of the tropics until the ship's carpenter had time to improvise a coffin. At El Callao they obtained a more appropriate container, and several days later the captain, furious at all the troubles this passenger had caused the shipping company and himself personally, unloaded him without a backward glance, surprised that not a soul was there to receive the body or cover the expenses he had incurred. Later he learned that the post office in these latitudes was not as reliable as that of far-off England, and that all his telegrams had vaporized en route. Fortunately for Longfellow, a customs lawyer who was a friend of the del Valle family appeared and offered to take charge, placing Marcos and all his paraphernalia in a freight car, which he shipped to the capital to the only known address of the deceased: his sister's house.... ❧

Comprehension Check

Complete the following items after you finish your first read.

1. How does Uncle Marcos try to win the hand of Cousin Antonieta?

2. What does Uncle Marcos make from the materials he brings back in "enormous boxes"?

3. What special power does Clara have that Marcos pretends to possess?

4. 🗐 **Notebook** To confirm your understanding, write a summary of "Uncle Marcos."

- -

RESEARCH

Research to Clarify Choose at least one unfamiliar detail from the text. Briefly research that detail. In what way does the information you learned shed light on an aspect of the story?

UNCLE MARCOS

Close Read the Text

1. This model, from paragraph 3 of the text, shows two sample annotations, along with questions and conclusions. Close read the passage, and find another detail to annotate. Then, write a question and your conclusion.

> **ANNOTATE:** These phrases have similar structures but present contrasting ideas.
>
> **QUESTION:** Why does the author use these similar phrases?
>
> **CONCLUDE:** The structure emphasizes the contrast and hints at the surprise of the successful lift-off.

ANNOTATE: This series of nouns indicates the reactions of the crowd.

QUESTION: Why does the author present the crowd's reaction in this way?

CONCLUDE: The series of nouns shows how different types of people respond. The nouns suggest their social roles.

> Against all logic, on the second try the bird lifted off without mishap and with a certain elegance, accompanied by the creaking of its skeleton and the roar of its motor. It rose flapping its wings and disappeared into the clouds, to a send-off of applause, whistlings, handkerchiefs, drumrolls, and the sprinkling of holy water.

2. For more practice, go back into the text and complete the close-read notes.

3. Revisit a section of the text you found important during your first read. Read this section closely and **annotate** what you notice. Ask yourself **questions** such as "Why did the author make this choice?" What can you **conclude**?

🔧 **Tool Kit**
Close-Read Guide and Model Annotation

- -

Analyze the Text

CITE TEXTUAL EVIDENCE
to support your answers.

📓 **Notebook** Respond to these questions.

1. Analyze Why might Uncle Marcos be "the only perfectly clear image" Clara remembers from her childhood? Explain.

2. Interpret What motivates Uncle Marcos to undertake the flying machine project? Explain your thinking.

3. Compare and Contrast In what ways is the barrel organ incident similar to and different from the incident with the mechanical bird?

4. Essential Question: *Are inventions realized through inspiration or perspiration?* What has this story taught you about the concept of invention?

≣ STANDARDS
Reading Literature
• Cite the textual evidence that most strongly supports an analysis of what the text says explicitly as well as inferences drawn from the text.

• Analyze how particular lines of dialogue or incidents in a story or drama propel the action, reveal aspects of a character, or provoke a decision.

Analyze Craft and Structure

Propelling the Action: Character A **character** is a personality that is part of a story. A character may be a person, an animal, or even an object. In all narratives, the **plot,** or sequence of related events, is moved by a conflict that characters face. The story involves the ways in which characters experience and solve the conflict.

- The **main character** is the most important character in the narrative, the one whose conflict drives the plot.

- **Character traits** are the qualities, attitudes, and values that a character has. For example, a character might be reliable, smart, selfish, or stubborn.

- A **round character** has many different traits, both good and bad. In contrast, a **flat character** is one-dimensional, displaying only a single trait.

- A **dynamic character** changes and learns. A **static character** does not change or learn.

Writers use a variety of techniques to portray characters. They describe what characters look like and how they behave. They reveal what characters want, feel, think, and say. **Dialogue**, or words characters say, is a tool most fiction writers use to help portray characters. Dialogue reflects the words as a character speaks them, and is set off with quotation marks. In this excerpt, Isabel Allende does not use dialogue in a traditional way. She refers to things characters say, but does not quote them directly.

Practice

CITE TEXTUAL EVIDENCE to support your answers.

📓 **Notebook Respond to these questions.**

1. **(a)** What happens to Nívea's household when Uncle Marcos visits? Cite details that support your response. **(b)** What does his effect on the household tell you about Uncle Marcos's character?

2. **(a)** What does Clara do repeatedly after her uncle disappears on the flying machine? **(b)** How does her reaction differ from those of other family members? **(c)** What does Clara's reaction show about her character and relationship to Uncle Marcos? Explain.

3. Allende does not quote characters directly. However, she sometimes tells the reader what they say. Cite an example of a statement Uncle Marcos makes. Explain what this statement shows about his character.

4. Reread sections of the text that describe Clara and Uncle Marcos. **(a)** Determine whether each character is round or flat. **(b)** Determine whether each character is static or dynamic. For both (a) and (b), explain your responses and cite textual details that support them.

UNCLE MARCOS

Concept Vocabulary

decipher	contraption	ingenuity
invincible	newfangled	improvisations

Why These Words? The concept vocabulary words are all related to cleverness and innovation. For example, Uncle Marcos manages to *decipher* an instruction manual written in English in order to build his flying machine. Severo must use his *ingenuity*, or original, clever thinking to restore Uncle Marcos's citizenship rights.

1. How does the concept vocabulary help the reader understand Uncle Marcos as an inventor?

2. What other words in the selection describe Uncle Marcos's inventions or inventiveness?

Practice

⊟ **Notebook** The concept vocabulary words appear in "Uncle Marcos." Complete each sentence with the correct word.

1. A person who prefers old-fashioned objects might not want something _____.

2. A spy might have to _____ a code to find the hidden message.

3. If things do not go according to plan, you might have to think quickly and make _____.

4. You might admire a creative person's _____ in solving problems.

5. People might call a strange or unusual machine a _____.

6. A superhero who is _____ has nothing to fear from a villain's attacks.

Word Study

Latin Suffix: -ity The Latin suffix *-ity* means "state or quality of being." The author of this story refers to Severo's legal *ingenuity*, or his quality of being *ingenious* (original, clever, and resourceful). Use what you know about the Latin suffix *-ity* to answer these questions.

1. How does the Latin suffix *-ity* help you understand the meaning of the word *ability* as it is used in paragraph 5?

2. Explain what the word *responsibility* means. Then, give an example of a situation in which a person demonstrates responsibility.

☰ STANDARDS

Language
• Demonstrate command of the conventions of standard English grammar and usage when writing or speaking.
• Determine or clarify the meaning of unknown and multiple-meaning words or phrases based on *grade 8 reading and content,* choosing flexibly from a range of strategies.
    b. Use common, grade-appropriate Greek or Latin affixes and roots as clues to the meaning of a word.

Conventions

Subject Complements One essential tool for Allende and other writers is the subject complement, which allows a writer to define or describe the subject of a sentence.

A **linking verb** connects its subject to a subject complement. A **subject complement** is a noun, a pronoun, or an adjective that follows a linking verb and tells something about the subject.

The most common linking verbs are forms of *be*, such as *am, is, are, was,* and *were.* Other verbs that function as linking verbs when they are followed by subject complements include *seem, look, feel, become, grow,* and *appear.* There are three types of subject complements:

- A **predicate noun** or **predicate pronoun** (also called **predicate nominatives**) follows a linking verb and identifies or renames the subject of a sentence.

- A **predicate adjective** follows a linking verb and describes the subject of a sentence.

PREDICATE NOUN	PREDICATE PRONOUN	PREDICATE ADJECTIVE
Ronnie *became* the <u>captain</u> of the team.	The winners *are* <u>they</u>.	The flight to Houston *seemed* <u>swift</u>.
The noun *captain* renames the subject, *Ronnie.*	*They* identifies the subject, *winners.*	*Swift* describes the subject, *flight.*

Read It

1. 📓 **Notebook** Identify the predicate noun, pronoun, or adjective in each sentence. Then, briefly describe its function in the sentence.

   a. The man who returned was really he, alive and well.

   b. Clara is a genuine fortune-teller.

   c. When Uncle Marcos leaves, Clara grows upset.

2. Reread paragraph 2 of "Uncle Marcos." Find and label at least one predicate noun and one predicate adjective.

Write It

1. Fill in each of the following sentences with a predicate noun or a phrase that includes a predicate noun.

   a. Uncle Marcos is a(n) _____.

   b. Clara is the _____.

2. Fill in each of the following sentences with a predicate adjective.

   a. When he works on his inventions, Uncle Marcos seems _____.

   b. The character of Clara appears _____.

UNCLE MARCOS

Writing to Sources

A critical review is a type of argument in which a writer states and supports an interpretation or evaluation of a literary work.

Assignment

Write a **critical review** in which you state, explain, and support your understanding of the character of Uncle Marcos. In your view, is Uncle Marcos a dreamer, a crackpot, an innovator, a phony, just an unusual person, or something else? Your critical review should include the following elements:

- a main claim in which you state your position about Uncle Marcos
- an explanation of specific ways in which author Isabel Allende shows what Uncle Marcos is like
- evidence, including quotations from the narrative, that supports your main claim
- reasons that clarify your claim or show why it is valid

As you write your review, be clear about the ways in which your ideas fit together. Use words and phrases that show how one idea leads to the next, and how your evidence connects to the ideas. For example, words and phrases such as *because, as a result,* and *consequently* show cause-and-effect relationships. Words and phrases such as *like, similarly,* or *on the other hand* show comparison and contrast.

Vocabulary and Conventions Connection Consider including several of the concept vocabulary words. Also, remember to use subject complements correctly to strengthen your writing.

decipher	contraption	ingenuity
invincible	newfangled	improvisations

Reflect on Your Writing

After you have written your critical review, answer these questions.

1. How does stating a claim and finding support for it help you write a critical review?

2. What was the most difficult part of writing your critical review?

3. Why These Words? The words you choose make a difference in your writing. Which words did you specifically choose to clearly convey the connections between your ideas and evidence from the text?

STANDARDS

Writing
Write arguments to support claims with clear reasons and relevant evidence.

b. Support claim(s) with logical reasoning and relevant evidence, using accurate, credible sources and demonstrating an understanding of the topic or text.
c. Use words, phrases, and clauses to create cohesion and clarify the relationships between claim(s), counterclaims, reasons, and evidence.

Speaking and Listening

Assignment

Prepare for a **class discussion** about how the episode involving Uncle Marcos and his mechanical bird draws on themes from the Greek myth of Icarus.

1. **Prepare to Participate in Class Discussion** Find a version of the myth of Icarus online or in the Independent Learning section of this unit. Read the myth and jot down some notes about the key events. Then, skim paragraphs 3 and 4 of "Uncle Marcos" to review the episode involving the mechanical bird. Think about connections you see between the two stories.

2. **Cite Specific Text Evidence** As you begin the discussion, refer to your notes so that you can support your ideas with evidence from the texts. Make sure you can answer the following questions during the discussion.

   - How is Uncle Marcos similar to and different from Icarus?
   - What passages from "Uncle Marcos" support your ideas?
   - Why might the author have chosen to draw on the myth of Icarus in her portrayal of Uncle Marcos?

3. **Evaluate Discussion Participation** As you and your classmates contribute to the discussion, listen to one another attentively. Use an evaluation guide like the one shown to analyze the quality of the discussion.

DISCUSSION PARTICIPATION GUIDE

Rate each statement on a scale of 1 (not demonstrated) to 5 (demonstrated).

☐ The participants were prepared for the discussion.

☐ The participants cited specific passages and examples from the texts to support ideas.

☐ The participants built on one another's ideas and expressed their own clearly.

☐ The participants posed questions that connected ideas.

☐ The participants responded to questions and comments with relevant evidence, observations, and ideas.

✏ EVIDENCE LOG

Before moving on to a new selection, go to your Evidence Log and record what you learned from "Uncle Marcos."

☰ STANDARDS

Reading Literature
Analyze how a modern work of fiction draws on themes, patterns of events, or character types from myths, traditional stories, or religious works such as the Bible, including describing how the material is rendered new.

Speaking and Listening
Engage effectively in a range of collaborative discussions with diverse partners on *grade 8 topics, texts, and issues,* building on others' ideas and expressing their own clearly.
  a. Come to discussions prepared, having read or researched material under study; explicitly draw on that preparation by referring to evidence on the topic, text, or issue to probe and reflect on ideas under discussion.
  c. Pose questions that connect the ideas of several speakers and respond to others' questions and comments with relevant evidence, observations, and ideas.

About the Author

Neil deGrasse Tyson
(b. 1958) is an American astrophysicist, author, and science communicator, as well as the current director of the Hayden Planetarium's Rose Center for Earth and Space. From 2006 to 2011, he hosted the educational science show *NOVA ScienceNow* on PBS. Tyson grew up in the Bronx and attended the Bronx High School of Science from 1972 to 1976, where he was the editor-in-chief of "Physical Science," the school paper, and also the captain of the wrestling team.

🔧 **Tool Kit**
First-Read Guide and Model Annotation

To Fly

Concept Vocabulary

As you conduct your first read of "To Fly," you will encounter these words. Before reading, note how familiar you are with each word. Then, rank the words in order from most familiar (1) to least familiar (6).

WORD	YOUR RANKING
myopic	
foresight	
naiveté	
prescient	
enable	
seminal	

After completing the first read, come back to the concept vocabulary and review your rankings. Mark changes to your original rankings as needed.

First Read NONFICTION

Apply these strategies as you conduct your first read. You will have an opportunity to complete the close-read notes after your first read.

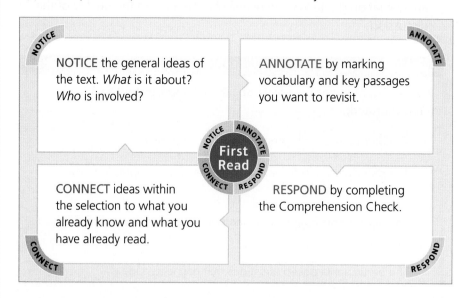

NOTICE the general ideas of the text. *What* is it about? *Who* is involved?

ANNOTATE by marking vocabulary and key passages you want to revisit.

CONNECT ideas within the selection to what you already know and what you have already read.

RESPOND by completing the Comprehension Check.

To Fly
from Space Chronicles
Neil deGrasse Tyson

BACKGROUND

The history of human flight is closely tied to the history of speed—flying has meant setting speed records. Heavy flying vehicles, like airplanes, have to move very quickly in order to stay in the air, and space shuttles have to travel at a very high speed called "escape velocity" to get into space.

SCAN FOR MULTIMEDIA

NOTES

1   In ancient days two aviators procured to themselves wings. Daedalus flew safely through the middle air, and was duly honored in his landing. Icarus soared upwards to the sun till the wax melted which bound his wings, and his flight ended in a fiasco. In weighing their achievements perhaps there is something to be said for Icarus. The classic authorities tell us, of course, that he was only "doing a stunt"; but I prefer to think of him as the man who certainly brought to light a serious constructional defect in the flying-machines of his day [and] we may at least hope to learn from his journey some hints to build a better machine.
—Sir Arthur Eddington, *Stars & Atoms* (1927)

2   For millennia, the idea of being able to fly occupied human dreams and fantasies. Waddling around on Earth's surface as majestic birds flew overhead, perhaps we developed a form of wing envy. One might even call it wing worship.

3   You needn't look far for evidence. For most of the history of broadcast television in America, when a station signed off for the night, it didn't show somebody walking erect and bidding farewell; instead it would play the "Star Spangled Banner" and show things that fly, such as birds soaring or Air Force jets whooshing by. The United States even adopted a flying predator as a symbol of its strength: the bald eagle, which appears on the back of the dollar bill, the quarter, the Kennedy half dollar, the Eisenhower dollar, and the Susan B. Anthony dollar. There's also one on the floor of the Oval Office in the White House. Our most famous superhero, Superman, can fly upon donning blue pantyhose and a red cape. When you die, if you qualify, you might just become an angel—and everybody knows that angels (at least the ones who have earned their wings) can fly. Then there's the winged horse Pegasus; the wing-footed Mercury; the aerodynamically unlikely Cupid; and Peter Pan and his fairy sidekick, Tinkerbell.

4   Our inability to fly often goes unmentioned in textbook comparisons of human features with those of other species in the animal kingdom. Yet we are quick to use the word "flightless" as a synonym for "hapless" when describing such birds as the dodo and the booby, which tend to find themselves on the wrong end of evolutionary jokes. We did, however, ultimately learn to fly because of the technological ingenuity afforded by our human brains. And of course, while birds can fly, they are nonetheless stuck with bird brains. But this self-aggrandizing line of reasoning is somewhat flawed, because it ignores all the millennia that we were technologically flightless.

5   I remember as a student in junior high school reading that the famed physicist Lord Kelvin, at the turn of the twentieth century, had argued the impossibility of self-propelled flight by any device that was heavier than air. Clearly this was a **myopic** prediction. But one needn't have waited for the invention of the first airplanes to refute the essay's premise. One merely needed to look at birds, which have no trouble flying and, last I checked, are all heavier than air.

6   If something is not forbidden by the laws of physics, then it is, in principle, possible, regardless of the limits of one's technological **foresight**. The speed of sound in air ranges from seven hundred to eight hundred miles per hour, depending

on the atmospheric temperature. No law of physics prevents objects from going faster than Mach 1,[1] the speed of sound. But before the sound "barrier" was broken in 1947 by Charles E. "Chuck" Yeager, piloting the Bell X-1 (a US Army rocket plane), much claptrap[2] was written about the impossibility of objects moving faster than the speed of sound. Meanwhile, bullets fired by high-powered rifles had been breaking the sound barrier for more than a century. And the crack of a whip or the sound of a wet towel snapping at somebody's buttocks in the locker room is a mini sonic boom, created by the end of the whip or the tip of the towel moving through the air faster than the speed of sound. Any limits to breaking the sound barrier were purely psychological and technological.

7   During its lifetime, the fastest winged aircraft by far was the space shuttle, which, with the aid of detachable rockets and fuel tanks, exceeded Mach 20[3] on its way to orbit. Propulsionless on return, it fell back out of orbit, gliding safely down to Earth. Although other craft routinely travel many times faster than the speed of sound, none can travel faster than the speed of light. I speak not from a **naiveté** about technology's future but from a platform built upon the laws of physics, which apply on Earth as they do in the heavens. Credit the Apollo astronauts who went to the Moon with attaining the highest speeds at which humans have ever flown: about seven miles per second at the end of the rocket burn that lifted their craft beyond low Earth orbit. This is a paltry 1/250 of one percent of the speed of light. Actually, the real problem is not the moat that separates these two speeds but the laws of physics that prevent any object from ever achieving the speed of light, no matter how inventive your technology. The sound barrier and the light barrier are not equivalent limits on invention.

8   The Wright brothers of Ohio are, of course, generally credited with being "first in flight" at Kitty Hawk, North Carolina, as that state's license-plate slogan reminds us. But this claim needs to be further delineated. Wilbur and Orville Wright were the first to fly a heavier-than-air, engine-powered vehicle that carried a human being—Orville, in this case—and that did not land at a lower elevation than its takeoff point. Previously, people had flown in balloon gondolas and in gliders and had executed controlled descents from the sides of cliffs, but none of those efforts would have made a bird jealous. Nor would Wilbur and Orville's first trip have turned any bird heads. The first of their four flights— at 10:35 A.M. eastern time on December 17, 1903—lasted twelve

© Pearson Education, Inc., or its affiliates. All rights reserved.

NOTES

naiveté (nah eev TAY) *n.* quality of innocent simplicity

---

1. **Mach** (mok) **1** speed of sound in dry air; sound travels faster in denser substances.
2. **claptrap** *n.* nonsensical talk.
3. **Mach 20** twenty times the speed of sound.

seconds, at an average speed of 6.8 miles per hour against a 30-mile-per-hour wind. The Wright Flyer, as it was called, had traveled 120 feet, not even the length of one wing on a Boeing 747.

9   Even after the Wright brothers went public with their achievement, the media took only intermittent notice of it and other aviation firsts. As late as 1933—six years after Lindbergh's historic solo flight across the Atlantic—H. Gordon Garbedian ignored airplanes in the otherwise **prescient** introduction to his book *Major Mysteries of Science*:

> Present day life is dominated by science as never before. You pick up a telephone and within a few minutes you are talking with a friend in Paris. You can travel under sea in a submarine, or circumnavigate the globe by air in a Zeppelin. The radio carries your voice to all parts of the earth with the speed of light. Soon, television will **enable** you to see the world's greatest spectacles as you sit in the comfort of your living room.

10   But some journalists did pay attention to the way flight might change civilization. After the Frenchman Louis Blériot crossed the English Channel from Calais to Dover on July 25, 1909, an article on page three of the *New York Times* was headlined "Frenchman Proves Aeroplane No Toy." The article went on to delineate England's reaction to the event:

> Editorials in the London newspapers buzzed about the new world where Great Britain's insular[4] strength is no longer unchallenged; that the aeroplane is not a toy but a possible instrument of warfare, which must be taken into account by soldiers and statesmen, and that it was the one thing needed to wake up the English people to the importance of the science of aviation.

11   The guy was right. Thirty-five years later, not only had airplanes been used as fighters and bombers in warfare but the Germans had taken the concept a notch further and invented the V-2 to attack London. Their vehicle was significant in many ways. First, it was not an airplane; it was an unprecedentedly large missile. Second, because the V-2 could be launched several hundred miles from its target, it basically birthed the modern rocket. And third, for its entire airborne journey after launch, the V-2 moved under the influence of gravity alone; in other words, it was a suborbital ballistic missile, the fastest way to deliver a bomb from one location on Earth to another. Subsequently, Cold War "advances" in the design of missiles enabled military power to target cities on

prescient (PREHSH uhnt) *adj.* having knowledge of things before they happen

enable (ehn AYB uhl) *v.* make possible

CLOSE READ

ANNOTATE: In paragraph 11, mark the word the author uses to refer to the writer of the passage quoted in paragraph 10.

QUESTION: Why does the author use this informal term?

CONCLUDE: What is the effect of this casual language?

---

4. **insular** (IHN suh luhr) *adj.* literally, related to being an island; figuratively, detached or isolated.

opposite sides of the world. Maximum flight time? About forty-five minutes—not nearly enough time to evacuate a targeted city.

12   While we can say they're suborbital, do we have the right to declare missiles to be flying? Are falling objects in flight? Is Earth "flying" in orbit around the Sun? In keeping with the rules applied to the Wright brothers, a person must be onboard the craft and it must move under its own power. But there's no rule that says we cannot change the rules.

13   Knowing that the V-2 brought orbital technology within reach, some people got impatient. Among them were the editors of the popular, family-oriented magazine *Collier's*, which sent two journalists to join the engineers, scientists, and visionaries gathered at New York City's Hayden Planetarium on Columbus Day, 1951, for its **seminal** Space Travel Symposium. In the March 22, 1952, issue of *Collier's*, in a piece titled "What Are We Waiting For?" the magazine endorsed the need for and value of a space station that would serve as a watchful eye over a divided world:

seminal (SEHM uh nuhl) *adj.* being the first of something that is later recognized as important

> In the hands of the West a space station, permanently established beyond the atmosphere, would be the greatest hope for peace the world has ever known. No nation could undertake preparations for war without the certain knowledge that it was being observed by the ever-watching eyes aboard the "sentinel in space." It would be the end of the Iron Curtains[5] wherever they might be.

14   We Americans didn't build a space station; instead we went to the Moon. With this effort, our wing worship continued. Never mind that Apollo astronauts landed on the airless Moon, where wings are completely useless, in a lunar module named after a bird. A mere sixty-five years, seven months, three days, five hours, and forty-three minutes after Orville left the ground, Neil Armstrong gave his first statement from the Moon's surface: "Houston, Tranquility Base here. The Eagle has landed."

15   The human record for "altitude" does not go to anybody for having walked on the Moon. It goes to the astronauts of the ill-fated Apollo 13. Knowing they could not land on the Moon after the explosion in their oxygen tank, and knowing they did not have enough fuel to stop, slow down, and head back, they executed a single figure-eight ballistic trajectory around the Moon, swinging them back toward Earth. The Moon just happened to be near apogee, the farthest point from Earth in its elliptical orbit. No other Apollo mission (before or since) went to the Moon during apogee, which granted the Apollo 13 astronauts the human

---

5. **Iron Curtains** figurative walls of secrecy and suspicion between the Soviet Union and non-communist countries during the Cold War.

altitude record. (After calculating that they must have reached about 245,000 miles "above" Earth's surface, including the orbital distance from the Moon's surface, I asked Apollo 13 commander Jim Lovell, "Who was on the far side of the command module as it rounded the Moon? That single person would hold the altitude record." He refused to tell.)

16   In my opinion, the greatest achievement of flight was not Wilbur and Orville's aeroplane, nor Chuck Yeager's breaking of the sound barrier, nor the Apollo 11 lunar landing. For me, it was the launch of Voyager 2, which ballistically[6] toured the solar system's outer planets. During the flybys, the spacecraft's slingshot trajectories stole a little of Jupiter's and Saturn's orbital energy to enable its rapid exit from the solar system. Upon passing Jupiter in 1979, Voyager's speed exceeded forty thousand miles an hour, sufficient to escape the gravitational attraction of even the Sun. Voyager passed the orbit of Pluto in 1993 and has now entered the realm of interstellar space. Nobody happens to be onboard the craft, but a gold phonograph record attached to its side is etched with the earthly sounds of, among many things, the human heartbeat. So with our heart, if not our soul, we fly ever farther. ❧

CLOSE READ

ANNOTATE: In paragraph 16, mark the point at which the author stops using scientific words and phrases and begins to use poetic, emotional language.

QUESTION: Why does the language change so dramatically at this point?

CONCLUDE: What is the effect of this change, especially in a concluding paragraph?

---

6. **ballistically** (buh LIHS tihk lee) *adv.* like a thrown object.

MEDIA CONNECTION

When I Look Up

💬 **Discuss It** How does viewing this video affect your thinking about space exploration?

Write your response before sharing your ideas.

SCAN FOR MULTIMEDIA

Comprehension Check

Complete the following items after you finish your first read.

1. According to Tyson, what idea occupied human fantasies for millennia?

2. According to Tyson, what two ideas did people once think were impossible, even though they do not defy any laws of physics?

3. In Tyson's opinion, what is the greatest achievement of human flight?

4. ⊟ **Notebook** Create a rough timeline showing when the inventions discussed in the article were first created. Make sure the order is correct, even if you do not have an exact date for every invention.

- -

RESEARCH

Research to Clarify Choose at least one unfamiliar detail from the text. Briefly research that detail. In what way does the information you learned shed light on an aspect of the essay?

Research to Explore Choose something that interested you from the text, and formulate a research question.

TO FLY

Close Read the Text

1. This model from the text shows two sample annotations, along with questions and conclusions. Close read the passage, and find another detail to annotate. Then, write a question and your conclusion.

ANNOTATE, QUESTION, Close Read, CONCLUDE

> ANNOTATE: These words and phrases have an informal, jokey quality.
>
> QUESTION: Why does the author use an informal, lighthearted tone?
>
> CONCLUDE: The author is presenting scientific information in a way that makes it entertaining for non-scientists.

> When you die, if you qualify, you might just become an angel—and everybody knows that angels (at least the ones who have earned their wings) can fly. Then there's the winged horse Pegasus; the wing-footed Mercury; the aerodynamically unlikely Cupid; and Peter Pan and his fairy sidekick, Tinkerbell.

ANNOTATE: This description applies a scientific term to a mythological figure.

QUESTION: Why does the author describe Cupid in this way?

CONCLUDE: The description is funny, and also reminds readers that scientific principles guide the technology of flight.

🔧 **Tool Kit**
Close-Read Guide and Model Annotation

2. For more practice, go back into the text, and complete the close-read notes.

3. Revisit a section of text you found important during your first read. **Annotate** what you notice. Ask **questions** such as "Why did the author make this choice?" What can you **conclude**?

- -

Analyze the Text

CITE TEXTUAL EVIDENCE to support your answers.

📝 **Notebook** Respond to these questions.

1. **Interpret** What is the author's attitude toward the achievements he describes? Explain your interpretation.

2. **Make a Judgment** Which of the achievements described in the article do you think is the most significant? Why? Cite details from the text to support your answer.

3. **Essential Question:** *Are inventions realized through inspiration or perspiration?* What have you learned about how inventions are created?

📋 STANDARDS

Reading Informational Text
• Analyze how a text makes connections among and distinctions between individuals, ideas, or events.
• Determine the meaning of words and phrases as they are used in a text, including figurative, connotative, and technical meanings; analyze the impact of specific word choices on meaning and tone, including analogies or allusions to other texts.
• Analyze in detail the structure of a specific paragraph in a text, including the role of particular sentences in developing and refining a key concept.

Language
Interpret figures of speech in context.

Analyze Craft and Structure

Text Structure: Expository Writing The word *exposition* means
"explanation." An **expository essay** is a brief work of nonfiction
that explains a topic. That explanation may involve the presentation of
information, discussion of ideas, or clarification of a process. In this essay,
Neil deGrasse Tyson presents information and ideas related to human
flight. He uses a variety of methods to make ideas and information clear
to readers.

- **Allusions** are references in a text to well-known people, places,
  characters, myths, events, or works of literature or art. These
  references appear without explanation. They are designed to help
  readers make connections and expand their thinking about the
  writer's ideas.

- **Comparisons and contrasts** present similarities and differences
  among two or more items or ideas. By showing how one thing is like
  or unlike another, an expository writer clarifies the qualities of each
  item.

- **Description** uses words and phrases that appeal to the senses. In
  expository writing, description can help readers understand a topic by
  "showing" what something looks like, how it sounds or moves, and
  even what it smells or tastes like.

- **Cause-and-effect** relationships show how one situation can result
  from another and then lead to yet another. These connections help
  readers understand how or why a situation developed as it did.

Practice

CITE TEXTUAL EVIDENCE
to support your answers.

📝 Notebook **Answer these questions.**

1. Reread paragraph 3. **(a)** What allusions does the author make? **(b)** What do
   these allusions have in common? **(c)** What idea do these allusions support?
   Explain.

2. Reread paragraph 4. **(a)** What two different things does the author compare
   and contrast? **(b)** What idea does this comparison-and-contrast help the author
   explain?

3. Reread paragraph 6. **(a)** What descriptive elements does this paragraph include?
   (b) What idea does the description help the author develop?

4. Reread paragraphs 11 to 13. **(a)** According to Tyson, under what circumstances
   was the German V-2 invented? **(b)** What was important about the V-2 at the
   time? **(c)** What changes in technology did the V-2 lead to or influence? Explain.
   (d) What idea does Tyson's example of the V-2 help develop or support?

TO FLY

Concept Vocabulary

enable	foresight	prescient
myopic	naivete	seminal

Why These Words? These concept words help to show the contrast between innovative and conventional ways of thinking. For example, in paragraph 5, the author criticizes Lord Kelvin's limited vision of flight as *myopic*. This word vividly reveals the author's view of Kelvin's mistake.

1. How does the concept vocabulary help the reader better understand the author's attitude toward invention and the future?

2. What other words in the selection connect to innovative or conventional thinking?

Practice

📄 **Notebook** The concept vocabulary words appear in "To Fly."

1. Write a paragraph in which you describe something that might *enable* someone to become a groundbreaking artist or musician. Use at least three of the concept vocabulary words in your paragraph.

2. Divide the concept vocabulary words into two categories: innovative thinking and conventional thinking. Explain why you placed each word in its category.

Word Study

Old English Prefix: *fore-* The prefix *fore-* means "before," "toward," or "front." In paragraph 6, the author notes that lack of *foresight*, or looking ahead, can be an obstacle to creating new inventions. Use what you know about the prefix *fore-* to answer these questions.

1. Where is a book's foreword located?

2. Where would you expect to find an animal's *foreleg*?

🔧 **WORD NETWORK**

Add words related to invention from the text to your Word Network.

STANDARDS

Language
• Demonstrate command of the conventions of standard English capitalization, punctuation, and spelling when writing.
  c. Spell correctly.
• Determine or clarify the meaning of unknown and multiple meaning words or phrases based on *grade 8 reading and content*, choosing flexibly from a range of strategies.
  b. Use common, grade-appropriate Greek or Latin affixes and roots as clues to the meaning of a word.

Conventions

Capitalization Capital letters signal the beginning of a sentence or quotation and identify proper nouns and proper adjectives. **Proper nouns** include the names of people, geographical locations, specific events and time periods, organizations, languages, documents, and religions. **Proper adjectives** are derived from proper nouns, as in *French* (from *France*) and *Canadian* (from *Canada*).

This chart shows examples of situations in which capitalization is required.

CAPITALIZE	EXAMPLES
the first letter of the first word in a sentence	The blue jay is a very aggressive bird. Wait! Can you give me back my pen?
the beginning of the first word in a quotation that is a complete sentence; the beginning of the first word in a line of dialogue	Einstein said, "Anyone who has never made a mistake has never tried anything new."
the pronoun *I*	After swimming, I felt tired.
proper nouns, including people's names, people's titles when used as part of their names, place names, and names of organizations	Elsa went sailing down the Hudson River with Ms. Liu and her Girl Scout troop.
proper adjectives, or adjectives formed from proper nouns	Many people of Brazilian background speak the Portuguese language.

Read It

1. Identify the capital letters in each sentence, and explain why each one is capitalized.
   a. Superman, a famous American superhero, has the power to fly.
   b. Neil deGrasse Tyson studied physics at Harvard and Columbia.
   c. I believe that *Collier's* published editorials about building a space station.
2. 🗒 **Notebook** In "To Fly," find examples of two types of capitalization, and explain why each word is capitalized.

Write It

🗒 **Notebook** Rewrite this paragraph, correcting errors in capitalization.

In this article, neil degrasse tyson starts by discussing birds and mythical flying figures, such as pegasus, mercury, and peter pan. he continues with the invention of the airplane by the wright brothers. Although tyson mainly focuses on american technology, he also discusses the german v-2 rocket. he writes, "their vehicle was significant in many ways."

TO FLY

Writing to Sources

In an argumentative essay, a writer states a position on a subject. He or she then defends or supports that position through the use of logical reasoning and relevant evidence.

Assignment

Tyson mentions the golden record that is attached to the side of the Voyager 2. That record includes music, voices, and other sounds that represent Earth and its occupants. Imagine that you are able to choose a sound to add to that record. What sound would it be? Write an **argumentative essay** in which you state and defend your choice. Follow these steps as you write:

- Clearly state your position, or claim, in an introductory paragraph. This should include both your choice of a sound and a broad reason for it.

- In the body of the essay, provide specific reasons for your choice, and support them with evidence from Tyson's essay, your own observations, or another source.

- Organize your reasons and evidence logically. Use transitional words and phrases, such as *because*, *instead*, and *after,* to clarify the relationships between your claims, your reasons, and the supporting evidence.

- Conclude with a strong closing statement that follows from and supports your argument.

Vocabulary and Conventions Connection Consider using several of the concept vocabulary words. Also, remember to use correct capitalization for proper nouns and proper adjectives.

enable	foresight	prescient
myopic	naivete	seminal

- -

Reflect on Your Writing

After you have written your essay, answer the following questions.

1. How might you revise your claim to make it stronger?

2. How might you revise the way you present your evidence to help it more strongly support your claim?

3. **Why These Words?** The words you choose make a difference in your writing. Which words did you specifically choose to clearly convey your ideas?

≡ STANDARDS

Writing
Write arguments to support claims with clear reasons and relevant evidence.

  b. Support claim(s) with logical reasoning and relevant evidence, using accurate, credible sources and demonstrating an understanding of the topic or text.
  e. Provide a concluding statement or section that follows from and supports the argument presented.

Speaking and Listening
- Present claims and findings, emphasizing salient points in a focused, coherent manner with relevant evidence, sound valid reasoning, and well-chosen details; use appropriate eye contact, adequate volume, and clear pronunciation.
- Integrate multimedia and visual displays into presentations to clarify information, strengthen claims and evidence, and add interest.

Speaking and Listening

Assignment

Work with a partner to create and deliver an **informative presentation** on one of the historic flying feats or scientific principles that Neil deGrasse Tyson discusses in the text.

1. **Research Your Topic** Choose a science-related topic mentioned in the text. Divide up tasks between partners. Be sure that you know enough about the topic that you are able to explain it in easy-to-understand language.

2. **Plan Your Presentation** Once you have completed the research, decide how to best present the information. You may find and add images, or create your own graphics, such as a table or chart. As you create the presentation, keep the following in mind:

   - Clearly state your main idea and supporting ideas.
   - Identify interesting and relevant details to support your key points.
   - Select images that add useful information or illustrate your ideas.

3. **Prepare Your Delivery** Practice your presentation with your partner. Include the following performance techniques.

   - Vary your speaking volume to emphasize key points. Use eye contact appropriately to connect with your audience.

   - Present images at appropriate points.

   - Invite questions from listeners, and work to clarify any information they may not understand.

4. **Evaluate Presentations** As your classmates deliver their presentations, listen carefully. Use an evaluation guide like the one shown to analyze classmates' presentations.

PRESENTATION EVALUATION GUIDE
Rate each statement on a scale of 1 (not demonstrated) to 5 (demonstrated).
☐ The information was well organized and easy to understand.
☐ The presenters connected with their audience by maintaining eye contact and varying the volume of their voices.
☐ Relevant details provided support for the main ideas.
☐ Images fit well with the information and were presented in a way that made sense for the subject.
☐ Presenters allowed time for the audience to ask questions.

✒ EVIDENCE LOG

Before moving on to a new selection, go to your Evidence Log and record what you learned from "To Fly."

WRITING TO SOURCES

• UNCLE MARCOS

• TO FLY

ACADEMIC VOCABULARY

As you craft your argument, consider using some of the academic vocabulary you learned in the beginning of the unit.

opponent
position
contradict
legitimate
dissent

🔧 **Tool Kit**
Student Model of an Argument

Write an Argument

You have just read two texts in which the authors explore the idea of human flight. In "Uncle Marcos," Uncle Marcos builds a flying machine and becomes a hero when he attempts to fly it over the mountains. In "To Fly," author Neil deGrasse Tyson discusses the development of human flight, from myths to airplanes and space travel. Now you will use your knowledge of these texts to explore your thoughts and write your own argument about human flight.

Assignment

Think about what flying means to people, both individually and collectively. Then, write an **argumentative essay** in which you make a claim that answers this question:

> **Which text—"Uncle Marcos" or "To Fly"—best describes the dream or fantasy of human flight?**

Be sure to clearly state your position and support it with logical reasoning and evidence from the texts.

Elements of an Argument

An **argument** is a logical way of presenting a viewpoint, belief, or stand on an issue. A well-written argument may convince the reader, change the reader's mind, or motivate the reader to take a certain action.

An effective argumentative essay about a literary work contains these elements:

- an analysis of the work, including its content and style
- a thesis statement or precise claim that expresses your interpretation of the work
- inclusion of a counterclaim, or alternate interpretation, and a discussion of why it is less convincing than yours
- textual evidence that supports your interpretation
- a logical organization, including a conclusion that follows from and supports your claim
- a formal style and objective tone appropriate for an academic purpose and audience
- error-free grammar, including correct use of gerunds and participles

Model Argument For a model of a well-crafted argument, see the Launch Text, "Inspiration Is Overrated!"

Challenge yourself to find all of the elements of an effective argument in the text. You will have an opportunity to review these elements as you prepare to write your own argument.

LAUNCH TEXT

Inspiration Is Overrated!

📋 **STANDARDS**

Writing
Write arguments to support claims with clear reasons and relevant evidence.

Prewriting / Planning

Write a Working Claim   You may already have a clear idea about which text you feel best portrays the dream of human flight. Start by writing a working claim. As you gather evidence that claim may shift or even change completely.

- **Working Claim:** _____

_____

Identify Types of Details   Your claim and supporting reasons determine the kinds of details you need to include. Consider these tips:

- **To analyze a text,** support your ideas with evidence from the selection.
- **To explain a personal response,** show how the work connects to your own experiences, observations, and ideas.
- **To refute an opposing point of view,** identify other interpretations of a text. Use the chart to gather textual details that support your position and could be used to refute, or argue against, a different opinion.

COUNTERCLAIM	RESPONSE WITH SUPPORTING EVIDENCE

Use Direct Quotations and Paraphrases   When you write about literature, include textual details that show the accuracy of your interpretation. You may use direct quotations or paraphrases.

- A **direct quotation** is the inclusion of exact words from the text. Use a direct quotation when the words are especially powerful or unique.
- A **paraphrase** is a restatement of an author's ideas in your own words. You may choose to use a paraphrase because the exact words are not particularly interesting or you have so many direct quotations that your own words get lost. Make sure your paraphrase accurately reflects the meaning of the original.

Formatting Direct Quotations   Shorter direct quotations appear within a sentence or paragraph. They are preceded by a comma or a colon. The page number on which the quotation appears is indicated in parentheses. Direct quotations that are four lines or longer are introduced with a colon, set apart, and indented ten spaces. The page number on which the quotation appears is always indicated in parentheses.

Direct Quotation in Running Text:
Rainsford is horrified when he realizes the truth of his situation: "The Cossack was the cat; he was the mouse" (232).

Direct Quotation Block Indented:
Rainsford breathes a sigh relief. Then, the horror hits him:

> Rainsford did not want to believe what his reason told him was true, but the truth was as evident as the sun that had by now pushed through the morning mists. The general was playing with him! (231)

EVIDENCE LOG

Review your Evidence Log and identify key details you may want to cite in your argument.

STANDARDS
Writing
Write arguments to support claims with clear reasons and relevant evidence.

a. Introduce claim(s), acknowledge and distinguish the claim(s) from alternate claims, and organize the reasons and evidence logically.
b. Support claim(s) with logical reasoning and relevant evidence, using accurate, credible sources and demonstrating an understanding of the topic or text.

Drafting

Present Your Reasoning In a strong argument, reasons are supported by evidence and organized in an order that makes sense. Use an outline to help you plan your reasons and the evidence that supports them.

Model: "Inspiration Is Overrated!"

CLAIM
Inspiration does not always produce successful inventions.

REASON
Many ideas for inventions never succeed.

EVIDENCE
One source says that only 3,000 products make money out of the 1.5 million products that have patents. Another says that only 1 in 5,000 products succeeds in the marketplace.

REASON
There is a reason many new inventions fail.

EVIDENCE
The author compares genius and invention by referring to the saying "genius is one percent inspiration and ninety-nine percent perspiration."

CONCLUSION
The conclusion restates and extends the claim: Successfully turning an idea into an invention requires a lot of hard work, not just inspiration.

Argument Outline

CLAIM

_____

REASON

_____

EVIDENCE

_____

REASON

_____

EVIDENCE

_____

CONCLUSION

Write a First Draft As you write, use your outline as a guide.

- Start by writing an introduction that clearly introduces your claim about which text best captures the dream of human flight.
- Confirm that you have presented sufficient evidence from the texts, as well as personal experience or observations, to support your claim.
- Present your reasons and evidence in an order that makes sense.
- End with a concluding statement or section that briefly summarizes or extends your argument.

STANDARDS
Writing
Write arguments to support claims with clear reasons and relevant evidence.
e. Provide a concluding statement or section that follows from and supports the argument presented.

LANGUAGE DEVELOPMENT: CONVENTIONS

Revising to Combine Sentences Using Gerunds and Participles

Gerunds and participles are **verbals**, or verb forms that are used as nouns or adjectives.

Identifying Gerunds A **gerund** is a verb form ending in *-ing* that acts as a noun. A **gerund phrase** is a gerund with modifiers or complements, all acting together as a noun. Like all nouns, gerunds and gerund phrases may be used in different parts of a sentence, as in these examples:

> **As a subject:** *Baking cookies* is Felice's hobby.
>
> **As a direct object:** Antoine enjoys *swimming*.
>
> **As a predicate noun:** David's greatest talent is *playing the piano*.
>
> **As the object of a preposition:** Greta never gets tired of *surfing*.

Identifying Participles A **participle** is a verb form that acts as an adjective. There are two kinds: present participles and past participles. A **participial phrase** is a participle with modifiers or complements, all acting together as an adjective.

> **Present participle:** The *chirping* canary sang sweetly.
>
> **Past participle in participial phrase:** The runner, *filled with hope*, raced toward the finish line.

Revising Sentences To combine sentences using gerunds and participles, first identify pairs of sentences that sound choppy and that relate to the same idea. Then, combine the sentences by using participles, gerunds, or participial or gerund phrases.

Read these choppy sentences: *The sisters like to draw and paint. They like to play together.* These sentences can be combined with two gerunds and a gerund phrase: *The sisters like **drawing, painting, and playing together.***

Read It

These sentences from the Launch Text contain gerunds and participles. Describe the function of each verbal in the sentence shown.

- *Each of these **forgotten** contraptions was probably someone's bright idea, a flash of inspiration **experienced while walking in the woods.*** **(past participle and past participial phrase)**
- ***Developing** something new that actually works—and that people want—can take years.* **(gerund)**

Write It

As you draft your argument, find pairs of sentences that deal with the same subject. If they are too choppy or repetitive, combine them using gerund or participial phrases.

SPELLING

Make sure to spell verbs used as gerunds or participles correctly.

- Remember that when a verb ends in e, the e should almost always be dropped before adding *-ing*. For example, the verb *hike* becomes the gerund *hiking*.

- The past participles of regular verbs are the same as the past tense, which ends in *-ed*. For example, *remembered* is both the past tense and the past participle of *remember*.

- Irregular verbs form the past tense differently. Many of these verbs also have special forms for the past participle, such as *forgotten*. Make sure to use the correct form as your participle.

STANDARDS

Language
- Demonstrate command of the conventions of standard English grammar and usage when writing or speaking.

  a. Explain the function of verbals in general and their function in particular sentences.

- Demonstrate command of the conventions of standard English capitalization, punctuation, and spelling when writing.

  c. Spell correctly.

Revising

Evaluating Your Draft

Use the following checklist to evaluate the effectiveness of your first draft. Then, use your evaluation and the instruction on this page to guide your revision.

FOCUS AND ORGANIZATION	EVIDENCE AND ELABORATION	CONVENTIONS
☐ Presents a clearly stated claim that is distinguished from other possible claims.	☐ Uses relevant, logical evidence and reasons to support the main claim.	☐ Attends to the norms and conventions of the discipline, especially correct use of gerunds and participles.
☐ Organizes information in a logical way that makes connections between claims, counterclaims, reasons, and evidence.	☐ Considers and discusses possible counterclaims.	
☐ Presents ideas in a clear and formal style.	☐ Includes language that helps make connections among claims, counterclaims, and supporting details.	
☐ Includes a conclusion that logically supports or extends the argument.		

⊹ WORD NETWORK

Include interesting words from your Word Network in your argument.

Revising for Focus and Organization

Conclusion Make sure that your concluding statement or section logically supports or extends your argument. You may wish to restate your claim and summarize the strongest reasons and evidence that support it. You may also introduce a final quotation or example. If you wish to extend your argument, make sure the connection between what you have written and your new idea is clear and logical. Use transition words and other language to make connections and help readers understand your train of thought.

Revising for Evidence and Elaboration

Use Language to Make Connections Make sure you are using transitions effectively in your argument. Add new transition words and phrases if necessary to make connections and clarify the relationship between ideas. Use words such as *because* and *therefore* to make connections that establish clearly how one event or idea led to another. Use words and phrases such as *such as* and *for example* to introduce evidence and examples. Use words such as *before* and *later* to clarify when events occurred.

STANDARDS

Writing
Write arguments to support claims with clear reasons and relevant evidence.

c. Use words, phrases, and clauses to create cohesion and clarify the relationships among claim(s), counterclaims, reasons, and evidence.

e. Provide a concluding statement or section that follows from and supports the argument presented.

PEER REVIEW

Exchange essays with a classmate. Use the checklist to evaluate your classmate's essay and provide supportive feedback.

1. Is the claim clearly stated and distinguished from other possible claims and counterclaims?

☐ yes ☐ no If no, suggest how the writer might improve it.

2. Are the reasons and evidence logical and relevant?

☐ yes ☐ no If no, explain what the author might add or remove.

3. Does the organization make clear connections among claims, counterclaims, reasons, and evidence?

☐ yes ☐ no If no, tell what you think might be missing.

4. What is the strongest part of your classmate's essay? Why?

_____

_____

_____

Editing and Proofreading

Edit for Conventions Reread your draft for accuracy and consistency. Correct errors in grammar and word usage. Make sure you have correctly combined sentences using gerunds and participles.

Proofread for Accuracy Read your draft carefully, looking for errors in spelling and punctuation. As you proofread, make sure that you have used the correct spelling for gerunds and other verbs ending in *-ing*. Also check that you have used the correct form of any irregular past participles, such as *lit* and *broken*.

Publishing and Presenting

Post your final essay to a class or school website so classmates can read and comment on your ideas. Consider the ways in which other students' arguments are similar to and different from your own.

Reflecting

Reflect on what you learned as you wrote your argument. What did you learn about how ideas for inventions are realized? What was the most challenging aspect of composing your argument? Did you learn something from reviewing yours and others' work that might inform your writing process in the future?

⊟ STANDARDS

Writing
• Write arguments to support claims with clear reasons and relevant evidence.
• With some guidance and support from peers and adults, develop and strengthen writing as needed by planning, revising, editing, rewriting, or trying a new approach, focusing on how well purpose and audience have been addressed.

Performance Task: Write an Argument **483**

ESSENTIAL QUESTION:

Are inventions realized through inspiration or perspiration?

Can hard work alone—or a great idea alone—result in a successful invention? How much of an invention's success results from creativity as opposed to hard work? You will work in a group to continue your exploration of the process of invention.

Small-Group Learning Strategies

Throughout your life, you'll continue to develop strategies that make you a better learner. In school, in your community, and in your career, you will continue to learn and work in teams.

Review these strategies and the actions you can take to practice them as you work in teams. Add ideas of your own for each step. Use these strategies during Small-Group Learning.

STRATEGY	ACTION PLAN
Prepare	• Complete your assignments so that you are prepared for group work. • Organize your thinking so you can contribute to your group's discussions. •
Participate fully	• Make eye contact to signal that you are listening and taking in what is being said. • Use text evidence when making a point. •
Support others	• Build off ideas from others in your group. • Invite others who have not yet spoken to do so. •
Clarify	• Paraphrase the ideas of others to ensure that your understanding is correct. • Ask follow-up questions. •

SCAN FOR MULTIMEDIA

CONTENTS

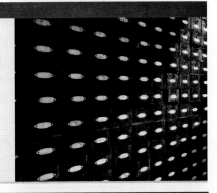
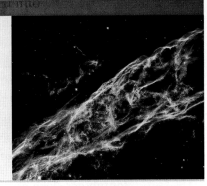

PERFORMANCE TASK

SPEAKING AND LISTENING FOCUS

Conduct a Debate

The Small-Group readings offer various ideas about the hard work and creative thinking that goes into inventions. After reading, your group will plan and conduct a debate on the Essential Question.

Working as a Team

1. Take a Position In your group, discuss the following question:

> **Is an invention typically created by a single inventor, or is an invention usually the result of many minds working together?**

As you take turns sharing your thoughts, be sure to provide information and examples to support your ideas. After all group members have shared, discuss your responses. Did other group members' ideas change your own response? Why or why not?

2. List Your Rules As a group, decide on the rules that you will follow as you work together. Samples are provided; add two more of your own. You may add or revise rules based on your experience together.

- Everyone should participate in group discussions.
- People should not interrupt.

- _____

  _____

- _____

  _____

3. Apply the Rules Practice working as a group. Share what you have learned about invention. Make sure each person in the group contributes. Take notes and be prepared to share with the class one thing that you heard from another member of your group.

4. Name Your Group Choose a name that reflects the unit topic.

Our group's name: _____

5. Create a Communication Plan Decide how you want to communicate with one another. For example, you might use online collaboration tools, email, or instant messaging.

Our group's decision: _____

_____

Making a Schedule

First, find out the due dates for the small-group activities. Then, preview the texts and activities with your group and make a schedule for completing the tasks.

SELECTION	ACTIVITIES	DUE DATE
Nikola Tesla: The Greatest Inventor of All?		
from The Invention of Everything Else		
25 Years Later, Hubble Sees Beyond Troubled Start		
Sounds of a Glass Armonica		

Working on Group Projects

As your group works together, you'll find it more effective if each person has a specific role. Different projects require different roles. Before beginning a project, discuss the necessary roles and choose one for each group member. Here are some possible roles; add your own ideas.

Project Manager: monitors the schedule and keeps everyone on task

Researcher: organizes research activities

Recorder: takes notes during group meetings

_____

_____

_____

_____

SCAN FOR
MULTIMEDIA

NIKOLA TESLA: THE
GREATEST INVENTOR OF ALL?

Comparing Texts

In this lesson, you will read and compare the
biographical work "Nikola Tesla: The Greatest
Inventor of All?" with an excerpt from *The
Invention of Everything Else,* a fictional account of
Tesla's life.

from THE INVENTION OF
EVERYTHING ELSE

About the Author

Vicky Baez (b. 1971) was
born in Albuquerque, New
Mexico. In elementary
school, one of Baez's
teachers gave exciting
science demonstrations that
instilled in her a love of the
subject, and she frequently
writes about science and
scientists. Her own science
library currently exceeds
1,000 books.

Nikola Tesla: The Greatest Inventor of All?

Concept Vocabulary

As you perform your first read, you will encounter these words.

engineer	generators	current

Base Words If these words are unfamiliar, check to see if any of them
contain a base word you know. Then, use context and your knowledge
of the "inside" word to find the meanings of the concept words. Follow
this strategy:

Unfamiliar Word: *equipment*

Familiar "Inside" Word: *equip,* which means "to supply with
necessary items for a particular purpose"

Context: At each place where he worked, [Tesla] designed and made
improvements to the **equipment.**

Conclusion: Tesla designed *equipment,* or items used for a purpose.

Apply your knowledge of base words and other vocabulary strategies to
determine the meanings of words you encounter during your first read.

First Read NONFICTION

Apply these strategies as you conduct your first read. You will have an
opportunity to complete a close read after your first read.

© Pearson Education, Inc., or its affiliates. All rights reserved.

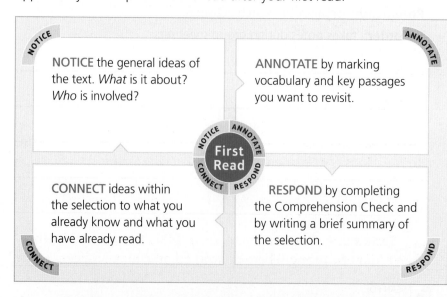

NOTICE the general ideas of
the text. *What* is it about?
Who is involved?

ANNOTATE by marking
vocabulary and key passages
you want to revisit.

First Read

CONNECT ideas within
the selection to what you
already know and what you
have already read.

RESPOND by completing
the Comprehension Check and
by writing a brief summary of
the selection.

STANDARDS

Reading Informational Text
By the end of the year, read and
comprehend literary nonfiction at
the high end of the grades 6–8 text
complexity band independently and
proficiently.

Language
• Demonstrate understanding
of figurative language, word
relationships, and nuances in word
meaning.

b. Use the relationship between
particular words to better
understand each of the words.

• Acquire and use accurately grade-
appropriate general academic and
domain-specific words and phrases;
gather vocabulary knowledge
when considering a word or phrase
important to comprehension or
expression.

Nikola Tesla:
The Greatest Inventor of All?

Vicky Baez

BACKGROUND

At the end of the nineteenth century, electricity was a new technology. At this time, very few people had access to electric lighting, and most people used coal, gas, and steam power for energy. Today, electricity has become a common utility because of inventors like Nikola Tesla and Thomas Edison.

SCAN FOR
MULTIMEDIA

1   Nikola Tesla was born in 1856 to a Serbian family in the country that is now called Croatia. When Tesla was young, he was able to do such complex math problems in his head that his teachers thought he was cheating. He finished high school in 3 years instead of 4.

2   He started college, but didn't finish. However, he learned enough to go to work. He moved several times over the next few years, each time getting a job as an electrician. At each place where he worked, he designed and made improvements to the equipment.

3   In 1884, he moved to New York City. He came with a letter of recommendation to Thomas Edison from one of his bosses. The letter is claimed to have said, "I know two great men and you are one of them; the other is this young man." Edison hired Tesla, who began as an electrical **engineer**. He quickly became very important to the company, solving some of its most difficult problems. Tesla was able to use his mind to imagine how different methods worked. Edison always made a lot of models and tried them out, which took a lot longer.

4   In 1885, Tesla and Edison had a falling out. Tesla told Edison he could improve some of Edison's motors and **generators**. Edison told him he would pay him $50,000 if he did. This was quite a lot of money at that time. Tesla worked hard and spent months on the task. When he succeeded, he asked Edison for the reward, but Edison told him he had been joking. He said, "Tesla, you don't understand our American humor." He offered Tesla a $10 raise on his $18 weekly pay. Tesla quit the job.

5   Tesla started his own company in 1887, Tesla Electric Light and Manufacturing. There he worked on making a system called

NOTES

Mark base words or indicate another strategy that helped you determine meaning.

engineer (ehn jih NEER) *n.*

MEANING:

generators (JEHN uhr ray tuhrz) *n.*

MEANING:

NOTES

Mark base words or indicate another strategy that helped you determine meaning.

current (KUR • uhnt) *n.*

MEANING:

"alternating **current**" to produce electricity. Thomas Edison thought his system, called "direct current," was better and safer. The two became rivals. They each gave talks about why his particular method was better. They had public demonstrations to show people how they created electricity. This rivalry was referred to as the "War of the Currents."

6   Another rival of Edison's, George Westinghouse, had also been trying to create an electrical system. He bought some of Tesla's inventions and paid him $2,000 a month to consult with him. Tesla spent all his money on new inventions and ideas. He invented the Tesla coil, which carried electricity without wires. You can still see a Tesla coil at some museums today. Tesla invented or helped develop a long list of devices, including X-ray machines, radio, wireless remotes, fluorescent lights, and the system of electricity that is still used today in our cities. He helped create a power plant in Niagara Falls that provided power all the way to New York City. He was given many awards and honorary degrees from universities all over the world.

7   Sadly, Tesla died without a cent. People forgot about him, and remembered Edison, whose companies still exist and have his name, like Consolidated Edison, the electric company that powers New York City. In the 1990s, people started to write about Tesla, and now he is becoming better known again. The owner of a new car company named it Tesla Motors because they make electric cars. Their first car used Tesla's design from 1882 for an electric car. ❧

Comprehension Check

Complete the following items after you finish your first read. Review and clarify details with your group.

1. Why did Tesla's teachers sometimes think he was cheating?

2. Why did Tesla leave Edison's company?

3. Why does Tesla Motors use Tesla's name?

4. 📓 **Notebook** Confirm your understanding of the biography by writing a short summary.

- -

RESEARCH

Research to Clarify Choose at least one unfamiliar detail from the biography. Briefly research that detail. In what way does the information you learned shed light on an aspect of the biography?

Close Read the Text

With your group, revisit sections of the text you marked during your first read. **Annotate** what you notice. What **questions** do you have? What can you **conclude**?

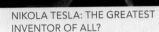

NIKOLA TESLA: THE GREATEST INVENTOR OF ALL?

Analyze the Text

> **CITE TEXTUAL EVIDENCE** to support your answers.

📓 **Notebook** Complete the activities.

1. **Review and Clarify** With your group, reread paragraph 3. Discuss the differences between Edison's and Tesla's approaches to invention. Whose approach, Edison's or Tesla's, do you think is better? Why?

2. **Present and Discuss** Discuss what you noticed in the selection, what questions you asked, and what conclusions you reached.

3. **Essential Question:** *Are inventions realized through inspiration or perspiration?* What has this selection taught you about invention? Discuss with your group.

LANGUAGE DEVELOPMENT

Concept Vocabulary

engineer	generators	current

Why These Words? The three concept vocabulary words are related. With your group, discuss the words, and determine what they have in common. Write another word related to this concept.

Practice

📓 **Notebook** Confirm your understanding of these words by using them in sentences. Include context clues that hint at meaning.

Word Study

Multiple-Meaning Words Many English words have more than one meaning. In "Nikola Tesla: The Greatest Inventor of All?," the word *current* refers to an *electrical current,* which is the flow of electricity through a wire. In this context, *current* is a technical word with a definition specific to the fields of science, electricity, and physics. Use a dictionary to look up other definitions of the word *current,* and record the meaning and the part of speech for each.

TIP

GROUP DISCUSSION
If you do not understand a group member's contribution, ask for clarification. Respond politely when others ask you for clarification, and try to state your point more simply and clearly.

🔗 **WORD NETWORK**

Identify words from the selection that relate to the concept of invention. Add these words to your Word Network.

☰ **STANDARDS**
Reading Informational Text
Analyze how a text makes connections among and distinctions between individuals, ideas, or events.
Language
• Determine or clarify the meaning of unknown and multiple-meaning words or phrases based on *grade 8 reading and content,* choosing flexibly from a range of strategies.

c. Consult general and specialized reference materials, both print and digital, to find the pronunciation of a word or determine or clarify its precise meaning or its part of speech.

NIKOLA TESLA: THE GREATEST
INVENTOR OF ALL?

Analyze Craft and Structure

Text Structure: Biographical Writing **Biographical writing** is a type of nonfiction in which the author tells about important events in the life of another person. Biographies provide factual information about the subject, and details and descriptions related to the person's life.

Most biographies are written in chronological order, describing key events in the subject's life. Individual paragraphs, however, may be organized differently, in order to provide information that supports a key idea. Here are some common paragraph structures:

- **chronological order:** the order in which events actually occur
- **comparison and contrast:** explanation and analysis of the similarities and differences between related subjects
- **cause and effect:** explanation of why something happens and how it affects other things

Practice

CITE TEXTUAL EVIDENCE
to support your answers.

📓 **Notebook** Use the chart to analyze the organization and development of ideas in the text. Model your analysis on the example. Then, answer the questions that follow.

PARAGRAPH	ORGANIZATION	DEVELOPMENT OF IDEAS
paragraph 1	chronological organization	• describes Tesla's early years • descriptive details provide information about early signs of Tesla's genius
paragraph 2		
paragraph 3		
paragraph 4		
paragraph 5		
paragraph 6		
paragraph 7		
paragraph 8		

1. What organizational strategy does the author use in paragraph 4? How does its organization link individuals, ideas, and events in the selection?

2. What organizational strategy does the author use in paragraphs 3 and 5? How does its organization help link ideas and events?

📋 STANDARDS

Reading Informational Text
• Analyze how a text makes connections among and distinctions between individuals, ideas, or events.
• Analyze in detail the structure of a specific paragraph in a text, including the role of particular sentences in developing and refining a key concept.

Conventions

Commas and Semicolons Effective writers use commas and semicolons correctly. Here are some guidelines for using commas and semicolons.

- A **comma (,)** is a punctuation mark that signals a brief pause.
- A **semicolon (;)** may be used to join two independent clauses.

✐ EVIDENCE LOG

Before moving on to a new selection, go to your Evidence Log and record what you learned from "Nikola Tesla: The Greatest Inventor of All?"

USE A COMMA	EXAMPLES
before a **coordinating conjunction** (*and, but, or, nor, for, so, yet*) that joins two independent clauses in a compound sentence	Tesla worked hard, **and** he invented many things.
between items in a series	He worked on **radio, fluorescent lights, and electric plants.**
between **coordinate adjectives,** adjectives of equal rank whose order may be switched	The **ingenious, inventive** products changed the world.
after introductory words, phrases, or clauses	**In his later years,** Tesla had little money.
to set off **nonrestrictive,** or nonessential, **phrases or clauses**	Edison's company, **which was in the United States,** hired Tesla.

USE A SEMICOLON	
to join independent clauses not connected by a coordinating conjunction	Edison did not pay Tesla $50,000**;** Tesla quit.
to separate independent clauses joined by adverbs such as *however* and *therefore*	Tesla had many great inventions**; however,** his fame faded over the years.

Read It

📓 **Notebook** Complete the following items by identifying a comma or semicolon in the selection paragraph and explaining the reason it is used in the sentence.

1. paragraph 1 (comma)
2. paragraph 3 (semicolon)
3. paragraph 5 (comma)
4. paragraph 7 (comma)

Write It

Correct each sentence by adding commas or semicolons as needed.

1. Tesla contributed many great electrical inventions to the world however he died a poor man.

2. Tesla invented or helped to develop X-ray machines wireless remotes fluorescent lights and the Tesla coil.

3. Edison preferred direct current he thought it was safer than alternating current.

COLLABORATION TIP
To ensure that your group understands the correct use of commas and semicolons in different grammatical situations, challenge members to come up with examples of each type of sentence modeled in the charts.

⊞ STANDARDS
Language
Demonstrate command of the conventions of standard English capitalization, punctuation, and spelling when writing

a. Use punctuation (comma, ellipsis, dash) to indicate a pause or break.

NIKOLA TESLA: THE
GREATEST INVENTOR OF ALL?

Comparing Texts

You will now read an excerpt from the novel *The Invention of Everything Else*. First, complete the first-read and close-read activities for the excerpt. Then, you will analyze the differences in how a subject is portrayed in a work of nonfiction and in a work of fiction.

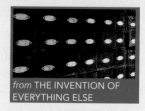

from THE INVENTION OF EVERYTHING ELSE

About the Author

Samantha Hunt (b. 1971) is an American novelist, essayist, and short story writer. Her award-winning stories and essays have appeared in many prestigious publications, including the *New Yorker,* the *New York Times Magazine,* and *Esquire.* In 2006, she won the National Book Foundation's *5 Under 35* award, which, each year, honors five young fiction writers for their excellence.

from The Invention of Everything Else

Concept Vocabulary

As you perform your first read of the excerpt from *The Invention of Everything Else*, you will encounter these words.

deficiencies	triumph	revolutionized

Context Clues If these words are unfamiliar to you, try using context clues—words and phrases that surround an unfamiliar word in a text to determine their meanings. There are various types of context clues that you may encounter as you read.

> **Related Details:** I maintain a small **infirmary** for injured and geriatric pigeons.
>
> **Restatement:** So **plentiful** was the supply that the jar was filled to the brim in no time.

Apply your knowledge of context clues and other vocabulary strategies to determine the meanings of unfamiliar words you encounter during your first read.

First Read FICTION

Apply these strategies as you conduct your first read. You will have an opportunity to complete a close read after your first read.

NOTICE *whom* the story is about, *what* happens, *where* and *when* it happens, and *why* those involved react the way they do.

ANNOTATE by marking vocabulary and key passages you want to revisit.

First Read

NOTICE · ANNOTATE · CONNECT · RESPOND

CONNECT ideas within the selection to what you already know and what you have already read.

RESPOND by completing the Comprehension Check and by writing a brief summary of the selection.

STANDARDS

Reading Literature
By the end of the year, read and comprehend literature, including stories, dramas, and poems, at the high end of grades 6–8 text complexity band independently and proficiently.

Language
Determine or clarify the meaning of unknown and multiple-meaning words or phrases based on grade 8 reading and content, choosing flexibly from a range of strategies.
  a. Use context as a clue to the meaning of a word or phrase.

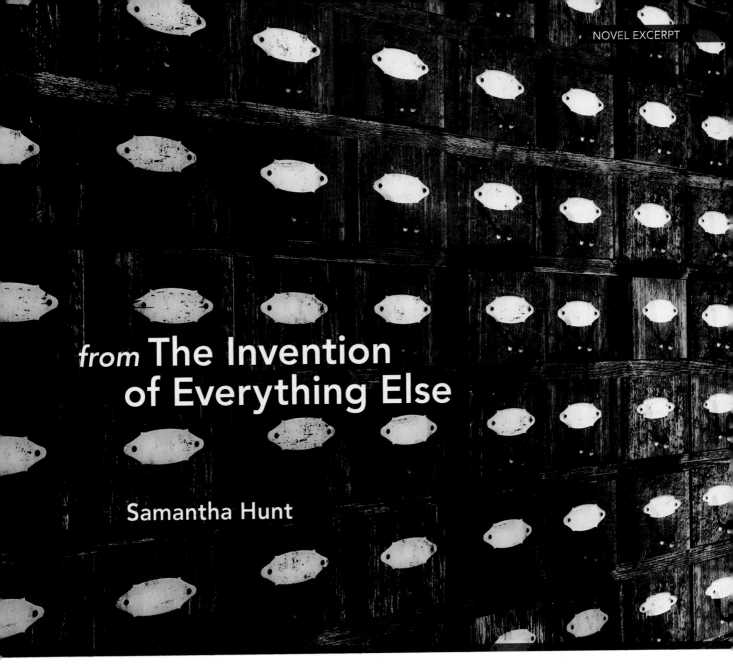

from **The Invention of Everything Else**

Samantha Hunt

BACKGROUND

In her novel, Samantha Hunt imagines the last days in the life of Nikola Tesla from the perspective of the famous inventor. This excerpt refers to Guglielmo Marconi, an inventor who sent the first wireless signal across an ocean and received a Nobel Prize for his work in 1911. However, he did so by using many key inventions that were initially developed by Nikola Tesla.

SCAN FOR MULTIMEDIA

NOTES

1   Lightning first, then the thunder. And in between the two I'm reminded of a secret. I was a boy and there was a storm. The storm said something muffled. Try and catch me, perhaps, and then it bent down close to my ear in the very same way my brother Dane used to do. Whispering. A hot, damp breath, a tunnel between his mouth and my ear. The storm began to speak. You want to know what the storm said? Listen.

2   Things like that, talking storms, happen to me frequently. Take for example the dust here in my hotel room. Each particle says something as it drifts through the last rays of sunlight, pale blades that have cut their way past my closed curtains. Look at this dust. It is everywhere. Here is the tiniest bit of a woman from Bath Beach who had her hair styled two days ago, loosening a few small flakes of scalp in the process. Two days it took her to arrive, but here she is at last. She had to come because the hotel where I live is like the sticky tongue of a frog jutting out high above Manhattan, collecting the city particle by wandering particle. Here is some chimney ash. Here is some buckwheat flour blown in from a Portuguese bakery on Minetta Lane and a pellicle of curled felt belonging to the haberdashery[1] around the corner. Here is a speck of evidence from a shy graft inspector. Maybe he lived in the borough of Queens. Maybe a respiratory influenza killed him off in 1897. So many maybes, and yet he is still here. And, of course, so am I. Nikola Tesla, Serbian, world-famous inventor, once celebrated, once visited by kings, authors and artists, welterweight pugilists,[2] scientists of all stripes, journalists with their prestigious awards, ambassadors, mezzo-sopranos,[3] and ballerinas. And I would shout down to the dining hall captain for a feast to be assembled. "Quickly! Bring us the Stuffed Saddle of Spring Lamb. Bring us the Mousse of Lemon Sole and the Shad Roe Belle Meunière! Potatoes Raclette! String Bean Sauté! Macadamia nuts! A nice bourbon, some tonic, some pear nectar, coffees, teas, and please, please make it fast!"

3   That was some time ago. Now, more regularly, no one visits. I sip at my vegetable broth listening for a knock on the door or even footsteps approaching down the hallway. Most often it turns out to be a chambermaid on her rounds. I've been forgotten here. Left alone talking to lightning storms, studying the mysterious patterns the dust of dead people makes as it floats through the last light of day.

4   Now that I have lived in the Hotel New Yorker far longer than any of the tourists or businessmen in town for a meeting, the homogeneity[4] of my room, a quality most important to any hotel décor, has all but worn off. Ten years ago, when I first moved in, I constructed a wall of shelves. It still spans floor to ceiling. The wall consists of seventy-seven fifteen-inch-tall drawers as well as a number of smaller cubbyholes to fill up the odd spaces. The

1. **haberdashery** *n.* store that sells men's clothing, including hats made from felt.
2. **welterweight pugilists** (PYOO juh lihsts) *n.* professional boxers of intermediate weight, between lightweight and middleweight.
3. **mezzo-sopranos** (MEHT soh suh PRAN ohz) singers.
4. **homogeneity** (hoh muh juh NEE uh tee) *n.* similar and uniform quality.

top drawers are so high off the ground that even I, at over six feet tall, am forced to keep a wooden step stool behind the closet door to access them. Each drawer is stained a deep brown and is differentiated from the others by a small card of identification taped to the front. The labels have yellowed under the adhesive. COPPER WIRE. CORRESPONDENCE. MAGNETS. PERPETUAL MOTION. MISC.

5   Drawer #42. It sticks and creaks with the weather. This is the drawer where I once thought I'd keep all my best ideas. It contains only some cracked peanut shells. It is too dangerous to write my best ideas down. "Whoops. Wrong drawer. Whoops." I repeat the word. It's one of my favorites. If it were possible I'd store "Whoops" in the safe by my bed, along with "OK" and "Sure thing" and the documents that prove that I am officially an American citizen.

6   Drawer #53 is empty, though inside I detect the slightest odor of ozone. I sniff the drawer, inhaling deeply. Ozone is not what I am looking for. I close #53 and open #26. Inside there is a press clipping, something somebody once said about my work: "Humanity will be like an antheap stirred up with a stick. See the excitement coming!" The excitement, apparently, already came and went.

7   That is not what I'm looking for.

8   Somewhere in one of the seventy-seven drawers I have a clipping from an article published in the *New York Times*. The article includes a photo of the inventor Guglielmo Marconi riding on the shoulders of men, a loose white scarf held in his raised left hand, flagging the breeze. All day thoughts of Marconi have been poking me in the ribs. They often do whenever I feel particularly low or lonely or poorly financed. I'll shut my eyes and concentrate on sending Marconi a message. The message is, "Marconi, you are a thief." I focus with great concentration until I can mentally access the radio waves. As the invisible waves advance through my head I attach a few words to each—"donkey," and "worm," and "limacine," which is an adjective that I only recently acquired the meaning of, *like a slug*. When I'm certain that the words are fixed to the radio waves I'll send the words off toward Marconi, because he has stolen my patents.[5] He has stolen my invention of radio. He has stolen my notoriety. Not that either of us deserved it. Invention is nothing a man can own.

9   And so I am resigned.

---

5. **patents** *n.* documents that give an individual the right to make or sell new inventions or products; patents prevent others from making, using, or selling the inventions or products for a set period of time.

10   Out the window to the ledge, thirty-three stories above the street, I go legs first. This is no small feat. I am no small man. Imagine an oversized skeleton. I have to wonder what a skeleton that fell thirty-three stories, down to the street below, would look like. I take one tentative glance toward the ground. Years ago power lines would have stretched across the block in a mad cobweb, a net, because years ago, any company that wanted to provide New York with electricity simply strung its own decentralized power lines all about the city before promptly going out of business or getting forced out by J. P. Morgan.[6] But now there is no net. The power lines have been hidden underground.

11   That's not why I've come here. I have no interest in jumping. I'm not resigned to die. Most certainly not. No, I'm resigned only to leave humans to their humanness. Die? No. Indeed, I've always planned to see the far side of one hundred and twenty-five. I'm only eighty-six. I've got thirty-nine more years. At least.

12   "HooEEEhoo. HooEEEhoo." The birds answer the call. Gray flight surrounds me, and the reverse swing of so many pairs of wings, some iridescent, some a bit duller, makes me dizzy. The birds slow to a landing before me, beside me, one or two perching directly on top of my shoulders and head. Mesmerized by their feathers—such engineering!—I lose my balance. The ledge is

6. **J.P. Morgan** powerful businessman who merged several electrical companies to create one massive company in 1891.

perhaps only forty-five centimeters wide. My shoulders lurch forward a bit, just enough to notice the terrific solidity of the sidewalks thirty-three stories down. Like a gasp for air, I pin my back into the cold stone of the window's casing. A few pigeons startle and fly away out over Eighth Avenue, across Manhattan. Catching my breath, I watch them go. I watch them disregard gravity, the ground, and the distance between us. And though an old feeling, one of wings, haunts my shoulder blades, I stay pinned to the window. I've learned that I cannot go with them.

13   Out on the ledge of my room, I maintain a small infirmary for injured and geriatric[7] pigeons. A few tattered boxes, some shredded newspaper. One new arrival hobbles on a foot that has been twisted into an angry knuckle, a pink stump. I see she wants nothing more to do with the hydrogen peroxide that bubbled fiercely in her wound last night. I let her be, squatting instead to finger the underside of another bird's wing. Beneath his sling the ball of his joint has finally stayed lodged in its orbit, and for this I am relieved. I turn my attention to mashing meal.

14   "Hello, dears." The air of New York this high up smells gray with just a hint of blue. I sniff the air. "It's getting chilly, hmm?" I ask the birds. "And what are your plans for the New Year tonight?" The hotel has been in a furor, preparing for the festivities all week. The birds say nothing. "No plans yet? No, me neither."

15   I stand, looking out into the darkening air. "HooEEEhoo?" It's a question. I stare up into the sky, wondering if she will show tonight. "HooEEEhoo?"

16   Having lived in America for fifty-nine years, I've nearly perfected my relationships with the pigeons, the sparrows, and the starlings of New York City. Particularly the pigeons. Humans remain a far greater challenge.

17   I sit on the ledge with the birds for a long while, waiting for her to appear. It is getting quite cold. As the last rays of sun disappear from the sky, the undersides of the clouds glow with a memory of the light. Then they don't anymore, and what was once clear becomes less so in the darkening sky. The bricks and stones of the surrounding buildings take on a deeper hue. A bird cuts across the periphery of my sight. I don't allow myself to believe it might be her. "HooEEEhoo?" Don't look, I caution my heart. It won't be her. I take a look just the same. A gorgeous checkered, his hackle purple and green. It's not her.

18   She is pale gray with white-tipped wings, and into her ear I have whispered all my doubts. Through the years I've told her of my childhood, the books I read, a history of Serbian battle songs, dreams of earthquakes, endless meals and islands, inventions,

NOTES

---

7. **geriatric** (jehr ee AT rihk) *adj.* elderly.

lost notions, love, architecture, poetry—a bit of everything. We've been together since I don't remember when. A long while. Though it makes no sense, I think of her as my wife, or at least something like a wife, inasmuch as any inventor could ever have a wife, inasmuch as a bird who can fly could ever love a man who can't.

19   Most regularly she allows me to smooth the top of her head and neck with my pointer finger. She even encourages it. I'll run my finger over her feathers and feel the small bones of her head, the delicate cage made of calcium built to protect the bit of magnetite[8] she keeps inside. This miraculous mineral powers my system of alternating-current electrical distribution. It also gives these birds direction, pulling north, creating a compass in their bodies, ensuring that they always know the way home.

20   I've not seen my own home in thirty-five years. There is no home anymore. Everyone is gone. My poor, torn town of Smiljan—in what was once Lika, then Croatia, now Yugoslavia. "I don't have wings," I tell the birds who are perched beside me on the ledge. "I don't have magnetite in my head." These **deficiencies** punish me daily, particularly as I get older and recall Smiljan with increasing frequency.

21   When I was a child I had a tiny laboratory that I'd constructed in an alcove of trees. I nailed tin candle sconces to the trunks so that I could work into the night while the candles' glow crept up the orange bark and filled my laboratory with odd shadows—the stretched fingers of pine needles as they shifted and grew in the wind.

22   There is one invention from that time, one of my very first, that serves as a measure for how the purity of thought can dwindle with age. Once I was clever. Once I was seven years old. The invention came to me like this: Smiljan is a very tiny town surrounded by mountains and rivers and trees. My house was part of a farm where we raised animals and grew vegetables. Beside our home was a church where my father was the minister. In this circumscribed[9] natural setting my ears were attuned to a different species of sounds: footsteps approaching on a dirt path, raindrops falling on the hot back of a horse, leaves browning. One night, from outside my bedroom window, I heard a terrific buzzing noise, the rumble of a thousand insect wings beating in concert. I recognized the noise immediately. It signaled the seasonal return of what people in Smiljan called May bugs, what people in America call June bugs. The insects' motions, their constant energy, kept me awake through the night, considering, plotting, and scheming. I roiled in my bed with the possibility these insects presented.

Mark context clues or indicate another strategy you used to help you determine connotations and denotations.

deficiencies (dih FIHSH uhn seez) *n.*

MEANING:

---

8. **magnetite** (MAG nuh tyt) *n.* type of iron that is strongly attracted by magnets.
9. **circumscribed** (suhr kuhm SKRYBD) *adj.* limited.

23   Finally, just before the sun rose, I sneaked outside while my family slept. I carried a glass jar my mother usually used for storing stewed vegetables. The jar was nearly as large as my rib cage. I removed my shoes—the ground was still damp. I walked barefoot through the paths of town, stopping at every low tree and shrub, the leaves of which were alive with June bugs. Their brown bodies hummed and crawled in masses. They made my job of collection quite easy. I harvested the beetle crop, sometimes collecting as many as ten insects per leaf. The bugs' shells made a hard click when they struck against the glass or against another bug. So plentiful was the supply that the jar was filled to brimming in no time.

24   I returned to my pine-tree laboratory and set to work. First, by constructing a simple system of gear wheels, I made an engine in need of a power supply. I then studied the insects in the jar and selected those that demonstrated the most aggressive and muscular tendencies. With a dab of glue on their thorax undersides, I stuck my eight strongest beetles to the wheel and stepped back. The glue was good; they could not escape its harness. I waited a moment, and in that moment my thoughts grew dark. Perhaps, I thought, the insects were in shock. I pleaded with the bugs, "Fly away!" Nothing. I tickled them with a twig. Nothing. I stomped my small feet in frustration and stepped back prepared to leave the laboratory and hide away from the failed experiment in the fronds of breakfast, when, just then, the engine began to turn. Slowly at first, like a giant waking up, but once the insects understood that they were in this struggle together their speed increased. I gave a jump of triumph and was immediately struck by a vision of the future in which humans would exist in a kingdom of ease, the burden of all our chores and travails would be borne by the world of insects. I was certain that this draft of the future would come to pass. The engine spun with a whirling noise. It was brilliant, and for a few moments I burned with this brilliance.

25   In the time it took me to complete my invention the world around me had woken up. I could hear the farm animals. I could hear people speaking, beginning their daily work. I thought how glad my mother would be when I told her that she'd no longer have to milk the goats and cows, as I was developing a system where insects would take care of all that. This was the thought I was tumbling joyfully in when Vuk, a boy who was a few years older than me, entered into the laboratory. Vuk was the urchin son of an army officer. He was no friend of mine but rather one of the older children in town who, when bored, enjoyed needling

Mark context clues or indicate another strategy you used to help you determine connotations and denotations.

triumph (TRY uhmf) *n.*
MEANING:

NOTES

Mark context clues or indicate another strategy you used to help you determine connotations and denotations.

revolutionized (rehv uh LOO shuh nyzd) *v.*

MEANING:

me, vandalizing the laboratory I had built in the trees. But that morning my delight was such that I was glad to see even Vuk. I was glad for a witness. Quickly I explained to him how I had just **revolutionized** the future, how I had developed insect energy, the source that would soon be providing the world with cheap, replenishable power. Vuk listened, glancing once or twice at the June bug engine, which, by that time, was spinning at a very impressive speed. His envy was thick; I could nearly touch it. He kept his eyes focused on the glass jar that was still quite full of my power source. Vuk twisted his face up to a cruel squint. He curled the corners of his fat lips. With my lecture finished, he nodded and approached the jar. Unscrewing the lid he eyed me, as though daring me to stop him. Vuk sank his hand, his filthy fingernails, down into the mass of our great future and withdrew a fistful of beetles. Before I could even understand the annihilation I was about to behold, Vuk raised his arm to his mouth, opened the horrid orifice, and began to chew. A crunching sound I will never forget ensued. Tiny exoskeletons mashed between molars, dark legs squirming for life against his chubby white chin. With my great scheme crashing to a barbarous end—I could never look at a June bug again—I ran behind the nearest pine tree and promptly vomited.

26   On the ledge the birds are making a noise that sounds like contentment, like the purr of the ocean from a distance. I forget Vuk. I forget all thoughts of humans. I even forget about what I was searching for in the wall of drawers until, staring out at the sky, I don't forget anymore.

27   On December 12, 1901, Marconi sent a message across the sea. The message was simple. The message was the letter *S*. The message traveled from Cornwall, England, to Newfoundland, Canada. This *S* traveled on air, without wires, passing directly through mountains and buildings and trees, so that the world thought wonders might never cease. And it was true. It was a magnificent moment. Imagine, a letter across the ocean without wires.

28   But a more important date is October 1893, eight years earlier. The young Marconi was seated in a crowded café huddled over, intently reading a widely published and translated article written by me, Nikola Tesla. In the article I revealed in exacting detail my system for both wireless transmission of messages and the wireless transmission of energy. Marconi scribbled furiously.

29   I pet one bird to keep the chill from my hands. The skin of my knee is visible through my old suit. I am broke. I have given AC electricity to the world. I have given radar, remote control, and

radio to the world, and because I asked for nothing in return, nothing is exactly what I got. And yet Marconi took credit. Marconi surrounded himself with fame, strutting as if he owned the invisible waves circling the globe.

30   Quite honestly, radio is a nuisance. I know. I'm its father. I never listen to it. The radio is a distraction that keeps one from concentrating.

31   "HooEEEhoo?"

32   There is no answer.

33   I'll have to go find her. It is getting dark and Bryant Park is not as close as it once was, but I won't rest tonight if I don't see her. Legs first, I reenter the hotel, and armed with a small bag of peanuts, I set off for the park where my love often lives.

34   The walk is a slow one, as the streets are beginning to fill with New Year's Eve revelers. I try to hurry, but the sidewalks are busy with booby traps. One gentleman stops to blow his nose into a filthy handkerchief, and I dodge to the left, where a woman tilts her head back in a laugh. Her pearl earrings catch my eye. Just the sight of those monstrous jewels sets my teeth on edge, as if my jaws were being ground down to dull nubs. Through this obstacle course I try to outrun thoughts of Marconi. I try to outrun the question that repeats and repeats in my head, paced to strike with every new square of sidewalk I step on. The question is this: "If they are your patents, Niko, why did Marconi get word—well, not word but letter—why did he get a letter across the ocean before you?" I walk quickly. I nearly run. Germs be damned. I glance over my shoulder to see if the question is following. I hope I have outpaced it.

> I do not want this question to catch me, and worse, I do not want the answer to this question to catch me.

35   New York's streets wend their way between the arched skyscrapers. Most of the street-level businesses have closed their doors for the evening. Barbizon Hosiery. Conte's Salumeria, where a huge tomcat protects the drying sausages. Santangelo's Stationery and Tobacco. Wasserstein's Shoes. Jung's Nautical Maps and Prints. The Wadesmith Department Store. All of them closed for the holiday. My heels click on the sidewalks, picking up speed, picking up a panic. I do not want this question to catch me, and worse, I do not want the answer to this question to catch me. I glance behind myself one more time. I have to find her tonight.

36   I turn one corner and the question is there, waiting, smoking, reading the newspaper. I pass a lunch counter and see the question sitting alone, slurping from a bowl of chicken soup. "If they are your patents, Niko, why did Marconi send a wireless letter across the ocean before you?"

37   The question makes me itch. I decide to focus my thoughts on a new project, one that will distract me. As I head north, I develop an appendix of words that begin with the letter *S*, words that Marconi's first wireless message stood for. ❧

Comprehension Check

Complete the following items after you finish your first read. Review and clarify details with your group.

1. Where does Tesla live? In what country did he originally live?

2. What does Tesla use the ledge outside his window for?

3. For what reason is Tesla angry with Marconi?

4. What question does Tesla try to outrun?

📓 **Notebook** Confirm your understanding of the text by writing a short summary.

- -

RESEARCH

Research to Clarify Choose at least one unfamiliar detail from the excerpt. Briefly research that detail. In what way does the information you learned shed light on an aspect of the story?

from THE INVENTION OF EVERYTHING ELSE

Close Read the Text

With your group, revisit sections of the text you marked during your first read. **Annotate** what you notice. What **questions** do you have? What can you **conclude**?

Analyze the Text

📓 **Notebook** Complete the activities.

1. **Review and Clarify** Reread paragraphs 21–25 of the excerpt. What is one of the first inventions Tesla made as a child? How does this **anecdote,** or short account, about his childhood experience with invention help to develop Tesla's character? What does it reveal about the nature of inventions? Discuss with your group.

2. **Present and Discuss** Discuss what you noticed in the selection, what questions you asked, and what conclusions you reached.

3. **Essential Question:** *Are inventions realized through inspiration or perspiration?* What have you learned about invention from reading this selection?

TIP

GROUP DISCUSSION
As you work with your group, make sure each member has an opportunity to contribute to the discussion. Be sensitive to the amount of time you spend speaking.

LANGUAGE DEVELOPMENT

Concept Vocabulary

deficiencies	triumph	revolutionized

Why These Words? The three concept vocabulary words are related. With your group, determine what the words have in common. Write your ideas, and add at least one other word that fits the category.

Practice

📓 **Notebook** Confirm your understanding of these words from the text by using each word in a sentence. Share your sentences with your group.

Word Study

Denotation and Connotation A word's **denotation** is its dictionary meaning. Synonyms have nearly identical denotations. A word's **connotation** is the idea or emotion associated with the word. Often, words have positive or negative connotations that affect how people respond to them. Synonyms often have different connotations. For example, the concept vocabulary word *triumph* and the word *win* are synonyms, but *triumph* has a more positive, stronger connotation than *win*, which is more neutral. With your group, find a synonym for each of the other concept vocabulary words, and discuss the connotations of each pair.

🔗 WORD NETWORK

Identify words from the selection that relate to the concept of invention. Add these words to your Word Network.

▤ STANDARDS

Language
• Determine or clarify the meaning of unknown and multiple-meaning words or phrases based on *grade 8 reading and content,* choosing flexibly from a range of strategies.

• Demonstrate understanding of figurative language, word relationships, and nuances in word meanings.

  c. Distinguish among the connotations of words with similar denotations.

Analyze Craft and Structure

Word Choice: Figurative Language In *The Invention of Everything Else*, the author uses **figurative language**—language not meant to be taken literally—to describe and compare things in imaginative ways. The chart defines several **figures of speech**, or types of figurative language, and provides an example for each type.

TYPE OF FIGURATIVE LANGUAGE	DEFINITION	EXAMPLE FROM THE TEXT
personification	comparison in which a nonhuman subject is given human characteristics	*The storm said something muffled. . . .* (paragraph 1)
simile	compares two unlike things using the words *like* or *as*	*She had to come because the hotel where I live is like the sticky tongue of a frog jutting out high above Manhattan, collecting the city particle by wandering particle. . . .* (paragraph 2)
metaphor	compares two unlike things by saying that one thing is the other	*Years ago power lines would have stretched across the block in a mad cobweb, a net, . . .* (paragraph 10)

Practice

CITE TEXTUAL EVIDENCE to support your answers.

Reread the excerpt and find other examples of figurative language. Gather your examples in the chart. With your group, analyze the ways in which the examples you noted deepen your understanding of the text and its subject, Nikola Tesla.

TYPE OF FIGURATIVE LANGUAGE	EXAMPLE FROM THE TEXT
personification	
simile	
metaphor	

STANDARDS

Reading Literature
• Determine the meaning of words and phrases as they are used in a text, including figurative and connotative meanings; analyze the impact of specific word choices on meaning and tone, including analogies or allusions to other texts.

Language
Demonstrate understanding of figurative language, word relationships, and nuances in word meanings.

a. Interpret figures of speech in context.

Conventions

Comparative and Superlative Forms of Adjectives and Adverbs

Most adjectives and adverbs have three degrees of comparison, helping writers easily compare the qualities or conditions of their subjects.

- The **positive** degree is used when no comparison is made: Tesla was a *great* inventor.
- The **comparative** is used when two things are being compared: Some people believe that Tesla was a *greater* inventor than Edison.
- The **superlative** is used when three or more things are being compared: Perhaps, Tesla was the *greatest* inventor of all.

FORMING COMPARATIVE AND SUPERLATIVE ADJECTIVES AND ADVERBS	
Use *-er* or *more* to form the **comparative** degree.	*taller, sooner, more inventive, more quietly*
Use *-est* or *most* to form the **superlative** degree.	*sharpest, fastest, most colorful, most creatively*

Irregular adjectives and adverbs have special forms that must be memorized. This chart shows some commonly used irregular adjectives and adverbs.

POSITIVE	COMPARATIVE	SUPERLATIVE
bad, badly	worse	worst
good, well	better	best
many, much	more	most
little (small amount of)	less	least

Read It

1. Identify the adjective or adverb in each sentence. Then, identify the degree of comparison it indicates: *positive, comparative,* or *superlative*.
   a. Toward the end of his life, Tesla seemed happiest feeding pigeons.
   b. Tesla's supporters were convinced he was doing the most exciting work ever in the field of electrical engineering.
   c. Rather than admit he had dropped out of school, Tesla found it easier to pretend he had drowned.
2. Find three adjectives and adverbs in *The Invention of Everything Else* and indicate the degree of comparison each reflects.

Write It

Notebook Write a brief paragraph about Tesla's feelings toward Marconi. Your paragraph should have at least one adjective or adverb for each degree of comparison. Include at least one irregular adjective or adverb in your paragraph.

STANDARDS
Language
Demonstrate command of the conventions of standard English grammar and usage when writing or speaking.

NIKOLA TESLA: THE GREATEST
INVENTOR OF ALL?

from THE INVENTION OF
EVERYTHING ELSE

Writing to Compare

In this feature you read two selections about the inventor Nikola Tesla. In the biographical work "Nikola Tesla: The Greatest Inventor of All?," you learned factual information about Tesla and his life. In *The Invention of Everything Else*, you read a historical fiction account in which the author, Samantha Hunt, uses her imagination in combination with historical facts to develop the character of Nikola Tesla.

Assignment

Write a **compare-and-contrast essay** in which you analyze the ways in which each text reveals an aspect of Tesla's life and personality.

You will work with your group to analyze the texts and gather information to use in your essay. Then, you will write your essays individually.

Planning and Prewriting

Compare Text Details Work with your group to analyze the ways in which Nikola Tesla is portrayed in a nonfiction text and a work of fiction. Work as a group to fill in the chart with details from both texts.

DETAILS FROM THE TEXT	NIKOLA TESLA: THE GREATEST INVENTOR OF ALL?	*from* THE INVENTION OF EVERYTHING ELSE
Events from Tesla's life		
Tesla's character traits and personality		
Details about important places in Tesla's life		
Details about Tesla's accomplishments		

📓 **Notebook** Respond to these questions.
- Which did you enjoy reading more? Which text more effectively portrayed Tesla? Which text provided more biographical detail?

Drafting

Form a Thesis Focus your thoughts by creating a thesis statement that explains the point of your comparison. Here is a sentence starter to help you begin:

Thesis: When you compare and contrast these two treatments of Nikola Tesla's life, it becomes clear that

_____

_____

_____ .

Organize Your Essay When you are satisfied with your thesis, determine how you should present the information. Develop an outline for your essay using the following strategies:

- Begin your essay by revealing your thesis and providing background for readers.

- Develop your comparison and contrast in one of two ways: Discuss one text and all its features in a series of paragraphs and then discuss the other text in the following paragraph. Alternatively, in each body paragraph, discuss one element as it is treated in both texts, and then discuss a second element, and so on.

- Create cohesion in your essay by using transitional words and phrases, such as *regardless*, *despite*, and *for this reason*, that connect your claims, reasons, and evidence.

- Conclude your essay with a paragraph in which you restate your thesis and summarize the main evidence that you presented in support of your thesis.

Review, Revise, and Edit

Add Details Review your draft and add supporting details where needed. Consider quoting materials from the texts as support. When you do so, be sure to use quotation marks and indicate the source of each quotation.

Use a Formal Style Once you are done drafting, review your essay to be sure you have maintained a formal style. Revise your writing to eliminate instances where you used informal language, such as contractions, slang, or clichés.

Proofread for Accuracy Carefully reread your essay. Fix spelling errors as well as any grammatical problems. Be sure to check all quoted material against the original source to be sure the quotes are accurate.

EVIDENCE LOG

Before moving on to a new selection, go to your Evidence Log and record what you have learned from reading "Nikola Tesla: The Greatest Inventor of All?" and *The Invention of Everything Else.*

STANDARDS

Writing
Write informative/explanatory texts to examine a topic and convey ideas, concepts, and information through the selection, organization, and analysis of relevant content.

- Draw evidence from literary or informational texts to support analysis, reflection, and research.

About the Author

Dennis Overbye (b. 1944) is a science writer specializing in physics and cosmology, the science of the origin and development of the universe. In 1998, he joined the staff of the *New York Times* as deputy science editor, then switched to full-time writing. His articles have appeared in *Time, Science,* the *Los Angeles Times,* and the *New York Times,* among others. In 2014, he was a finalist for the Pulitzer Prize for Explanatory Reporting. Overbye lives in New York City with his wife, daughter, and two cats.

25 Years Later, Hubble Sees Beyond Troubled Start

Concept Vocabulary

As you perform your first read of "25 Years Later, Hubble Sees Beyond Troubled Start," you will encounter these words.

dismay	controversy	outcry

Context Clues Sometimes you need to infer the meaning of an unfamiliar word by looking for context clues in the surrounding words.

Example from the selection:

> When the Hubble was finally deployed, NASA's **spinmasters** were instantly at the top of their game, <u>hailing it as the greatest advance in astronomy since Galileo.</u>

If you didn't know the meaning of the term *spinmasters,* you might infer from the underlined clues that *spinmasters* provide positive reviews to the public in order to boost the reputation of a business or organization.

First Read NONFICTION

Apply these strategies as you conduct your first read. You will have an opportunity to complete a close read after your first read.

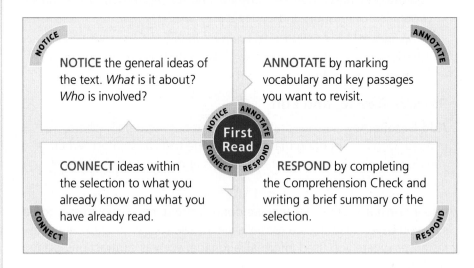

NOTICE the general ideas of the text. *What* is it about? *Who* is involved?

ANNOTATE by marking vocabulary and key passages you want to revisit.

CONNECT ideas within the selection to what you already know and what you have already read.

RESPOND by completing the Comprehension Check and writing a brief summary of the selection.

☰ STANDARDS

Reading Informational Text
By the end of the year, read and comprehend literary nonfiction at the high end of the grades 6–8 text complexity band independently and proficiently.

Language
Determine or clarify the meaning of unknown and multiple-meaning words or phrases based on *grade 8 reading and content,* choosing flexibly from a range of strategies.

a. Use context as a clue to the meaning of a word or phrase.

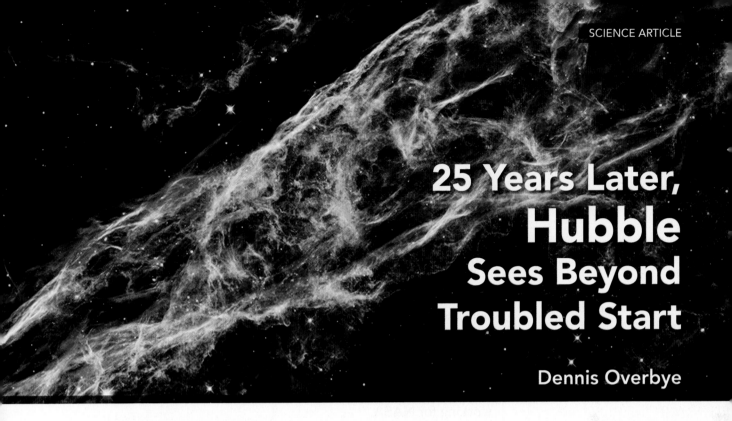

25 Years Later, Hubble Sees Beyond Troubled Start

Dennis Overbye

BACKGROUND

Lyman Spitzer Jr. (1914–1997), whose ideas inspired the creation of the Hubble Space Telescope, achieved great success as an astrophysicist. He studied space astronomy, star clusters, and the physics of stars. Not only did he propose the creation of a space telescope, he did so a decade before the first satellite had been launched.

SCAN FOR
MULTIMEDIA

NOTES

1   Against all odds, it's 25 years in space and counting for the Hubble Space Telescope this month.[1]

2   Few icons of science have had such a perilous existence, surviving political storms, physical calamities, and the simple passage of time in the service of cosmic exploration.

3   In 1946, the astronomer Lyman Spitzer, Jr., had a dream. A telescope in space, above the unruly atmosphere, would be able to see stars unaffected by the turbulence that blurs them and makes them twinkle. It would be able to see ultraviolet and infrared emissions that are blocked by the atmosphere and thus invisible to astronomers on the ground.

4   It took more than three decades for the rest of the astronomical community, NASA, and Congress to buy into this dream, partly as a way to showcase the capabilities of the space shuttle, still in development then, and the ability of astronauts to work routinely in space. By the time the telescope was launched into space from the space shuttle *Discovery* on April 25, 1990, it had been almost canceled at least twice and then delayed following the explosion of the shuttle *Challenger* in 1986.

---

1. **this month** This article was published in April 2015.

5   When the Hubble was finally deployed, NASA's spinmasters were instantly at the top of their game, hailing it as the greatest advance in astronomy since Galileo.[2]

6   And it might have been except for one problem: The telescope couldn't be focused. Instead, within days it became a laughingstock—a "technoturkey," in the words of some of its critics.

7   Designed using spy satellite technology, Hubble had an eight-foot mirror, just small enough to fit into the space shuttle cargo bay.

8   But because of a measuring error during a testing process that was hurried to save money, that big mirror wound up misshapen, polished four-millionths of an inch too flat, leaving the telescope with blurry vision. It was the kind of mistake, known as a spherical aberration, that an amateur astronomer might make, and it was a handful of astronomers who first recognized the flaw—to the disbelief and then the **dismay** of the engineers and contractors working for NASA.

9   For bright objects, astronomers could correct for the flaw with image processing software. But for the fainter parts of the universe, the Hubble needed glasses.

10   NASA scientists shrugged off their heartbreak and worked to figure out a way to provide corrective lenses.

11   Three years later, the space shuttle *Endeavour* and a repair crew led by Story Musgrave—astronaut, pilot, surgeon, spacewalker and Zen gardener—rode to the rescue.

12   In five tense days of spacewalks, they replaced the telescope's main camera and installed tiny mirrors designed to correct the Hubble's vision.

13   The rest of the universe snapped into crystalline focus. And NASA could stop holding its breath.

14   The Hubble was the first big-deal telescope of the Internet age, and its cosmic postcards captivated the world. Trained on a patch of sky known as the Hubble Ultra Deep Field in 2010, the telescope's keen eye discerned swarms of baby galaxies crawling out of the primordial[3] darkness as early as only 600 million years after the Big Bang.

15   And it took one of the first visible-light photos of a distant planet, Fomalhaut b, orbiting its star.

16   In perhaps its most iconic image, called "Pillars of Creation," the Hubble recorded baby stars burning their way out of biblical-looking mountains of gas and dust in a stellar nursery known as the Eagle nebula.

---

2. **Galileo** Galileo Galilei (1564–1642) was an Italian scientist and scholar who was the first person to use a telescope to observe space.
3. **primordial** *adj.* ancient; from the beginning of time.

Mark context clues or indicate another strategy you used that helped you determine meaning.

dismay (diss MAY) *n.*

MEANING:

17   These postcards were not without **controversy**. The Hubble's camera records in black and white, through filters that isolate the characteristic light from different atoms, such as sulfur, hydrogen, and oxygen. Then the different layers are assigned whatever colors look good to the eye and best show off the underlying astrophysics rather than their natural colors.

18   "Pillars of Creation," for example, is presented in earth tones of green and brown and is oriented to look like a Turner landscape,[4] while the natural emissions from the nebula are shades of red.

19   Technological hiccups have also continued. In 1999, four of the six gyroscopes that keep the telescope pointed failed, and the Hubble went into "safe mode." A crew was hastily dispatched to replace the gyros. That was the first of what would be three trips to the telescope by John M. Grunsfeld, an astronaut, astronomer, and now NASA's associate administrator for science, who would win the sobriquet "Hubble Repairman" for his feats.

20   The telescope has been reborn again and again over the years, thanks to the efforts of astronaut servicing crews. Astronauts wearing the equivalent of boxing gloves have gradually learned how to do things the telescope's designers had never dared dream of, fiddling with its innards, replacing circuit boards and performing the equivalent of eye surgery and computer repairs in space.

21   The Hubble was hitting its stride, getting better and better, when the *Columbia* space shuttle disintegrated in 2003, killing all seven astronauts on board. That harkened the end of NASA's space shuttle dreams.

22   The agency's administrator, Sean O'Keefe, canceled what was to be the final Hubble servicing mission on the grounds that it was too risky. Without it, the telescope would be doomed to die in orbit within two or three years when its batteries and gyros failed again.

23   The decision was announced and defended by Dr. Grunsfeld, who was then NASA's chief scientist. "Being an astronaut, there are not a lot of things that have really shocked me in my life," Dr. Grunsfeld recalled later. "But I don't think anybody could ever prepare themselves for, you know, trying to bury something that they have said, 'Hey, this is worth risking my life for.'"

24   Mr. O'Keefe's decision ignited a national **outcry**. Schoolchildren offered to send their pennies to NASA to help pay for the telescope.

NOTES

Mark context clues or indicate another strategy you used that helped you determine meaning.

controversy (KON truh vuhr see) *n.*

MEANING:

Mark context clues or indicate another strategy you used that helped you determine meaning.

outcry ((OWT kry) *n.*

MEANING:

---

4. **Turner landscape.** J.M.W Turner was an artist famed for his use of color.

25   Behind the scenes, however, Dr. Grunsfeld and other astronomers and NASA engineers were working on ways to save the Hubble, perhaps by sending robots to work on it.

26   The robotic approach was eventually rejected by a National Academy of Sciences panel, but it had served as a placeholder to keep the teams of engineers together. In the end, Mr. O'Keefe resigned, and his successor, Michael Griffin, reinstated a servicing mission.

27   In 2009, Dr. Grunsfeld led one last mission to the Hubble. He was the last human to touch the telescope, patting it as the shuttle *Atlantis* prepared to let it go again. But that does not mean the telescope has ceased to touch humanity. On the contrary, it continues to deliver news about this thing we are all part of—a universe—but barely understand.

28   Earlier this spring, astronomers announced that the Hubble had seen a sort of cosmic mirage known as an Einstein ring, in which they could view multiple reruns of a star that died in a stupendous supernova explosion more than nine billion years ago on the other side of the cosmos.

29   NASA is making a big deal of the Hubble anniversary, with a weeklong symposium[5] in Baltimore, where the Space Telescope Science Institute is based.

30   "This is a celebration partly about the telescope and partly about NASA," Dr. Grunsfeld said, "but much of it is a celebration of people doing science."

31   The Hubble today is more powerful than its designers ever dreamed, and it has a good chance of living long enough to share the universe with its designated successor, the James Webb Space Telescope, due to be launched in 2018. The Hubble's longevity is something few would have imagined 10 years ago, yet NASA is already planning a 30th-anniversary celebration in 2020, Dr. Grunsfeld said.

32   After a quarter-century, the telescope's future and promise are still as big as the sky and our ignorance of what lies behind it. ❧

---

5. **symposium** *n.* conference where experts discuss a certain topic.

Comprehension Check

Complete the following items after you finish your first read. Review and clarify details with your group.

1. When was the Hubble Space Telescope launched into space?

2. What advantage does a telescope in space have over one located on the ground?

3. A *laughingstock* is the subject of a joke or an object of ridicule. According to the article, what flaw made Hubble a "laughingstock"?

4. What is Hubble's most recent image?

5. 🗐 **Notebook** Confirm your understanding of the article by writing a short summary.

RESEARCH

Research to Clarify Choose at least one unfamiliar detail from the text. Briefly research that detail. In what way does the information you learned shed light on an aspect of the article?

Research to Explore Conduct research on an aspect of the text you find interesting. For example, you may want to learn more about the Hubble's designated successor, the James Webb Space Telescope, due to be launched in 2018.

25 YEARS LATER, HUBBLE SEES
BEYOND TROUBLED START

TIP

GROUP DISCUSSION

Take time to review the meanings of unfamiliar words and technical terms before discussing the article with your group.

⬡ WORD NETWORK

Identify words from the article that relate to the concept of invention. Add these words to your Word Network.

☰ STANDARDS

Language
Determine or clarify the meaning of unknown and multiple-meaning words or phrases based on *grade 8 reading and content*, choosing flexibly from a range of strategies.

b. Use common, grade-appropriate Greek or Latin affixes and roots as clues to the meaning of a word.

c. Consult general and specialized reference materials, both print and digital, to find the pronunciation of a word or determine or clarify its precise meaning or its part of speech.

Close Read the Text

With your group, revisit sections of the text you marked during your first read. **Annotate** what you notice. What **questions** do you have? What can you **conclude**?

Analyze the Text

> **CITE TEXTUAL EVIDENCE**
> to support your answers.

📓 **Notebook** Complete the activities.

1. **Review and Clarify** With your group, reread paragraphs 8–9 of the article. Discuss the specific problem that the Hubble had. What does this problem show about the nature of invention?

2. **Present and Discuss** Discuss what you noticed in the selection, what questions you asked, and what conclusions you reached.

3. **Essential Question:** *Are inventions realized through inspiration or perspiration?* What has this article taught you about invention? Discuss with your group.

LANGUAGE DEVELOPMENT

Concept Vocabulary

dismay	controversy	outcry

Why These Words? The concept vocabulary words from the text are related. With your group, determine what the words have in common. Write your ideas and add another word that fits the category.

Practice

📓 **Notebook** Confirm your understanding of the concept vocabulary words by using each in a sentence. Provide context clues for the words.

Word Study

Latin Root: -vers- The word *controversy* contains the Latin root *-vers-* which means "to turn." It also includes a variation of the Latin prefix *contra-*, which means "against" or "in opposition." In the article, the author explains that the images from Hubble were the subject of a *controversy* because people had different opinions on their accuracy and usefulness. Based on the context and the Latin word parts, you can infer that a *controversy* is when people "turn against" each other. Use a dictionary to find the definitions of the following words that include the root *-vers-*: *reverse, subversive,* and *converse.* Briefly explain how the root *-vers-* contributes to the meaning of each word.

Analyze Craft and Structure

Author's Purpose: Diction and Tone An author's purpose for writing is the reason he or she writes. For example, an author may write to inform, to persuade, or to entertain. In "25 Years Later, Hubble Sees Beyond Troubled Start," Dennis Overbye's purpose for writing can be inferred by studying his diction and tone.

Diction, or word choice, has a great impact on readers. Writers choose what information to convey and how to say it. Examining diction can help you identify an author's tone and purpose.

Tone is an author's attitude toward his or her subject and audience. Tone is created by an author's diction. Tone can usually be described using adjectives, such as *humorous, argumentative,* or *academic.* Identifying tone can also help you identify author's purpose.

Here is an example of how to analyze diction and tone:

PASSAGE	ANALYSIS OF DICTION	ANALYSIS OF TONE
The telescope has been reborn again and again over the years, thanks to the efforts of astronaut servicing crews.	"reborn," "thanks to the efforts" This passage conveys information but in an informal way.	grateful; positive

TIP

COLLABORATION

Some members of your group may have different ideas about the tone of the article. Reading a passage aloud may help you come to agreement.

STANDARDS

Reading Informational Text
• Determine an author's point of view or purpose in a text and analyze how the author acknowledges and responds to conflicting evidence or viewpoints.

Practice

CITE TEXTUAL EVIDENCE to support your answers.

Use this chart to analyze Dennis Overbye's diction and tone in "25 Years Later, Hubble Sees Beyond Troubled Start." Then, share your analysis with your group, and work together to determine Overbye's purpose for writing. The first row has been completed as an example.

PASSAGE	ANALYSIS OF DICTION	ANALYSIS OF TONE
Against all odds, it's 25 years in space and counting for the Hubble Space Telescope this month. Few icons of science have had such a perilous existence, surviving political storms, physical calamities, and the simple passage of time in the service of cosmic exploration.	"it's 25 years … and counting" / "icons" / "service of" / "perilous" / "calamity" This passage uses contrasting language—informal words in Paragraph 1 and formal, difficult words in Paragraph 2.	dramatic; admiring
Paragraph 8		
Paragraphs 19 and 20		
Paragraph 31		
Author's Purpose		

25 YEARS LATER, HUBBLE SEES
BEYOND TROUBLED START

Conventions

Dashes and Ellipses

- An **ellipsis (. . .)** shows something is missing from a quoted passage. It can also show a pause or an interruption in speech.
- A **dash (—)** shows a strong, sudden break in thought or speech.

This chart shows some common reasons why authors use an ellipsis or a dash.

USE AN ELLIPSIS	EXAMPLES
to show the reader that you have chosen to leave out a word or words from a quoted passage	As the inscription on the Statue of Liberty says, "Give me your tired, your poor. . . ."
to indicate a pause or an interruption in speech	The scientist said, "When I saw the telescope's pictures, I . . . I couldn't speak."

USE A DASH	EXAMPLES
to show the reader that there is a strong, sudden interruption in thought or speech	"I can't believe—hey, look at the meteor!—how gorgeous the night sky is."
in place of *in other words*, *namely*, or *that is* before an explanation	The astronaut wanted one thing—to explore space in his lifetime.
to set off nonrestrictive elements (modifiers or other elements that are not essential to the meaning of the sentence) when there is a sudden break in thought	Albert Einstein—the physicist who developed the theory of relativity—became an American citizen in 1940.

Read It

Work with your group to complete each of the following items.

1. The following quotations are passages from the news article. Use an ellipsis to omit a portion of each quotation without altering the meaning.

   a. "Few icons of science have had such a perilous existence, surviving political storms, physical calamities, and the simple passage of time in the service of cosmic exploration."

   b. "The telescope has been reborn again and again over the years, thanks to the efforts of astronaut servicing crews."

2. Review the selection, and find at least two sentences in which the author uses dashes. Record the sentence, and determine the reason the author used dashes based on the information in the chart.

Write It

📓 **Notebook** Write a brief paragraph in which you explain what you learned from the news article about the Hubble Space Telescope. In your paragraph, use an ellipsis and a dash in at least three of the ways indicated in the chart.

⊞ STANDARDS

Language
Demonstrate command of the conventions of standard English capitalization, punctuation, and spelling when writing.

a. Use punctuation to indicate a pause or break.
b. Use an ellipsis to indicate an omission.

Speaking and Listening

Assignment

With your group, conduct a **debate** in which you respond to one of the following propositions, or statements of opinion:

☐ **Proposition 1:** Learning about the universe with a space telescope, such as Hubble, is a worthwhile pursuit that should be endorsed and well funded.

☐ **Proposition 2:** The Hubble's flaws prevent it from providing humans with accurate and useful information about the universe.

Project Plan Decide which proposition your group will debate. With your group, determine which members will argue for the proposition and which members will argue against it. Choose a moderator to keep time and see that the debaters remain orderly and don't speak out of turn. Keep the following instructions in mind.

Preparing for the Debate

- Reread the article, and identify information from the selection that supports your proposition. Then, conduct research to find additional evidence to support your proposition, or argument.
- Analyze your evidence, and note specific details that support your proposition. Based on these notes, make logical connections between the evidence and your proposition. These connections are your reasons for arguing the position.
- Create a thesis, or statement of your position, from your notes. Present this thesis during your opening statement.
- Prior to the debate, prepare to address your opponents' arguments, or the **counterclaims** to your position, by thinking about the topic from the opposite perspective and considering the arguments that they might make.

Taking Part in the Debate

- During the debate, each participant should build on and respond to the arguments presented by the previous speaker.
- Use supporting evidence from the selection and from your research.
- Listen carefully to the opposing side during the debate so you can address their arguments and make counterclaims.
- Listen carefully and evaluate your opponents' arguments to see if they make sense. Identify when they do not present enough evidence to support their views or when the evidence they present is not well connected to their arguments.

EVIDENCE LOG

Before moving on to a new selection, go to your Evidence Log and record what you learned from "25 Years Later, Hubble Sees Beyond Troubled Start."

STANDARDS

Speaking and Listening
- Engage effectively in a range of collaborative discussions (one-on-one, in groups, and teacher-led) with diverse partners on *grade 8 topics, texts, and issues,* building on others' ideas and expressing their own clearly.

  a. Come to discussions prepared, having read or researched material under study; explicitly draw on that preparation by referring to evidence on the topic, text, or issue to probe and reflect on ideas under discussion.
  b. Follow rules for collegial discussions and decision-making, track progress toward specific goals and deadlines, and define individual roles as needed.
  c. Pose questions that connect the ideas of several speakers and respond to others' questions and comments with relevant evidence, observations, and ideas.
  d. Acknowledge new information expressed by others, and, when warranted, qualify or justify their own views in light of the evidence presented.

- Delineate a speaker's argument and specific claims, evaluating the soundness of the reasoning and relevance and sufficiency of the evidence and identifying when irrelevant evidence is introduced.

About the Musician

William Zeitler (b. 1954) earned his music degree from the California Institute of the Arts. He is a pianist, composer, and the author of a book on the history of the glass armonica. He is also one of the world's few professional armonica players and has released five albums of original armonica music.

Sounds of a Glass Armonica

Media Vocabulary

The following words will be useful to you as you analyze, discuss, and write about the video.

zoom: enlarge, magnify, or close in on an image	• Elements within the lens create the camera's zoom effect. • Zooming in on an image emphasizes its importance.
video clip: a short video, often part of a larger recording, that can be used on a website	• The term "video clip" is used to mean any video shorter than the length of a traditional program. • A video clip can contain video, audio, animation, graphics, or any other content.
focus: to aim the camera so that it creates a distinct image	• A shot that is out of focus can seem mysterious and eerie. • Some photographers prefer sharply focused images and bright colors.

First Review MEDIA: VIDEO

Review the video using these strategies. Take note of time codes as you watch the video so that you can revisit sections you find interesting or important.

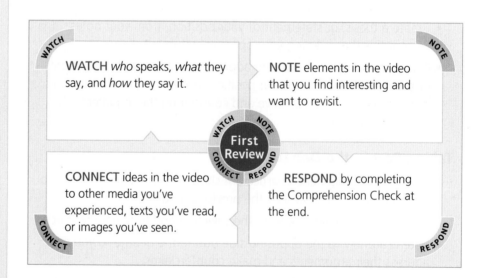

WATCH *who* speaks, *what* they say, and *how* they say it.

NOTE elements in the video that you find interesting and want to revisit.

CONNECT ideas in the video to other media you've experienced, texts you've read, or images you've seen.

RESPOND by completing the Comprehension Check at the end.

▐ **STANDARDS**

Reading Informational Text
By the end of the year, read and comprehend literary nonfiction at the high end of the grades 6–8 text complexity band independently and proficiently.

Language
Acquire and use accurately grade-appropriate general academic and domain-specific words and phrases; gather vocabulary knowledge when considering a word or phrase important to comprehension or expression.

Sounds of a Glass Armonica

BACKGROUND

Although Benjamin Franklin is well known for his role in the founding of the United States, he was also one of the era's foremost scientists. Among his numerous inventions were the "Franklin stove," the lightning rod, bifocals, the rocking chair, and a musical instrument called the armonica that premiered in 1762. At first Franklin named the instrument the "glassychord," but he soon changed it to *armonica*—based on the Italian word *armonia*, which means "harmony."

SCAN FOR
MULTIMEDIA

NOTES

Comprehension Check

Complete the following items after you finish your first review. Review and clarify details with your group.

1. What produces sound in the glass armonica?

2. What is the purpose of the bowl of water shown in the video?

3. What famous composer wrote for the glass armonica?

MEDIA VOCABULARY

Use these words as you discuss and write about the video.

zoom
video clip
focus

WORD NETWORK

Identify words from the video that relate to the concept of invention. Add these words to your Word Network.

STANDARDS

Speaking and Listening
Engage effectively in a range of collaborative discussions with diverse partners on *grade 8 topics, texts, and issues,* building on others' ideas and expressing their own clearly.

Close Review

Watch the video or parts of it again. Write any new observations that seem important. What **questions** do you have? What can you **conclude**?

Analyze the Media

CITE TEXTUAL EVIDENCE to support your answers.

Complete the activities.

1. **Present and Discuss** Choose the section of the video you found most interesting or powerful. Share your choice with the group, and explain what you noticed in the video, the questions it raised for you, and the conclusions you reached about it.

2. **Review and Synthesize** With your group, review the whole video. What did you learn about how the armonica was invented? What do you think went into the design process?

3. **Essential Question:** *Are inventions realized through inspiration or perspiration?* What has this video revealed about whether inventions are realized through inspiration or perspiration? Discuss with your group.

SOUNDS OF A GLASS ARMONICA

Research

Assignment

Create a **multimedia presentation** highlighting a homemade or unusual musical instrument. Choose from the following topics:

☐ Research and present information on another unusual musical instrument, such as the steel drum, the zither, or the theremin.

☐ Research and present information on a "homemade" instrument, such as the comb kazoo, the chopo choor, or the reed flute.

Set Project Goals Work with your group to form a plan for your presentation. Decide which instrument to focus on, what information and multimedia you will need, and the best way to present your information. Decide which group member will be responsible for each part of the presentation.

Conduct Research Begin the research process by finding details about the instrument your group chose—how it works, its origins, notable musicians who have played it, and memorable songs that feature it. Then, consider the types of multimedia that will best help your audience to visualize and understand how the instrument works and sounds. Since the presentation is about a musical instrument, you will need to include some audio components. For example, you might use audio or video recordings of the instrument being played, or you may choose to play the instrument yourself during the class presentation.

Organize Your Information It is important to sequence, or organize, your information effectively in a multimedia presentation. You must integrate text, visuals, and audio in a seamless, easy-to-follow manner. You will also have to consider the best time for information to be presented digitally, by a speaker, and through live performance. Once you have organized a sequence, rehearse your presentation with your group. Then, try rearranging the elements of your presentation, and practice presenting them in a different order. This will help you to determine whether you have selected the best organization for your presentation.

Use a chart like this to organize your ideas.

PRESENTER	SCRIPT	MEDIA

📝 EVIDENCE LOG

Before moving on to a new selection, go to your Evidence Log and record what you learned from the video.

☰ STANDARDS

Writing
Conduct short research projects to answer a question, drawing on several sources and generating additional related, focused questions that allow for multiple avenues of exploration.

Speaking and Listening
• Engage effectively in a range of collaborative discussions with diverse partners on *grade 8 topics, texts, and issues,* building on others' ideas and expressing their own clearly.

a. Come to discussions prepared, having read or researched material under study; explicitly draw on that preparation by referring to evidence on the topic, text, or issue to probe and reflect on ideas under discussion.
b. Follow rules for collegial discussions and decision-making, track progress toward specific goals and deadlines, and define individual roles as needed.

• Integrate multimedia and visual displays into presentations to clarify information, strengthen claims and evidence, and add interest.

 **Tool Kit**
Collaboration Checklist

Conduct a Debate

Assignment

The selections in this section have provided various perspectives on the subject of invention—the processes involved, the people behind them, and the inventions themselves. With your group, pair up with another group to conduct a **debate** in which each team takes a position on the Essential Question:

> Are inventions realized through inspiration or perspiration?

Plan With Your Group

Support your position with evidence and examples from reading, viewing, and analyzing the selections in this part of the unit. Use the chart to list your ideas. For each selection, identify evidence that relates to whether inventions are realized through inspiration or perspiration. Use the evidence to begin planning the argument you will make in the debate.

TITLE	SUPPORTING EVIDENCE
Nikola Tesla: The Greatest Inventor of All?	
from The Invention of Everything Else	
25 Years Later, Hubble Sees Beyond Troubled Start	
Sounds of a Glass Armonica	

Gather Evidence and Media Examples As a group, discuss your notes and ideas. Identify specific examples from the selections to support your group's position. As a group, assess whether you have sufficient evidence to support your position.

STANDARDS
Speaking and Listening
• Engage effectively in a range of collaborative discussions with diverse partners on *grade 8 topics, texts, and issues,* building on others' ideas and expressing their own clearly.

  a. Come to discussions prepared, having read or researched material under study; explicitly draw on that preparation by referring to evidence on the topic, text, or issue to probe and reflect on ideas under discussion.
  b. Follow rules for collegial discussions and decision-making, track progress toward specific goals and deadlines, and define individual roles as needed.

• Delineate a speaker's argument and specific claims, evaluating the soundness of the reasoning and relevance and sufficiency of the evidence and identifying when irrelevant evidence is introduced.

Organize Your Ideas As a group, develop an outline for your argument. Clearly identify the claims you will make and the reasons and evidence that support them. Prepare for your opponents' arguments by considering their counterclaims to your position. Consider how you can respond, and have evidence ready to support your responses.

Set Debate Rules Assign one member of each group to moderate the debate and assign a designated time limit for each response. To show respect for your opponents, keep your responses within the designated time limit. Plan the discussion so you do not get cut off by the moderator when making a point.

Rehearse With Your Group

Practice With Your Group Within your group, practice delivering the points you will make in the debate. As each member practices his or her delivery, have other group members role-play as opponents. This will help you to identify places you need to strengthen your argument.

CONTENT	DEBATE TECHNIQUE	PRESENTATION TECHNIQUES
☐ Claims are presented clearly and supported by reasons and evidence.	☐ Each speaker keeps within the allotted time limit.	☐ Each speaker argues persuasively and confidently.
☐ Counterclaims are anticipated and addressed effectively.	☐ Points are clear and organized.	☐ Each speaker speaks clearly and makes eye contact with the person he or she is addressing.

Fine-Tune the Content Review your evidence to be sure it supports your claims. If your claim is not fully supported, work with your group members to find information that better supports your claim.

Improve Your Debate Technique As you review your outline, consider whether you have connected all of your ideas in the clearest way possible. If you are concerned you might be missing a connection, ask your teacher for guidance on how to better connect your ideas.

Present and Evaluate

As you listen to other groups' debates, evaluate how well they meet the checklist requirements. After the debate, discuss whether other groups' claims were well supported by reasons and evidence. Then, discuss and reflect on any new information you gained from the process and whether it changed your initial views on the subject.

▤ STANDARDS

Speaking and Listening
• Engage effectively in a range of collaborative discussions with diverse partners on *grade 8 topics, texts, and issues,* building on others' ideas and expressing their own clearly.

  c. Pose questions that connect the ideas of several speakers and respond to others' questions and comments with relevant evidence, observations, and ideas.
  d. Acknowledge new information expressed by others, and, when warranted, qualify or justify their own views in light of the evidence presented.

• Present claims and findings, emphasizing salient points in a focused, coherent manner with relevant evidence, sound valid reasoning, and well-chosen details; use appropriate eye contact, adequate volume, and clear pronunciation.

ESSENTIAL QUESTION:

Are inventions realized through inspiration or perspiration?

There is a story behind every invention, and the ideas, knowledge, and experiences that contributed to each one are different. In this section, you will complete your study of invention by exploring an additional selection related to the topic. Then, you will share what you have learned with your classmates. To choose a text, follow these steps.

Look Back Think about the selections you have already read. What more do you want to know about the topic of invention?

Look Ahead Preview the selections by reading the descriptions. Which one seems most interesting and appealing to you?

Look Inside Take a few minutes to scan through the text you chose. Make another selection if this text doesn't meet your needs.

Independent Learning Strategies

Throughout your life, in school, in your community, and in your career, you will need to rely on yourself to learn and work on your own. Review these strategies and the actions you can take to practice them during Independent Learning. Add ideas of your own for each category.

STRATEGY	ACTION PLAN
Create a schedule	• Understand your goals and deadlines. • Make a plan for what to do each day. •
Practice what you have learned	• Use first-read and close-read strategies to deepen your understanding. • After you read, evaluate the usefulness of the evidence to help you understand the topic. • Consider the quality and reliability of the source. •
Take notes	• Record important ideas and information. • Review your notes before preparing to share with a group. •

SCAN FOR
MULTIMEDIA

CONTENTS

Choose one selection. Selections are available online only.

PERFORMANCE-BASED ASSESSMENT PREP

Review Evidence for an Argument

Complete your Evidence Log for the unit by evaluating what you have learned and synthesizing the information you have recorded.

SCAN FOR MULTIMEDIA

First-Read Guide

Use this page to record your first-read ideas.

🔧 **Tool Kit**
First-Read Guide and
Model Annotation

Selection Title: _____

NOTICE

NOTICE new information or ideas you learn about the unit topic as you first read this text.

ANNOTATE

ANNOTATE by marking vocabulary and key passages you want to revisit.

First Read
NOTICE · ANNOTATE · CONNECT · RESPOND

CONNECT ideas within the selection to other knowledge and the selections you have read.

RESPOND by writing a brief summary of the selection.

CONNECT

RESPOND

▤ STANDARD
Reading Read and comprehend complex literary and informational texts independently and proficiently.

Close-Read Guide

Use this page to record your close-read ideas.

Selection Title: _____

Close Read the Text

Revisit sections of the text you marked during your first read. Read these sections closely and **annotate** what you notice. Ask yourself **questions** about the text. What can you **conclude**? Write down your ideas.

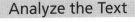

Analyze the Text

Think about the author's choices of patterns, structure, techniques, and ideas included in the text. Select one, and record your thoughts about what this choice conveys.

QuickWrite

Pick a paragraph from the text that grabbed your interest. Explain the power of this passage.

_____

_____

_____

_____

_____

_____

_____

_____

_____

_____

_____

▤ STANDARD
Reading Read and comprehend complex literary and informational texts independently and proficiently.

Share Your Independent Learning

Prepare to Share

Are inventions realized through inspiration or perspiration?

Even when you read something independently, your understanding continues to grow when you share what you have learned with others. Reflect on the text you explored independently and write notes about its connection to the unit. In your notes, consider why this text belongs in this unit.

Learn From Your Classmates

Discuss It Share your ideas about the text you explored on your own. As you talk with your classmates, jot down ideas that you learn from them.

Reflect

Review your notes, and mark the most important insight you gained from these writing and discussion activities. Explain how this idea adds to your understanding of the topic of invention.

▤ STANDARDS

Speaking and Listening
Engage effectively in a range of collaborative discussions with diverse partners on *grade 8 topics, texts, and issues,* building on others' ideas and expressing their own clearly.

Review Evidence for an Argument

At the beginning of this unit you took a position on the following question:

> **Which invention described in this unit has had the biggest impact on humanity?**

✎ EVIDENCE LOG

Review your Evidence Log and your QuickWrite from the beginning of the unit. Has your position changed?

☐ YES	☐ NO
Identify at least three pieces of evidence that convinced you to change your mind.	Identify at least three new pieces of evidence that reinforced your initial position.
1.	**1.**
2.	**2.**
3.	**3.**

State your position now: _____

_____

_____

Identify a possible counterclaim: _____

_____

_____

Evaluate the Strength of Your Evidence Consider your argument. Do you have enough evidence to support your claim? Do you have enough evidence to refute a counterargument? If not, make a plan.

☐ Do more research   ☐ Talk with my classmates

☐ Reread a selection   ☐ Ask an expert

☐ Other: _____

☰ STANDARDS

Writing
Write arguments to support claims with clear reasons and relevant evidence.

a. Introduce claim(s), acknowledge and distinguish the claim(s) from alternate or opposing claims, and organize the reasons and evidence logically.
b. Support claim(s) with logical reasoning and relevant evidence, using accurate, credible sources and demonstrating an understanding of the topic or text.

SOURCES

- WHOLE-CLASS SELECTIONS
- SMALL-GROUP SELECTIONS
- INDEPENDENT-LEARNING SELECTION

PART 1
Writing to Sources: Argument

In this unit, you read about various inventors and inventions, real and imaginary. In some cases, the inventors described seem like uniquely gifted individuals who also work hard. In other cases, inventors are presented as workers presented with a challenge who use what they know to solve practical problems.

Assignment

Write an **argument** in which you state and defend a claim about the following question:

> **Which invention described in this unit has had the biggest impact on humanity?**

Take a position on this question based on the knowledge you gained from reading and analyzing the selections in the unit. Use examples from the selections you read and viewed to support your claim, and organize your ideas so that they flow logically and are easy to follow. Address and refute counterclaims to limit dissent and ensure your argument is well received. Use an appropriately formal tone.

WORD NETWORK

As you write and revise your argument, use your Word Network to help vary your word choices.

STANDARDS

Writing
Write arguments to support claims with clear reasons and relevant evidence.

a. Introduce claim(s), acknowledge and distinguish the claim(s) from alternate or opposing claims, and organize the reasons and evidence logically.
b. Support claim(s) with logical reasoning and relevant evidence, using accurate, credible sources and demonstrating an understanding of the topic or text.
c. Use words, phrases, and clauses to create cohesion and clarify the relationships among claim(s), counterclaims, reasons, and evidence.
d. Establish and maintain a formal style.
e. Provide a concluding statement or section that follows from and supports the argument presented.

Reread the Assignment Review the assignment to be sure you fully understand it. The task may reference some of the academic words presented at the beginning of the unit. Be sure you understand each of the words given below to complete the assignment correctly.

Academic Vocabulary

opponent	contradict	dissent
position	legitimate	

Review the Elements of Effective Argument Before you begin writing, read the Argument Rubric. Once you have completed your first draft, check it against the rubric. If one or more of the elements is missing or not as strong as it could be, revise your essay to add or strengthen that element.

Argument Rubric

	Focus and Organization	Evidence and Elaboration	Conventions
4	The introduction engages the reader and establishes a position in a compelling way. The position is supported by logical reasons and relevant evidence, and opposing claims are addressed. The reasons and evidence are organized logically so that the argument is easy to follow. Transitions clearly show the relationships among ideas. The conclusion follows from and supports the rest of the argument.	The sources of evidence are relevant and credible. The tone of the argument is formal and objective. Words are carefully chosen and suited to the audience and purpose.	The argument consistently uses standard English conventions of usage and mechanics.
3	The introduction is somewhat engaging and states the position clearly. The claim is supported by reasons and evidence, and opposing claims are acknowledged. Reasons and evidence are organized so that the argument is easy to follow. Transitions show the relationships among ideas. The conclusion restates the claim.	The sources are relevant. The tone of the argument is mostly formal and objective. Words are generally suited to the audience and purpose.	The argument demonstrates general accuracy in standard English conventions of usage and mechanics.
2	The introduction states a claim. The claim is supported by some reasons and evidence, and opposing claims may be briefly acknowledged. Reasons and evidence are organized somewhat logically. A few sentence transitions are used to orient readers. The conclusion relates to the claim.	Some sources are relevant. The tone of the argument is occasionally formal and objective. Words are somewhat suited to the audience and purpose.	The argument demonstrates some accuracy in standard English conventions of usage and mechanics.
1	The claim is not clearly stated. The claim is not supported by reasons and evidence, and opposing claims are not addressed. Reasons and evidence are disorganized and the argument is difficult to follow. No transitions are used. The conclusion does not restate the claim.	Reliable and relevant evidence is not included. The tone of the argument is informal. The vocabulary is ineffective.	The argument contains mistakes in standard English conventions of usage and mechanics.

PART 2
Speaking and Listening: Speech

Assignment
After completing the final draft of your argument, use it as the foundation for a three- to five-minute **speech.**

Take the following steps to make your speech lively and engaging.

- Go back to your argument and annotate the most important claims and supporting details.
- Refer to your annotated text to guide your speech and keep it focused.
- Use appropriate eye contact, adequate volume, and clear pronunciation when speaking.
- Deliver your speech with conviction.

Review the Rubric Before you deliver your speech, check the rubric. If one or more of the elements is weak, revise your presentation.

STANDARDS

Speaking and Listening
- Delineate a speaker's argument and specific claims, evaluating the soundness of the reasoning and relevance and sufficiency of the evidence and identifying when irrelevant evidence is introduced.
- Present claims and findings, emphasizing salient points in a focused, coherent manner with relevant evidence, sound valid reasoning, and well-chosen details; use appropriate eye contact, adequate volume, and clear pronunciation.

	Content	Organization	Presentation Techniques
3	The introduction engages the reader and establishes a claim in a compelling way. The presentation has strong, valid reasons and evidence to support the claim and answers counterclaims. The conclusion follows from and supports the rest of the argument.	Ideas progress logically, with clear transitions among ideas so that listeners can easily follow the argument.	The speaker maintains effective eye contact and speaks clearly and with adequate volume. The speaker presents with strong conviction and energy.
2	The introduction establishes a claim. The presentation includes some valid reasons and evidence to support the claim and acknowledges counterclaims. The conclusion offers some insight into the claim and restates important information.	Ideas progress logically with some transitions between ideas. Listeners can mostly follow the speaker's argument.	The speaker sometimes maintains effective eye contact and speaks somewhat clearly and with adequate volume. The speaker presents with some conviction and energy.
1	The introduction does not clearly state a claim. The presentation does not include reasons or evidence to support a claim or acknowledge counterclaims. The conclusion does not restate important information about a claim.	Ideas do not progress logically. Listeners have difficulty following the argument.	The speaker does not maintain effective eye contact or speak clearly with adequate volume. The speaker presents without conviction or energy.

Reflect on the Unit

Now that you've completed the unit, take a few moments to reflect on your learning. Use the questions below to think about where you succeeded, what skills and strategies helped you, and where you can continue to grow in the future.

Reflect on the Unit Goals

Look back at the goals at the beginning of the unit. Use a different colored pen to rate yourself again. Think about readings and activities that contributed the most to the growth of your understanding. Record your thoughts.

Reflect on the Learning Strategies

💬 **Discuss It** Write a reflection on whether you were able to improve your learning based on your Action Plans. Think about what worked, what didn't, and what you might do to keep working on these strategies. Record your ideas before a class discussion.

Reflect on the Text

Choose a selection that you found challenging, and explain what made it difficult.

Describe something that surprised you about a text in the unit.

Which activity taught you the most about invention? What did you learn?

SCAN FOR
MULTIMEDIA

RESOURCES

CONTENTS

Marking the Text: Strategies and Tips for Annotation

When you close read a text, you read for comprehension and then reread to unlock layers of meaning and to analyze a writer's style and techniques. Marking a text as you read it enables you to participate more fully in the close-reading process.

Following are some strategies for text mark-ups, along with samples of how the strategies can be applied. These mark-ups are suggestions; you and your teacher may want to use other mark-up strategies.

✱	Key Idea
!	I love it!
?	I have questions
◯	Unfamiliar or important word
----	Context Clues

Suggested Mark-Up Notations

WHAT I NOTICE	HOW TO MARK UP	QUESTIONS TO ASK
Key Ideas and Details	• Highlight key ideas or claims. • Underline supporting details or evidence.	• What does the text say? What does it leave unsaid? • What inferences do you need to make? • What details lead you to make your inferences?
Word Choice	• Circle unfamiliar words. • Put a dotted line under context clues, if any exist. • Put an exclamation point beside especially rich or poetic passages.	• What inferences about word meaning can you make? • What tone and mood are created by word choice? • What alternate word choices might the author have made?
Text Structure	• Highlight passages that show key details supporting the main idea. • Use arrows to indicate how sentences and paragraphs work together to build ideas. • Use a right-facing arrow to indicate foreshadowing. • Use a left-facing arrow to indicate flashback.	• Is the text logically structured? • What emotional impact do the structural choices create?
Author's Craft	• Circle or highlight instances of repetition, either of words, phrases, consonants, or vowel sounds. • Mark rhythmic beats in poetry using checkmarks and slashes. • Underline instances of symbolism or figurative language.	• Does the author's style enrich or detract from the reading experience? • What levels of meaning are created by the author's techniques?

CLOSE READING

* Key Idea
! I love it!
? I have questions
◯ Unfamiliar or important word
---- Context Clues

In a first read, work to get a sense of the main idea of a text. Look for key details and ideas that help you understand what the author conveys to you. Mark passages that prompt a strong response from you.

Here is how one reader marked up this text.

NOTES

MODEL

INFORMATIONAL TEXT

from Classifying the Stars

Cecilia H. Payne

1   Sunlight and starlight are composed of waves of various lengths, which the eye, even aided by a telescope, is unable to separate. We must use more than a telescope. In order to sort out the component colors, the light must be dispersed by a prism, or split up by some other means. For instance, sunbeams passing through rain drops are transformed into the myriad-tinted rainbow. The familiar rainbow spanning the sky is Nature's most glorious demonstration that light is composed of many colors.

2   The very beginning of our knowledge of the nature of a star dates back to 1672, when Isaac Newton gave to the world the results of his experiments on passing sunlight through a prism. To describe the beautiful band of rainbow tints, produced when sunlight was dispersed by his three-cornered piece of glass, he took from the Latin the word *spectrum*, meaning an appearance. The rainbow is the spectrum of the Sun. . . .

3   In 1814, more than a century after Newton, the spectrum of the Sun was obtained in such purity that an amazing detail was seen and studied by the German optician, Fraunhofer. He saw that the multiple spectral tints, ranging from delicate violet to deep red, were crossed by hundreds of fine dark lines. In other words, there were narrow gaps in the spectrum where certain shades were wholly blotted out. We must remember that the word spectrum is applied not only to sunlight, but also to the light of any glowing substance when its rays are sorted out by a prism or a grating.

First-Read Guide

Use this page to record your first-read ideas.

Selection Title: _____ Classifying the Stars _____

> You may want to use a guide like this to organize your thoughts after you read. Here is how a reader completed a First-Read Guide.

NOTICE

NOTICE new information or ideas you learned about the unit topic as you first read this text.

Light = different waves of colors. (Spectrum)

Newton - the first person to observe these waves using a prism.

Faunhofer saw gaps in the spectrum.

ANNOTATE

ANNOTATE by marking vocabulary and key passages you want to revisit.

Vocabulary
   myriad
   grating
   component colors

Different light types = different lengths

Isaac Newton also worked theories of gravity.

<u>Multiple spectral tints?</u> "colors of various appearance"

Key Passage:
Paragraph 3 shows that Fraunhofer discovered more about the nature of light spectrums: he saw the spaces in between the tints.

First Read

NOTICE · ANNOTATE · CONNECT · RESPOND

CONNECT

CONNECT ideas within the selection to other knowledge and the selections you have read.

I remember learning about prisms in science class.

Double rainbows! My favorite. How are they made?

RESPOND

RESPOND by writing a brief summary of the selection.

Science allows us to see things not visible to the naked eye. What we see as sunlight is really a spectrum of colors. By using tools, such as prisms, we can see the components of sunlight and other light. They appear as single colors or as multiple colors separated by gaps of no color. White light contains a rainbow of colors.

TOOL KIT: CLOSE READING

CLOSE READING

Close Read · ANNOTATE · QUESTION · CONCLUDE

* **Key Idea**
! **I love it!**
? **I have questions**
◯ **Unfamiliar or important word**
---- **Context Clues**

MODEL

INFORMATIONAL TEXT

NOTES

from **Classifying the Stars**

Cecilia H. Payne

explanation of sunlight and starlight

What is light and where do the colors come from?

*
1   Sunlight and starlight are composed of waves of various lengths, which the eye, even aided by a telescope, is unable to separate. We must use more than a telescope. In order to sort out the component colors, the light must be dispersed by a prism, or split up by some other means. For instance, sunbeams passing through rain drops are transformed into the myriad-tinted rainbow. The familiar rainbow spanning the sky is Nature's most glorious demonstration that light is composed of many colors.

This paragraph is about Newton and the prism.

What discoveries helped us understand light?

*
2   The very beginning of our knowledge of the nature of a star dates back to 1672, when Isaac Newton gave to the world the results of his experiments on passing sunlight through a prism. To describe the beautiful band of rainbow tints, produced when sunlight was dispersed by his three-cornered piece of glass, he took from the Latin the word *spectrum*, meaning an appearance. The rainbow is the spectrum of the Sun. . . .

Fraunhofer and gaps in spectrum

*
3   In 1814, more than a century after Newton, the spectrum of the Sun was obtained in such purity that an amazing detail was seen and studied by the German optician, Fraunhofer. He saw that the multiple spectral tints, ranging from delicate violet to deep red, were crossed by hundreds of fine dark lines. In other words, there were narrow gaps in the spectrum where certain shades were wholly blotted out. We must remember that the word spectrum is applied not only to sunlight, but also to the light of any glowing substance when its rays are sorted out by a prism or a grating.

Close-Read Guide

Use this page to record your close-read ideas.

Selection Title: _Classifying the Stars_

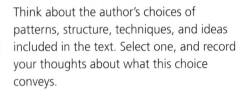

You can use the Close-Read Guide to help you dig deeper into the text. Here is how a reader completed a Close-Read Guide.

Close Read the Text

Revisit sections of the text you marked during your first read. Read these sections closely and **annotate** what you notice. Ask yourself **questions** about the text. What can you **conclude?** Write down your ideas.

Paragraph 3: Light is composed of waves of various lengths. Prisms let us see different colors in light. This is called the spectrum. Fraunhofer proved that there are gaps in the spectrum, where certain shades are blotted out.

More than one researcher studied this and each built off the ideas that were already discovered.

Analyze the Text

Think about the author's choices of patterns, structure, techniques, and ideas included in the text. Select one, and record your thoughts about what this choice conveys.

The author showed the development of human knowledge of the spectrum chronologically. Helped me see how ideas were built upon earlier understandings. Used dates and "more than a century after Newton" to show time.

QuickWrite

Pick a paragraph from the text that grabbed your interest. Explain the power of this passage.

The first paragraph grabbed my attention, specifically the sentence "The familiar rainbow spanning the sky is Nature's most glorious demonstration that light is composed of many colors." The paragraph began as a straightforward scientific explanation. When I read the word "glorious," I had to stop and deeply consider what was being said. It is a word loaded with personal feelings. With that one word, the author let the reader know what was important to her.

TOOL KIT: CLOSE READING

Argument

When you think of the word *argument,* you might think of a disagreement between two people, but the word has another meaning, too. An argument is a logical way of presenting a belief, conclusion, or stance. A good argument is supported with reasoning and evidence.

Argument writing can be used for many purposes, such as changing a reader's opinion or bringing about an action or a response from a reader.

Elements of an Argumentative Text

An **argument** sets forth a belief or stand on an issue. A well-written argument may convince the reader, change the reader's mind, or motivate the reader to take a certain action.

An effective argument contains these elements:

- a precise claim
- consideration of alternate claims, or opposing positions, and a discussion of their strengths and weaknesses
- logical organization that makes clear connections among claim, reasons, and evidence
- valid reasoning and evidence
- a concluding statement or section that follows from and supports the argument
- formal and objective language and tone
- error-free grammar, including accurate use of transitions

Celebrities Should Try to Be Better Role Models

A lot of Celebrities are singers or actors or actresses or athletes. Kids spend tons of time watching Celebrities on TV. They listen to their songs. They read about them. They watch them play and perform. No matter weather the Celebrities are good people or bad people. Kids still spend time watching them. The kids will try to imitate what they do. Some of them have parents or brothers and sisters who are famous also.

Celebrities don't seem to watch out what they do and how they live. Some say, *"Why do I care? It's none of you're business"!* Well, that's true. But it's bad on them if they do all kinds of stupid things. Because this is bad for the kids who look up to them.

Sometimes celebrity's say they wish they are not role models. *"I'm just an actor!" "I'm just a singer"!* they say. But the choice is not really up to them. If their on TV all the time, then kids' will look up to them, no matter what. It's stupid when Celebrities mess up and then nothing bad happens to them. That gives kids a bad lesson. Kids will think that you can do stupid things and be fine. That is not being a good role model.

Some Celebrities give money to charity. That's a good way to be a good role model. But sometimes it seems like Celebrities are just totally messed up. It's hard always being in the spotlight. That can drive Celebrities kind of crazy. Then they act out.

It is a good idea to support charities when you are rich and famous. You can do a lot of good. For a lot of people. Some Celebrities give out cars or houses or free scholarships. You can even give away your dresses and people can have an auction to see who will pay the most money for them. This can help for example the Humane Society. Or whatever charity or cause the celebrity wants to support.

Celebrities are fun to watch and follow, even when they mess up. I think they don't realize that when they do bad things, they give teens wrong ideas about how to live. They should try to keep that under control. So many teens look up to them and copy them, no matter what.

The claim is not clearly stated in the introduction or elsewhere.

Some of the ideas in the essay do not relate to the stated position or focus on the issue.

The word choice in the essay is not effective and lends it an informal tone.

The progression of ideas is not logical or well controlled.

Errors in spelling, capitalization, punctuation, grammar, usage, and sentence boundaries are frequent. The fluency of the writing and effectiveness of the essay are affected by these errors.

The conclusion does not clearly restate the claim.

TOOL KIT: WRITING

MODEL

ARGUMENT: SCORE 2

Celebrities Should Try to Be Better Role Models

Most kids spend tons of time watching celebrities on TV, listening to their songs, and reading about them. No matter how celebrities behave—whether they do good things or bad—they are role models for kids. They often do really dumb things, and that is not good considering they are role models.

Sometimes celebrity's say they wish they were not role models. *"I'm just an actor!"* or, *"I'm just a singer!"* they say. But the choice is not really up to them. If they are on TV all the time, then kids' will look up to them. No matter what. It's really bad when celebrities mess up and then nothing bad happens to them. That gives kids a false lesson because in reality there are bad things when you mess up. That's why celebrities should think more about what they are doing and what lessons they are giving to kids.

Some celebrities might say, *"Why do I care? Why should I be bothered?"* Well, they don't have to. But it's bad on them if they do all kinds of stupid things and don't think about how this affects the kids who look up to them. Plus, they get tons of money, much more even than inventors or scientists or other important people. Being a good role model should be part of what they have to do to get so much money.

When you are famous it is a good idea to support charities. Some celebrities give out cars, or houses, or free scholarships. They even sometimes give away their dresses and people have an auction to see who will pay the most money for them. This can help for example the Humane Society, or whatever charity or cause the celebrity wants to support.

Sometimes it seems like celebrities are more messed up than anyone else. That's in their personal lives. Imagine if people wanted to take pictures of you wherever you went, and you could never get away. That can drive celebrities kind of crazy, and then they act out.

Celebrities can do good things and they can do bad things. They don't realize that when they do bad things, they give teens wrong ideas about how to live. So many teens look up to them and copy them, no matter what. They should make an effort to be better role models.

The introduction does not state the argument claim clearly enough.

Errors in spelling, grammar, and sentence boundaries decrease the effectiveness of the essay.

The word choice in the essay contributes to an informal tone.

The writer does not make use of transitions and sentence connections.

Some of the ideas in the essay do not relate to the stated position or focus on the issue.

The essay has a clear conclusion.

TOOL KIT: WRITING

ARGUMENT: SCORE 3

Celebrities Should Try to Be Better Role Models

Kids look up to the celebrities they see on TV and want to be like them. Parents may not *want* celebrities to be role models for their children, but they are anyway. Therefore, celebrities should think about what they say and do and live lives that are worth copying. Celebrities should think about how they act because they are role models.

"I'm just an actor!" or, *"I'm just a singer!"* celebrities sometimes say. *"Their parents and teachers are the ones who should be the role models!"* But it would be foolish to misjudge the impact that celebrities have on youth. Kids spend hours every day digitally hanging with their favorite stars. Children learn by imitation, so, for better or worse, celebrities are role models. That's why celebrities should start modeling good decision-making and good citizenship.

With all that they are given by society, celebrities owe a lot back to their communities and the world. Celebrities get a lot of attention, time, and money. Often they get all that for doing not very much: acting, singing, or playing a sport. It's true; some of them work very hard. But even if they work very hard, do they deserve to be in the news all the time and earn 100 or even 1000 times more than equally hard-working teachers, scientists, or nurses? I don't think so. After receiving all that, it seems only fair that celebrities take on the important job of being good role models for the young people who look up to them.

Celebrities can serve as good role models is by giving back. Quite a few use their fame and fortune to do just that. They give scholarships, or even build and run schools; they help veterans; they visit hospitals; they support important causes such as conservation, and women's rights. They donate not just money but their time and talents too. This is a great way to be a role model.

Celebrities should recognize that as role models, they have a responsibility to try to make good decisions and be honest. Celebrities should step up so they can be a force for good in people's lives and in the world.

The writer's word choice is good but could be better.

The introduction mostly states the claim.

The ideas relate to the stated position and focus on the issue.

The sentences are varied and well controlled and enhance the effectiveness of the essay.

The progression of ideas is logical, but there could be better transitions and sentence connections to show how ideas are related.

The conclusion mostly follows from the claim.

TOOL KIT: WRITING

WRITING

MODEL

ARGUMENT: SCORE 4

Celebrities Should Try to Be Better Role Models

Like it or not, kids look up to the celebrities they see on TV and want to be like them. Parents may not *want* celebrities to be role models for their children, but the fact is that they are. With such an oversized influence on young people, celebrities have a responsibility to think about what they say and do and to live lives that are worth emulating. In short, they should make an effort to be better role models.

Sometimes celebrities say they don't want to be role models. "I'm just an actor!" or "I'm just a singer!" they protest. "Their parents and teachers are the ones who should be guiding them and showing them the right way to live!" That is all very well, but it would be foolish to underestimate the impact that celebrities have on children. Kids spend hours every day digitally hanging out with their favorite stars. Children learn by imitation, so for better or worse, celebrities act as role models.

Celebrities are given a lot of attention, time, and money. They get all that for doing very little: acting, singing, or playing a sport very well. It's true some of them work very hard. But even if they work hard, do they deserve to be in the news all the time and earn 100 or even 1,000 times more than equally hardworking teachers, scientists, or nurses? I don't think so.

With all that they are given, celebrities owe a lot to their communities and the world. One way they can serve as good role models is by giving back, and quite a few celebrities use their fame and fortune to do just that. They give scholarships or even build and run schools; they help veterans; they entertain kids who are sick; they support important causes such as conservation and women's rights. They donate not just money but their time and talents too.

Celebrities don't have to be perfect. They are people too and make mistakes. But they should recognize that as role models for youth, they have a responsibility to try to make good decisions and be honest about their struggles. Celebrities should step up so they can be a force for good in people's lives.

The writer has chosen words that contribute to the clarity of the essay.

The writer clearly states the claim of the argument in the introduction.

The essay is engaging and varied.

There are no errors to distract the reader from the fluency of the writing and effectiveness of the essay.

The writer uses transitions and sentence connections to show how ideas are related.

The writer clearly restates the claim and the most powerful idea presented in the essay.

Argument Rubric

	Focus and Organization	Evidence and Elaboration	Conventions
4	The introduction is engaging and states the claim in a compelling way. The claim is supported by clear reasons and relevant evidence. Reasons and evidence are logically organized so that the argument is easy to follow. The conclusion clearly restates the claim and the most powerful idea.	Sources are effectively credible and accurate. The argument demonstrates an understanding of the thesis by providing strong examples. The tone of the argument is formal and objective.	The argument intentionally uses standard English conventions of usage and mechanics. The argument effectively uses words, phrases, and clauses to clarify the relationships among claim(s) and reasons.
3	The introduction is mostly engaging and states the claim. The claim is mostly supported by logical reasons and evidence. Reasons and evidence are organized so that the argument is mostly easy to follow. The conclusion mostly restates the claim.	Sources are mostly credible and accurate. The argument mostly demonstrates an understanding of the thesis by providing adequate examples. The tone of the argument is mostly formal and objective.	The argument mostly demonstrates accuracy in standard English conventions of usage and mechanics. The argument mostly uses words, phrases, and clauses to clarify the relationships among claim(s) and reasons.
2	The introduction somewhat states the claim. The claim is supported by some reasons and evidence. Reasons and evidence are organized somewhat logically with a few transitions to orient readers. The conclusion somewhat relates to the claim.	Some sources are relevant. The argument somewhat demonstrates an understanding of the thesis by providing some examples. The tone of the argument is occasionally formal and objective.	The argument demonstrates some accuracy in standard English conventions of usage and mechanics. The argument somewhat uses words, phrases, and clauses to clarify the relationships among claim(s) and reasons.
1	The claim is not clearly stated. The claim is not supported by reasons and evidence. Reasons and evidence are disorganized and the argument is difficult to follow. The conclusion does not include relevant information.	There is little or no reliable, relevant evidence The argument does not demonstrate an understanding of the thesis and does not provide examples. The tone of the argument is informal.	The argument contains mistakes in standard English conventions of usage and mechanics. The argument does not use words, phrases, and clauses to clarify the relationships among claim(s) and reasons.

TOOL KIT: WRITING

Informative/Explanatory Texts

Informative and explanatory writing should rely on facts to inform or explain. Informative writing can serve several purposes: to increase readers' knowledge of a subject, to help readers better understand a procedure or process, or to provide readers with an enhanced comprehension of a concept. It should also feature a clear introduction, body, and conclusion.

Informative/explanatory texts present facts, details, data, and other kinds of evidence to give information about a topic. Readers turn to informative and explanatory texts when they wish to learn about a specific idea, concept, or subject area, or when they want to learn how to do something.

An effective informative/explanatory text contains these elements:

- a topic sentence or thesis statement that introduces the concept or subject
- relevant facts, examples, and details that expand upon a topic
- definitions, quotations, and/or graphics that support the information given
- headings (if desired) to separate sections of the essay
- a structure that presents information in a direct, clear manner
- clear transitions that link sections of the essay
- precise words and technical vocabulary where appropriate
- formal and objective language and tone
- a conclusion that supports the information given and provides fresh insights

INFORMATIVE: SCORE 1

Kids, School, and Exercise: Problems and Solutions

In the past, children ran around and even did hard physical labor. Today most kid's just sit most of the time. They don't know the old Outdoor Games. Like tether ball. and they don't have hard chores to do. Like milking the cows. But children should be Physically Active quite a bit every day. That doesn't happen very much any more. Not as much as it should anyway.

Even at home when kid's have a chance to run around, they choose to sit and play video games, for example. Some schools understand that it's a problem when students don't get enough exercise. Even though they have had to cut Physical Education classes. Some also had to make recess shorter.

But lots of schools are working hard to find ways to get kid's moving around again. Like they used to long ago.

Schools use volunteers to teach kid's old-fashioned games. Old-fashioned games are an awesome way to get kid's moving around like crazy people.

Some schools have before school activities. Such as games in the gym. Other schools have after school activities. Such as bike riding or outdoor games. They can't count on kid's to be active. Not even on their own or at home. So they do the activities all together. Kids enjoy doing stuff with their friends. So that works out really well.

If you don't exercise you get overweight. You can end up with high blood pressure and too much colesterol. Of course its also a problem if you eat too much junk food all the time. But not getting enough exercise is part of the problem too. That's why schools need to try to be part of the solution.

A break during class to move around helps. Good teachers know how to use exercise during classes. There are all kinds of ways to move in the classroom that don't mean you have to change your clothes. Classes don't have to be just about math and science.

Schools are doing what they can to get kids moving, doing exercise, being active. Getting enough exercise also helps kid's do better in school. Being active also helps kids get strong.

There are extensive errors in spelling, capitalization, punctuation, grammar, usage, and sentence boundaries.

Many of the ideas in the essay do not focus on the topic.

The word choice shows the writer's lack of awareness of the essay's purpose and tone.

The essay's sentences are not purposeful, varied, or well controlled. The writer's sentences decrease the effectiveness of the essay.

The essay is not well organized. Its structure does not support its purpose or respond well to the demands of the prompt.

The essay is not particularly thoughtful or engaging.

TOOL KIT: WRITING

WRITING

MODEL

INFORMATIVE: SCORE 2

Kids, School, and Exercise: Problems and Solutions

In the past, children ran around a lot and did chores and other physical work. Today most kid's sit by a TV or computer screen or play with their phones. But children should be active for at least 60 minutes a day. Sadly, most don't get nearly that much exercise. And that's a big problem.

Some schools understand that it's a problem when students don't get enough exercise. Even though they have had to cut Physical Education classes due to budget cuts. Some also had to make recess shorter because there isn't enough time in the schedule. But they are working hard to find creative ways that don't cost too much or take up too much time to get kid's moving. Because there's only so much money in the budget, and only so much time in the day, and preparing to take tests takes lots of time.

Schools can use parent volunteers to teach kid's old-fashioned games such as kick-the-can, hopscotch, foursquare, tetherball, or jump rope. Kid's nowadays often don't know these games! Old-fashioned games are a great way to get kid's moving. Some schools have before school activities, such as games in the gym. Other schools have after school activities, such as bike riding or outdoor games. They can't count on kid's to be active on their own or at home.

A break during class can help students concentrate when they go back to work. There are all kinds of ways to move in the classroom. And you don't have to change your clothes or anything. Wiggling, stretching, and playing a short active game are all good ideas. Good teachers know how to squeeze in time during academic classes like math and language arts.

Not getting enough exercise is linked to many problems. For example, unhealthy wait, and high blood pressure and colesterol. When students don't' get enough exercise, they end up overweight.

Physical activity also helps kid's do better in school. Kids who exercise have better attendance rates. They have increased attention span. They act out less. They have less stress and learn more. Being active also helps muscles and bones. It increases strength and stamina.

Schools today are doing what they can to find a solution by being creative and making time for physical activity before, during, and after school. They understand that it is a problem when kid's don't get enough exercise.

Not all the ideas in the essay focus on the topic.

The writer uses some transitions and sentence connections.

Some of the ideas in the essay are reasonably well developed. Some details and examples add substance to the essay.

Some ideas are well developed. Some examples and details are well chosen and specific and add substance to the essay.

Some details are specific and well chosen.

There are errors in spelling, punctuation, grammar, usage, and sentence boundaries that decrease the effectiveness of the essay.

The essay is not well organized. Its organizing structure does not support its purpose well or respond well to the demands of the prompt.

INFORMATIVE: SCORE 3

Kids, School, and Exercise: Problems and Solutions

A 2008 report said school-age children should be physically active for at least 60 minutes a day. Sadly, most children don't get nearly that much exercise. Lots of schools have cut Physical Education classes because of money and time pressures. And there's less recess than there used to be. Even at home when kids have a chance to run around, many choose screen time instead. No wonder so many of us are turning into chubby couch potatoes!

Not getting exercise is linked to many problems, for example unhealthy weight, and high blood pressure and cholesterol. Studies show physical activity also helps students do better in school: it means better attendance rates, increased attention span, fewer behavioral problems, less stress, and more learning. Being active helps develop strong muscles and bones. It increases strength and stamina.

Many schools around the country get that there are problems when students are inactive. They are working hard to find creative solutions that don't cost too much or take up precious time in the school schedule.

Some schools are using parent volunteers to teach kids active games such as kick-the-can, hopscotch, foursquare, tetherball, or jump rope. These games are more likely to get kids moving than just sitting gossiping with your friends or staring at your phone. Some schools have before school activities such as run-around games in the gym. Other schools have after school activities such as bike riding or outdoor games. They can't count on kids to be active on their own.

There are all kinds of fun and healthy ways to move in the classroom, without changing clothes. An active break during class can help students concentrate when they go back to work. Creative teachers know how to squeeze in active time even during academic classes. Wiggling, stretching, and playing a short active game are all good ideas.

Schools today understand that it is a problem when kids don't get enough exercise. They are doing what they can to find a solution by being creative and making time for physical activity before, during, and after school.

The essay is fairly thoughtful and engaging.

Almost all the ideas focus on the topic.

The ideas in the essay are well developed, with well-chosen and specific details and examples.

The writer uses transitions and connections, such as *"Not getting exercise is linked…"* *"Many schools …"* *"Some schools…"* *"Other schools…"*

Ideas in the essay are mostly well developed.

Words are chosen carefully and contribute to the clarity of the essay.

TOOL KIT: WRITING

WRITING

INFORMATIVE: SCORE 4

Kids, School, and Exercise: Problems and Solutions

In 2008, the U.S. Department of Health and Human Services published a report stating that all school-age children need to be physically active for at least 60 minutes a day. Sadly, most children don't get nearly the recommended amount of exercise. Due to budget cuts and time pressure, many schools have cut Physical Education classes. Even recess is being squeezed to make room for more tests and test preparation.

The writer explains the problem and its causes.

Lack of exercise can lead to many problems, such as unhealthy weight, high blood pressure, and high cholesterol. Physical activity helps develop strong muscles and bones, and it increases strength and stamina. Studies show physical activity leads to better attendance rates, increased attention span, fewer behavioral problems, less stress, and more learning. When kids don't get enough physical activity, a lot is at stake!

The writer clearly lays out the effects of the problem.

Many schools around the country are stepping up to find innovative solutions—even when they don't have time or money to spare. Some have started before-school activities such as active games in the gym. Others have after-school activities such as bike riding or outdoor games. Just a few extra minutes a day can make a big difference!

The writer turns to the solution. The essay's organizing structure supports its purpose and responds to the demands of the prompt.

Some schools try to make the most of recess by using parent volunteers to teach kids active games such as kick-the-can, hopscotch, foursquare, tetherball, or jump rope. Volunteers can also organize races or tournaments—anything to get the kids going! At the end of recess, everyone should be a little bit out of breath.

The writer includes specific examples and well-chosen details.

Creative educators squeeze in active time even during academic classes. It could be a quick "brain break" to stretch in the middle of class, imaginary jump rope, or a game of rock-paper-scissors with legs instead of fingers. There are all kinds of imaginative ways to move in the classroom, without moving furniture or changing clothes. And research shows that an active break during class can help students focus when they go back to work.

The progression of ideas is logical and well controlled.

Details and examples add substance to the essay.

Schools today understand the problems that can arise when kids don't have enough physical activity in their lives. They are meeting the challenge by finding opportunities for exercise before, during, and after school. After all, if students do well on tests but end up unhealthy and unhappy, what is the point?

The essay is thoughtful and engaging.

Informative Rubric

	Focus and Organization	Evidence and Elaboration	Conventions
4	The introduction is engaging and sets forth the topic in a compelling way. The ideas progress logically. A variety of transitions are included to show the relationship among ideas. The conclusion follows from the rest of the essay.	The topic is developed with relevant facts, definitions, details, quotations, and examples. The tone of the essay is formal. The vocabulary is precise and relevant to the topic, audience, and purpose.	The essay uses standard English conventions of usage and mechanics.
3	The introduction is somewhat engaging and sets forth the topic in a way that grabs readers' attention. The ideas progress somewhat logically. Some transitions are included to show the relationship among ideas. The conclusion mostly follows from the rest of the essay.	The topic is developed with some relevant facts, definitions, details, quotations, and other examples. The tone of the essay is mostly formal. The vocabulary is generally appropriate for the topic, audience, and purpose.	The essay demonstrates general accuracy in standard English conventions of usage and mechanics.
2	The introduction sets forth the topic. More than one idea is presented. A few transitions are included that show the relationship among ideas. The conclusion does not completely follow from the rest of the essay.	The topic is developed with a few relevant facts, definitions, details, quotations, or other examples. The tone of the essay is occasionally formal. The vocabulary is somewhat appropriate for the topic, audience, and purpose.	The essay demonstrates some accuracy in standard English conventions of usage and mechanics.
1	The topic is not clearly stated. Ideas do not follow a logical progression. Transitions are not included. The conclusion does not follow from the rest of the essay.	The topic is not developed with reliable or relevant evidence. The tone is informal. The vocabulary is limited or ineffective.	The essay contains mistakes in standard English conventions of usage and mechanics.

TOOL KIT: WRITING

Narrative

Narrative writing conveys an experience, either real or imaginary, and uses time order to provide structure. Usually its purpose is to entertain, but it can also instruct, persuade, or inform. Whenever writers tell a story, they are using narrative writing. Most types of narrative writing share certain elements, such as characters, setting, a sequence of events, and, often, a theme.

Elements of a Narrative Text

A **narrative** is any type of writing that tells a story, whether it is fiction, nonfiction, poetry, or drama.

An effective nonfiction narrative contains these elements:

- an engaging beginning in which characters and setting are established
- characters who participate in the story events
- a well-structured, logical sequence of events
- details that show time and place
- effective story elements such as dialogue, description, and reflection
- a narrator who relates the events from a particular point of view
- use of language that brings the characters and setting to life

An effective fictional narrative usually contains these elements:

- an engaging beginning in which characters, setting, or a main conflict is introduced
- a main character and supporting characters who participate in the story events
- a narrator who relates the events of the plot from a particular point of view
- details that show time and place
- narrative techniques such as dialogue, description, and suspense
- use of language that vividly brings to life characters and events

NARRATIVE: SCORE 1

Mind Scissors

There's a bike race. Right away people start losing. But me and Thad were winning. Thad is the kid who always wins is who is also popular. I don't like Thad. I pumped pumping hard at my pedals, I knew the end was coming. I looked ahead and all I could see was Thad, and the woods.

I pedaled harder and then I was up to Thad. That was swinging at me, I swerved, I kept looking at him, I was worried!

That's stick had untied my shoelace and it was wrapped around my pedal! But I didn't know it yet.

We were out of the woods. I still wanted to win, I pedaled even faster. than my pedals stopped!

I saw with my mind the shoelace was caught in my pedal. No worries, I have the superpower of mind scissors. That's when my mind looked down and I used my mind scissors. I used the mind scissors to cut the shoelace my right foot was free.

That's how I became a superhero. I save people with my mind scissors now.

The story's beginning is not clear or engaging.

The narrative does not include sensory language and precise words to convey experiences and to develop characters.

Events do not progress logically. The ideas seem disconnected, and the sentences do not include transitions.

The narrative contains mistakes in standard English conventions of usage and mechanics.

The conclusion does not connect to the narrative.

TOOL KIT: WRITING

WRITING

NARRATIVE: SCORE 2

Mind-Scissors

When I was a baby I wound up with a tiny pair of scissors in my head. What the doctors couldn't have predicted is the uncanny ability they would give me. This past summer that was when I discovered what I could do with my mind-scissors.

Every summer there's a bike race. The kid who always wins is Thad who is popular.

The race starts. Right away racers start losing. After a long time pumping hard at my pedals, I knew the end was coming. I looked ahead and all I could see was Thad, and the woods.

I pedaled harder than ever. I was up to Thad. I turned my head to look at him. He was swinging a stick at me, I swerved, I kept looking at him, boy was I worried.

We were now out of the woods. Still hopeful I could win, I pedaled even faster. Suddenly, my pedals stopped!

Oh no! Thad's stick had untied my shoelace and it was wrapped around my pedal!

I was going to crash my bike. That's when my mind looked down. That's when I knew I could use my mind-scissors. I used the mind scissors to cut the shoelace my right foot was free.

That's how I won the race.

The story's beginning introduces the main character.

Events in the narrative progress somewhat logically, and the writer use some transition words.

The writer uses some description in the narrative.

The narrative demonstrates some accuracy in standard English conventions of usage and mechanics.

The words vary between vague and precise. The writer uses some sensory language.

The conclusion is weak and adds very little to the narrative.

TOOL KIT: WRITING

Mind-Scissors

When I was a baby I wound up with a tiny pair of scissors in my head. Lots of people live with pieces of metal in their heads. We just have to be careful. What the doctors couldn't have predicted is the uncanny ability they would give me.

Every summer there's a bike race that ends at the lake. The kid who always wins is Thad Thomas the Third, who is popular. This past summer that was about to change. It's also when I discovered what I could do with my mind-scissors.

The race starts. Right away racers start falling behind. After what seemed an eternity pumping hard at my pedals, I knew the end had to be in sight. I looked ahead and all I could see was Thad, and the opening to the woods—the last leg of the race.

I felt like steam was coming off my legs. I could see Thad's helmet. I turned my head to flash him a look. Only, Thad was the one who was gloating! And then I saw it—he was holding a stick he had pulled off a low-hanging branch.

He jabbed it toward me. I swerved out of the way. I kept pedaling, shifting my eyes to the right, to see what he was going to do.

But I waited too long. Then Thad made a slashing motion. Then he tossed the stick aside, yelled, "Yes!" and zoomed forward.

What happened? I felt nothing. We were now out of the woods and into the clearing before the finish line. Still hopeful I could win, I pedaled even faster. Suddenly, there was a jerk. My pedals had stopped!

I looked down. Oh no! My shoelace was wrapped around my pedal! Thad's stick had untied it!

I looked for a place to crash. That's when my head started tingling. I looked down at the shoelace. I concentrated really hard. I could see the scissors in my mind, floating just beside the pedal. Snip! The shoelace broke and my foot was free.

Thad was too busy listening to his fans cheer him on as I rode past him. Thanks to the mind-scissors, I won.

The story's beginning is engaging and clearly introduces the main character and situation.

Events in the narrative progress logically, and the writer uses transition words frequently.

The writer uses precise words and some sensory language to convey the experiences in the narrative and to describe the characters and scenes.

The writer uses some description and dialogue to add interest to the narrative and develop experiences and events.

The narrative demonstrates accuracy in standard English conventions of usage and mechanics.

The conclusion follows from the rest of the narrative.

TOOL KIT: WRITING

WRITING

MODEL

NARRATIVE: SCORE 4

Mind-Scissors

As long as I wear my bike helmet, they say I'll be okay. Lots of people live with pieces of metal in their heads. We just have to be careful. When I was a baby I wound up with a tiny pair of scissors in mine. What the doctors couldn't have predicted is the uncanny ability they would give me.

> The story's beginning is engaging and introduces the main character and situation in a way that appeals to a reader.

Every summer there's a bike race that ends at the lake. The kid who always wins is Thad Thomas the Third, who is popular, but if you ask me, it's because he knows how to sweet-talk everyone. This past summer that was about to change. It's also when I discovered what I could do with my mind-scissors.

> The writer uses techniques such as dialogue and description to add interest to the narrative and to develop the characters and events.

The race starts. Right away, racers start falling behind. After what seemed an eternity pumping hard at my pedals, I knew the end had to be in sight. I looked ahead and all I could see was Thad and the opening to the woods—the last leg of the race.

> Events in the narrative progress in logical order and are linked by clear transitions.

I put my stamina to the test—pedaling harder than ever, I felt like steam was coming off my legs. Thad's red helmet came into view. As I could sense I was going to overtake him any second, I turned my head to flash him a look. Only, to my befuddlement, Thad was the one who was gloating! And then I saw it—he was holding a stick he had pulled off a low-hanging branch.

> Writer uses vivid description and sensory language to convey the experiences in the narrative and to help the reader imagine the characters and scenes.

He jabbed it toward me. I swerved out of the way. Was he trying to poke me with it? I kept pedaling, shifting my eyes to the right, to see what he was going to do.

But I waited too long. Thad made a slashing motion. Then he tossed the stick aside, yelled, "Yes!" and zoomed forward.

> The writer uses standard English conventions of usage and mechanics.

What happened? I felt nothing. We were now out of the woods and into the clearing before the finish line. Still hopeful I could win, I pedaled even faster. Suddenly, there was a jerk. My pedals had stopped!

I looked down. Oh no! My shoelace was wrapped around my pedal! Thad's stick had untied the shoelace!

I coasted as I looked for a place to crash. That's when my head started tingling. I got this funny notion to try something. I looked down. I had the tangled shoelace in my sights. I concentrated really hard. I could see the scissors in my mind, floating just beside the pedal. Snip! The shoelace broke and my right foot was free.

Thad was busy motioning his fans to cheer him on as I made my greatest effort to pedal back up to speed. Guess who made it to the finish line first?

> Writer's conclusion follows from the events in the narrative.

Narrative Rubric

	Focus and Organization	Development of Ideas/Elaboration	Conventions
4	The introduction is engaging and introduces the characters and situation in a way that appeals to readers. Events in the narrative progress in logical order and are linked by clear transitions. The conclusion effectively follows from and reflects on the narrated experiences or events.	The narrative effectively includes techniques such as dialogue and description to add interest and to develop the characters and events. The narrative effectively includes precise words and phrases, relevant descriptive details, and sensory language to convey experiences and events. The narrative effectively establishes voice through word choice, sentence structure, and tone.	The narrative intentionally uses standard English conventions of usage and mechanics. The narrative effectively varies sentence patterns for meaning, reader interest, and style.
3	The introduction is somewhat engaging and clearly introduces the characters and situation. Events in the narrative progress logically and are often linked by transition words. The conclusion mostly follows from and reflects on the narrated experiences or events.	The narrative mostly includes dialogue and description to add interest and develop experiences and events. The narrative mostly includes precise words and sensory language to convey experiences and events. The narrative mostly establishes voice through word choice, sentence structure, and tone.	The narrative mostly demonstrates accuracy in standard English conventions of usage and mechanics. The narrative mostly varies sentence patterns for meaning, reader interest, and style.
2	The introduction occasionally introduces characters. Events in the narrative progress somewhat logically and are sometimes linked by transition words. The conclusion adds very little to the narrated experiences or events.	The narrative includes some dialogue and descriptions. The words in the narrative vary between vague and precise, and some sensory language is included. The narrative occasionally establishes voice through word choice, sentence structure, and tone.	The narrative demonstrates some accuracy in standard English conventions of usage and mechanics. The narrative occasionally varies sentence patterns for meaning, reader interest, and style.
1	The introduction does not introduce characters and an experience or there is no clear introduction. The events in the narrative do not progress logically. The ideas seem disconnected and the sentences are not linked by transitions. The conclusion does not connect to the narrative or there is no conclusion.	Dialogue and descriptions are not included in the narrative. The narrative does not incorporate sensory language or precise words to convey experiences and to develop characters. The narrative does not establish voice through word choice, sentence structure, and tone.	The narrative contains mistakes in standard English conventions of usage and mechanics. The narrative does not vary sentence patterns for meaning, reader interest, and style.

RESEARCH

Conducting Research

You can conduct research to gain more knowledge about a topic. Sources such as articles, books, interviews, or the Internet have the facts and explanations that you need. Not all of the information that you find, however, will be useful—or reliable. Strong research skills will help you find accurate information about your topic.

Narrowing or Broadening a Topic

The first step in any research is finding your topic. Choose a topic that is narrow enough to cover completely. If you can name your topic in just one or two words, it is probably too broad. Topics such as mythology, hip hop music, or Italy are too broad to cover in a single report. Narrow a broad topic into smaller subcategories.

When you begin to research, pay attention to the amount of information available. If there is way too much information on your topic, you may need to narrow your topic further.

You might also need to broaden a topic if there is not enough information for your purpose. A topic is too narrow when it can be thoroughly presented in less space than the required size of your assignment. It might also be too narrow if you can find little or no information in library and media sources. Broaden your topic by including other related ideas.

Generating Research Questions

Use research questions to focus your research. Specific questions can help you avoid wasting time. For example, instead of simply hunting for information about Peter Pan, you might ask, "What inspired J. M. Barrie to write the story of Peter Pan?" or "How have different artists shown Peter Pan?"

A research question may also lead you to find your topic sentence. The question can also help you focus your research plan. Write your question down and keep it in mind while you hunt for facts. Your question can prevent you from gathering unnecessary details. As you learn more about your topic, you can always rewrite your original question.

Consulting Print and Digital Sources

An effective research project combines information from multiple sources. It is important not to rely too heavily on a single source. The creativity and originality of your research depends on how you combine ideas from many places. Plan to include a variety of these resources:

- **Primary and Secondary Sources:** Use both primary sources (firsthand or original accounts, such as interview transcripts and newspaper articles) and secondary sources (accounts that are not created at the time of an event, such as encyclopedia entries).

- **Print and Digital Resources:** The Internet allows fast access to data, but print resources are often edited more carefully. Plan to include both print and digital resources in order to guarantee that your work is accurate.

- **Media Resources:** You can find valuable information in media resources such as documentaries, television programs, podcasts, and museum exhibitions.

- **Original Research:** Depending on your topic, you may wish to conduct original research to include among your sources. For example, you might interview experts or eyewitnesses or conduct a survey of people in your community.

Evaluating Sources It is important to evaluate the credibility and accuracy of any information you find. Ask yourself questions such as these to evaluate other sources:

- **Authority:** Is the author well known? What are the author's credentials? Does the source include references to other reliable sources? Does the author's tone win your confidence? Why or why not?

- **Bias:** Does the author have any obvious biases? What is the author's purpose for writing? Who is the target audience?

- **Currency:** When was the work created? Has it been revised? Is there more current information available?

> ### Using Online Encyclopedias
>
> Online encyclopedias are often written by anonymous contributors who are not required to fact-check information. These sites can be very useful as a launching point for research, but should not be considered accurate. Look for footnotes, endnotes, or hyperlinks that support facts with reliable sources that have been carefully checked by editors.

RESEARCH

Using Search Terms

Finding information on the Internet is easy, but it can be a challenge to find facts that are useful and trustworthy. If you type a word or phrase into a search engine, you will probably get hundreds—or thousands—of results. However, those results are not guaranteed to be relevant or accurate.

These strategies can help you find information from the Internet:

- Create a list of topic keywords before you begin using a search engine. Use a thesaurus to expand your list.
- Enter six to eight keywords.
- Choose unique nouns. Most search engines ignore articles and prepositions. Verbs may lead to sources that are not useful. Use modifiers, such as adjectives, when necessary to specify a category. For example, you might enter "ancient Rome" instead of "Rome."
- Use quotation marks to focus a search. Place a phrase in quotation marks to find pages that include exactly that phrase. Add several phrases in quotation marks to narrow your results.
- Spell carefully. Many search engines correct spelling automatically, but they cannot catch every spelling error.
- Scan search results before you click them. The first result isn't always the most useful. Read the text and notice the domain before make a choice.
- Consult more than one search engine.

Evaluating Internet Domains

Not everything you read on the Internet is true, so you have to evaluate sources carefully. The last three letters of an Internet URL identify the site's domain, which can help you evaluate the information of the site.

- **.gov**—Government sites are sponsored by a branch of the United States federal government and are considered reliable.
- **.edu**—Information from an educational research center or department is likely to be carefully checked, but may include student pages that are not edited or monitored.
- **.org**—Organizations are nonprofit groups and usually maintain a high level of credibility but may still reflect strong biases.
- **.com** and **.net**—Commercial sites exist to make a profit. Information might be biased to show a product or service in a good light.

Taking Notes

Use different strategies to take notes:

- Use index cards to create notecards and source cards. On each source card, record information about each source you use—author, title, publisher, date of publication, and relevant page numbers. On each notecard, record information to use in your writing. Use quotation marks when you copy exact words, and indicate the page number(s) on which the information appears.
- Photocopy articles and copyright pages. Then, highlight relevant information. Remember to include the Web addresses of printouts from online sources.
- Print articles from the Internet or copy them directly into a "notes" folder.

You will use these notes to help you write original text.

Source Card

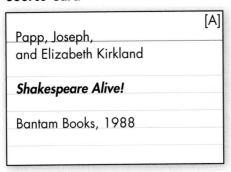

Notecard

Quote Accurately Responsible research begins with the first note you take. Be sure to quote and paraphrase your sources accurately so you can identify these sources later. In your notes, circle all quotations and paraphrases to distinguish them from your own comments. When photocopying from a source, include the copyright information. Include the Web addresses of printouts from online sources.

Reviewing Research Findings

You will need to review your findings to be sure that you have collected enough accurate and appropriate information.

Considering Audience and Purpose

Always keep your audience in mind as you gather information. Different audiences may have very different needs. For example, if you are writing a report for your class about a topic you have studied together, you will not need to provide background information in your writing. However, if you are writing about the topic for a national student magazine, you cannot assume that all of your readers have the same information. You will need to provide background facts from reliable sources to help inform those readers about your subject. When thinking about your research and your audience, ask yourself:

- Who are my readers? For whom am I writing?
- Have I collected enough information to explain my topic to this audience?
- Do I need to conduct more research to explain my topic clearly?
- Are there details in my research that I can leave out because they are already familiar to my audience?

Your purpose for writing will also affect your research review. If you are researching to satisfy your own curiosity, you can stop researching when you feel you understand the answer completely. If you are writing a research report that will be graded, you need to think about your assignment. When thinking about whether or not you have enough information, ask yourself:

- What is my purpose for writing?
- Will the information I have gathered be enough to achieve my purpose?
- If I need more information, where might I find it?

Synthesizing Sources

Effective research writing is more than just a list of facts and details. Good research synthesizes—gathers, orders, and interprets—those elements. These strategies will help you synthesize effectively:

- Review your notes. Look for connections and patterns among the details you have collected.
- Organize notes or notecards to help you plan how you will combine details.
- Pay close attention to details that emphasize the same main idea.
- Also look for details that challenge each other. For many topics, there is no single correct opinion. You might decide to conduct additional research to help you decide which side of the issue has more support.

Types of Evidence

When reviewing your research, also think about the kinds of evidence you have collected. The strongest writing combines a variety of evidence. This chart describes three of the most common types of evidence.

TYPE OF EVIDENCE	DESCRIPTION	EXAMPLE
Statistical evidence includes facts and other numerical data used to support a claim or explain a topic.	Statistical evidence are facts about a topic, such as historical dates, descriptions about size and number, and poll results.	Jane Goodall began to study chimpanzees when she was 26 years old.
Testimonial evidence includes any ideas or opinions presented by others. Testimonies might be from experts or people with special knowledge about a topic.	Firsthand testimonies present ideas from eyewitnesses to events or subjects being discussed.	Goodall's view of chimps has changed: "When I first started at Gombe, I thought the chimps were nicer than we are. But time has revealed that they are not. They can be just as awful."
	Secondary testimonies include commentaries on events by people who were not directly involved.	Science writer David Quammen points out that Goodall "set a new standard, a very high standard, for behavioral study of apes in the wild."
Anecdotal evidence presents one person's view of the world, often by describing specific events or incidents.	An anecdote is a story about something that happened. Personal stories can be part of effective research, but they should not be the only kind of evidence presented. Anecdotes are particularly useful for proving that broad generalizations are not accurate.	It is not fair to say that it is impossible for dogs to use tools. One researcher reports the story of a dog that learned to use a large bone as a back scratcher.

Incorporating Research Into Writing

Avoiding Plagiarism

Whether you are presenting a formal research paper or an opinion paper on a current event, you must be careful to give credit for any ideas or opinions that are not your own. Presenting someone else's ideas, research, or opinion as your own—even if you have phrased it in different words—is *plagiarism*, the equivalent of academic stealing, or fraud.

Do not use the ideas or research of others in place of your own. Read from several sources to draw your own conclusions and form your own opinions. Incorporate the ideas and research of others to support your points. Credit the source of the following types of support:

- Statistics
- Direct quotations
- Indirectly quoted statements of opinions
- Conclusions presented by an expert
- Facts available in only one or two sources

When you are drafting and revising, circle any words or ideas that are not your own. Follow the instructions on pages R32 and R33 to correctly cite those passages.

Reviewing for Plagiarism Take time to review your writing for accidental plagiarism. Read what you have written and take note of any ideas that do not have your personal writing voice. Compare those passages with your resource materials. You might have copied them without remembering the exact source. Add a correct citation to give credit to the original author. If you cannot find the questionable phrase in your notes, think about revising your word choices. You want to be sure that your final writing reflects your own thinking and not someone else's work.

Quoting and Paraphrasing

When including ideas from research into your writing, you will decide to quote directly or paraphrase.

Direct Quotation Use the author's exact words when they are interesting or persuasive. You might decide to include direct quotations in these situations:

- to share a strong statement
- to reference a historically significant passage
- to show that an expert agrees with your position
- to present an argument to which you will respond

Include complete quotations, without deleting or changing words. If you need to leave out words for space or clarity, use ellipsis points to show where you removed words. Enclose direct quotations in quotation marks.

Paraphrase A paraphrase restates an author's ideas in your own words. Be careful to paraphrase accurately. Beware of making sweeping generalizations in a paraphrase that were not made by the original author. You may use some words from the original source, but a good paraphrase does more than simply rearrange an author's phrases, or replace a few words with synonyms.

Original Text	"Some teens doing homework while listening to music and juggling tweets and texts may actually work better that way, according to an intriguing new study performed by two high-school seniors." *Sumathi Reddy, "Teen Researchers Defend Media Multitasking"*
Patchwork Plagiarism phrases from the original are rearranged, but they too closely follow the original text.	An intriguing new study conducted by two high-school seniors suggests that teens work better when they are listening to music and juggling texts and tweets.
Good Paraphrase	Two high-school students studied homework habits. They concluded that some people do better work while multitasking, such as studying and listening to music or checking text messages at the same time.

Maintaining the Flow of Ideas

Effective research writing is much more that just a list of facts. Maintain the flow of ideas by connecting research information to your own ideas. Instead of simply stating a piece of evidence, use transitions to connect information you found from outside resources and your own thinking. The transitions in the box on the page can be used to introduce, compare, contrast, and clarify.

Choosing an effective organizational strategy for your writing will help you create a logical flow of ideas. Once you have chosen a clear organization, add research in appropriate places to provide evidence and support.

Useful Transitions

When providing examples:

for example   for instance   to illustrate   in [name of resource], [author]

When comparing and contrasting ideas or information:

in the same way   similarly   however   on the other hand

When clarifying ideas or opinions:

in other words   that is   to explain   to put it another way

RESEARCH

ORGANIZATIONAL STRUCTURE	USES
Chronological order presents information in the sequence in which it happens.	historical topics; science experiments; analysis of narratives
Part-to-whole order examines how several categories affect a larger subject.	analysis of social issues; historical topics
Order of importance presents information in order of increasing or decreasing importance.	persuasive arguments; supporting a bold or challenging thesis
Comparison-and-contrast organization presents similarities and differences.	addressing two or more subjects

Formats for Citing Sources

When you cite a source, you acknowledge where you found your information and you give your readers the details necessary for locating the source themselves. Within the body of a paper, you provide a short citation, a footnote number linked to a footnote, or an endnote number linked to an endnote reference. These brief references show the page numbers on which you found the information. Prepare a reference list at the end of a research report to provide full bibliographic information on your sources. These are two common types of reference lists:

- A bibliography provides a listing of all the resources you consulted during your research.
- A works-cited list indicates the works your have referenced in your writing.

The chart on the next page shows the Modern Language Association format for crediting sources. This is the most common format for papers written in the content areas in middle school and high school. Unless instructed otherwise by your teacher, use this format for crediting sources.

Focus on Citations When you revise your writing, check that you cite the sources for quotations, factual information, and ideas that are not your own. Most word-processing programs have features that allow you to create footnotes and endnotes.

Identifying Missing Citations These strategies can help you find facts and details that should be cited in your writing:

- Look for facts that are not general knowledge. If a fact was unique to one source, it needs a citation.
- Read your report aloud. Listen for words and phrases that do not sound like your writing style. You might have picked them up from a source. If so, use you notes to find the source, place the words in quotation marks, and give credit.
- Review your notes. Look for ideas that you used in your writing but did not cite.

MLA (8th Edition) Style for Listing Sources

Book with one author	Pyles, Thomas. *The Origins and Development of the English Language.* 2nd ed., Harcourt Brace Jovanovich, 1971. [Indicate the edition or version number when relevant.]
Book with two authors	Pyles, Thomas, and John Algeo. *The Origins and Development of the English Language.* 5th ed., Cengage Learning, 2004.
Book with three or more authors	Donald, Robert B., et al. *Writing Clear Essays.* Prentice Hall, 1983.
Book with an editor	Truth, Sojourner. *Narrative of Sojourner Truth.* Edited by Margaret Washington, Vintage Books, 1993.
Introduction to a work in a published edition	Washington, Margaret. Introduction. *Narrative of Sojourner Truth,* by Sojourner Truth, edited by Washington, Vintage Books, 1993, pp. v–xi.
Single work in an anthology	Hawthorne, Nathaniel. "Young Goodman Brown." *Literature: An Introduction to Reading and Writing,* edited by Edgar V. Roberts and Henry E. Jacobs, 5th ed., Prentice Hall, 1998, pp. 376–385. [Indicate pages for the entire selection.]
Signed article from an encyclopedia	Askeland, Donald R. "Welding." *World Book Encyclopedia,* vol. 21, World Book, 1991, p. 58.
Signed article in a weekly magazine	Wallace, Charles. "A Vodacious Deal." *Time,* 14 Feb. 2000, p. 63.
Signed article in a monthly magazine	Gustaitis, Joseph. "The Sticky History of Chewing Gum." *American History,* Oct. 1998, pp. 30–38.
Newspaper article	Thurow, Roger. "South Africans Who Fought for Sanctions Now Scrap for Investors." *Wall Street Journal,* 11 Feb. 2000, pp. A1+. [For a multipage article that does not appear on consecutive pages, write only the first page number on which it appears, followed by the plus sign.]
Unsigned editorial or story	"Selective Silence." Editorial. *Wall Street Journal,* 11 Feb. 2000, p. A14. [If the editorial or story is signed, begin with the author's name.]
Signed pamphlet or brochure	[Treat the pamphlet as though it were a book.]
Work from a library subscription service	Ertman, Earl L. "Nefertiti's Eyes." *Archaeology,* Mar.–Apr. 2008, pp. 28–32. *Kids Search,* EBSCO, New York Public Library. Accessed 7 Jan. 2017. [Indicating the date you accessed the information is optional but recommended.]
Filmstrips, slide programs, videocassettes, DVDs, and other audiovisual media	*The Diary of Anne Frank.* 1959. Directed by George Stevens, performances by Millie Perkins, Shelley Winters, Joseph Schildkraut, Lou Jacobi, and Richard Beymer, Twentieth Century Fox, 2004. [Indicating the original release date after the title is optional but recommended.]
CD-ROM (with multiple publishers)	Simms, James, editor. *Romeo and Juliet.* By William Shakespeare, Attica Cybernetics / BBC Education / Harper, 1995.
Radio or television program transcript	"Washington's Crossing of the Delaware." *Weekend Edition Sunday,* National Public Radio, 23 Dec. 2013. Transcript.
Web page	"Fun Facts About Gum." ICGA, 2005–2017, www.gumassociation.org/index.cfm/facts-figures/fun-facts-about-gum. Accessed 19 Feb. 2017. [Indicating the date you accessed the information is optional but recommended.]
Personal interview	Smith, Jane. Personal interview, 10 Feb. 2017.

All examples follow the style given in the MLA Handbook, 8th edition, published in 2016.

MODEL

Evidence Log

Unit Title: Discovery

Perfomance-Based Assessment Prompt:
Do all discoveries benefit humanity?

My initial thoughts:
Yes - all knowledge moves us forward.

As you read multiple texts about a topic, your thinking may change. Use an Evidence Log like this one to record your thoughts, to track details you might use in later writing or discussion, and to make further connections.

Here is a sample to show how one reader's ideas deepened as she read two texts.

Title of Text: Classifying the Stars   Date: Sept. 17

CONNECTION TO THE PROMPT	TEXT EVIDENCE/DETAILS	ADDITIONAL NOTES/IDEAS
Newton shared his discoveries and then other scientists built on his discoveries.	Paragraph 2: "Isaac Newton gave to the world the results of his experiments on passing sunlight through a prism." Paragraph 3: "In 1814 . . . the German optician, Fraunhofer . . . saw that the multiple spectral tints . . . were crossed by hundreds of fine dark lines."	It's not always clear how a discovery might benefit humanity in the future.

How does this text change or add to my thinking? This confirms what I think.   Date: Sept. 20

Title of Text: Cell Phone Mania   Date: Sept. 21

CONNECTION TO THE PROMPT	TEXT EVIDENCE/DETAILS	ADDITIONAL NOTES/IDEAS
Cell phones have made some forms of communication easier, but people don't talk to each other as much as they did in the past.	Paragraph 7: "Over 80% of young adults state that texting is their primary method of communicating with friends. This contrasts with older adults who state that they prefer a phone call."	Is it good that we don't talk to each other as much? Look for article about social media to learn more about this question.

How does this text change or add to my thinking?   Date: Sept. 25
Maybe there are some downsides to discoveries. I still think that knowledge moves us forward, but sometimes there are negative effects.

Word Network

A word network is a collection of words related to a topic. As you read the selections in a unit, identify interesting theme-related words and build your vocabulary by adding them to your Word Network.

Use your Word Network as a resource for your discussions and writings. Here is an example:

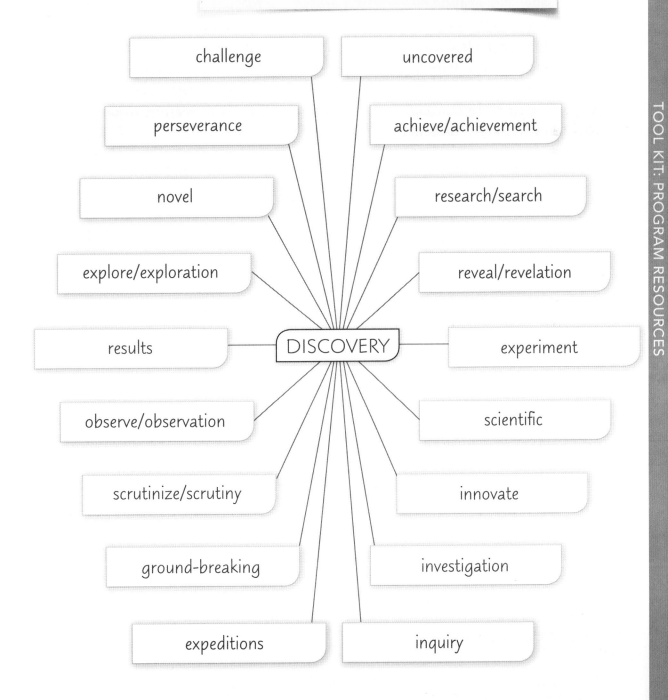

ACADEMIC / CONCEPT VOCABULARY

Academic vocabulary appears in **blue type**.

Pronunciation Key

Symbol	Sample Words	Symbol	Sample Words
a	_at, catapult, Alabama_	oo	_boot, soup, crucial_
ah	_father, charms, argue_	ow	_now, stout, flounder_
ai	_care, various, hair_	oy	_boy, toil, oyster_
aw	_law, maraud, caution_	s	_say, nice, press_
awr	_pour, organism, forewarn_	sh	_she, abolition, motion_
ay	_ape, sails, implication_	u	_full, put, book_
ee	_even, teeth, really_	uh	_ago, focus, contemplation_
eh	_ten, repel, elephant_	ur	_bird, urgent, perforation_
ehr	_merry, verify, terribly_	y	_by, delight, identify_
ih	_it, pin, hymn_	yoo	_music, confuse, few_
o	_shot, hopscotch, condo_	zh	_pleasure, treasure, vision_
oh	_own, parole, rowboat_		

A

accomplish (uh KOM plihsh) _v._ carry out; finish or complete

achieve (uh CHEEV) _v._ succeed in doing something you want to do

aesthetic (ehs THEHT ihk) _adj._ sensitive to art and beauty

annotated (AN uh tayt ihd) _adj._ containing explanatory notes

anxiously (ANGK shuhs lee) _adv._ in a nervous or worried way

apprehension (ap rih HEHN shuhn) _n._ fearful feeling about what will happen next

art (ahrt) _v._ archaic form of the verb _be,_ used with _thou_

assimilate (uh SIHM uh layt) _v._ absorb, as a culture or ideas; make part of oneself

attribute (uh TRIHB yoot) _v._ indicate the cause of; give the origin of

audio (AW dee oh) _adj._ relating to the sound of a film

awakenings (uh WAY kuhn ihngz) _n._ acts of waking up from sleep

B

beaming (BEEM ihng) _v._ smiling broadly with happiness

bickering (BIHK uhr ihng) _n._ arguing over unimportant things

C

candid (KAN dihd) _adj._ very honest; informal; unposed

cautiously (KAW shuhs lee) _adv._ carefully, to avoid danger

chronological (kron uh LOJ uh kuhl) _adj._ arranged in a sequence that follows the time order of events

clarity (KLAR uh tee) _n._ state of thinking clearly

close-up (KLOHS uhp) _n._ camera shot taken from a short distance

confidently (KON fuh duhnt lee) _adv._ with the belief that one will succeed

contradict (kon truh DIHKT) _v._ say the opposite of what has been said; disagree

contraption (kuhn TRAP shuhn) _n._ machine that seems strange or unnecessarily complicated

contrast (KON trast) _n._ amount of difference between bright and dark elements in filming and viewing

controversy (KON truh vuhr see) _n._ quarrel or dispute

current (KUR uhnt) _n._ flow of electricity

D

decipher (dih SY fuhr) _v._ succeed in interpreting or understanding something

declaration (dehk luh RAY shuhn) _n._ announcement; formal statement

deficiencies (dih FIHSH uhn seez) *n.* lackings; missing essentials

despised (dih SPYZD) *v.* hated; scorned

deterioration (dih tihr ee uh RAY shuhn) *n.* process of becoming worse

determination (dih tuhr muh NAY shuhn) *n.* quality of pursuing a goal even when it is difficult

dictate (DIHK tayt) *v.* give orders to control or influence something

dismay (dihs MAY) *n.* strong feeling of disappointment

dissent (dih SEHNT) *n.* difference in belief or opinion; disagreement

documentation (dok yuh muhn TAY shuhn) *n.* printed information; proof

E

enable (ehn AY buhl) *v.* make possible

encapsulation (ehn kap suh LAY shuhn) *n.* choice of which scenes to capture, or display, in panels

engineer (ehn jih NEER) *n.* person with scientific training who designs and builds machines, products, or systems

enumerate (ih NOO muh rayt) *v.* specify, as in a list; count

exemption (ehg ZEHMP shuhn) *n.* permission not to do or pay for something that others are required to do or pay

F

fair (fair) *adj.* beautiful; lovely

fatigue (fuh TEEG) *n.* physical or mental exhaustion

focus (FOH kuhs) *v.* aim the camera so that it creates a distinct image

forbidden (fuhr BIHD uhn) *v.* not permitted

foreboding (fawr BOH dihng) *n.* sudden feeling that something bad is going to happen

foresight (FAWR syt) *n.* knowledge or insight gained by looking toward the future

frail (frayl) *adj.* delicate; weak

G

generators (JEHN uh ray tuhrz) *n.* machines that produce electricity

gratifying (GRAT uh fy ihng) *adj.* satisfying; pleasing

H

horizon (huh RY zuhn) *n.* the distant line where the sky appears to meet the surface of the earth

humiliation (hyoo mihl ee AY shuhn) *n.* feeling of shame or embarassment

hysterically (hihs TEHR ihk lee) *adv.* in a way that shows uncontrolled emotion

I

icons (Y konz) *n.* symbols or graphic representations, often used in charts and on digital screens

immense (ih MEHNS) *adj.* very large; huge

implemented (IHM pluh mehnt ihd) *adj.* carried out; put into effect

impose ((ihm POHZ) *v.* force a law, idea, or belief on someone by using authority

improvisations (ihm pruh vy ZAY shuhnz) *n.* things that are created without any preparation

infographic (ihn foh GRAF ihk) *n.* image used to present information, data, or knowledge quickly and clearly

ingenuity (ihn juh NOO uh tee) *n.* quality of being original and clever

insistent (ihn SIHS tuhnt) *adj.* demanding that something should happen

inspire (ihn SPYR) *v.* stimulate to some creative or effective effort

integrate (IHN tuh grayt) *v.* bring together different parts

intentions (ihn TEHN shuhnz) *n.* purposes for or goals of one's actions

intervene (ihn tuhr VEEN) *v.* interfere with; take action to try to stop a dispute or conflict

introspective (ihn truh SPEHK tihv) *adj.* thoughtful; inward-looking

intuition (ihn too IHSH uhn) *n.* ability to see the truth of something immediately without reasoning

invincible (ihn VIHN suh buhl) *adj.* impossible to defeat

J

justifiable (juhs tuh FY uh buhl) *adj.* able to be defended as correct; reasonable and logical

L

labels and captions (LAY buhlz) (KAP shuhnz) n. short descriptive words or phrases that provide information

legitimate (luh JIHT uh miht) *adj.* allowed; legal; valid

M

majestic (muh JEHS tihk) *adj.* very grand; dignified; king-like

mandates (MAN dayts) *n.* orders or commands

misrepresentations (mihs rehp rih zehn TAY shuhnz) *n.* false statements

misunderstandings (mihs uhn duhr STAND ihngz) *n.* failures in coming to agreements; minor disputes

mounting (MOWN tihng) *adj.* increasing gradually; building up

myopic (my OP ihk) *adj.* nearsighted; unable to see clearly; showing a lack of understanding

N

naiveté (nah eev TAY) *n.* quality of innocent simplicity

narration (na RAY shuhn) *n.* commentary that accompanies a film

nervously (NUR vuhs lee) *adv.* in a manner that shows worry or fear

newfangled (NOO fang uhld) *adj.* invented only recently and, therefore, strange-seeming

notable (NOH tuh buhl) *adj.* worth noticing; important

numerous (NOO muhr uhs) *adj.* very many; existing in large numbers

O

obligations (ob lih GAY shuhnz) *n.* debts to someone due to past promises or favors

observation (ob suhr VAY shuhn) *n.* act of watching carefully to obtain information

opponent (uh POH nuhnt) *n.* person on the other side in a game, debate, argument, etc.

outcry (OWT kry) *n.* strong expression of anger in reaction to an event

P

pan (pan) *n.* vertical or horizontal camera motion used to follow a subject

panel (PAN uhl) *n.* individual frame of a graphic novel depicting a single moment

parallel (PAR uh lehl) *adj.* similar and happening at the same time

patronized (PAY truh nyzd) *v.* treated someone as inferior

peak (peek) *n.* highest level

performance (puhr FAWR muhns) *n.* entertainment presented before an audience, such as music or a drama

persecuted (PUR suh kyoo tihd) *v.* treated unfairly and cruelly

persistent (puhr SIHS tuhnt) *adj.* continuing; lasting, especially in the face of difficulty

personal account (PUR suh nuhl) (uh KOWNT) *n.* account of a personal experience, told from the first-person point of view

position (puh ZIH shuhn) *n.* point of view or stand taken on an issue

prescient (PREHSH uhnt) *adj.* having knowledge of things before they happen

principle (PRIHN suh puhl) *n.* moral rule or set of ideas about right or wrong that influences individuals to behave in a certain way

pronounce (pruh NOWNS) *v.* say a word in the correct way; officially announce

psychological (sy kuh LOJ ih kuhl) *adj.* of the mind; mental

purposeful (PUR puhs fuhl) *adj.* having a clear aim or goal

pursue (puhr SOO) *v.* continue doing an activity over a period of time

Q

quarrels (KWAWR uhlz) *n.* arguments; disagreements

R

rational (RASH uh nuhl) *adj.* able to make decisions based on reason rather than emotion; sensible

rectify (REHK tuh fy) *v.* correct; set right

regression (rih GREHSH uhn) *n.* return to a previous, less advanced state

restraining (rih STRAY nihng) *v.* holding back; controlling one's emotions

restrictions (rih STRIHK shuhnz) *n.* limitations; rules that limit activities

retort (rih TAWRT) *n.* witty, sharp reply

revolutionized (rehv uh LOO shuh nyzd) *v.* drastically changed; improved

rigid (RIHJ ihd) *adj.* stiff and unbending

S

sacrifices (SAK ruh fys ihz) *n.* acts of giving up needs or desires for a purpose

seminal (SEHM uh nuhl) *adj.* being the first of something that is later recognized as important

sheepishly (SHEEP ihsh lee) *adv.* in an embarrassed way

speculate (SPEHK yuh layt) *v.* make a guess about something unknown

speech balloon (speech) *(buh* LOON) *n.* display of what a character is speaking or thinking

spiral (SPY ruhl) *n.* winding circle around a central point

status quo (STAT uhs kwoh) *n.* existing state or condition at a particular time

straggled (STRAG uhld) *v.* hung in messy strands

subconscious (suhb KON shuhs) *n.* mental activity that occurs without someone's being aware of it

suspicion (suh SPIHSH uhn) *n.* feeling of doubt or mistrust

sustain (suh STAYN) *v.* maintain or keep up

sychronization, sync (sihng kruh nih ZAY shuhn) (sihngk) *n.* coordination of motion and sound

symmetrical (sih MEH trih kuhl) *adj.* having the same form on both sides of a dividing line

T

tackling (TAK lihng) *v.* dealing with or handling a problem or situation

tendency (TEHN duhn see) *n.* inclination; way of behaving that is likely or becoming common

tension (TEHN shuhn) *n.* nervous, worried, or excited condition that makes relaxation impossible

theorize (THEE uh ryz) *v.* form an explanation based on observation and reasoning; speculate

traumatized (TRAW muh tyzd) *adj.* severely hurt; suffering serious emotional injury

tress (trehs) *n.* a woman's or girl's hair

triumph (TRY uhmf) *n.* victory; success

U

unleashed (uhn LEESHT) *v.* released; set loose on the world

urgently (UR juhnt lee) *adv.* in a manner that requires immediate attention

V

verify (VEHR uh fy) *v.* prove to be true

video clip (VIHD ee oh) (klihp) *n.* short video, often part of a larger recording, that can be used on a website

volume and pacing (VOL yoom) (PAYS ihng) n. softness or loudness of one's voice and the rate at which one speaks

W

wearily (WEER uh lee) *adv.* in a tired way

Z

zoom (zoom) *v.* enlarge, magnify, or close in on an image

VOCABULARIO ACADÉMICO/ VOCABULARIO DE CONCEPTOS

El vocabulario académico está en **letra azul**.

A

accomplish / lograr *v.* alcanzar una meta; terminar

achieve / lograr *v.* tener éxito en algo que se quiere hacer

aesthetic / estético *adj.* sensible al arte y la belleza

annotated / comentado *adj.* marcado con notas explicativas

anxiously / ansiosamente *adv.* de manera nerviosa o con preocupación

apprehension / aprensión *s.* sentimiento de temor hacia lo que va a suceder

art / sois *v.* forma arcaica del verbo *ser*, usado con *vos*

assimilate / asimilar *v.* absorber una cultura o ideas

attribute / atribuir *v.* indicar la causa de; dar el origin de

audio / sonoro *adj.* relativo al sonido de una película

awakenings / despertares *s.* actos de despertarse

B

beaming / sonriente *adj.* que sonríe con alegría

bickering / reñir *v.* discutir por cosas sin importancia

C

candid / franco *adj.* muy honesto; informal, sin pretensiones

cautiously / cautelosamente *adv.* cuidadosamente, para evitar el peligro

chronological / cronológico *adj.* clasificado en una secuencia que sigue el orden en que ocurrieron eventos

clarity / claridad *s.* estado en el que se piensa claramente

close-up / primer plano *s.* toma de cámara a corta distancia

confidently / confiadamente *adv.* con la certeza de que se tendrá éxito

contradict / contradecir *v.* decir lo opuesto a lo que se ha dicho; discrepar

contraption / artilugio *s.* máquina que parece extraña o innecesariamente complicada

contrast / constraste *s.* cantidad de diferencia entre los elementos brillantes y oscuros de una película

controversy / controversia *s.* desacuerdo o disputa

current / corriente *s.* flujo de electricidad

D

decipher / descifrar *v.* interpretar o comprender algo desconocido

declaration / declaración *s.* anuncio; revelación formal

deficiencies / deficiencias *s.* insuficiencias; falta de lo esencial

despised / detestó *v.* odió; aborreció

deterioration / deterioro *s.* proceso de empeorar

determination / determinación *s.* cualidad de perseguir una meta aun cuando sea difícil

dictate / dictar *v.* dar órdenes para controlar o influir sobre algo

dismay / desaliento *s.* consternación o pena

documentation / documentación *s.* información impresa; prueba

E

enable / posibilitar *v.* permitir; hacer posible

encapsulation / encapsulación *s.* elección de escenas importantes para capturar, o mostrar, en paneles

engineer / ingeniero *s.* persona con entrenamiento científico que diseña y construye máquinas, productos o sistemas

enumerate / enumerar *v.* especificar en forma de lista; contar

exemption / exención *s.* permiso de no hacer o pagar por algo que los demás deben hacer o pagar

F

fair / hermoso *adj.* precioso; bonito

fatigue / fatiga *s.* agotamiento físico o mental

focus / enfocar *v.* apuntar la cámara para que forme una imagen nítida

forbidden / prohibido *v.* no permitido

foreboding / presagio *s.* ansiedad repentina de que va a suceder algo malo

foresight / previsión *s.* visiónfuturo; consideración o provisión para el futuro

frail / frágil *adj.* delicado; débil

G

generators / generadores *s.* máquinas que producen electricidad

gratifying / gratificante *v.* que satisface o complace

H

horizon / horizonte *s.* la línea distante donde el cielo parece unirse a la superficie terrestre

humiliation / humillación *s.* sentimiento de vergüenza o turbación

hysterically / histéricamente *adv.* de forma que muestra emociones descontroladas

I

icons / íconos *s.* símbolos o representaciones gráficas que se usan con frecuencia en tablas y en pantallas digitales

immense / inmenso *adj.* muy grande; enorme

implemented / implementó *v.* llevó a cabo; realizó

impose / imponer *v.* obligar a otros a seguir una ley o idea por fuerza de autoridad

improvisations / improvisaciones *s.* cosas que se crean sin ninguna preparación

infographic / infografía *s.* imagen que se usa para presentar información y conocimientos de manera rápida y sencilla

ingenuity / ingenio *s.* calidad de ser original y listo

insistent / insistente *adj.* que exige que algo ocurra

inspire / inspirar *v.* estimular para lograr algún esfuerzo creativo o efectivo

integrate / integrar *v.* abolir la segregación; unir diferentes partes

intentions / intenciones *s.* propósitos o metas de las acciones de alguien

intervene / intervenir *v.* interferir con; tomar acción para tratar de detener una disputa o conflicto

introspective / introspectivo *adj.* reflexivo; introvertido

intuition / intuición *s.* capacidad de ver la verdad de algo inmediatamente, sin razonarlo

invincible / invencible *adj.* imposible de vencer

J

justifiable / justificable *adj.* capaz de ser defendido como correcto, razonable y lógico

L

labels and captions / rótulos y leyendas *s.* frases cortas y descriptivas que proveen información

legitimate / legítimo *adj.* permitido; legal; válido

M

majestic / majestuoso *adj.* muy grande; digno; de reyes

mandates / mandatos *s.* órdenes

misrepresentations / distorsiones *s.* declaraciones falsas

misunderstandings / malentendidos *s.* fracasos al intentar llegar a un acuerdo; disputas menores

mounting / creciente *adj.* que incrementa gradualmente; que se acumula

myopic / miope *adj.* que no puede ver bien de lejos; que ve sin claridad; falto de comprensión

N

naiveté / ingenuidad *s.* cualidad de la simplicidad inocente

narration / narración *s.* comentario que acompaña a una película

nervously / nerviosamente *adv.* mostrando preocupación o temor

newfangled / moderno *adj.* recién inventado y, a consecuencia, de aspecto extraño

notable / destacado *adj.* que merece atención; importante

numerous / numeroso *adj.* muchos; que existe en gran cantidad

O

obligations / obligaciones *s.* deudas que se le deben a alguien por promesas o favores pasados

observation / observación *s.* acto de mirar con atención para obtener información

opponent / oponente *s.* persona del otro lado del juego, debate, argumento, etc.

oughts / deberes *s.* obligaciones; compromisos

outcry / clamor *s.* expresión fuerte de protesta en contra de un evento

P

pan / paneo *s.* movimiento horizontal o vertical de la cámara

panel / viñeta *s.* cada uno de los recuadros de una novela gráfica en el que se representa una escena

parallel / paralelo *adj.* similar y que sucede al mismo tiempo

patronized / condescendió *v.* trató a alguien como inferior

peak / pico *s.* nivel más alto

penned / enjauló *v.* encerró a alguien como a un animal; encarceló

performance / representación *s.* entretenimiento musical, dramático o de otro tipo que se presenta ante un público

persecuted / acosó *v.* trató con injusticia y crueldad

persistent / persistente *adj.* duradero; que perdura, especialmente ante las dificultades

personal account / relato personal *s.* relato de una experiencia personal contado desde el punto de vista de primera persona

position / posición *s.* punto de vista tomado respecto de algo

prescient / profético *adj.* teniendo conocimiento de las cosas antes de que pasen

principle / principio *s.* regla moral o conjunto de ideas que influye sobre el comportamiento de individuos

pronounce / pronunciar *v.* decir una palabra de forma correcta; anunciar oficialmente

psychological / psicológico *adj.* de la mente; mental

purposeful / significante *adj.* que tiene una meta u objetivo claro

pursue / perseguir *v.* continuar una acción por un período de tiempo

Q

quarrels / peleas *s.* discusiones; desacuerdos

R

rational / racional *adj.* capaz de tomar decisiones basado en la razón; sensato

rectify / rectificar *v.* corregir; reparar

regression / regresión *s.* retroceso a un estado anterior menos avanzado

restraining / restringiendo *v.* reteniendo; controlando las emociones

restrictions / restricciones *s.* limitaciones; reglas que limitan las actividades

retort / réplica *s.* respuesta ingeniosa y brusca

revolutionized / revolucionó *v.* que cambió de forma drástica; mejoró

rigid / rígido *adj.* tieso e inflexible

S

sacrifices / sacrificios *s.* actos de abandonar las necesidades o deseos para lograr un propósito

seminal / trascendental *adj.* que es el primero o el más antiguo de algo

sheepishly / avergonzadamente *adv.* de manera vergonzosa

speculate / especular *v.* adivinar sobre lo desconocido

speech balloon / globo de diálogo *s.* espacio donde se contienen las palabras o pensamientos de un personaje

spiral / espiral *s.* círculos alrededor de un punto central

status quo / statu quo *s.* estado o condición de las cosas en un momento dado

straggled / desaliñó *v.* colocó de forma desaliñada o desordenada

subconscious / subconsciente *s.* actividad mental que ocurre sin que la persona la perciba

suspicion / sospecha *s.* sentimiento de duda; falta de confianza

sustain / sostener *v.* mantener o seguir el ritmo

sychronization, sync / sincronización *s.* coordinación de movimiento y sonido

symmetrical / simétrico *adj.* que tiene la misma forma a ambos lados de la recta que lo divide

T

tackling / afrontando *v.* lidiando con un problema o situación

tendency / tendencia *s.* inclinación; comportamiento probable o que se vuelve común

tensión / tensión *s.* estado de nerviosismo, preocupación o emoción que hace imposible la relajación

theorize / teorizar *v.* formar una explicación con base en la observación y razonamiento; especular

traumatized / traumatizado *adj.* herido o golpeado emocionalmente; gravemente afectado

tress / mechón *s.* cabello de una niña o mujer

triumph / triunfo *s.* victoria; éxito

U

unleashed / desató *v.* soltó; dio rienda suelta a

urgently / urgentemente *adv.* que requiere de atención inmediata

V

verify / verificar *v.* demostrar que es cierto

video clip / videoclip *s.* video corto, que suele ser parte de una grabación de mayor extensión, y que se puede usar en sitios web

volume and pacing / volumen y velocidad *s.* nivel de la voz y rapidez con que se habla

W

wearily / cansino *adv.* con aire cansado

Z

zoom / hacer zoom *v.* agrandar, magnificar o aumentar una imagen

LITERARY TERMS HANDBOOK

ALLITERATION *Alliteration* is the repetition of initial consonant sounds. Writers use alliteration to draw attention to certain words or ideas, to imitate sounds, and to create musical effects.

ALLUSION An *allusion* is a reference to a well-known person, event, place, literary work, or work of art. Allusions connect literary works to a larger cultural heritage. They allow the writer to express complex ideas without spelling them out. Understanding what a literary work is saying often depends on recognizing its allusions and the meanings they suggest.

ANALOGY An *analogy* makes a comparison between two or more things that are similar in some ways but otherwise unalike.

ANECDOTE An *anecdote* is a brief story about an interesting, amusing, or strange event. Writers tell anecdotes to entertain or to make a point.

ARGUMENT An *argument* is a logical way of presenting a belief, conclusion, or stance. A good argument must include at least one *claim* and be supported with reasoning and *evidence* that is *relevant*, or related, to the subject. If an author's beliefs and feelings are too prominent, the argument is less convincing and may seem *biased* or one-sided.

AUTHOR'S INFLUENCES An *author's influences* include his or her heritage, culture, and personal beliefs.

AUTHOR'S POINT OF VIEW The attitudes and approach that an author takes to a piece of informational writing shows the *author's point of view*, or the *author's perspective*.

AUTHOR'S PURPOSE An *author's purpose* is his or her main reason for writing. For example, an author may want to entertain, inform, or persuade the reader. Sometimes an author is trying to teach a moral lesson or reflect on an experience. An author may have more than one purpose for writing.

AUTHOR'S STYLE *Style* is an author's typical way of writing. Many factors determine a writer's style, including diction; tone; use of characteristic elements such as figurative language, dialect, rhyme, meter, or rhythmic devices; typical grammatical structures and patterns, typical sentence length, and typical methods of organization. Style comprises every feature of a writer's use of language.

AUTOBIOGRAPHY An *autobiography* is the story of the writer's own life, told by the writer. Autobiographical writing may tell about the person's whole life or only a part of it.

Because autobiographies are about real people and events, they are a form of nonfiction. Most autobiographies are written in the first person.

BIOGRAPHY A *biography* is a form of nonfiction in which a writer tells the life story of another person. Most biographies are written about famous or admirable people. Although biographies are nonfiction, the most effective ones share the qualities of good narrative writing.

BLURB A *blurb* is a short description of a piece of literature, often found on the back cover of a book.

CAUSE-AND-EFFECT ESSAY A *cause-and-effect essay* examines the relationship between events. Effective essays contain clearly stated thesis statements, with examples, evidence, and logic to support them.

CHARACTER A *character* is a person or an animal that takes part in the action of a literary work. The main, or *major*, character is the most important character in a story, poem, or play. A *minor* character is one who takes part in the action but is not the focus of attention.

Characters are sometimes classified as flat or round. A *flat character* is one-sided and often stereotypical. A *round character*, on the other hand, is fully developed and exhibits many traits—often both faults and virtues. Characters can also be classified as dynamic or static. A *dynamic character* is one who changes or grows during the course of the work. A *static character* is one who does not change.

CHARACTERIZATION *Characterization* is the act of creating and developing a character. Authors use two major methods of characterization—*direct* and *indirect.* When using *direct* characterization, a writer states the *character's traits*, or characteristics.

When describing a character *indirectly,* a writer depends on the reader to draw conclusions about the character's traits. Sometimes the writer tells what other participants in the story say and think about the character.

CHRONOLOGICAL ORDER Writers often sequence events in narratives using *chronological order*, so that one event proceeds to the next in the order in which they actually happened.

CHARACTER TRAITS *Character traits* are the qualities, attitudes, and values that a character has or displays—such as dependability, intelligence, selfishness, or stubbornness.

CLAIM A *claim* is a reasonable conclusion based on evidence. A *counterclaim* is an opposing position to a claim. Strong, specific, *narrow claims* are usually more effective than *broad claims* because they are easier to support with evidence.

CLIMAX The *climax,* also called the turning point, is the high point in the action of the plot. It is the moment of greatest tension, when the outcome of the plot hangs in the balance.

COMPARE-AND-CONTRAST ESSAY An essay in which an author lays out the differences and similarities between two subjects is called a *compare-and-contrast essay.*

Compare-and-contrast essays can be organized using *point-by-point organization,* in which one aspect of both subjects is discussed, and then another aspect, and so on. *Block-method* organization presents all the details of one subject, and then all details about the next subject.

CONFLICT A *conflict* is a struggle between opposing forces. Conflict is one of the most important elements of stories, novels, and plays because it causes the action. There are two kinds of conflict: external and internal. An *external conflict* is one in which a character struggles against some outside force, such as another person. Another kind of external conflict may occur between a character and some force in nature.

An *internal conflict* takes place within the mind of a character. The character struggles to make a decision, take an action, or overcome a feeling.

CONNECTIONS Transition words show *clear connections* among claims, reasons, and evidence. *Unclear connections* can confuse and weaken arguments.

CONNOTATIONS The *connotation* of a word is the set of ideas associated with it in addition to its explicit meaning. The connotation of a word can be personal, based on individual experiences. More often, cultural connotations—those recognizable by most people in a group—determine a writer's word choices.

DENOTATION The *denotation* of a word is its *dictionary* meaning, independent of other associations that the word may have. The denotation of the word *lake,* for example, is "an inland body of water." "Vacation spot" and "place where the fishing is good" are connotations of the word *lake.*

DESCRIPTION A *description* is a portrait, in words, of a person, place, or object. Descriptive writing uses images that appeal to the five senses—sight, hearing, touch, taste, and smell.

DIALOGUE A *dialogue* is a conversation between characters. In poems, novels, and short stories, dialogue is usually set off by quotation marks to indicate a speaker's exact words.

In a play, dialogue follows the names of the characters, and no quotation marks are used.

DIARY A *diary* is a type of autobiographical writing. Entries to a diary or journal are made periodically over time.

DICTION *Diction* is a writer's or speaker's word choice. Diction is part of a writer's style and may be described as formal or informal, plain or fancy, ordinary or *technical,* sophisticated or down-to-earth, old-fashioned or modern.

DICTIONARY A *dictionary* is a reference resource that provides a word's meaning, its part of speech, pronunciation, and etymology.

DRAMA A *drama* is a story written to be performed by actors. Although a drama is meant to be performed, one can also read the script, or written version, and imagine the action. The *script* of a drama is made up of dialogue and stage directions. The *dialogue* is the words spoken by the actors. The *stage directions,* usually printed in italics, tell how the actors should look, move, and speak. They also describe the setting, sound effects, and lighting.

Dramas are often divided into parts called *acts.*

The acts are often divided into smaller parts called *scenes.*

DRAMA REVIEW A *drama review* is an evaluation of a dramatic performance. The writer's analysis and opinions are supported with examples.

ESSAY An *essay* is a short nonfiction work about a particular subject. Most essays have a single major focus and a clear introduction, body, and conclusion.

There are many types of essays. An *informal essay* uses casual, conversational language. A *historical essay* gives facts, explanations, and insights about historical events. An *expository essay* explains an idea by breaking it down. A *narrative essay* tells a story about a real-life experience. An *informational essay* explains a process. A *persuasive essay* offers an opinion and supports it. An *explanatory essay* is a short piece of nonfiction in which the author explains, defines, or interprets ideas, events, or processes. A *reflective essay* is a brief prose work in which an author presents his or her thoughts or feelings—or reflections—about an experience or an idea.

In an *argumentative essay* the writer states and supports a claim, based on factual evidence and logical reasoning. *Problem-and-solution essays* identify problems and make arguments, or claims about solutions.

EXAMPLE An *example* is a fact, idea, or event that supports an idea or insight.

EXPOSITION In the plot of a story or a drama, the *exposition,* or introduction, is the part of the work that introduces the characters, setting, and basic situation.

EXPLANATORY TEXT *Explanatory text* explains a process or provides directions.

EXPOSITORY WRITING *Expository writing* is a work that presents information, discusses ideas, or explains a process.

FACTS AND DETAILS *Facts and details* are forms of evidence a writer uses to support a thesis or opinion. Facts can be proven to be true.

FANTASY A *fantasy* is highly imaginative writing that contains elements not found in real life. Examples of fantasy include stories that involve supernatural elements, stories that resemble fairy tales, stories that deal with imaginary places and creatures, and science-fiction stories.

FICTION *Fiction* is prose writing that tells about imaginary characters and events. Short stories and novels are works of fiction. Some writers base their fiction on actual events and people, adding invented characters, dialogue, settings, and plots. Other writers rely on imagination alone.

FIGURATIVE LANGUAGE *Figurative language* is writing or speech that is not meant to be taken literally. The many types of figurative language are known as *figures of speech.* Common figures of speech include metaphor, personification, and simile. Writers use figurative language to state ideas in vivid and imaginative ways.

FORESHADOWING *Foreshadowing* is the author's use of clues to hint at what might happen later in the story. Writers use foreshadowing to build their readers' expectations and to create suspense.

FREE VERSE *Free verse* is poetry not written in a regular, rhythmical pattern, or meter. The poet is free to write lines of any length or with any number of stresses, or beats. Free verse is therefore less constraining than *metrical verse,* in which every line must have a certain length and a certain number of stresses.

GENRE A *genre* is a division or type of literature. Literature is commonly divided into three major genres: poetry, prose, and drama. Each major genre is, in turn, divided into lesser genres, as follows:

1. *Poetry:* lyric poetry, concrete poetry, dramatic poetry, narrative poetry, epic poetry
2. *Prose:* fiction (novels and short stories) and nonfiction (biography, autobiography, letters, essays, and reports)
3. *Drama:* serious drama and tragedy, comic drama, melodrama, and farce

HISTORICAL FICTION In *historical fiction,* real events, places, or people are incorporated into a fictional, or made-up, story.

HUMOR *Humor* is writing intended to evoke laughter or entertain. It can also be used to convey a serious theme.

IMAGERY *Imagery* is the use of vivid word pictures writers use to appeal to the five senses.

IMAGES *Images* are words or phrases that appeal to one or more of the five senses. Writers use images to describe how their subjects look, sound, feel, taste, and smell. Poets often paint images, or word pictures, that appeal to your senses. These pictures help you to experience the poem fully.

INFERENCE Making an educated guess about a character based on how he or she thinks, acts, or speaks is *making an inference*. Making an inference is sometimes referred to as *reading between the lines*.

INFORMATIVE TEXT *Informative text* provides information on a subject.

IRONY *Irony* is a contradiction between what happens and what is expected. There are three main types of irony. *Situational irony* occurs when something happens that directly contradicts the expectations of the characters or the audience. *Verbal irony* occurs when what is said is the exact opposite of what is meant. said. In *dramatic irony,* the audience is aware of something that the character or speaker is not.

JOURNAL A *journal* is a daily, or periodic, account of events and the writer's thoughts and feelings about those events. Personal journals are not normally written for publication, but sometimes they do get published later with permission from the author or the author's family.

LETTERS A *letter* is a written communication. In personal letters, the writer shares information and his or her thoughts and feelings with one other person or group. Although letters are not normally written for publication, they sometimes are published with the permission of the author or the author's family.

LOGICAL FALLACIES *Logical fallacies* are errors in reasoning that weaken an argument. Here are some examples: *Overgeneralization* is a false conclusion that ignores evidence to the contrary. A *slippery slope* assumes that B, C, and D, will happen because of A. *Ad populum* appeals to the audience's basic beliefs of right and wrong.

LYRIC POEM A *lyric poem* is a highly musical verse that expresses the observations and feelings of a single *speaker*. It creates a single, unified impression.

MAIN IDEA The *main idea* is the *central idea* or most important point in a text. To determine an *implied central* idea, make *inferences* based on what is known.

MEDIA Stories and information are shared using different forms of *media*. Books, magazines, film, television, and ebooks are all forms of media. A *multimedia presentation* contains a combination of words, images, sounds, and video.

MEDIA ACCOUNTS *Media accounts* are reports, explanations, opinions, or descriptions written for television, radio, newspapers, and magazines. While some media accounts report only facts, others include the writer's thoughts and reflections.

MEMOIR A *memoir* is a type of autobiography that focuses on a particularly meaningful period or series of events in the author's life. A memoir is typically written from the first-person point of view in which the author, or narrator, takes part in the story's events. The author will refer to himself or herself using the pronoun I.

METAPHOR A *metaphor* is a figure of speech in which something is described as though it were something else. A metaphor, like a simile, works by pointing out a similarity between two unlike things.

METER The *meter* of a poem is its rhythmical pattern. This pattern is determined by the number of *stresses,* or beats, in each line. To describe the meter of a poem, read it while emphasizing the beats in each line. Then, mark the stressed and unstressed syllables, as follows:

My făth | ĕr wás | thĕ fírst | tŏ héar |

As you can see, each strong stress is marked with a slanted line (´) and each unstressed syllable with a horseshoe symbol (˘). The weak and strong stresses are then divided by vertical lines (|) into groups called feet.

MONOLOGUE A *monologue* is a lengthy speech given by a character that expresses that character's point of view.

MOOD The *mood* is the feeling created in a reader by a piece of writing. Writers create mood by using imagery, word choice, and descriptive details.

MOTIVE A *motive* is a reason that explains or partially explains a character's thoughts, feelings, actions, or speech. Writers try to make their characters' motives, or *motivations*, as clear as possible. If the motives of a main character are not clear, then the character will not be well understood.

Characters are often driven by *external motivations* or needs, such as food and shelter. *Internal motivations* that drive characters are feelings, such as fear, love, and pride. Motives may be obvious or hidden.

MYTH A *myth* is a fictional tale that explains the actions of gods or heroes or the origins of elements of nature. Myths are part of the oral tradition. They are composed orally and then passed from generation to generation by word of mouth. Every ancient culture has its own mythology, or collection of myths. Greek and Roman myths are known collectively as *classical mythology.*

NARRATION *Narration* is writing that tells a story. The act of telling a story is also called narration. A story told in fiction, nonfiction, poetry, or even in drama is called a *narrative.*

NARRATIVE A *narrative* is a story. A narrative can be either fiction or nonfiction. Novels and short stories are types of fictional narratives. Biographies and autobiographies are nonfiction narratives. Poems that tell stories are also narratives. An author uses *narrative pacing* to regulate the speed and flow of information in a text.

NARRATIVE POEM A *narrative poem* is a story told in verse. Narrative poems often have all the elements of short stories, including characters, conflict, and plot.

NARRATOR A *narrator* is a speaker or a character who tells a story. The narrator's perspective is the way he or she sees things. A *third-person narrator* is one who stands outside the action and speaks about it. A *first-person narrator* is one who tells a story and participates in its action.

NONFICTION *Nonfiction* is prose writing that presents and explains ideas or that tells about real people, places, objects, or events. Autobiographies, biographies, essays, reports, letters, memos, and newspaper articles are all types of nonfiction.

NOVEL A *novel* is a long work of fiction. Novels contain such elements as characters, plot, conflict, and setting. The writer of novels, or novelist, develops these elements. In addition to its main plot, a novel may contain one or more subplots, or independent, related stories. A novel may also have several themes.

ONOMATOPOEIA *Onomatopoeia* is the use of words that imitate sounds. *Crash, buzz, screech, hiss, neigh, jingle,* and *cluck* are examples of onomatopoeia. *Chickadee, towhee,* and *whippoorwill* are onomatopoeic names of birds.

Onomatopoeia can help put the reader in the action of a poem.

OPINION An *opinion* is a person's judgment or belief. It may be supported by factual evidence, but it cannot be proved.

ORGANIZATION The *organization*, or structure of a text, depends on the topic and the author's purpose and reason for writing.

OXYMORON An *oxymoron* (pl. *oxymora*) is a figure of speech that links two opposite or contradictory words, to point out an idea or a situation that seems contradictory or inconsistent but on closer inspection turns out to be somehow true.

PARALLELISM *Parallelism* is the use of similar grammatical forms or patterns to express similar ideas. Parallelism adds rhythm and balance to writing and strengthens the connections among an author's ideas.

PARAPHRASE To *paraphrase* is to restate something you read or heard in your own words.

PERSONIFICATION *Personification* is a type of figurative language in which a nonhuman subject is given human characteristics.

PERSUASION *Persuasion* is used in writing or speech that attempts to convince the reader or listener to adopt a particular opinion or course of action. Newspaper editorials and letters to the editor use persuasion, as do advertisements and campaign speeches given by political candidates. Writers use a variety of persuasive techniques to argue their point of view. **Appeals to authority** use the statements of experts. **Appeals to emotion** use words that convey strong feelings. **Appeals to reason** use logical arguments supported by facts.

PLAYWRIGHT A *playwright* is a person who writes plays. William Shakespeare is regarded as the greatest playwright in English literature.

PLOT *Plot* is the sequence of events in a story. In most novels, dramas, short stories, and narrative poems, the plot involves both characters and a central conflict. The plot usually begins with an exposition that introduces the setting, the characters, and the basic situation. This is followed by the **inciting incident,** which introduces the central conflict. The conflict then increases during the **rising action,** until it reaches a high point of interest or suspense, the **climax.** The climax is followed by the **falling action,** or events that happen after the central conflict is resolved. The story's final outcome, in which remaining conflicts are resolved or left open, is the **resolution** or **denouement.**

Some plots do not have all of these parts. For example, some stories begin with the inciting incident and end with the resolution.

See **Conflict.**

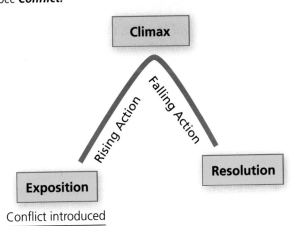

Conflict introduced

POETRY *Poetry* is one of the three major types of literature, the others being prose and drama. Most poems make use of highly concise, musical, and emotionally charged language. Many also make use of imagery, figurative language, and special devices of sound such as rhyme. Major types of poetry include **lyric poetry, narrative poetry,** and **concrete poetry.**

POINT OF VIEW *Point of view* is the perspective, or vantage point, from which a story is told. It is either a narrator outside the story or a character in the story. **First-person point of view** is told by a character who uses the first-person pronoun "I."

The two kinds of **third-person point of view,** limited and omniscient, are called "third person" because the narrator uses third-person pronouns such as "he" and "she" to refer to the characters. There is no "I" telling the story.

In stories told from the **omniscient third-person point of view,** the narrator knows and tells about what each character feels and thinks.

In stories told from the **limited third-person point of view,** the narrator relates the inner thoughts and feelings of only one character, and everything is viewed from this character's perspective.

PRESENTATION An *oral presentation* is a verbal form of presentation and can include other **visual presentation** forms such as charts, diagrams, illustrations, and photos. Video clips and slide-shows are included in **digital presentations,** which are created partly or entirely on a computer.

PROSE *Prose* is the ordinary form of written language. Most writing that is not poetry, drama, or song is considered prose. Prose is one of the major genres of literature and occurs in two forms—fiction and nonfiction.

QUOTATION *Quotations* are exact statements from personal interviews or conversations with the subjects of a narrative.

REPETITION *Repetition* is the use, more than once, of any element of language—a sound, word, phrase, clause, or sentence. Repetition is used in both prose and poetry.

RESOLUTION The *resolution* is the outcome of the conflict in a plot.

RESPONSES Any reaction to a set of events is called a *response*. **Internal responses** reveal a character's thoughts. **External responses** are actions.

RETELLING A *retelling* of a story can be either written or oral and should include a clear sequence of events and narrative techniques such as dialogue and descriptions.

RHYME *Rhyme* is the repetition of sounds at the ends of words. Poets use rhyme to lend a songlike quality to their verses and to emphasize certain words and ideas. Many traditional poems contain **end rhymes,** or rhyming words at the ends of lines.

Another common device is the use of **internal rhymes,** or rhyming words within lines. Internal rhyme also emphasizes the flowing nature of a poem.

RHYTHM *Rhythm* is the pattern of stressed and unstressed syllables in spoken or written language.

SCENE A *scene* is a section of uninterrupted action in the act of a drama.

SCIENCE FICTION *Science fiction* combines elements of fiction and fantasy with scientific fact. Many science-fiction stories are set in the future.

SENSORY LANGUAGE *Sensory language* is writing or speech that appeals to one or more of the five senses.

SETTING The *setting* of a literary work is the time and place of the action. The setting includes all the details of a place and time—the year, the time of day, even the weather. The place may be a specific country, state, region, community, neighborhood, building, institution, or home. Details such as dialects, clothing, customs, and modes of transportation are often used to establish setting. In most stories, the setting serves as a backdrop—a context in which the characters interact. Setting can also help to create a feeling, or atmosphere.

SHORT STORY A *short story* is a brief work of fiction. Like a novel, a short story presents a sequence of events, or plot. The plot usually deals with a central conflict faced by a main character, or protagonist. The events in a short story usually communicate a message about life or human nature. This message, or central idea, is the story's theme.

SIMILE A *simile* is a figure of speech that uses *like* or *as* to make a direct comparison between two unlike ideas. Everyday speech often contains similes, such as "pale as a ghost," "good as gold," "spread like wildfire," and "clever as a fox."

STAGE DIRECTIONS *Stage directions* are notes included in a drama to describe how the work is to be performed or staged. Stage directions are usually printed in italics and enclosed within parentheses or brackets. Some stage directions describe the movements, costumes, emotional states, and ways of speaking of the characters.

STAGING *Staging* includes the setting, lighting, costumes, special effects, music, dance, and so on that go into putting on a stage performance of a drama.

SUMMARY A *summary* is a concise, complete, and accurate overview of a text.

SYMBOL A *symbol* is anything that stands for or represents something else. Symbols are common in everyday life. A dove with an olive branch in its beak is a symbol of peace. A blindfolded woman holding a balanced scale is a symbol of justice. A crown is a symbol of a king's or queen's status and authority.

SYMBOLISM *Symbolism* is the use of symbols. Symbolism plays an important role in many different types of literature. It can highlight certain elements the author wishes to emphasize and also add levels of meaning.

THEME The *theme* is a central message, concern, or purpose in a literary work. A *universal theme* can usually be expressed as a generalization, or a general statement, about human beings or about life. The theme of a work is not a summary of its plot. The theme is the writer's central idea. A *stated theme* is directly expressed. An *implied theme* is suggested by what happens to the characters.

Although a theme may be stated directly in the text, it is more often presented indirectly. When the theme is stated indirectly, or implied, the reader must figure out what the theme is by looking carefully at what the work reveals about people or about life.

THESAURUS A *thesaurus* is a reference resource that provides synonyms and antonyms of words.

TONE The *tone* of a literary work is the writer's attitude toward his or her audience and subject. The tone can often be described by a single adjective, such as *formal* or *informal, serious* or *playful, bitter,* or *ironic.* Factors that contribute to the tone are word choice, sentence structure, line length, rhyme, rhythm, and repetition.

TOPIC A text's *central idea* is its *topic.* The sentence that states the author's main idea about a topic is the *topic sentence* and is often the first sentence of the paragraph.

UNIVERSAL THEME A *universal theme* is a message about life that is expressed regularly in many different cultures and time periods. Folk tales, epics, and romances often address universal themes like the importance of courage, the power of love, or the danger of greed.

VOICE The unique *voice* of an author is created using sentence length, word choice, and tone. A writer can adjust his or her voice to the type of writing and audience.

WORD CHOICE An author's *word choice*—sometimes referred to as *diction*—is an important factor in creating the tone or mood of a literary work. Authors choose words based on the intended audience and the work's purpose.

MANUAL DE TÉRMINOS LITERARIOS

ALLITERATION / ALITERACIÓN La *aliteración* es la repetición de los sonidos consonantes iniciales. Los escritores usan la aliteración para llamar la atención sobre determinadas palabras o ideas, para imitar sonidos y para crear efectos de musicalidad.

ALLUSION / ALUSIÓN Una *alusión* es una referencia a una persona, lugar, hecho, obra literaria u obra de arte muy conocida. Las alusiones relacionan las obras literarias con una herencia cultural más extensa. Permiten al escritor expresar ideas complejas sin explicarlas con gran lujo de detalles. Comprender lo que dice una obra literaria a menudo depende de poder reconocer sus alusiones y los significados que sugieren.

ANALOGY / ANALOGÍA Una *analogía* establece una comparación entre dos o más cosas que son parecidas en algunos aspectos, pero se diferencian en otros.

ANECDOTE / ANÉCDOTA Una *anécdota* es un relato breve sobre un hecho interesante, divertido o extraño. Los escritores cuentan anécdotas con el fin de entretener o decir algo importante.

ARGUMENT ARGUMENTO Un *argumento* es una manera lógica de presentar una creencia, una conclusión o una postura. Un buen argumento debe incluir una *afirmación* y se respalda con razonamientos y *evidencias* que sean *relevantes*; es decir, que se relacionen con el tema. Si las creencias y el sentir del autor son obvios, el argumento es menos convincente y resulta *sesgado* o parcial.

AUTHOR'S INFLUENCES / INFLUENCIAS DEL AUTOR Las *influencias de un autor* son su herencia, su cultura y sus creencias personales.

AUTHOR'S POINT OF VIEW / PUNTO DE VISTA DEL AUTOR La actitud y postura que revela el autor de un texto informativo muestra el *punto de vista del autor*, o la *perspectiva del autor*.

AUTHOR'S PURPOSE / PROPÓSITO DEL AUTOR El *propósito del autor* es su razón principal para escribir. Por ejemplo, el autor puede tener como objetivo entretener, informar o persuadir al lector. En ocasiones el autor intenta dar una lección o hacer una reflexión sobre una experiencia. El autor puede tener más de un propósito para escribir.

AUTHOR'S STYLE / ESTILO DEL AUTOR El *estilo* de un autor es la manera típica en que escribe. Muchos factores determinan el estilo de un escritor, entre ellos la dicción, el tono, el uso que hace de elementos característicos como el lenguaje retórico, el dialecto, la rima, la métrica o los recursos rítmicos; las estructuras y patrones gramaticales típicos, la longitud de las oraciones y los métodos típicos de organización. El estilo comprende todas las características del uso del lenguaje de un escritor.

AUTOBIOGRAPHY / AUTOBIOGRAFÍA Una *autobiografía* es la historia de la vida del escritor contada por él mismo. Una autobiografía puede contar toda la vida de una persona o solo parte de ella.

Como las autobiografías tratan de personas y hechos reales, son una forma de no-ficción. La mayoría de las autobiografías están escritas en primera persona.

BIOGRAPHY / BIOGRAFÍA Una *biografía* es una forma de no-ficción en la que un escritor cuenta la vida de otra persona. La mayoría de las biografías tratan de personas famosas o admirables. Aunque las biografías son formas de no-ficción, las más efectivas comparten las cualidades de los buenos relatos.

CAUSE-AND-EFFECT ESSAY / ENSAYO DE CAUSA Y EFECTO Un *ensayo de causa y efecto* analiza la relación entre distintos sucesos. Los ensayos eficaces contienen una tesis clara, respaldada por ejemplos, evidencia y lógica.

CHARACTER / PERSONAJE Un *personaje* es una persona o animal que participa en la acción en una obra literaria. El personaje principal, o *protagonista*, es el personaje más importante del relato, poema u obra de teatro. Un personaje *secundario* es el que forma parte de la acción, pero no es el centro de la atención.

Los personajes se clasifican a veces como complejos o chatos. Un *personaje chato* muestra solo un rasgo y a menudo representa un estereotipo. Un *personaje complejo*, por el contrario, está totalmente desarrollado y muestra muchos rasgos diferentes, tanto faltas como virtudes.

Los personajes también se pueden clasificar como dinámicos o estáticos. Un *personaje dinámico* cambia o crece en el curso de la obra. Un *personaje estático* no cambia.

CHARACTERIZATION / CARACTERIZACIÓN La *caracterización* es el acto de crear y desarrollar un personaje. Los autores usan dos métodos principales de caracterización: *directa* e *indirecta*.

En una caracterización *directa*, el escritor expresa los *rasgos*, o características, *del personaje*.

Cuando describe a un personaje de manera *indirecta*, el escritor depende del lector para que saque conclusiones sobre los rasgos del personaje. Algunas veces, el autor cuenta lo que otros participantes del relato dicen y piensan del personaje.

CHARACTER TRAITS / RASGOS DEL PERSONAJE Los *rasgos de los personajes* son los atributos, actitudes y valores que un personaje tiene o exhibe, como la confiabilidad, la inteligencia, el egoísmo o la obstinación.

CHRONOLOGICAL ORDER / ORDEN CRONOLÓGICO
Los escritores suelen ordenar los sucesos en las narraciones utilizando el *orden cronológico*, de manera que un suceso precede al siguiente en el orden en el que tuvieron lugar.

CLAIM / AFIRMACIÓN
Una *afirmación* es una conclusión razonable que se basa en evidencia. Un *contraargumento* es una postura opuesta a la afirmación. Las *afirmaciones limitadas* son fuertes y específicas, por lo que suelen ser más eficaces que *las afirmaciones amplias* porque se pueden respaldar más fácilmente con evidencia.

CLIMAX / CLÍMAX
El *clímax,* también llamado punto de inflexión, es el punto máximo en la acción de la trama. Es el momento de mayor tensión, cuando el resultado de la trama pende de un hilo.

COMPARE-AND-CONTRAST ESSAY / ENSAYO DE COMPARACIÓN Y CONTRASTE
Se conoce como *ensayo de comparación y contraste* al ensayo en el que el autor expone las diferencias y similitudes entre dos asuntos.

Los ensayos de comparación y contraste pueden utilizar una *organización de punto por punto* en la que primero se trata un aspecto de los dos asuntos, después otro y así sucesivamente. También se puede emplear una *organización de método de bloques* en la que primero se presentan todos los detalles de uno de los asuntos, seguidos por los detalles del otro asunto.

CONFLICT / CONFLICTO
Un *conflicto* es una lucha entre fuerzas opuestas. El conflicto es uno de los elementos más importantes de cuentos, novelas y obras de teatro porque causa la acción.

Hay dos tipos de conflicto: externos e internos. Un *conflicto externo* es aquel en el que un personaje lucha contra una fuerza externa, por ejemplo, otra persona. Otro tipo de conflicto externo puede ocurrir entre un personaje y alguna fuerza de la naturaleza.

Un *conflicto interno* tiene lugar dentro de la mente de un personaje, el cual lucha para tomar una decisión, realizar una acción o superar un sentimiento.

CONNECTORS / CONECTORES
Los nexos o conectores son palabras que muestran *conexiones claras* entre las afirmaciones, las razones y las evidencias. Por el contrario, las *conexiones confusas* pueden complicar y debilitar los argumentos.

CONNOTATION / CONNOTACIÓN
La *connotación* de una palabra es el conjunto de ideas que se asocian a ella, además de su significado explícito. La connotación de una palabra puede ser personal, esto es, basarse en experiencias personales. Más a menudo, las connotaciones culturales, es decir, las que la mayoría de un grupo reconoce, determinan la elección de palabras que hace el autor.

DENOTATION / DENOTACIÓN
La *denotación* de una palabra es su significado en un *diccionario*, independientemente de otras asociaciones que la palabra suscita. Por ejemplo, la denotación de la palabra *lago* es "cuerpo de agua tierra adentro". "Lugar de vacaciones" y "lugar donde la pesca es buena" son connotaciones de la palabra *lago*.

DESCRIPTION / DESCRIPCIÓN
Una *descripción* es un retrato en palabras de una persona, un lugar o un objeto. La escritura descriptiva utiliza imágenes que apelan a los cinco sentidos: la vista, el oído, el tacto, el gusto y el olfato.

DIALOGUE / DIÁLOGO
Un *diálogo* es una conversación entre personajes. En poemas, novelas y cuentos, el diálogo en inglés usualmente se resalta con comillas para indicar las palabras exactas del hablante.

En una obra de teatro, el diálogo sigue a los nombres de los personajes y no se usan comillas.

DIARY / DIARIO
Un *diario* es un tipo de texto autobiográfico. Las entradas de un diario se hacen de manera periódica a lo largo del tiempo.

DICTION / DICCIÓN
La *dicción* comprende la elección de palabras que hace el autor o el hablante. La dicción es parte del estilo de un escritor y se puede describir como formal o informal, sencilla o elevada, coloquial o *técnica*, sofisticada o centrada, antigua o moderna.

DICTIONARY / DICCIONARIO
Un *diccionario* es una obra de referencia que ofrece información sobre el significado de una palabra, su categoría gramatical y su etimología.

DRAMA / DRAMA
Un *drama* es una historia escrita para ser representada por actores. Aunque la intención del drama es su representación, también se puede leer el guion, o versión escrita, e imaginar la acción. El *guion* de un drama está constituido por el diálogo y las acotaciones. El *diálogo* son las palabras que dicen los actores. Las *acotaciones*, por lo general impresas en cursivas, dicen cómo se ven, se mueven y hablan los actores. También describen la ambientación, los efectos sonoros y la iluminación.

Con frecuencia, los dramas se dividen en partes llamadas *actos*.

Los actos se dividen a menudo en partes más pequeñas llamadas *escenas*.

THEATRICAL CRITICISM / CRÍTICA TEATRAL
La *crítica teatral* es una evaluación de una representación dramática. El análisis y las opiniones del escritor se respaldan con ejemplos.

ESSAY / ENSAYO Un *ensayo* es una obra breve de no-ficción sobre un tema en particular. La mayoría de los ensayos tienen un único punto central importante y una introducción, cuerpo y conclusión claras.

Hay muchos tipos de ensayos. Un *ensayo informal* usa lenguaje casual, coloquial. Un *ensayo histórico* brinda hechos, explicaciones y perspectivas de hechos históricos. Un *ensayo expositivo* explica una idea al descomponerla. Un *ensayo narrativo* cuenta una historia sobre una experiencia de la vida real. Un *ensayo informativo* explica un proceso. Un *ensayo persuasivo* ofrece una opinión y la apoya. Un *ensayo explicativo* es una pieza breve de no-ficción en la que el autor explica, define o interpreta ideas, eventos o procesos. Un *ensayo reflexivo* es una breve obra en prosa en la cual el autor presenta sus pensamientos o sentimientos (o reflexiones) sobre una experiencia o idea. En un *ensayo argumentativo* el escritor manifiesta y respalda una afirmación, basándose en evidencias y en razones lógicas. Los *ensayos de problema y solución* identifican un problema y presentan un argumento o afirmación sobre sus soluciones.

EXAMPLE / EJEMPLO Un *ejemplo* es un hecho, idea o suceso que respalda una opinión o percepción.

EXPOSITION / EXPOSICIÓN En la trama de un cuento o de un drama, la *exposición*, o introducción, es la parte de la obra donde se presenta a los personajes, la ambientación y la situación básica.

EXPLANATORY TEXT / TEXTO EXPLICATIVO Un *texto explicativo* explica un proceso o da instrucciones.

EXPOSITORY WRITING / ESCRITURA EXPOSITIVA La *escritura expositiva* es aquella que presenta información, discute ideas o explica un proceso.

FACTS AND DETAILS / HECHOS Y DETALLES Los *hechos y detalles* son un tipo de evidencia que el escritor usa para respaldar una tesis u opinión. Los hechos son datos cuya veracidad se puede demostrar.

FANTASY / LITERATURA FANTÁSTICA La *literatura fantástica* son escritos de gran imaginación que contienen elementos que no se encuentran en la vida real. Ejemplos de la literatura fantástica son los cuentos que incluyen elementos sobrenaturales, historias que recuerdan a los cuentos de hadas o las que tratan de lugares y criaturas imaginarias, y los relatos de ciencia ficción.

FICTION / FICCIÓN Una obra de *ficción* es un escrito en prosa que cuenta algo sobre personajes y hechos imaginarios. Los cuentos y las novelas son obras de ficción. Algunos escritores basan sus obras de ficción en hechos y personas reales, a los que agregan personajes, diálogos, ambientaciones y tramas de su propia invención. Otros autores dependen solo de su imaginación.

FIGURATIVE LANGUAGE / LENGUAJE FIGURADO El *lenguaje figurado* es un escrito o discurso que no se debe interpretar literalmente. Los muchos tipos de lenguaje figurado son conocidos como *figuras retóricas*. Las figuras retóricas comunes incluyen la metáfora, la personificación y los símiles. Los escritores usan el lenguaje figurado para expresar sus ideas de forma vívida y creativa.

FORESHADOWING / PREFIGURACIÓN La *prefiguración* es el uso que hace un autor de claves que sugieren hechos que van a suceder. Los escritores usan la prefiguración para desarrollar las expectativas de los lectores y crear suspenso.

FREE VERSE / VERSO LIBRE El *verso libre* es una forma poética en la que no se sigue un patrón, o métrica, regular ni rítmico. El poeta es libre de escribir los versos de cualquier longitud o con cualquier cantidad de énfasis o ritmos. Por consiguiente, el verso libre es menos restrictivo que el *verso métrico*, en el que cada verso debe tener una longitud determinada y un cierto número de acentos.

GENRE / GÉNERO Un *género* es una categoría o tipo de literatura. La literatura se divide por lo general en tres géneros principales: poesía, prosa y drama. Cada uno de estos géneros principales se divide a su vez en géneros más pequeños. Por ejemplo:

1. *Poesía*: poesía lírica, poesía concreta, poesía dramática, poesía narrativa y poesía épica
2. *Prosa*: ficción (novelas y cuentos) y no-ficción (biografía, autobiografía, cartas, ensayos, artículos)
3. *Drama*: drama serio y tragedia, comedia dramática, melodrama y farsa

HISTORICAL FICTION / FICCIÓN HISTÓRICA En la *ficción histórica* se incorporan hechos, lugares o personas reales a un relato ficticio o inventado.

HUMOR / HUMOR El *humor* es la escritura que tiene la intención de despertar la risa o entretener. También se puede usar para transmitir un tema serio.

IMAGERY / IMAGINERÍA La *imaginería* es el uso que hacen los escritores de imágenes vívidas creadas con palabras para apelar a los cinco sentidos.

IMAGES / IMÁGENES Las *imágenes* son las palabras vívidas que los autores usan para apelar a uno o más de los cinco sentidos. Los escritores usan imágenes para describir cómo se ven, suenan, sienten, gustan y huelen sus personajes. Los poetas a menudo pintan imágenes, o dibujos con palabras, que despiertan los sentidos. Estas imágenes ayudan a experimentar plenamente el poema.

INFERENCE / INFERENCIA Se conoce como *hacer una inferencia* al acto de hacer una conjetura o deducción sobre un personaje basándose en la manera en la que dicho personaje piensa, se comporta o habla. También se conoce como *leer entre líneas*.

INFORMATIVE TEXT / TEXTO INFORMATIVO Un *texto informativo* ofrece información sobre un tema.

IRONY / IRONÍA La *ironía* es una contradicción entre lo que se espera y lo que ocurre. Hay tres tipos principales de ironía. La *ironía situacional* se da cuando ocurre algo que contradice directamente las expectativas de los personajes o de la audiencia. La *ironía verbal* tiene lugar cuando lo que se dice es justo lo opuesto a lo que se quiere decir. En la *ironía dramática*, la audiencia sabe algo que el personaje o el que habla no sabe.

JOURNAL / DIARIO Un *diario* es un relato diario o periódico de sucesos y de los pensamientos y sentimientos que el escritor tiene sobre esos sucesos. Por lo general, los diarios personales no se escriben para publicarse, pero algunas veces se publican más tarde con la autorización del autor o de la familia del autor.

LETTERS / CARTAS Una *carta* es una comunicación escrita. En las cartas personales, el escritor comparte información y sus pensamientos y sentimientos con otra persona o grupo. Aunque las cartas por lo general no se escriben para su publicación, a veces se publican con la autorización del autor o de la familia del autor.

LOGICAL FALLACIES / FALACIAS LÓGICAS Las *falacias lógicas* son errores en el razonamiento que debilitan el argumento. Estos son algunos ejemplos: La *sobregeneralización* es una conclusión que no toma en cuenta una evidencia opuesta o contraria. En la *presuposición* se asume que B, C y D sucederán como consecuencia de A. Un *argumento ad populum* apela a las creencias fundamentales que tiene el público sobre lo que está bien y lo que está mal.

LYRIC POEM / POEMA LÍRICO Un *poema lírico* es una sucesión de versos de mucha musicalidad que expresan las observaciones y sentimientos de un único *hablante*. Crea una impresión única y unificada.

LOGICAL FALLACIES / FALACIAS LÓGICAS Las falacias lógicas son errores en el razonamiento que debilitan el argumento. Estos son algunos ejemplos: La *sobregeneralización* es una conclusión que no toma en cuenta una evidencia opuesta o contraria. En la *presuposición* se asume que B, C y D sucederán como consecuencia de A. Un *argumento ad populum* apela a las creencias fundamentales que tiene la audiencia sobre lo que están bien y lo que está mal.

MAIN IDEA / IDEA PRINCIPAL La *idea* principal es la *idea central*; es decir, el objetivo más importante de un texto. Se deben hacer *inferencias* basándose en lo que se sabe para poder determinar la *idea central implícita*.

MEDIA / MEDIOS DE COMUNICACIÓN Las historias y la información se divulgan a través de distintos *medios de comunicación*. Los libros, las revistas, las películas, la televisión y los libros electrónicos son medios de comunicación. Una *presentación multimedia* es el resultado de la combinación de palabras, imágenes, sonidos y video.

MEDIA ACCOUNTS / INFORMES DE MEDIOS DE COMUNICACIÓN Los *informes de los medios de comunicación* son reportes, explicaciones, opiniones o descripciones escritos para televisión, radio, periódicos y revistas. Aunque algunos informes de medios de comunicación se refieren solo a hechos, otros incluyen los pensamientos y reflexiones del escritor.

MEMOIR / MEMORIAS Un libro de *memorias* es un tipo de autobiografía que se centra en un período o serie de eventos particularmente significativos de la vida del autor. Por lo general, las memorias se escriben desde el punto de vista de la primera persona, en la que el autor, o narrador, forma parte de los eventos de la historia. El autor se refiere a sí mismo usando el pronombre *yo*.

METAPHOR / METÁFORA Una *metáfora* es una figura retórica en la que se describe algo como si fuera otra cosa. Una metáfora, al igual que el símil, destaca una similitud entre dos cosas disímiles.

METER / MÉTRICA La *métrica* de un poema es su patrón rítmico. Este patrón queda determinado por el número de *acentos,* o ritmos, en cada línea. Para describir la métrica de un poema en inglés, léelo enfatizando los acentos en cada línea. Luego, marca las sílabas acentuadas y las no acentuadas, como sigue:

Mҳ fáth | ĕr wás | thĕ fírst | tŏ héar |

Como puedes ver, en inglés cada acento fuerte se marca con una rayita inclinada, (´) y cada sílaba no acentuada con un símbolo de herradura (ˇ). Luego, los acentos débiles y fuertes se dividen con rayas verticales (|) en grupos llamados pies.

MONOLOGUE / MONÓLOGO Un *monólogo* es un parlamento extenso de uno de los personajes en el que dicho personaje expresa su punto de vista.

MOOD / ATMÓSFERA La *atmósfera* es la sensación que un texto produce en el lector. Los escritores crean la atmósfera mediante el uso de imaginería, su elección de palabras y los detalles descriptivos.

MOTIVE / MOTIVO Un *motivo* es una razón que explica del todo o parcialmente los pensamientos, sentimientos, acciones o discurso de un personaje. Los escritores tratan de hacer que los motivos, o *motivaciones*, de sus personajes sean lo más claros posible. Si los motivos de un personaje principal no están claros, entonces el personaje no será bien entendido.

A menudo, a los personajes los mueven *motivos externos*; es decir, necesidades como la alimentación y el cobijo. También los mueven *motivos internos*; es decir, sentimientos como el miedo, el amor y el orgullo. Los motivos pueden ser obvios o escondidos.

MYTH / MITO Un *mito* es un relato de ficción que explica las acciones de los dioses, los héroes o los orígenes de los elementos de la naturaleza. Los mitos forman parte de la tradición oral. Se componían oralmente y luego pasaban de boca en boca, de una generación a otra. Todas las culturas antiguas tienen su propia mitología, o recopilación de mitos. Los mitos griegos y romanos son conocidos en su conjunto como **mitología clásica**.

NARRATION / NARRACIÓN Una **narración** es un escrito que cuenta una historia. El acto de contar una historia de forma oral también se llama narración. Una historia contada en forma de ficción, no-ficción, poesía o incluso en forma de drama es un **relato**.

NARRATIVE / RELATO Se llama **relato** a la historia que se narra. Puede ser de ficción o de no-ficción. Las novelas y los cuentos son tipos de relatos de ficción. Las biografías y las autobiografías son relatos de no-ficción. Los poemas que cuentan historias también son relatos.

Los autores usan el **ritmo narrativo** para controlar la velocidad y el flujo de información de un texto.

NARRATIVE POEM / POEMA NARRATIVO Un **poema narrativo** es una historia contada en verso. Los poemas narrativos a menudo tienen todos los elementos de los cuentos, incluyendo los personajes, el conflicto y la trama.

NARRATOR / NARRADOR Un **narrador** es el hablante o el personaje que cuenta una historia. La perspectiva del narrador es la forma en que ve las cosas. Un **narrador en tercera persona** permanece fuera de la acción y habla de ella. Un **narrador en primera persona** es quien cuenta la historia y participa en su acción.

NONFICTION / NO-FICCIÓN La **no-ficción** es un escrito en prosa que presenta y explica ideas o cuenta algo acerca de personas, lugares, objetos o hechos reales. Las autobiografías, biografías, ensayos, informes, cartas, memorándums y artículos de periódico son tipos de no-ficción.

NOVEL / NOVELA Una **novela** es una obra extensa de ficción. Las novelas contienen elementos como personajes, trama, conflicto y ambientación. El escritor de novelas, o novelista, desarrolla estos elementos. Además de su trama principal, una novela puede contener una o más tramas secundarias, es decir, historias relacionadas independientes. Una novela también puede tener varios temas.

ONOMATOPOEIA / ONOMATOPEYA La **onomatopeya** es el uso de palabras que imitan sonidos. **Crash, pío-pío, tica-tac** y **psss** son ejemplos de onomatopeyas. **Cu-cú** es un nombre onomatopéyico de un pájaro.

La onomatopeya puede ayudar a meter al lector en la acción de un poema.

OPINION / OPINIÓN Una **opinión** es un juicio de valor o la creencia de una persona. Puede respaldarse con evidencias basadas en hechos, pero no se puede demostrar.

ORGANIZATION / ORGANIZACIÓN La **organización** o estructura de un texto depende del tema y del propósito o razón que tenga el escritor para escribir.

OXYMORON / OXÍMORON Un **oxímoron** (pl. **oxímora**) es una figura retórica que relaciona dos palabras opuestas o contradictorias para resaltar una idea o situación que parece contradictoria o incongruente, pero que, al analizar con más detalle, resulta tener algo de cierto.

PARALLELISM / PARALELISMO **Paralelismo** es el uso de formas o patrones gramaticales similares para expresar ideas parecidas. El paralelismo añade ritmo y equilibrio a la escritura y fortalece las relaciones entre las ideas del autor.

PARAPHRASE / PARÁFRASIS La **paráfrasis** es reescribir o volver a contar con nuestras propias palabras algo que hemos leído u oído.

PERSONIFICATION / PERSONIFICACIÓN La **personificación** es un tipo de figura retórica en la que se dota a una instancia no humana de características humanas.

PERSUASION / PERSUASIÓN La **persuasión** es un recurso escrito u oral por el que se intenta convencer al lector u oyente de que adopte una opinión en particular o actúe de determinada manera. Los editoriales de los periódicos y las cartas al editor utilizan la persuasión. También lo hacen los anuncios y los discursos de campaña que dan los candidatos políticos.

Los escritores emplean distintas técnicas persuasivas para defender sus opiniones. Las **apelaciones a la autoridad** usan lo que han dicho diversos expertos. Las **apelaciones a las emociones** usan palabras que transmiten sentimientos profundos. Las **apelaciones a la razón** utilizan argumentos lógicos fundamentados con datos.

PLAYWRIGHT / DRAMATURGO Un **dramaturgo** es una persona que escribe obras de teatro. William Shakespeare es reconocido como el mejor dramaturgo de la literatura inglesa.

PLOT / TRAMA o ARGUMENTO La **trama** o **argumento** es la secuencia de los sucesos de una historia. En la mayoría de las novelas, dramas, cuentos y poemas narrativos, la trama implica tanto a los personajes como al conflicto central. La trama por lo general empieza con una exposición que introduce la ambientación, los personajes y la situación básica. A ello le sigue el **suceso desencadenante**, que introduce el conflicto central. Este conflicto aumenta durante la **acción ascendente** hasta que alcanza el punto más alto de interés o suspenso, llamado **clímax**. Al clímax le sigue la **acción descendente**, o los sucesos que ocurren después de que se haya resuelto el conflicto central. El final de la historia, en el que se resuelven los conflictos que quedaban pendientes o se dejan abiertos, conforma el **desenlace,** o **resolución**.

Algunas tramas no tienen todas estas partes. Por ejemplo, algunas historias comienzan con el suceso desencadenante y terminan con el desenlace.

Ver **Conflicto.**

Presentación del conflicto

POETRY / POESÍA La *poesía* es uno de los tres géneros literarios más importantes. Los otros dos son la prosa y el drama. La mayoría de los poemas están escritos en un lenguaje altamente conciso, musical y emocionalmente rico. Muchos también hacen uso de imágenes, figuras retóricas y recursos especiales de sonido, como la rima. Los tipos principales de poesía incluyen la *poesía lírica*, la *poesía narrativa* y la *poesía concreta.*

POINT OF VIEW / PUNTO DE VISTA El *punto de vista* es la perspectiva, o enfoque, desde la cual se narran o describen los hechos. Es un narrador externo a la historia o un personaje del relato. El *punto de vista en primera persona* lo cuenta un personaje que usa el pronombre en primera persona "yo".

Los dos tipos de *punto de vista en tercera persona*, limitado y omnisciente, se llaman "tercera persona" porque el narrador usa pronombres de la tercera persona como "él" o "ella" para referirse a los personajes. No hay un "yo" que cuente la historia.

En los relatos contados desde el *punto de vista omnisciente en tercera persona*, el narrador sabe y cuenta lo que cada personaje siente y piensa.

En los relatos contados desde el *punto de vista limitado en tercera persona*, el narrador relata los pensamientos y sentimientos internos de solo un personaje, y todo se ve desde la perspectiva de este personaje.

PRESENTATION / PRESENTACIÓN Las *presentaciones orales* son un tipo de presentación verbal que puede incluir *presentaciones visuales* como tablas, diagramas, ilustraciones y fotos. Los videoclips y las presentaciones de diapositivas son parte de las llamadas *presentaciones digitales*, que se crean en parte o en su totalidad con computadora.

PROSE / PROSA La *prosa* es la forma común del lenguaje escrito. La mayoría de los escritos que no son poesía, drama, ni canciones, se consideran prosa. La prosa

es uno de los géneros literarios más importantes y puede ser de dos formas: de ficción y de no-ficción.

QUOTE / CITA Las *citas* son enunciados exactos tomados de entrevistas y conversaciones personales con los individuos de una narración.

REPETITION / REPETICIÓN La *repetición* es el uso de cualquier elemento del lenguaje —un sonido, una palabra, una frase, una cláusula, o una oración— más de una vez. La repetición se usa tanto en prosa como en poesía.

RESPONSE / RESPUESTA Se conoce como *respuesta* a la reacción a un conjunto de sucesos. Las *respuestas internas* revelan los pensamientos del personaje. Las *respuestas externas* son acciones.

RESOLUTION / RESOLUCIÓN La *resolución* es el resultado del conflicto de una trama.

RETELL / VOLVER A CONTAR Las historias se pueden *volver a contar* de manera escrita u oral. Al volverse a contar una historia, se debe seguir una secuencia clara de los sucesos y utilizar técnicas narrativas como el diálogo y la descripción.

RHYME / RIMA La *rima* es la repetición de sonidos al final de las palabras. Los poetas usan la rima para prestar un atributo musical a sus versos y para enfatizar determinadas palabras e ideas. Muchos poemas tradicionales contienen *rimas finales*, o palabras que riman al final de los versos.

Otro recurso común es el uso de *rimas internas*, o palabras que riman dentro de los versos. La rima interna también enfatiza la naturaleza fluida de un poema.

RHYTHM / RITMO El *ritmo* es el patrón de sílabas acentuadas y no acentuadas en el lenguaje hablado o escrito.

SCENE / ESCENA Una *escena* es una sección de acciones ininterrumpidas en la representación de un drama.

SCIENCE FICTION / CIENCIA FICCIÓN La *ciencia ficción* combina elementos de ficción y fantasía con información científica. Muchos relatos de ciencia ficción están ambientados en el futuro.

SENSORY LANGUAGE / LENGUAJE SENSORIAL El *lenguaje sensorial* es un escrito o discurso que apela a uno o más de los cinco sentidos.

SETTING / AMBIENTACIÓN La *ambientación* de una obra literaria es la época y el lugar en el que se desarrolla la acción. Incluye todos los detalles del lugar y la época (el año, la hora del día, incluso el clima). El lugar puede ser un país, estado, región, comunidad, barrio, edificio, institución o casa específicos. Los detalles como dialectos, vestuario, costumbres y medios de transporte se usan a menudo para establecer la ambientación. En la mayoría de los relatos, la ambientación sirve como telón de fondo para la acción: un contexto en el que los personajes interactúan.

La ambientación también puede ayudar a crear un sentimiento o atmósfera.

SHORT STORY / CUENTO Un *cuento* es una obra breve de ficción. Como en la novela, un cuento presenta una secuencia de eventos, o trama. La trama por lo general trata de un conflicto central que enfrenta un personaje principal o protagonista. Los eventos de un cuento por lo general comunican un mensaje sobre la vida o la naturaleza humana. Este mensaje, o idea central, es el tema del cuento.

SIMILE / SÍMIL Un *símil* es una figura retórica en la que se usa la palabra *como* para establecer una comparación entre dos ideas disímiles. El habla cotidiana a menudo contiene símiles, como "pálido como un fantasma", "bueno como el oro", "se expandió como el fuego" y "astuto como un zorro".

STAGE DIRECTIONS / ACOTACIONES Las *acotaciones* son notas que se incluyen en una obra de teatro para describir cómo debe ser actuada o puesta en escena. Estas instrucciones suelen aparecer en cursivas y entre paréntesis o corchetes. Algunas acotaciones describen los movimientos, vestuario, estados emocionales y formas de hablar de los personajes.

STAGING / PUESTA EN ESCENA La *puesta en escena* incluye la ambientación, la iluminación, el vestuario, los efectos especiales, la música, el baile, etc. que forman parte de poner en un escenario la representación de un drama.

SUMMARY / RESUMEN Un *resumen* es una visión concisa, completa y precisa de un texto.

SYMBOL / SÍMBOLO Un *símbolo* es algo que representa otra cosa. Los símbolos son comunes en la vida diaria. Una paloma con una rama de olivo en el pico es un símbolo de paz. Una mujer con los ojos vendados que sostiene una balanza es un símbolo de la justicia. Una corona es un símbolo del estatus y la autoridad de un rey o una reina.

SYMBOLISM / SIMBOLISMO El *simbolismo* es el uso de los símbolos. El simbolismo desempeña un papel importante en muchos tipos diferentes de literatura. Puede destacar determinados elementos que el autor quiera enfatizar y también añadir niveles de significado.

THEME / TEMA El *tema* es el mensaje central, preocupación o propósito de una obra literaria. El *tema universal* puede expresarse como generalización, o enunciado general, sobre los seres humanos o sobre la vida. El tema de una obra no es un resumen de su trama. Es la idea central del autor. Un *tema explícito* es aquel que se expresa directamente. Un *tema implícito* se insinúa en lo que les sucede a los personajes.

Aunque el tema se puede expresar directamente en el texto, se presenta con más frecuencia de manera indirecta. Cuando se expresa indirectamente, o está implícito, el lector debe averiguar cuál es el tema analizando con cuidado lo que la obra revela sobre la gente o sobre la vida.

THESAURUS / TESAURO Un *tesauro* es una obra de referencia que incluye los sinónimos y los antónimos de las palabras.

TONE / TONO El *tono* de una obra literaria es la actitud del escritor hacia su tema y su audiencia. A menudo, el tono se puede describir con un solo adjetivo, como *formal* o *informal*, *serio* o *divertido*, *amargo* o *irónico*. Los factores que contribuyen al tono son la elección de las palabras, la estructura de las oraciones, la longitud de las líneas, la rima, el ritmo y la repetición.

TOPIC or ISSUE / TEMA o ASUNTO La *idea central* de un texto es su *tema o asunto*; es decir, nos indica de qué trata el texto. La oración que nos ofrece la idea principal del autor es la *oración temática* y suele ser la primera oración del párrafo.

UNIVERSAL THEME / TEMA UNIVERSAL Un *tema universal* es un mensaje sobre la vida que se expresa regularmente en muchas culturas y periodos diferentes. Las leyendas populares, la novela épica y los romances a menudo tratan temas universales como la importancia del valor, el poder del amor y el peligro de la avaricia.

VOICE / VOZ La *voz* distintiva de un autor se crea mediante la extensión de las oraciones, la elección de las palabras y el tono. El escritor puede modificar su voz según el tipo de texto y la audiencia.

WORD CHOICE / ELECCIÓN DE LAS PALABRAS La *elección de las palabras* que hace un autor (a veces conocida como *dicción*) es un factor importante en la creación del tono o atmósfera de la obra literaria. Los autores eligen las palabras con base en la audiencia a la que se dirigen y el propósito de la obra.

GRAMMAR HANDBOOK

PARTS OF SPEECH

Every English word, depending on its meaning and its use in a sentence, can be identified as one of the eight parts of speech. These are nouns, pronouns, verbs, adjectives, adverbs, prepositions, conjunctions, and interjections. Understanding the parts of speech will help you learn the rules of English grammar and usage.

Nouns A **noun** names a person, place, or thing. A **common noun** names any one of a class of persons, places, or things. A **proper noun** names a specific person, place, or thing.

Common Noun	Proper Noun
writer, country, novel	Charles Dickens, Great Britain, *Hard Times*

Pronouns A **pronoun** is a word that stands for one or more nouns. The word to which a pronoun refers (whose place it takes) is the **antecedent** of the pronoun.

A **personal pronoun** refers to the person speaking (first person); the person spoken to (second person); or the person, place, or thing spoken about (third person).

	Singular	Plural
First Person	I, me, my, mine	we, us, our, ours
Second Person	you, your, yours	you, your, yours
Third Person	he, him, his, she, her, hers, it, its	they, them, their, theirs

A **reflexive pronoun** reflects the action of a verb back on its subject. It indicates that the person or thing performing the action also is receiving the action.

I keep *myself* fit by taking a walk every day.

An **intensive pronoun** adds emphasis to a noun or pronoun.

It took the work of the president *himself* to pass the law.

A **demonstrative** pronoun points out a specific person(s), place(s), or thing(s).

this, that, these, those

A **relative pronoun** begins a subordinate clause and connects it to another idea in the sentence.

that, which, who, whom, whose

An **interrogative pronoun** begins a question.

what, which, who, whom, whose

An **indefinite pronoun** refers to a person, place, or thing that may or may not be specifically named.

all, another, any, both, each, everyone, few, most, none, no one, somebody

Verbs A **verb** expresses action or the existence of a state or condition.

An **action verb** tells what action someone or something is performing.

gather, read, work, jump, imagine, analyze, conclude

A **linking verb** connects the subject with another word that identifies or describes the subject. The most common linking verb is *be*.

appear, be, become, feel, look, remain, seem, smell, sound, stay, taste

A **helping verb,** or **auxiliary verb,** is added to a main verb to make a verb phrase.

be, do, have, should, can, could, may, might, must, will, would

Adjectives An **adjective** modifies a noun or pronoun by describing it or giving it a more specific meaning. An adjective answers the questions:

What kind?	*purple* hat, *happy* face, *loud* sound
Which one?	*this* bowl
How many?	*three* cars
How much?	*enough* food

The articles *the, a,* and *an* are adjectives.

A **proper adjective** is an adjective derived from a proper noun.

French, Shakespearean

Adverbs An **adverb** modifies a verb, an adjective, or another adverb by telling *where, when, how,* or *to what extent.*

will answer *soon, extremely* sad, calls *more* often

Prepositions A **preposition** relates a noun or pronoun that appears with it to another word in the sentence.

Dad made a meal *for* us. We talked *till* dusk. Bo missed school *because of* his illness.

Conjunctions A **conjunction** connects words or groups of words. A **coordinating conjunction** joins words or groups of words of equal rank.

bread *and* cheese, brief *but* powerful

Correlative conjunctions are used in pairs to connect words or groups of words of equal importance.

both Luis *and* Rosa, *neither* you *nor* I

Subordinating conjunctions indicate the connection between two ideas by placing one below the other in rank or importance. A subordinating conjunction introduces a subordinate, or dependent, clause.

> We will miss her *if* she leaves. Hank shrieked *when* he slipped on the ice.

Interjections An **interjection** expresses feeling or emotion. It is not related to other words in the sentence.

> ah, hey, ouch, well, yippee

PHRASES AND CLAUSES

Phrases A **phrase** is a group of words that does not have both a subject and a verb and that functions as one part of speech. A phrase expresses an idea but cannot stand alone.

Prepositional Phrases A **prepositional phrase** is a group of words that begins with a preposition and ends with a noun or pronoun that is the **object of the preposition.**

> before dawn   as a result of the rain

An **adjective phrase** is a prepositional phrase that modifies a noun or pronoun.

> Eliza appreciates the beauty **of a well-crafted poem.**

An **adverb phrase** is a prepositional phrase that modifies a verb, an adjective, or an adverb.

> She reads Spenser's sonnets **with great pleasure.**

Appositive Phrases An **appositive** is a noun or pronoun placed next to another noun or pronoun to add information about it. An **appositive phrase** consists of an appositive and its modifiers.

> Mr. Roth, **my music teacher,** is sick.

Verbal Phrases A **verbal** is a verb form that functions as a different part of speech (not as a verb) in a sentence. **Participles, gerunds,** and **infinitives** are verbals.

A **verbal phrase** includes a verbal and any modifiers or complements it may have. Verbal phrases may function as nouns, as adjectives, or as adverbs.

A **participle** is a verb form that can act as an adjective. Present participles end in *-ing;* past participles of regular verbs end in *-ed.*

A **participial phrase** consists of a participle and its modifiers or complements. The entire phrase acts as an adjective.

> Jenna's backpack, **loaded with equipment,** was heavy.
> **Barking incessantly,** the dogs chased the squirrels out of sight.

A **gerund** is a verb form that ends in *-ing* and is used as a noun.

A **gerund phrase** consists of a gerund with any modifiers or complements, all acting together as a noun.

> **Taking photographs of wildlife** is her main hobby. [acts as subject]
> We always enjoy **listening to live music.** [acts as object]

An **infinitive** is a verb form, usually preceded by *to,* that can act as a noun, an adjective, or an adverb.

An **infinitive phrase** consists of an infinitive and its modifiers or complements, and sometimes its subject, all acting together as a single part of speech.

> She tries **to get out into the wilderness often.** [acts as a noun; direct object of *tries*]
> The Tigers are the team **to beat.** [acts as an adjective; describes *team*]
> I drove twenty miles **to witness the event.** [acts as an adverb; tells why I drove]

Clauses A **clause** is a group of words with its own subject and verb.

Independent Clauses An independent clause can stand by itself as a complete sentence.

> George Orwell wrote with extraordinary insight.

Subordinate Clauses A subordinate clause cannot stand by itself as a complete sentence. Subordinate clauses always appear connected in some way with one or more independent clauses.

> George Orwell, **who wrote with extraordinary insight,** produced many politically relevant works.

An **adjective clause** is a subordinate clause that acts as an adjective. It modifies a noun or a pronoun by telling *what kind* or *which one.* Also called relative clauses, adjective clauses usually begin with a **relative pronoun:** *who, which, that, whom,* or *whose.*

> "The Lamb" is the poem **that I memorized for class.**

An **adverb clause** is a subordinate clause that, like an adverb, modifies a verb, an adjective, or an adverb. An adverb clause tells *where, when, in what way, to what extent, under what condition,* or *why.*

The students will read another poetry collection **if their schedule allows.**

When I recited the poem, Mr. Lopez was impressed.

A **noun clause** is a subordinate clause that acts as a noun.

William Blake survived on **whatever he made as an engraver.**

SENTENCE STRUCTURE

Subject and Predicate A **sentence** is a group of words that expresses a complete thought. A sentence has two main parts: a *subject* and a *predicate*.

A **fragment** is a group of words that does not express a complete thought. It lacks an independent clause.

The **subject** tells *whom* or *what* the sentence is about. The **predicate** tells what the subject of the sentence does or is.

A subject or a predicate can consist of a single word or of many words. All the words in the subject make up the **complete subject.** All the words in the predicate make up the **complete predicate.**

Complete Subject	Complete Predicate
Both of those girls	have already read *Macbeth*.

The **simple subject** is the essential noun, pronoun, or group of words acting as a noun that cannot be left out of the complete subject. The **simple predicate** is the essential verb or verb phrase that cannot be left out of the complete predicate.

Both of those girls | **have** already **read** *Macbeth*.
[Simple subject: *Both;* simple predicate: *have read*]

A **compound subject** is two or more subjects that have the same verb and are joined by a conjunction.

Neither the horse nor the driver looked tired.

A **compound predicate** is two or more verbs that have the same subject and are joined by a conjunction.

She **sneezed and coughed** throughout the trip.

Complements A **complement** is a word or word group that completes the meaning of the subject or verb in a sentence. There are four kinds of complements: *direct objects, indirect objects, objective complements,* and *subject complements.*

A **direct object** is a noun, a pronoun, or a group of words acting as a noun that receives the action of a transitive verb.

We watched the **liftoff.**
She drove **Zach** to the launch site.

An **indirect object** is a noun or pronoun that appears with a direct object and names the person or thing to which or for which something is done.

He sold the **family** a mirror. [The direct object is *mirror.*]

An **objective complement** is an adjective or noun that appears with a direct object and describes or renames it.

The decision made her **unhappy.**
[The direct object is *her.*]
Many consider Shakespeare the greatest **playwright.** [The direct object is *Shakespeare.*]

A **subject complement** follows a linking verb and tells something about the subject. There are two kinds: *predicate nominatives* and *predicate adjectives.*

A **predicate nominative** is a noun or pronoun that follows a linking verb and identifies or renames the subject.

"A Modest Proposal" is a **pamphlet.**

A **predicate adjective** is an adjective that follows a linking verb and describes the subject of the sentence.

"A Modest Proposal" is **satirical.**

Classifying Sentences by Structure

Sentences can be classified according to the kind and number of clauses they contain. The four basic sentence structures are *simple, compound, complex,* and *compound-complex.*

A **simple sentence** consists of one independent clause.

Terrence enjoys modern British literature.

A **compound sentence** consists of two or more independent clauses. The clauses are joined by a conjunction or a semicolon.

Terrence enjoys modern British literature, but his brother prefers the classics.

A **complex sentence** consists of one independent clause and one or more subordinate clauses.

Terrence, who reads voraciously, enjoys modern British literature.

A **compound-complex sentence** consists of two or more independent clauses and one or more subordinate clauses.

Terrence, who reads voraciously, enjoys modern British literature, but his brother prefers the classics.

Classifying Sentences by Function

Sentences can be classified according to their function or purpose. The four types are *declarative, interrogative, imperative,* and *exclamatory.*

GLOSSARY: GRAMMAR HANDBOOK

SENTENCE STRUCTURE continued

A **declarative sentence** states an idea and ends with a period.

An **interrogative sentence** asks a question and ends with a question mark.

An **imperative sentence** gives an order or a direction and ends with either a period or an exclamation mark.

An **exclamatory sentence** conveys a strong emotion and ends with an exclamation mark.

PARAGRAPH STRUCTURE

An effective paragraph is organized around one **main idea,** which is often stated in a **topic sentence.** The other sentences support the main idea. To give the paragraph **unity,** make sure the connection between each sentence and the main idea is clear.

Unnecessary Shift in Person

Do not change needlessly from one grammatical person to another. Keep the person consistent in your sentences.

Max went to the bakery, but **you** can't buy mints there. [shift from third person to second person]

Max went to the bakery, but **he** can't buy mints there. [consistent]

Unnecessary Shift in Voice

Do not change needlessly from active voice to passive voice in your use of verbs.

Elena and I **searched** the trail for evidence, but no clues **were found.** [shift from active voice to passive voice]

Elena and I **searched** the trail for evidence, but we **found** no clues. [consistent]

AGREEMENT

Subject and Verb Agreement

A singular subject must have a singular verb. A plural subject must have a plural verb.

Dr. Boone uses a telescope to view the night sky.

The **students use** a telescope to view the night sky.

A verb always agrees with its subject, not its object.

Incorrect: The best part of the show were the jugglers.

Correct: The best part of the show was the jugglers.

A phrase or clause that comes between a subject and verb does not affect subject-verb agreement.

His **theory,** as well as his claims, **lacks** support.

Two subjects joined by *and* usually take a plural verb.

The **dog** and the **cat are** healthy.

Two singular subjects joined by *or* or *nor* take a singular verb.

The **dog** or the **cat is** hiding.

Two plural subjects joined by *or* or *nor* take a plural verb.

The **dogs** or the **cats are** coming home with us.

When a singular and a plural subject are joined by *or* or *nor,* the verb agrees with the closer subject.

Either the **dogs** or the **cat is** behind the door.

Either the **cat** or the **dogs are** behind the door.

Pronoun and Antecedent Agreement

Pronouns must agree with their antecedents in number and gender. Use singular pronouns with singular antecedents and plural pronouns with plural antecedents.

Doris Lessing uses **her** writing to challenge ideas about women's roles.

Writers often use **their** skills to promote social change.

Use a singular pronoun when the antecedent is a singular indefinite pronoun such as *anybody, each, either, everybody, neither, no one, one, or someone.*

Judge **each** of the articles on **its** merits.

Use a plural pronoun when the antecedent is a plural indefinite pronoun such as *both, few, many, or several.*

Both of the articles have **their** flaws.

The indefinite pronouns *all, any, more, most, none,* and *some* can be singular or plural depending on the number of the word to which they refer.

Most of the *books* are in **their** proper places.

Most of the *book* has been torn from **its** binding.

USING VERBS

Principal Parts of Regular and Irregular Verbs

A verb has four principal parts:

Present	Present Participle	Past	Past Participle
learn	learning	learned	learned
discuss	discussing	discussed	discussed
stand	standing	stood	stood
begin	beginning	began	begun

Regular verbs such as *learn* and *discuss* form the past and past participle by adding *-ed* to the present form. **Irregular verbs** such as *stand* and *begin* form the past and past participle in other ways. If you are in doubt about the principal parts of an irregular verb, check a dictionary.

The Tenses of Verbs

The different tenses of verbs indicate the time an action or condition occurs.

The **present tense** expresses an action that happens regularly or states a current condition or a general truth.

> Tourists **flock** to the site yearly.

Daily exercise **is** good for your heallth.

The **past tense** expresses a completed action or a condition that is no longer true.

> The squirrel **dropped** the nut and **ran** up the tree.
> I **was** very tired last night by 9:00.

The **future tense** indicates an action that will happen in the future or a condition that will be true.

> The Glazers **will visit** us tomorrow.
> They **will be** glad to arrive from their long journey.

The **present perfect tense** expresses an action that happened at an indefinite time in the past or an action that began in the past and continues into the present.

> Someone **has cleaned** the trash from the park.
> The puppy **has been** under the bed all day.

The **past perfect tense** shows an action that was completed before another action in the past.

> Gerard **had revised** his essay before he turned it in.

The **future perfect tense** indicates an action that will have been completed before another action takes place.

> Mimi **will have painted** the kitchen by the time we finish the shutters.

USING MODIFIERS

Degrees of Comparison

Adjectives and adverbs take different forms to show the three degrees of comparison: the *positive*, the *comparative*, and the *superlative*.

Positive	Comparative	Superlative
fast	faster	fastest
crafty	craftier	craftiest
abruptly	more abruptly	most abruptly
badly	worse	worst

Using Comparative and Superlative Adjectives and Adverbs

Use comparative adjectives and adverbs to compare two things. Use superlative adjectives and adverbs to compare three or more things.

> This season's weather was **drier** than last year's.
> This season has been one of the **driest** on record.
> Jake practices **more often** than Jamal.
> Of everyone in the band, Jake practices **most often.**

USING PRONOUNS

Pronoun Case

The **case** of a pronoun is the form it takes to show its function in a sentence. There are three pronoun cases: *nominative, objective,* and *possessive.*

Nominative	Objective	Possessive
I, you, he, she, it, we, you, they	me, you, him, her, it, us, you, them	my, your, yours, his, her, hers, its, our, ours, their, theirs

Use the **nominative case** when a pronoun functions as a *subject* or as a *predicate nominative.*

> **They** are going to the movies. [subject]
> The biggest movie fan is **she.** [predicate nominative]

Use the **objective case** for a pronoun acting as a *direct object,* an *indirect object,* or the *object of a preposition.*

> The ending of the play surprised **me.** [direct object]
> Mary gave **us** two tickets to the play. [indirect object]
> The audience cheered for **him.** [object of preposition]

Use the **possessive case** to show ownership.

> The red suitcase is **hers.**

Diction The words you choose contribute to the overall effectiveness of your writing. **Diction** refers to word choice and to the clearness and correctness of those words. You can improve one aspect of your diction by choosing carefully between commonly confused words, such as the pairs listed below.

accept, except

Accept is a verb that means "to receive" or "to agree to." *Except* is a preposition that means "other than" or "leaving out."

> Please **accept** my offer to buy you lunch this weekend.
>
> He is busy every day **except** the weekends.

affect, effect

Affect is normally a verb meaning "to influence" or "to bring about a change in." *Effect* is usually a noun meaning "result."

> The distractions outside **affect** Steven's ability to concentrate.
>
> The teacher's remedies had a positive **effect** on Steven's ability to concentrate.

among, between

Among is usually used with three or more items, and it emphasizes collective relationships or indicates distribution. *Between* is generally used with only two items, but it can be used with more than two if the emphasis is on individual (one-to-one) relationships within the group.

> I had to choose a snack **among** the various vegetables.
>
> He handed out the booklets **among** the conference participants.
>
> Our school is **between** a park and an old barn.
>
> The tournament included matches **between** France, Spain, Mexico, and the United States.

amount, number

Amount refers to overall quantity and is mainly used with mass nouns (those that can't be counted). *Number* refers to individual items that can be counted.

> The **amount** of attention that great writers have paid to Shakespeare is remarkable.
>
> A **number** of important English writers have been fascinated by the legend of King Arthur.

assure, ensure, insure

Assure means "to convince [someone of something]; to guarantee." *Ensure* means "to make certain [that something happens]." *Insure* means "to arrange for payment in case of loss."

> The attorney **assured** us we'd win the case.
>
> The rules **ensure** that no one gets treated unfairly.
>
> Many professional musicians **insure** their valuable instruments.

bad, badly

Use the adjective *bad* before a noun or after linking verbs such as *feel, look,* and *seem.* Use *badly* whenever an adverb is required.

> The situation may seem **bad**, but it will improve over time.
>
> Though our team played **badly** today, we will focus on practicing for the next match.

beside, besides

Beside means "at the side of" or "close to." *Besides* means "in addition to."

> The stapler sits **beside** the pencil sharpener in our classroom.
>
> **Besides** being very clean, the classroom is also very organized.

can, may

The helping verb *can* generally refers to the ability to do something. The helping verb *may* generally refers to permission to do something.

> I **can** run one mile in six minutes.
>
> **May** we have a race during recess?

complement, compliment

The verb *complement* means "to enhance"; the verb *compliment* means "to praise."

> Online exercises **complement** the textbook lessons.
>
> Ms. Lewis **complimented** our team on our excellent debate.

compose, comprise

Compose means "to make up; constitute." *Comprise* means "to include or contain." Remember that the whole comprises its parts or is composed of its parts, and the parts compose the whole.

> The assignment **comprises** three different tasks.
>
> The assignment is **composed** of three different tasks.
>
> Three different tasks **compose** the assignment.

different from, different than

Different from is generally preferred over *different than,* but *different than* can be used before a clause. Always use *different from* before a noun or pronoun.

> Your point of view is so **different from** mine.
>
> His idea was so **different from** [or **different than**] what we had expected.

farther, further

Use *farther* to refer to distance. Use *further* to mean "to a greater degree or extent" or "additional."

> Chiang has traveled **farther** than anybody else in the class.
>
> If I want **further** details about his travels, I can read his blog.

fewer, less

Use *fewer* for things that can be counted. Use *less* for amounts or quantities that cannot be counted. *Fewer* must be followed by a plural noun.

Fewer students drive to school since the weather improved.

There is **less** noise outside in the mornings.

good, well

Use the adjective *good* before a noun or after a linking verb. Use *well* whenever an adverb is required, such as when modifying a verb.

I feel **good** after sleeping for eight hours.

I did **well** on my test, and my soccer team played **well** in that afternoon's game. It was a **good** day!

its, it's

The word *its* with no apostrophe is a possessive pronoun. The word *it's* is a contraction of "it is."

Angelica will try to fix the computer and **its** keyboard.

It's a difficult job, but she can do it.

lay, lie

Lay is a transitive verb meaning "to set or put something down." Its principal parts are *lay, laying, laid, laid*. *Lie* is an intransitive verb meaning "to recline" or "to exist in a certain place." Its principal parts are *lie, lying, lay, lain*.

Please **lay** that box down and help me with the sofa.

When we are done moving, I am going to **lie** down.

My hometown **lies** sixty miles north of here.

like, as

Like is a preposition that usually means "similar to" and precedes a noun or pronoun. The conjunction *as* means "in the way that" and usually precedes a clause.

Like the other students, I was prepared for a quiz.

As I said yesterday, we expect to finish before noon.

Use **such as,** not **like,** before a series of examples.

Foods **such as** apples, nuts, and pretzels make good snacks.

of, have

Do not use *of* in place of *have* after auxiliary verbs such as *would, could, should, may, might,* or *must.* The contraction of *have* is formed by adding *-ve* after these verbs.

I **would have** stayed after school today, but I had to help cook at home.

Mom **must've** called while I was still in the gym.

principal, principle

Principal can be an adjective meaning "main; most important." It can also be a noun meaning "chief officer of a school." *Principle* is a noun meaning "moral rule" or "fundamental truth."

His strange behavior was the **principal** reason for our concern.

Democratic **principles** form the basis of our country's laws.

raise, rise

Raise is a transitive verb that usually takes a direct object. *Rise* is intransitive and never takes a direct object.

Iliana and Josef **raise** the flag every morning.

They **rise** from their seats and volunteer immediately whenever help is needed.

than, then

The conjunction *than* is used to connect the two parts of a comparison. The adverb *then* usually refers to time.

My backpack is heavier **than** hers.

I will finish my homework and **then** meet my friends at the park.

that, which, who

Use the relative pronoun *that* to refer to things or people. Use *which* only for things and *who* only for people.

That introduces a restrictive phrase or clause, that is, one that is essential to the meaning of the sentence. *Which* introduces a nonrestrictive phrase or clause—one that adds information but could be deleted from the sentence—and is preceded by a comma.

Ben ran to the park **that** just reopened.

The park, **which** just reopened, has many attractions.

The man **who** built the park loves to see people smiling.

when, where, why

Do not use *when, where,* or *why* directly after a linking verb, such as *is.* Reword the sentence.

Incorrect: The morning is when he left for the beach.

Correct: He left for the beach in the morning.

who, whom

In formal writing, use *who* only as a subject in clauses and sentences. Use *whom* only as the object of a verb or of a preposition.

Who paid for the tickets?

Whom should I pay for the tickets?

I can't recall to **whom** I gave the money for the tickets.

your, you're

Your is a possessive pronoun expressing ownership. *You're* is the contraction of "you are."

Have you finished writing **your** informative essay?

You're supposed to turn it in tomorrow. If **you're** late, **your** grade will be affected.

Capitalization

First Words

Capitalize the first word of a sentence.

Stories about knights and their deeds interest me.

Capitalize the first word of direct speech.

Sharon asked, "**D**o you like stories about knights?"

Capitalize the first word of a quotation that is a complete sentence.

Einstein said, "**A**nyone who has never made a mistake has never tried anything new."

Proper Nouns and Proper Adjectives

Capitalize all proper nouns, including geographical names, historical events and periods, and names of organizations.

Thames **R**iver   **J**ohn **K**eats   the **R**enaissance

United **N**ations   **W**orld **W**ar II   **S**ierra **N**evada

Capitalize all proper adjectives.

Shakespearean play   **B**ritish invaision

American citizen   **L**atin **A**merican literature

Academic Course Names

Capitalize course names only if they are language courses, are followed by a number, or are preceded by a proper noun or adjective.

Spanish   **H**onors **C**hemistry   **H**istory 101

geology   **a**lgebra   **s**ocial **s**tudies

Titles

Capitalize personal titles when followed by the person's name.

Ms. Hughes   **D**r. Perez   **K**ing George

Capitalize titles showing family relationships when they are followed by a specific person's name, unless they are preceded by a possessive noun or pronoun.

Uncle Oscar   Mangan's **s**ister   his **a**unt Tessa

Capitalize the first word and all other key words in the titles of books, stories, songs, and other works of art.

Frankenstein   "**S**hooting an **E**lephant"

Punctuation

End Marks

Use a **period** to end a declarative sentence or an imperative sentence.

We are studying the structure of sonnets.
Read the biography of Mary Shelley.

Use periods with initials and abbreviations.

D. H. Lawrence   Mrs. Browning

Mt. Everest   Maple St.

Use a **question mark** to end an interrogative sentence.

What is Macbeth's fatal flaw?

Use an **exclamation mark** after an exclamatory sentence or a forceful imperative sentence.

That's a beautiful painting!   Let me go now!

Commas

Use a **comma** before a coordinating conjunction to separate two independent clauses in a compound sentence.

The game was very close, but we were victorious.

Use commas to separate three or more words, phrases, or clauses in a series.

William Blake was a writer, artist, and printer.

Use commas to separate coordinate adjectives.

It was a witty, amusing novel.

Use a comma after an introductory word, phrase, or clause.

When the novelist finished his book, he celebrated with his family.

Use commas to set off nonessential expressions.

Old English, of course, requires translation.

Use commas with places and dates.

Coventry, England   September 1, 1939

Semicolons

Use a **semicolon** to join closely related independent clauses that are not already joined by a conjunction.

Tanya likes to write poetry; Heather prefers prose.

Use semicolons to avoid confusion when items in a series contain commas.

They traveled to London, England; Madrid, Spain; and Rome, Italy.

Colons

Use a **colon** before a list of items following an independent clause.

Notable Victorian poets include the following: Tennyson, Arnold, Housman, and Hopkins.

Use a colon to introduce information that summarizes or explains the independent clause before it.

She just wanted to do one thing: rest.

Malcolm loves volunteering: He reads to sick children every Saturday afternoon.

Quotation Marks

Use **quotation marks** to enclose a direct quotation.

"Short stories," Ms. Hildebrand said, "should have rich, well-developed characters."

An **indirect quotation** does not require quotation marks.

Ms. Hildebrand said that short stories should have well-developed characters.

Use quotation marks around the titles of short written works, episodes in a series, songs, and works mentioned as parts of collections.

"The Lagoon"   "Boswell Meets Johnson"

Italics

Italicize the titles of long written works, movies, television and radio shows, lengthy works of music, paintings, and sculptures.

Howards End   *60 Minutes*   *Guernica*

For handwritten material, you can use underlining instead of italics.

<u>The Princess Bride</u>   <u>Mona Lisa</u>

Dashes

Use **dashes** to indicate an abrupt change of thought, a dramatic interrupting idea, or a summary statement.

I read the entire first act of *Macbeth*—you won't believe what happens next.

The director—what's her name again?—attended the movie premiere.

Hyphens

Use a **hyphen** with certain numbers, after certain prefixes, with two or more words used as one word, and with a compound modifier that comes before a noun.

seventy-two
self-esteem
president-elect
five-year contract

Parentheses

Use **parentheses** to set off asides and explanations when the material is not essential or when it consists of one or more sentences. When the sentence in parentheses interrupts the larger sentence, it does not have a capital letter or a period.

He listened intently (it was too dark to see who was speaking) to try to identify the voices.

When a sentence in parentheses falls between two other complete sentences, it should start with a capital letter and end with a period.

The quarterback threw three touchdown passes. (We knew he could do it.) Our team won the game by two points.

Apostrophes

Add an **apostrophe** and an *s* to show the possessive case of most singular nouns and of plural nouns that do not end in *-s* or *-es*.

Blake's poems   the mice's whiskers

Names ending in *s* form their possessives in the same way, except for classical and biblical names, which add only an apostrophe to form the possessive.

Dickens's   Hercules'

Add an apostrophe to show the possessive case of plural nouns ending in *-s* and *-es*.

the girls' songs   the Ortizes' car

Use an apostrophe in a contraction to indicate the position of the missing letter or letters.

She's never read a Coleridge poem she didn't like.

Brackets

Use **brackets** to enclose clarifying information inserted within a quotation.

Columbus's journal entry from October 21, 1492, begins as follows: "At 10 o'clock, we arrived at a cape of the island [San Salvador], and anchored, the other vessels in company."

Ellipses

Use three ellipsis points, also known as an **ellipsis**, to indicate where you have omitted words from quoted material.

Wollestonecraft wrote, "The education of women has of late been more attended to than formerly; yet they are still . . . ridiculed or pitied. . . ."

In the example above, the four dots at the end of the sentence are the three ellipsis points plus the period from the original sentence.

Use an ellipsis to indicate a pause or interruption in speech.

"When he told me the news," said the coach, "I was . . . I was shocked . . . completely shocked."

Spelling

Spelling Rules

Learning the rules of English spelling will help you make **generalizations** about how to spell words.

Word Parts

The three word parts that can combine to form a word are roots, prefixes, and suffixes. Many of these word parts come from the Greek, Latin, and Anglo-Saxon languages.

The **root word** carries a word's basic meaning.

Root and Origin	Meaning	Examples
-leg- (-log-) [Gr.]	to say, speak	*legal, logic*
-pon- (-pos-) [L.]	to put, place	*postpone, deposit*

A **prefix** is one or more syllables added to the beginning of a word that alter the meaning of the root.

Prefix and Origin	Meaning	Example
anti- [Gr.]	against	*antipathy*
inter- [L.]	between	*international*
mis- [A.S.]	wrong	*misplace*

A **suffix** is a letter or group of letters added to the end of a root word that changes the word's meaning or part of speech.

Suffix and Origin	Meaning and Example	Part of Speech
-ful [A.S.]	full of: *scornful*	adjective
-ity [L.]	state of being: *adversity*	noun
-ize (-ise) [Gr.]	to make: *idolize*	verb
-ly [A.S.]	in a manner: *calmly*	adverb

Rules for Adding Suffixes to Root Words

When adding a suffix to a root word ending in *y* preceded by a consonant, change *y* to *i* unless the suffix begins with *i*.

ply + -able = pliable   happy + -ness = happiness

defy + -ing = defying   cry + -ing = crying

For a root word ending in *e*, drop the *e* when adding a suffix beginning with a vowel.

drive + -ing = driving   move + -able = movable

SOME EXCEPTIONS: traceable, seeing, dyeing

For root words ending with a consonant + vowel + consonant in a stressed syllable, double the final consonant when adding a suffix that begins with a vowel.

mud + -y = muddy   submit + -ed = submitted

SOME EXCEPTIONS: mixing, fixed

Rules for Adding Prefixes to Root Words

When a prefix is added to a root word, the spelling of the root remains the same.

un- + certain = uncertain   mis- + spell = misspell

With some prefixes, the spelling of the prefix changes when joined to the root to make the pronunciation easier.

in- + mortal = immortal   ad- + vert = avert

Orthographic Patterns

Certain letter combinations in English make certain sounds. For instance, *ph* sounds like *f*, *eigh* usually makes a long *a* sound, and the *k* before an *n* is often silent.

pharmacy   n**eigh**bor   **k**nowledge

Understanding **orthographic patterns** such as these can help you improve your spelling.

Forming Plurals

The plural form of most nouns is formed by adding -*s* to the singular.

computer**s**   gadget**s**   Washington**s**

For words ending in *s*, *ss*, *x*, *z*, *sh*, or *ch*, add -*es*.

circus**es**   tax**es**   wish**es**   bench**es**

For words ending in *y* or *o* preceded by a vowel, add -*s*.

key**s**   patio**s**

For words ending in *y* preceded by a consonant, change the *y* to an *i* and add -*es*.

cit**ies**   enem**ies**   troph**ies**

For most words ending in *o* preceded by a consonant, add -*es*.

echo**es**   tomato**es**

Some words form the plural in irregular ways.

women   oxen   children   teeth   deer

Foreign Words Used in English

Some words used in English are actually foreign words that have been adopted. Learning to spell these words requires memorization. When in doubt, check a dictionary.

sushi   enchilada   au pair   fiancé

laissez faire   croissant

INDEX OF SKILLS

Research

Speaking and Listening

Writing

INDEX OF AUTHORS AND TITLES

The following authors and titles appear in the print and online versions of Pearson Literature.

ADDITIONAL SELECTIONS: AUTHOR AND TITLE INDEX

The following authors and titles appear in the Online Literature Library.

ACKNOWLEDGMENTS AND CREDITS

Acknowledgments

The following selections appear in Grade 8 of *my*Perspectives. Some selections appear online only.

Albion Press. "Words Do Not Pay," Excerpt from *In a Sacred Manner I Live: Native American Wisdom,* edited by Neil Philip. (The Albion Press Ltd., 1997).

Associated Press (Reprint Management Services). "Scientists Build Robot That Runs, Call It 'Cheetah'" used with permission of The Associated Press Copyright ©2015. All rights reserved.

BBC Worldwide Americas, Inc. *The Holocaust* ©BBC Worldwide Learning.

Carmen Balcells Agencia Literaria. "Uncle Marcos" from *The House of the Spirits* by Isabel Allende. Published by Jonathan Cape. Reprinted by permission of Carmen Balcells Agencia Literaria.

CBS News. "Saving the Children," ©CBS News.

Chabad Lubavitch Center. "Irena Sendler: Rescuer of the Children of Warsaw" by Chana Kroll; Used with permission.

Charlotte Sheedy Literary Agency, Inc. "Hanging Fire," Copyright ©1978, 1997 by Audre Lorde – from the collection BLACK UNICORN by Audre Lorde.

CNN. "Remembering a Devoted Keeper of Anne Frank's Legacy," From CNN.com, March 19, 2015 ©2015 Turner Broadcast Systems, Inc. All rights reserved. Used by permission and protected by the Copyright Laws of the United States. The printing, copying, redistribution, or retransmission of this Content without express written permission is prohibited.

Curtis Brown Ltd. "The Unknown Citizen." Copyright ©1940 by W. H. Auden, renewed. Reprinted by permission of Curtis Brown, Ltd.

ENSLOW PUBLISHING, LLC. "Quiet Resistance," *Courageous Teen Resisters* by Ann Byers, ©2010 by Enslow Publishers, Inc. and reprinted with permission.

Essinger, James. "Ada Lovelace: A Science Legend" by James Essinger, from *Huffington Post,* December 29, 2014. Used with permission of the author.

Flora Roberts, Inc. Entire Play from *Diary of Anne Frank* by Frances Goodrich and Albert Hackett, Copyright ©1956 by Albert Hackett, Frances Goodrich Hackett, and Otto Frank. Copyright renewed 1984 by Albert Hackett. Used by permission of Flora Roberts, Inc.

Funders and Founders. "The Types of Intelligences Infographic based on Howard Gardner's Theory of Multiple Intelligences"; http://fundersandfounders.com/9-types-of-intelligence/ by Mark Vital and Anna Vital. Used with permission of Funders and Founders.

Georges Borchardt Literary Agency. "Friends All of Us" from *Neruda and Vallego: Selected Poems* translated by Robert Bly. Translation Copyright ©1971, 1993 by Robert Bly. Reprinted by permission of Georges Borchardt, Inc., for Robert Bly.

Hannigan Salky Getzler Agency. "Harriet Tubman: Conductor of the Underground Railroad" reprinted by the permission of HSG Agency as agent for the author. Copyright ©1954, 1982, 2006 by Ann Petry.

Hear Africa Foundation. Hear Africa gives permission to Pearson Education for "Stories of Zimbabwean Women."

Houghton Mifflin Harcourt Publishing Co. Excerpt from *In a Sacred Manner I Live: Native American Wisdom,* edited by Neil Philip. Copyright ©1997 by The Albion Press Ltd. Reprinted by permission of Clarion Books, an imprint of Houghton Mifflin Harcourt Publishing Company. All rights reserved; Excerpted from *Flowers for Algernon* by Daniel Keyes. Copyright ©1966, 1959 and renewed 1994, 1987 by Daniel Keyes. Reprinted by permission of Houghton Mifflin Harcourt Publishing Company. All rights reserved; "Circles" from *The People, Yes* by Carl Sandburg. Copyright 1936 by Houghton Mifflin Harcourt Publishing Company. Copyright © renewed 1981 by Carl Sandburg. Reprinted by permission of Houghton Mifflin Harcourt Publishing Company. All rights reserved; Excerpt from *The Invention of Everything Else: A Novel* by Samantha Hunt. Copyright ©2008 by Samantha Hunt. Used by permission of Houghton Mifflin Harcourt Publishing Company. All rights reserved.

ITN Source. *Amazing Man Draws NYC from Memory* © ITN Source.

Jukin Media. *Dear Graduates—A Message From Kid President* Courtesy Jukin Media, Inc.

LA Times. "Soda's a Problem but Bloomberg Doesn't Have the Solution" by Karin Klein, from *LA Times,* March 15, 2013. Copyright ©2013 Los Angeles Times. Reprinted with Permission.

Little, Brown and Co. (UK). From *I Know Why the Caged Bird Sings* by Maya Angelou. Copyright ©1997. Used with permission of Little, Brown Book Group.

Mayer, John. "Is Personal Intelligence Important?" by John D. Mayer, *Psychology Today* blog, May 6, 2014; Used with permission of the author.

McIntosh & Otis. "Winter Hibiscus," Copyright ©1993 by Minfong Ho. Reprinted by permission of McIntosh & Otis, Inc.

Mok, Kimberly. "Fermented Cow Dung Air Freshener Wins Two Students Top Science Prize," ©Kimberly Mok.

Mungoshi, Jesesi. From *The Setting Sun and the Rolling World* by Charles Mungoshi, ©1989. Used with permission of Jesesi Mungoshi.

National Geographic Creative. *Girl's Rite of Passage* ©National Geographic Creative.

National Geographic Magazine. "Barrington Irving, Pilot and Educator" from National Geographic: Explorers, http://www.national-geographic.com/explorers/bios/barrington-irving/. NG Staff/National Geographic Creative.

Nobel Media AB. "Elie Wiesel Nobel Acceptance Speech," Copyright © The Nobel Foundation (1986). Source: Nobelprize.org.

Parekh, Divya. "Why Is Emotional Intelligence Important for Teens?" by Divya Parekh. Used with permission of the author.

PARS International Corporation. "A Great Adventure in the Shadow of War," From *Newsweek,* September 13, 2004 ©2004 IBT Media. All rights reserved. Used by permission and protected by the Copyright Laws of the United States. The printing, copying, redistribution, or retransmission of this Content without express written permission is prohibited; "Three Cheers for the Nanny State" from *The New York Times,* March 25, 2013 ©2013 The New York Times. All rights reserved. Used by permission and protected by the Copyright Laws of the United States. The printing, copying, redistribution, or retransmission of this Content without express written permission is prohibited; "25 Years Later, Hubble Sees Beyond Troubled Start" from *The New York Times,* April 24, 2015 ©2015 The New York Times. All rights reserved. Used by permission and protected by the Copyright

Laws of the United States. The printing, copying, redistribution, or retransmission of this Content without express written permission is prohibited.

Penguin Books, Ltd. (UK). From *The Diary of a Young Girl: The Definitive Edition* by Anne Frank, edited by Otto H. Frank and Mirjam Pressler, translated by Susan Massotty (Viking, 1997) copyright © The Anne Frank-Fonds, Basle, Switzerland, 1991. English translation copyright © Doubleday a division of Bantam Doubleday Dell Publishing Group Inc., 1995. Reproduced by permission of Penguin Books Ltd.; From THE COMPLETE MAUS by Art Spiegelman (Penguin Books, 2003). Copyright © Art Spiegelman, 1973, 1980, 1981, 1982, 1983, 1984, 1985, 1986, 1989, 1990, 1991. Reproduced by permission of Penguin Books Ltd.; "Einstein's Brain and Enhancing Our Intelligence" from *The Future of the Mind* by Michio Kaku (Penguin, 2015) Copyright © Michio Kaku, 2014. Reproduced by permission of Penguin Books Ltd.

Peppe, Holly. *Got 30 Dollars in my Pocket* Courtesy Barrington Irving.

Random House Group Ltd., Permissions Department. From *The Invention of Everything Else* by Samantha Hunt. Published by Harvill Secker. Reprinted by permission of The Random House Group Limited.

Random House UK Limited. "Uncle Marcos" from *The House of the Spirits* by Isabel Allende. Published by Jonathan Cape. Reprinted by permission of The Random House Group Limited.

Random House, Inc. Excerpt(s) from *I Know Why the Caged Bird Sings* by Maya Angelou, Copyright ©1969 and renewed 1997 by Maya Angelou. Used by permission of Random House, an imprint and division of Penguin Random House LLC. All rights reserved. Any third party use of this material, outside of this publication, is prohibited. Interested parties must apply directly to Penguin Random House LLC for permission; Entire Play from *Diary of Anne Frank* by Frances Goodrich and Albert Hackett, copyright ©1956 by Albert Hackett, Frances Goodrich Hackett, and Otto Frank. Copyright renewed 1984 by Albert Hackett. Used by permission of Random House, an imprint and division of Penguin Random House LLC. All rights reserved. Any third party use of this material, outside of this publication, is prohibited. Interested parties must apply directly to Penguin Random House LLC for permission; Excerpt(s) from *The Diary of a Young Girl: The Definitive Edition* by Anne Frank, edited by Otto H. Frank and Mirjam Pressler, translated by Susan Massotty, translation Copyright ©1995 by Doubleday, a division of Random House LLC. Used by permission of Doubleday, an imprint of the Knopf Doubleday Publishing Group, a division of Penguin Random House LLC. All rights reserved. Any third party use of this material, outside of this publication, is prohibited. Interested parties must apply directly to Penguin Random House LLC for permission; Graphic Novel excerpt from *The Complete Maus: A Survivor's Tale* by Art Spiegelman, Maus, Volume I copyright ©1973, 1980, 1981, 1982, 1983, 1984, 1985, 1986 by Art Spiegelman; Maus, Volume II copyright ©1986, 1989, 1990, 1991 by Art Spiegelman. Used by permission of Pantheon Books, an imprint of the Knopf Doubleday Publishing Group, a division of Penguin Random House LLC. All rights reserved. Any third party use of this material, outside of this publication, is prohibited. Interested parties must apply directly to Penguin Random House LLC for permission; "The Unknown Citizen," copyright ©1940 and renewed 1968 by W. H. Auden; from *W. H. Auden Collected Poems* by W. H. Auden. Used by permission of Random House, an imprint and division of Penguin Random House LLC. All rights reserved. Any third party use of this material, outside of

this publication, is prohibited. Interested parties must apply directly to Penguin Random House LLC for permission; "What Happened During the Ice Storm" from *The One-Room Schoolhouse: Stories About the Boys* by Jim Heynen, copyright ©1993 by Jim Heynen. Used by permission of Alfred A. Knopf, an imprint of the Knopf Doubleday Publishing Group, a division of Penguin Random House LLC. All rights reserved; "Einstein's Brain and Enhancing Our Intelligence" excerpt(s) from *The Future of the Mind: The Scientific Quest to Understand, Enhance, and Empower the Mind* by Michio Kaku, copyright ©2013 by Michio Kaku. Used by permission of Doubleday, an imprint of the Knopf Doubleday Publishing Group, a division of Penguin Random House LLC. All rights reserved. Any third party use of this material, outside of this publication, is prohibited. Interested parties must apply directly to Penguin Random House LLC for permission.

Ricketson, James. *Phillipe Petit Tightrope Walk on The Sydney Harbour Bridge* 1973 - Part 2 © James Ricketson.

Scholastic, Inc. "I'll Go Fetch Her Tomorrow" from *Hidden Like Anne Frank* by Marcel Prins and Peter Kenk Steehuis, translated by Laura Watkinson. Copyright ©2001 by Marcel Prins and Peter Henk Steenhuis. Translation by Laura Watkinson copyright ©2014 by Scholastic, Inc. Reprinted by permission of Scholastic Inc.; From *Through My Eyes* by Ruby Bridges. Copyright ©1999 by Ruby Bridges. Reprinted by permission of Scholastic, Inc.

Simon & Schuster Inc. "Uncle Marcos" from *The House of the Spirits* by Isabel Allende. Copyright ©1982. Used with permission of Simon & Schuster, Inc.; "Blue Nines and Red Words" reprinted with the permission of Free Press, a Division of Simon & Schuster, Inc., from *Born on a Blue Day: Inside the Extraordinary Mind of an Autistic Savant* by Daniel Tammet. Copyright © 2006 by Daniel Tammet. Originally published in Great Britain in 2006 by Hodder & Stoughton. All rights reserved.

Sneve, Virginia. "The Medicine Bag" from *Grandpa Was a Cowboy & an Indian and Other Stories* by Virginia Driving Hawk Sneve. Used with permission.

Stone, SidneyAnne. "Ban the Ban!" from *Huffington Post,* May 12, 2013, by SidneyAnne Stone. Used with permission of the author.

The Andrew Lownie Literary Agency Ltd. "Blue Nines and Red Words" from *Born on a Blue Day* by Daniel Tammet. Copyright ©2009. Used with permission of Andrew Lownie Literary Agency.

The Daily News. "Quinceanera Birthday Bash Preserves Tradition, Marks Passage to Womanhood," Copyright ©July 28, 2012, Author: Natalie St. John, in *The Daily News.*

The Moth. The Moth Presents: Aleeza Kazmi © The Moth.

Toronto Star Newspapers Limited. Sounds of a Glass Armonica ©Mike Kelly/GetStock

University of Arizona Press. From *For a Girl Becoming* by Joy Harjo. ©2009 Joy Harjo and Mercedes McDonald. Reprinted by permission of the University of Arizona Press.

University of Queensland Press. From *Follow the Rabbit-Proof Fence* by Doris Pilkington. Copyright ©1996. Used with permission of University of Queensland Press.

Vega, Eddie. "Translating Grandfather's House" by Eddie Vega, from *Cool Salsa: Bilingual Poems on Growing Up Latino in the United States,* edited by Lori M. Carlson, Introduction by Oscar Hijuelos. Used with permission of Eddie Vega.

W. W. Norton & Co. "Hanging Fire." Copyright ©1978 by Audre

Lorde, from *The Collected Poems of Audre Lorde* by Audre Lorde. Used by permission of W.W. Norton & Company, Inc.; "To Fly" from *Space Chronicles: Facing the Ultimate Frontier* by Neil deGrasse Tyson, edited by Avis Lang. Copyright ©2012 by Neil deGrasse Tyson. Used by permission of W.W. Norton & Company.

WGBH Stock Sales. *Got 30 Dollars in my Pocket* Courtesy of the WGBH Media Library & Archives.

William Morris Endeavor Entertainment, LLC. Excerpted from *Flowers for Algernon* by Daniel Keyes. Copyright ©1966, 1959, and renewed 1994, 1987 by Daniel Keyes. Reprinted by permission of WME Entertainment, LLC.

Writers House. "Heartbeat" Copyright ©2005 David Yoo. Reprinted with permission of the author.

Wylie Agency. From *Maus* by Art Spiegelman. Copyright ©1973, 1980, 1981, 1982, 1983, 1984, 1985, 1986 by Art Spiegelman, used by permission of The Wylie Agency.

Zest Books. "Just Be Yourself!," reprinted from *Dear Teen Me: Authors Write Letters to Their Teen Selves* by E. Kristin Anderson and Miranda Kenneally, published by Zest Books © 2012; "You Are the Electric Boogaloo," reprinted from *Dear Teen Me: Authors Write Letters to Their Teen Selves* by E. Kristin Anderson and Miranda Kenneally, published by Zest Books, © 2012.

Credits

Photo locators denoted as follows Top (T), Center (C), Bottom (B), Left (L), Right (R), Background (Bkgd)

Cover: Lee Powers/Stone/Getty Images

vi Encyclopedia/Corbis; **viii** Josselin Dupont/Moment/Getty Images; **xii** David Malan/Photographer's Choice RF/Getty Images; **xiv** Ruslan Grumble/Shutterstock; **2** Encyclopedia/Corbis; **3** (BC) Paul Bruins Photography/Moment Open/Getty Images, (BCR) Christina Havis/EyeEm/Getty Images, (BR) Tetsuya Tanooka/a.collectionRF/Getty Images, (C) Amos Morgan/Photodisc/Getty Images, (CBR) Image Source/Photodisc/Getty Images, (CR) Library of Congress/Science Faction/Getty Images, (T) Michael Shay/Stockbyte/Getty Images, (TC) Kiselev Andrey Valerevich/Shutterstock, (TL) Claudia Kunin/The Image Bank/Getty Images, (TR) John Parrot/Stocktrek Images/Getty Images; **6** Michael Shay/Stockbyte/Getty Images; **11** (B) National Geographic Creative, (T) Claudia Kunin/The Image Bank/Getty Images; **12** (TL) Claudia Kunin/The Image Bank/Getty Images, (TR) National Geographic Creative; **13, 22, 24, 26, 28** (L), **32** (T) Claudia Kunin/The Image Bank/Getty Images; **17** Roberto A Sanchez/Getty Images; **28** (R), **29, 31, 32** (B) National Geographic Creative; **34** Michael Shay/Stockbyte/Getty Images; **41** (T), **44, 46** Kiselev Andrey Valerevich/Shutterstock, (B) Paul Bruins Photography/Moment Open/Getty Images, (C) Amos Morgan/Photodisc/Getty Images; **45** Photo by Katherine Warde; **48** Olaf Speier/Alamy; **54** Danita Delimont/Gallo Images/Getty Images; **55** (B) ©Eddie Vega, (T) Everett Collection Historical/Alamy; **56** Amos Morgan/Photodisc/Getty Images; **58** Danita Delimont/Gallo Images/Getty Images; **66** ©Jesesi Mungoshi; **67** Paul Bruins Photography/Moment Open/Getty Images; **72** Paul Bruins Photography/Moment Open/Getty Images; **74** Paul Bruins Photography/Moment Open/Getty Images; **79** (B) Tetsuya Tanooka/a.collectionRF/Getty Images, (BR) Christina Havis/EyeEm/Getty Images, (C) Image Source/Photodisc/Getty Images, (T) John Parrot/Stocktrek Images/Getty Images, (TR) Library of Congress; **88** Josselin Dupont/Moment/Getty Images; **89** (B) Dave Bartruff/Danita Delimont Photography/Newscom, (BC) Miquel Benitez/REX/Newscom, (BCL) Anne Frank Fonds Basel/Premium Archive/Getty Images, (BCR) DC Premiumstock/Alamy, (BL) Historical/Corbis, (C) Heritage Images/Glow Images, (CBR) Charlie Riedel/AP Images, (CL) Anne Frank Fonds Basel/Getty Images, (CR) Harvey Meston/Staff/Getty Images, (T) Age Fotostock/Alamy, (TC) Leo La Valle/epa/Corbis, (TL) John Cairns/Alamy, (TR) Pictorial Press Ltd/Alamy; **92** Age Fotostock/Alamy; **97** (B) Historical/Corbis, (BC) Anne Frank Fonds Basel/Premium Archive/Getty Images, (T) John Cairns/Alamy, (TC) Anne Frank Fonds Basel/Getty Images; **98** (B) Print Collector/Hulton Archive/Getty Images, (T) Hulton-Deutsch Collection/Corbis, (B) John Cairns/Alamy; **99** Galerie Bilderwelt/Hulton Archive/Getty Images; **100** (BL, CL) Nancy R. Schiff/Archive Photos/Getty Images, (TL) Anne Frank Fonds Basel/Getty Images, (TR) Historical/Corbis; **101, 105, 152, 154, 156** (TL), **157, 177, 188, 190, 192, 194** (L), **197** (TL), **200** (T), **212** Anne Frank Fonds Basel/Getty Images; **110** Bettmann/Corbis; **119** Desk/AFP/Getty Images; **127** Richard Sowersby/REX/Newscom; **134** UPPA/Photoshot/Newscom; **139** Ralph Crane/The Life Picture Collection/Getty Images; **145** CSP_RonaldWilfredJansen/AGE Fotostock; **150** Reuters Photographer/Reuters/Corbis; **156** (BL), (CL) Nancy R. Schiff/Archive Photos/Getty Images; **156** (TR), **194** (R), **196** (BL), **199, 200** (B) Historical/Corbis; Hulton Archive/Getty Images; **169** Leo La Valle/epa/Corbis; **196** (BC) Rieke Hammerich/Alamy, (BR) Hulton-Deutsch Collection/Corbis; **196** (T), **197** (BL) Bettmann/Corbis; **197** (BR) GPO/Hulton Archive/Getty Images, (TR) Richard Boot/Alamy; **202** Age Fotostock/Alamy; **209, 223, 226, 228** Heritage Images/Glow Images; **209, 213, 218, 220** Leo La Valle/epa/Corbis; **222** Ulf Andersen/Hulton Archive/Getty Images; **230** Aurora Photos/Alamy; **245** (B) Dave Bartruff/Danita Delimont Photography/Newscom, (BC) Miquel Benitez/REX/Newscom, (C) Charlie Riedel/AP Images, (CB) DC Premiumstock/Alamy, (T) Pictorial Press Ltd/Alamy, (TC) Harvey Meston/Staff/Getty Images; **254** Noah Seelam/Getty Images; **255** (B) Universal History Archive/Getty Images, (BR) Rawpixel/Shutterstock, (C) Paul Mayall/Paul Mayall imageBROKER/Newscom, (CL) Blend Images/Brand X Pictures/Getty Images, (CR) AP Images, (T) Jerry Horbert/Shutterstock,(TC) Washington State Historical Society/Art Resource, New York, (TL) MA1/MA1 Wenn Photos/Newscom, (TR) Jed Jacobsohn/

Sports Illustrated/Getty Images; **258** Jerry Horbert/Shutterstock; **263** (C) Blend Images/Brand X Pictures/Getty Images, (T) MA1/MA1 Wenn Photos/Newscom; **265, 270, 272, 274** MA1/MA1 Wenn Photos/Newscom; **276** (B) Copyright Bowdoin College, (TL) Blend Images/Brand X Pictures/Getty Images; **277, 282, 284, 286, 294** Blend Images/Brand X Pictures/Getty Images; **296** Jerry Horbert/Shutterstock; **303** (B) ©The Moth, (C) Paul Mayall/Paul Mayall imageBROKER/Newscom, (T) Washington State Historical Society/Art Resource, New York; **306** Library of Congress, Prints & Photographs Division, LC-USZC4-5785; **307, 310, 312** Washington State Historical Society/Art Resource, New York; **314** Tom Kidd/Alamy; **315, 320, 322** Paul Mayall/Paul Mayall imageBROKER/Newscom; **324, 325, 327** ©The Moth; **331** (B) Universal History Archive/Getty Images, (BC) Rawpixel/Shutterstock, (T) Jed Jacobsohn/Sports Illustrated/Getty Images, (TC) AP Images; **340** David Malan/Photographer's Choice RF/Getty Images; **341** (B) Lucien Aigner/Corbis, (BC) Magann/YAY Media AS/Alamy, (BR) Vladyslav Starozhylov/Shutterstock, (T) DrAfter123/DigitalVision Vectors/Getty Images, (TC) Puckillustrations/Fotolia, (TL) Neil Lockhart/Shutterstock, (TR) Nopgraphic/Fotolia; **344, 390** DrAfter123/DigitalVision Vectors/Getty Images; **349, 350, 351, 380, 382, 388** Neil Lockhart/Shutterstock; **366** ABC Pictures/Photofest; **373** Everett Collection; **378** ClassicStock/Superstock; **384** (B) Ari Perilstein/Getty Images, (T) Neil Lockhart/Shutterstock; **397** (B) Magann/YAY Media AS/Alamy, (T) Puckillustrations/Fotolia; **400** Gerard Julien/AFP/Getty Images; **401, 408, 410** Puckillustrations/Fotolia; **404** Shutterstock; **412** J.L. Cereijido/epa/Corbis; **416, 418** Magann/YAY Media AS/Alamy; **417** (B) Library of Congress, Prints & Photographs Division, LC-USZ62-115064, (T) Anthony Barboza/Getty Images; **419** Olha Lavrenchuk/Shutterstock; **429** (B) Lucien Aigner/Corbis, (BC) Vladyslav Starozhylov/Shutterstock, (T) Nopgraphic/Fotolia; **438** Ruslan Grumble/Shutterstock; **439** (B) Pan Xunbin/Shutterstock, (BC) NASA/ESA/Hubble Heritage Team, (BCR) Fyle/Fotolia, (C) Imagophotodesign/Shutterstock, (CBR) Charles Krupa/AP Images, (CL) World History Archive/Alamy, (CR) AP Images, (T) Laborant/Shutterstock, (TC) Richard T. Nowitz/Corbis, (TL) MorganStudio/Shutterstock, (TR) Bill Pierce/The Life Images Collection/Getty Images; **442** Laborant/Shutterstock; **447** (B) World History Archive/Alamy, (T) MorganStudio/Shutterstock; **449** MorganStudio/Shutterstock; **455** Peter vd Rol/Shutterstock; **458, 460, 462** MorganStudio/Shutterstock; **464** Mike Coppola/Getty Images; **465, 472** World History Archive/Alamy; **474, 476** World History Archive/Alamy; **478** Laborant/Shutterstock; **485** (B) Mike Kelly/GetStock.com, (BC) NASA/ESA/Hubble Heritage Team, (TC) Imagophotodesign/Shutterstock, (T) Richard T. Nowitz/Corbis; Photo by Celine M Grouard; **488** (L) Richard T. Nowitz/Corbis; **488** (R) Imagophotodesign/Shutterstock; **489, 491, 492, 508** Richard T. Nowitz/Corbis; **494** (TL) Richard T. Nowitz/Corbis, (TR) Imagophotodesign/Shutterstock, (B) Marion Ettlinger/Corbis; **495, 505, 506** Imagophotodesign/Shutterstock; **498** Andrew Meyerson/Shutterstock; **510** Terry Ashe/The LIFE; Images Collection/Getty Images; **511, 516, 518** NASA/ESA/Hubble Heritage Team; **521, 523** Mike Kelly/GetStock.com; **527** (B) Pan Xunbin/Shutterstock, (BC) Fyle/Fotolia, (C) Charles Krupa/AP Images, (T) Bill Pierce/The Life Images Collection/Getty Images.

Credits for Images in Interactive Student Edition Only

Unit 1

Africa Studio/Shutterstock; AP Images; Christopher Dennis; Everett Historical/Shutterstock; Jedrzej Kaminski/EyeEm/Getty images; Ken Charnock/Getty Images; Natalie St. John copyright 2013; North Wind Picture Archives;

Unit 2

Courtesy CNN; Czarek Sokolowski/AP Images; Hulton-Deutsch Collection/Corbis; Jason Kempin/Getty Images; Piotr Latacha/Shutterstock; Wjarek/Shutterstock; ©Nancy Newberry; ©United States Holocaust Memorial Museum, Courtesy of Bloeme Evers-Emden. THE VIEWS OR OPINIONS EXPRESSED IN THIS (BOOK/ARTICLE/EXHIBIT/OTHER), AND THE CONTEXT IN WHICH THE IMAGES ARE USED, DO NOT NECESSARILY REFLECT THE VIEWS OR POLICY OF, NOR IMPLY APPROVAL OR ENDORSEMENT BY, THE UNITED STATES HOLOCAUST MEMORIAL MUSEUM;

Unit 3

The Underground Railroad, 1893 (oil on canvas), Webber, Charles T. (1825–1911)/Cincinnati Art Museum, Ohio, USA/Subscription Fund Purchase/Bridgeman Art Library; Walter Daran/The LIFE Images Collection/Getty Images; ZUMA Press,Inc./Alamy;

Unit 4

Anthony Barboza/Getty Images; Divya Parekh; Evan Agostini/AP Images; Kmiragaya/Fotolia; ©2013, The University of New Hampshire;

Unit 5

David Levenson/National Basketball Association/Getty Images; Kimberley Mok; Michael Nicholson/Corbis.